Constructing Inequality

Constructing Inequality

The Fabrication of a Hierarchy
of Virtue among the Etoro

RAYMOND C. KELLY

Ann Arbor

THE UNIVERSITY OF MICHIGAN PRESS

Copyright © by the University of Michigan 1993
All rights reserved
Published in the United States of America by
The University of Michigan Press
Manufactured in the United States of America

1996   1995   1994   1993   4   3   2   1

A CIP catalogue record for this book is available from the British Library.

Library of Congress Cataloging-in-Publication Data

Kelly, Raymond C. (Raymond Case), 1942–
     Constructing inequality : the fabrication of a hierarchy of virtue
among the Etoro / Raymond C. Kelly.
          p.   cm.
     Includes bibliographical references and index.
     ISBN 0-472-09528-5 (alk. paper). — ISBN 0-472-06528-9 (pbk. :
alk. paper)
     1. Etoro (Papua New Guinea people)—Social conditions. 2. Etoro
(Papua New Guinea people)—Economic conditions. 3. Subsistence
economy—Papua New Guinea. 4. Bride price—Papua New Guinea.
5. Social status—Papua New Guinea. 6. Sex role—Papua New Guinea.
7. Papua New Guinea—Social conditions. 8. Papua New Guinea—
Economic conditions.   I. Title.
DU740.42.K437   1993
305.8999′12—dc20   93-14258
                                                                    CIP

For my daughters,
Kathryn E. and Gwendolyn I. O. Kelly

Acknowledgments

The data on which this study is based were collected during the course of field research funded by a grant and predoctoral fellowship from the National Institute of Mental Health, whose support I gratefully acknowledge. Mary Pfender provided valuable research assistance during the period of data collection (April 1968 to July 1969). I likewise appreciate the efforts of those who contributed to my field research through advice, suggestions, discussion, and/or correspondence, particularly Roy Rappaport, Marshall Sahlins, and Edward Schieffelin. I am especially grateful to the Etoro for making me a part of their lives for fifteen months and for their many kindnesses. The assistance of Illawi was invaluable and the recollection of his friendship remains bright after nearly twenty-five years.

The broad outlines of the theoretical approach to the understanding of social inequality developed in this book were initially broached in an article published in 1976, "Witchcraft and Sexual Relations: An Exploration in the Social and Semantic Implications of the Structure of Belief." This article forms the core of chapter 3, and I appreciate the willingness of the American Anthropological Association to allow me to make use of it here. In this paper I concluded that "the production of an elementary system of inequality based on age and sex" was attributable to an interplay between beliefs pertaining to witchcraft and sexual relations (Kelly 1976:51). These beliefs constitute the basis of the *moral hierarchy* and the *prestige/stigma system* that are given explicit theoretical formulation in the present work. An unpublished paper (Kelly n.d.) concerned with the analysis of covariation between types of male prestige systems, on one hand, and the degree of elaboration of beliefs concerning female pollution (i.e., stigma), on the other hand, represents an intermediate step in the development of these ideas. A synopsis of this paper can be found in Ortner and Whitehead (1981:20–21). I have benefited from discussions with both Ortner and Whitehead over the past fifteen years, and the dialogue between their papers and mine is also reflected in the present work.

The protracted gestation period of this book makes it unfeasible to mention all those who have contributed to the development of the ideas presented herein. However, I would additionally like to single out Bruce

Knauft and Eileen Cantrell, with whom I have had many stimulating exchanges of ideas. I have likewise learned much from the students in my course Social Inequality in Tribal Societies.

Eileen Cantrell, Peter Dwyer, Jim Hagen, Dorothy Hodgson, Bruce Knauft, Sherry Ortner, Michael Peletz, Harriet Whitehead, and Michael Wood have read earlier or later drafts of all or part of the book and offered many valuable comments and suggestions. I would particularly like to express my appreciation to Eileen Cantrell, Bruce Knauft, Michael Peletz, and Harriet Whitehead for their comprehensive and exceptionally detailed comments. I am grateful to the secretaries in the Anthropology Department at the University of Michigan for typing successive drafts of the manuscript.

Contents

Introduction

What is the principal locus for the production of inequality in human society? This is a question that has been pondered since the Enlightenment by philosophers, nineteenth-century social theorists, and their modern descendants. Locke ([1690] 1978) and Rousseau ([1755] 1938) posited a very substantial degree of equality in a "state of nature" as a counterpart to the concept that inequality in society is socially constructed (Beteille 1981:62–64). The comparison of historically known constructions revealed both their arbitrary (non-naturalistic) character and their status as temporally limited productions subject to causal explanation in terms of institutional features. This effectively raised the issue. The concept that an explanation could be formulated in terms of a central locus for the social production of inequality, constituting the internal equivalent of a prime mover, is largely attributable to Marx's persuasive analysis of social inequality in nineteenth-century capitalist society. This concept more narrowly defined the focal issue and thus shaped the nature of the debate that continues to the present.

Consideration of comparatively egalitarian premodern tribal societies— in which the forms of hierarchy associated with the nation-state and industrialized world economy were indigenously absent (and comparatively attenuated at the time of study)—has been of central importance in this debate, because these societies provide an ideal testing ground for general theories addressing the causes of social inequality. All such theories explicitly or implicitly "predict" the social and economic configuration of this category of societies, since whatever produces more elaborated forms of social inequality (e.g., private property) should logically be absent or attenuated when these elaborated forms are not present. The ethnography of "egalitarian" or "simple" or "nonhierarchical" societies thus came to occupy the place in the structure of the argument formerly occupied by the philosophically postulated "state of nature."[1] It has been the distinctive task of anthropology to provide detailed ethnographic accounts of these comparatively egalitarian societies that represent test cases for theoretical formulations concerning the locus for the production of inequality and the sources of its elaboration in the course of sociocultural evolution. In more general terms, addressing fundamental questions pertaining to inequality may be regarded as one of anthropology's most basic intellectual charges (cf. Diamond 1974).

Since the early 1970s, issues pertaining to gender inequality and the universality of male domination have increasingly occupied anthropological attention. (See Strathern 1988; Ortner and Whitehead 1981; Ortner 1990; Mukhopadhyay and Higgins 1988; and Flanagan 1989 for recent reviews of this extensive literature.) The most prominent effect of this, when viewed in relation to long-term trends in the study of social inequality, has been to focus analytic scrutiny upon the inegalitarian rather than the egalitarian features of the least-stratified societies. This reinforced a somewhat earlier parallel trend in Marxian analysis of premodern tribal societies (see Terray 1972 and his discussion of the earlier work of Meillassoux) and eventuated in the deconstruction of a comparatively utopian vision of egalitarian society. Although the egalitarian qualifications of selected ethnographic cases continue to be debated (Ortner 1990), a major shift has nevertheless occurred in that the locus for the production of social inequality in the erstwhile egalitarian societies has become a focal issue.

This contrasts markedly with the central issue that preoccupied the proponents of the concept of egalitarian societies, i.e., the socioeconomic conditions conducive to the maintenance of egalitarian features. This previously dominant perspective is particularly well represented by Fried (1967:35), who argues that "at the heart of an egalitarian society is a fundamentally egalitarian economy." The central features of such an economy include a lack of surplus production, an absence of "valuables" or tokens possessing exchange value, very limited accumulation, distribution governed by the principle of sharing (or generalized reciprocity), and communal and unrestricted access to the resources essential to subsistence food production. The nature of the question Fried sought to answer (concerning the enabling conditions for a comparatively egalitarian form of organization) is readily apparent in the form of his argument. Moreover, the issues addressed do not differ significantly from those considered by Engels ([1884] 1942). The shift that occurred in the seventies thus entailed a significant change in the sociology of knowledge. A shift in the basic question under consideration engendered a recontextualization of extant ethnographic data as well as the generation of new data and revised analyses, interpretations, and theoretical formulations. For reasons that are as yet not entirely clear, utopian ethnographic allegory lost much of its prior appeal, and the inequalities present in simple societies were highlighted.[2]

The most comprehensive and influential current model of the erstwhile egalitarian societies is that developed by Collier and Rosaldo (1981) and Collier (1988). Although these societies have been relabeled "simple" societies or "brideservice societies," the group of ethnographic cases that constitutes the analytic set remains largely unchanged (Collier 1988:3). They are perhaps most readily characterized as those societies in which age, gender, and personal characteristics are the predominant bases of social differentiation (Sahlins 1958:1).[3] They consequently manifest comparable forms and dimensions of social inequality and constitute a set of cases that can be employed to test general theoretical formulations concerning the central locus for the production of inequality. The basic postulate of Collier's theoretical position is that "marriage . . . organizes social inequality" (Collier 1988:vii) and thus constitutes the central locus, or internal prime mover, that generates the distinctive forms of social inequality that characterize brideservice, equal bridewealth, and unequal bridewealth societies (i.e., types of societies distinguished by different forms of marriage). In essence Collier's theoretical position presupposes that all significant social inequalities are grounded in marital practice—predicated upon the institutional forms of marriage in place—and are either directly generated by these forms and practices or built up upon core relations of social inequality that are so generated. Thus marriage organizes relations of production and is the source of the inequalities entailed by the latter. Collier's formulation draws on the prior work of Meillassoux (1972, 1973a, 1973b, 1981) in this respect (Collier 1988:4) and thus constitutes a synthesis of feminist and neo-Marxian perspectives.

The present work is squarely within the well-established intellectual tradition pertaining to the study of social inequality that I have outlined. The first of two primary objectives is to critically evaluate current anthropological theories of social inequality in simple societies against the relevant data derived from an apposite ethnographic case, the Etoro. The theory that underwrites the brideservice model is the most prominent focus of this evaluation. Moreover, the Etoro have been specifically nominated by Collier (1988:258) as an ethnographic case to which the brideservice model could fruitfully be applied. It is my contention that a close examination of the Etoro case reveals basic flaws both in the brideservice model and in the theory of social inequality that informs it. The basic proposition that marriage is the central locus for the production of inequality entails misplaced causality. A theoretical reformulation is thus required, and the development of this alternative to the brideservice model is the second primary objective of the book.

Both an extended critical evaluation of the brideservice model and the proposed theoretical reformulation are presented in the concluding chapter. The six preceding chapters are principally devoted to providing a comprehensive account of social inequality, and of the interplay between egalitarian and inegalitarian features, within the Etoro sociocultural system. The eight ethnographically described societies of the Strickland-Bosavi region are also discussed in order to establish a comparative framework that enhances the analysis and interpretation of the Etoro data. The central theoretical arguments developed are a direct outgrowth of this analysis and interpretation, and theoretical discussion is thus largely reserved for the conclusions. Only a brief sketch will be provided here. Readers who wish to be more fully apprised of this theoretical position at the onset can read the concluding chapter before turning to the ethnographic analysis and interpretation that provide the foundation for it.

The main outlines of Etoro social organization and subsistence food production have previously been described (Kelly 1977, 1988; Dwyer 1982, 1983, 1985a, 1985b, 1985c, 1990), and the plan of the current work is thus to focus on those aspects of the cultural and socioeconomic system that are germane to social inequality. Social inequality can be minimally defined as social differentiation accompanied by differential moral evaluation (following Berreman 1981 and Fallers 1973). In practice, morally evaluated social differentiation is almost invariably accompanied by differences in prestige (and stigma), privilege (and debility), and culturally pertinent advantage (and disadvantage), although it is analytically useful to unbundle these. The principal ethnographic objective of the book is to exhaustively describe and analyze all social inequalities irrespective of the extent to which they have figured in current theoretical formulations. Thus the morally denigrated, stigmatized, and socially disadvantaged category of the witch is extensively analyzed, even though the inequalities associated with assignment to this category are not organized by marriage or derived from the means and relations of production.

A condensed chapter summary will provide a guide to what follows. The first chapter delineates the Strickland-Bosavi region in terms of linguistic affinities, recent history, and commonalities and variations in the socioeconomic organization of the eight cultural groups within it that have been ethnographically described. This lays the groundwork for consideration of regional variation that informs the subsequent analysis of Etoro production, distribution (including exchange), and consumption that is undertaken in chapter 2.

All of the eight Strickland-Bosavi tribes are classifiable as "brideservice societies" in terms of Collier's typology, insofar as bachelors are not dependent on senior males for accumulation of the valuables included in marriage payments (see Collier 1988:19). Marriage payments are present in some cases but not others. However, there is a uniform emphasis on the reciprocal exchange of women, and marriage payments, when present, do not alter the obligation to provide women in reciprocation for those received. Although marriage is typologically similar in these respects among all eight tribes, there are notable differences in the larger social and economic context in which it is enmeshed. These are attributable to variations in the division of labor and in the extent to which conjugal sociality is encouraged or discouraged by the interior design of the longhouses that are common throughout the region.

The longhouses of the Strickland-Bosavi tribes display two main themes in terms of spatially formulated groupings and distinctions. In one basic type of longhouse design, eating, sleeping, and socializing areas are all gender-segregated, so that the internal solidarity of each gender is promoted and conjugal sociality notably attenuated in this context. In the other type of design, the longhouse contains a communal section containing family hearths so that husbands and wives (and men and women more generally) socialize and share meals. This counterbalances the gender-segregated sleeping quarters and male-exclusive socializing areas in the rear of the dwelling. Integration and division of the genders are thus countervailing principles of social life within the longhouse, and marriage constitutes the central mechanism through which the otherwise divided genders are communally integrated. The character of marriage as both an institution and a social relationship thus differs significantly in accordance with these variations in longhouse design.

The Strickland-Bosavi tribes also differ significantly in terms of the gendered division of labor. These differences are accompanied by concomitant variation in the exchange of labor and/or the products of labor between males and females. The Etoro represent one basic pattern. Husbands and wives predominantly exchange labor, working together cooperatively to coproduce sago and garden crops in which their respective labor contributions are intermingled. This conjugally organized male-female coproduction contrasts with the gender-exclusive organization of major productive domains (such as sago processing) among the Kamula (Wood 1982).[4] In the latter case, it is the products of labor rather than labor itself which are exchanged between spouses (and males and females more generally). The remaining Strickland-Bosavi tribes either approximate one or the other of these contrasting forms of the division of labor or combine elements of both. These graded variations in the gendered division of labor and modes of conjugal exchange are theoretically significant with respect to evaluating Collier's central thesis that marriage organizes inequality. The contrast between the Etoro and Kamula cases that emerges from the regional comparison carried out in this chapter is further developed along these lines in the concluding chapter.

Among the Etoro a division of labor characterized by conjugally organized coproduction is matched with a longhouse design that provides for familial dining within the gender-inclusive communal section of the dwelling. Husbands and wives thus work together at complementary components of subsistence food production and subsequently share meals in which they jointly consume what they have jointly produced. In contrast, the Kamula longhouse is of the uniformly gender-segregated type, and this combines

with the gender-exclusive organization of major productive domains so that
husbands and wives do not work together (in most contexts) and likewise do
not eat together. They exchange the products of their separate labor and
consume these with others of their own gender. The Etoro and Kamula thus
contrast in terms of the organization of social space as well as in terms of the
organization of subsistence food production, distribution (including exchange), and consumption that is keyed by the division of labor. However,
longhouse design and the mode of organization of subsistence food production are not analogously aligned in parallel among other Strickland-Bosavi
tribes. Thus conjugally based male-female coproduction is combined with
the gender-segregated type of longhouse design among the Onabasulu and
Kaluli so that conjugal sociality is predominantly realized in sago processing
and gardening, and in garden houses (Ernst 1978). Regional comparison thus
brings out the distinctive features of the Etoro case with respect to the larger
socioeconomic context in which conjugal relations and the institution of
marriage are embedded. The contrasting Kamula case provides a theoretically productive comparative counterpoint that serves as one of several means
of broadening the critical evaluation of Collier's (1988) and Collier and
Rosaldo's (1981) thesis that marriage organizes inequality in brideservice
societies.

The subsistence economy of the Etoro is examined in more detail in the
second chapter, in the context of a comparison of the economies of the
Strickland-Bosavi tribes as a group. Throughout the region, subsistence food
production entails varied combinations of large- and small-game hunting,
trapping, fishing, foraging, sago processing, swidden agriculture, and pig
husbandry. There are altitudinal variations in the availability of aquatic resources, large versus small game, naturally occurring sago stands, and areas
suited to the propagation of sago. Banana cultivation and the yields and
efficiency of sago processing are also affected by altitude. Variations in the
mix of subsistence components that make up the economy of each cultural
group are generally intelligible in terms of these altitudinally determined
ecological differences. However, there are differences between similarly
situated tribes that cannot be explained in this way and appear to be attributable to the gendered division of labor. An environmentally suitable resource
such as sago may be underutilized when fuller utilization would create or
exacerbate an imbalance in the proportional contributions of male and female
labor, or entail a rearrangement of the division of labor in order to alleviate
the magnification of an imbalance in these contributions.

Comparative analysis of the division of labor is of particular interest.
Available data show that the division of labor that obtains within a particular
subsistence activity is variable from tribe to tribe but that the range of variation is relatively confined in most instances. The labor expended in the

hunting of large game (wild pig, cassowary, and wallaby) is nearly all male labor, while women may participate significantly in the procurement of small game through hunting, trapping, and foraging. Women contribute more than three-fourths of the labor involved in sago processing and more than half of that involved in gardening in all cases. The Kamula economy combines a reliance on large-game hunting and sago processing, each of which is undertaken by task groups that are typically gender exclusive. In contrast, the Etoro economy is more heavily weighted toward small- rather than large-game procurement and entails a more balanced dependence on swidden agriculture and sago processing. These major subsistence activities all entail conjugal coproduction, and Etoro male contributions to both gardening and sago processing are at the high end of the scale for the region as a whole. Subsistence food production thus entails cooperation, joint effort, and shared interests on the part of Etoro husbands and wives.

An organization of starch staple production that entails the exchange of labor between a male and female provides a much stronger inducement to marriage (and remarriage) on the part of women than one in which women produce a starch staple (i.e., sago) without male labor inputs, and are self-sufficient in this respect. Moreover, the exchange of labor requires a stable association between coworkers extending over a gardening cycle, while an exchange of the products of labor can be instantaneous and involve different parties from one occasion to the next. Coproduction also provides an impetus to joint consumption on the part of those whose labor is intermingled in the foods produced. Differences in the specific mode of the gendered division of labor thus have a broad range of differential effects upon conjugal relations and social relations between males and females more generally. These differences in the division of labor are relevant to the critique of the brideservice model presented in the concluding chapter.

While the Kamula division of labor is culturally formulated in terms of a naturalistic concept of gendered capabilities, the Etoro division of labor is not a locus for the formulation of gender differentiation. On the contrary, gender differences are effaced in the realm of production since some women hunt and bachelors garden and process sago on their own in conjunction with male initiation. Although there are two male-exclusive subsistence activities (large-game hunting and fish poisoning) and a notion of gendered capabilities with respect to the extensive tree felling involved in garden clearance, women as well as men are seen to chase game, climb and fell trees, and check traps, while men as well as women plant and weed gardens and sometimes perform all the tasks involved in sago processing. Gender differences are thus blurred rather than highlighted in Etoro subsistence food production.

Quantitative data pertaining to Etoro male and female labor inputs are also presented in chapter 2. These show that the division of labor entails more hours of male than female labor per week. The exchange of labor between the genders thus favors women in this respect.

Patterns of food consumption are quite egalitarian in terms of nutritional values, although certain spiritually significant game animals are reserved for senior men by a system of food taboos. Starch staple production is readily expandable, and these foods are available to individuals in essentially whatever quantity they desire. Animal protein is in more limited supply and is less amenable to increased production. Over the course of a lifetime, women are slightly favored over men with respect to consumption of animal protein, but this constitutes only a minor deviation from nutritional equality in consumption.

The Etoro economy thus evidences a number of egalitarian features with respect to production and consumption. However, men predominate in the distribution of those products that are given to extrafamilial kin and co-resident community members. Men thus build social relations and attain prestige through generosity in a way that women do not. This is largely attributable to the division of labor and the division of prestige value accorded to the products of labor. As is typically the case in simple societies, the producer holds distributional rights over the products of his or her own labor (Collier 1988:30). Men thus hold distributional rights over fish and the large game that they alone hunt and trap. Men predominate in the procurement of midsize game and thus in the distribution of these game animals as well. Since prestige enhancing generosity is culturally defined in terms of distributing game to all coresidents, men are in a position to earn prestige by distributing the products of their own labor. Although there is thus an economically derived inequality between the genders with respect to prestige, this is not attributable to appropriation of the products of female labor. Prestige is earned through individual effort, and the male attainment of prestige is consequently not dependent upon female labor. Moreover, generosity is but one component of the prestige system, and the others are unrelated to the economy. I will return to this point momentarily.

Although the producer holds distributional rights over the products of his or her own labor in simple societies, the identity of the producer is only unambiguous when production is strictly individualistic. When labor is combined in group hunting or conjugal coproduction, the allocation of distributional rights is governed by cultural conventions and is not entirely the pragmatic product of labor inputs. In the Etoro case, the "producer" is culturally defined as the individual who completes the process of production. Distributional rights over items coproduced by husbands and wives are allocated accordingly. Women thus hold distributional rights over starch staples (sago and root crops) that are predominantly distributed to family members, while men hold distributional rights over domesticated pigs and certain cultivated foods such as marita pandanus that are subject to extrafamilial distribution. Nearly all the pigs that are jointly reared by husband and wife are deployed in affinal exchange in which half the animal (one side of pork) is given to the wife's brother or father so that the kinship interests of the wife as well as the husband are served. Sides of pork received in exchange are distributed to coresident agnates and matrilateral siblings, each of whom shares his portion with his wife.

Although men hold distributional rights over pigs whose production entails a female labor component, the exercise of these rights is not a significant source of prestige attainment. The reasons for this are twofold. First, the prestige value of domesticated pigs is less than that of game because game is offered up by powerful spirit entities while domestic pigs are entirely mundane and lack any ambrosial qualities. Second, the extrafamilial distribution of pigs lacks several of the central dimensions of generosity as culturally defined. Neither the giving of a side of pork to an affine nor the distribution of one received in exchange entails the communitywide sharing that is the hallmark of such generosity. Unlike game, the pork distributed is not a product of the distributor's skill and effort, but of that of his affine. These transactions in pork are consequently not particularly prestige enhancing but rather entail fulfillment of reciprocal obligations.

It is noteworthy that those who hold the most prestigious statuses—spirit mediums and respected senior men who serve as community leaders (i.e., *tafidilos*)—own fewer pigs than equivalently aged peers who lack such statuses. Although *tafidilos* are renowned for generosity in game distribution, some of them own no pigs at all. The means and relations of pig production (entailing a significant female labor contribution) thus constitute only a minor exception to the central point noted above: that male prestige attainment is not dependent upon female labor or appropriation of the products of female labor. Although distributional rights over pigs enable men to engage in system-maintaining affinal exchanges, these exchanges are of an obligatory nature and consequently are not a vehicle for prestige enhancement. (The centrality of elective social action to prestige will be explicitly taken up a little further along in this introduction.)

The detailed account of Etoro social relations of subsistence food production, distribution, and consumption presented in chapter 2 provides a basis for assessing economic sources and dimensions of social inequality. The gendered division of labor constitutes a form of social differentiation that is morally evaluated by the division of value accorded to labor. The division of labor is thus a source of social inequality, but the differential moral evaluation that engenders this is derived from the cosmological system rather than from economic processes per se. The starch staples that are the principal products of female labor are mundane, while the fish and game that are the products of male labor are made available by the spirits and betoken the beneficence of the latter. Women's labor is merely work, while men's labor entails communion with the supernatural and is grounded in a spiritual affinity. In this respect, the economy represents a domain of relations upon which cosmologically based inequalities have been inscribed.

An evaluation of the Etoro economy in terms of labor expenditure and the allocation of material rewards leads to the conclusion that women are favored over men since women perform fewer hours of labor per week and have somewhat superior access to available animal protein. From this vantage point, it could be concluded that the gendered division of labor institutes an exchange of labor, and the products of labor, that eventuates in a measure of female appropriation of the fruits of male effort. This conclusion is amplified by consideration of the cultural value of the items given and received, since women obtain a more valuable product (game) in exchange for a less valuable one (starch staples) as well as devoting fewer hours to the production of the foods they exchange. However, an evaluation of the results of the division of labor in terms of a metric of prestige rather than material rewards is conducive to quite different conclusions. The tasks accorded to men eventuate in the production and communitywide distribution of culturally prized foods and in the attainment of prestige through the acts of generosity this entails. The tasks accorded to women eventuate in the production of mundane staples that are not prized and are subject to familial distribution that is not productive of prestige. Although women are somewhat advantaged in terms of material rewards they are markedly disadvantaged in terms of prestige. Moreover, it is evident that differential prestige is not accompanied by differential economic privilege. Prestige is not associated with reduced work or enhanced consumption. While subsequent chapters reveal that prestige and certain forms of privilege and prerogative do go hand in hand, these culturally pertinent advantages are noneconomic in character.

The male attainment of prestige through generosity in the distribution of game is grounded in the division of labor rather than appropriation of distributional control over the products of female labor. There is no prestige-enhancing use to which another person's labor can be directly applied and thus no benefit to be gained from the labor of another person other than a reduction of one's own workload. Moreover, the gendered division of labor imposes constraints upon the substitution of female for male labor in subsistence food production. A man with two wives thus nearly doubles his labor expenditure in gardening and sago processing and consequently has less rather than more time to devote to prestige-enhancing endeavors. Although women have restricted opportunities to earn prestige, the male attainment of prestige is dependent upon male rather than female labor. The Etoro subsistence economy also lacks several important sources of inequality present in other tribal economic systems, in that surpluses cannot be deployed to gain control over persons or the productive process, and relations of economic indebtedness are entirely absent. These and other comparatively egalitarian features of the Etoro economy are summarized at the conclusion of chapter 2 in conjunction with an examination of Woodburn's (1982) recent reformulation of the concept of egalitarian societies.

Consideration of the data presented in chapter 2 is conducive to the conclusion that the economic organization of subsistence food production is not a central locus for the production of social inequality. The social relations that govern the deployment of labor and allocation of the products of labor are principally relations of conjugality, siblingship, affinity, and community membership, whose formulation is external to and independent of the labor process. Moreover, relations of (subsistence food) production are not a source of relations of control over other persons that can be exercised in other areas of social life. Although the division of labor institutes an exchange of labor and the products of labor between male and female coproducers, neither party gains control over the other. In this respect, the principal effect of the division of labor is thus to provide an economic inducement to marriage (cf. Levi-Strauss 1971). This is somewhat asymmetrical in that women are dependent upon male labor for forest clearance preparatory to cultivation, while men are not comparably dependent upon women for performance of a task that they regard themselves as unable to undertake. However, this asymmetry in one economic inducement to marriage is counterbalanced by other economic and noneconomic inducements so that marriage is highly desirable for both men and women, albeit for somewhat different reasons. More importantly, female dependence upon males for forest clearance does not constitute a basis for a husband's or father's exercise of authority over the person of his wife or daughter due to the social substitutability intrinsic to a network of kin relations. Other kinsmen can perform this task.

Although the division of labor constitutes a form of morally evaluated social differentiation, the resultant inequalities are not generated by relations of production but are inscribed upon those relations by values that have their source within the cosmological system. Thus both the (kinship-based) formulation and (cosmologically grounded) valuation of relations of production are external to and independent of the labor process.

The gendered division of labor provides males and females with unequal opportunities to attain prestige through generosity and in this respect constitutes a locus for the production of inequality. However, the means and relations of the production and allocation of prestige and moral superiority are more broadly linked to the perpetuation of life across generations. Generosity is manifested not only in the provision of growth-inducing food (i.e., game) but also in the transmission of a life force embodied in male semen

(as will be explained further along). Stigma, the negative reciprocal of prestige, is associated with witchcraft that entails the selfish appropriation of this
life force. Confirmed witches occupy the lowest rung of the prestige hierarchy, while spirit mediums and *tafidilos* occupy the highest. Spirit mediums
contribute to the perpetuation of life by curing potentially lethal witchcraft-
induced illness. *Tafidilos* are respected senior men who are free of the taint
and stigma of witchcraft and who have made generous contributions to the
perpetuation of life through donations of semen and game over the years.
An understanding of moral hierarchy and the interrelated system of prestige
production and allocation is critical to the elucidation of Etoro social inequality, but both of these are principally grounded in cosmological formulations
pertaining to the transmission of life force rather than being grounded in
economic process. Only one dimension of prestige production is contingent
upon the relations of subsistence food production (organized by the gendered
division of labor). Moreover, other dimensions of the prestige hierarchy
cannot be explicated as derivatives of this. This is at variance with the
expectations of the Marxian theory of social inequality founded on the key
proposition that all social inequalities are grounded in the dynamics of a
particular mode of production and are either directly generated by this or
built on core relations of inequality that are so generated. (See Wolf 1981 for
a particularly clear presentation of the centrality of this proposition to the
Marxian approach.) The absence of covariation between inequalities of prestige and inequalities of material advantage (in the form of reduced labor
inputs and privileged consumption) is also problematic from a Marxian perspective. Although consideration of Etoro relations of production provides
an essential precursor to the subsequent evaluation of Collier's formulation,
such consideration only very partially elucidates Etoro social inequality.

    As was noted earlier, social inequality can be minimally defined as
social differentiation accompanied by differential moral evaluation. This
minimal degree of inequality pertaining to a set of morally evaluated social
categories is characteristically amplified by corresponding differences in the
distribution of prestige (and stigma), privilege (and debility), and other culturally pertinent advantages (and disadvantages). However both the extent
to which various forms of advantage are elaborated and the degree to which
all of these are perfectly aligned with the hierarchical order implicit in morally evaluated social differentiation are variable and require specific ethnographic documentation. Elucidating the cultural construction of the Etoro
scheme of morally evaluated social differentiation is the principal objective
of chapter 3. Evaluating the distribution of prestige, stigma, privilege, debility, advantage, and disadvantage is a central theme that runs through chapters
4, 5, and 6.

    Etoro metaphysical formulations—pertaining to the fundamental causes and processes of being and becoming—delineate the physical and spiritual components of the person, successive transformations of these constitutional components over the life course, and the positive and negative contributions of specified human and supernatural agents to the life-cycle processes of procreation, growth, maturation, senescence, and death. These metaphysical formulations thus comprehend not only the reproduction of mature social persons but also their dissolution and death. Social categories are simultaneously delineated and valorized in terms of differences in physical and spiritual constitution, in terms of stages in the transformation of these constitutional components, and in terms of the role played by members of one category in the life-cycle transformations of others. Males and females differ in physical and spiritual constitution and particularly in their contributions to reproduction. Although the corporeal components of bone and flesh are respectively derived from paternal semen and maternal blood, semen is also a source of the animating principle of an individual's spiritual constitution. Males are depleted by the transmission of this life force to others in both heterosexual and homosexual relations and thus undergo senescence, decline, and death in order to bring about the conception, growth, and maturation of the succeeding generation. A number of social categories of males are differentiated in terms of the roles they play in receiving and transmitting life force at different stages of the life cycle. Prereproductive, reproductive, and postreproductive females are likewise differentiated as social categories in terms of their contributions to the perpetuation of life across generations. Witches extract the life force of others, causing illness and death, while spirit mediums seek to cure, thwart, and combat witchcraft.

Differential moral qualities are implicit components of the defining characteristics of each social category of persons. Senior men who have brought about the growth and maturation of others at the expense of their own vitality are intrinsically generous. Spirit mediums seek to protect life, while witches seek to appropriate it in an ongoing contest between the forces of good and evil. The cosmological system thus provides the foundation for a scheme of social differentiation in which moral evaluation is intrinsically embedded. Social inequality is thus fabricated as a moral hierarchy or hierarchy of virtue.

There are two aspects of virtue, exemplified by the difference between virtuousness and virtuosity. Generosity is a virtue in the Etoro system of moral evaluation, and senior men are intrinsically virtuous as a result of their substantial contributions to the perpetuation of life. Virtue is thus assigned or ascribed to this social category of men (with grown children and mature inseminees) on the basis of the completion of acts that are normative and obligatory rather than elective. However, individuals also differ in the extent to which they have engaged in the generous distribution of growth-inducing game to others. These differences in merit or distinction (i.e., in virtuosity) are based upon skill and effort in hunting, as well as a propensity to regularly distribute the proceeds of the hunt to coresidents. Some men hunt more frequently and for longer hours than others and also regularly engage in the widespread distribution of game to coresidents of the longhouse community (rather than adopting a more restricted distribution at a garden house). There is a choice involved both in the effort devoted to hunting and in the mode of distribution. Distinction with respect to the virtue of generosity is thus a result of achievement within a framework of elective social action. In this study, prestige is defined as the esteem accorded to distinction in the attainment of virtues that are achieved in this way. While the system of moral evaluation can thus be defined as the component of the value system that delineates virtues and their opposites (such as generosity and self-aggrandizement), the prestige system pertains to the achievable virtues or aspects of virtue that differentiate individuals (as opposed to the virtues or aspects of virtue that are ascribed to a categorical social status). The system of moral evaluation thus provides the basis for two distinct but interrelated foundations of social inequality, a moral hierarchy and a prestige system, or, more accurately, a prestige/stigma system.

Prestige is accorded to individuals on the basis of distinction in the performance of culturally valued activities that are imbued with virtue, while stigma is likewise earned by the performance of morally despicable acts of witchcraft. Although witches constitute a category of persons who possess a distinctive spiritual constitution that enables them to perform supernatural acts of witchcraft, the deployment of these powers to bewitch someone is nevertheless regarded as the product of a conscious choice. The performance of witchcraft is thus an elective social act. The counteractions employed by mediums are elective as well. Healing and thwarting witchcraft are quintessential examples of culturally valued activities imbued with virtue. Thus spirit mediumship is at the apex of the prestige/stigma hierarchy.

The prestige/stigma system provides universal metrics applicable to all members of the social system. Since game is procured by men, women, and children, everyone can be evaluated in terms of distinction in the breadth and frequency of game distribution (even though the outcome is significantly prefigured by the division of labor). Although the distribution of prestige tends to covary with the moral hierarchy of ascribed virtue in certain respects, there is no one-to-one relation between these. Moreover, the degree of covariation that obtains is not a product of the system of moral evaluation per se but is contingent upon extrinsic factors. Thus the division of labor is instrumental to producing a significant degree of alignment between the moral hierarchy and the prestige hierarchy (with respect to game distribution). In other respects these are not perfectly aligned. Spirit mediums are young men (who are bachelors at the inception of their careers) and thus occupy only a moderately positive position in the moral hierarchy of ascribed virtue. However, mediums occupy the highest rung of the prestige hierarchy, followed closely by *tafidilos*. Although *tafidilos* are elder senior men, this achieved status does not encompass all members of this gendered life-cycle category. It is restricted to elder senior men who are free of the taint and stigma of witchcraft, who have made generous distributions of growth-inducing game to coresidents over the years, and who are pivotal figures in many aspects of the social life of the community. The witch represents both the lowest category in the moral hierarchy (delineated by spiritual constitution and role in life-cycle transformations) and also a stigmatized status in the prestige/stigma hierarchy. The witch/nonwitch distinction is a universal metric of evaluation and anyone, irrespective of age and gender, may be a witch. A witchcraft accusation both recruits an individual to this category in the moral hierarchy and simultaneously accords the individual a stigmatized status that negates prestige. The bottom rungs of both hierarchies are thus congruent.

The relative positions of statuses in both hierarchies are shown diagrammatically below. This also brings out a notable structural difference between them: the prestige/stigma hierarchy is binary and lacks an intermediate status,

Moral Hierarchy		*Prestige/Stigma Hierarchy*	
Moral Standing			Social Standing
high	Senior men ($\geq$ age 46)	Spirit mediums *Tafidilos*	high
	Ever-married men ($<$ age 46) Initiated bachelors ($\geq$ age 20)		
neutral	Married women of reproductive age Children Postreproductive married women ($\geq$ age 50) Uninitiated adolescent males (age 14–19) Prereproductive married women Unremarried widows Divorcées		
low	Witches *Sa:gos*	Witches *Sa:gos*	low

while the moral hierarchy entails a continuum of gradations that includes a point of moral neutrality. While women are included within the graded moral hierarchy, the only status they are eligible to occupy in the prestige/stigma hierarchy is that of witch. The statuses of spirit medium, *tafidilo* and *sa:go* (or superwitch) are all male-exclusive. Although women can earn prestige through game distribution, they are ineligible for the statuses that concretize prestige attainment.

Investigation of the cosmological foundations of the system of moral evaluation not only elucidates the fabrication of a moral hierarchy (of morally evaluated social differentiation) but also elucidates the bases for earning prestige and the morally just deserts of stigma. Examination of the system of moral evaluation thus provides a productive point of departure for examination of the prestige system. It likewise provides a useful entrée into the investigation of privilege, since privilege is constituted as socially legitimated advantage and the same cosmological principles that inform moral evaluation also underwrite the legitimation of advantage. Chapter 3 thus lays the groundwork for a systematic inquiry that proceeds from the delineation of morally evaluated social differentiation to consideration of the distribution of prestige (stigma), privilege (debility), and other culturally pertinent advantages (and disadvantages).

Specification of the cosmological foundations of morally evaluated social differentiation raises several important questions. If the grounding of social inequality is essentially ideological, in what sense is that ideology hegemonic? Moreover, are the critical valuations that provide the basis of moral hierarchy shared or contested? These questions are addressed in the last section of chapter 3, through the analysis of gendered interpretations of myths that provide a commentary on fundamental cosmological doctrines of male sexual and spiritual depletion. This inquiry leads to the conclusion that these doctrines are not contested but rather constitute the underlying premise of what is contested, namely the question of whether male sexual and spiritual depletion is a result of male lust or the sexually predatory nature of women. It is thus attribution of responsibility for the ultimately fatal loss of male vitality that is at issue. The basis of male moral superiority is conceded by the terms of the debate, since the mutually acknowledged male depletion underwrites the concept of intrinsic male generosity. What is contested is whether women are morally neutral (insofar as men are responsible for their own depletion and death) or morally negative (as active agents of depletion that are analogues of the witch). The fundamental doctrine that provides the basis of the moral hierarchy is thus shared. The cosmologically grounded ideology is hegemonic both because the core principles of it are uncontested and because it is institutionalized. Both men and women live in a social world shaped by it.

While the cosmologically grounded moral hierarchy of ascribed virtue constitutes the main focus of chapter 3, chapters 4 and 5 are directed to elucidation of the prestige/stigma hierarchy based on achieved distinction. The stigmatized social status of the witch is examined in chapter 4, and the prestigious statuses of spirit medium and *tafidilo* are considered in the following chapter.

There are two central components of statuses in the prestige/stigma hierarchy. They are both earned through elective social action and bestowed upon an individual by the members of society as an acknowledged social standing. Selected individuals are thus assigned the prestigious status of *tafidilo* or the stigmatized status of witch by others on the basis of achieved distinction in the attainment of commendable virtue or morally despicable vice, respectively. From a cultural perspective, the elements of earned distinction and societal recognition are equally present in both instances.

However, no one aspires to attain the stigmatized status of witch, and the elective acts that constitute a prerequisite are inscrutable insofar as they have taken place upon an invisible plane of existence. The analysis of stigma thus necessarily focuses on the manner in which it is assigned, the issue of control over this process, and the question of the social characteristics of the individuals accorded a stigmatized status. The intriguing question of what an individual actually does to earn this status is largely inaccessible to analysis because societal labeling recontextualized the individual's prior life history, and retrospective accounts serve to validate the categorization. Alienation insures that the individuals assigned stigma will currently manifest the requisite traits of being ungenerous, ill-tempered, and lacking in a community-spirited nature. Witches also appear to be prone to interpersonal conflict since they are the respondents in conflicts generated by others and are typically blamed for whatever goes amiss (i.e., the disappearance of a pig).

In contrast, those who are accorded *tafidilo* status are generous, good-natured, community-spirited individuals who have positive social relations with their coresidents. The Etoro say that a *tafidilo* should ideally possess the following qualities: the ability to command respect, articulateness (such that "people listen when he talks"), physical strength and endurance, courage in battle, generosity, and a reputation as an enthusiastic worker in communal enterprises and a conformist with regard to cultural rules and values. However, a number of these qualities are ascribed to the status itself. A *tafidilo* commands respect by virtue of being a *tafidilo*, and people "listen when he talks" for the same reason. Retrospective accounts may validate his courage in battle and the past performance of feats of strength. The processes of labeling and ex post facto attribution thus operate in this instance as well. However, the characteristics of a *tafidilo* are also empirically manifested through social action in the present and are consequently amenable to analysis in a way that the deeds of a witch are not. Generosity, for example, can be measured. The earned aspect of prestige can thus be investigated. It is the bestowed aspect that remains somewhat opaque, since this is a matter of public opinion. A man is a *tafidilo* if people say that he is; there is no formal process of designation or investiture. This contrasts with the complex and lengthy formal procedure involved in definitively establishing that an individual is responsible for bringing about a particular death by witchcraft, and is veritably a witch. Although analysis highlights the earned aspect of prestige and the socially assigned aspect of stigma, it is important to recognize that both aspects are relevant to each of these statuses. Prestige and stigma are the reciprocal components of a conceptually unified system.

An authenticated witchcraft accusation recruits an individual to membership in a morally reviled category and simultaneously assigns a stigmatized status that imposes marked disabilities. The accuser may justifiably and legitimately execute the witch without incurring any actual risk of retaliation. Alternatively, the accuser may, at his option, demand compensation in lieu of retribution. This is the more prevalent course of action. However, the accused's life is then placed in jeopardy as surety for compensation, the payment of which intrinsically entails an admission of guilt. The accused draws on his kinsmen for support but in so doing puts strains upon these relations that have a cumulative effect. Two-thirds of the accusations are within the longhouse community, and these almost invariably lead to the witch's migration to another community where he or she has diminished kin support and is very likely to attract a subsequent accusation. Available data indicate that a once-accused witch is often accused again and again and eventually executed. Nineteen percent of all recorded accusations (8 of 42) during a four-year period were resolved through execution. Assignment to the stigmatized status of witch thus entails the likely prospect of a short and distinctively unhappy life punctuated by repeated social conflict that is accompanied by progressively diminished support. In the end, the closest kin of a witch who has been subject to multiple accusations welcome the denouement that rids them of an otherwise permanent social liability.

An authenticated witchcraft accusation also negates the prospect of prestige attainment. A known witch will not be nominated for apprenticeship by an established medium and is likewise precluded from achieving *tafidilo* status. An accusation against an established medium or *tafidilo* (or a member of either's immediate family) may prompt migration to another community, leading to temporary or permanent loss of the functional positions of established practitioner and community leader, respectively. A witchcraft accusation thus has the capacity to strip away the central prerogatives that accrue to individuals who have achieved these prestigious statuses. Such accusations are also politically significant in that they figure in succession to the positions of senior resident medium and leading *tafidilo* of a longhouse community.

The assignment of stigma and disability in the form of a witchcraft accusation constitutes an arena of power with respect to social inequality. Chapter 4 focuses on the central questions this raises. What is the nature of the complex process through which accusations are formulated, authenticated, confirmed, and ultimately resolved by execution or payment of compensation? What influences are exerted by the next of kin of the deceased victim, public opinion, *tafidilos,* and mediums in determining the identity of the witch responsible for a death? How are accusations distributed among socially differentiated categories of persons, and to what extent does this distribution conform to the contours of the cosmologically grounded moral hierarchy?

Identification of a witch is initiated by the deceased's next of kin who places two names before an oracle. The selection of suspects is influenced by the deathbed testimony of the deceased and by public opinion, which is in turn influenced by *tafidilos* and the preliminary information derived from a spirit inquest conducted by the senior resident medium. The entranced medium's spirits authenticate the results of a second, publicly performed oracle and confirm the identity of the witch responsible for the death. The medium's spirits may also authorize and legitimate execution of the witch.

The distribution of accusations by age and gender favors women and seniors, in that males as a group are disproportionately accused and individuals over the age of 40 are infrequently subject to an accusation. Adolescent males (aged 14 to 20) and young women (aged 16 to 20) are both subject to a high rate of accusations. These patterns are congruent with the moral hierarchy and the role of these respective age and gender categories in the system of life-force transmission that informs it. However, males aged 31 to 40 are subject to the highest incidence of accusations (relative to their representation in the population), and this is incongruent with the moral hierarchy. This aspect of the distribution of accusations is a product of male control over the machinery through which accusations are formulated and authenticated, combined with status competition. Some of these accusations are directed against established mediums, while all of them disqualify those accused from subsequent attainment of *tafidilo* status (excepting those accusations that are unauthenticated).

Male control over the resolution of accusations (as well as their formulation) has significant repercussions with respect to gender inequality. When a woman is accused, compensation is paid by her husband and brother (or father). Women are consequently rendered dependent upon these men by the complex of beliefs and practices relating to the formulation and resolution of witchcraft accusations. The domain of witchcraft is thus a central locus for the production of male control and female dependence that extends into other domains of social life. However, the domain of witchcraft is at the same time an integral component of the prestige/stigma system.

One of the principal objectives of chapter 5 is to elucidate the means by which individuals achieve the prestigious statuses of medium and *tafidilo* and their subsequent progression from novice or aspirant to eventual retiree. Recently initiated bachelors (aged 19 to 20) are nominated for mediumship by the spirits of an established practitioner and commence an apprenticeship under him if they elect to answer the call. Available data indicate that more than half of the eligible young men are offered the opportunity to become mediums, but declinations and attrition among novices subsequently reduce the ranks of mediums so that they comprise 18.5 percent of men aged 21 to 45. Mediums generally cease to practice in their early to middle forties, typically relinquishing their position in favor of a protégé they have trained. Mediums related as mentor and protégé usually coreside. The presence of two mediums in a community who are not so related is infrequent and of short duration. Competition is intrinsic to relations between mediums and is contained only by the mentor-protégé relationship (although it occasionally occurs in that context as well). Mediums can be linked directly or indirectly to both the formulation and authentication of nearly all witchcraft accusations directed against mediums and members of their families. Such accusations play a role in succession to the position of senior resident medium in some instances. The senior resident medium has jurisdiction over determination of the identity of the witch responsible for any deaths that occur within the community. Only his spirits can legitimately authenticate an accusation and legitimately authorize execution. A protégé serves as a second, coparticipating in cures and ratifying the pronouncements of his mentor with respect to witchcraft.

While mediums as a group occupy the apex of the prestige hierarchy—as a consequence of the life-giving and life-sustaining role of their spirits—senior resident mediums also constitute a socially powerful elite. The prerogative of authenticating accusations confers substantial influence in the assignment of stigma, and the prerogative of authorizing execution likewise enables senior mediums to play a significant role in giving direction to lethal violence. Moreover, mediums possess spiritual authority in that the spirits of which they are vessels express revealed truth. Séances provide a forum for interpretively constructing the meaning of current events and enunciating prophecies that influence subsequent social action. Mediums also represent and recreate the cosmology that underwrites the moral hierarchy and prestige hierarchy. The ultimate virtue of contributing to the perpetuation of life across generations is most perfectly realized by the life-giving and life-sustaining role of their spirits. The most active of these in curing and detecting witchcraft is a woman, the medium's spirit wife. The implications of this cosmological construction of the spirit order are also examined in this chapter. However, it may be noted here that this ingenious construction is indicative of a medium's capacity to shape basic tenets of belief. It is implausible that anyone else would formulate spiritual power as invested in a woman who is not only under male control, but specifically under the control of her medium husband. The spirit wife is helpful, cooperative, loyal, trustworthy, and diligent in furthering the enterprises of the latter.

Tafidilos are active, respected senior men of the age group containing individuals whose children and inseminees are typically fully grown. This status is achieved through the accumulation of prestige and the avoidance of stigma and serves as a prerequisite for assuming a leadership role in a longhouse community. More than half (58 percent) of the men aged 46 to 60 are regarded as *tafidilos,* while a few exceptional individuals achieve this status as early as their late thirties or remain sufficiently vigorous to retain it beyond the age of 60.

Tafidilo status is achieved by attaining prestige through generosity in the frequent distribution of growth-inducing game to coresidents and is maintained in the same manner. An elder *tafidilo* who ceases to hunt and trap is no longer regarded as such. There are generally one or two *tafidilos* per longhouse community, and the leading *tafidilo* is typically the man who distributes the greatest quantity of game to coresidents. In one documented instance this amounted to more than half the total bag weight of the game consumed by community members over the course of a year. Most senior men are capable of achieving *tafidilo* status because the requisite skills are largely a product of experience, and hunting productivity also increases in accordance with increased effort. Senior men devote more hours to hunting than others and also achieve a higher rate of return. Men who have previously been accused of witchcraft are excluded from the ranks of *tafidilos* and also rarely engage in the distribution of game to coresidents. Prominence in game distribution is indexical with respect to most of the qualities a *tafidilo* should ideally possess. An individual who achieves distinction in this regard is, by definition, generous and hardworking, and likewise by definition possesses continued vigor and endurance in later middle age, conforms to key cultural values, and commands respect. As noted earlier, many of the requisite qualities are also artifacts of the status itself. A *tafidilo* commands respect by virtue of being a *tafidilo,* and by the same token "people listen when he talks."

Tafidilos are prominent in the organization of collective community enterprises such as communal gardening, longhouse construction, and preparations for hosting *kosa* ceremonies. They also coordinate multicommunity endeavors such as male initiation and raids directed against the longhouses of other tribes. A *tafidilo* leads by example and devotes more effort than others to longhouse construction and tree felling preparatory to cultivation. A *tafidilo* undertakes the dangerous role of covering the rear of a retreating raiding party and is likewise in the forefront of battle when armed conflict occurs between Etoro longhouse communities.

When there are several *tafidilos* in a community, they share the organizational prerogatives, with the younger man taking precedence in those activities requiring strength and endurance and the older man taking precedence in the remainder (e.g., selecting sites for communal gardens). The more active man is recognized as the leading *tafidilo*. In contrast to relations among mediums, there is no evidence of competition among *tafidilos*. The latter are never subject to an authenticated witchcraft accusation. However, an accusation against a *tafidilo's* wife or child may lead to his migration to another community, and such accusations thus sometimes play a role in succession to the position of community leader. But in these instances there is no evidence linking the beneficiary to the formulation of the accusation. Succession normally occurs through the death or retirement of the more senior *tafidilo*. The median age of the 32 males who died during a four-year sample period is only 38 so that the number of eligibly aged men (who are 46 to 60) is not great, and the mortality rate among them is high.

Although most men who survive to the eligible age attain *tafidilo* status and routinely succeed to the position of leading *tafidilo*, those included in the latter category are the members of an elite comprising only 7.9 percent of the male population over the age of 20. Senior resident mediums comprise 5.6 percent of this same population. The leading *tafidilos* and senior resident mediums constitute a power elite that exercises significant influence over important events in the social life of their communities. An extremely select group of men graduate from senior resident medium to *tafidilo* status and are members of this elite throughout their adult lives. The protégés of such men may also serve as senior resident mediums in several communities so that they possess very considerable influence. However, high mortality makes the probability of achieving and sustaining such a position of influence extremely low. Moreover, those individuals who do attain such a position invariably experience a comedown connected in one way or another to a witchcraft accusation against a family member or protégé.

The privileges, prerogatives, and other culturally pertinent advantages enjoyed by spirit mediums and *tafidilos* are also investigated in chapter 5. The principal advantages of both statuses are the prestige intrinsically associated with them and the prerogatives derived from serving in the respective positions of senior resident medium and community leader. Influence in shaping the course of events within a community is intrinsic to these positions, and those who occupy them are prominent in all decision-making processes pertaining to social conflict and to the assignment of stigma. In contrast, mediums and *tafidilos* who have the acknowledged status but lack these positions are not influential (i.e., junior mediums and *tafidilos* who have recently migrated to another community).

Spirit mediums are economically undifferentiated from other men their age with respect to production, distribution, and consumption, with the sole exception of their organization and direction of fish poisoning (i.e., one productive activity). *Tafidilos* are prominent in the organization of production, and in distribution, but do not enjoy privileged consumption. A prestigious status confers almost no material benefits in practice. Mediums are entitled to be polygynous but are not in fact more likely to have two wives than other men of the same age. *Tafidilos* are more likely to have several wives than other men of the same age, but none of the leading *tafidilos* of longhouse communities was in fact polygynous. Polygyny on the part of *tafidilos* is very strongly correlated with the temporary or permanent loss of the position of community leader due to migration following a witchcraft accusation directed against a wife or child. Neither mediums nor *tafidilos* are significantly less likely to themselves be accused of witchcraft than other men of the same age. *Tafidilos* are not advantaged in this respect because no men over the age of 40 were subject to an authenticated witchcraft accusation during the four-year sample period (during which there were a total of 42 accusations). Mediums are not significantly advantaged because they tend to engineer witchcraft accusations against each other and thus are accused as often as other men of the same age. Prestige is not translated into material benefits or other advantages apart from the prerogatives intrinsic to the positions of senior resident medium and leading *tafidilo*.

Chapter 6 is concerned with the production and circulation of wealth in the form of shell valuables that are acquired in external trade, constitute an accumulable medium of exchange, and are deployed internally in bridewealth, compensation, and ceremonial payments. Examination of the circulation of wealth in these social payments constitutes an extension of the general inquiry into the distribution of advantage noted above. Moreover, there are a number of theoretical formulations that posit a causal interconnection between control over such forms of wealth and social inequality. Chapter 6 thus constitutes a precursor to the critical evaluation of theories of social inequality in chapter 7. The data presented provide the grounds for evaluating Meillassoux's (1964) contention that control over matrimonial goods engenders control over social reproduction that ensures both dependence on the part of junior males and their concomitant subjugation to the authority of the elders. Collier and Rosaldo (1981:288) further extend this formulation in proposing that bridewealth requirements determine conjugal as well as junior/

senior relations of production that in turn engender social inequality. These formulations are consistent with a long-standing received wisdom dating back to Engels ([1884] 1942): when transactions in valuables are integral to a social system, unequal accumulation and/or relations of dependence and indebtedness are inevitable.

In the Etoro case, shell valuables are acquired through external trade carried out almost exclusively by recently initiated bachelors. A young man provides a little more than half of his own bridewealth payment (in terms of total value) and derives another quarter of it from the contributions of other bachelors. Items locally procured or manufactured by these bachelors are exchanged for shell valuables in the Highlands; the latter are then used to obtain more highly valued lowland products (e.g., tree oil) from neighboring Strickland-Bosavi tribes that are in turn exchanged for a greater quantity of shell valuables in the Highlands. This circuit can be continued indefinitely until the groom's expected contribution to his own bridewealth is accumulated. Junior males rather than senior males thus control matrimonial goods. They also obtain them through their own efforts and are not dependent upon either female labor or senior males' provision of the items initially employed in trade. Bridewealth requirements therefore do not engender dependence and subjugation to authority on the part of junior males and do not shape relations of production.

The Etoro are consequently classified as a "brideservice" (rather than an "equal bridewealth") society in terms of Collier's (1988) typology. As was noted earlier, the Etoro are designated as one of a number of ethnographic cases to which the brideservice model might fruitfully be applied (Collier 1988:258). The Etoro are thus included in a category that encompasses the erstwhile "egalitarian societies." This classification is appropriate. The extent to which the brideservice model elucidates social inequality in the Etoro and other cases is addressed in the concluding chapter.

The pool of shell valuables initially accumulated by a young man is not replenished by trade later in life. It is deployed to provide the bulk of his own bridewealth payment, to contribute to the social payments of others, and to obtain essential commodities (salt and axes) procured through external trade. The internal circulation of wealth entails contributions to these social payments (bridewealth, witchcraft compensation, and homicide compensation) and their subsequent redistribution to a number of recipients. This total cycle of accumulation and redistribution of valuables contains the possibility for a systematic redistribution of wealth. This potentiality is realized in that individuals contribute to social payments largely in accordance with their ability to do so but receive in redistribution more nearly in proportion to their representation in the population than in proportion to past contributions. Younger men (aged 21 to 40), who have the most substantial holdings of shell valuables, thus donate somewhat more than they receive on each cycle of accumulation and redistribution. The pool of shell valuables a bachelor accumulates in trade is thus progressively diminished over time by this redistributive process and by the conversion of shell valuables into imported commodities. The principal beneficiaries of the redistribution of wealth are women; they receive about 11 percent of the shell valuables when death compensation is distributed to the kin of the deceased. Women retain these valuables for personal adornment so that they do not return to the circulating pool of valuables deployed in social payments except through inheritance. Elder senior men (aged 41 to 60) are also beneficiaries of this redistribution of wealth insofar as they receive somewhat more than they donate to social payments. However, they do not recoup their earlier losses as young men because these losses constitute a larger percentage of substantial holdings while the gains are registered as a smaller percentage of significantly diminished holdings (further eroded by conversion) so that the latter remain at a low level. Inheritance is nominal since elderly men possess very few valuables. The life-cycle pattern entailing the accumulation of shell valuables before marriage followed by progressive depletion that decelerates in later middle age largely parallels the life-cycle pattern that obtains with respect to the transmission of life force. Moreover, shell valuables are symbolic analogues of semen.

The obligation to accumulate witchcraft compensation is diffused over the entire adult male population by the jural minority of women and uninitiated males. Although men over the age of 40 are virtually immune from witchcraft accusations, they are responsible for paying compensation on behalf of wives, sisters, daughters, and adolescent sons. The obligation to contribute to such compensations is likewise broadly diffused. This significantly diminishes the extent to which shell valuables are effectively transferred from witches to nonwitches through payment of witchcraft compensation. However, there is a redistribution of modest proportions. *Tafidilos,* who contribute less than others to witchcraft compensation, are the principal beneficiaries. This enables them to make unsolicited token contributions to the bridewealth payments of distant kin and thereby manifest generosity. *Tafidilos* do not possess larger holdings of shell valuables than other men of the same age but deploy them differently, frequently contributing to bridewealth and infrequently contributing to witchcraft compensation. *Tafidilos* thus engage in prestige-enhancing generosity and accumulate prestige rather than wealth (or the salt, axes, pigs, and Western trade goods into which shell valuables can be converted). This is consistent with the general conclusion that those who attain the prestigious statuses of spirit medium and *tafidilo* do not enjoy any material advantages.

The Etoro case contradicts the received wisdom that wealth inevitably breeds inequality in the form of unequal accumulation and/or relations of dependence and indebtedness. Wealth is concentrated in the hands of junior males rather than in the hands of those who have attained prestigious statuses. Inequalities of prestige are counterbalanced rather than amplified by this countervailing distribution of wealth (and by a largely egalitarian distribution of material benefits more generally). The production of wealth is not grounded in the appropriation of the products of female labor; instead females are the recipients of wealth produced through male effort. In sum, the production and circulation of wealth does not constitute a central locus for the production of social inequality. The Etoro sociocultural system is predominantly economically egalitarian. It is virtue, moral superiority, and prestige rather than material advantages that are unequally distributed.

This book is devoted to the objective of providing a comprehensive account of all aspects of social inequality within the Etoro sociocultural system and is not limited to presenting only those data that can be mapped onto extant theories of social inequality. As noted earlier, the data and analyses presented in the chapters summarized here provide the basis for both a critical evaluation of the brideservice model and the development of an alternative theory concerning the central locus for the production of social inequality in the erstwhile "egalitarian societies." The fundamental inequalities of the Etoro sociocultural system are inscribed in the cosmologically grounded moral hierarchy and the prestige/stigma hierarchy. The inequalities pertaining to the stigmatized status of witch and the prestigious status of spirit medium are neither organized by marriage nor generated by the means and relations of production. Moreover, theoretical formulations that take the prestige system as a point of departure in the analysis of social inequality (e.g., Ortner and Whitehead 1981) have failed to distinguish the moral hierarchy from the prestige hierarchy and have ignored the integral role of stigma in the cultural conceptualization of prestige systems. Omitting consideration of stigma also leads to a failure to appreciate the dimensions of the arena of power intrinsic to the assignment of stigma and debility. Inequalities derived from the organization and channeling of lethal violence can thus be tied to the prestige/stigma system so that violence does not enter into the analysis of social inequality as an acultural component of human (or male) nature. Those are some of the ingredients of the theoretical reformulation presented in the concluding chapter.

CHAPTER 1

The Strickland-Bosavi Tribes

The Etoro are one of eight ethnographically described cultural groups within the Bosavi language family, a linguistic unit that extends southward from the southern rim of the New Guinea Highlands toward the Fly River estuary and is largely bounded by the Strickland River on the west and the Tagari-Gigio-Kikori tributary sequence in the east (see map 1). The Etoro, Onabasulu, Kaluli, Kasua, Kamula, Bedamini, Gebusi, and Samo are similar in economy, social organization, and ritual, and represent historically linked variants of a regional sociocultural system that is interconnected by trade networks and intermarriage between neighboring groups.

Consideration of regional variation informs the analysis of Etoro production, distribution, and exchange of foodstuffs and shell valuables that is presented in subsequent chapters. This regional approach also supplies comparative grounds for evaluating a number of theoretical arguments concerning the relationship between economic organization and inequality in the concluding chapter. The main objective of chapter 1 is thus to lay the groundwork for what follows by providing a general introduction to the region in terms of linguistic affinities, contact history, and the commonalities and variations in sociocultural organization. In introducing the latter, I will focus on variations in the floor plans of the large longhouses that constitute residential, social, and ceremonial centers of community life in all eight cases. The connections between social differentiation, the division and organization of labor, and longhouse design that make this particular comparative analysis a useful point of departure will emerge in the course of the discussion. I will refer to the eight cultural groups with which I am concerned as the Strickland-Bosavi tribes, using "tribe" as a synonym for "sociocultural group" and employing this geographic designation to refer to a regional cluster within a larger linguistic entity.

The Bosavi language family encompasses languages with more than 20 percent shared basic vocabulary (Shaw 1986:52). The percentages of shared basic vocabulary between adjacent, named cultural groups are shown in table 1.1 (based on data reported in Shaw 1986:53).[1] The familiar New Guinea

27

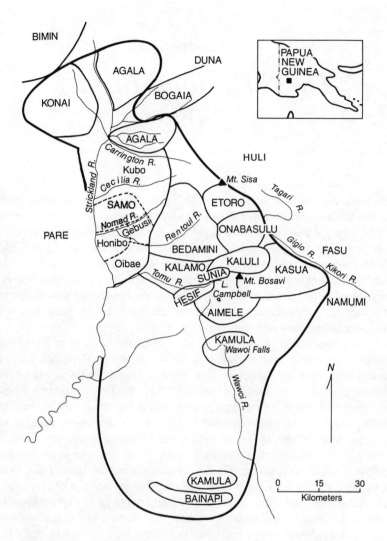

Map 1. The Constituents of the Bosavi Language Family and Adjacent
Linguistic Groups. (Based on Shaw 1990:3)

TABLE 1.1

The Percentage of Shared Basic Vocabulary between Adjacent, Named Cultural
Groups of the Strickland-Bosavi Region (percentage of shared cognates between
adjacent pairs)

	Named Cultural Groups (percentage of shared cognates)	Approximate Number of Speakers in 1981	Total for Subfamily
Strickland Plain subfamily	Konai (67)	450 350	
	Agala (78)		
	Kubo (90)	600	
	Samo (90)	550	
	Gebusi (92)	500	
	Honibo (94)	200	
	Oibae (79)	200	
	Kalamo (71)	300	
	Hesif (35)	200	3,350
Papuan Plateau subfamily	Bedamini (67)	3,800	
	Etoro (58)	750	
	Onabasulu (64)	500	5,050
Bosavi watershed subfamily	Kaluli (70)	1800	
	Sunia (56)	300	
	Kasua (61)	450	
	Aimele (38)	400	
	Kamula (41)	600	
	Bainapi	400	3,950

pattern of dialect chains is evident from these data. A marked reduction in the percentage of shared cognates along this continuum provides a natural division between the Strickland Plain subfamily and the remainder of the cultural groups in this region. Consideration of a broader range of factors provides grounds for a tentative and comparatively more arbitrary division of the latter into the Papuan Plateau and Bosavi Watershed subfamilies (Shaw 1986:55–56). The eight ethnographically described Strickland-Bosavi tribes thus include the Samo and Gebusi of the Strickland Plain subfamily; the Bedamini, Etoro, and Onabasulu of the Papuan Plateau subfamily; and the Kaluli, Kasua, and Kamula of the Bosavi Watershed subfamily. The percentage of shared basic vocabulary between these eight tribes is shown in table 1.2 (also based on data reported in Shaw 1986:53). Although the ethnographers of these respective tribes have in some instances presented a slightly different picture of the linguistic relationships between them,[2] the data provided by Shaw (1986) provide a useful overview of the general pattern of linguistic and cultural affinities between and among these groups. There are notable similarities between (1) the Samo and Gebusi, (2) the Etoro and Bedamini, and (3) the Kaluli, Kasua, and Kamula. The Onabasulu share affinities with both the second and third groupings such that any definitive classification of them appears somewhat arbitrary. However, they are culturally somewhat more akin to the Kaluli, Kasua, and Kamula.

There is a relatively marked linguistic discontinuity along the northern and western borders of the Bosavi language family. The percentages of shared cognates between neighboring cultural groups are: (1) Agala and Bogaia, 17 percent, (2) Konai and Bimin, 15 percent, and (3) Kubo and Pare 25 percent. In the east, the linguistic discontinuity is also notable, but somewhat less marked. The percentage of shared cognates between the Kasua and adjacent Namumi is 31 percent.[3]

Linguistic criteria thus provide a relatively clear-cut basis for establishing the tribes of the Strickland-Bosavi region as a set for the purposes of

TABLE 1.2

The Percentage of Shared Basic Vocabulary in the Languages
of the Ethnographically Described Strickland-Bosavi Tribes

Samo							
90	Gebusi						
36	42	Bedamini					
34	37	67	Etoro				
31	34	52	58	Onabasulu			
36	37	46	48	64	Kaluli		
30	32	38	41	52	64	Kasua	
24	28	29	31	32	44	55	Kamula

controlled comparison. Although the Strickland-Bosavi tribes are linguistically related to cultural groups beyond the borders of the region, these cultural groups are less closely related to the Strickland-Bosavi tribes than the latter are to each other and have thus been classified as components of different language families. The languages of the Strickland-Bosavi tribes appear to have diverged from a common stock within a time period that is on the order of several millenia. The cultural groups of the Bosavi language family that have been ethnographically described are similar in economy, social organization, and ritual (Knauft 1985b) and represent historically linked variants of a regional sociocultural system that display transformations of a set of common themes.

Although the Strickland-Bosavi region was first penetrated by exploratory patrols in 1911, regular interaction with patrol officers and missionaries did not commence until more than 50 years later. The early exploratory patrols of Staniforth Smith (1911), Henry Ryan (1913), and Jack Hides and Jim O'Malley (1935) have been described and analyzed in considerable detail by Schieffelin and Crittenden (1991). Smith's party reached the Kikori River at the point where it forms a border between the Kasua and Fasu territories (ibid.:39), while Ryan's patrol traversed Kasua and/or Kamula territory (ibid.). Hides and O'Malley crossed the center of the Strickland-Bosavi region, from the Strickland to the Kikori, passing through the territories of the Honibo, Oibae, Bedamini, Etoro, and Onabasulu (ibid.:54–87). These early exploratory patrols were generally perceived as the incursions of nonautochthonous spirit beings with whom any direct interaction was intrinsically dangerous (Kelly 1977:26; Schieffelin and Crittenden 1991:73–83). They were watched from a distance, avoided by the residents of communities they stumbled upon, and, in some instances, attacked. From the indigenes' viewpoint, all the interactions that occurred were hostile. Some of these eventuated in the loss of lives (Schieffelin and Crittenden 1991:73–83).

Colonial administration in the Strickland-Bosavi region commenced with the construction of an airstrip and patrol post at Nomad, in Samo territory, in late 1961 (Shaw 1990:4) and the beginning of annual patrols to the Papuan Plateau from the Komo patrol post (in Huli territory, in the Southern Highlands) in 1964. Although there was a census patrol into Kaluli territory from the Lake Kutubu patrol post (35 miles to the east) in 1958 (Schieffelin 1976:15), most tribes were first censused in the 1965-to-1967 period, and this marks the inception of regular administrative patrolling in which an effort was made to visit the main communities of each tribe at least once a year. The Asian Pacific Christian Mission (APCM) established two stations, with airstrips, near Nomad and in the eastern part of Kaluli territory in 1963 and 1967, respectively (Shaw 1990:5; Schieffelin 1976:7). In the latter part of the 1960s, mission substations staffed by native pastors were established at additional locations, including the Etoro community of Bobole (a substation of the APCM at Komo). During the period from late 1966 to 1980, anthropologists commenced extended residence among the Kaluli (1966), Etoro (1968), Onabasulu (1969), Samo (1969), Bedamini (1972), Kasua (1973), Kamula (1975), and Gebusi (1980). With the exception of the Kasua and Kamula, anthropological study preceded significant missionary and administrative influence.

Although there were sporadic contacts between the people of the Strickland-Bosavi region and exploratory patrols between 1935 and the early to middle 1960s, flight was a common response to the news of these patrols' entry into an area. The vast majority of the regional population, therefore, never saw an Australian (or other representative of Western culture) during this period but only heard tell of them as strange mythic beings. In the Etoro case, occasional overflights by airplanes (including aerial photography runs) constituted a more widely shared direct experience of the impingement of something external and unknown. This strange new "flying thing," enormous and noisy, produced fearful wonderment and foreboding. What if it should alight? A song composed by an Etoro man in early 1968 begins, "The flying thing has landed now; at Komo the native police play soccer on the airstrip." This perhaps marked the beginning of Etoro consciousness that a new era had begun, and an initial understanding of the threat to autonomy that it portended. A pattern through which the episodic unintelligible events of earlier times might be interpreted was beginning to take shape as the contents of the "flying thing" were finally revealed: a colonial administration implemented at the community level by the periodic visits of a patrol officer accompanied by armed native police.

Several important developments preceded the inception of administrative and missionary influence in the early to middle 1960s. Trade relations were significantly altered, and introduced diseases reduced the population of many tribes. Both the Kasua and Kamula were connected by trade routes to more contacted areas to the south and gained access to steel tools in the 1930s and 1940s (Freund 1977:68–75; Wood 1982:10). Stone axes, which were traditionally exported southward, were no longer needed in these areas, while steel axes derived from them were sought by the more remote Strickland-Bosavi tribes. This and analogous developments in the Southern Highlands in the 1950s led to extensive rearrangement of trade networks and trade items that also altered the composition of marriage and compensation payments among many tribes of the region (Kelly 1977:11; Ernst 1978; Ernst 1984:59–100; Freund 1977:68–75; Schieffelin 1976:15–16). Steel tools flowed into the area very slowly, effectively replacing stone counterparts among the Kaluli, Etoro, and Samo by the late 1940s, middle 1950s, and early 1960s, respectively (Schieffelin op. cit.; Kelly op. cit.; Shaw 1990:5). Steel axes and bush knives (which arrived still later) reduced labor inputs in gardening. Traditional patterns of bridewealth accumulation do not appear to have been altered by the rearrangement of trade items and networks. However, the changes noted here provide a backdrop for more specific consideration of these developments in subsequent discussion.

Introduced diseases began to enter the region in the late 1930s, and their impact accelerated in the 1940s and continued through the 1960s (Kelly 1977:28–31). The population and population density of each of the ethnographically known tribes of the Strickland-Bosavi region are shown in table 1.3, together with estimates of the extent of depopulation produced by introduced diseases (in those cases where this information is provided in the sources). Depopulation significantly increased some of the economic resources available to the smaller populations present at the time of study. In some instances, the number of sago palms per capita doubled as populations were halved. The incidence of witchcraft and sorcery accusations (which are made on the occasion of most adult deaths throughout the region) was amplified. In the case of the Etoro and Kaluli, withdrawal from border areas produced a marked decline in intertribal raiding (Kelly 1977:19–20, 28). Changes in the age structure of the population created a temporary shortage of marriageable women, widened the age differential between spouses, and increased the incidence of widowhood and remarriage among the Etoro (Kelly 1977:169–72).

While the Etoro were thus materially affected by external impingements prior to the inception of direct administrative and missionary influence in the

TABLE 1.3

The Population Density of the Strickland-Bosavi Tribes

Cultural Group	Population	Census Date	Density per Square Mile	Estimated Population Decline	Estimated Precontact Density
Etoro	386	1968	4.8	50%	9.6
Onabasulu	390	1969	1.8	60%	4.5
Kaluli	1,200	1966	5.0	14%	5.8
Kasua	438	1974	6.7	27%	9.2
Kamula	657	1975	<1.0 E*	?	?
Bedamini	3,800	1973	13.1	?	?
Gebusi	450	1973	6.9	25%	9.2
Samo	650	1971	1.6	?	?

Sources: Etoro, Kelly 1977:18, 28; Onabasulu, Ernst 1984:39, 44; Kaluli, Schieffelin and Crittenden 1991:59 and Schieffelin 1971:9 and 1976:7, 15; Kasua, Freund 1977:24, 174; Kamula, Wood 1982:5, 12; Bedamini, Sørum, n.d.:28; Gebusi, Knauft 1985a:1, 20; and Samo, Shaw 1974a:1 and 1990:2.
*E = estimated from map area and census figures.

early to middle 1960s, their responses to these were entirely indigenous, internal adjustments. Later, in the 1970s, missionaries would attack the institution of polygyny (Dwyer 1990:6), and this would resonate with traditional Etoro views that an individual ought not to have more than one of anything that another person lacked, and with the shortage of marriageable women, to sharply reduce polygynous unions. However, at the time of study in 1968–69, this form of linkage between direct influences and the indirect consequences of demographic changes had not taken place. This applies equally to all cultural groups of the region except the Kasua and the Kamula, who had already entered this secondary stage of cultural transformation when they were ethnographically described. Elsewhere traditional beliefs and practices predominated at the time of ethnographic reportage, modified only by internally wrought adjustments. Although the Kamula began to exchange crocodile skins for Western goods with internally based traders in the early 1960s (Wood 1982:30), no other tribe experienced similar engagement with commercial interests prior to study. Only a very small number of men had gone to work on plantations elsewhere in New Guinea as contract laborers and subsequently returned. The very small amounts of money present before study had not yet been incorporated into bridewealth or compensation payments.

Administrative influence has generally waned throughout the region since the late 1970s, as a result of cutbacks in the staffing of patrol posts and a consequent reduction in the frequency of patrols. However, the influence of the missions has steadily increased up to the present. Both forms of influence are localized and decrease with distance from government and mission stations.

Prior to depopulation, overall population densities of about 5 to 10 persons per square mile prevailed throughout most of the Strickland-Bosavi region north of the Tomu River (see table 1.3). The important exception to this generalization is the very numerous and comparatively densely settled Bedamini population, which exceeds 13 persons per square mile despite a highly probable but unknown extent of population decline (see Sørum n.d.:33). The Bedamini are also the only group in the region that has a known history of territorial expansion (see Knauft 1985a:8–9, 237–40). In contrast to this northern sector, the population density of the Tomu River area, the lower southern slopes of Mt. Bosavi and southward (including the southern half of the area on map 1), appears to have always been low, probably on the order of 1 to 2 persons per square mile. Although the extent of depopulation in this southern sector is unknown, there is no reason to expect that it would exceed that estimated for the northern tribes. There is consequently an observable tendency toward a population gradient as one moves outward from the higher altitude areas proximate to Mt. Sisa and Mt. Bosavi. Thus the

Bedamini (at 13.1 persons per square mile) are more densely settled than the Gebusi (at 6.9), and the latter are more densely settled than the Honibo (at 2.1), Samo (at 1.6), and Oybae (at 1.1), while the density of the Tomu River area falls to less than 1 person per square mile (Knauft 1985a:9; Shaw 1990:2; see map 1 for locations). Although this pattern is less definitive further east, Etoro and Kaluli density exceeds that of the Onabasulu, whose tribal territory is at somewhat lower elevation, and the population density of all the northern groups (Etoro, Kaluli, Onabasulu, and Kasua) is greater than that of the Kamula further south.

In general, tribal territories that include or are proximate to lower montane forest (which begins at about 800 to 900 meters) tend to support higher precontact densities than those located exclusively in the lowland rain forest. The lowland Gebusi population, which constitutes an exception to this generalization, has been augmented by immigration from the adjacent high-density Bedamini territory (Knauft 1985a:237–40). While further research is needed with regard to the very marked disparities in population density throughout the region (i.e., a 20-fold difference between the Bedamini and the adjacent Tomu River area), the plentiful game resources of the transitional zone between rain forest and lower montane forest are likely to be one of the factors responsible. Ecologically based demographic differences may also be amplified by asymmetrical raiding.

The Etoro, Onabasulu, Kaluli, Kasua, Kamula, Bedamini, Gebusi, and Samo all reside in longhouses that are internally divided into separate men's and women's sections in accordance with a culturally specific floor plan that varies from tribe to tribe (as will be discussed in some detail further along). These longhouses have an average population of 27 to 70 persons as shown below (omitting the Kasua and Kamula, whose communities have been most altered by contact-induced changes).

Cultural Groups	*Average Longhouse*	*Sources*
	Population	
Etoro	35	Kelly 1977:138
Bedamini	60	Sørum n.d.:42
Gebusi	27	Knauft 1985a:21
Samo	27	Shaw 1974a:1; 1982:417
Onabasulu	43	Ernst 1984:146
Kaluli	70	Schieffelin 1971:1

The residents of the longhouse community are typically members of a number of small, dispersed patrilineal groups that are interrelated by siblingship, marriage, and kin ties arising from marriages. In some communities of a tribe, a single patrilineal group may be numerically dominant and this tendency is more pronounced among the Bedamini and especially the Samo (where a patrifilial extended family constitutes the core of the house group; see Shaw 1974a:2).

Sister exchange, and the more general notion of reciprocity in marriage transactions, is an espoused ideal throughout the region (and the parties to a sister exchange often coreside). Marriage payments are made at the time a bride is transferred among the Etoro, Kaluli, Onabasulu, Kasua, Kamula, and Eastern Bedamini (bordering the Etoro) but not among the Central and Western Bedamini, Gebusi, and Samo. The Central Bedamini, who are intermediate in an east-to-west chain along which marriage payments diminish, present gifts to prospective affines during betrothal (Sørum n.d.:146). Further west, the Samo lack both betrothal and marriage payments but provide compensation when elopement disrupts a planned reciprocal exchange of women (Shaw 1972:41). Likewise, the Gebusi, who otherwise lack compensation payments (as well as bridewealth), sometimes make a small payment (e.g., one pig) to wife-givers when demographic circumstances preclude the possibility of a reciprocal marriage in future (Knauft 1985a:170). In those ethnographic cases where marriage payments are customarily made to wife-givers for every marriage, they do not diminish the obligation to reciprocate by providing a woman in exchange. This emphasis on reciprocal exchange is embodied in a preference for FZSD marriage among the Etoro and Bedamini. Moreover, there are continuing reciprocal exchanges of foodstuffs (typically pork and/or game) between affines in all cases. Outstanding imbalances in exchange—justified by a concept of continued indebtedness to wife-givers— are found only among the Kamula (Wood 1982:101).

Overall, the constellation of features manifested in the region indicates a very strong emphasis on the reciprocal exchange of women modified by a tendency to provide compensatory gifts when this is not or cannot be realized. This appears to constitute a shared cultural base and one may speculate that marriage payments evolved from these compensatory gifts in the ethnographic cases in which they are present. As explained in chapter 6, all Etoro transactions involving shell valuables are compensatory in nature and are directed toward alleviating the emotional distress (i.e., grief or anger) of the recipient. The bridewealth payment addresses the father's grief upon the marriage of his daughter, while witchcraft compensation addresses the grief and anger of the deceased victim's next of kin. The east-to-west marriage payment gradient noted above can also be related to the position of the respective cultural groups in a regional trade network, and this may partly account for the differential development of bridewealth. The regional comparative perspective adopted here thus provides an instructive contextualization for analysis of the production and circulation of wealth among the Etoro that is taken up in chapter 6.

All eight ethnographically known Strickland-Bosavi tribes perform variants of an all-night ritual that is formally similar in costume, dance step, and song and constitutes one of the principal occasions for large intercommunity gatherings (Knauft 1985b). The Kaluli variant has been analyzed in depth by Schieffelin (1976) and Feld (1982) as a central cultural institution. In every case it is a major component of the ceremonial repertoire. All-night séances conducted by spirit mediums are also a common feature of community life throughout the region (Schieffelin 1977, 1985b; Knauft 1985a; Shaw 1990; Sørum 1980). Knauft (1985b:323) points out that "everywhere, séances addressed issues of [supernaturally induced] sickness and curing, the undertaking of collective subsistence activity, witchcraft or sorcery, and armed conflict." Within this overall framework of commonality in the complex that encompasses spirit mediumship and supernatural attack, there are also notable differences between cultural groups in witchcraft and sorcery concepts and in the distribution of accusations by age, gender, and community of residence that will be noted in chapter 4. While mediums play an important role in organizing collective social action in all tribes, as Knauft notes, secular leadership positions (from which mediums are typically excluded) are also present among the Etoro and Bedamini (Sørum 1984:320; Kelly 1988:146–47).

All eight tribes "practiced a single stage initiation or celebratory transition into manhood" (Knauft 1985b:323), but these traditional initiations appear to have been much more central to the sociocultural systems of the Samo (Shaw 1982), Kamula (Wood 1982:218–65), Bedamini (Sørum 1982, n.d.), and Gebusi (Cantrell n.d.) than to those of the Kaluli (Schieffelin 1982), Onabasulu (Ernst n.d.), and Etoro. The traditional Kamula and Samo variants included female coinitiates, and Shaw (1990) analyzes the initiatory complex as an embodiment of the cultural system as a whole. Overall, the region displays a pattern of permutational variation within a framework of broader similarities that makes it an especially fruitful context for controlled comparison, and for the utilization of comparative methods to elucidate selected aspects of particular cultural systems. Spirit mediumship, secular leadership, and the distinctions between witch/nonwitch and novice/initiate are all important aspects of social differentiation, and these will be a focus of discussion in chapters 3, 4, and 5.

The longhouse communities of the Strickland-Bosavi tribes are residential, social, and ceremonial centers for populations that disperse over substantial areas to hunt, trap, forage, process sago palms, and cultivate swidden gardens. Single-family and communal gardens are widely scattered through the secondary forest surrounding the longhouse, and family groups generally divide their time between small garden houses and the longhouse community. Temporary shelters are also constructed in conjunction with sago processing

and extended hunting expeditions. Social life thus entails an oscillation between smaller, single- or multiple-family work-group dwellings and the communal longhouse. This general pattern prevails throughout the region, although there are variations between cultural groups in the distance between
work-group dwellings and the longhouse (which are as much as a day's walk
apart in the case of the low-population-density Kamula [Wood 1982:50]).

There has also been a tendency toward the construction of some single-
or multiple-family dwellings adjacent to selected longhouses during the era
of administrative and/or missionary influence (Freund 1977:46; Ernst
1984:139; Knauft 1985a:26). This settlement pattern tends to be found in the
larger communities of a tribe, while the traditional, isolated, solitary longhouse is more typical of smaller communities. Among the Samo, 24 traditional longhouse communities were consolidated into seven "villages" by
administrative directive during the later 1960s (Shaw 1982:417). However,
these "villages" are simply a cluster of three or four traditional longhouses
in close proximity. These contact-induced changes have altered the character
of the longhouse community in some cases, but the pattern of movement
between dispersed garden houses and community center persists. (The average longhouse populations presented earlier do not appear to have been
materially affected by these changes at the time of study in the ethnographic
cases included, excepting the Kaluli; see Schieffelin and Crittenden
1991:59.)

Ernst (1978:190, 193) has made the interesting observation that the Onabasulu family emerges as a visible social group in the context of sago
processing and gardening (and in the shelters and dwellings associated with
these activities), while the longhouse is divided into male and female spaces
that foster a broader sociality among same-sex groupings. This contrast is
applicable to all of the Strickland-Bosavi tribes in some degree, although
there is considerable variation in the organization of gender-exclusive and
communal (mixed-gender) spaces among the varied longhouse designs of
these tribes. These variations in spatial organization (depicted in fig. 1.1) are
particularly germane both to social differentiation and to features of gender
segregation pertinent to the organization of production and consumption.
They will thus be considered in some detail.

The distribution of the spatially formulated groupings and distinctions
that obtain in the floor plans of the Strickland-Bosavi tribes is shown in table
1.4. Male-exclusive socializing areas and gender-segregated sleeping quarters are common features indicative of a pervasive emphasis on gender-based
distinctions and same-sex social categories and groupings. However, the
eight tribes can be divided into two groups with respect to the presence or
absence of a communal, gender-inclusive socializing area that contains family hearths. The absence of these features—which integrate the otherwise

TABLE 1.4

Social Differentiation and Spatial Groupings in Strickland-Bosavi Longhouse Design

Cultural Group	Male-Exclusive Socializing Space	Female-Exclusive Socializing Space	Gender-Inclusive Socializing Space	Family Hearths	Gender-Segregated Sleeping Quarters	Conjugal Pair Proximity	Menstrual Confinement Room or House	Bachelors' Designated Space	Widows' and/or Single Women's Designated Space
Etoro	+	–	+	+	+	+	–	+	+
Bedamini	+	–	+	+	+	?	–	–	–
Gebusi	+	–	+	?	+	–	–	–	–
Samo	+	–	+	–	+	–	+	+	?
Onabasulu	+	+	–	–	+	+	?	+	+
Kaluli	+	+	–	–	+	+	+	+	+
Kasua	+	+	–	+	+	+	?	+	+
Kamula	+	+	–	–	+	–	–	+	+

Sources: Etoro, Kelly 1977:23; Bedamini, Sørum 1982:275–76 and van Beek 1987:app. C; Gebusi, Knauft 1985a:23; Samo, Shaw 1990:36; Onabasulu, Ernst 1984:138; Kaluli, Schieffelin 1976:33; Kasua, Freund 1977:40; and Kamula, Wood 1982:83.
+ = present, – = absent, ? = not addressed in sources.

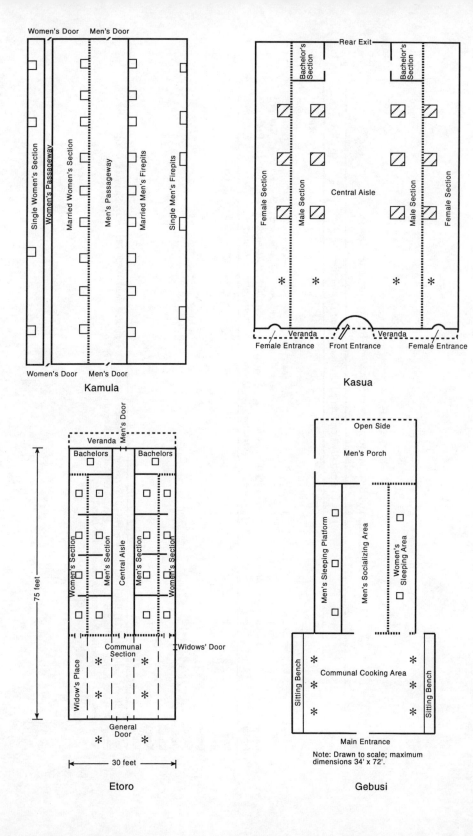

Kamula

Kasua

Etoro

Gebusi

Note: Drawn to scale; maximum dimensions 34' x 72'.

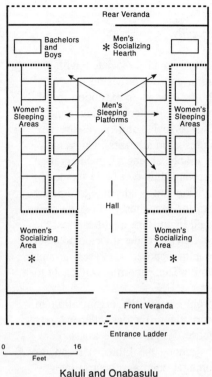

Kaluli and Onabasulu

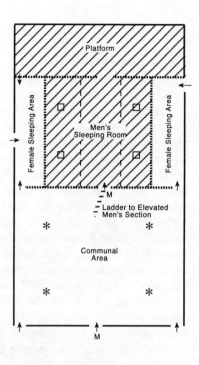

Bedamini

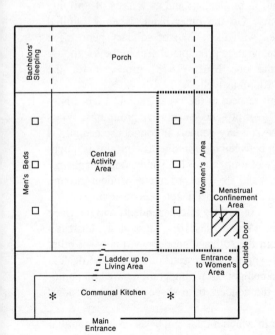

Samo

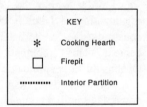

KEY

*   Cooking Hearth

☐   Firepit

··············   Interior Partition

Fig. 1.1 Longhouse design among the Strickland-Bosavi tribes. (Sources: Kamula, Wood 1982:83; Kasua, Freund 1977:40; Kaluli, Shieffelin 1976:33; Onabasulu, Ernst 1984:138; Bedamini, van Beek 1987: app. C; Etoro, Kelly; 1977:23; Gebusi, Knauft 1985a:23; Samo, Shaw 1990:36.)

divided genders when they are present—tends to be associated with the elaboration of concepts of menstrual pollution and the provision of special quarters for menstruating women (although one case is an exception to this generalization). In all instances in which these counterbalancing gender-integrative features are absent, female-exclusive socializing spaces are provided (as well as the male-exclusive spaces present in all cases). Conversely, female-exclusive socializing spaces are invariably absent when integration of the genders is spatially encouraged. There are thus two basic themes in these longhouse designs. In one, gender division and gender integration are countervailing principles of social life within the longhouse. This pattern is applicable to the Etoro, Bedamini, Gebusi, and (with some qualifications) the Samo. The second basic theme is the elaboration of gender division so as to promote the internal solidarity of conceptually opposed same-sex groups within the context of the longhouse community. This pattern is applicable to the Kamula, Kasua, Kaluli, and Onabasulu.[4]

The extent to which the family is prominent in the organization of subsistence food production (as in Ernst's formulation) varies independently with respect to these two themes in longhouse design. Where this is combined with the gender-integrative theme, as among the Etoro, it resonates with an already-present emphasis on the conjugal bond as a central integrative force that unites what gender distinction divides. In other words, the husband-wife relation is focal both in production and as a basis of unifying social order within the community. On the other hand, when a familial organization of labor is combined with the theme of solidary genders, it constitutes the counterbalancing integrative principle absent in the longhouse context. This combination is the one Ernst (1978) proposed for the Onabasulu. It is applicable to the Kaluli as well.

An alternative possibility with respect to the organization of labor is to downplay familial cooperation in favor of gender-exclusive groupings. When this is combined with the theme of solidary genders in longhouse design, as among the Kamula, the opposition between male and female groups is unmediated by any countervailing source of unification. Men and women exchange the products of their separate labors and are rendered interdependent through this exchange. However, men and women need not depend upon specific others, husbands and wives are not exclusively interdependent, and marriage becomes nonessential in this respect (Wood 1987:10). Although the husband-wife relation joins individuals from the solidary genders, virtually all other socioeconomic forces are aligned with the latter division so that the deck is stacked against the realization of a countervailing integration based on conjugal relations. Exchange between the genders both shapes and overshadows husband-wife relations.

The final combination is one in which a dual emphasis on both familial and single-gender production is combined with the gender-integrative theme in longhouse design. Here the countervailing forces of gender division and integration are played out in both the social spaces of the longhouse and the organization of production. This is the pattern found among the Gebusi and Bedamini. Although similar in some respects, the Samo are sufficiently distinctive in others to set them aside. The same applies to the Kasua due to the fact that certain features are not addressed in the single source available. My purpose here is not to create a classification into which all cases can be placed, but to preview some of the main contrasts I seek to develop in the more detailed discussion that follows. The matrix presented below is thus included primarily to orient the reader to this discussion.

The longhouses of the Onabasulu, Kaluli, Kasua, and Kamula are divided into exclusive men's and women's sections and lack any interior space in which all residents of both sexes can intermingle on a daily basis (Ernst 1984:138; Schieffelin 1976:33; Freund 1977:40; Wood 1982:83). These male and female spaces are separated by a shoulder-height partition that a standing person can peer and talk over, so that a husband and wife (and others) can communicate. However, more congenial, close social and conversational interaction is restricted to same-sex coresidents. In contrast, the longhouses of the Etoro, Bedamini, Gebusi, and Samo all contain a communal section in the front of the house in which men and women can interact, talk, and share food. In the Etoro case, each family regularly utilizes one of the four cooking hearths in the communal section. The family larder of sago is hung on an adjacent house post, and game may be stored on a smoking rack which is suspended about four feet above the fire. The hearth is often shared with another family, usually that of a sibling (e.g., the families of a pair of brothers or a brother and sister). This arrangement of space provides scope for family aggregation during meals. Essentially the same pattern obtains among the Bedamini (Sørum 1984:326) and Gebusi (Cantrell, personal communication).

Etoro husbands and wives typically sit together during the main later-afternoon meal (while children tend to circulate). Both the husband and wife cook, and they often offer each other selected morsels of any special foods they may have collected during the day as well as cooked portions of game the husband has already divided between them. Bite-sized morsels are frequently given to others seated nearby as well. Although the predominant tone is one of broader communal sociality and general conversation, in which the conjugal relation is only one of many kinds of relations between interacting individuals, families are merged into a more encompassing sense of community rather than being divided between spatially segregated same-sex groups. Moreover, this communal sociality entails the integration of men and women, in this significant context of food sharing, in addition to emphasizing

		Organization of Subsistence Food Production		
		Familial Organization of Production	Dual Emphasis on Familial and Single Gender Organization of Production	Gender Exclusive Organization of Major Productive Domains
Themes of Longhouse Design	Countervailing Principles of Gender Division and Integration	ETORO	GEBUSI BEDAMINI	
	Internal Solidarity of Conceptually Opposed Genders	ONABASULU KALULI		KAMULA

the cohesiveness of same-sex groupings in other contexts and in the spatial organization of the rear portion of the house.

This is distinctively different from the pattern Ernst describes for the Onabasulu, although the contrast between small work groups in which the family is prominent and the broader and more encompassing sociality of the longhouse still holds. The individuals who spend a week or so at a garden house are often the pair of brothers or brother and sister and their spouses and children who share a hearth (cf. Sørum 1984:326) so that the family (or extended family) does emerge more noticeably in these productive contexts, as Ernst suggests. An Etoro garden house contains a communal section in the front and male and female sleeping quarters in the rear, but these are usually separated only by several stacked logs that form a 1-and-a-half to 2-foot-high partition within a total interior space of about 10 by 12 feet. Sexual segregation is nominal in the context of these cramped quarters. The longhouse context differs in that same-sex socializing often prevails outside of meal-times, particularly in the evening after the main meal.

The rear portion of the Etoro longhouse is divided into men's and women's sleeping quarters separated by floor-to-ceiling partitions that provide complete visual segregation and privacy for each gender, although normal conversation is audible through the partition, as are the séances conducted by mediums in the men's quarters. The men's section includes ample space for socializing, while the women's section lacks this. However, the women may remain in the communal section after the men have retired to the men's section, and the communal section therefore sometimes doubles as a place for women's socializing in the evening. Nevertheless, it is not specifically demarcated for this purpose and is not comparable to the men's private social space. In the Kaluli and Onabasulu longhouses, two-thirds of what would be the communal section of an Etoro, Bedamini, Gebusi, or Samo longhouse constitutes two separate women's socializing areas, while the men's socializing area is in the rear of the house, about 45 feet away. Same-sex dining and socializing is a pronounced feature of community social life, and there is no interior space in which the family can sit together.

In the Etoro, Bedamini, Kaluli, Onabasulu, and Kasua floor plans, the men's section is centrally located and the women's sections flank it on both sides, so that the women are effectively divided into two discrete sleeping groups, while the men are divided into two sleeping groups that share a common space between them (the men's socializing area). The women's section is consolidated on the right side of the Gebusi and Samo longhouse, while the men's section occupies the center and left-hand side. In the Kamula case, the sections are reversed, so that the women are on the left.[5]

The Samo longhouse is distinctive in that the women's section is entered through an anteroom that serves as a menstrual confinement area. Although the concept of menstrual pollution is relatively unelaborated in comparison to the New Guinea Highlands, the Samo do regard this as a key to the necessity of gender-segregated sleeping quarters (Shaw 1990:161). Moreover, the communal kitchen is proximate to the menstrual confinement area, while the rear porch that serves as the center for male-exclusive socializing is at the opposite end of the structure, purposefully located at maximum remove. Women prepare food and serve it to their husbands on large trays (Shaw 1990:35–37), suggesting gender-segregated clusters during meals. However, the central activity area, which is open to the men's sleeping section (but walled off from the women's), is not reserved for men and "can be frequented by anyone" (ibid.). There is an apparent contradiction between the fact that most interior space is shared, while menstrual pollution necessitates separate sleeping quarters (of which more below). In the Gebusi longhouse design, which is internally divided in the same way as the Samo longhouse (with the exception of the menstrual confinement room), this central area is normally reserved for male socializing, as it is in the Etoro and Bedamini longhouses (which differ from the Gebusi only in that there are two women's sleeping sections rather than one). This men's socializing area can be occupied by women on certain ceremonial occasions (Knauft n.d.:22) but is normally off limits. The exclusion of women from this area in everyday life is a matter of etiquette rather than a rigid taboo. The large rear porch of the Samo, Bedamini, and Gebusi longhouses is entirely male-exclusive, and men often gather there to talk. The smaller rear veranda of the Etoro long-house is little used for socializing and functions primarily as a platform for bowmen in the defense of the longhouse against raiding parties (Kelly 1977:21). However, the important contrast to be noted here is that Etoro, Bedamini, and Gebusi gender-segregated sleeping quarters and male-exclusive socializing areas are not justified in terms of concern with men-strual pollution as they are among the Samo.

Among the Etoro, Bedamini, and Gebusi there is no elaboration of a concept of menstrual pollution. As Sørum (1984:326) points out, menstrual blood is not regarded differently from other bodily wastes. These are all polluting in a sense but are not a focus of concern. Women tend to remain in their sleeping quarters for a day or two during menstruation (ibid.; Kelly 1976:46; Cantrell n.d.). In the Etoro case, this is typical but does not seem to be mandatory. If a woman does not experience discomfort she may go about her usual activities, although she would probably not join in communal meals. Both the short duration and nonmandatory nature of the time women spend in their quarters suggest that the concept of menstrual "confinement" or "seclusion" is an inappropriate categorization of these behavior patterns. Although the Etoro, Bedamini, and, to a lesser extent, the Gebusi all regard heterosexual relations as a depletion of male vitality due to loss of semen, female persons are not polluting, and regular daily interaction between men and women is not inhibited by pollution concepts (Kelly 1976:42; Sørum 1984:326; Knauft n.d.:21–22). The provision of a gender-inclusive commu-nal section in the longhouse is consistent with this.

In contrast, the concept of menstrual pollution is well-developed among the Kaluli. Schieffelin (1976:67) provides an extensive list of pollution beliefs:

> If a menstruating woman eats a fresh [unsmoked] animal caught in a trap, future [deadfall] traps will not fall; if the animal was caught with a dog, the dog will lose his ability to find a scent. Similarly, bananas and pandanus, if eaten by a menstruating woman, will cease to bear. Other people in the longhouse avoid going to their gardens if they hear that a woman has come into her period, and the woman herself must leave the longhouse and move to a shack some distance away for the duration. If she should cook or step over food, those who eat it, particularly her husband, will become ill with a cough and possibly die.

As in many areas of the Highlands, prolonged close contact with women is viewed as detrimental to male health and vitality even when women are not menstruating, due to an implicit concept of residual contamination. The permanent spatial segregation of men and women within the longhouse is thus mandated by the continuous nature of women's debilitating effects on male well-being (ibid.:67, 123).

Kamula concepts of menstrual pollution are very similar to those of the Kaluli. A woman goes into seclusion in a menstrual house separate from the longhouse for the duration of her period and may not eat any food other than sago. It is said that if menstruating women were to eat pig men would lose their knowledge of how to hunt pigs, and this outcome exemplifies the general consequences of the consumption of prohibited foods (Wood 1982:86–87). Despite this seclusion, the women's section of the longhouse is perceived to be contaminated by residual menstrual pollution capable of causing men to become ill (ibid.). As in the Kaluli case, this logically necessitates a gender-segregated dwelling that includes no communal section in which men and women would regularly intermingle. Indeed the residual effects of lingering menstrual contamination are sufficiently potent that men repair to an area away from the longhouse to undertake the making of drums, bows, and paddles, so that their work will not be spoiled (ibid.).[6]

There is thus a significant contrast between the Kaluli and Kamula, on one hand, and the Etoro, Bedamini, and Gebusi, on the other, with respect to the presence of a concept of menstrual pollution and its implications for gender segregation both in the longhouse and in the organization of production and consumption. The Samo are intermediate and appear to lack the axiom of continuing residual contamination that is associated with a detached menstrual confinement house located away from the longhouse (so as to segregate the most potent source of contamination). The absence of this belief is also consistent with the fact that the longhouse includes shared as well as gender-segregated spaces. These intermediate features of the Samo configuration are distinctive within the region. The Samo also differ from the Etoro, Bedamini, Kaluli, Onabasulu, and Kamula in that insemination is not an integral feature of male maturation and an ideologically central aspect of the larger cosmology (Shaw 1990:17). (This aspect of Kasua culture has not been investigated.)

The longhouses of the Kamula, Kasua, Kaluli, Onabasulu, Etoro, and Samo all include a specified area within the men's sleeping quarters for bachelors. (This feature is absent among the Gebusi and Bedamini.) Among the Kamula the unmarried men's sleeping section along the outer wall on the right side is paralleled by the unmarried women's sleeping section similarly located along the left outer wall. Thus married persons are conceptually and spatially opposed to single persons, with the former central and the latter peripheral (Wood 1982:82). The male-female contrast is one of right to left (or vice versa), and the front-to-rear axis is undifferentiated in terms of social space. In the case of the Etoro, Kaluli, Onabasulu, and Kasua floor plans, males are central and unified while females are spatially peripheral and divided. The right and left sides of these longhouses are undifferentiated mirror images of each other, and the front-to-rear axis is associated with the distinction between married and unmarried. Among the Etoro and Kasua, widows sleep toward the front of the house (Freund 1977:45), while "important senior women and unmarried girls" sleep in the women's socializing section at the front of the Kaluli longhouse (Schieffelin 1976:35).

The Etoro marital opposition is clearly formulated, in spatial terms, as one between never-married men and previously married women (i.e., bachelors and widows). The Etoro longhouse has small side doors that are especially for widows, who cannot enter through the front door or cross the central passageway (*kamu*) that runs the length of the dwelling. Widows also sit along the outer walls of the communal section. These restrictions pertaining to widows are related to the ideology that heterosexual relations entail depletion of a male life force, embodied in semen, leading to weakness, senescence, and, ultimately, death. A widow thus bears a certain responsibility for her husband's demise (Kelly 1976:49–50). Equally important, however, is the fact that most widows are also in mourning (since they would otherwise remarry, if not of advanced age, and thus cease to be widows). That widows are both peripheral and socially set aside—in terms of the space allocated for their eating, sitting, and sleeping and the doors provided for their use—is consistent with these two interrelated aspects of their social condition (i.e., mourning and responsibility for husband's death).

The cultural sense of the Etoro opposition between never-married men and previously married women can perhaps be more accurately conveyed by designating the former as male virgins, rather than merely bachelors. Although brought to maturity through insemination by older men, the bachelors are (at least in theory) virgins with respect to heterosexual relations and the spiritual depletion this entails (through progressive debilitation of the breath soul due to loss of semen; see Kelly 1976). They represent the acme of male vitality and a reservoir of the precious life force that men have transmitted to one another down through the generations. Opposite them, at the other end of the longhouse, are widows who epitomize the consequences of heterosexual depletion, i.e., male death. Moreover, the front of the longhouse is at ground level while the rear rests on piles, some twenty-five feet above the downslope of a ridge. Spirit mediums conduct séances in the space near the bachelors' sleeping platforms, and the spirits enter through the adjacent rear door to the veranda. The front-to-rear spatial opposition is thus one of low to high and profane to sacred, as well as an opposition of widows to bachelors and of familial social and sexual solidarity (re: family hearths) to male homosocial and homosexual solidarity (re: male-exclusive quarters). The countervailing principles of male-female integration and gender division are spatially represented along the same front-to-rear axis as the widow-to-bachelor opposition.

It is important to emphasize the conceptual complementarity of these two principles. Although the conjugal relation leads to male death through depletion, it also brings forth the next generation so that life continues (and death is transcended). Like European concepts of virginity, bachelorhood represents an elevated symbolic moment in the life cycle that one passes through. The symbolic elaboration of a concept of female virginity does not entail a devaluation of marriage, and this is equally applicable to the comparable elaboration of Etoro bachelorhood. Moreover, while widows epitomize the deadly consequences of heterosexual depletion from the standpoint of the bachelors, the bachelors represent remarriage and resumed reproduction to the widows, since nearly half of the latter marry bachelors on completion of mourning. The widows are sexually experienced and perceived by the bachelors to be sexually aggressive. The virginal bachelors are sexually inexperienced and, being concerned with losing their precious vital essence, are passive responders to female advances. But more often than not, they succumb. (The marital consequences are discussed later, see note 24 of chap. 2.) I mention this drama of lost male virginity here because the conceptual oppositions posed by the symbolic architecture of the longhouse appear too stark and sharply drawn when presented in the abstract, outside of the dynamics of practice through which they are mediated. The opposition between widows and bachelors is also definitively overcome when they intermarry, and the conjugal relation thus unites these same-sex groupings. This is yet another manifestation of the general theme identified earlier.

Conjugal relations are a very central integrative principle in Etoro community organization. Although male-female opposition and male solidarity are spatially formulated, marriage joins men and women in family units and thus establishes a countervailing gender integration that has its spatial locus at the family hearth. Moreover, each husband-wife pair occupies adjacent sleeping platforms, separated only by the thin sago-mat partition that divides the men's and women's sleeping quarters. Conjugal links thus crosscut gender segregation at every point. Although sexual relations between spouses are precluded by the partition that separates their sleeping platforms, conversation is not. There is a kind of conjugal intimacy and Victorian eroticism in these sleeping arrangements. This can be brought out more clearly by relating the oscillation between longhouse and garden house residence to Etoro taboos concerning heterosexual relations (cf. Weiner 1988:11–15). Heterosexual relations are prohibited during the first several months of garden preparation and throughout the time period devoted to sago processing (Kelly 1976:43). These are precisely the times when a family would reside away from the longhouse at a small garden house or sago-processing shelter. Conjugal sexual intimacy is thus prohibited during the period when interpersonal intimacy and joint effort in subsistence food production are greatest. Conversely, sexual relations between spouses are permitted during periods

that coincide with longhouse residence, when the homosocial solidarity of a
unified group of males is most prominent. The general theme of countervailing familial and same-sex solidarity is unmistakable here. The organization
of sexuality works against any individual tendency to overemphasize one or
the other. Since heterosexual relations are prohibited in the vicinity of the
longhouse (as well as in gardens), married couples must go off to the forest
together to copulate during the period of longhouse residence. A man is
prohibited from offering food or smoke from his pipe to other men during the
remainder of the day (Kelly 1976:4) and is thus socially isolated from the
male group. This encourages the couple to spend an extended period of time
together, rather than returning promptly to the longhouse. An impetus to
conjugal solidarity is thus established during the period when this otherwise
tends to be submerged in a broader communal sociality and when same-sex
social relations are prominent. The fact that husbands and wives sleep next
to each other, separated only by a sago-mat partition, is another dimension
of this general pattern.

Although men are spatially central and unified in the Etoro longhouse
design while women are divided and spatially peripheral, women are conjugally linked to the male core by the arrangement of adjacent sleeping platforms, and their division into two groups is an artifact of this. The absence
of a female socializing space is also consistent with the emphasis on conjugal
linkages that crosscut gender division. The Etoro longhouse design is the
only one of the eight that provides both family hearths and conjugal-pair
proximity in sleeping arrangements (although the culturally similar
Bedamini, for whom specific data on sleeping arrangements are lacking,
may also manifest both of these features). Among the Kamula, Kasua,
Kaluli, and Onabasulu, interior eating and socializing spaces are gender-
segregated. Among the Kamula, Gebusi, and Samo, conjugal-pair proximity
in the gender-segregated sleeping quarters is absent, as male and female
sections are separated by a central activity area. Among the Kamula, Kaluli,
and, to a lesser extent, the Samo, gender segregation is amplified by the
concept of menstrual pollution. The lack of concern with this in the Etoro
case is evidenced by the fact that a man sleeps adjacent to his wife during
her period. This is precluded in all other cases (with the possible exception
of the Bedamini). All these contrasts show that Etoro longhouse architecture
provides greater spatial support for the husband-wife relation than that of
other Strickland-Bosavi tribes (with the possible exception of the Bedamini).
The Kamula occupy the other end of the spectrum with respect to spatial
provision for conjugal solidarity.

The preceding discussion of longhouse architecture provides a general
contextual background for consideration of social differentiation and the
organization of production, distribution, and consumption in subsequent

chapters. As noted earlier, the organization of subsistence food production varies independently with respect to the two main themes of longhouse design. In the Etoro case, there is an emphasis on the cooperation and joint effort of husbands and wives, who often work together at the same tasks or at complementary tasks. Ernst has likewise emphasized the familial basis of Onabasulu food production. Although the family has no spatial locus within the longhouse, it emerges as a prominent social group in this productive context. Schieffelin (1976:26) also reports that a Kaluli man "tends to think of his life with his wife, on reflection, in terms of the situations in which he worked cooperatively with her. . . ." This contrasts markedly with the Kamula, among whom there is an emphasis on male-exclusive hunting and female-exclusive sago processing (although there is a greater degree of cooperative work organization in gardening). I will draw on the contrast between the Etoro and Kamula at a number of points throughout this work, as these comparisons bring many features of Etoro socioeconomic organization into sharper focus.

Among the Etoro, the "relations of production" are primarily the relations between husbands and wives and between conjugal pairs linked by siblingship and other kin relations in communal productive endeavors. These focal conjugal relations are embedded in a broader matrix of life-force transmission that culturally defines reproduction. One of the objectives of the preceding discussion has been to convey some of the main contours of these more encompassing domains in which the husband-wife relation is enmeshed. The social relations of distribution and consumption are likewise the familial, kin, and communal relations that obtain within a longhouse that spatially formulates a system of relations between conjugal work groups, and between the genders that the sexual division of labor divides. The division and organization of labor and the social relations of subsistence food production, distribution, and consumption are the specific foci of chapter 2.

The Social Relations of Etoro Food Production, Distribution, and Consumption in Comparative Perspective

Prior analyses of the relationship between economy and inequality in simple societies have proceeded in two quite different directions. One perspective has emphasized the aspects of economic organization that are conducive to egalitarian relations. This perspective is well represented by Fried's (1967:35) conclusion that "at the heart of an egalitarian society is a fundamentally egalitarian economy," and by his delineation of the enabling economic conditions. Woodburn's (1982) formulation of a contrast between immediate return and delayed return systems (as ideal types) likewise entails an effort to specify the economic prerequisites of egalitarian social relations and egalitarian ideology. In contrast, the second perspective focuses on the inegalitarian relations that obtain in simple societies—between men and women and between junior and senior males—and seeks to elucidate the role of economic organization in generating these inequalities. This perspective is well represented by Collier and Rosaldo (1981) and Collier (1988), who see marriage as playing a pivotal role in the organization of obligations that shape the relations of production and distribution that eventuate in inequalities of prestige and privilege. In noting the difference between her perspective and that of Fried, Collier (1988:30) concludes by saying

> I do not stress the egalitarian nature of social relations in brideservice societies. Rather I focus on the social bases of inequalities in prestige and privilege.

In my view, neither of these perspectives provides a balanced account of both the egalitarian and inegalitarian aspects of simple societies. More-

53

over, economic organization is selectively rather than comprehensively examined, since the explanatory objective entails focusing on selected aspects
of the economy that play a role in egalitarian relations among adult men, on
one hand, or inegalitarian relations between senior and junior males and men
and women, on the other hand.

The account presented in this chapter thus attempts to chart a middle
course and to provide a more balanced and comprehensive account of these
divergent aspects of economic organization. However, elucidating the central
locus for the production of inequality is the main goal of this work, and it is
thus more closely aligned with the explanatory objectives of the second
perspective than the first. The central question, with respect to an analysis
of the economy, is thus to determine what role economic organization plays
in the production of social inequalities. (Subsistence food production, distribution, and consumption are addressed in this chapter while the production
and circulation of wealth are addressed in chap. 6.) In answering this question, it is possible to conclude that there are no significant inequalities in
labor inputs or in consumption, and that the economy is egalitarian in these
respects. At the same time, it is also possible to conclude that economic
organization is instrumental to the generation of inequalities in the distribution of prestige. Similarly, one may note that opportunities to attain prestige
through generosity are open to women and junior males as well as senior
males, while at the same time noting that, in practice, such prestige predominantly accrues to the latter. The central question posed in this chapter is thus
consistent with the objectives of a balanced account, even though the larger
goal of this work concerns elucidation of the sources of social inequality.

It is evident from the preceding discussion that this chapter is constituted
as a general inquiry into the relationship between economy and inequality
rather than an effort to map Etoro economic data onto preexisting theoretical
models in which the economic basis of social inequality is presupposed.
Although these models direct attention to certain issues, and the data relevant
to them, the plan of the chapter is to discover what emerges from a comprehensive consideration of data pertaining to production, distribution, and consumption and then subsequently consider the extent to which these data fit
preexisting theoretical conceptions or require reformulations. This reduces
potential distortions arising from selectivity in data presentation and the
consequences of prior assumptions. Moreover, the Etoro data were collected
in 1968–69 so that they were not generated in relation to current theories of
inequality (which were formulated subsequently). The data are thus well
suited to the mode of presentation and inductive theoretical approach
adopted. Comparative analysis of the eight ethnographically described
Strickland-Bosavi tribes is employed in order to contextualize the Etoro case,
establish productive contrasts, and lay the groundwork for consideration of

covariation between economic features (eg., the division of labor) and the organization of social inequality. The main contours of this comparative inquiry into the relationship between economy and inequality have been described in the introduction in order to provide a guide to what follows.

The subsistence economy of the Strickland-Bosavi region entails varied combinations of hunting, trapping, fishing, foraging, sago processing, swidden agriculture, and pig husbandry. These variations are of considerable importance in understanding the division of labor, the organization of production, and the distribution of rights of access to economic resources in any particular ethnographic case and thus provide a very instructive background to analysis of the Etoro economy. The means of securing the animal protein component of the diet are markedly affected by altitude, and a discussion of these effects provides a useful point of departure in consideration of regional variation.

HUNTING, TRAPPING, FISHING, AND FORAGING

The primary forest on the upper slopes of Mt. Sisa and Mt. Bosavi, above 1,200 meters, is rich in small- and medium-sized forest mammals. In the Etoro case, these animals are procured through daylong or multiple-day hunting trips and through the seasonal utilization of an extensive network of traplines (Dwyer 1982). The latter consist of a picket fence interspersed with deadfalls at intervals of 10 to 15 meters. A single trapline may extend for as much as 300 meters, and a longhouse community near the margin of the primary forest maintains about one trapline for each seven residents (Dwyer 1982:536–37; Kelly 1977:37). These traplines are repaired and reused annually and thus represent an asset that provides a return on labor expended in prior years (re: Woodburn 1982). Access to both hunting territories and trapping sites is governed by lineage membership, and discussion of rights to take game animals (and fish) is one of relatively few contexts in which lineage membership is specifically invoked.

Not all Etoro lineage territories abut primary forest. Those that fall in the second tier, at about 700 to 800 meters, evidence a different pattern of resource exploitation that is linked to differences in faunal composition. This is evident in Dwyer's (1985c) comparisons of the contributions of nondomesticated animals to the diet of two Etoro communities at 800 and 1,100 meters (see table 2.1).[1] In the high-altitude community, trapping and daylong hunts in the primary forest supply 35 percent and 48 percent, respectively, of the game mammals that account for more than half of the animal protein in the diet. The balance of the game mammals is derived from foraging (or "casual encounter") (17 percent) and robbing dogs (2 percent) (Dwyer 1985c:105). At lower elevations baited deadfalls that are widely scattered throughout the secondary forest are the primary means of capture of game mammals (and increase the take of small mammals as well), while foraging is second in importance. Daylong (or multiple-day) hunting expeditions are rarely undertaken in the secondary forest (the exception being occasional wild pig hunts, discussed further along). Instead, hunting is opportunistic and takes place within the context of foraging activities. Animals are procured when they are spotted by individuals en route to gardens or sago stands, or in the course of trips undertaken for the purpose of collecting tree ferns and pandanus, searching for bush hen eggs, or collecting seasonally available wild nuts, mushrooms, and the like (Kelly 1977:40–41). Widely dispersed deadfalls, cassowary snares, and small fish traps are checked in the course of these rounds as well. This marked shift from focused hunting of midsize game to generalized foraging at lower elevations is evident in both the decreased contribution of game mammals and the increased contribution of collectibles in the diet (see table 2.1). The dietary importance of birds' eggs, which are a widely dispersed resource, is particularly indicative of the foraging mode. At the lower altitude community of Namosado, collecting megapode, cassowary, and other eggs provided about half as much protein as trapping mammals (i.e., 1.56 grams and 3.17 grams, respectively) and constituted the second most important means of securing protein from nondomestic sources (Dwyer 1985c:111–12; see also Kelly 1977:34).

The second major shift that occurs with decline in altitude is in the availability of fish, eels, and crayfish. This is reflected in table 2.1 but is particularly well brought out by Ernst's (1984) discussion of Onabasulu subsistence at the Orogaiye community, located on the Papuan Plateau be-

TABLE 2.1

Altitudinal Differences in Etoro Animal Protein Sources

	Quantity (in grams/person/day)	
Source of Protein	Bobole 1,100 m	Namosado 800 m
Game mammals	6.0	3.84
Domestic pigs	3.0	3.0 E
Cassowaries	.5 E	.5 E
Small mammals	.25 E	.66
Other: fish, crayfish, frogs, lizards, birds, eggs, terrestrial crabs, spiders, beetle larvae, moth larvae, other insects	1.0 E	2.93
Total	10.75	10.93

Source: Based on data in Dwyer 1985c; see n. 1.

E = estimated.

tween Mt. Sisa and Mt. Bosavi at about 700 meters. Crayfish are available in "remarkably vast quantities" in November and December and in "smaller but considerable quantities throughout the year" (Ernst 1984:110). Eels are speared by torchlight. Cone-shaped bamboo fish traps are interspersed along a weir constructed of branches, mud, rocks, and a spanning log bridge extending across a small stream. These sets of fish traps appear to be aquatic equivalents of high-altitude traplines set for forest mammals (or vice versa). Multiple-day fish-poisoning expeditions entailing the coordinated labor of a group of persons are also undertaken. The Onabasulu fish-poisoning method requires the preparation of large quantities of concentrated derris-root fish poison in wood-frame-supported bark troughs extending across a major stream. The troughs are simultaneously emptied, and the poison released is sufficient to stun fish over a three-kilometer stretch of the stream. Ernst (1984:109) estimates the catch from one such multiple-day expedition at 45 kilograms, shared among eight men (and an unknown number of spouses and dependents). A portion of the catch was smoked, as is done with the large quantities of forest mammals taken during hunting expeditions, and in traplines during the early period of their seasonal operation.

The sites suited to fish poisoning are those stretches of a larger stream that flow over comparatively level terrain, so that the concentration of fish poison will penetrate to the bottom and not be swept too rapidly downstream. A deep pool may also be suitable if several days without rain have reduced the rate of inflow and outflow so that fish poison can accumulate. These favorable locations are limited in number and are more prevalent at lower elevations where rivers and streams descend more gradually. Access to these sites is governed by lineage membership, although the work party that shares the catch will normally include affinal and matrilateral kin who are coresident at the same longhouse community (Ernst 1984:107–9).

The Etoro also engage in fish-poisoning expeditions that require the labor of half a dozen men for the better part of a day. Etoro methods differ from those of the Onabasulu in that dams and diversion channels are employed to seal off a 30-to-100-meter stretch of river in order to reduce both the quantity and velocity of water and provide for the buildup of sufficient concentrations of poison (see Kelly 1977:38–40 for a more complete description of these procedures). This more labor-intensive method is necessary because Etoro territory is considerably more steeply sloped than the center of the Papuan Plateau where the majority of Onabasulu communities are located. (The use of long-standing fish traps set in weirs is also precluded by swift currents and flash floods.) Etoro fish-poisoning sites require not only favorable locations but also a labor investment, by prior generations, in the construction of the diversion channels that provide a means to reroute a substantial volume of water around the dammed area. As in the Onabasulu case, access is governed by lineage membership. Moreover, fish poisoning is directed by spirit mediums and requires the prior approval of the ghosts and ancestral spirits whose souls occupy the bodies of the larger fish that are sought (see Kelly 1977:61). To take these fish from the territory of another lineage without the participation of agnates and the spiritual authorization of their forebears would be a serious offense at several levels.

The general effects of altitude on the different types of nondomesticated animal resources exploited throughout the Strickland-Bosavi region are illustrated by the data presented in table 2.2, which extends the earlier comparison between Bobole and Namosado to other communities for which comparable data are available.[2] Aquatic resources, and the bird eggs, reptiles, and insects that are procured through generalized foraging comprise 13 percent of total nondomesticated animal protein at 1,100 meters, 34 to 51 percent at 350 to 800 meters, and as much as 83 percent at 250 meters (during a short sample period). Virtually all the items in this category can be taken as readily by women as by men so that the deviations from this potentiality that are manifested by some cultural groups can be regarded as a consequence of

TABLE 2.2

The Proportion of Different Types of Nondomesticated Animal Protein
Procured by Five Strickland-Bosavi Communities at Different Altitudes
(expressed as percentage of total for sample period)

	Bobole Etoro (1,100 m, 52-week sample)	Namosado Etoro (800 m, 3-week sample)	Kaburusato Etoro (775 m, 52-week sample)	Gofabi Bedamini (350 m, 3-week sample)	Fagamaiu Kasua (250 m, 1.5-week sample)
Wild pig and cassowary	6.5	6.3	35.6	49.7	17.4
Mammals	80.6	56.7	13.9	16.4	
Other: eels, fish, crayfish, frogs, lizards, snakes, birds, eggs, terrestrial crabs, spiders, beetle larvae, moth larvae, grasshoppers, caterpillars, dragonflies	12.9	37.0	50.5	33.9	82.6
Total	100%	100%	100%	100%	100%

Sources: Bobole and Namosado Etoro, Dwyer 1985c; Kaburusato Etoro, Kelly 1977:34; Gofabi Bedamini, van Beek 1987:app. B; and Fagamaiu Kasua, Freund 1977:324; see n. 2.

arbitrary features of the division of labor (as discussed further along). In contrast, large game (wild pig and cassowary) are almost entirely procured by men in all cases. These large game (and particularly wild pig) are comparatively scarce at 1,100 meters but constitute a source of protein roughly equal in importance to aquatic resources and the products of foraging at lower elevations. When the sample period during which game procurement is measured is of relatively brief duration, the proportional contribution of large game animals tends to be somewhat understated (Namosado Etoro and Fagamaiu Kasua) or overstated (Gofabi Bedamini) (see note 2). However, the general tendency toward the increased availability of large game at lower elevations (best illustrated by the Kaburusato Etoro and Gofabi Bedamini in table 2.2) is supported by the descriptive accounts of other cultural groups in the region, particularly the Kamula (discussed below).

Small to midsize forest mammals constitute the third main category of game. These are by far the most important resource at higher altitude locations proximate to primary forest, where they are the focus of directed hunting and trapping. At lower altitude they typically decline in importance, being displaced by the more readily available large game that often constitute a prime objective of focused hunting carried out by men. In secondary forest many small and midsize mammals are opportunistically procured during garden clearance and in the course of generalized foraging, i.e., by the same general methods employed to obtain reptiles, bird eggs, and insects. As much as 38 percent of these forest mammals may consequently be taken by women (van Beek 1987:app. B). The Bedamini case indicates that half of the nondomesticated animal protein in the diet can potentially be supplied by small and midsize mammals, reptiles, bird eggs, insects, and aquatic resources that women procure in substantial quantity (representing about one-third of total bag weight for these items). Although this potentiality is not realized in many instances due to features of the division of labor, women make significant contributions to the supply of nondomesticated animal protein in all cases. This is one of the notable features of the economies of the Strickland-Bosavi region.

It is important to note that the environmentally based general tendencies in resource availability outlined above are not neatly manifested in every case. Bedamini, Kamula, and Samo men devote considerable effort to hunting large game (particularly pigs), thereby increasing the proportional contribution of such game to the diet. The Kasua, Gebusi, and midaltitude Etoro pursue large game much less frequently and direct greater effort toward procuring the other resources that are environmentally available.

Foraging, often carried out jointly by husbands and wives, is the principal mode of game procurement among the Gebusi (at 300 meters) (Knauft 1985a:18–19; personal communication). The items obtained are essentially the same as those listed in the second and third categories of table 2.2. The larger, slower flowing rivers present at this altitude support many more species of fish than those at higher elevation, as well as crayfish, eels, and turtles. All of these aquatic resources are extensively utilized. In contrast, large-game hunting—entailing daylong and multiple-day hunting expeditions carried out by several men—is only quite infrequently undertaken in uninhabited forest to the south, even though such hunts generally yield "one or more wild pigs or cassowaries" (Knauft 1985a:19).

The Samo, who occupy a comparable tropical forest environment at the same altitude as the Gebusi, exploit a very similar range of resources through foraging, fish poisoning, and the deployment of small fish traps (Shaw 1990:45–46). However, the Samo differ from the Gebusi in that they frequently engage in collective hunting expeditions during the December-to-May period (when garden work is minimal). Groups of men accompanied by dogs pursue wild pigs, cassowary, and smaller game for several days, camping at overnight shelters. The hunt proceeds without regard to territorial boundaries, although the catch is shared with owners of the territory on which it was taken (ibid.). The lower altitude tropical forest provides the Samo and Gebusi with comparable opportunities for systematic hunting of large game animals, but these two cultural groups differ markedly in the extent to which they avail themselves of these opportunities.

The Etoro communities at lower elevations (700 to 800 meters) have access to a comparable resource zone in the uninhabited southern portion of Etoro territory at 450 to 700 meters. However, like the Gebusi, the Etoro only undertake large-game hunting expeditions infrequently. These are impromptu affairs rather than a regular component of the seasonal round of activities. At Kaburusato, daylong wild pig hunts carried out by three to five men were organized on only two occasions during a 15-month period. Both were unsuccessful. However, four wild pigs were taken opportunistically during a 52-week sample period. Three of these were ambushed in gardens that they had previously invaded, and the fourth was surprised at a sago stand by the work party arriving to complete processing of the palm that had attracted the pig to the site. Some men locate their gardens further from the longhouse in areas frequented by wild pigs in order to enhance the prospects for obtaining these animals. In effect, the garden itself functions as a baited trap. This technique is still fundamentally opportunistic (in contrast to focused hunting), although an effort is made to expand the number of opportunities that arise. Cassowaries are also taken with snares rather than by hunting. The midaltitude Etoro community of Kaburusato thus obtained significant quantities of the large game animals that are environmentally available in this zone, although foraging combined with checking widely dispersed deadfalls and snares was the principal mode of game procurement in terms of labor expenditure. At Namosado, the same mode of game procurement produced different proportions of large and midsize game (although these differences are partially attributable to different sampling methods).[3] This emphasis on foraging is reflected in the substantial dietary contribution of megapode, cassowary, and other eggs in both communities (noted earlier).

The Kamula, who reside on the lower south slopes of Mt. Bosavi from about 300 meters to 650 meters, engage in extensive large-game hunting. Wood (1982:58–59) notes that multiple-day hunts carried out by a number of groups of several men each procured 16 pigs, 5 cassowaries, and 2 wallabies in preparation for a ritual. When the arrival of the guests was delayed for two weeks, the exercise was repeated and yielded 16 pigs and 3 cassowaries. Rifles were used, and this very likely affected returns. Nevertheless, the pattern of communitywide multiple-day hunting expeditions directed to the procurement of large game for ritual occasions is traditional, and other data indicate that a proficient hunter may shoot as many as 8 pigs a year with a bow and arrow (ibid.:71).

The Kamula also engage in communal hunts in which women act as "beaters," flushing game toward a point surrounded on three sides by water. Men wait at the cul de sac to shoot the pigs that are driven toward them (ibid.:52). When game is not being accumulated for ritual purposes, men hunt alone (currently with a rifle), stalking wallabies, pigs, and cassowaries with the aid of a dog or employing blinds set up near a recently processed sago palm or where wild fruit drops attract these animals. Kamula hunting is focused on these large game animals—pigs, cassowaries, and wallabies. Neither deadfalls nor cassowary snares are mentioned as means of taking game. Foraging also appears to contribute a comparatively small proportion of the nondomesticated animal protein in the diet. The items collected reportedly are limited to megapode and cassowary eggs, sago grubs (beetle larvae), and sugary-tasting ants (ibid.).

The Kamula also make extensive use of aquatic resources and employ both of the fishing methods described earlier with respect to the Onabasulu (e.g., fish traps set in weirs and derris-root poisoning, carried out without damming by large groups of people). They also employ a third method entailing bailing a dammed section of a stream. Crayfish collecting and the shooting or spearing of fish attracted to fruit baits littered on the bottom of shallow areas are reported. Crocodiles are speared from canoes. Fishing with hook and line and the use of scoop nets and large purchased nets that are stretched across streams represent modern methods that are also practiced. Wood (1982:51–52) does not mention whether or not fishnets were fabricated traditionally, as they were among the Gogodala and other lowland Southwest New Guinea groups (Landtman 1927:146). However, it is evident that sys-

tematic exploitation of aquatic resources and large-game hunting were a main
focus of the Kamula's traditional means of procuring nondomestic animal
protein, with foraging being of comparatively limited importance.

Large-game hunting, small-game hunting, trapping, foraging, and the
various means of exploiting aquatic resources entail different organizations
of production and different modes of food distribution and consumption.
Foraging is intrinsically conducive to an individualistic form of production
and consumption insofar as the food resources sought are dispersed, distributed in quantities that one person can readily carry, and in many instances
obtainable in amounts commensurate with a single individual's daily food
requirements. Thus an individual might visit a small stream to collect
crayfish, pick a handful of wild greens further down the trail, stop by last
year's garden to gather a few banana leaves, and return to the longhouse to
cook the crayfish and greens encased in sago flour wrapped with a banana
leaf. The communal meal at which this food was consumed might then be
characterized by many small exchanges between individual foragers on the
order of "have a piece of this crayfish" and "umm, really good, try a bite of
my mouse."

This picture presents a marked contrast to one in which a successful
Kamula large-game hunter

> enters the longhouse in modest silence and drops the bundle [of butchered pig]
> in the passageway near his fireplace. Usually single men divide the meat into two
> piles, one for the men and the other for the women. The men's meat is cut up
> into smaller pieces and each male living in the men's section of the house is given
> a piece or else it is hung above the man's fireplace to await his arrival. Meat is
> also distributed to all the women who cook and feed it to their immediate family
> (including their husbands, sons and brothers who may have already received
> meat from the intra-male distribution). If it was a pig that was shot, later that
> evening or the next evening the skin, parts of the intestines and sago are cooked
> in tree bark by the men. The cooked food is divided amongst all the men who
> then usually give some of it to their wife and family. (Wood 1982:53)

Here the mode of procuring game involves cooperative as well as individual
hunting, while distribution entails both a division of uncooked meat into
male and female shares (that are then individually portioned out) and a
subsequent exchange of a male-prepared pork-rind-and-tripe dish against a
female-prepared meat dish. Communal meals are also characterized by extensive sharing of cooked food between members of the same sex (Wood
1982:44), and these would be expected to entail further exchanges of the
type described above, e.g., "try a piece of this liver" and "have a taste of
loin." Irrespective of whatever transpires earlier, eating itself is distinctly
communal in character in all these longhouse societies.

These two forms of animal protein procurement differ not only in terms of cooperative versus individualistic endeavor and communal distribution of the uncooked product versus none, but also in terms of the division of labor by sex and age. In large-game hunting, the division of labor is much more marked. Although Kamula women occasionally hunt in groups using dogs to track and corner game, which is then bludgeoned to death (Wood 1987:9; 1982:52), hunting is a predominantly male activity and is ideologically conceived as "an exclusively male activity" (Wood 1982:52). This exclusivity is realized to the extent that women are prohibited from using bows and arrows (and currently guns as well). In contrast, foraging is conducive to an attenuated division of labor. In theory, all of the varied activities that constitute foraging can be accomplished by individuals of either sex, and many can be pursued by children as well as adults. Foraging thus presents the theoretical possibility of virtually no division of labor by age and sex or, alternatively, of innumerable permutations.

The contrast being drawn here is one between ideal types. In the Kamula case, the game drives involving female beaters and male bowmen encompass a sexual division of labor internal to the task, showing that the Kamula view of hunting as "exclusively male" is not an entirely accurate representation of the facts. Moreover, large-game hunting clearly admits of forms of organization that are not limited to males. The fact that Kamula women occasionally kill a pig when they hunt with dogs amplifies this point. It would thus be difficult to put forward a convincing argument to the effect that the environmentally given type and distribution of game necessitates a "man the hunter" division of labor, although it can be said that these ecological factors readily accommodate a male predominance in hunting (that can also be ideologically highlighted). Similarly, a dispersed distribution of small quantities of collectible foods and small game animals accommodates individualistic foraging and creates a potentiality for an attenuated division of labor by age and sex without necessitating this particular organization of effort. Indeed, the point of this discussion is to lay the groundwork for an analysis of the Etoro organization of labor that attempts to bring out cultural emphases by displaying them against the backdrop of an ecologically informed range of possibilities. Regional comparison also contributes to an appreciation of this range of possibilities. Thus available data suggest that the Gebusi approximate the foraging ideal type adduced in the preceding discussion (see Knauft 1985a:16–20), although—like the Etoro—the Gebusi appear to favor companionship in food-getting activities even when this entails a duplication of effort that reduces returns per person.

The ecological conditions of Etoro foraging largely correspond to those described earlier. Eggs, fledgling birds, crayfish, minnows, lizards, snakes, insect larvae, small mammals, and many game mammals are both widely dispersed and procured in meal-sized quantities. This is equally applicable to the wild greens, tubers, mushrooms, and (some) nuts collected in the course of the same foraging expeditions. Only certain wild nuts and some frogs are seasonally found in sufficient concentrations to make collection by more than one person fruitful.

An ecological pull toward individualistic foraging is thus present, but this runs up against the cultural view that it is undesirable for an individual ever to be alone. Every myth and tale of witchcraft portrays the unfortunate victim as having gone off alone, typically to hunt or gather, and the notion that an individual alone is especially susceptible to witchcraft attack is an often enunciated article of faith. Being alone in the course of food-getting activities is minimized, although not entirely avoided, by several accommodations. First, a good deal of foraging takes place en route to sago stands and gardens and on the return trip to the longhouse. For example, when a sago palm is to be processed, several men will proceed to the site to fell and split the palm. Several women arrive an hour or two later to begin their part of the work. The two parties may well take different trails to the site and yet others on the return. Moreover, it is common for individuals to split off from the work group for a portion of the trip to harvest from gardens, check a deadfall, visit a small fish weir, or collect tree ferns, bamboo shoots, and other wild foods. At the end of the day, a whole section of the secondary forest between the sago stand and longhouse will have been thoroughly combed for edibles, although each participant will have spent little time alone.

More far-ranging trips are undertaken by men to collect megapode eggs in forests at some distance from the longhouse and current gardens, to check isolated deadfalls, cassowary snares, and traplines, to harvest breadfruit nuts and pandanus in distant groves, to check the whereabouts of semidomesticated pigs that forage unattended in the bush, and to engage in opportunistic hunting and collecting of whatever turns up along the way. These half-day or longer expeditions may be undertaken alone, but quite often an 8- to 12-year-old "younger brother" or "cross-cousin" will be recruited for companionship and to decrease the perceived danger of an attack by a witch. Or two young men may go together. While foraging (and the associated activities listed above) does intrinsically promote dispersed individual effort on the part of adult workers, the capacity that children have for this activity makes it possible to accommodate culturally desired companionship and sociality with less wastage of labor due to reduplication of effort than would otherwise be the case. In communal gardening, labor economies are realized in the reduced fencing needed per plot (Kelly 1977:54). In foraging, joint effort entails the inefficient deployment of labor. The fact that the Etoro favor joint effort in both cases indicates that sociality and companionship in food getting rank higher on their scale of values than labor efficiency.

All Etoro—male and female, young and old—engage in foraging and in the associated activities of harvesting from old gardens and checking traps and snares. However, adult men spend many more hours engaged in these activities than do women and children. Nearly all the foraging carried out by women takes place in the context of trips to sago stands and current gardens that are generally located within a twenty-minute walk from the longhouse. When more distant sites are taken into cultivation, the work group will reside at a garden house for extended periods of time, and the radius within which women travel is even more restricted. Women's foraging is thus limited to the areas proximate to the longhouse and garden house.

In contrast, men's foraging activities are concentrated in a radius that extends outward from current gardens and currently utilized sago stands to a distance of about two hours' walk from the longhouse. The resources available in this zone include marita pandanus, breadfruit nuts, and Tahitian chestnuts planted in gardens many years earlier, as well as tree ferns and wild nut trees, whose locations are kept in mind. A brief review of the relevant Etoro gardening practices will make it clear why these important foods are located at some distance from the longhouse. Marita pandanus and breadfruit trees are planted in one relatively small section of a garden in which either sweet potatoes or a combination of taro and bananas predominates. The root crops are generally completely harvested by the ninth month (and I use the designation "current gardens" to refer to those still producing these starch staples). Bananas first become available in the twelfth to fifteenth calendar month, depending on the variety, while the earliest of seven varieties of pandanus is said to begin to bear in twenty lunar months and the latest in thirty-four lunar months after planting. Full production is probably not attained until four or five years after planting, but the trees are said to bear seasonally for a lifetime. Breadfruit nut trees are said to begin to bear in eight to ten years and to yield seasonally for thirty to forty-five years. Tahitian chestnuts, which are planted in or near gardens, are said to begin bearing more than 20 years later and to continue beyond an individual's lifetime. Wild *kisipe* and *morape* nut trees are not planted but are, of course, left standing in areas taken under cultivation. Thus some of the most wide-branching and heavily producing trees are in former gardens. Breadfruit nuts, Tahitian chestnuts, *kisipe* and *morape* nuts are available in succession, providing a nearly year-round supply (Kelly 1977:45–46). Pandanus is eaten almost daily for three months, often for three more months, and occasionally during the remainder of the year. (Both nuts and pandanus are important components of the diet as sources of oil and, in the case of pandanus, vegetable protein as well.)

Regular harvesting trips to gardens cultivated five to fifty years ago are thus required. The most recent of these gardens would be adjacent to a former longhouse site, since a new longhouse is constructed about every four years. Tree ferns, which are available in quantity about five years after a garden is abandoned to fallow succession, would be collectible in the same area. Other former gardens are scattered throughout several lineage territories where residents of the longhouse lived earlier in their lives.[4] Although some nuts, pandanus, and tree ferns are available in former gardens near the longhouse, these proximate resources are quickly exhausted, and the bulk of the harvesting takes place further afield.

During the height of the pandanus season, two men from the longhouse (or a man and a boy) make daily harvesting trips of about two to four hours' duration, returning with one or two fully loaded net bags of pandanus weighing about thirty pounds. The fruits are split and cored and the fleshy parts to which the kernels are attached are then steam cooked, all of this being done by the men. After cooking, the oily red kernels are shucked into a large trough and kneaded, with water added from time to time. This juice is then thickened with baked sago to produce a sauce of about the consistency of tomato paste. It may be eaten with sweet potatoes, taro, sago, or by itself. The amount of pandanus sauce prepared by the men is sufficient to be shared out among all members of the longhouse community (averaging thirty-five persons). The preparation of this dish takes several hours, and an hour or more may also be spent at the pandanus grove clearing undergrowth and cutting saplings and nearby trees that offer root and light competition as the secondary forest regenerates. This, plus the two to four hours' travel and harvesting time, makes a very full day's work. However, the next day another man or pair of men will take their turn provisioning the community.

Tree ferns are also collected in large quantities and shared out to all members of the community, particularly when there is pork to be cooked with them. Bananas are sometimes shared as well, since a single plant may yield forty pounds and there is often some urgency to harvest the ripening fruit before it is lost to fruit bats. The bananas that a man has planted in a section of his garden (or plot) may thus yield in quantities that exceed the immediate needs of himself and his family.

All these long-bearing crops—bananas,[5] pandanus, breadfruit, and Tahitian chestnut trees—are planted, maintained over time, and harvested predominantly by men. Moreover, they are all distributed to coresidents rather than being consumed solely by a man's immediate family. In the case of pandanus, a special dish is prepared for the entire community, while in other instances bananas and various nuts may be shared among some coresident kinsmen, but not inclusively among all community residents. In contrast, the sweet potatoes, taro, and garden greens that are harvested from current gardens—mostly by women—are primarily consumed by the family units that produce them within the demarcated plots they own in communal gardens. The same applies to sago, which is produced from individually owned palms.

Sometimes male distribution of vegetable foods extends beyond the confines of the community. Thus Kaburusato was once the beneficiary of a large net bag full of taro brought by a man from another community, who enthused about his bumper crop. He reportedly delivered equivalent bags to three other communities as well. Ernst (1984:121) notes that one Onabasulu man planted a large monocrop garden of sugar cane that far exceeded the annual needs of his entire community, and it is likely that this was destined for wider distribution. Generosity in the distribution of food, the widespread provision of special treats (such as nuts), and the preparation of communally consumed dishes are all male attributes. This association of generosity with men is consistent with the pattern noted by Collier and Rosaldo (1981:282–83), but here extends to vegetable foods as well as game animals (although the capture of game is only preponderantly rather than exclusively male).

Harvesting and foraging go hand in hand. Thus women harvest in current gardens almost daily and forage in the area between these and the longhouse. Men harvest in older gardens further afield and forage within a wider radius of the longhouse. Anyone who encounters an animal will attempt to capture it, but men have many more such encounters since they spend more hours foraging and cover less-traveled areas. The principal hunting implement is a long-handled ax which is used to cut trees in which game has taken refuge and to dig out holed up animals, the handle being used for this purpose. Hunting is carried out by walking through the forest, often accompanied by a dog (Dwyer 1983:147). The method is the same whether hunting is the main objective or incidental to foraging, and irrespective of whether the area searched for game is primary or secondary forest. (The bow and arrow is used only in hunting wild pigs and in shooting birds from blinds, both of which are infrequent activities.) Women who forage in the zone proximate to the longhouse are well equipped to dig out terrestrial animals with a digging stick, and the bulk of the game taken in the secondary forest, both in traps and by opportunistic hunting, is terrestrial. (The bandicoots *Echymipera kalubu* and *E. rufescens* and the large rat *Uromys caudimaculatus* account for 63.5 percent of the edible weight of game taken at the lower altitude community of Namosado [Dwyer 1985c:111], and these were also the most common game animals seen at Kaburusato.) Before the introduction of the steel ax and bush knife, women used a stone ax/adze to clear underbrush and cut small trees in garden preparation and thus would have been as well equipped as men to go after arboreal game. In 1968–69, women would be more likely to be carrying a bush knife while en route to a garden, and would sing out for someone with an ax if an animal was treed or arboreal game spotted. However, women will cut trees under these circumstances if an ax is available and no men are within earshot. Both young women and young men in their teens and twenties will climb trees to rob nests and check promising-looking holes; older persons of both sexes tend to forego this, though men persist longer than women. The point here is that there is very little difference in male and female foraging, including the opportunistic "hunting" this entails (i.e., digging out holed animals). The key difference is that men forage in more productive areas for many more hours, and this accounts for the fact that men procure the bulk of the game and of certain types of collectibles (e.g., nuts).

The division of labor by sex is not ideologically marked among the Etoro in a number of respects. There is very little notion of male and female tools, male-exclusive and female-exclusive tasks, male and female crops, or nega- tive influences stemming from the intrusion of one gender into the domain of the other. It is not the food-getting activities that males and females perform that are bound up with the cultural elaboration of gender. Ernst (1978:193) notes that Onabasulu adults of both sexes know "how to perform the entire repertoire, male and female, of most productive tasks" and that axes and digging sticks are used by both sexes (ibid.:196). This is equally true of the Etoro. It is a common occurrence to see a woman use an ax in clearing undergrowth and saplings in garden preparation, and the digging stick is routinely used by all in planting. Although men bring in firewood (which must be dried in the longhouse before use) and generally split it, women will split wood if they need some and none is at hand, whether or not there are men present that could be called upon to do this. Only men hunt with the bow and arrow, but this type of hunting is very infrequent. Although there are clearly certain tasks that are normally done by men and by women, respec- tively, in both gardening and sago processing, men sometimes put in gardens or process sago on their own (as discussed in later sections).

Fish poisoning is an exception to the general pattern of a division of labor that does not entail male-exclusive and female-exclusive tasks, in that there is a definite idea that women should not enter the water during fish poisoning. Women are thus debarred from the construction of dams and breakwaters, the beating of the derris-root poison, and the collection of the stunned fish. The only task women may perform is the collection of leaves and moss used to plug the holes between stones. All the work in fish poison- ing is nominally allotted to men, and women undertake the collection of leaves and moss on their own volition. Women need not accompany fish- poisoning expeditions at all, but they usually do since these occasions offer diversion, excitement, and the pleasant sociality of a day spent by the river. Being in the company of the greatest number of people, male and female, is usually the preferred choice among alternatives. Once there, women tend to pitch in and make at least a token contribution to the enterprise, since cooperative effort is also culturally valued in its own right.

The degree of male exclusivity associated with the main tasks of fish poisoning is clearly connected to the fact that it is a spiritual as well as a subsistence activity. The fish taken are the corporeal abode of the spirits of the dead, and the operation is directed by a spirit medium who secures the permission of the *Kesame* spirits during a séance conducted the night before the operation commences. If few fish are taken, this reflects poorly on the medium, and an additional séance is necessary to explain what went wrong (see Kelly 1977:61–62). The Gebusi are similar to the Etoro in that spirit mediums are actively involved in fish poisoning and females are excluded (Knauft, personal communication). Among both the Onabasulu (Ernst 1984:108–10) and Kamula (Wood 1982:51, 68), women take a greater part in the work of fish poisoning, and in both cases there is no mention of organization of the activity by spirit mediums. Etoro men perform a number of tasks that fall to women among neighboring groups, and this is a feature that we will return to later in the discussion.

The absence of a clear-cut sexual division of labor in practice applies to hunting and trapping as well as foraging. Although traplines are rebuilt for seasonal use by men, checking traps, collecting the captured game, resetting traps, and making necessary repairs to the traps and fence line are tasks "widely shared by men, women and children" (Dwyer 1982:537). Dwyer (1983:151, 156) also reports that two of thirty-one Etoro hunters in his sample were women who accompanied their husbands on multiple-day hunting expeditions to the primary forest, that both sexes "chase game, climb or fell trees," and that nine of fifteen captures of the large and formidable tree kangaroo (*D. dorianus*) were made by these two husband-wife teams.[6] However, setting cassowary snares, which requires the permission of the *Sigisato* spirits, is only carried out by men.

Although the primary forest is a place connected with male *Sigisato* spirits, in which taboos preclude the utterance of words referring to sago, fish, gardens, other low-altitude phenomena, and women, it is not a place forbidden to women (Dwyer 1990:14). What is critical is that a defined order be maintained by proper behavior and proper language, irrespective of the gender of the persons involved (ibid.). Several stories relate the unfortunate consequences of a failure to maintain this order. In one of these, a woman goes on a hunting expedition to the primary forest with her husband but thoughtlessly brings a forbidden variety of sago. She is killed by a *Sigisato* spirit and buried in the mud (in the same way that sago itself is buried for storage). However, there is no suggestion in this tale that the woman herself was out of place. Her husband is bewildered when he cannot find her at the overnight shelter they had constructed before he set out to hunt, and he weeps when he discovers her loss (revealed by a *Sigisato* in the form of a bird). In the second myth, a woman utters a shocking blasphemy (taking the name of the *Sigisato* spirits in vain in a sexual connection) during a fish-poisoning expedition and is instantly dismembered by these spirits. All useful things in nature—vines, cooking leaves, firewood, greens—speak ominously to the people of the woman's community, and their longhouse is then struck by lightning (controlled by *Sigisatos*) on their return. Only two spirit mediums survive. They engage the *Sigisatos* in a battle in which the latter take the form of game animals—pigs, pythons, and cassowaries (just as they earlier took the form of useful flora). Although these animals are brought down by the mediums' arrows, the two mediums are ultimately killed by innumerable pebbles and thorns shot into them by the *Sigisatos*.

In these stories, the wrath of the *Sigisatos* is evoked by transgressive behavior that occurs in the course of productive activity: hunting and fish poisoning. Although both activities are normally carried out by men and the verbal/behavioral transgressions are committed by women, there is no concept that the presence of female persons is in any way inimical to male efforts or male enterprise. Women are not out of place in these contexts. But some women may say and do things that are out of place. Since there are no comparable stories about male transgressions, one may conclude that Etoro oral literature portrays women as tending to lack a proper respect for the spirits and thus prone to careless error and transgression. But this alleged character flaw is not seen as necessitating the exclusion of a female presence from the domain of male productive activity.

It should be pointed out that women are not called upon to perform any labor whatsoever in these areas, and there is no question of any appropriation or mystification of their efforts. Rather, women are *permitted* to participate, provided that they behave appropriately, as these cautionary tales instruct them. Moreover, it is not a husband's (or other man's) task to bring about the proper behavior of women when they act in male domains. Women's transgressions are directly punished by the *Sigisato* spirits without any need for direct male intervention or control (though innocent parties may suffer together with the transgressor when the ultimate blasphemy is uttered). This absence of a need for direct male control is related to the fact that men are not dependent on a female labor contribution to carry out hunting and fish poisoning, since men have taken it upon themselves to do all the work that is required.[7] However, this has important consequences with respect to food distribution that will be elucidated further along.

It is important to note that the discussion has progressed from practice to myth, and that in practice men may perform the tasks normally allotted to women and vice versa entirely without incident. Ernst's (1978:194) point that an Onabasulu conceptual dichotomy between male and female that is significant in other domains of the sociocultural system (most notably in the spatial partitions of the longhouse) "is a false and tenuous one *in the realm of the productive economy*" is well taken. In other words, a male/female opposition is good to think in a number of conceptual contexts, but it is *least* realized in the actualities of productive activity. This is particularly well illustrated by the fact that women hunt in the primary forest although the word for woman cannot be uttered there. Relations of production do not mirror a conceptual gender opposition in practice and are clearly not the locus for the production of gender differentiation. In short, it is principally in stories about food-getting activities, rather than in these activities themselves, that gender distinctions emerge. These stories may be seen as upholding a conceptual order that is not palpable to actors. One might then say that it is just because the sexual division of labor is marked by frequent role reversals and an absence of task exclusivity that the Etoro feel a need to maintain an order based on words and things (that are out of place in the primary forest), and that they tell stories suggesting that those who violate this order will be punished by *Sigisato* spirits.[8]

Although the set of conceptual oppositions that "male" and "female" enter into will be discussed later, it may be noted here that the fundamental Etoro opposition is homosexuality : heterosexuality :: growth, strength, and vitality : senescence, weakness, and death (Kelly 1977:24; cf. Sørum 1984). Male and female then figure into this set in a secondary sense, in that male is associated with homosexuality and female with heterosexuality. Male is further associated with "high" and female with "low," as is expressed in the siting and layout of the longhouse (Kelly 1976; cf. Sørum 1984:334). Thus women are one of the things associated with "low" that cannot be named in the primary forest. However, there is very little extension of this basic oppositional set into other domains, probably because the homosexual/ heterosexual contrast does not easily map onto the attributes of things in the world. Thus while dogs are classified as male and homosexual because they lick one another's genitals, this principle does not lend itself to a general classification of fauna and flora (including garden crops). There is consequently no cosmic and encompassing dual organization in which "male : female" stands at the apex. It is the transmission of life force between generations rather than gender that is employed to conceptually order the world, and the cultural formulation of gender attributes is specified in the context of this life-force ideology (Kelly 1976; cf. Sørum 1984).

Thus far the discussion of Etoro economic organization has focused on the means of procuring nondomesticated animal protein, including foraging, hunting, trapping, and fish poisoning. Consideration has been given to the intrinsic, ecologically grounded tendencies toward individualistic effort and an attenuated division of labor that foraging per se entails, and to the cultural construction of a distinctive Etoro version of this activity. Companionship and joint effort are engineered (against the grain) and an artificial spatial division of labor is constructed such that women forage near the longhouse and men further afield, in a donut-shaped zone that surrounds and encompasses the spatial domain of most female activity.[9] Men forage longer hours in a more productive area and account for a markedly disproportionate share of the game animals garnered through both hunting and foraging, while the smaller, individually consumed items such as crayfish and frogs are procured in more equivalent quantities by both sexes. Men consequently predominate in the distribution of game, which is portioned out to coresidents who then share it with their families to the extent consistent with food taboos.[10] Other foods that are widely distributed are mostly harvested from old gardens that are in the male domain, so that male generosity is further accentuated.

However, there is no male exclusivity in these areas of food getting and food giving and no cultural ideology that capturing game plays an important role in the delineation of masculinity.[11] Indeed the logic of the system is one that holds a potentiality for both gender blurring and invidious comparison, rather than being grounded in exclusion. To a large extent women either do the same things as men, as in foraging, or are free to participate in the activities allotted to men, i.e., hunting and, with restricted participation, fish poisoning. Stories convey the idea that women are prone to the egregious introduction of disorder when they participate in these nominally male productive domains, and must take care to behave properly. However, in actual practice their inclusion and participation are welcomed. The general tenor of male-female relations in these productive activities, as in gardening and sago processing, is one of cooperation, joint effort, and complementarity. Thus the potentiality for invidious comparison, whereby women might be seen to forage in the same way as men, but less effectively, was not realized in the sense that (to my knowledge) no disparaging remarks were ever made.[12] No one comments on differential success in taking game, either among men, among women, or between men and women. However, game distribution provides the basis for an individual's publicly acknowledged reputation for generosity, and this does constitute an arena of comparative evaluations (as discussed further along).

The alternative, more egalitarian possibility of blurred genders (as opposed to invidious comparison) is an emergent quality of the division of labor as this is realized in practice. Thus women are seen to be capable of chasing game, climbing and felling trees, and repairing traps, while men are likewise seen to be capable of processing sago and weeding gardens. Gender-linked attributes are effaced or blurred in the realm of work, and the contributions one gender makes to tasks normally allotted to the other are appreciated rather than denigrated. It is interesting in this connection that an Etoro myth envisions the possibility of a man magically producing children, growing breasts, donning women's attire, and joining the women in their sago-processing tasks. This attempt to transcend the division of labor in reproduction (as well as production) will tell us much about Etoro conceptions of what is fundamental to maleness and femaleness. The point to be noted here is that the Etoro find it necessary to explicitly address this question, suggesting that distinctive maleness and femaleness are not rooted in a perceived "natural" order of gendered capabilities or in the experience of everyday life in some obvious and unquestionable way that requires no explanation. While work is the mainstay of life experience on a day-to-day basis, this experience does not convey the notion that men and women are uniquely and distinctively different.

It is important to note that the Etoro spatial division of labor in foraging is not amenable to functional explanations. The null hypotheses that could be put forward to account for the near-home foraging of women and the far-ranging foraging of men include female vulnerability to raiding parties, tending nonbipedal children, efforts to control female sexuality, and the need to carry heavy loads long distances. However, none of these is plausible since young women can flee from raiding parties as readily as men do, either have no children to tend (as yet) or could easily leave them with a kinswoman, can readily carry heavy loads, and have ample opportunities for adulterous trysts near the longhouse on the days when their husbands are engaged in far-ranging foraging but other men are not. Even more telling, however, is the fact that Kamula women engage in the more wide-ranging foraging carried out by Etoro men. Thus Kamula women collect cassowary and bush hen eggs, which are found outside the zone of habitations and current gardens, in addition to beetle larvae, fruits, wild greens, honey, and sugary-tasting ants (Wood 1982:52). However, in the Kamula case, foraging makes a relatively slight contribution to the diet, compared to large-game hunting and various means of exploiting aquatic resources, and does not entail the collection of foods that are widely shared. A comparison of the Etoro and Kamula with respect to the place of far-ranging foraging in the sexual division of labor thus suggests that this task may be arbitrarily allotted to either gender. However, men predominate in the food-getting activities that eventuate in the distribution of food to others in both instances, and men thus have a superior opportunity to attain prestige through generosity.

The Etoro organization of harvesting, foraging, hunting, trapping, and fish poisoning generates differential prestige in that men are in a position to generously distribute game, fish, pandanus sauce, and the like while women infrequently have the opportunity to do so. Since differences in prestige are a central aspect of inequality, it is especially important to understand the cultural meaning of generosity. This may best be grasped by examining the role of generosity in the community in terms of a specific example.

Ibo (aged 46) was the *tafidilo* or respected senior man of Kaburusato (a status to be explored more fully in subsequent chapters). He was an assiduous hunter of midsize game and was also proficient in snaring cassowaries. During the fifteen-month fieldwork period he shot three wild pigs at his garden, trapped two cassowaries, and procured a variety of smaller game animals that he shared with other members of the longhouse community. In all, he provided 56 percent of the game consumed by the community (measured in terms of live weight). Only Weliba (aged 34), who provided the other wild pig and the other two cassowaries consumed during this period, came close to matching his contribution to the community's dining pleasure. However, this contribution was much more than merely gustatory, since Ibo provisioned occasions during which a culturally valued sense of social community was realized in the sharing of a relative abundance of especially favored foods among all coresidents (excepting those to whom the type of game distributed was taboo). The narrower concerns of individuals, of families, and of close kin relations were all transcended at these repasts in which all eligible coresidents shared equally, irrespective of their kin relation to Ibo (or lack thereof). The more encompassing sociality of community was thus engendered.

The reproduction and reaffirmation of broader forms of sociality is a central component of what I have termed "generosity." It is this accomplishment—achieved through elective social action—that is accorded prestige. Generosity is the abnegation of individual self-interest in favor of relational and communal sociality. The contrastive quality in the Etoro worldview is thus the despised individualistic selfishness of the witch, who grows large by consuming the bodies and life force of his or her coresidents and thereby inverts these values. Likewise, a witch consumes game privately rather than bringing it to the longhouse to be shared with others, a potentiality that is easily realized without detection. The Etoro are also adept at preserving meat by smoking and are not compelled to share in order to fulfill self-interests that would otherwise be defeated by spoilage. Moreover, sharing game with a few garden house coresidents is a socially acceptable option. Since the Etoro are well aware of these alternatives, generosity in distributing game to the community as a whole is seen as a positive act toward others rather than the realization of self-interest by alternative means.

In giving meat to others and subsequently receiving meat in return, an exchange value is created over and above the consumption value intrinsic to the game animal, namely the social value of having given and received. ("Exchange value" will be used in this sense throughout this work; cf. Sahlins 1972:82–84.) To fail to share is to consume this exchange value and its relational potential as well as the game itself. The creation of exchange value and its use in the reproduction of broader relational and communal forms of sociality are the key elements of generosity. To share game with community members thus constitutes a form of generosity, while sharing with family members within the domestic unit does not, insofar as the latter does not entail a realization of exchange value in the broader sphere. Although sharing with family members is expected, it is not accorded prestige. The generosity through which one earns prestige is linked to the realization of community as a form of sociality and entails the transcendence of compulsory or obligatory provisioning.

Although the sharing of game should be reciprocated, there is no calculation of an accumulation of credits that must be repaid and indeed virtually no likelihood that a proficient hunter such as Ibo will ever receive in equal measure on other occasions. The nature of the distribution itself also tends to depersonalize the transaction between the successful hunter and the recipients of game. A pig or cassowary is butchered and portioned out to other hunters residing in the community in a routine fashion such that each hunter's share includes some of all the various parts of the animal (which the recipient then allocates in the same way among family members who constitute the hearth group). There is no scope for favoring some families over others and, given the invariance of the mode of distribution, anyone may carry it out. Generally the butchering and division are done by a group of men which may or may not include the successful hunter. The shares received are an entitlement of community membership in which the element of a personal gift from hunter to recipient is effaced. What the successful hunter accumulates is thus the prestige that derives from generosity (in the sense explained), not credits to be repaid in meat at some future date, or to be repaid in some other way. Likewise, the recipients are under no obligation other than the general obligation to share game with coresidents that was in place prior to this specific distribution. These features are important components of the broader sociality that is achieved through the sharing of game with community members.

The depersonalization of hunting success is also accentuated by the connection between game and spirits. The *Sigisato* spirits are nonancestral forest spirits linked to lineages through the co-ownership and co-occupancy of lineage territories. They are the guardians of the game the Etoro procure, and they occupy the bodies of the cassowaries that are snared (see Dwyer 1990:11–26; Kelly 1977:61–64). The *Sigisatos* thus give up their "pigs" and "dogs" (as various small game animals are construed) and in the case of cassowaries yield up their own flesh for human consumption. The fish that are poisoned are likewise the corporeal abode of the *Kesames,* spirits of the dead. Spiritual direction, communicated in dreams and in séances, is a prerequisite to the setting of cassowary snares and to fish-poisoning operations, so that *Kesame* and *Sigisato* spirits can vacate these particular corporeal forms and assume others (see Kelly 1977:61–64). Hunting success is spiritually derived (as is success in fish poisoning) and therefore is not entirely attributable to the skill of an individual hunter (or of the medium who directs a fish-poisoning operation). The hunter only mediates a transaction in which the spirits provide game to community members. The game is as much a gift from the spirits as a contribution from a particular hunter. The depersonalized mode of distribution and the fact that the shares coresidents receive are regarded as an entitlement are both consistent with this.

The snaring of a cassowary (or successful fish poisoning) betokens the goodwill and beneficence of the spirits. A séance that builds upon and amplifies the sense of community that has been achieved through food sharing is typically conducted after the meal in order to communicate with and pay homage to these spirits. The Durkheimian conflation of communal solidarity with powerful spiritual entities is clearly in evidence on these occasions. However, human generosity is the vehicle for the realization of the spirits' beneficence as well as the achievement of community. Thus if Ibo's personal role as the giver of game has been effaced, his role as the facilitator of community and mediator of the community's receipt of spiritual goodwill has been accentuated. What I have termed "generosity" thus has a spiritual quality. It is the spirit of community in the Durkheimian sense.[13] The cultural meaning of generosity thus hinges on the creation of exchange value through sharing, the realization of community by an encompassing disposition of exchange value, and the concomitant generation of spiritual values that arise out of this realization of community. It is easy to see why generosity in this sense is esteemed.

Having elucidated the underpinnings of the relation between generosity and prestige, we may return to the question of how the organization of production engenders differential opportunities to achieve the latter. It is evident that the division of labor represents a division of the potentiality for attaining prestige through generosity. Etoro men predominate in all subsistence activities that eventuate in the distribution of food to individuals outside their immediate family. Women are not excluded from distributing food to a wider range of kinspersons and coresidents but have fewer opportunities to do so. Since generosity is readily amenable to comparative evaluation by the recipients of things given, men appear to be more generous than women. Indeed men *are* more generous. However, this is an artifact of a division of labor that provides unequal opportunities to distribute foods widely.

These differential opportunities that the division of labor affords to men and women to engage in the extrafamilial distribution of game can be more precisely specified. Wild pigs are exclusively taken by men, since only men possess the bows and arrows employed to dispatch them when they are encountered in the course of other activities (i.e., surprised at a sago stand or in a garden they have invaded). Cassowaries are also exclusively procured by men, who have been granted permission to set snares by *Sigisato* spirits.

Sigisatos appear to men (but not women) in dreams and convey this permission; they may also convey it via spirit mediums. Fish are likewise poisoned by men after spirit permission has been obtained from the *Kesames* by a spirit medium. These are the principal game animals that are of sufficient size (or available in sufficient quantity in the case of fish) to distribute to all community members at Kaburusato. These three male-exclusive sources of nondomesticated animal protein contributed 44.6 percent of the total consumed at this community. Bush hen eggs and wood grubs are predominantly procured in the zone further from gardens and habitations, in which men forage. These make up another 35.8 percent of total nondomesticated animal protein consumed at Kaburusato (but these plus large game and fish constitute less than 20 percent of the total at Bobole). Frogs, fledgling birds, moles, mice, minnows, and insects are obtained by females as often as males, but these small items provide no scope for generosity (in the sense defined) and are shared with family members by both genders. Thus, the only game animals regularly procured by women that are suitable for extrafamilial distribution are forest mammals (weighing about two pounds a piece, on average). They represent 13.9 percent of nondomesticated animal protein at Kaburusato but over 80 percent of this at Bobole. Women capture a fair proportion of them. However, at Kaburusato these are generally taken by women in the course of garden clearance and are distributed to others at garden houses rather than at the longhouse.[14] Distribution is thus typically restricted to family members, but may also include brother, brother's wife, and husband's sister and her husband, who are likely to share a garden house with a female ego. At Bobole, several women hunted forest mammals, and many had access to the forest mammals they retrieved from family-operated traplines as well as those taken during garden clearance. Animals obtained in gardens were frequently consumed there (as at Kaburusato), while women often distributed the proceeds of traps to female kin when their husbands were absent from the village (Dwyer 1990:124). The women who hunted distributed game to coresidents of the longhouse community. Thus, at Kaburusato women had few opportunities to distribute game widely at the longhouse, but also did not avail themselves of these, electing restricted distribution at a garden house instead. At Bobole the opportunities were considerably greater since forest mammals were the main item available for distribution to coresidents. However, only the two women who hunted appear to have engaged in the prestigious form of distribution.

Wild pigs, cassowaries, and fish can be eaten by everyone except widows and the male and female children of deceased men below the ages of 17 and 12, respectively. These large game and fish procured exclusively by men are thus well suited for a widespread distribution to community members. Thirteen of twenty-one forest mammals can also be consumed by everyone except the restricted categories noted above, and these are the ones most frequently obtained.

A number of factors conspire to markedly curtail female generosity (in the sense defined) in game distribution. These include not possessing bows and arrows and the spatial division of foraging zones, as well as the spiritual permission required for fish poisoning and cassowary snaring. The spiritual restrictions are of particular interest insofar as they pertain to activities in which women could otherwise rather easily engage. Thus, while women are seen to be capable of chasing game, climbing and felling trees, and repairing traps, as men do, they are comparatively infrequently in a position to distribute game to individuals other than family members and rarely in a position to provision a communitywide distribution (particularly at Kaburusato). Women who take part in hunting expeditions to the high forest are the exception, but only one of the two women at Bobole who participated in these expeditions did so on a regular basis and procured substantial quantities of game (Dwyer 1983).

Van Beek (1987:145–53, app. B) provides very detailed data concerning the distribution of small and midsize game by Bedamini men, women, boys, and girls. The items involved are forest mammals, fish, crayfish, snakes, lizards, and insects procured by adults and children of both genders. These data are of considerable interest in revealing the forms of sharing engaged in by men, women, boys, and girls, respectively, when they have the *same* things to share. It is notable that everything is shared with others to some extent, including items as small as grasshoppers, dragonflies, and spiders. However, consumption by the individual who procured the item ranges from 30 to 85 percent for the smallest items (various insects) and from 17 to 81 percent for larger items (ibid.:app. B). There is "no significant difference between the male and female part of the community in general in the amount of game kept for themselves and given to others" (ibid.:147). Adult men and women both procure substantial quantities of small and midsize game (see note 10) and share out nearly the same proportion of their take (52 percent and 48 percent, respectively). However, patterns of distribution differ. While all four age-sex categories give portions of their catch to men, women, boys, and girls, each of these categories distributes game to others in somewhat different proportions.

Boys give significantly more to their peer-group and give very little to girls. Contrarily, girls give a considerable portion of their catch to adult women and virtually nothing to adult men. The women distribute mainly to children without differentiating significantly between the sexes (except in the case of mammals)[15] and tend to give little to other adult women. Lastly, the distribution behavior of men does not show a marked trend, though they tend to share their catch somewhat less with other adult men and girls. (van Beek 1987:148)

Adult men give somewhat less to girls because this may convey connotations of sexual interest when it involves nonfamily members. However, men give somewhat more of these types of game to adult women (e.g., wives and sisters) than to adult men, and their individual consumption is the lowest of all four groups. Overall, their distribution is more generalized than that of any other category, and Bedamini men thus tend to conform to the ideal of generosity with respect to midsize as well as large game.

Men also publicly display their game on returning to the community and consequently are open to direct requests for a share that, in accordance with cultural etiquette, cannot be refused (ibid.:152). In contrast, women conceal what they obtain.

The animals are taken home in the netbag, carefully wrapped in leaves. Only when sitting in the hearth room, the day's catch is unpacked together with other harvest of the day (bananas, tubers, etc.) and unwrapped. The game is then quietly distributed to children of the household present around the fireplace. (ibid.:153)

This mode of sharing "circumvents the ethics of general . . . distribution" (ibid.). Thus, while Bedamini women are not selfish from an etic standpoint, in that their individual consumption is not high, they clearly are not generous in terms of emic conceptions of generosity.

This conclusion is equally applicable to Etoro women. Although I lack data comparable in level of detail to those collected by van Beek with respect to the distribution of small and midsize game, my observations are very consistent with the general patterns he reports.[16] While male extrafamilial sharing of midsize game is highly conspicuous, the female counterpart is rarely observed at the longhouse. Thus, men earn prestige through generosity in the distribution of both large and midsize game to nonfamily members. Women, who also procure midsize game such as forest mammals, distribute this game in a manner that is not productive of prestige.

The preceding discussion raises important issues concerning the extent to which generosity is part of a "male prestige system" that imposes hegemonic values upon both male and female actors (see Ortner and Whitehead 1981:10–16 and the critique of this concept in Yanagisako and Collier 1987:27–28). Available data indicate that generosity is as much esteemed by women as by men. It is through this generosity (in the sense defined) that women are provisioned with game not procured by their husbands. Yet women do not engage in this form of generosity themselves. To a very large extent, the division of labor ensures that they lack the wherewithal to do so. However, when they do procure forest mammals that might be more widely distributed, they circumvent the expectations of the hegemonic ethic of generosity by concealing them (or distributing them at garden houses). The concealment shows that women are equally subject to these expectations. If favoring their children in distribution were culturally valued and approved behavior for women, then one would expect it to be done openly in a manner commensurate with male conspicuousness in displaying and generously distributing game. This suggests that the prestige system encodes values equally applicable to both men and women (and in this sense is not a *male* prestige system, although males earn the prestige). There is not a separate set of values for the distribution of midsize game applicable to a domestic domain, implicitly delineated by a woman's obligation to feed her family, in contrast to those values applicable to a public domain, implicitly delineated by a man's obligation to distribute meat widely (contra Collier and Rosaldo 1981:281; Collier 1988:17). On the contrary, there are general cultural values that impinge upon the distribution of large, midsize, and small game irrespective of the gender of the individual who procures it. Thus, among the Etoro, small game is subject to familial distribution by both men and women. Large game is widely distributed because it is large game, not because the distributor is male. (The gender of the distributor is a product of the division of labor.) Midsize game can potentially be distributed either way, but familial distribution does not conform to the ideal of generosity and is not prestige-enhancing. The concealment of midsize game by Bedamini women reported by van Beek is thus to be interpreted as a choice not to engage in the prestigious form of distribution on occasions when these women possessed the wherewithal to do so. Concealment signals that nonfamily members should not request or expect to receive a share. If a woman were fulfilling a generally recognized and invariant obligation to feed her children, then the obligatory nature of the distribution would render such a signal unnecessary. The concept of gendered obligations—of wife and husband to family and group (respectively)—that is employed by Collier and Rosaldo (1981) thus misconstrues the mechanisms that eventuate in male attainment of prestige through generosity, particularly the division of labor that accords men distributional control over the types of game that are required to be widely distributed. This problem of misplaced causality is taken up in the concluding chapter.

It should be noted that Bedamini men as well as women sometimes elect the nonprestigious mode of distributing midsize game. By residing at a garden house periodically, a man can restrict the distribution of his small and midsize game to family members and also consume more of it himself (van Beek 1987:156). In so doing a man eschews a prestige-producing distribution. This option applies equally to the Etoro. However, Ibo frequently brought midsize as well as large game to the longhouse while in residence at his gardening dwelling, where he might readily have distributed it exclusively to family members without residents of the longhouse even being aware that this had occurred. Thus, men elect prestigious and nonprestigious modes of distribution of midsize game on different occasions and differ in the frequency with which they choose one mode over the other.

This element of choice is a critical component of the prestige earned through generosity. Prestige is achieved through *elective* social action rather than being ascribed on the basis of intrinsic hunting ability that mechanically eventuates in obligatory widespread distribution of the game procured. Differences between men in the attainment of prestige through generosity are not only a product of differences in ability but also a product of differences in the time devoted to hunting and differences in the frequency with which game is brought to the longhouse rather than distributed at garden dwellings. Generosity takes place against a background of clear recognition by everyone that private consumption is an alternative easily accomplished without detection while restricted sharing at a garden house is a socially acceptable option. Generosity is not compelled but elected, and the prestige derived from generosity is bestowed, in the form of esteem, by community members who benefit from this choice. Moreover, the female pattern of familial distribution provides part of the background that highlights male generosity. In short, this pattern provides the comparative counterpoint against which generosity is assessed. The potential for invidious comparison is realized with respect to distribution. Thus women are not conceptually external to the prestige/stigma system even though they generally do not earn prestige and are ineligible for *tafidilo* status. The fact that women regularly procure midsize game but characteristically do not elect the prestige-enhancing (generous) mode of distribution naturalizes male attainment of prestige through generosity and thus contributes to legitimation of the male monopoly on *tafidilo* status. Cultural constructions of gender provide the basis for female self-conceptions that are conducive to the underutilization of these distributional opportunities, as will be elucidated in subsequent chapters.

Among the Etoro, large game is distributed to all coresident hunters of the longhouse community (and thus to all hearth groups), small game is distributed only among members of the procurer's hearth group, and midsize game brought to the longhouse is generally distributed to some but not all hunters in the community, since the quantity is often insufficient for an encompassing distribution. The range over which distribution takes place is thus commensurate with the quantity of game available. However, this general relationship between quantity at hand and range of distribution does not hold with respect to sago. Sago flour is produced from a single palm in quantities sufficient to feed the longhouse community for days but is predominantly subject to distribution among those who participated in its production, i.e., the family-based hearth group or pair of families who share a hearth. Sago is widely distributed to nonfamily members only when the community hosts a *kosa* ceremony. Women provide three-fourths of the labor in sago production and hold distributional rights over sago flour. Thus a husband cannot take sago from the family larder to employ in trade without his wife's permission, and only women give sago to nonfamily members who drop by sago-processing operations (as described more fully in a later section of this chapter). With the exception of these gifts, which account for only about 5 percent of the sago produced, sago is subject to a familial mode of distribution in which its exchange value is not realized. In other words, sago is intrinsically suited to a mode of distribution in which the producer gives the surplus over and above her own family's immediate requirements to other women of the community and receives sago from them when they process a palm in turn. If this were done, women would conform to the ethic of generosity by provisioning the community at large and would additionally amplify the network of social relations between and among women. Thus while the division of labor in animal protein procurement represents a division of the potentiality for earning prestige through generosity, it cannot be said that the division of labor leaves women with no products suitable for an encompassing distribution to community members. However sago, unlike game, lacks spiritual qualities. The differences between these foods in terms of the role they respectively play in the reproduction of the next generation will be elucidated in the next chapter. However, it can be noted here that a cosmologically derived division of value accorded to the products of labor engenders differences in their potential to serve as vehicles for prestige enhancement.

The Etoro conform to the general behavioral pattern that Collier and Rosaldo (1981:281) describe for brideservice societies in that women feed their families while men distribute game to group members. The preceding discussion addresses the issue of what accounts for this. I have argued that extrafamilial distribution is the product of a prestige system in which generosity (defined in relation to such distribution) is esteemed. Insofar as individuals hold rights of disposal over the products of their own labor, the division of labor entails an allocation of distributional rights. The division of labor thus affords men superior opportunities to engage in prestige-enhancing distributions, since men are the procurers of most of the products suited to extrafamilial distribution. However, the secondary question that arises from this explanation is why women engage in a familial mode of distribution with respect to products compatible with a more widespread distribution. Women hold rights of disposal over the sago they process (although this involves some male labor inputs), and over the midsize game they procure, so that the familial mode of distribution can be regarded as one that women elect. In the case of sago flour, the reasons for this are rooted in the second aspect of the division of labor, namely the division of value accorded to the products of labor. This division of value is attributable to the same cosmological principles that inform the prestige system, as will be elucidated in subsequent chapters. While women as producers control the distribution of the products of their own labor, men control the cosmological system that culturally defines "producer" and "labor" and encodes the values accorded to these products. Although these aspects of the general framework for elucidating social inequality remain to be developed, they are mentioned here to contextualize the data and observations presented thus far.

It is important to emphasize that differential access to the attainment of prestige through generosity is grounded in the division of labor itself rather than appropriation of the products of labor. By and large, the foods that men distribute are the products of male labor. This labor adds substantially to the total hours of work men perform in food production and contributes to an overall imbalance whereby men do more work than women. (This will be more fully explored after all aspects of subsistence have been considered.) While men attain more prestige through generosity than do women, they also undertake more hours of labor in order to achieve this result. Thus male generosity is not artificial. Moreover, there is considerable difference between individuals in the effort they expend in hunting, cassowary trapping, and foraging. The men who put in the most hours (such as Ibo) procure and distribute the largest quantities of game. Dwyer's data (1983:155) show that senior males in their early forties to mid-fifties hunt 1.61 to 1.72 hours longer each hunting day than young men aged 16 to 25 (for two separate data sets, respectively) and that the older hunters are also 2.9 to 5.89 times more successful in terms of kilograms of game procured per hour. (The values for men aged 26 to 40 are intermediate.) The older men whose hunting plays a major role in provisioning the longhouse are thus rewarded, in terms of prestige, in a manner commensurate with their efforts (and their skill, which is largely a product of past efforts in the form of experience).

However, there are a few instances in which men distribute foods that were produced with some component of female labor that is only partially recognized. The old gardens from which men harvest pandanus, breadfruit nuts, bananas, Tahitian chestnuts, and tree ferns were originally taken under cultivation by both men and women, although men do the subsequent work of maintaining nut and pandanus groves in production over the years by clearing underbrush and cutting encroaching trees as well as the work of harvesting, transporting (and in the case of pandanus, preparing) the food. The fact that these items are seen as male contributions to the food supply is offset by the fact that sago is viewed as a predominantly female contribution to the food supply, although men contribute labor to the initial stages of sago production. The "producer," who holds distributional rights, is defined as the individual who completes the process of production. Women thus distribute the sago they produce just as men distribute nuts and pandanus. Although more than 95 percent of this sago is deployed in provisioning family units, women do give sago to other kin both within and outside the community (as is described in more detail in the section on sago processing). There are thus parallels in men's and women's control over the distribution of products that were not solely produced by either. However, men's distribution of nuts and (especially) pandanus to extrafamilial kin takes place in the context of communal meals and contributes to the realization of community sociality in the manner described earlier, while women give raw sago to kin in dyadic contexts. The exchange value women thereby create is deployed relationally rather than communally, in transactions that are not witnessed by an audience. In contrast, men's generosity is conspicuous by virtue of its communal character.

Although the distribution of domesticated pork is an infrequent occurrence (compared to the sharing of game animals), these distributions invariably take place in ritual and ceremonial contexts and are thus of particular importance to the issue of appropriation. A brief review of the main features of pig husbandry (described in detail in Kelly 1988) will provide a basis for analyzing deployment in relation to labor contributions.

Most pigs are reported to be jointly owned by a husband and wife or by a young man and his widowed mother, although a few are solely owned by either men or women (Kelly 1988:132). The animals are semidomesticated and spend their adult lives foraging in the bush unattended. During this comparatively lengthy period, social bonds established earlier are maintained by periodically feeding and scratching these free-ranging pigs when they are encountered in the course of daily activities or searched out for this purpose. Most of this is done by men during their more frequent and far-ranging foraging expeditions. It is likewise the male co-owner who spends entire days searching for a pig that has not been encountered for more than a week, causing concern that it may have died or been stolen or that it might become feral. The husband also retrieves a mature pig when it is to be slaughtered and deployed in a social transaction. He then kills, butchers, and cooks the animal (with the help of other men) and presents sides of pork or smaller portions to others, depending on the occasion. The general rule that distribution of a food item is in the hands of the person who completed the process of production holds here as it does with respect to sago processing and pandanus grove maintenance and harvesting. Thus the husband serves as distributor despite the co-owning wife's labor contribution at a much earlier point in time.

During the first three months after weaning, piglets are fed and fondled so that each will establish a permanent attachment to its owners. The piglets are constantly in the company of family members at the longhouse and accompany them during garden making and sago processing, beginning to learn to forage for themselves on these occasions. Although men devote considerable time to petting and feeding the piglets at this stage, in order to establish the bonds that will ensure approachability for the next one to two years (or more), women and girls spend more time keeping track of the animals since the latter remain within the domain proximate to the longhouse, gardens, and sago stands within which women's activities are largely confined. An estimated 5 percent of the annual tuber crop is fed to pigs (Kelly 1988:119), and 58 percent of the labor in producing this is contributed by women (amounting to .34 hours a week of female labor as opposed to .24 hours a week of male labor, based on total gardening effort, presented later in the chapter).

About a third of the shoats reared are acquired in trade from the Huli for either a black palm bow or about eighteen pounds of sago flour. In the latter case, the sago would embody about 7 hours of female labor and 2.25 hours of male labor. However, the trading expedition to acquire the shoat(s) would take four days, entailing at least 24 hours of walking time, so that the male labor contribution significantly outweighs the female labor contribution in pig acquisition when sago flour is traded (while all the labor is male when black palm bows are employed in the exchange). Similarly, men usually go in a group (after dark) to capture the almost-weaned shoats of a semidomesticated sow that has given birth in the bush, in order to bring these to the longhouse for the initial period of domestication. Sometimes a female co-owner will accompany her husband and other men. However, pigs are mostly acquired by men. They are then reared by men and women for the next three months, with the women doing more of the tending. For several additional months, the shoats stay close to the longhouse and are fed occasionally but not tended. Men (and to a lesser extent women as well) subsequently maintain regular contact with the free-ranging adult pigs for a protracted period until slaughter. Men are involved in all phases of the pig life cycle, and overall, their labor contribution in pig husbandry is somewhat greater than that of women. However, men are also prominent at the point of acquisition of a shoat and, more importantly, complete the process of pig production. This, together with male assumption of responsibility for pig rearing, plays a role in the allocation of use and exchange values when a pig is deployed. This issue of responsibility requires further explication.

The owner of a mature pig that dies of natural causes is prohibited from consuming domesticated pork (as opposed to wild pig) until he or she slaughters another pig and shares it with others (see Kelly 1988:135–36). But if virtually all pigs are jointly owned (*ua*) by husband and wife, who then will undergo this prohibition? The Etoro say that either the husband or wife may undertake the burden of this prohibition, as is consistent with their joint ownership. However, in practice it is nearly always the husband who does so. Thus at Kaburusato half the men could not consume domestic pork at any given time (during a fifteen-month period), while no women were under this prohibition. At the neighboring community of Turusato, the same 50-percent level of prohibition obtained, but in the case of one couple the wife had assumed the burden. One consequence of this prohibition is that most domesticated pork is consumed by women (and children). However, the more important point in the present context is that assumption of this responsibility both confers and legitimates men's superior rights in jointly owned pigs. Since men are the primary caretakers of mature pigs (to which this potential prohibition applies), it is logical that men should incur the consequences when a pig dies. But then, by the same logic, they should receive the credit when a pig survives to be slaughtered and deployed in a social transaction. The male role in bringing a pig to maturity is also highlighted and shown to be crucial by the sheer existence of this prohibition. Moreover, this male role in pig rearing parallels and resonates with the importance of the male role in bringing boys to the completion of manhood through insemination.[17] The emphasis on the completion of a maturation process that this prohibition encodes is clearly informed by the cosmology of life-force transmission (to be detailed in chap. 3).

In the case of pigs, however, the Etoro inject an element of choice into the assumption of this role as primary caretaker and completer of a pig's maturation. A woman can acquire a shoat through trade, inheritance, or as a gift from her brother, and become its sole owner and primary caretaker. A wife may also assume this primary caretaker role with respect to a jointly owned pig. In the former instance, the woman alone will bear the burden of the prohibition on pork consumption if the pig dies and will distribute the pork if the pig survives to be slaughtered at maturity. In the latter instance, the wife would be the logical person to assume the responsibility for an untimely porcine demise, but this could still be assumed by her husband by mutual agreement (just as a wife can assume this burden when her husband is primary caretaker). In practice, very few women choose to be sole owners of pigs (although they possess the sago with which to procure shoats in trade) or to undertake the risks and rewards of overseeing the completion of maturation. Men's superior distributional rights are thus doubly legitimated, by the fact that men assume responsibility and by the fact that women nearly always reject it, of their own volition. Finally, half the pigs slaughtered serve to remove some man's prohibition on pork consumption and are thus more specifically linked to the male co-owner. With all these aspects of the over-determined nature of men's superior distributional rights in mind, we can now turn to the issue of deployment.

Pigs are deployed in bridewealth payments, witchcraft and death compensation, affinal exchange, mortuary ceremonies, and divinations pertaining to witchcraft accusations (see Kelly 1988). Pigs are not transacted live and are not contributed to another person's social payments, so the single pig included in a bridewealth or compensation payment is provided by the groom or compensator himself. A husband therefore cannot donate co-owned family pigs to another man's transaction. Nearly all of the pigs that are jointly owned by a husband and wife are deployed in affinal and cross-cousin exchange, with others being used infrequently to provision a man's deceased father's or brother's mortuary feast and the associated divination, or as part of a witchcraft compensation should a family member be accused. Since affinal exchange is the predominant use to which pigs are put, the main venue for sharing pork to lift the prohibition described above, and the critical context with respect to the allocation of social credit between co-owning husbands and wives, I will focus on these transactions.

A pig destined for affinal exchange is split at the backbone and rib cage so as to create two sides of pork, each consisting of a foreleg, shoulder, rib cage, and hindquarter. These two sides of pork are cooked and then publicly presented, with fanfare, to two affines or other kinsmen related by marriage (while the co-owners retain the head and entrails for their own consumption). This division of the pig into two halves provides a Solomonic resolution of any potential divergence of interest arising out of co-ownership. Typically, one side of pork is given to the wife's brother or her father and the other to the husband's sister's husband (or one of his cross-cousins). Most of these gifts are reciprocated the following year, although the return can be completed as early as the next day (see Kelly 1977:222–28 for a more detailed account of these exchanges). The initial exchange is always in the direction of a wife-giver, so that the side of pork given to a husband's sister's husband is a return for that he received earlier as a wife's brother. All the transactions take place within a context of established and ongoing exchanges of women between lineages.

A wife's joint ownership of a pig and her indigenous kinship interests are taken into account by typically giving half the animal to her brother or father. The wife perceives this as a transaction in the relational domain of kinship, and her brother (or father) acknowledges it in the same vein, thereby crediting her labor contribution and co-ownership. At the same time, the husband perceives the gift as also part of an exchange relationship between lineages within the context of a more encompassing structure of intergroup relations, and this is also acknowledged by the recipient. These two aspects of this exchange, which give it a double meaning, are mutually compatible.

The other side of pork is deployed by the husband to repay his sister's husband (for an earlier gift he received as a wife's brother) or to keep up other exchange relations by being given to a cross-cousin or mother's brother. The wife may well have no coinciding kinship interest in this transaction, unless the husband's sister's husband is her lineage brother due to classificatory sister exchange.

At this juncture the husband and wife, as co-owners and coproducers, have each realized the exchange value of one half of a pig. The husband can also coincidentally realize a higher order exchange value (pertaining to interlineage exchange relations) in his wife's kin-based transaction, while she often cannot coincidentally realize a kinship interest in his transaction. This asymmetry stems from the fact that men exchange women by arranging marriages and thereby create a more encompassing structure of intergroup relations in which they have an enduring interest. Men, as the creators of this structure of exchange, realize the exchange value that is structurally derived (in addition to the value that is kinship based). In other words, these values do not adhere in the pig, or in the giving and receiving itself, but in the structure of intergroup exchange relations that makes the affinal exchange of pigs meaningful at a higher level. There is a production of structure and meaningfulness as well as the production of a pig. Thus while there is no appropriation of a product of female labor in the usual sense, there is an appropriation of the production of meaningfulness that allows men to derive additional values from affinal exchange that women cannot realize. Men also "appropriate" their daughters in arranging marriages in order to create and perpetuate a structure of intergroup exchange relations. But here, too, labor and economic production are not at issue. The theoretical differences between these two divergent views of appropriation are critical. In one view, articulated by Modjeska (1982) and Josephides (1985), pig production and the subsequent appropriation of a product of female labor are seen as the central locus of the production of inequality. In the other view, advanced herein, men's control of marriage, their creation of an exchange system, and their appropriation of the production of meaningfulness are the sources of inequality. These theoretical differences, which are partly attributable to differences in the types of systems being analyzed, will be taken up in the conclusions.

When a reciprocal side of pork is received for one given earlier, it is cut up and distributed by the husband. The husband's role as distributor is attributable to his superior rights of ownership in the original pig for which this constitutes a return. The husband gives portions to his coresident agnates and matrilateral siblings. This affinally derived pork may not be shared with coresident affines, although the distributor and his "brothers" are obliged to share it with their wives. Men are thus the givers of the pork that is actually eaten within the community and women receive pork from their husbands, by virtue of their relationship as a wife, while men receive from other men by virtue of siblingship. (Unmarried women receive from fathers, brothers, deceased husband's brothers, etc.) The pork that a woman receives from her husband may be seen as the share to which she is entitled as co-owner and coproducer of other pigs deployed in affinal exchanges. The pig a woman helps produce is thus given to her brother (and her husband's affines), and the reciprocal sides of pork received by her husband are distributed in smaller portions to his "brothers," who later make comparable returns in which the wife shares. The wife thus realizes the full consumption value of the pork she helped produce, with the returns on her labor being spread out over time (providing a desirable pattern of regular opportunities to consume meal-sized quantities of pork).

As often as not, a husband does not realize the consumption value of the pig he coproduced because he is prohibited from consuming pork half the time as a consequence of high mortality among free-ranging mature pigs (see Kelly 1988:138, 178). To forego consumption is the price of seniority of ownership, and a man therefore cannot distribute his pig and eat it too. However, his role as distributor, earned through assumption of the risk of prohibition, enables him to derive a second set of exchange values by giving portions of the side of pork to his "brothers." In the end, he will have given pork to his affines, cross-cousins, agnates, and matrilateral siblings, in accordance with the significant contours of the larger social system. And he will have provisioned a festive meal in which all coresident "brothers" and their wives have shared pork. Typically, a coresident affine will have received a side of pork at the same time and shared it with his "brothers," so that everyone in the community simultaneously consumes pork.

However, neither the giving of a side of pork to affines nor the distribution of one received in exchange entails the provisioning of communitywide sharing that is the epitome of generosity as culturally defined. Only half the community is provisioned in such distribution. Moreover, fulfilling reciprocal obligations to affines and distributing pork received from them to coresident brothers are both obligatory rather than elective and lack the component of choice that is central to the prestige derived from the distribution of game (i.e., both the choice to hunt and the choice to share). In addition, the pork distributed is not a product of the individual effort and skill of the person who distributes it, as in the case of game, but of the effort and skill of his affine. Although the affinal donor may be credited with the creation of exchange value, this is not deployed in an encompassing distribution that transcends close kin relations but is instead given to a single individual (e.g., wife's brother). The latter then realizes the residual exchange value of the side of pork received by sharing it with his "brothers." The dimensions of this distribution are comparable to a distribution of midsize game in that some but not all coresident men are given shares. In contrast, all coresident men would receive shares of a wild pig. However, the most critical difference between game distribution and the distribution of affinal pork turns on allocation of the credit for generosity and thus the allocation of prestige value. In the affinal exchange of pork, the prestige value inherent in the production of exchange value and its utilization in the reproduction of broader relational and communal forms of sociality is split between two men. In contrast, the producer and distributor of a game animal are one and the same. The production (or engendering) and the distribution (or sharing) components of the prestige value derived from generosity thus accrue to the same individual. Finally, domestic pork is not rendered up by the *Sigisato* spirits and thus lacks the spiritual quality of game. Séances do not typically accompany its consumption. These transactions in pork are consequently not prestige-enhancing in the same way as game distribution, although they do entail a deployment of exchange value (in the sense defined) that amplifies central social relationships. The prestige that accrues to each of the two participants is of a lesser and somewhat different order. It is of interest in this respect that the same senior men (in the early forties to mid-fifties age category) that predominate in game procurement and distribution own only about one-third as many pigs as younger men, while some *tafidilos* at times own no pigs at all (Kelly 1988:144, 148).

As noted above, the husband deploys exchange value in distributing an affinally given pig to his "brothers." His wife is a recipient of pork, but not a distributor, and consequently has no access to this deployment of exchange value. However, that is attributable to the cultural fact that she has elected not to assume the role of primary caretaker of one or more pigs that entails the risk of being prohibited from consuming pork. The assumption of this role is open to a woman, and if she successfully brings a pig to maturity she would serve as distributor of the sides of pork received in return. (I did not witness such a distribution but was told this was anticipated in the case of two pigs solely owned by women, one given as a shoat by a brother and the other acquired as a shoat in trade.)

The fact that half the married men cannot eat pork means that the distribution outlined above proceeds from the recipient of an affinally given side of pork to his coresident "brothers," who then as often as not give the entire portion to their wife and children. The distributor himself may also give away an entire side of pork without consuming a morsel. This constitutes a prominent display of self-abnegation in sharing, similar to that involved in generosity (in the strict sense of the term) and serves to accentuate the male reputation in this regard. Conversely, the women are seen to enjoy this favored food, which they consume in double measure since their husbands have taken on the prohibition for which, by joint ownership, they also share potential responsibility. Thus, men get the credit for selflessly provisioning a food distribution, while the women get the pork. This outcome is culturally viewed as a product of prior male and female choices in the assumption of responsibility for pig rearing. The culturally constituted traits of men and women are thus enacted and publicly revealed in social practice. Men are self-sacrificing and generous; women are the beneficiaries of male generosity and are more interested in consumption than in exchange values (cf. Strathern 1972:132–52). This enactment of gendered traits resonates with the cosmology of life-force transmission, in which men are seen to generously and self-sacrificingly transmit life force to others at the expense of their own debilitation, senescence, and ultimate demise in order to ensure the perpetuation of life (as discussed in the next chapter; see also Kelly 1976). It is important to recognize that this cosmology not only credits men with the reproduction of the social order through generosity but charges them with this responsibility. This is internalized and acted upon. Men do not merely appear to be generous and community-spirited but are truly so. The efforts they devote to provisioning the community and reproducing broader forms of sociality represent the realization of a culturally constituted self-image rather than a strategically motivated self-interest.

The production, distribution, and consumption of semidomesticated pigs have been discussed in some detail because pigs are invariably deployed in a ritual or ceremonial context and because their production entails both male and female labor. However, it is important not to overrate the significance of pigs in this sociocultural system. Game is distributed much more frequently and has a spiritual significance that semidomesticated pigs entirely lack. Moreover, sides of pork are only one of three items involved in affinal exchange, the other two being a quantity of smoked marsupials (ideally seventeen animals) and large banana-leaf-wrapped packages of sago grubs. Both of these are produced entirely by male labor. The grubs (beetle larvae) are incubated in a sago palm cut for this purpose, and the smoked game is procured during extended hunting expeditions in the primary forest, sometimes combined with more intensive use of established traplines (which are reset daily during the period the men camp in the vicinity). The sago grubs and smoked game are given to the same relatives by marriage who receive sides of pork and are reciprocated in kind (see Kelly 1977:222; Kelly 1988:125, 177; cf. Ernst 1978).

In earlier discussion of the division of labor, we saw that the "practice" of production does not provide actors with a sense that men and women are uniquely and distinctively different. In contrast, it is evident here that both the regular distribution of game, pandanus sauce, etc., and the special occasions on which domestic pork is distributed do provide a palpable experience of significantly greater male generosity toward others in the realization of a communitarian ethic and the reproduction of the social order.

Having discussed male and female labor contributions in the production of the foods men distribute, we can return to the issue that prompted this inquiry, namely the source of differential access to the achievement of prestige through food distribution. The critical point here is that the attainment of prestige through generosity is primarily grounded in the division of labor itself—and in distributional rights over products embodying the labor of others that follow directly from the division of labor—rather than being based upon men's unilateral appropriation of distributional rights over products produced primarily by female labor. The Etoro thus stand in marked contrast to the Highlands New Guinea social systems in which men attain prestige by deploying pigs that are largely produced by female labor (in the form of the female contribution to the cultivation of sweet potatoes for fodder). One of the central corollaries of this difference is that Etoro men are not dependent upon a female labor contribution in order to achieve prestige in this arena of social life (or in others) and consequently have no need to exert control over female labor inputs (Kelly n.d.; Ortner and Whitehead 1981:20–21; Feil 1987:179–81). Etoro men simply go about the business of performing the tasks allotted to them and, by dint of their own labor, acquire wild pig, cassowary, small forest mammals, birds, clutches of eggs, sago grubs, fish, and wild nuts that they deploy both to provision their immediate family and to distribute more widely to coresidents, and on the occasions of affinal exchange, to relatives by marriage in other communities. As a result of labor that is more than nine parts male and one part female, they acquire cultivated nuts, pandanus, and tree ferns that are likewise deployed. Finally, by virtue of being the primary caretakers of semidomesticated pigs that are jointly owned with and partly tended by their wives—together with the customary rules of exchange and distribution just described—they come to be the distributors of exchange pork at the point of consumption. While this final instance of distributional prerogative is rooted in more than the division of labor alone (and anticipates the Highlands configuration), in the other instances distributional rights do arise rather directly from the division of labor itself. The person who procures or produces something also distributes it. The fact that unmarried men, who have no direct claim on female labor, readily acquire and distribute all the foods discussed above, including domestic pig, shows that male attainment of prestige through generosity is not dependent or contingent upon female labor contributions. Men do not need wives to be generous (contra Collier 1988:209).

STARCH STAPLE PRODUCTION

The principal vegetable foods consumed by the people of the Strickland-Bosavi region are sago, bananas (including plantains), taro, pandanus, sweet potatoes, yams, and a variety of greens. The proportional contribution of each of these items to the diet varies considerably among cultural groups. Among the Gebusi, bananas are the starch staple, constituting 65 to 70 percent of this portion of the diet (based on the percentage of days that bananas were the principal starch consumed). Sago is second in importance, contributing 25 to 30 percent, while root crops (principally taro) make up the remaining 5 to 10 percent (Knauft 1985a:17). The neighboring Samo rely more extensively on sago, which is the dietary staple (Shaw 1990:44). Bananas (plantains) are the principal garden crop, said to be "of considerable importance" in the diet, while taro is a variety food (ibid.:42). Although proportional contributions are not reported, these data suggest that sago supplies somewhat more than half of dietary starch, bananas provide the bulk of the remainder, and the contribution of taro is comparable to the lower estimate noted for the Gebusi (i.e., 5 percent). Among the Bedamini, bananas are the staple, while "taro, yam, sweet potato and sago are important subsidiary crops" (Sørum 1980:274). In the Kamula case, sago is the predominant staple, constituting 85 to 90 percent of dietary starch intake by weight (Wood 1982:40, 71; Wood, personal communication), while bananas and taro make up the remainder. Freund's detailed dietary study of the Kasua (1977:314–31) indicates that sago provides an average (for two communities) of 84.7 percent of dietary starch intake by weight, while the average percentage contributions of the other starchy components of the diet are taro (4.7 percent), bananas (5.6 percent), sweet potatoes (3.2 percent), and yams (1.9 percent). Sago is the starch staple among the Kaluli, bananas are the most important garden crop, and all the crops characteristic of the region are also grown, but the proportional distribution of these dietary components is not reported (Schieffelin 1975; Schieffelin 1976:32). Among the Onabasulu, sago makes up 45 to 50 percent of the vegetable diet, while the importance of sweet potatoes, bananas, and taro varies with altitude (Ernst 1984:115, 120). Sweet potato gardens predominate at higher elevations, and taro-banana gardens are more prevalent at lower altitudes. A similar pattern is evident among the Etoro. At Kaburusato (775 meters), sago constituted an estimated 55 to 60 percent of the starch component of the diet (based on the percentage of days sago was the principal starch consumed). The proportion of sweet potato to taro-banana gardens was 80 percent to 20 percent (Kelly 1977:61). The percentage of land in cultivation devoted to sweet potatoes is reduced in lower altitude Etoro communities in favor of taro and bananas, and increased at higher altitudes. At Bobole (1,100 meters), sweet potatoes provided an estimated 42, 48, 66, and 90 percent of dietary starch for each of the four longhouses clustered there (Dwyer 1985b:50). The two house groups with the lowest reliance on sweet potato devoted the most days to sago processing (Dwyer 1990:66) and filled out their diet with taro and yams (bananas being of little importance). Eighty-five percent of the land in cultivation was devoted to sweet potatoes and the remainder to these taro and yam gardens (Dwyer 1990:223). Overall, Dwyer (1990:68, 223) estimates that sago constituted 32 percent of the starch component of the diet at Bobole (in terms of caloric intake), with the proportion rising to about 50 percent for some families. The sweet potato component is estimated to be 59 percent, while taro and yams account for the remaining 9 percent (ibid.).

Pandanus is a very important part of the diet at both Kaburusato and Bobole, but no estimates of its caloric or weight contribution have been made (and pandanus is not included in the proportional contributions to the starch diet discussed above). Perhaps the best index is Dwyer's (1990:62) rough estimate that 4,000 to 5,000 trees occupying ten hectares were maintained by Bobole residents (109 people), while twenty hectares of land were devoted to sweet potato cultivation per annum (Dwyer 1985b:50). These holdings of thirty-seven to forty-six trees per capita are consistent with the fact that pandanus is eaten almost daily for three months, regularly for three months, and occasionally during other times of the year. None of the other cultural groups in the region utilize pandanus to this extent.

The available data surveyed here indicate that sago supplies 20 to 90 percent of dietary starch across the region, with the Gebusi and Bedamini at the low end of this range, the Samo, Etoro, and Onabasulu in the middle, the Kamula and Kasua at the high end, and the position of the Kaluli uncertain within the middle to high end of the range (table 2.3).[18]

Bananas are a particularly important crop among all the cultural groups residing below 600 meters. Bananas are the starch staple among those groups with the least reliance on sago (Gebusi and Bedamini) and are a leading crop (together with taro) among those with the greatest reliance on sago (Samo, Kasua, and Kamula). Sweet potatoes contribute little to the diet of all these lower altitude groups and are the primary crop only among the Etoro and Northern Onabasulu, where they are codominant with sago as the starch staple.

In the Etoro and Onabasulu cases, there is considerable internal variation in the mix of staples which correlates with altitudinal differences. This is probably partly due to the effects of temperature on both banana yields and the efficiency of sago starch production. A mean monthly temperature below 70 degrees Fahrenheit retards the rate of commercial banana growth and delays fruiting (Simmonds 1966:132), with these effects progressively increasing as temperature declines. At Kaburusato (775 meters), the rate of leaf production of the better plants in an experimental plot was only .7 per week, less than the one leaf a week expected of bananas growing under ideal climatic conditions. (Nutrient deficiencies primarily affect leaf size rather than reducing the rate of leaf production.) During the cloud season, the daily mean temperature frequently falls below 70 degrees and this probably accounts for the retarded growth rate of bananas at this altitude. While bananas could readily be grown (despite the delayed fruiting), they would not be the ideal choice of starch staple as they are at the lower elevations that characterize Gebusi and Bedamini territory. Moreover, bananas would be much more suitable for the Southern Onabasulu community of Orogaiye, where the monthly mean minimum averages 70 degrees Fahrenheit (21 degrees Celsius) and the monthly mean temperature is in the high 70s (28.2 degrees Celsius) (Ernst 1984:24). Among the Southern Onabasulu, taro-banana gardens account for 60 percent of the land in production, and sweet potato gardens make up the remaining 40 percent, while the proportions among the Northern Onabasulu are similar to those recorded for the Kaburusato Etoro—80 percent sweet potato gardens and 20 percent taro-banana gardens (Ernst 1984:120). At Bobole, the cooler temperatures associated with an altitude 300 to 400 meters higher than Kaburusato and Orogaiye probably played a

TABLE 2.3

Percentage Contribution of Sago, Bananas, and Root Crops to the Starchy Component of the Diet among the Strickland-Bosavi Tribes in Relation to Environmental Variables

Cultural Group	Sago	Bananas	Root Crops	Altitudinal Zone of Occupation (in meters)	Annual Rainfall (in inches)	Range of Annual Rainfall (in inches)
Samo	50–60 E	35–45 E	5 E	90–120	150	116–212
Gebusi	25–30	65–70	5–10	100–200	164	116–212
Bedamini	20–25 E	50–60 E	20–25 E	250–600	236	?
Etoro	32–60	1–8	32–67	700–1,100	230	197–263
Southern Onabasulu	45–50	15–17	35–39	500–800	260	?
Kaluli	50–60 E	20–25 E	20–25 E	700–1200	197	?
Kasua	85	6	9	250–750	210	?
Kamula	85–90		5–7 E	50–400	?	?

Sources of dietary information: Samo, Shaw 1990:42, 44; Gebusi, Knauft 1985a:17; Bedamini, Sørum 1980:274; Etoro, Kelly 1977:61 and Dwyer 1985b:50 and 1990:68, 223; Southern Onabasulu, Ernst 1984:115, 120; Kaluli, Schieffelin 1975 and 1976:32; Kasua, Freund 1977:314–31; and Kamula, Wood 1982:40, 71 and personal communication.
Sources of rainfall data: Samo, Shaw 1990:40; Gebusi, Knauft 1985a:16; Bedamini, Sørum 1980:273; Etoro, Kelly 1977:32 and Dwyer 1990:23; Southern Onabasulu, Ernst 1984:22; and Kaluli and Kasua, Freund 1977:26.
E = estimated on the basis of ethnographic description reported in the text.

role in making bananas a minor crop. A definite altitudinal gradient in the importance of bananas is thus evident throughout the region, and this appears to be related to the effects of altitude on temperature. The reasons why bananas are heavily utilized in preference to other crops where they can productively be grown will be taken up shortly.

The period of maturation of sago palms is affected by temperature and soil moisture. Palms growing in permanent swamps in the warmer climates near sea level attain maturity in ten years, while those that are only seasonally submerged require twenty years (Ohtsuka 1983:93–94). Cooler temperatures likewise retard maturation. When maturation is delayed, fewer palms are available for processing at any given time. However, the main difficulty posed by slow-maturing palms is that they are more time-consuming to process due to increased fibrousness and/or the toughness of the fibers that are interlaced through the pith. Etoro territory is steeply sloped, and there are few permanent swamps. Most sago palms are planted in depressions along small streams and are subject to root and light competition from surrounding trees. Although annual rainfall is high and the soil is almost continuously moist, Etoro sago palms do not grow under the permanent swamp conditions that are ideal and this, combined with the lower temperatures encountered at 700 to 1,100 meters, results in slower maturation and reduced yields per person-hour of labor compared to lower altitude areas of New Guinea (see n. 20). Some palms are considered to be too "hard" to be worth processing in their entirety, and the uppermost and lowermost sections are left for sago beetle grubs to develop for later harvesting (Kelly 1977:35). Dwyer (1990:64) reports that Bobole residents considered sago palms growing at 700 to 800 meters to possess the most desirable qualities, and the majority of the sago palms utilized by members of this community were processed during one- or two-week expeditions to these lower altitudes. This lack of desirable sago close at hand made it difficult to combine sago processing with other subsistence activities (Dwyer 1985b:58), as was typically the case at Kaburusato (Kelly 1977:51–52), and probably played a role in the generally lower degree of sago utilization at Bobole.

The marked variations in the degree of sago exploitation and reliance on sweet potatoes among the four longhouses at Bobole (with constant altitude) are partly due to historical circumstances of clustering near a mission, so that longhouses had not been moved within the usual wide radius for ten years and house groups differed in their access to favorable sago resources, access to proximate garden land, and so forth (see Dwyer 1985b). Nevertheless, it is evident that such variability is intrinsic to the Etoro economy, rather than being a unique product of missionization, since each family has a wide variety of subsistence options and may shift from a heavy reliance on sago one year to a greater dependence on gardening the next, also choosing between a sweet potato or taro-banana garden (in the case of the lower altitude Etoro communities). These options are discussed as individuals plan gardening commitments for the months ahead. At Bobole, those with superior access to well-fallowed garden land engaged in more extensive sweet potato gardening (combining this with greater use of traplines), while newcomers lacking equivalent gardening opportunities relied more heavily on sago production (combined with comparatively greater hunting, which was not impaired by long absences for sago working as was trap checking). (See Dwyer 1985b for a more detailed account of these variations.)

In other areas of New Guinea (and elsewhere), sago processing has been found to be more than twice as efficient as gardening in terms of calories produced per hour of labor (Townsend 1974; Ohtsuka 1977; Ellen 1979:49–51). Available data indicate that this advantage is reduced in the Etoro case, due to the increased difficulty of processing fibrous palms, to something on the order of a 1.4 to 1 efficiency advantage in favor of sago processing (see n. 21). Even though the labor-saving advantage of sago processing is not as great among the Etoro as it is elsewhere, it is still a significant advantage. An interesting question then arises: why didn't the Etoro at Kaburusato rely more heavily on sago processing in 1968–69? Their failure to do so cannot have been due to any constraints on the availability of sago palms, since mature palms were abundant as a result of depopulation (Kelly 1977:137) and some went to seed without being processed. While dietary preferences may have played a role to some extent, the division of labor appears to have been a more important factor. Although the underutilization of sago palms increased total labor expenditure in subsistence, all of this increase added to male rather than female labor since men do much less work in sago processing than in gardening. (The precise labor contributions of each gender to these activities will be presented later in this section.) In other words, greater use of available sago palms would have reduced male labor considerably, while increasing female labor only slightly, if at all (since there is less total work to produce equivalent calories of starch even though women do a larger share of this work). The economic mix of gardening and sago processing that did prevail contributed to an overall division of labor in which men devoted more hours per week to subsistence than women (as will be documented further along), while greater sago utilization would have contributed to equalization of the labor inputs of each gender. It is probable that sago utilization at Kaburusato in 1968–69 had been expanded to some extent compared to the period before depopulation, but full utilization (and realization of the attendant labor savings) was clearly not achieved.

The economic mix of starch staples has an important bearing on male and female labor inputs throughout the Strickland-Bosavi region, since the sexual division of labor varies according to subsistence activity. Available data indicate that women do 76 to 100 percent of the work in sago processing, while gardening labor is more equally divided between men and women in all ethnographic cases for which information is available (detailed in a later section of this chapter). The fact that the Bedamini and Gebusi rely on bananas as their starch staple is thus indicative of an economic mix that appears to be comparatively more favorable to women, while the Kamula's and Kasua's heavy reliance on sago betokens economies in which female labor inputs would be expected to be considerably greater than male labor inputs (although no precise figures are available). That the Samo appear to consume twice as much sago as the neighboring Gebusi suggests a parallel conclusion. There is no reason to expect that sago (which can readily be planted) is less suited to the Bedamini and Gebusi environment than to that of the Samo, Kasua, and Kamula. Moreover, all five of these cultural groups are within the altitudinal zone where sago processing would be expected to be twice as efficient as gardening in terms of labor inputs. Although Bedamini population density (of 13.1 persons per square mile) may have exceeded the point at which sago could be a starch staple (due to the restricted environmental contexts suitable for its growth), no other cultural group significantly exceeds the population density of the Kasua (at 6.7 persons per square mile), among whom sago constitutes 85 percent of the starchy component of the diet. Differences in the extent of sago utilization therefore do not seem to be entirely reducible to demographic and ecological factors.

While further research is clearly needed, it appears likely that the mix of starch staples in the subsistence economies of the Strickland-Bosavi tribes has at least as much to do with the overall division of labor—and the interrelations between the gender system and the economy—as with ecological factors. As noted above, a heavy reliance on sago is indicative of substantially greater female than male labor inputs in starch staple production. Moreover, concepts of menstrual pollution are present in three of the four cases in which sago comprises more than 50 percent of the starch diet (i.e., Samo, Kaluli, and Kamula), while no data on this point are available in the fourth case (the Kasua). This indicates that elevated levels of female labor inputs in starch production covary with concepts of menstrual pollution in the Strickland-Bosavi region as they do elsewhere in New Guinea. It can thus be postulated that movement toward a greater degree of sago utilization—which reduces total labor inputs due to the higher efficiency of production—is impeded by the sexual division of labor.

But why wouldn't the sexual division of labor in sago processing simply be adjusted so as to entail more male and less female labor? The only answer that can be offered is that available data (to be presented later) show no covariation between the sexual division of labor in sago processing and the extent of sago utilization. In other words, expanded sago utilization appears to lead to concepts of menstrual pollution rather than adjustment of the division of labor. Or a relatively inflexible division of labor may lead to underutilization of sago resources despite the superior efficiency of production. These formulations can only be tentative given available data, and I propose them in hopes of stimulating further research. However, the available data do suggest that the division of labor is slow to change. If this is so, then neither the introduction of steel tools nor the increased sago resources per capita brought about by depopulation are likely to have significantly altered the division of labor in the Strickland-Bosavi region. Some limited changes reported with respect to Kamula agricultural production will be noted in subsequent discussion of that sector of the regional economies.

The characteristic pattern of cultivation in the region is one in which gardening procedures maximize yields per unit of labor rather than per unit of land (Kelly 1977:61; Wood 1982:48; Knauft 1985a:18; Ernst 1984:121; Schieffelin 1975:34). Among the Etoro,

> Sites which require the least effort in fencing and cutting timber are preferred. Large communal gardens also reduce fencing labor. Clearing time is decreased by felling tree crowns on top of each other and thus allowing the energy released by falling trees to do the work of removing branches. Cutting the trees six weeks or so after clearing undergrowth provides for the initial germination of weeds which do not flourish in full sun and later reduces labor expenditure in weeding since few grasses are present. Time consuming tasks of burning, mounding and soil preparation are avoided. (Kelly 1977:61)

While all of these gardening techniques are widely employed, the Kamula, Samo, Bedamini, and Gebusi go one step further by omitting to fence most of their gardens. Among the Gebusi, Bedamini, and Samo, only the plots devoted to root crops are fenced, while the banana gardens (sometimes interplanted with taro in the Gebusi and Bedamini cases) are not (Knauft 1985a:18; van Beek 1987:20; Shaw 1990:42). None of the Kamula taro-banana gardens were fenced, although the people said this would be done if intrusions by the many wild pigs in the area reached intolerable levels (Wood 1982:48). Bananas are relatively immune to the depredations of pigs, and both the Gebusi and Kamula appear to regard the loss of a portion of the taro crop to pigs as preferable to the added labor of fencing taro-banana gardens. Van Beek (1987:19) reports that the interplanted taro in Bedamini banana gardens is intended for the consumption of domesticated pigs. Omitting fence construction reduces male labor inputs inasmuch as fencing is always a male task. The choice of staple crop thus has an effect on male and female labor requirements similar to that noted with respect to the degree of reliance on sago.

Banana yields are most strongly affected by nutrient uptake during the first three months after planting (Simmonds 1966:39). A single weeding in this early period is thus sufficient to ensure a crop, even though fruiting does not occur for twelve to fifteen months at 800 meters. This characteristic of bananas accounts for the fact that they produce reasonable (if not maximal) yields while growing in Etoro gardens that have been choked with weeds for six to nine months. The banana plants overtop the weeds (re: light competition) and obtain sufficient nutrients in the critical early period of growth to produce a crop. Competition for soil moisture is not a concern in the high-rainfall regimes of the region. The unfenced and lightly weeded banana gardens of the Gebusi, Bedamini, and Samo thus represent the least labor-intensive gardening methods in the region. Samo weeding, which occurs several weeks after planting, is limited to the area immediately adjacent to each banana stalk. As in the Etoro case, weedy undergrowth is rampant by the time of harvest (Shaw 1990:44). The limited weeding done by the Samo reduces female labor inputs, since weeding is an exclusively female task in this society. (Bedamini banana-gardening techniques also entail little weeding [Sørum n.d.:71]; Kamula gardens in which taro is interplanted with bananas may require more complete weeding.)

The particular characteristics of bananas make them an ideal crop for non-labor-intensive gardening, and this is probably one of the factors that accounts for the reliance on bananas as a starch staple among the Gebusi and Bedamini, and as a major crop among all the lower altitude groups that utilize sago as the primary starch staple (e.g., the Kasua, Kamula, and Samo). Extrapolation from Etoro data suggests that unfenced and lightly weeded banana gardens would require only about 60 percent of the labor (in person-hours per acre) expended in fenced and weeded sweet potato gardens. However, yields per unit of land may not be comparable.

Consideration of Etoro subsistence patterns within a regional context leads to the conclusion that the Etoro economy entails comparatively greater labor inputs. The sago palms that occur primarily as a nondomesticated food resource at lower altitudes are essentially a crop in the Etoro case. All sago stands are said to have been created by past or recent planting. The palms are also maintained by periodically cutting back the encroaching forest (with both of these tasks being performed by men). Sago processing is also more time-consuming than at lower elevations due to the fibrous qualities of slow-maturing palms (adding primarily to female labor). Bananas are environmentally unsuited as a staple crop, prompting a reliance on root crops (principally sweet potatoes) that require fenced gardens, increasing male labor, and more thorough weeding, increasing both male and female labor (as this task is shared in the Etoro case). The inclusion of large quantities of pandanus in the diet entails the maintenance of very extensive pandanus groves (also adding to male labor). An environmentally induced focus on small rather than large game in higher altitude Etoro communities entails significantly greater labor expenditure (primarily on the part of men), as returns in edible weight per hour are less (Dwyer 1983:165). The extent of easily exploitable riverine resources is reduced, and favorable fish-poisoning sites that occur naturally at lower elevations are created by the construction of diversion channels in the Etoro case (entailing added male labor). Both the fish-poisoning sites and the traplines constructed in the primary forest (by men, with female assistance in maintenance) represent a long-term labor investment, and access to both is governed by lineage membership. Lineage-owned territories do not govern access to the large game hunted by the Kamula, Kasua, and Samo. The Etoro also appear to keep greater numbers of domesticated pigs than other cultural groups in the region (e.g., 1.32 per capita for the Etoro, .61 for the Kamula, and .28 for the Bedamini [Kelly 1988:119; Wood 1982:62; van Beek 1987:25]). The substitution of a larger proportion of domestic pigs for hunted wild pigs increases labor inputs, and pig husbandry entails somewhat more male than female labor in the Etoro case. In all these respects, the Etoro subsistence economy represents a more labor-intensive version of the general range of economies found throughout the region. In contrast to the patterns of intensification characteristic of the New Guinea Highlands (Waddel 1972; Modjeska 1982; Josephides 1983; Feil 1987:230–32), most of the additional labor is male rather than female labor. The total division of labor also reflects this, as will be documented later in this chapter.

The preceding outline of subsistence combinations in the Strickland-Bosavi region provides a backdrop for consideration of the Etoro division of labor in sago processing and gardening from a comparative perspective. As noted above, Etoro men devote a greater number of hours to food production than do women. They also perform tasks that fall to women among neighboring groups. A comparative perspective thus provides an important ground for developing an understanding of these features of the subsistence economy and their relation to the primary theoretical focus of this work, namely the locus of the production of inequality.

SAGO PROCESSING

Women do 76 percent or more of the work in sago processing throughout the Strickland-Bosavi region. Nevertheless, there is considerable variation among cultural groups in the extent of male involvement in this component of the economy, as is displayed in table 2.4. The Kamula delineate one end of the spectrum, in which women normally do all the tasks involved in the process, although "occasionally a man will assist his wife by chopping the sago tree down, splitting it open and pulping the pith" (Wood 1982:40). Among the Etoro, who delineate the other end of the spectrum, the men normally cut down, section, and split the palm, construct the troughs, and shred (or pulp) the pith, leaving only the final (though most time-consuming) task of beating, washing, and kneading the sago to their wives. Occasionally Etoro men do the entire job (although this only occurs when the sago is to be exported in trade). Despite the fact that Etoro men customarily undertake certain sago-processing tasks left to women in other ethnographic cases, women's labor inputs constitute 76 percent of the total. In the three societies in which men only cut and split open the palm (i.e., Gebusi, Bedamini, and Samo), female labor inputs would be about 96 percent of the total (based on extrapolation from Etoro data). Among the Kasua, where men only fell the palm, the comparable figure would be about 99 percent. The Kaluli are similar to the Etoro, while the Onabasulu fall somewhere in between the Etoro and the Samo, Gebusi, and Bedamini. The customary division of labor is the same among the Etoro at Kaburusato and at Bobole (Dwyer 1990:65), despite the significant differences between these communities in their reliance on sago as a starch staple. Indeed, the Kaburusato Etoro are not that dissimilar from the Kamula in terms of the predominant importance of sago in the diet, although the allocation of tasks is maximally contrastive. A comparison of the Gebusi and Kasua makes the same point from the opposite direction, in that the allocation of tasks is very similar while the dependence on sago is maximally divergent. In other words, it is clear that the allocation

TABLE 2.4

The Sexual Division of Labor in Sago Processing: A Comparison
of the Strickland-Bosavi Tribes

Cultural Group	Sago Processing Tasks					Percentage Contribution of Sago to Dietary Starch
	Cut Palm	Trim, Split, and Debark Log	Construct Troughs	Shred Pith	Beat, Wash, and Knead Pith	
Etoro	M	M	M&F	M	F	32–60
Kaluli	M	M	?	M	F	50–60 E
Onabasulu	M	M	M	M&F	F	45–50
Gebusi	M	M	F	F	F	25–30
Samo	M	M	F	F	F	50–60 E
Bedamini	M	M	F	F	F	20–25 E
Kasua	M	F	F	F	F	85
Kamula	F	F	F	F	F	85–90

Sources: Etoro, Kelly 1977:51 and Dwyer 1990:65; Kaluli, Schieffelin 1976:74; Onabasulu, Ernst 1984:115; Gebusi, Cantrell n.d.:88; Samo, Shaw 1990:44; Bedamini, Sørum n.d.:73; Kasua, Freund 1977:33–35; and Kamula, Wood 1982:40.
M = Male, F = Female, E = estimated.

of tasks among men and women bears no relationship to the total amount of labor required (as reflected in the proportional contribution of sago to the diet, and thus the monthly frequency of sago processing). In other words, there is no tendency toward an increased male labor contribution when sago is extensively utilized. This documents a point noted earlier with respect to underutilization of sago and a failure to take advantage of the superior labor efficiency of sago processing in certain instances.

The division of labor has more to do with the general nature of relations between husbands and wives (and men and women) than with the allocation of hours of work per se. This can be brought out by a comparison of the Etoro and Kamula. In the Kamula case, sago processing is a female domain. Several women go to a sago stand and work together in felling, trimming, sectioning, and splitting the palm. Each woman then constructs her own trough and proceeds individually with the main tasks of processing the sago. However, the women sing in unison while they beat the sago and it is evident that female bonding and camaraderie are engendered (Wood 1982:65). The lines of one of these songs is "my son, I am making sago, you bring me meat" (Wood 1982:37, 40–41). Thus an exchange of female-produced sago and male-procured game is clearly conceptualized. Women have definite rights of disposal over the sago that they wholly produce, and they distribute it in transactions that Wood (1982:43–44) characterizes in terms of exchange. This exchange occurs among women: "for example, if a daughter makes sago while her mother fishes the two may exchange part of their respective products" (ibid.). Women give sago to their sons and husbands (and to their widowed fathers, unmarried brothers, and husband's unmarried brothers) as cooked food. These transactions are not ideologically justified, in the sense that no cultural explanation of male entitlement is put forward. However, the provision of this sago is seen as creating an obligation on the part of the male recipient to reciprocate by providing meat, and this is clearly articulated (as in the aforementioned song). A woman is also reported to have responded to her brother's request for some of the fresh sago she was carrying by asking "where is your meat" (Wood 1982:55). The men, on their part, relate a cautionary tale to newly married young men in which a dissatisfied wife whose husband failed to hunt feeds the man his own son (ibid.). Reciprocity is also enforced by a woman's capacity to obviate her son's or brother's hunting ability through a curse (ibid.:55–56). Overall, Wood (ibid.:57, 65) sees women as possessing substantial means of exerting control over men's labor (including refusal to cook for a husband) and thus ensuring the desired return of meat for the sago they provide. However, the existence of these sanctions indicates that an equitable exchange is not intrinsic to this organization of production. Moreover, a man who does not hunt because his hunting has been cursed is relieved of performing the task that is the main male contribution to the division of labor, although his social standing is perhaps impaired.

While the Kamula division of labor in sago processing promotes the solidarity of women and provides a basis for exchange relations between men and women (and among women) that are characterized by calculation of the state of reciprocity, the Etoro organization of this component of production entails a complementarity of male and female roles that promotes conjugal solidarity and eventuates in a product in which the labor of husbands and wives is intermingled, undercutting the possibility for both a clear-cut exchange of gendered products and for precise calculations of reciprocity. A detailed description will provide a basis for developing a sense of the forms of sociality that are embedded in this organization of production.

A sago-processing work group invariably includes a minimum of two women and one man, since both male and female labor are required and a woman would not want to work alone during the times the male contingent is not present at the site. This minimum group would usually consist of a man, his wife, and an unmarried daughter (aged 13 to 16); a husband and his two wives; or a man and wife and an unremarried widow who normally worked with them in sago processing and gardening. More frequently, the work group would exceed the minimum size and consist of two families related by the ties of siblingship and/or affinity that typically link residents of a longhouse community, e.g., the parties to a "sister"-exchange (see Kelly 1977:144–61).

The men initiate the operation by felling the sago palm, removing the sharp thorns from along the trunk, and cutting the fronds from the upper section. The sago heart is harvested from the growth point at the top of the palm, and the fronds are searched for a large edible grasshopper, with eight to twelve of these typically being found. The men also clear the general area in which the work is to be performed to the extent necessary to create a pleasant, sunlit open space that also facilitates ease of movement as the work proceeds. Since the work will typically take five to seven days and rain is inevitable, a shelter is constructed from the sago fronds to provide a place to rest, smoke, socialize, and cook lunch during the periods between exertions. The men then proceed with final preparations for the main work by cutting a seven-to-eight-foot section from the sago log, splitting this open and removing the rind-like bark from the upper half to expose the inner pith. The troughs in which the shredded sago pith will be beaten and washed are usually constructed by the men as well, although the women, or men and women together, may complete this task. This largely depends upon whether or not the women have arrived at the site by this point in the preparations. They will either have spent a leisurely morning at the longhouse or have gone to nearby gardens to weed or clear undergrowth, since it takes the men several hours to complete the preparatory tasks. If the women arrive before the troughs are constructed, they will proceed with this task while the men finish splitting the sago log, or they may work with the men if the task is underway.

The sago pith is shredded by the men with a triangular-faced stone tool hafted as an adze. A man sits astride or within the split sago log and strikes the face of the unworked pith so as to shear off and pulverize a thin section with each blow. These are struck in rapid succession, at a rate averaging twenty-one strokes a minute, and a man tires after a twenty- or thirty-minute shift. He will then be spelled by his workmate (or, if working alone, will rest for five or ten minutes). The work is arduous, and perspiration beads the brow, but at this rapid pace only several hours are required to shred sufficient pith to keep the women supplied for the remainder of the afternoon and the following morning.

The complementarity of male and female effort is accentuated by this division of labor, in which the men shred pith for the women to beat and wash (a sequence that also characterizes Kaluli sago processing but is typically absent among all the other groups compared, although Onabasulu men do some of the shredding and Kamula men occasionally assist in this). After the first day, the men and women will generally go to the site together (around 8:00 A.M.), and the women will finish beating a trough-full of pith left over from the previous day while the men shred a new batch. This is consciously engineered, since it would be easy to organize the labor such that the men finished shredding a one day's supply of pith before the women's arrival, departing at that time. In other words, the work is organized so that the men's and women's time at the site will overlap substantially, despite the intrinsically sequential order of their tasks. Although the men finish at around 11:30 A.M., well before the women, they generally remain at the site until after the midday meal. They often collect firewood to build up the fire so they can roast sweet potatoes, visiting a nearby garden to harvest these if this was not done en route to the sago stand. After a shared meal, the men may or may not remain at the site depending upon whether there are other things they need to do, such as felling trees in a nearby garden. Some time may be spent cutting back the encroaching forest around the margins of the sago stand. However, most often men forage in the general vicinity part of the time, returning to the sago stand around 3:00 in the afternoon. The women generally finish the day's work between 3:00 P.M. and 5:30 P.M.

The women's part of the work begins with collecting the shredded pith in net bags and carrying it to their respective troughs, constructed of the curved basal portion of a sago frond. Water from a nearby stream is added, and the pith is beaten with a stick four-and-a-half feet long and tapering from three-quarters of an inch at the grip to one-half inch at the tip. The beating proceeds at a rate of averaging seventeen strokes a minute for about twenty to forty minutes, with pauses to add water and turn the pith. After the initial beating is completed, more water is added to leach out the starch. The sago is kneaded and the water squeezed out by the handful, with the washed portion separated out to the high end of the trough. This washing and squeezing is repeated twice more, and the sago pith is then beaten a second time and again washed thrice before being discarded for a new batch. If the sago pith is "soft," fewer steps may be required. The watery suspension of sago starch flows out through a tight-mesh straw bag into a settling trough, where it eventually settles out. A woman stops from time to time to wait for this settling so that she can scoop the clear water out of the top of the trough to make room for that being continuously added, often taking this opportunity to retire to the shelter for a rest. Each woman has a separate beating trough (though they may drain into opposite ends of the same collecting trough).

With no one to spell them and no one awaiting completion of their portion of the work to proceed (as in the case of the men's shredding task), the women's pace is steady but unhurried and punctuated with necessary rests. If there is a continuous drizzle, as is typical during the cloud season, the warmth and comfort of the fire that is kept burning in the shelter provides a welcome respite. During these rests and at the midday meal, a family or two closely related families would share a time of private conversation, away from the longhouse setting where a large number of people are always present. The garden house provides a similar context. The contrastive forms of sociality that characterize the longhouse, on one hand, and the sago stand shelter and garden house, on the other, were noted in chapter 1. The point to be emphasized here is that Etoro sago processing is organized so that husbands and wives work together as a companionable interdependent unit. Their labor is also intermingled in the final product, although in unequal proportions. In contrast, sago processing is essentially a female domain of productive activity among those cultural groups where men do no more than cut and split the palm in the morning of the first day of the enterprise and leave the women to spend the week completing the remainder of the task. The Kamula, Kasua, Samo, Bedamini, and Gebusi manifest this single-gender organization of production.

At Kaburusato, a family processes sago six to twelve times a year (with this activity more concentrated during certain periods, see Kelly 1977:49).[19] Labor expenditure averages 6.72 hours a week, with female labor accounting for 76 percent of this.[20] Although the sexual division of labor is more unbalanced in terms of female effort in sago processing than in gardening, the former is a more efficient means of producing a starch staple[21] so that women actually spend fewer hours per week in sago processing (5.11) than in gardening (6.73).

Women's superior labor contribution in sago processing is recognized in their control over the disposition of sago other than that required for family meals. Thus, while a husband is free to take sago as needed for his own consumption (from the family larder hung in bags in the communal section of the longhouse), only women give uncooked sago to others. This is particularly noticeable at sago stands. Individuals who are traveling along paths in the vicinity of a sago stand often stop by to visit with the work party. More often than not, they offer to spell one of the latter at their task (either a man or woman, depending on the gender of the passerby). Before the visitor departs, he or she is frequently given two to four pounds of fresh sago (although there is no one-to-one relation between volunteered labor and these gifts, since broader reciprocities are involved). Such gifts of sago are always made by the women. Likewise, a husband would not utilize sago in trade without his wife's agreement. Two bundles of sago (weighing about eighteen pounds) can be traded to the Huli for a shoat. Normally, the animal is said to belong jointly (*ua*) to the man and woman who produced the sago, e.g., a husband and wife or a widowed mother and her son. However, on one occasion when a young woman traveled with her husband to Huli country to conduct this trade, it was said that the pig she acquired through her own transaction was wholly hers, while the one acquired by her husband belonged to both of them. Here again, women's superior labor contribution is recognized in superior rights of ownership in the products of her labor. Normally, the male effort expended in the four-day trip to carry out this exchange would more than offset the larger share of female effort in producing the sago so that each of the co-owners would have made substantial contributions to the acquisition.

As explained earlier, a husband's and wife's respective interests in a jointly owned pig are both realized in an affinal exchange of pork, so that difficulties pertaining to a divergence of interest do not arise. However, such a divergence of interest is foreseen in the case of bachelors, and a bachelor may find it necessary to process sago on his own if he wishes to use it in trade to acquire a pig, since the nature of his relationship to the woman with whom he might process sago does not guarantee that she will benefit from the eventual deployment. This occurred in the case of a bachelor (Nogobe, aged 26) who formed a work group in sago processing and gardening with his unmarried FFBSS (Selagu) and the latter's 14-year-old half-sister (Saffara), and 50-year-old widowed mother (Yebua). Although Nogobe derived the sago he consumed on a regular basis from Yebua's stock (which he helped produce), he undertook sago processing on his own when this was to be employed in trade. In contrast, his FFBSS and age-mate Selagu utilized some of this stock of sago (provided by Yebua) to trade for a shoat on the same expedition. This shows that the widow had effective rights of disposal over the uncooked sago vis-à-vis her two male coproducers. The bachelor was able to draw on this stock for meals, but had no right to claim a portion of this sago for trade despite the fact that he had helped to produce it. Consideration of the degree of congruence in the kinship interests of a pig's co-owners is also evident here. If the shoat the widowed mother and her son jointly owned were later given to the mother's brother (in affinal exchange), the kinship interest of these co-owners would clearly coincide. However, had the widow become co-owner of a shoat with her deceased husband's FBSS (Nogobe), these interests would not coincide, making eventual deployment problematic.

The fact that sago is jointly produced by wife and husband (and by women and men more generally) makes it somewhat unsuitable for conceptualization as one component of an exchange of male and female products, even though a wife holds distributional rights as a result of having completed the process of production. A husband (or son) thus incurs no formulated obligation to hunt in order to reciprocate for the sago he receives (as in the Kamula case), because he helped to produce it. Men do make reciprocal contributions to the food supply through fish poisoning, hunting, trapping, foraging, and the collection of nuts and pandanus—and they hold distributional rights over these products—but the general tenor of both male and female contributions is one of pooling resources rather than exchanging gendered products. Female labor is intermingled with male labor (in unequal proportions) in the production of nuts and pandanus, in the produce of current gardens, and in domesticated pigs and trapped game as well as in sago processing. Moreover, women also procure game through foraging and, in the case of some women, hunting as well. The absence of task exclusivity in the sexual division of labor is consistent with a notion of pooling resources, although it would fit awkwardly with a Kamula-like conception of exchange that entailed precise calculations of the state of reciprocity in transactions involving gendered products.

Etoro husband-wife relations entail an exchange of labor within the framework of a sexual division of labor, and the products of that labor consequently embody joint effort. Distributional rights over them are assigned to the party who completed the process of production and are thus rendered individual rather than joint. This enables women to make gifts of sago to others and receive like gifts in return and similarly enables men to deploy sides of pork to fulfill affinal exchange obligations and receive sides of pork in return. The manner in which the wife's joint interest and husband's distributional rights both enter into these transactions has been described in some detail and need not be reiterated. What is significant in the present context is that the husband's distributional rights do not eradicate the wife's joint interest, which continues to be recognized in various ways. The assignment of distributional rights therefore does not eventuate in gendered products but rather allows one party to deploy joint products. As a result, the contributions of husband and wife to the meals they share at the family hearth have the character of a pooling of resources rather than an exchange of gendered products. What was jointly produced is jointly consumed. However, the concept of an exchange of products over which husband and wife hold distributional rights continues to be useful in elucidating certain aspects of conjugal reciprocity, since large game (for example) is not jointly produced but is distributed among all hunters in the community who then distribute it among family members.

Although the Etoro generally lack a conception of gendered products, there is a connection drawn between the male provision of game and female childbearing. After a woman gives birth to a child, her husband is expected to provide her with lavish quantities of small game. This is expressed in myth, where the identity of the unknown father of a child is revealed to be a totemic python by the fact that the latter surrounds the woman with heaps of small game animals (see Kelly 1977:111). There is a general notion that the conjugal relationship entails a woman's obligation to bear children and a man's reciprocal obligation to supply his wife with game in recognition of her childbearing. There is somewhat of a parallel here with the Kamula theme that a wife whose husband does not provide her with game will feed him his son, chopped up to appear to be wallaby. However, the Kamula emphasize that game is given in exchange for sago rather than in recognition of the woman's reproductive role. The Etoro lack cautionary tales of this type. Etoro ideology focuses on the pitfalls of failing to share game with co-residents of the longhouse community rather than failing to procure it for a spouse. To consume unshared game is seen as an attribute of a witch and to appear stinting in the distribution of midsize game is said to invite bewitchment should the disgruntled recipients, or those persons omitted, include an individual who, unbeknownst to the distributor, possesses these powers. This ideology is consistent with generalized reciprocity at the community level rather than balanced reciprocity between spouses.

The symbolic significance of the husband's provision of game in recognition of his wife's childbearing also figured in the only domestic conflict that occurred during the fifteen months I was in the field. During the course of a communal meal in the longhouse, Wadome complained softly but audibly that her husband, Tuni, was not giving her an equivalent portion of the cooked marsupial he was dividing between them as they sat cross-legged facing each other. When he ignored this entirely, she complained loudly of his stinginess and then, drawing back one of her legs, gave him a sturdy kick in the midsection. Silence fell over the gathering as everyone looked aghast at the couple, who were glaring at each other. Wadome's "brothers"—six young men in all—silently exchanged glances and then rose and walked out of the longhouse as a group. A man would never strike a woman in the presence of a "brother" (I was told later), and thus Tuni was being granted permission to retaliate for the blow that had been struck against him. Having done nothing but fix his wife with an angry stare up to this point, he now rose to do what expectations seemingly made unavoidable and attempted to cuff Wadome on the side of the head, once with each hand. These blows were delivered with little force and, since Wadome deflected them with her arms, were significant in what they expressed rather than in their physical effect. Wadome burst into tears and ran into the women's section of the longhouse, where she wailed at full volume for several hours. Those remaining hurried to finish eating and go elsewhere, while voicing general disapproval of conjugal conflict (literally translatable as "husband-wife fighting is bad"). No one spoke to Tuni, and it was not until some time later that some of the women went to sympathize with Wadome. Later, at my house, it was said that women virtually never strike their husbands, "brothers" thus have no cause to withdraw their protection, husbands consequently do not strike their wives, and "this sort of thing just doesn't happen." No data that came to my attention during the fieldwork period contradicted this generalization. The social composition of an Etoro community is such that half the men of any woman's generation will be her "brothers," and many true affines core-side. This seems to provide an effective deterrent to conflict between spouses, with rare exceptions such as the event described above.

The underlying cause of this conjugal conflict was rooted in the fact that Wadome had not yet given birth to a child, although being about 24 years of age and thus somewhat beyond the age at which most women first give birth (i.e., 20). She thus appears to have read a deeper meaning into Tuni's division of the cooked marsupial, taking her somewhat-less-than-equal share to be a rebuke. When Tuni failed to rectify the distribution, confirming her interpretation, she loudly called attention to his stinginess, which, given the relation of generosity to male prestige, was the culturally appropriate counterinsult. It is thus evident that female fecundity and male generosity in the provision and distribution of game are counterposed in Etoro thinking, within a framework that should entail generalized reciprocity (rather than a consideration of present fecundity, as in this conflict). Hence the consensus view in the community that both parties behaved badly; Tuni should have shared equally and Wadome went too far in kicking him.

GARDENING

In gardening as in sago working, Etoro husbands and wives work together toward the fulfillment of common subsistence objectives, either as an individual family unit in their own garden or collectively with other families in a large communal garden. Although several bachelors sometimes cultivate a garden on their own, the work group typically includes both men and women, predominantly husbands and wives. The labor requirements per task and the male and female contribution to these (excluding bachelor gardens) are shown in table 2.5.[22]

The men begin a garden by cutting a swath through the forest around the perimeter of the site and building a stacked log fence from the felled timber. (See Kelly 1977:45–61 and Dwyer 1990:27–54 for more detailed accounts of gardening; only those features relevant to the division of labor are discussed here.) While this is in progress, the women clear the undergrowth within the area to be enclosed. When this clearing is completed in a section of the garden, that area will be planted to provide a somewhat earlier crop. Men and women share the tasks of collecting planting material from old gardens (e.g., sweet potato vines and banana ratoons), transporting this to the garden and planting it. In the earlier phase of the garden, women spend somewhat more time than men in planting sweet potatoes, but this is balanced out at later stages by men's efforts in preparing ash beds for the planting of seeds, in their planting of longer bearing crops near brush piles, and in a general filling-out of the garden with variety crops. After the staple crop has been planted in a section of the garden and has taken root, the trees are felled in this area by the men.

At the point when fencing, clearing undergrowth, planting, and felling trees are completed, male and female labor contributions are very nearly equal (see table 2.5). Husbands and wives will have been working simultaneously in different areas of the garden the majority of the time (although the men always have some tree felling to do at the end), and this tends to

TABLE 2.5

The Sexual Division of Labor in Etoro Gardening

Task	Man-hours per Acre	Woman-hours per Acre	Total Person-Hours per Acre
Fencing	120	0	120
Felling trees	128	0	128
Clearing undergrowth	0	256	256
Planting	65	65	130
Weeding	173	347	520
Total	486	668	1,154
Percentage	42.1%	57.9%	100%

eventuate in an equalization of their efforts. Husbands and wives also contribute to each other's task in order to facilitate this. Thus a wife may cut saplings with an ax while clearing undergrowth (rather than leaving most of these for her husband), and the latter may likewise help in the clearing of the low undergrowth (usually left to his wife) to speed completion so that the planting can commence. Each helps the other with what needs to be done in order to advance the enterprise at this stage. Dwyer (1990:38) captures the tone of conjugal cooperation quite accurately in his account. A husband and wife are

> the ideal working combination and, at Bobole, the family was a conspicuous unit in the recurring round of making, maintaining and harvesting gardens. They departed together in the morning, worked alongside each other throughout the day—sometimes at different tasks, sometimes at the same task—and often returned together in the afternoon, the woman carrying the day's harvest, the man with firewood.

Nearly all of the imbalance in male and female labor contributions in gardening is attributable to the task of weeding the garden, since women do two-thirds of this work, and it amounts to 45 percent of the total labor in gardening. Overall, men and women devote an average of 4.9 and 6.73 hours per week to gardening, respectively, so that the female labor contribution amounts to 58 percent of the total.[23] (This excludes harvesting, which is combined with foraging in terms of labor time and is included in figures for the latter presented subsequently; see n. 22.)

In gardening work and in sago processing, the labor force primarily consists of males aged 15 to 60 and females aged 13 to 60, with boys of 13 to 14, girls of 11 to 12, and elderly individuals making smaller contributions. The different ages at which males and females begin to do work comparable to that of an adult is a function of the division of labor. Younger girls are physically capable of performing the less arduous tasks allotted to women, while younger boys are not physically capable of doing the more demanding work allotted to men. For example, a boy and girl of 13 are both capable of weeding, while neither can effectively fell trees. In the Etoro case, both are eager to emulate adults of their gender but only girls are capable of effectively doing so. Boys do cut trees but are short-winded and quickly become exhausted. It is thus the division of labor that creates the illusion of retarded male development that the Etoro attribute to the negative influence of the womb on male (but not female) growth and that they seek to rectify by insemination undertaken to ensure the maturation and strengthening of boys (see Kelly 1976).

Young men in their early twenties who have matured physically attribute their strength and energy to insemination and specifically say that this enables them to fell trees for hours on end without tiring (Kelly 1976:46). They take pride in demonstrating this and readily join in communal gardens as well as making some gardens on their own. As a result, bachelors participate in a larger number of gardens than any other class of individuals. On average, bachelors participated in 5.8 gardens and married men in 3.4 gardens over a two-year period (including gardens in production at the inception of my fieldwork).

Sawa (aged 26) was the most industrious bachelor at Kaburusato. He joined with others in a total of nine gardens, including one that he and three other bachelors made on their own. His younger brother Illawe, also a bachelor (aged 20), participated in seven of these gardens plus one he also made on his own. These brothers joined gardens initiated by two father's brothers (three gardens), two sisters' husbands, a mother's brother, a mother's sister's son, and a father's sister's son (with a variety of other kinsmen and kinswomen also being coparticipants). Their gardening relations linked them to four (of eleven) longhouse communities. However, they did not join in gardening with the fathers of the girls to whom they were betrothed, although Sawa married near the end of the period under discussion. A man's relationship to his wife's parents (*nesuā*) is one of formality and respect from the time of betrothal until the birth of the couple's first child (or sometime sooner), and he can speak to them only through a third party during this period (Kelly 1977:213, 221). Gardening together is awkward given the cooperative nature of the relations among coworkers; a betrothed girl's parents are generally avoided and there is consequently no labor service contributed to a future wife's father in the form of gardening assistance. The wife's father is thus conspicuously absent from the roster of close relatives with whom a bachelor gardens. (However, married men frequently garden with affines, including wife's parents, and commence to do so not long after conjugal relations are established.) Likewise, a physically mature young man does not repay his inseminator, to whom he is indebted for his strength, by contributing labor to the latter's garden. Although his inseminator may be among those he joins (e.g., ZH), this is no different from his coparticipation with other close relatives debarred from serving in this capacity. There is a diffuse sense of obligation to senior kinsmen generally, but this is also reciprocated by them. These two young men thus helped virtually all their close male kin as well as their two sisters and two widows of a recently deceased father's brother who reared them after their own father's death.

Sawa and Illawe also cultivated several bachelor gardens in which they (and other bachelors) performed all the tasks on their own except weeding, in which they were assisted to some extent by one sister. The number of garden plots established produced yields far in excess of their own dietary needs, and they encouraged their kin to harvest the surplus for the latter's own use. In other words, they displayed a culturally laudable generosity toward their kin in this facet of food production, as is characteristic of bachelors generally. This was reciprocated in a variety of ways (e.g., their mother's brother invited them to collect bush hen eggs from his lineage territory when these were unusually abundant). Although senior men hunt longer hours with greater effectiveness than young men in this age group, the game the former procure is distributed within the hunter's longhouse community so that a young man is not in a position to benefit from the hunting of older male kin in other communities whom he has assisted in gardening. However, the larger share of gardening work that young men perform is offset by the more extensive hunting of older men within a framework of generalized reciprocity. Widows are actually the principal beneficiaries of the extra work bachelors perform, and older men benefit by the alleviation of additional work they would otherwise be obligated to do on behalf of deceased brothers' wives, rather than in a reduction of their normal workload. These features will emerge as the discussion proceeds.

The Etoro division of labor in gardening entails a more substantial male labor component than is the case among the neighboring Onabasulu. Onabasulu men fell trees, fence the garden, and help in the collection and transport of planting material while women clear the undergrowth, plant, and weed (Ernst 1984:130–34). The fact that planting and (especially) weeding are done by the women rather than being shared by both sexes would shift a substantial portion of the total labor required from the men to the women (compared to the Etoro distribution given in table 2.5). The female labor contribution would be on the order of 70 to 75 percent.

Among the Samo, the women clear the underbrush while the men cut small trees, at this stage, and fell the upper story cover after the crop is planted. Both men and women plant while women weed (and later harvest the main crop) (Shaw 1990:42–44). As noted earlier, the Samo's banana gardens are not fenced, reducing male labor, and weeding is only partial, reducing female labor. If one assumes that tree felling, clearing undergrowth, and planting require the same number of hours per acre as they do in the Etoro case, and that partial weeding entails only one-third the time (and fencing is omitted), Samo banana gardening would require a total of 687 person-hours per acre, and 72 percent of the total labor would be female labor. While little weight should be given to this specific number, it is evident that clearing undergrowth is more time-consuming than felling trees, so that female labor inputs are greater than male labor inputs at this juncture. If the planting is equally divided, then the fact that women do all the weeding—however limited this may be—can only further unbalance labor inputs. Shaw (1990:43 et passim) emphasizes the point that women's central cultural role

is as "producers" while men's central role is as "protectors." Thus in gardening "as in all subsistence activity, some of the men are assigned to watch
the periphery of the area, guarding against bush spirits that might threaten
the laborers" (ibid.). The fact that men watch while women work supports
the conclusion that a high proportion of the total labor expenditure is female
labor, whatever the precise figure may be.

The data that would be needed to extend these comparisons to additional
groups are not reported in sufficient detail. However, Wood (1982:48, 50)
notes that traditionally Kamula men did all the tree felling and undergrowth
clearing that required an ax, while women carried out the clearing and weeding (and planting?) that could be done by hand. This division of labor parallels that of the Onabasulu except that gardens are unfenced and this male task
is omitted. Wood (1982:50) reports that currently, "a [Kamula] man would
make a garden with his wife assisting in clearing, planting and weeding."
Elsewhere (Wood 1987:8) he describes the division of labor as one in which
women weed and harvest gardens, with no mention being made of their
efforts in clearing and planting. If labor inputs in Kamula gardens are the
same as those in Etoro gardens, then weeding alone would constitute just a
little over half (50.3 percent) of the total labor required to make an unfenced
garden (leaving aside harvesting). If a wife's assistance in clearing and planting typically amounted to one quarter of the work entailed, women's overall
labor contribution would be 59.7 percent. It thus appears that Kamula women
do more than half the work in gardening as well as all the work in sago
processing (although additional data are clearly needed in order to assess
gardening contributions more accurately).

The introduction of steel axes has made it possible for unmarried
Kamula young women and widows to make gardens "without recourse to
male labor," although usually a brother will help out (Wood 1982:50). Here
we see the absence of task exclusivity in the sexual division of labor that
appears to be characteristic of the region. However, it should be kept in mind
that the Kamula rely heavily on sago (which women produce on their own)
and that the garden a Kamula woman (or group of women) might make would
not need to be large if sago provides the bulk of caloric intake. A rejection
of the sexual division of labor such as this entails no change in the total labor
required if the original sexual division of labor is equal and each gender can
perform the tasks of the other with the same efficiency. Thus, a woman
gardening on her own would do half as much weeding as would be required
gardening with a male partner and apply the time saved to clearing, planting,
and felling trees. Since women evidently do some clearing and planting,
fencing is not required, and women fell sago palms, all the tasks would be
familiar. Additional data, including a more precise assessment of proportional contributions to the conventional division of labor in gardening would

be needed to determine whether female labor inputs are decreased or increased when Kamula women garden on their own. If women do 60 percent of the work when gardening with men, as I have roughly estimated, their total labor expenditure would be reduced by gardening alone.

Given the fact that Kamula women hunt and forage, the men's contribution to sago processing is nil, and men's contribution to gardening appears to be somewhat less than half (making independent gardens a viable alternative for women), Kamula women are within comparatively easy reach of attaining economic self-sufficiency. In other words, the Kamula sexual division of labor in subsistence is substantially unbalanced and therefore approaches the point at which a woman does not need a male partner in order to constitute a viable economic unit in subsistence food production. More specifically, a woman does not need a husband, especially insofar as she can exchange sago for game with her brothers and receive assistance in making the small gardens required from these same male kinsmen. Thus, Wood concludes that among the Kamula, as among the Mundurucu, "males and females, as collectivities, depend upon each other for subsistence, but individual men and women do not depend upon each other" (Murphy and Murphy 1980:190, cited in Wood 1987:10). It is noteworthy in this respect that 8.7 percent of Kamula widows below the age of 40 had not remarried and were not expected to do so, while an additional 4.7 percent of women over age 25 had never married (Wood 1982:110–11).

In contrast, the Etoro division of labor is unbalanced in the direction of greater male (rather than female) labor inputs so that women are not within easy reach of self-sufficiency. Marriage is economically advantageous for women for the same reason. In addition, the absence of gendered products, produced exclusively by males and females, constitutes an impediment to exchange between a broader range of cross-sex kin that would make it unnecessary to have a spouse. Although economic self-sufficiency might be possible hypothetically, Etoro women do not envision the task of felling a third of an acre of trees annually as within their capabilities and thus perceive themselves to be dependent upon male labor. All widows whose children are not old enough to comprise a viable economic unit consequently seek to attach themselves to a family work group or to constitute a work group with a bachelor (often related as a "son"). A widow may reside in any longhouse community she chooses and enter into any cooperative work group she elects. Widows also generally seek to remarry, and a younger widow will characteristically attempt to establish a sexual relationship with a bachelor in order to exert de facto control over her marital destiny by inducing him to offer for her. In contrast to the Kamula, all widows below the age of 40 are expected to remarry and the rate of remarriage indicates that this expectation is fulfilled (Kelly 1977:301). In addition, a number of widows aged 41 to 60 also remarry (ibid.:309). Although men arrange widow remarriages to create desired kin relations within and between lineages (ibid. 229–55), widows beyond childbearing age hold no potentiality for achieving these ends, lineage objectives are not engaged, and no effort is made to arrange unions for these women.[24] Moreover, these older widows generally have grown sons and daughters with whom they might readily garden and process sago. They can thus quite easily choose to remain unmarried if they so desire, and the fact that they actively seek remarriage in most instances is significant. In contrast, the Kamula division of labor makes the avoidance of remarriage on the part of widows readily understandable. A parallel comparison may also be drawn with respect to teenage girls. Although marriages are arranged in the Etoro case, a girl elects the time at which she enters into matrimony and may delay this if she wishes (ibid. 214). However, all girls are married by the age of 16 (ibid. 304). Again, the contrast with the Kamula is noteworthy. Although many noneconomic factors have a bearing on the desirability of the married state, the point I seek to make here is that the Etoro division of labor is conducive to a general preference for matrimony on the part of women as well as men.

Although Etoro bachelors look forward to marriage, they are capable of performing the full range of subsistence tasks and do not perceive themselves to be dependent upon female labor. The gardens that bachelors make on their own constitute an expression of their sense of self-sufficiency, since these young men are encouraged to join in communal gardens and do so to an extent that is more than sufficient to fulfill their needs for garden produce. Bachelor gardens are not only unnecessary in this respect but also require the performance of tasks that would be done by women in communal gardens. A specific comparison between these two gardening options will bring out the difference.

It is easy for bachelors and widows to achieve an equitable exchange of labor in communal gardens because male labor in tree felling and fencing is quite close to being equivalent to female labor in clearing undergrowth (see table 2.5). The work of planting is equally divided, so that this could either be shared or done by each separately in their demarcated plots within the enclosed area. Each would then weed and harvest his or her own plot. Here the bachelor would do half the total weeding of the two plots combined, rather than the one-third typically done by married men. However, in a bachelor garden he would need to clear the undergrowth as well, rather than doing additional tree felling and fencing in exchange for this work of clearing, as occurs in a communal garden. (If a sister were to help with the weeding, this would be equally available in either case.) What a bachelor achieves in making a garden with other bachelors is thus an expression of self-sufficiency and a rejection of the division of labor in this facet of subsistence. It might thus be said, in counterpoint to the Kamula, that Etoro bachelors make gardens "without recourse to female labor," although often a sister helps with the weeding. In both instances this constitutes a symbolic statement of self-sufficiency and independence as well as a form of food production.

A widow needs to exchange her labor in clearing undergrowth for male labor in fencing and felling trees, while a bachelor has no necessity to enter into this exchange. (This is equally true in the case of a married man, but for the different reason that a wife supplies all the female labor needed to form a viable economic unit, as discussed below.) This asymmetry points up the superior value of male labor in the context of this exchange. This is probably balanced out in the sago processing that this same widow and bachelor would be likely to jointly undertake. These cooperative arrangements between widows and bachelors are essentially contractual relations that are both freely entered into and easily dissoluble so that they provide insights into the sexual division of labor that are not as readily discerned in examining the relation between husbands and wives. These contractual relations also point up the fact that the conventional sexual division of labor between spouses in gardening is advantageous to women in terms of the allocation of tasks and advantageous to men with respect to the allocation of labor time. This is also applicable to sago processing.

The potential inclusion of a widow within a family work group remains to be discussed. As noted above, a married man does not need any additional female labor, since he already has a wife to perform the tasks allotted to women. Moreover, the inclusion of a widow within the gardening group will necessitate an expansion of the area under cultivation and thus entail added male labor in fencing and felling trees. This is offset by the widow's assumption of most of the weeding the husband would otherwise do, so that an exchange of labor is effected. In other words, the husband will spend as many hours in the garden as he otherwise would have, but with his efforts concentrated in the tasks of fencing, felling trees, and planting. However, the exchange of the arduous labor of felling trees for the light labor of weeding is burdensome, and it is the man's kin relationship to the widow that facilitates her inclusion within the gardening group. Often she is his deceased brother's wife, whom he is obligated to assist by performing the male tasks his brother would otherwise have performed.

In the Etoro socioeconomic system, there is no benefit to be gained from the labor of another person other than a reduction of one's own workload, because there is no significant use to which expanded agricultural or sago production beyond subsistence needs can be put. This contrasts with the Highlands, where a man might deploy an added widow's labor to increase sweet potato production and support a larger number of pigs that could be deployed in prestige-enhancing ceremonial exchange. The Etoro both lack this prestige system and are not in a position to expand pig production in this way, as their system of pig husbandry is based on forage, rather than fodder (Kelly 1988) and is therefore largely disconnected from agricultural production. A man will typically have as many pigs as he needs to fulfill his affinal exchange obligations, and the addition of a widow to his gardening group cannot be translated into increased holdings in any event. Although sago flour can be deployed in trade to obtain shoats, a wife can easily produce the small amount needed to acquire one or two shoats annually. The additional labor of a widow would be superfluous. Thus while "pig production and the social relation of pig production, circulation and consumption [are] the strategic points for understanding inequality in the Highlands," as Modjeska (1982:93) argues, the social relations of pig production are not a key locus for the production of inequality in the Etoro case. Although men do receive some credit for generosity in the distribution of pork received in exchange for jointly produced semidomesticated pigs (as described earlier), the locus for the production of inequalities in the attainment of prestige through generosity is grounded in the division of labor rather than appropriation of distributional control over the products of female labor. Moreover, the "generosity" derived from distributing affinal pork is of a lower order than that derived from the distribution of game. The more general point which this difference reflects is that *the Etoro male prestige system is not dependent upon female labor. There is consequently no prestige-enhancing use to which additional female labor can be put.*

The inclusion of a widow within a family work group thus entails a redistribution of tasks that is burdensome for the husband. Polygyny has precisely the same economic consequences. A man with one wife has all the female labor he needs to fulfill his subsistence needs. Since the latter are constant, an additional wife will only increase his workload without any compensating benefits. Although a second wife or widow can assume some of the lighter tasks he might otherwise do in exchange for the added labor, the degree of substitutability of female for male labor is limited to the tasks that men and women both perform, such as weeding and planting. The Etoro ideology which holds that a man with two wives is likely to die young as a result of the double dose of sexual (i.e., life-force) depletion thus reflects the disadvantages of polygyny in terms of the male workload. The preceding discussion also explains why widows seek to remarry and why more than 70 percent of them wed single men (bachelors, widowers, and divorcés), although nearly all of them could be claimed by married men on the basis of leviratic rights if these men wanted an additional wife. A widow cannot easily operate as an independent agent in subsistence food production because she needs to exchange her labor for male labor in performing the more arduous tasks, while her labor has no value beyond its substitutability and is not in demand. The most satisfactory arrangement is matrimony, in which the full range of reciprocities between spouses is engaged and the exchange of labor is assured.

The potentialities and limits that are inherent in this system, in which one person's labor can be substituted for another's, remain to be explored. As the system is constituted, there is one sequence of substitutions that could hypothetically be employed to augment the frequency of prestige-enhancing distributions of game. A senior man might gain the assistance of a bachelor in performing the tree felling and fencing he assumed by the inclusion of a widow in his gardening project, while the widow took over the weeding and planting he might otherwise do. The senior man might then devote greater efforts to hunting while being largely relieved of gardening responsibilities, repaying the bachelor through the distribution of game but attaining prestige through generosity in these distributions. A series of substitutions would thus enable this hypothetical individual to divert his efforts to more prestige-enhancing activities. However, this does not occur, and it is important to understand why. First, the inclusion of a bachelor, in addition to a widow, requires another expansion of the area under cultivation so that he can be provided with a plot. The tree felling and fencing that the bachelor performs are then done in exchange for the clearing carried out by the widow, so that each of them gains a plot within the garden. The senior man who initiated the garden thus does not need to assume additional tree-felling and fencing chores, but as a result the widow does not undertake the planting or weeding he would ordinarily do. His workload and tasks remain the same as they would be if he and his wife had made a garden by themselves.

What the initiator of a communal garden does accomplish is the facilitation of a culturally valued communal mode of production in which people work together. More specifically, he creates a framework within which widows and bachelors can readily pool their efforts in accordance with the sexual division of labor and join with married couples in a shared productive enterprise. Since widows, bachelors, and indeed all residents of the community can move to another longhouse or to smaller garden houses at any time, a community's continued social existence is dependent upon this successful facilitation of cooperative effort. Individuals acknowledge the role of a *tafidilo* or respected senior man in engendering a longhouse community—through the organization of the construction of the dwelling itself and the organization of communal gardening—when they describe their residence as "living at Ibo's place." The intrinsic anarchical quality of the domestic mode of production (Sahlins 1972:95–99) is thus transcended by the establishment of communal production, and the social relations of community are amplified through these social relations of production. The credit that accrues to the *tafidilo* is not misplaced. Moreover, the prestige associated with this status is rooted in bringing about the realization of a communitarian ethic, not in the substitution of other persons' labor for his own, or in the appropriation of distributional control over the products of another's labor. Rather than off-loading his gardening responsibilities, Ibo more than fulfilled them, starting early and continuing after others had quit for the day. His assiduous hunting (described earlier) entailed added labor with no benefit from labor substitution. The occasions on which he provisioned the sharing of food among all coresidents represented another facet of his general role in engendering the social relations of community.

THE DIVISION OF LABOR

The total number of hours Etoro males and females expend weekly in subsistence tasks is presented in table 2.6. Although women do somewhat more work than men in root crop gardening and considerably more work in sago processing, this is more than offset by male labor expenditure in maintaining and harvesting nut and pandanus groves, foraging, hunting, trapping, and fish poisoning, so that overall, the male contribution to subsistence effort amounts to 56 percent of the total. Consideration of the effects of the introduction of steel tools and the potential consequences of a reduced reliance on sago prior to depopulation indicate that the distribution of male and female effort has changed very little from that which obtained during the precontact era.[25]

As noted earlier, foraging is part of all trips to gardens and sago stands where work is in progress and is also carried out in the course of expeditions that include harvesting. In the table, the hours of labor devoted to sago processing and gardening incorporate travel time, so that some foraging is encompassed under those headings. Gardening effort is likewise reduced by the classification of harvesting with foraging. The 5 percent of the sweet potato crop that is devoted to feeding shoats during the early period of domestication is included in total gardening labor. The efforts men make to check on free-ranging mature pigs and maintain their approachability by periodic feeding take place in the context of foraging. Women's efforts in tending pigs in the early months entail taking them to gardens and sago stands so that they can begin to learn to forage for their own food, and these efforts are encompassed within the time spent on these other activities. Most of the firewood utilized is carried to the longhouse by men in the form of eight-foot logs, which are stored inside so that they can dry thoroughly before being split and used. This firewood is picked up on the way back to the longhouse, and the labor time entailed is thus included within the figures for other tasks as well. The maintenance of nut and pandanus groves (by men) is incorporated in harvesting trips. All aspects of subsistence are thus included in the hours of labor presented, although it is not possible to accurately break down these figures into more specific tasks due to the fact that so many of these tasks are carried out in combination.

Cooking, which is an aspect of food production in the broadest sense, also deserves discussion. Cooking is carried out by men, women, and children. Balls of sago, sweet potatoes, cooking bananas, and nuts are roasted on the coals by the person who will consume them. When packets of sago or garden vegetables are steam cooked, the men split the firewood and make the fire to heat the stones, while the women wash the tubers or wrap the sago in banana leaves (with meat and/or greens inside) and place this in the earth oven. The men's part of the job is more time-consuming. Men also undertake the task of preparing pandanus sauce (as described earlier). Men butcher, cook, and distribute game and domestic pork. The fact that men are prominent in the distribution of foods that are widely shared entails heavy involvement in the preparation of these foods. Although no time studies were made and no precise figures are available, male labor expenditure in food preparation would substantially exceed female labor expenditure for this reason.

Most craft and tool production is carried out by men, who make bows, arrows, cassowary-bone implements, and sago pounders, and sharpen steel axes and bush knives (as in the recent past they would have sharpened stone tools). Women produce string from the inner bark of trees and make net bags used by all. Men and women each make their own attire with the exception of a woven string loincloth women make for men (that is now being replaced by purchased cloth). Nearly all the work in longhouse and garden house construction is done by men, although women help to collect sago leaves for thatch. Trade, which entails lengthy trips to Onabasulu and Huli territory, is carried out almost entirely by the men. In the past, this trade was essential to the procurement of stone tools necessary for subsistence, salt which was

TABLE 2.6

The Sexual Division of Labor in Etoro Subsistence Food Production

Task	Man-hours per Week	Woman-hours per Week	Total Person-hours per Week
Sago processing	1.61	5.11	6.72
Gardening	4.90	6.73	11.63
Harvesting, hunting, trapping, and fish poisoning	14.36	4.67	19.03
Total	20.87	16.51	37.38
Percentage	55.8%	44.2%	100%

otherwise lacking in the diet, and shoats that supplemented those bred locally. Currently, trade is equally important in acquiring shoats, steel tools, and commercially produced salt from the Huli. The shell valuables that are deployed in bridewealth and compensation payments are also acquired through this trade (discussed more fully in chap. 6).

Although no quantified data are available concerning the number of hours men and women devote to trade, construction, craft and tool production, and cooking, the inclusion of these tasks in an overall calculation of labor expenditure by gender would add much more to the male than to the female column. The addition of weekly all-night séances, through which a medium and male chorus maintain beneficial relations with the spirits, would add many hours to the male side as well. Within this broader framework of the reproduction of the social system (as opposed to economic production, distribution, and consumption per se), it is important to also include the efforts that women devote to bearing, nursing, and tending small children.[26] As noted earlier, the conjugal relationship is seen by the Etoro as entailing a woman's obligation to bear children and a man's reciprocal obligation to provision his wife with game in recognition of her childbearing. The greater male contribution to subsistence is counterbalanced by the female's recognized contribution in this respect. However, a woman who fails to bear children not only fails in her conjugal obligation but also drains her husband's productive energies without reciprocating, just as she drains his spiritual vitality through sexual depletion without the reciprocation of producing a child. Moreover, only a wife can complete the exchange that the Etoro envision as an essential part of the division of labor, whereas an unmarried girl, widow, sister, or other kinswoman cannot.

The complementarity and joint effort that are intrinsic to the Etoro sexual division of labor are conducive to feelings of mutuality and shared interests on the part of husbands and wives that are readily apparent in their daily interactions. There is no elaboration of sanctions to ensure the fulfillment of reciprocal obligations, as in the Kamula case. I neither observed nor learned of any instances in which services were withheld by either spouse. There were no disagreements that arose between married couples concerning the division of labor. However, disgruntlement, tension, and conflict did surface with respect to Wadome's childlessness (as described earlier). In another instance, a wife initiated an adulterous relation with her husband's brother's son that appeared to be motivated by her childlessness (and the thought that the problem might be attributable to her husband's deficiencies rather than her own). Her actions were consistent with the interpretation that she hoped to become pregnant so as to forestall her husband's plan to take a second wife in order that he might have the children she had failed to bear. This is the customary recourse. Between married couples it was not issues of work but of childlessness that were the source of difficulties. However, outside of marriage the division of labor did become an issue on one occasion. Yebua wanted her son Selagu and her deceased husband's FBSS Nogobe to initiate a garden. However, they procrastinated, creating a situation in which additional sago processing would be necessary to fill a foreseeable gap in garden yields, and thus increasing Yebua's workload. Yebua announced that she would not process sago until they began the garden, and this produced the desired result. Yebua's subsequent refusal to allow Nogobe to utilize the work group's jointly produced sago to trade for a shoat (described earlier) was related to this earlier disagreement. This sequence of events shows that disputes concerning the balance of effort within the sexual division of labor can arise (although this dispute also entailed issues of who was giving direction to the work group's efforts). However, such disputes are confined to the contractual relations between widows and bachelors and are significantly absent from the relations between husbands and wives. In sum, available data indicate that the division of labor is both mutually satisfactory and a source of positive affect when the components of marriage and children that it encompasses are present.

As noted earlier, the Etoro sexual division of labor in gardening and sago processing is advantageous to women in terms of the allocation of tasks and advantageous to men in terms of the allocation of labor time. In effect, there is an exchange of arduous work for more tedious and time-consuming work. In harvesting, foraging, hunting, trapping, and fish poisoning the sexual division of labor is advantageous to women in terms of the allocation of time and advantageous to men in terms of the allocation of tasks, since this work eventuates in the procurement of foods that are widely distributed, providing a vehicle for the attainment of prestige through generosity. Here men readily take on additional hours of work in order to fulfill their self-image as generous and community-spirited individuals, and to earn the prestige that accompanies this. A few women also hunt regularly and play an acknowledged role in the provision of game to the community, but most forego this potentiality and the added labor this entails. Nevertheless, Nowalia (a woman in the mid-30s-to-early-40s age class), ranks third on Dwyer's list of thirty-six Bobole hunters in terms of the number of hours expended in hunting (Dwyer 1983:168–71, based on the combined totals reported in appendices I to IV). Although Nowalia and her husband Maga (in the early-40s-to-mid-50s age category) usually hunt together, each also hunts separately on some occasions (ibid.). It is of interest that Nowalia and Maga have four children aged 12, 9, 6, and 3 (Dwyer, personal communication). Having young children is therefore not a deterrent to female hunting. Tending children is not confined to nuclear family members.

Is the Etoro division of labor egalitarian? To answer this question, it would be necessary to establish a standard against which the Etoro case might be measured. As a point of departure, one might envision a hypothetical absence of any division of labor, in which each person performed exactly the same tasks and was entirely self-sufficient. Although this would be perfectly egalitarian, it would be a hardship for older persons, particularly older women who cannot easily perform the more arduous tasks. The bachelor gardens discussed earlier provide a glimpse of the social consequences of self-sufficiency and point up the fact that an absence of division (and exchange) of labor favors young men and is not a neutral arrangement. This form of egalitarian organization of labor would therefore not be entirely equitable. An alternative that would remedy these inequities could be constructed on the basis of an exchange of labor in which each person performed the task that he or she could most readily do. The Etoro approximate this in that young men take on a larger share of the difficult work of cutting trees, which they can do more easily than others, and older men engage in more extensive hunting in which the skill acquired through years of experience produces greater returns per hour. The tasks that women perform are ones that are time-consuming but not arduous. I think it can be argued that this overall pattern is equitable as a division of types of work per se. However, since this organization of work is based on complementarity rather than homogeneity, issues of the rates of exchange between types of labor and the social rewards for labor also arise. In the Etoro case, men would need to work an additional 1.75 hours per week in sago processing and an additional .92 hours a week in gardening in order to equalize the division of labor in these subsistence activities by substituting this amount of male labor for female labor. If the sexual division of labor in harvesting, foraging, hunting, trapping, and fish poisoning were similarly equalized, women would need to devote 4.85 more hours per week to these activities. There is thus an "exchange" of 2.67 hours of female work in gardening and sago processing for 4.85 hours of male work in harvesting, foraging, hunting, trapping, and fish poisoning. If one leaves aside the social rewards for different types of work (in order to factor them out), I think it can be argued that the rate of exchange is quite favorable to women.

This line of reasoning thus leads to the conclusion that the division of types of work and the exchange of one form of labor for another are not, in and of themselves, inequitable and productive of differences that engender inequality. However, the social value accorded to different types of work is not the same, and thus inequalities emerge. As noted in the introduction, inequality can be defined as social differentiation accompanied by differential privileges, prestige, and moral evaluation. Men are not privileged in consumption,[27] and they are not privileged in the sense that they do less work or easier work. However, differential prestige and moral evaluation are accorded to men since the food-getting activities they undertake eventuate in the communitywide distribution of food and in the attainment of prestige through the acts of generosity this distribution entails. The source of inequality is thus isolable as pertaining to the ascription of cultural value. It does not arise from the division of work per se or from the allocation of the consumable products of labor but from the division of value accorded to labor and to the products of different forms of labor.

The point of articulation between economic process and cultural value can also be specified as lying particularly within the realm of distribution, rather than that of production or consumption. In distribution there is a potentiality to create exchange value (in the sense specified earlier) by giving a thing and later receiving an identical thing in return. Broader forms of sociality can be engendered by the deployment of this exchange value, and it is these broader forms of sociality that are accorded cultural value. Moreover, the dynamic of this value-creating process can also be specified as the Durkheimian moment of social effervescence, at which the achievement of community suffuses individuals with a sense of transcendent spiritual value. It is by this alchemy that the lead of bits of food is transmuted into the gold of prestige (by the conversion of exchange value into spiritual value). Although economic process supplies the lead, the conversion is contingent upon a value-creating process that is external to the economy. Within the economic sphere, the division of labor is instrumental to male predominance in the extrafamilial distribution of valued foods. This, in turn, is the source of the exchange value that is convertible into spiritual value, yielding prestige. These are the lineaments of the production of inequality in terms of differential prestige. However, this is only one form of prestige. Other forms of prestige, which are remote from economic process, remain to be examined (e.g., spirit mediumship). The question of the interrelation between these diverse sources and forms of prestige can then be addressed.

The proposition that female starch staple production subsidizes male attainment of prestige—which is central to Collier and Rosaldo's (1981) and Collier's (1988) analysis of social inequality in brideservice societies—is only marginally applicable to economic systems that are characterized by male-female coproduction of starch staples. This is evident from the figures presented above and the earlier discussion of bachelor gardens. A bachelor who does not engage in an exchange of labor with a widow takes only half as much land under cultivation. He thus devotes only half as much labor to tree felling and fencing and applies this labor saving to clearing undergrowth and additional weeding, so that the added labor expenditure works out to only .92 hours a week. Processing sago on his own would add another 1.75 hours per week, bringing the total to the 2.67 hours noted above. However, a bachelor's added labor expenditure would actually be only two-thirds of this (1.78 hours) because the figures for labor expenditure that provide the basis for these calculations take the support of dependent children (i.e., nonproductive consumers) into account. A wife's labor therefore provides a small subsidy by freeing up 1.78 hours a week that a husband would otherwise need to devote to providing his own starch staples and .89 hours a week that he would otherwise need to devote to providing for dependent children (calculated as two .5 consumers per couple). However, a self-sufficient bachelor who devoted the same number of hours per week to prestige production as a married man would only have to increase his labor expenditure by about 8.5 percent (from 20.87 to 22.65 hours). It is thus evident that the lack of a wife does not constitute a significant impediment to a bachelor's attainment of prestige through generosity in the distribution of game. The fact that younger hunters procure less than a fourth (22.8 percent) as many kilograms of game per hour as senior men in their early 40s to mid-50s is the critical factor, since a young bachelor would need to more than quadruple the time devoted to hunting to achieve comparable results, and his total labor expenditure would thus increase to unrealistic levels. The difference between young men and older men in this aspect of prestige attainment is thus largely attributable to hunting skill acquired through years of experience, not to the labor subsidy a wife provides.

Within the framework of the Etoro economy, there is no benefit to be gained from the labor of another person other than a reduction of one's own workload. But the actual extent of this potential benefit that can be realized in practice is very small as a percentage of total labor expenditure. This is an egalitarian feature of the Etoro economy. The fact that junior and senior males have essentially equivalent opportunities to earn prestige through game distribution is also a significant egalitarian feature of the Etoro economy. Moreover, a bachelor does not need a wife in order to facilitate his efforts to earn prestige, not only because the potential labor subsidy is small but because he can form a production team with a widowed "mother" and exchange the arduous labor of tree felling for the tedious labor of weeding, thereby gaining this subsidy (which qualifies as such only if one leaves aside differences in the energy expenditure of male and female tasks and focuses on person-hours). Widows are eager to enter into such arrangements, since they regard the labor exchange as essential. They are available because a married man has all the female labor he requires and cannot make use of the labor of a second wife or attached widow in order to divert more time to earning prestige. All of these features of the Etoro economy pose serious problems for the brideservice model formulated by Collier and Rosaldo (1981) and Collier (1988). However, it is important to note that many of these features are attributable to male-female coproduction of starch staples and to the exchange of labor, rather than the products of labor, this entails.

If women exclusively produced sago and men exclusively hunted large game
(as approximated in the Kamula case), then the exchange of these gendered
products would at the same time entail female subsidization of male prestige
attainment. The magnitude of the subsidy would be half the number of hours
women devote to sago production, or a figure on the order of seven hours a
week.

The Etoro productive economy is quite gender egalitarian by comparative standards in that the division of labor does not entail task exclusivity and
an attendant concept of gendered capabilities. There are very few tasks that
men perform that women do not at least occasionally undertake and vice
versa. The division of labor therefore does not instantiate the proposition
that men and women are uniquely and distinctively different (although it
does propose that they can exchange different types of work to mutual
benefit). The lack of task exclusivity is significant in that the avenues of
prestige attainment outlined above are not closed to women. Women can
hunt, play an acknowledged role in the provision of game to the community,
be the sponsors of the widespread distribution of food, and achieve prestige
in this way. Moreover, there is scope within the division of labor for them
to take on substantial hunting without exceeding the labor time men devote
to subsistence tasks. Although women do not hunt large game and cannot
participate in fish poisoning in the same way as men, so that a perfect equality
of opportunity does not obtain, it is nevertheless important to recognize that
there are opportunities open to women and that this aspect of the prestige
system is not male exclusive. In higher altitude Etoro communities, where
large game and fish constitute only a small proportion of the nondomesticated
animal protein in the diet, a more comparable equality of opportunity prevails.

Moreover, the attainment of prestige through generosity is not dependent upon female labor nor restricted to those who have wives. A woman
does not need a wife in order to hunt, nor does a bachelor. There are thus
significant differences between the Etoro and the brideservice societies portrayed and analyzed by Collier and Rosaldo (1981) and Collier (1988) with
respect to the interrelations between marriage, economic organization, and
social inequality. The theoretical significance of these differences is explored
at length in the conclusions, and one of the main objectives of the present
chapter is to lay the groundwork for this.

The openness of the prestige system noted above does not eventuate in
equality in the distribution of prestige. While women can hunt and provision
a prestige-enhancing distribution of game, this rarely occurs. Senior men in
the early-40s-to-mid-50s age category also predominate over younger men
in the attainment of prestige through generosity, since they hunt somewhat
longer hours and with considerably greater effectiveness. Although prestige

is earned through elective social action open to females and young men, as well as to senior males, it largely accrues to the latter. The individual choice that is intrinsic to prestige systems (as opposed to systems of ascribed status) is instrumental to the comparative evaluation of differences between individuals in prestige. In other words, it is central to the prestige system as constituted that game procurement is not a prerogative of senior men or an activity from which others are debarred. The exceptional woman who hunts and the comparatively paltry results achieved by young male hunters thus serve to highlight, magnify, and naturalize the superior prestige attainment of senior males. The same general phenomenon is apparent with respect to the fact that women rarely engage in the prestigious mode of distribution of the midsize game they regularly procure and that women rarely elect to become the senior owner and eventual distributor of semidomesticated pigs by assuming responsibility for the pig's maturation (and undertaking the potential burden of a prohibition on pork consumption if the pig dies). The construction of inequality in the Etoro case is thus subtle in that it turns on a concept of elective social action in domains of activity that are relatively unrestricted, accompanied by outcomes in which females and young men compare quite unfavorably to senior men in their early 40s to mid-50s.

In my account I have attempted to capture this cultural sense of an absence of arbitrary restrictions and of an approximation of equal opportunity that informs social actors' perception of the "natural" superiority of this category of senior men. However, the empirical manifestations of this in terms of generosity in game distribution are, of course, culturally preconditioned outcomes. Age and gender categories are delineated with respect to a cosmology of life-force transmission that shapes self-image, motivation, and perception of capabilities on the part of each socially differentiated category of actors. Prestige thus accrues to individuals who do in fact make superior contributions to the realization of community, while at the same time this prestige is measured in terms of an activity that senior men are inclined to engage in more frequently, and one in which their experience confers a high rate of success (cf. Collier 1988:200). However, an ascribed age status or having a wife does not mechanically confer superior opportunities to earn prestige, due to enabling conditions external to the individual, as Collier (ibid.:202–10) supposes. On the contrary, these opportunities are underexploited by women and younger men as a result of internalized self-conceptions that impinge on motivation and are self-limiting. The cultural construction of age and gender categories analyzed in the next chapter will elucidate these self-conceptions.

If the Etoro economy is measured against the standard of "from each according to his or her ability, to each according to his or her need," it conforms quite closely. The division of labor takes differential abilities pertaining to age and sex into account, and consumption is in accord with nutritional requirements. The economy does not deviate from egalitarian ideals in these respects. Moreover, differential prestige is not accompanied by differential economic privileges. The process that is instrumental to the generation of prestige necessarily entails a widespread distribution of food. Thus, the inequalities of prestige that obtain are part of a prestige-driven mode of distribution that also promotes equality of consumption. Finally, it should be noted that the achievement of community and the spiritual values this engenders are necessarily experienced by all and thus shared by all. What men (and a few women) create through the deployment of exchange value is a social product of general benefit to men and women alike. More-over, these are occasions when social differences are submerged and an egalitarian ethos is most strongly experienced through food sharing. Para-doxically, inequalities of prestige arise out of the palpable experience of equality in community, as a sense of appreciation for those who made it possible.

ECONOMIC SOURCES OF INEQUALITY

The central question to which this work is addressed is a fundamental one: what is the locus of the production of inequality in the Etoro sociocultural system? Much of what has been written on the subject of the source of inequality derives from the Marxian position that all social inequalities are ultimately grounded in the internal dynamics of a particular mode of produc-tion and are either directly generated by this or built up on core relations of inequality that are so generated. (Wolf [1981:55] provides a particularly clear statement of this root-cause argument.) Likewise, Fried (1967:35) states unequivocally that "at the heart of an egalitarian society is a fundamentally egalitarian economy." Accumulation is very limited, distribution is governed by the principle of generalized reciprocity (Sahlins 1972:193), access to resources is communal and unrestricted, and conflict over productive prop-erty is rare to nonexistent. Woodburn's (1982) recent analysis of egalitarian societies is grounded in similar economic prerequisites, but provides a more comprehensive and detailed consideration of the connection between econ-omy and society as this pertains to the issue of inequality. His position can usefully be reviewed here in relation to the Etoro data.

The Etoro economy is a delayed-return system in terms of Woodburn's (ibid.) classification in that fish-poisoning sites, traps, snares, traplines, gar-dens, sago stands, and nut and pandanus groves all represent sources of food production in which labor is invested in order to provide returns over time. Management of the environment includes the selective cutting of trees for firewood along forest trails so as to establish groves of fruiting trees in which game animals are concentrated at certain (predictable) times of year (Kelly 1977:37). Even opportunistic foraging along forest trails therefore entails realization of the benefits of prior labor investment. Longhouses and garden dwellings also entail a labor investment from which benefits are realized over time. Techniques for storing sago flour and smoking meat are well developed. Both the stone tools used until circa 1955 and the steel tools used currently are imported and represent an investment with long-term returns. Finally, the Etoro social system is one in which "rights [are] held by men over their female kin who are then bestowed in marriage on other men" (Woodburn 1982:433), these rights being seen by Woodburn as assets managed in a way that "has similar social implications to delayed yields on labour" (ibid.:432). These implications or consequences are that social relations and social groupings entail binding commitments between persons and "jurally-defined relationships through which crucial goods and services are transmitted" (ibid.:433). The economic system thus entails ownership, management, and transmission of assets, and extensive interdependencies between individuals and groups grounded in kinship, descent, and marriage alliance. Although it is not useful for our present theoretical purposes to assimilate rights in women to a bundle of economic assets, Woodburn's formulation is otherwise useful in bringing out the economic aspects of certain features of Etoro social organization, and the extent to which transmission of assets and coproduction engender interdependencies. However, it should be noted at the outset that the Etoro lack the extensive dependencies presumed to be associated with delayed-return systems. They correspond much more closely to the egalitarian immediate-return systems in Woodburn's typology in this respect. This calls into question Woodburn's fundamental thesis that egalitarian features are contingent upon the disengagement of persons from property.

In the Etoro case, productive resources are owned by individuals and patrilineages, and access to these resources is governed by a combination of individual inheritance and lineage and community membership. Sago palms and the regrowth from cut palms are individually owned and are transmitted by inheritance to both sons and daughters (Kelly 1977:140). However, sago palms can be planted, so that access does not entirely depend upon transmission from parents. Sago is also abundant, and palms are frequently given to a wide variety of kinsmen for the asking (ibid. 1977:140). Since access is both diverse and diffused over a broad range of kin ties, holder-heir conflicts are nonexistent and no intergenerational inequalities are generated. Moreover, inheritance is an entitlement and does not engender any sense of dependence or indebtedness of child to parents. More generally, the Etoro subscribe to the view that a person who has more of something than he or she needs must share the surplus with any kinsman who requests it and that the recipient is not indebted to the donor in any way that exceeds the preexisting mutual obligations between kin. This conception was applied to valued steel axes only recently introduced into the economy. No individual could own two axes so long as any one of his kinsmen lacked one. He would have no grounds for refusing a request for the second ax. Likewise, the young man who helped me to bring in firewood parceled out the shillings he received as a wage to his kin, keeping only one coin for himself each weekly payday. Later in my fieldwork, when he became more familiar with money, he asked me to hold his wages and give him one larger denomination bill on those occasions when he was traveling to the patrol post and trade store, so that the money would be a thing he only had one of and therefore was not required to share. These examples illustrate Etoro values regarding the sharing of items possessed in multiple. Given these values, sago palms are easily acquired by anyone who needs one and lacks a mature palm that is ready to cut. Ownership and inheritance of sago palms therefore do not create dependencies that bring about inequality. Likewise, tools are not monopolized, and ownership of tools does not engender control over the process of production.

Although sons are favored over daughters to some extent in the transmission of sago palms, daughters are allotted substantial resources. The fact that both men and women possess extensive holdings of these important assets is a significant gender-egalitarian feature of the Etoro economy. Female ownership provides that women are not dependent upon their husbands or brothers for access to a means of starch staple production. Since men and women are both quite capable of processing sago without assistance, a basis for economic autonomy is established by individual ownership. In other words, each gender enters into the division of labor and the productive process on an equal footing. Moreover, women as well as men can give mature sago palms to their kin. Although sago palm utilization entails marked delayed-return features due to the long maturation period, this component of the economy does not foster the development of dependencies between parents and child, husband and wife, or brother and sister that Woodburn's formulation anticipates.

Marita pandanus, breadfruit, and Tahitian chestnut trees are also individually owned. Since these resources are maintained over time by men, they tend to be transmitted in inheritance from men to their brothers and sons. However, they are regularly planted, and an individual can therefore readily acquire personal holdings independent of inheritance. An individual can plant sago palms, pandanus, and nut trees on the territory of any lineage where he is currently gardening and residing, so that holdings are widely dispersed and individual ownership of these productive assets is counterposed to collective ownership of lineage assets (discussed below), offsetting potential lineage-based dependencies. The absence of a consolidated set of dependencies vested in a single key relationship (to parents, to agnates, or to spouse) is a general feature of the Etoro socioeconomic system.

Since pandanus is shared among coresidents of the longhouse community during the period of seasonal abundance, in accordance with the principle of generalized reciprocity, consumption is relatively detached from production and ownership of these delayed-return assets. The fact that some individuals have more extensive holdings than others thus has little bearing on consumption (except during the off-season, when small quantities are harvested and consumed by family units). Likewise, women are not dependent upon any particular man (e.g., husband or son) for access to this food (which is an essential source of vegetable protein in the diet). It is important to recognize that male attainment of prestige through generosity in the distribution of pandanus to all coresidents provides the main incentive for the maintenance of thousands of trees that yield abundant supplies. The enhancement of female autonomy is a consequence of this prestige-stimulated mode of production and distribution, and potential dependencies are thereby undercut. This is equally true with respect to the distribution of game animals (cf. Collier 1988:17).

A lineage and the *Sigisato* spirits associated with it are co-owners of a territory of one to two square miles that contains fish-poisoning sites, sections of primary forest (in the northern-tier territories) that provide favorable locations for traplines and hunting, and secondary forest in which hunting, trapping, and foraging can be carried out and swidden gardens cut. Male and female agnates have equivalent rights to lineage-owned resources (Kelly 1977:91). A female agnate can not only garden anywhere within her lineage territory at her own discretion but can also grant usufructuary privileges to others without any need to seek the approval of other lineage members. A woman and her husband can thus initiate a large communal garden on her lineage territory and invite whomever they wish to join them. A male agnate can do the same. No individual holds exclusive rights of stewardship over any section of lineage land, and there is consequently no intergenerational transmission of such rights, eliminating any potential for parental control, dependencies, feelings of indebtedness, and holder-heir conflicts. (Communal gardening also precludes the establishment of any discrete individual connection to land previously cultivated.) Lineage membership is acquired through a relation to an ancestor mediated by a male parent, and membership confers access to lineage-held assets. The productiveness of these assets is attributed to nonancestral *Sigisato* spirits who are co-owners (with the exception of fish, linked to *Kesames,* or spirits of the dead). There is consequently a conceptual diversion of the source of bounty and fruitfulness away from the patrifilial and ancestral connections through which lineage membership is secured. One is indebted to *Sigisatos* rather than to one's father or patrilineal ancestor. The spiritual cosmology thus not only fails to provide metaphoric support for patriarchial values but also negates the concept of filial indebtedness. Effective access to economic assets is attributable to spirits, not parents. Property rights fail to create dependency in the manner that Woodburn's formulation anticipates, and this is a consequence of both the organization of intergenerational transmission and the cosmology through which indebtedness is culturally formulated. This cosmology both depersonalizes hunting success and de-emphasizes the parental role in transmission of access to hunting territory.

The fish, game, bush hen eggs, and other collectibles found within the confines of a lineage territory are the property of lineage members. Nonagnatic residents of a longhouse community are granted customary rights to take rodents, snakes, lizards, frogs, birds, and bird eggs from the lineage territory on which the longhouse is located, but require specific permission to engage in the purposeful hunting and trapping of wild pigs, cassowaries, and forest mammals (e.g., midsize and large game), to poison fish, and to collect wood grubs (Kelly 1977:143). Thus, while all game may be taken by casual encounter on the territory of a lineage where an individual resides, the extensive traplines employed by the Etoro are almost always established on one's own lineage territory. Although male and female agnates have equivalent rights to take game from their lineage territory, no single individual can grant these rights to others. A female agnate therefore cannot authorize her husband to establish deadfalls, set cassowary snares, or poison fish. These activities require the spiritual authorization of the *Sigisato* and *Kesame* spirits (as explained earlier), and the request would need to be put to these spirits when they spoke through an entranced medium in the context of a séance at which all coresidents (including a number of agnates) would be likely to be present. It is thus Etoro beliefs concerning the relation between game and lineage spirits that effectively restrict access to these resources.

Since the taking of game is also the receipt of a spiritual offering, there is a strong tendency for men to engage in intensive hunting and trapping on their own lineage territory, where they receive game from their own *Sigisato* spirits. However, a man can easily do this while residing at a longhouse on any one of a half-dozen or more neighboring lineage territories, so that choice of residence is not constrained by this. Thus a man who resides at a longhouse on his wife's (or other kinsperson's) lineage territory will normally commute a mile or so to his own lineage territory for hunting and trapping, while gardening and sago processing are carried out in closer proximity to the longhouse. A little more than half the adult men reside in longhouses outside their lineage territories (Kelly 1977:165). Despite lineage claims to game animals, an individual can readily move from one longhouse to another "without economic penalty and without sacrificing . . . vital interests"

(Woodburn 1982:435). About 10 percent of the population changes residence each year (Kelly 1977:136), a rate comparable to the 13 percent that Lee reports for the !Kung (cited in Woodburn 1982:435). Many families participate in the gardens of two longhouse communities, and all divide their time between a longhouse and a garden house. As in the case of the egalitarian systems Woodburn analyzes, this extensive freedom of movement is antithetical to authority relations. It also undercuts the potentiality for more subtle forms of parental constraint. Even a child of eight may move to another longhouse for weeks at a time to be with an age-mate. The only person one cannot very easily move away from is one's spouse. There is no formulated obligation to coreside with any specific kinsmen or affines, and mutual obligations between kin do not entrain dependence but rather provide alternative sources of social support and economic cooperation (as in communal gardening).

Since an individual acquires hunting and trapping rights through lineage membership in the same way that rights to garden land are acquired, no dependencies are generated by intergenerational transmission of these rights (for the reasons explained above). All large and midsize game should be brought to the longhouse where an individual resides and shared out among coresidents. This applies equally to agnatic and nonagnatic members of the community, and the latter are not beholden to the former since both provision the community (see Kelly 1977:141). As with pandanus, a woman is not dependent upon any particular man to supply her. However, the distribution of game typically proceeds from men to other men, who then redistribute their portion among family members (including mothers, wives, daughters, and/or deceased brothers' wives, etc., depending upon the developmental cycle of each domestic group). Thus women receive meat through their relationships to men. Nevertheless, it is an entitlement and there are no acceptable grounds on which it might be withheld, so that dependency is not engendered by this mode of distribution. Although the Etoro socioeconomic system is characterized by many delayed-return features, there is a considerable degree of lack of dependency "on *specific* other people for access to basic requirements" (Woodburn 1982:434), although Woodburn associates this lack of dependency with egalitarian immediate-return systems.

However, the most singular obligations are toward one's spouse, because this is the one relationship that (polygyny aside) is not amenable to social substitutability. An individual has many "fathers," "mothers," "brothers," "sisters," "mother's brothers," and so forth, who can be a source of assistance (in giving a sago palm for example). There is a diffusion of mutual obligation over a broad range of kin, and the potential substitutability this establishes has the same consequences that Woodburn notes with respect to a generalized obligation to share and residential mobility. It undercuts the potential for both obligations to specific persons and authority relations. However, the husband-wife relationship is specifically marked off as distinctive in terms of the specificity of obligations both in the realm of sexuality and reproduction and in the division of labor. A spouse is the only culturally sanctioned heterosexual partner and source of legitimate offspring. Likewise, an individual cannot fail to honor the obligation to exchange labor with a spouse within the framework of the division of labor without violating the terms of the relationship. Unlike other relations, an alternative kinsperson cannot be substituted at will. This binding commitment between spouses is also distinctive in the egalitarian systems that are the focus of Woodburn's generalizations. However, the Etoro appear to differ in that marriages are a matter of group concern and are both carefully arranged to create and maintain intergroup relations and virtually indissoluble after the birth of a child (Kelly 1977:255–59). Substitutability through divorce is thus highly restricted. In addition, while Etoro women are rendered autonomous in certain respects by their ownership of sago palms and their access to game, pork, and pandanus through generalized sharing, they perceive themselves to be dependent upon male labor in tree cutting and fencing in order to engage in agricultural production. Swidden agriculture thus tends to create a degree of female dependence upon men that is absent in a nonintensive foraging (or hunting-and-collecting) economy, and this dependence is amplified by stone as opposed to steel tool technology. (Recall that Kamula women's independent gardening is a recent development linked to the advent of steel tools.) Thus Woodburn is correct in identifying a lesser degree of binding commitment in nonagricultural economies. However, the dependency of an Etoro woman upon specific men is diluted by social substitutability (as is exemplified by widows). Moreover, this dependency does not stem from the delayed-return features of agriculture, or the ownership of assets this entails, but from the specific labor requirements of agricultural production in a swidden regime.

In considering the degree of obligation to specific individuals in the Etoro sociocultural system, it is particularly important to note that there are no special obligations toward wife's parents in the distribution of game inasmuch as these have figured prominently in the analysis of the institution of marriage and gender inequalities in "brideservice societies" (Collier and Rosaldo 1981; Collier 1988). A hunter's wife's parents do not receive either larger portions or "best cuts" (Collier 1988:16). Instead, all coresidents share as equals, with an effort made to provide some of each part of an animal to all recipients if the game animal is large enough to make this at all feasible. Wife's parents share in the same way as others if they coreside. Distribution is modified by food taboos in the case of many midsize game animals, but the discriminant categories do not encompass affinal considerations (see Kelly 1977:43). The obligations of a man toward his affines that entail presentations of food are confined to the clearly demarcated context of affinal exchange (discussed earlier). Moreover, gifts of sides of pork, packages of sago grubs, and smoked game are all reciprocated, so that they do not constitute payments but are the components of perfectly equivalent exchange. These features have important implications for Collier's analysis that will be taken up in the conclusions. The point to be noted here is that the Etoro manifest a generalized obligation to share that is unmodified by special considerations for the hunter's wife's parents.

The Etoro are similar to the egalitarian societies Woodburn describes in that hunting success is depersonalized. Routinized forms of food distribution, carried out within a framework of generalized reciprocity, undercut any potential for patron-client relations. Although a successful hunter can attain prestige through generosity, he cannot create indebtedness (as explained earlier). Prestige does not entail economic privilege and is not convertible into forms of economic control over others. Thus there is no tendency for proficient hunters to have more wives than other men (and, indeed, both Ibo and Weliba, whose hunting success was described earlier, are monogamous). There is likewise no tendency for proficient hunters to be spirit mediums. Spirit mediums do have the capacity to influence witchcraft accusations (as will be discussed in chap. 4), but there are no economic prerequisites or correlates of this social position. This indicates that the means and relations of production are extensively disassociated from the inequalities that pertain to spirit mediumship. Finally, hunting success is germane to attainment of the status of *tafidilo*, or respected elder. However, this status is accorded to nearly all men between the ages of about 45 and 60 who have avoided the taint of a recent witchcraft accusation. Moreover, it is the men in this age group (early 40s to mid-50s) who tend to hunt longer hours and with a higher rate of success so that there is an intrinsic correlation between *tafidilo* status and the provision of substantial quantities of game to the community. It is probably the case that *tafidilo* status also stimulates assiduous hunting to fulfill cultural expectations. In sum, the social differentiation that pertains to the *tafidilo*/non-*tafidilo* distinction is related to age and prior witchcraft accusations as well as generosity in game distribution, and is thus only partially linked to economic production. Both the Hadza and !Kung associate each camp with a respected mature man (Woodburn 1982:444–45) in the same way that the Etoro sometimes associate a longhouse community with a *tafidilo*. Although the status of *tafidilo* remains to be discussed more fully in subsequent chapters, it may be noted here that the traits of modesty, generosity, and community-spirited egalitarianism that characterize the Etoro *tafidilo* parallel the characteristics of !Kung camp leaders (Lee 1979:350 cited in Woodburn 1982:445). Here again we see that the Etoro social system has much in common with the social systems of the egalitarian societies that are characterized by immediate-return economies, even though the Etoro economy is definitely not of this type.

This shows that the "disengagement of people from property" (Woodburn 1982:447) is not essential to the development of egalitarian features, in that the Etoro manifest such features but lack the expected disengagement. What is critical is the manner in which the relations of persons to property are socially organized, and the cultural values that govern distribution. The individual ownership and intergenerational transmission of rights to economic assets need not engender the dependency of children if there are alternative means of obtaining these assets. The lineage ownership of hunting and trapping territories also creates no dependencies when rights to these assets are acquired by lineage membership. Agnates share equally in these resources, and co-ownership promotes equality rather than a constraining dependence. Although one territory may differ from another in the resources available, this only produces the differences in the composition of the diet noted at the beginning of this chapter and does not engender inequality between lineages. While individual mobility is indeed an important aspect of egalitarian society, as Woodburn points out, the lineage and individual ownership of economic assets does not constrain mobility. In a comparatively rich environment, the distances between exploitable resources are not great, and it is easy to live in any one of a variety of communities and still be only a half-hour's walk from one's lineage territory. Woodburn is correct in pointing out that delayed-return features correlate with the ownership of economic assets and thus an engagement of persons with property, but the causal chain that links the latter to inequality is not borne out in the Etoro case for the reasons noted above. Moreover, the ownership of economic assets does not preclude the presence of cultural values emphasizing sharing through generalized reciprocity. Particularly notable here is the sharing of pandanus derived from cultivated, individually owned trees. Here the Etoro go far beyond the sharing of food surpluses that naturally obtain when a large game animal is killed, since considerable effort is expended to *create* surpluses far in excess of individual family needs *in order that* communitywide sharing can be realized. Cultural values thus shape production, distribution, and consumption rather than being shaped by delayed-return features of the economy. Woodburn recognizes the importance of cultural values but sees these as ultimately derived from the degree of engagement or disengagement of persons with property that is attributable to the delayed-return/immediate-return distinction (ibid.:448).

The Etoro economy is conducive to egalitarian relations both among men and between men and women in a number of respects detailed in the preceding discussion. In addition, the Etoro economy lacks certain features that are integral to inegalitarian systems in that (1) surpluses cannot be deployed to gain control over persons or the productive process; (2) there is no prestige- or privilege-enhancing use to which another person's labor can be put; and (3) relations of economic indebtedness are entirely absent. The only outlets for the domestic group's subsistence surplus are generalized distribution to the community or the fulfillment of perfectly reciprocal exchange obligations toward relatives by marriage. The former entails sharing as equals and the latter exchanging as equals. Moreover, these exchanges are entirely noncompetitive in contrast to other areas of New Guinea (cf. Woodburn 1982:446).

The sole source of social inequality rooted in the subsistence economy per se is that attributable to differences in the attainment of prestige through generosity in provisioning the community with game. This differential prestige is present to some degree in all comparatively egalitarian systems (see Woodburn 1982:442) and thus appears to be the unavoidable minimum degree of inequality that arises out of economic process. Prestige is accorded to those who contribute to the realization of sharing among equals, the transcendence of the anarchy intrinsic to the domestic mode of production, and the achievement of a communitarian ethos that is of equal benefit to all. Moreover, the attainment of this form of prestige is not dependent upon the labor of others, since the foods distributed are predominantly the products of the distributor's own labor. Men are therefore not economically dependent upon other men, or upon women, either to attain this form of prestige or to fulfill cultural expectations with regard to their economic role.

The division of labor engenders a degree of interdependence between men and women, and this is slightly asymmetrical in that men perceive themselves to be capable of performing the full range of subsistence tasks while women do not perceive themselves to be capable of easily performing the arduous labor of felling a third of an acre of large trees. Some degree of interdependence between men and women attributable to the sexual division of labor is also present in all ethnographically reported cases. The Etoro subsistence economy is thus comparable to the subsistence economies of the most egalitarian societies. It is somewhat more egalitarian than some of these standard-setting cases in the absence of task exclusivity in the division of labor (especially in hunting) and in the fact that a generalized obligation to share is unmodified by special prerogatives accorded to the hunter's wife's parents. This economic expression of an asymmetrical relation of indebtedness is absent in the Etoro case. The Etoro subsistence economy is perhaps somewhat less egalitarian with respect to the asymmetrical dependence of women upon men in the gardening component of the economy.

Overall, the Etoro subsistence economy may be characterized as one that is positively conducive to egalitarian relations and that provides only minimal grounds for the development, amplification, or expression of social differences. If all social inequalities are generated by the means and relations of production or are built on core relations of inequality that are so generated, as the Marxian position supposes, then one might expect that there would be little to add to the material presented in this chapter in order to provide a comprehensive account of inequality in Etoro society. But this is not at all the case. The social distinction between witch and nonwitch constitutes the most radical difference within the Etoro scheme of social differentiation, but one entirely disconnected from the productive process. As yet we also know very little about spirit mediums, whose economic role is slight in comparison to their engagement in the domain of witchcraft. Likewise the social category of *tafidilos* cannot be defined without reference to this domain. Although we have had occasion to allude to the Etoro cosmology of life-force transmission and the role that this plays in Etoro conceptualization of economic interrelations connected with the division of labor, the central role of this cosmology in the cultural formulation of social differences pertaining to age, gender, and the category of the witch remains unexplored. Clearly there is a powerful locus of the production of social inequality that is not economically grounded and is not elucidated by taking the means and relations of production as a point of departure in the analysis.[28] The following chapter thus addresses this cosmological domain.

CHAPTER 3

Moral Hierarchy: The Cultural Construction of Social Inequality

Social inequality can be analytically distinguished from social differentiation per se and may be minimally defined as social differentiation accompanied by differential moral evaluation (cf. Berreman 1981:4). Inequalities pertaining to morally evaluated social categories (that constitute a scheme of social differentiation) are characteristically amplified by corresponding differences in the distribution of prestige (and stigma), privilege (and debility), and culturally pertinent advantage (and disadvantage). This definition presupposes that social differentiation is logically prior to inequality and constitutes an analytically separable foundation upon which an edifice of social advantage may—or may not—be constructed and, to varying degrees, elaborated. Thus, all Etoro are members of one of twenty-three named patrilineal descent groups that are perfectly equivalent from a systemwide perspective in terms of prestige, privilege, and moral quality. Although an individual's evaluation of his (or her) own lineage differs from his (or her) evaluation of other lineages, each lineage is equivalent in possessing members who assign comparable values to the own group/other group distinction. It is the same difference in each case. Social classification in terms of lineage membership thus constitutes a cultural scheme of social differentiation that lacks the differential values that betoken inequality. Indeed, this prominent feature of the cultural landscape is positively egalitarian, and one of the advantages of the distinction between social differentiation and inequality is that it promotes the identification of egalitarian features and their inclusion within the analysis of a cultural system as a whole.

This minimal definition also offers the heuristic advantage of posing several straightforward questions. What are the elements of moral worthiness (or denigration), of prestige (or stigma), and of social privilege (or debility) that are culturally assigned to differentiated social categories? What beliefs, concepts, and cosmological principles engender the disposition of cultural value that is inscribed in differential moral evaluation and prestige? What social, ritual, and material advantages (or disadvantages) accrue to these culturally evaluated categories? The sequence of these questions implicitly leaves open the possibility that culturally delineated and morally evaluated differences may or may not be accompanied by privileges (especially those that take the form of material advantages), and this also is heuristically useful. The fact that the prestige derived from food distribution is unaccompanied by privileged consumption in the Etoro case provides an illustrative instance of the utility of this distinction. That prestige and privilege may not uniformly covary and that different social categories may be advantaged in different respects also have important theoretical implications for our understanding of the potentially unconsolidated character of inequality in comparatively egalitarian social systems. The proposed line of inquiry makes the degree of alignment and consolidation of diverse constituents an open question.

Although the minimal definition of inequality presented above provides heuristically and analytically useful distinctions, it fails to directly specify one of the most prominent features of the phenomenon, namely systematicity. The cultural schemes of differentiation (and social classification) present in any particular ethnographic case are invariably articulated within a more encompassing system: the cultural meanings that delineate and inform local conceptions of prestige, stigma, moral worthiness, denigration, and prerogative are not only the integrated components of a coherent system as well but also provide the grounds for social differentiation itself (Kelly 1976). Inequality as a cultural system, analyzed from the native (hegemonic) point of view, tends toward approximation of the proverbial seamless whole. That systematicity and internal coherence are unusually well developed in cultural formulations that not only constitute but also legitimate inequality is not surprising. These cultural formulations are nothing if not persuasive, since they are built up on a fragile foundation of value judgments (evaluations) that must have the character of unquestionable self-evident truths if the system is to persist and stand the test of time. Moreover, the doctrine recruits its own propagators.

With inequality as with witchcraft, the ideological system as a whole deftly provides answers to the questions posed by its internal logic, is regularly confirmed by individual experience in certain respects, and is often based on mystical elements that transcend experience (and are not subject to disconfirmation) in other respects (Evans-Pritchard [1937] 1976:201–2). Evans-Pritchard's classic study of Azande witchcraft provides a useful model for the analysis of inequality in that it explicates the systematicity and coherence of an ideology that makes it compellingly persuasive to social actors (in a variety of structural positions) and at the same time maintains an analytic distance appropriate to the consideration of legitimation. A degree of skepticism is clearly warranted. Moreover, witchcraft beliefs constitute a system of differential moral evaluation par excellence, while accusations entail the assignment of stigma, the negative reciprocal of prestige. When witchcraft (and/or other forms of supernatural attack carried out by human agents) is a component of the cultural system, as it is among the Etoro and other Strickland-Bosavi tribes, it is invariably integral to social inequality. (This articulation is particularly well elucidated in E. Goody 1970.) Consideration of witchcraft beliefs and the more encompassing system of which they form a part thus goes a long way toward answering one of the basic questions posed earlier, namely: what beliefs, concepts, and cosmological principles engender the disposition of cultural value that is inscribed in differential moral evaluation and prestige? The anthropological study of witchcraft thus not only provides a general model for explicating the systematicity and coherence of ideologies of inequality more generally but is also directly germane to the symbolic mechanisms of cultural valuation in the ethnographic cases at hand.

The principal objective of the first part of this chapter is to analyze inequality as a compelling culturally formulated system by elaborating the themes introduced in the preceding discussion. I will begin by examining the physical and spiritual constitution of the person and the extended, ritually mediated processes by which a person attains physical and spiritual completion. This will entail consideration of the larger cosmological system through which social differentiation—based on differences in physical and spiritual constitution—is simultaneously given both cultural definition and moral evaluation.[1] These constitutional differences culturally delineate and valorize gender categories as well as distinctions based on life-cycle position (i.e., age), role in the sexual transmission of life force (encompassing marital status), and the presence or absence of an inherent characterological predisposition to harm others (i.e., witchcraft). The latter part of the chapter addresses gendered perspectives, informed by the actor's point of view, and analyzes the features that render the cosmologically grounded ideology hegemonic.

The critical importance of witchcraft beliefs and accusations will emerge throughout this chapter, since these impinge on virtually every aspect of social differentiation and inequality. However, several key points should be noted at the outset. The Etoro espouse a unitary concept of witchcraft that is entirely undifferentiated with respect to age and sex. The *mugwabe* is the singular and exclusive human agent capable of carrying out supernatural attacks that cause sickness and death. Anyone—male or female, newborn, adult, or aged—may possess the mutation of the soul (*tohorora*) that provides both the supernatural means and predisposition to harm others. Moreover, both spirit mediums and *tafidilos* may possess a *tohorora,* and neither is immune from witchcraft accusation. In these respects, the Etoro *mugwabe* is strongly egalitarian *in concept.*

The ideology of witchcraft posits a radical difference between two classes of human beings. Those who possess a *tohorora* are inherently prone to malicious self-aggrandizement through consumption of the life force of other persons. This characterological predisposition to selfishness and to inversion of the values that are central to generosity is held to be expressed in social life as well as supernatural attack. (Such expressions are a source of suspicions that may be translated into accusations.) In contrast, a normal person—who lacks this mutation of the soul—is perceived to be governed by relational (rather than individualistic) motivation and is characterologically predisposed to be helpful, generous, and supportive toward others. Thus, when I asked third parties why Sawa helped Wabulu to fell trees in the latter's garden, the answer was "because Wabulu is his mother's brother." The impulse to generosity in assisting others is believed to be an inherent component of human nature that is given direction by relational motivation. Only a failure to manifest such impulses requires a deeper explanation, namely a defective spiritual constitution. A witch is "different inside."

The concepts of relational motivation, normative predisposition, and the selfish and individualistic spiritually deformed witch that lacks both are all important components of the culturally standardized schemes of interpretation the Etoro employ to interpret the motives and psychological states of other actors. The sense of these concepts can perhaps be most readily conveyed to the reader by adducing their counterparts in certain areas of American culture. If a foreign ethnographer asked an American, "Why did you go to your mother's funeral," the American might well respond, "Because she is my mother!" and add perhaps, "It would be unthinkable to do otherwise." Such statements reflect the view that the relationship itself prompts an individual to act and that there is a strong compulsion to act in accordance with normative cultural expectations. If the informant added, "What kind of [defective] person do you think I am?" this would parallel the Etoro view that only a witch, who is "different inside" would do anything else. Moreover, the Etoro believe that a discrepancy between the ostensible public meaning of social action and the actor's emotional state betokens the spiritual deformity of a witch. For example, only a witch would be capable of enacting outward manifestations of grief on the occasion of a community member's death while inwardly concealing quite different feelings. A witch feigns grief and conceals anger, while a normal person gives these full expression in culturally standardized displays. Like the Kaluli *gisaro,* the Etoro *kosa* celebrates the public expression of continuing grief and sorrow over the loss of a deceased relative (see Schieffelin 1976; Feld 1982). Moreover, all Etoro social payments are intended to empathetically alleviate emotional distress.

These social payments include witchcraft and death compensation (to mourning next of kin), bridewealth (for the father who weeps on the occasion of his daughter's marriage), and ceremonial payments to those reduced to tears by the *kosa* performer's songs. (These payments constitute the circulation of wealth discussed in chap. 6.) Thus, witchcraft beliefs are central to a cultural theory of motivation that also informs social payments, all of which address the recipient's publicly manifested emotional state. The witch whose emotional states are concealed pursues individualistic, antisocial expression of illegitimate desires. However, the main point here is that the concept of a singular, undifferentiated evil agent is consistent with an equally undifferentiated cultural constitution of human nature.

The difference between a witch and a normal person is thus a difference in the very core of being. Yet this difference that segregates two classes of persons crosscuts and overrides all other principles of social differentiation. The most fundamental differences between human beings are, in all cases, attributable to their spiritual constitution. While individual spiritual constitutions vary in terms of the quantity of life force (*hame*) present at various stages of the life cycle, and male and female spirit doubles (*ausulubo*) possess the physical characteristics of their respective genders, these differences , are minor compared to the difference between those who possess a *tohorora* and those who do not. The stark difference may perhaps best be conveyed by saying that the Etoro wholly reject the Judeo-Christian concept that there is good and evil in everyone. An individual who lacks a *tohorora* is totally incapable of evil, and one who possesses it can, at best, only repress an inherently evil predisposition to harm others. The execution of those who fail to do so is not infrequently supported by their closest kin. Indeed, the latter sometimes take it upon themselves to carry out this culturally necessary act. This is justified by the cultural fact that a witch is a nonrelational person whose being is a rejection of kinship itself.

Although the singular *mugwabe* is a conceptually egalitarian construct, the larger cosmological system of which it forms a part creates metaphoric associations between witchcraft and social categories differentiated by age and gender, creating an implicit system of inequality that is juxtaposed with the explicitly egalitarian concept of a singular evil agent. This construction of associational interconnections between witchcraft and social differentiation will be thoroughly examined in the following pages. However, it is important to note that these symbolically formulated inequalities, based on metaphoric association, are constructed against the background of an egalitarian concept of witchcraft that formulates a radical distinction between witch and nonwitch that overrides age and gender differences.

Which of these divergent cultural visions is realized in practice, through actual witchcraft accusations, and thus given dramatic validation in these prominent events of individual life experience? In other words, are accusations patterned with respect to social differentiation, or are they age and gender neutral? And who controls the complex and involved process through which accusations are formulated? These critical questions will be addressed in the next chapter.

METAPHYSICAL FOUNDATIONS: FUNDAMENTAL CAUSES AND PROCESSES OF BEING

Etoro thought and cosmology are ordered by a central and fundamental concept: that life and death are complementary and reciprocal aspects of a larger process whereby a spiritual "life force" is transmitted from one human being to another. The life-cycle processes of conception, growth, maturation, senescence, and death are attributed to the acquisition, augmentation, depletion, and loss of life force in these transactions. In each instance, a recipient's growth entails a donor's depletion, such that one individual flourishes while another declines. Acts of sexual intercourse and acts of witchcraft are the two modes of interaction through which this transmission of life force is effected and "life" and "death" are the reciprocal terms of the transaction in each case. Relations between sexual partners are comparable to those between witch and victim by virtue of this analogic conjunction, and the idioms in which each sphere of interaction is (respectively) grounded therefore stand in a metaphoric relation to each other. This juxtaposition of witchcraft and sexual relations enriches the cultural meaning of each, in that sexual intercourse is informed by the idiom of witchcraft and vice versa. Moreover, this provides a mechanism for projecting the characteristics of actors in one domain upon their analogic counterparts in the other, so that socially differentiated categories and the relations between them are culturally delineated. Differential moral evaluations are thus affixed to age and gender categories that are also shaped with respect to the system of life-force transmission.

The Etoro believe every human being to be possessed of two discrete spiritual aspects: the *ausulubo,* an immaterial spirit double, and the *hame,* a life-force or animating principle. Both are imparted to a child (at and before birth, respectively) by a *Sigisato* spirit associated with his or her lineage, and both are (jointly) immortal, persisting beyond the grave in the form of a *Kesame* or spirit of the dead. These spiritual aspects are significant to the present analysis insofar as they are affected by witchcraft and sexual relations and will be examined from that perspective.

The *ausulubo* replicates the possessor's physical body in form but lacks corporeal substance. The same term is employed with reference to an individual's shadow, reflected image, and the echo of his or her voice, and these may be conceived as visible (or aural) manifestations of the *ausulubo.* All three are characterized by qualities of duplication and separability which are essential attributes of this spiritual aspect.

The *ausulubo* is normally contained within the owner's physical body but possesses a capacity for conscious independent activity under certain circumstances. The average individual's spirit double may wander only in dreams; its movements tend to be restricted to the immediate vicinity, and it does not normally venture into the spirit realms frequented by mediums. In contrast, the *ausulubo* of a medium may go on extended excursions to a variety of spirit worlds while he sleeps, during a séance, or even while his body carries out a normal routine of daily activities (although in a somewhat distracted manner). A witch (*mugwabe*) is likewise capable of leading a double life, and acts of witchcraft are generally perpetrated by an *ausulubo* operating apart from the body of its owner. The spirit double is invisible to an individual in his or her normal state, and the witch can therefore carry out nefarious activities without being seen or identified by the victim or others present at the time.[2] However, objects employed by the *ausulubo* of a witch (e.g., an ax) can be seen, and the sound of twigs snapping as the invisible spirit double approaches through the forest is also audible. In addition, the witch's *ausulubo* (which differs from that of normal individuals) gives off a pale glow, or *moropa,* that betrays the presence of a witch without revealing the witch's identity.

The commission of an act of witchcraft entails the infliction of some injury upon the spirit double of the victim. In the typical case, some foreign object is thrust or impelled into the *ausulubo* of an individual, causing illness. The witch may then proceed to dismember the *ausulubo* of the weakened victim, limb by limb, on successive nights. These parts are either consumed by the witch or hidden for later consumption. Removal of the heart and liver (of the *ausulubo*) causes the final demise (and this may occur without the intervening dismemberment).

When the spirit double is injured, illness afflicts the corresponding part of the corporeal body; this provision applies to witch as well as victim. Thus a witch whose *ausulubo* has been burned with a torch or firebrand in the course of an act of witchcraft can later be identified by the analogous burns on his or her physical body. An arrow shot into the heart of the witch's spirit double will likewise kill the witch. Events such as these occur only in myths and legends but are nevertheless indicative of the perceived relationship between the soundness of the *ausulubo* and that of its corporeal counterpart. It is also important to note that acts of witchcraft are perpetrated upon the *ausulubo* of the victim by that of the witch, such that the entire transaction takes place on what may be called the *ausulubo* "plane of existence."

The *hame* is the second major component of an individual's spiritual constitution. The *hame* embodies the animating principle and vital energy of human existence. It is formless, like the wind, and is manifested in breath (designated by the same term) in much the same way that the *ausulubo* is manifested in a person's shadow or reflection. Strength, vigor, and vitality emanate from the *hame*. However, it lacks consciousness as well as form and is incapable of operating as an independent entity apart from the corporeal body and *ausulubo,* which are mutually animated by it. This dual role is evident in accounts of witchcraft. When a witch dismembers the limbs of his victim's spirit double, the corporeal limbs are weakened by the loss of both their essence and their vitality (corresponding to elements of the *ausulubo* and *hame,* respectively). Although the *hame* is thereby diminished, it nevertheless continues to provide a reduced quantity of vital energy to the corporeal flesh that remains—for it is immanent in both the physical and spirit body.

A *Sigisato* spirit animates a fetus by implanting a nascent *hame* within it (and, at birth, imparts an *ausulubo* to the child). At the moment of death, the residual *hame* is exhaled with the last breath and is subsequently merged with the *ausulubo* to form a single entity which persists as a *Kesame,* or spirit of the dead. The *ausulubo*—which has previously been maimed, dismembered, and consumed by a witch—is somehow reconstituted and united with the analogously traumatized *hame* through a mysterious supernatural process described by a special verb (*keketosa*), elucidated by the paraphrase "many things become one." However, the manner in which this is effected is said to be beyond human understanding. The evil spiritual aspect that distinguishes a witch from normal individuals is segregated in this process and ascends to the heavens to become a star, glowing with the pale light of the *moropa.* Thus purified of evil, the witch's *hame-ausulubo* descends to the river and associated underworld which is the domain of the *Kesames.* The countless stars visible on a clear night betoken the pervasiveness of witchcraft from time immemorial to the present. However, like the lower jaws of slain wild pigs that glimmer in the firelight from the interior walls of the men's section within the longhouse, many of these stars are also trophies. They mark the innumerable occasions when the death of a witchcraft victim has been reciprocated by the execution of a witch and evil thereby exiled to the far reaches of the heavens. It is also noteworthy that the radical distinction between witch and nonwitch is dissolved in the afterlife, where equality reigns. The execution of a witch thus redeems his or her soul and reestablishes equality.

The degree of strength and vitality which emanates from the *hame* varies during the course of an individual's lifetime. The *hame* may be conceived, in this respect, as a reservoir of life force which can be augmented or diminished. This occurs in two ways—through witchcraft and through sexual intercourse. When a witch removes a limb from an individual's *ausulubo* and consumes it, the witch incorporates a portion of the victim's life force and thereby augments the strength of his or her own *hame,* while depleting that of the victim. The witch grows uncommonly large and acquires added physical strength and vigor through this appropriation. The children he or she begets "as a witch" are also physically large and are themselves identifiable as *kagomano* or witch-children by this quality. (This is one of two ways witchcraft is acquired, as is discussed further below).[3]

The corresponding diminution of the victim's life force is evident from the weakened condition accompanying illness and is also registered by labored breathing, short-windedness, coughing, chest pains, and the like. Breath is a physical manifestation of the *hame* that reflects its spiritual condition, and respiratory difficulties are taken to be indicative of depletion of the *hame*'s reservoir of life force. Labored breathing and short-windedness are onomatopoeically referred to as *hame hah hah,* and this condition is generally recognized as the outward sign of a concomitant spiritual disability. It is, moreover, a consequence of sexual intercourse as well as a result of bewitchment.

Every adult male possesses a limited quantity of life force that resides in his body as a whole but is especially concentrated in his semen. A portion of this is expended in each act of sexual intercourse, so that a man's reservoir of life force is gradually depleted over the course of his lifetime. The vital energy that emanates from the *hame* is correspondingly diminished, rendering the subject enervated and enfeebled. An elderly man—who was once strong and vigorous—is thus short-winded and suffers *hame hah hah* when climbing hills or engaging in other strenuous activity. The Etoro also point out that this selfsame shortness of breath is experienced upon completion of the sexual act itself; the temporary condition becomes general as semen is progressively lost.

The life force that a man expends in sexual intercourse is transferred, through the process of conception, to the children he begets (or, in the absence of conception, is lost). This serves to augment the nascent *hame* implanted in each child by the *Sigisato* spirits and contributes to their early growth. Among the Gebusi, a male child is fed his father's semen at the age of about eighteen to twenty-four months in order to ensure his early growth (Cantrell n.d.: chap. 5). This takes place at a private family ritual carried out by the parents in a secluded area of the forest. The father obtains the semen by masturbation and mixes this with ant eggs and a salty substance obtained from the bottom of streams. A female child receives a mixture of the stream-bottom substance and certain insect larvae that does not contain human bodily fluids, since it is believed that she requires only her mother's breast milk for growth (ibid.). The ritual takes place at the time a child is beginning to walk and is intended to promote a successful transition from infancy to childhood, just as the subsequent insemination of boys effects a transition to manhood (ibid.). Although I did not inquire into the transition from infancy to childhood in the Etoro case, the Gebusi practices reported by Cantrell are entirely consistent with the basic premises of Etoro thought regarding life-cycle transitions, and it is not unlikely that the Etoro employ a similar means of transferring life force to male infants.

Prepubescent boys are inseminated by their elders so as to provide them with semen (which they do not yet have the capacity to produce in their bodies), and also to supply the life force or vital energy they require in order to grow, mature, and develop manly strength. The *hame* of the youth is augmented by this acquisition (while that of his inseminator is depleted). The growth-inducing properties attributed to semen are clearly expressed in these beliefs.

It is evident here that witchcraft and sexual relations are mutually embedded in a single conceptual system insofar as they constitute the two modes of interaction through which life force is transmitted from one human being to another. The interconnection is particularly well illustrated by the aforementioned belief that the child of a witch will be physically large. This follows from the fact that the parent has appropriated the life force of others through acts of witchcraft and is thus capable of transmitting an enriched infusion of this to his or her offspring in the process of conception. The witch-child grows large in the womb as a consequence of this. To explain why a large infant is the child of a witch clearly requires an understanding of the ideology of sexual relations as well as the ideology of witchcraft, for the two interpenetrate. However, the relation goes deeper than this insofar as acts of intercourse are in some respects equivalent to acts of witchcraft such that each stands in a metaphoric relation to the other. The semantic implications of this will be elucidated after beliefs concerning sexual relations and the physical and spiritual constitution of the person are more fully explored.

The association of sexual intercourse with impairment of the *hame* is expressed in a number of restrictions that govern male-female relations and circumscribe the postcopulatory interaction of a man with his fellows. A man who has had intercourse with a woman must refrain from offering food or tobacco smoke (from his bamboo pipe) to another man throughout the remainder of the day. Should an individual consume such food or inhale smoke from the pipe of a copulator he will experience *hame hah hah* and, in the latter case, a coughing spell as well.

Women are at all times enjoined from stepping over men's personal possessions, pipes and tobacco, and especially food and the items employed in its cooking and consumption. Thus a woman must never step over split firewood or sit on the woodpiles at the front of the longhouse. If a man consumes a morsel of food cooked over such firewood (or smokes tobacco which has likewise been subjected to this negative influence) he will suffer *hame hah hah* and a general lack of strength while pursuing his daily activities. Should a woman step over his ax, it will rapidly become dull when used.

A man must avoid seeing or coming into contact with a newborn child for seventeen days. If he fails to do so he will suffer especially severe *hame hah hah* and may die as a consequence. In addition, the father of the child should not offer food or smoke from his pipe to any male for seven days. The growth of a youth would be forestalled by consumption of such food or smoke; an adult man would experience *hame hah hah*. In all these above instances, the enjoined behavior is *tobi,* i.e., stringently forbidden or taboo.

The Etoro do not espouse any beliefs concerning female pollution or the contamination of objects through the addition of impure substances or essences which would account for the negative effects attributed to violation of these regulations, and I would suggest that the regulations are best interpreted as extensions of the basic concept of depletion discussed above. When a woman steps over an object it "passes between her thighs" and this is a symbolic equivalent of intercourse.[4] An object such as an ax thus loses its cutting edge, or essential property, in the same way that a man loses the essential property of his masculinity in copulation, i.e., his semen. The pipe smoke of a man who has recently copulated, and food, firewood, and other items subjected to symbolic intercourse all have the same effect on a man who internalizes them as intercourse itself; they are capable of transmitting the depletion signified by *hame hah hah*. These objects are, in some sense, negatively charged with respect to masculinity, and they have the capacity to drain or negate the life force of a male who consumes them or comes into close contact with them. A newborn child has the most powerful antithetical effect as a consequence of having lain within the womb for such an extended period. It is an especially potent carrier of depletion, which can be transmitted to males by the mere sight of it.

The Etoro note that males attain physical maturity later than females and are particularly concerned to promote and insure male growth and development through insemination. As was mentioned earlier, the division of labor amplifies this perception of differential rates of maturation since a girl can carry out an adult woman's tasks at an earlier age than a boy can perform adult men's work. Like an elderly man, a boy is short-winded and experiences labored breathing when he fells trees. The underlying cause of this retarded male development that so concerns the Etoro is the birth of men from women; later maturation is a consequence of the adverse effects upon males of close contact with the depleting powers of femininity in the womb— adverse effects that the early-maturing female offspring never experience. The fact that food received from the father of a newborn child forestalls the growth of boys (but not girls) is consistent with this notion. The cumulative depletion of the father is manifested in the event of birth itself since a child possesses life force as a direct consequence of his father's loss of it. The state of a male parent after birth is comparable in nature to that of a man after copulation (although intensified in degree).

Although women have a weakening influence upon men (directly or indirectly) under certain specific conditions of actual and symbolic intercourse, they are not a source of pollution and therefore do not pose a continuous threat to male well-being. The absence of any beliefs concerning menstrual pollution was noted in chapter 1. Thus, while intercourse is depleting, the female persona is not contaminating and men therefore need not avoid contact with women per se. It follows that the general tenor of male-female relations is neither constrained nor hedged with anxiety. Men and women intermingle and interact freely in gardening, in sago working, and in the communal portion of the longhouse at meals and during the course of daily activities. Women are careful to observe the prohibition on stepping over certain items (noted above), but this does not restrict or constrain their movements since food is normally kept out of the way in net bags hung from walls or house posts and men's possessions are similarly placed or are stored in the men's quarters. If a woman does accidentally step across food, men would refrain from eating it but would not be vexed by the incident (except perhaps in the case of highly valued game or pork). Should a man's pipe be affected, he would set it aside for several days (and borrow another) but would be unlikely to discard it unless particularly concerned about his health at the time. Although the owner of the pipe might express mild irritation, other men tend to regard the situation as a humorous one. Jests made in such contexts stem from the prevalent view that a man who is truly strong (*keloi*) can withstand the weakening influence of women without noticeable ill effects. This view is also relevant to the male attitude toward marriage and polygyny. A man who has two wives and nevertheless remains vigorous in spite of the resultant double dose of depletion (through intercourse) takes pride in his demonstrated strength and vitality and is admired for this by others.

Male attitudes toward heterosexual intercourse itself are charged with ambivalence and ambiguity. Men privately nurture variable degrees of anxiety concerning the debilitating effects of copulation. However, they can quite effectively alleviate such anxiety by engaging in the very act that they fear— and not experiencing the negative consequences believed to follow from it. A man thereby develops self-confidence in his residual vitality that is at once comforting and highly precarious. His attitude will shift rapidly to one of deep concern if he feels enervated or develops a cough or other respiratory sign of depletion. The virginal bachelors likewise view heterosexual intercourse with trepidation while at the same time wanting to demonstrate their vitality by engaging in it without ill effects.

The opposite poles of male ambivalence are well illustrated by the events of an adulterous liaison (as related to me by an informant). A young man in his early 20s was secretly trysting with his father's brother's wife. The woman was childless and apparently initiated the affair in an attempt to rectify this and thus forestall her husband's plan to take a second wife. When the sexual relation was discovered, the young man temporarily fled to another community to avoid his uncle's wrath, returning after several days when compensation (of one mother-of-pearl shell) had been arranged by his father. At the time this was publicly paid, the cuckolded husband made a speech in which he vividly described the depleting effects of intercourse to his brother's son and other young men present at the time. Toward the conclusion of this harangue, he dramatically lifted his wife's skirt and exposed her genitals for all to behold. Several young men (including my informant) retched forthwith, and the adulterous young man himself became queasy and visibly discomfited. Older men turned their faces aside with expressions of disgust, while the chastened wife wept from shame and repudiation. The point of this tale is that the spontaneous vomiting clearly indicated a very real and deepseated anxiety, while the adulterous liaison documents the capacity to disregard it, at least temporarily. (The parties to the transgression continued to coreside without further incident.)

Men are protected from undue depletion (and anxiety pertaining to same) by prolonged periods of enjoined abstinence. Heterosexual relations are narrowly circumscribed with respect to permitted times (and places) of occurrence. In all, copulation is prohibited (*tobi*) for an estimated 205 to 260 days a year. The specific proscriptions and the imputed results of their violation are:

1. Throughout the period from the commencement of a new garden until the trees have been felled (at the end of the fourth month). If this taboo is violated, the crops will not mature properly, yields will be poor, and pigs will ravage the garden.
2. From the time a sago palm is cut until processing is completed (lest yields be poor).
3. Whenever deadfalls or snares have been set for wild pigs, marsupials, or cassowaries (else little or nothing will be caught).
4. During any period when sago grubs are maturing in an unprocessed palm cut for this purpose. If this restriction is not observed, the growth of any youth who consumes the grubs will be stunted.
5. When a new longhouse is under construction (else the project will be beset with difficulties).

6. While a trading party from the longhouse is carrying out an expedition and for four days prior to its departure (or little of what is sought will be obtained).

These prohibitions are linked to virtually all major aspects of the productive economy—gardening, sago processing, and trapping are nearly tantamount to subsistence. Exchange and construction are not omitted. Moreover, these activities tend to be segregated in time so that there is relatively little overlap between one proscribed period and another. This imposes very substantial limitations on the frequency of heterosexual relations, and there is, moreover, indirect evidence of general adherence to the prohibitions. Eight of ten births which occurred within the tribe during a fifteen-month period took place over a short span of three and one-half months. Although the economic preoccupations of all ten parents at the times of conception are not precisely known, the distribution of births is predictable in terms of the seasonal cycle of subsistence activity. (The birthrate itself is also rather low.)

Heterosexual intercourse should take place only in the forest, never within a garden, in a garden dwelling, in the longhouse, or the general vicinity of the longhouse. (Even in the forest one cannot be entirely at ease, for the Etoro maintain that death adders are offended by the noxious odor of intercourse and are particularly likely to strike a couple thus engaged.) Violation of the prohibition on copulation in and around the longhouse is a serious offense which may provoke public rebuke and expulsion from the community. The following incident is a case in point.

A widow and an older bachelor (aged 28) had been carrying on an affair, sporadically, for over a year. This was a subject of gossip and private disapproval but no public action. It is not uncommon for younger widows to solicit the attentions of marriageable bachelors; indeed, this is frequently a prelude to remarriage. However, when the couple was discovered violating the locational prohibitions by copulating at the spring near the longhouse, and subsequently within the men's section (!) of the longhouse, the community was outraged. The close kin of the transgressors were impelled by public opinion to put a stop to this immoral behavior. When the community foregathered for the usual afternoon meal (several days after the latest and most flagrant offense), the widow and bachelor were set upon and pummeled by three close kinsmen[5] to the accompaniment of a chorus of recriminations and verbal abuse from the remaining members of the longhouse. Both ran off to take refuge (separately) with kinsmen at other locations. The bachelor returned about three days later and resumed his residence at the community after a public statement of contrition; the widow remained elsewhere. As was mentioned earlier (chap. 2, n. 24), this widow had alienated the married women of the community.

The prohibition of heterosexual relations in the environs of the long-house is also enforced upon the canine population. On several different occasions, the members of the longhouse community where I resided spent the better part of the day throwing stones at a bitch in heat and her coterie of male admirers in order to drive them into the forest.[6] The women were especially vigilant in this effort to ensure proper behavior on the part of the dogs. In the first incident described above, the women were also most adamant in demanding that strong measures be taken to reestablish moral behavior. These data are significant in that they connote female (and especially married women's) acceptance of and adherence to the norms described herein.

These locational restrictions emphasize the fact that heterosexuality has no place within the community (or in inhabited areas) and is properly conducted only in the wild. It is fundamentally antisocial behavior in the strict sense of the term, inasmuch as "society" is conceived as communal social life that transcends a narrow conjugal solidarity (of which heterosexuality is a part). The postpartum and postcopulatory taboos noted above accentuate this theme inasmuch as they proscribe the customary sharing of food and tobacco which is one of the central moral values of community life. Heterosexuality segregates a man and places him outside of society, and especially, outside the social community of males.

The imputed effects that are said to follow from the violation of the (activity-related) temporal prohibitions are also instructive. Copulation diminishes the yields of gardens, sago palms, traps, and trading expeditions just as it diminishes a man's life force and depletes his *hame*. The central belief that is (once again) expressed here is also explicitly enunciated with respect to the undesirable effects said to result from copulation in gardens. The Etoro maintain that heterosexual intercourse in a garden will cause the crops to wither and die. The general consequences of heterosexuality are death and depletion. However, this is only one component of a complementary opposition between heterosexuality and homosexuality, for the Etoro also maintain that homosexual relations in a garden will cause the crops to grow, flourish, and yield bountifully.

One of the conceptual cornerstones of Etoro cosmology is the view that accretion at one point in the system entails depletion elsewhere. Life cannot be created ex nihilo, and the birth (and growth) of one generation is inextricably linked to the senescence and death of its predecessor. Life and death are complementary and reciprocal aspects of a larger process. In the context of this general concept, the gradual depletion of life force that men experience in heterosexual intercourse is, at the same time, a precondition for the perpetuation of life through birth. The transference of life force is similarly a precondition for the growth and maturation of boys into men.

Boys differ most importantly from men in that they completely lack the most critical and essential attribute of manhood, i.e., semen. The Etoro believe, moreover, that semen does not occur naturally in boys and must be "planted" in them. If one does not plant sweet potato vines, then surely no sweet potatoes will come up in the garden and, similarly, semen must be planted in boys if they are to possess it as men. Moreover, all aspects of manliness are seen as consequences of this acquisition. A youth is continually inseminated from about age 10 until he reaches his early 20s. This period is also marked by rapid growth in stature, increased physical strength and endurance, the sprouting of facial and body hair, and the development of masculine skills and characteristics such as hunting ability and courageousness in war. These empirically observable changes are uniformly regarded as the direct results of insemination. (This is accomplished orally. The boy manipulates the man to the point of ejaculation and consumes the semen. The above effects are only realized through ingestion and therefore are not applicable to heterosexual relations; women do not acquire strength or other male attributes in this way.)

The recipient of semen in homosexual intercourse experiences beneficial effects which are the exact converse of the negative effects suffered as a consequence of loss of semen in heterosexual intercourse. While the *hame* of a man is weakened and depleted by copulation, the *hame* of a youth is correspondingly strengthened by insemination. Prior to this boys are short-winded and tire readily; afterward they possess strength and endurance. These effects are thought to be cumulatively manifested over the maturation period, but are also apparent on specific occasions. For example, young men say they are able to fell trees in a new garden for hours on end without tiring after they have consumed semen.

These and other beliefs (discussed in preceding pages) are all relatable to a general equation whereby receiving semen : life, growth, and vitality :: losing semen : weakness, senescence, and death. However, receiving semen is also culturally associated with homosexuality and the loss of it with heterosexuality, such that the former is to life as the latter is to death. This opposition is expressed in myth and also in the previously cited beliefs that heterosexual relations in a garden will cause the crops to wither and die while homosexual relations will cause them to flourish and yield bountifully. Although informants report that loss of semen in both types of intercourse is equally enervating, the negative effects adhere only to heterosexual relations in formal ideology. Thus there are no rules that prohibit a man from offering food or smoke to others after homosexual relations, and there are no prohibitions that circumscribe such relations with respect to time and place. Men and boys may properly engage in sexual relations in the men's section of the longhouse (and in gardens) on any day of the year. Indeed, this is essential if the youths are to grow and attain manhood.[7]

The personal characteristics that a youth develops as he matures are believed to correspond to those of his inseminator. If a man is strong (*keloi*), vigorous in his advanced years, a proficient hunter and trapper, and/or a courageous warrior, then his protégé will possess identical qualities and abilities upon attaining manhood. Witchcraft is also transmitted in this manner. The semen of a witch is said to contain minute frogs and worms which are the seed of witchcraft. Acquisition of these predisposes the *ausulubo* of a witch to develop a mutant evil spiritual aspect—the *tohorora*. This distinguishes a witch from normal individuals and endows one with the extraordinary capabilities that enable him or her to perform acts of witchcraft. (Transmission of witchcraft between women is discussed below.) The *tohorora* is located or concentrated in the heart and liver and gives off a cold, phosphorescent light (the *moropa*) that is sometimes visible when a witch is active at night. This can also be seen when the heart of an executed witch is cut out in order to confirm his or her guilt. The organ (which is displayed on a stake) is said to glow like an ember with the light of the *moropa*. The frogs and worms that are the seed of witchcraft are visibly present in the auricles and ventricles, respectively. However, the acquisition of these frogs and worms is not sufficient, in itself, to engender the development of the *tohorora;* the seed of witchcraft must also be nurtured by the malice and ill will in a person's heart. The individual thus bears the ultimate responsibility for the mutation of his soul that makes him or her a witch.[8] In this sense, the capability to perform acts of witchcraft is achieved rather than ascribed.

LIFE-CYCLE TRANSITIONS AND CATEGORIES

Youths are initiated into manhood in their teens or early 20s when they are physically mature (although not fully bearded). At intervals of about five years, all young men who have reached this stage of development go into seclusion at a lodge which is especially constructed for this purpose in an isolated area near the margin of the primary forest on the upper slopes of Mt. Sisa. They must not see or be seen by women. Details of activities at the seclusion lodge and at the subsequent emergence ceremony are sketchy as neither took place during my fieldwork. However, accounts of previous occasions indicate that most men of the tribe participate to some extent. The previous group of initiates (now fully mature but not yet married) reside at the lodge with the neophytes, while others visit it periodically for several days at a time. These bachelor mentors and youths spend much of their time hunting and trapping. Bachelor gardens and male sago processing provide the remainder of their sustenance, so that male self-sufficiency is complete. Throughout this period, all the men residing at the lodge go about nude and, it is said, with their penises erect. This is part of a general celebration of masculinity (and especially that recently attained by the initiates).

A generalized insemination of the youths by older men also takes place at the seclusion lodge, with the resident bachelor mentors playing a leading role. This is important in that it makes it impossible to retrospectively determine who may have transmitted the seed of witchcraft to whom. If a young man is named as a witch, his principal inseminator is not necessarily implicated. Similarly, any attempt to identify a particular individual as the source of witchcraft in a specific instance implicates many young men, some of whom are likely to be close kinsmen of the individual drawing the inference. Confirmed witches are excluded from the seclusion lodge proceedings, and the men who participate are presumed to be free of witchcraft. Young men who are subsequently accused are thought to have secretly consorted with witches outside this context. The generalized transmission of semen from mature initiated men to the neophytes also emphasizes the spiritual community of all males, who share a common pool of life force that has been passed from one generation of men to the next down through the ages (cf. Whitehead 1986).

Little information is available concerning the beliefs and activities of women pertaining to female maturation, as it is difficult, in the context of Etoro culture, for a male anthropologist to develop an informant relationship (or have frequent private conversations) with a female. Moreover, each sex is supposed to be totally ignorant of the private, gender-exclusive activities of the other, and men generally respond to inquiries by saying that "only the women know what the women do." However, women are thought to engage in some form of homosexual activities and to transmit the seed of witchcraft in this way.[9] Men appear to be genuinely ignorant concerning the processes of female maturation and do not know whether this occurs naturally or as a consequence of transmission of substance. Some informants thought it plausible that girls obtained menstrual blood from mature women in the same way that boys obtained semen from men; others pointed out that females possess blood from birth (even though they do not menstruate until later), while boys completely lack semen. The *Sigisato* spirits determine the sex of a child by implanting a male or female *ausulubo* within it. Gender differences are therefore grounded in the spiritual constitution of the person. The female *hame* is considered to be weak and underdeveloped, so that women are always short-winded in comparison with men in their prime. However, women, boys, and elderly men all share this same condition so that age and gender differences are only quantitative (rather than qualitative) with respect to the life-force component of spiritual constitution.

The fact that Etoro male ideology does not encompass a coherent account of female growth and maturation is part of a larger pattern in which the female contribution to the reproduction of complete persons is represented as an initial contribution that is transcended. A child is the product of a union of semen and menstrual blood whose flesh, blood, and skin are derived from the maternal contribution while the bone and hair (that endure after death) are derived from the paternal contribution. The *ausulubo* and nascent *hame* are implanted by a male *Sigisato* of the father's lineage, and the *hame* is augmented by the father's semen. The meat provided by men (primarily) promotes the growth of healthy flesh, blood, and skin. Inasmuch as game is ultimately derived from the male *Sigisato* spirits, the initial contribution of maternal blood to a child's physical constitution is progressively masculinized with time.[10] Similarly, it is the provision of an abundant supply of game to the mother of a newborn infant that promotes an adequate supply of mother's milk, so that women are vehicles for the transmission of male nurturance (at least in male ideology). Mother's milk is regarded as an especially nutritious growth-inducing food, like game, but has no spiritual or mystical properties. The starch staples are thought to alleviate hunger rather than to make significant contribution to growth. These are the foods that embody a predominant female labor contribution and the ones most closely associated with women. In sum, a mother contributes to her child's initial physical but not spiritual constitution, and this initial contribution of flesh, blood, and skin is progressively augmented and overshadowed by a predominantly male provision of growth-inducing game. Moreover, the unique contribution of female parturition is a stillborn infant lacking the *hame* or animating component of the soul derived from a male *Sigisato* spirit and augmented by the father's semen. Women are only credited with the capability of giving birth to lifeless flesh and thus, paradoxically, give birth to death rather than life. This conception is developed in the myth accounting for the origin of witchcraft, and hence of death and lost immortality (discussed further along).

If the growth and augmentation of blood is derived from game supplied by men and made available by male *Sigisato* spirits, then even the female reproductive substance is not wholly a female contribution. However, the main thrust of male ideology is to regard menstrual blood in itself (i.e., unmixed with semen) as inconsequential so that its origin is not of concern. Menstrual blood entirely lacks supernatural properties, in contrast to semen. Its lack of any intrinsic potency is consistent with the absence of menstrual taboos. Hence a woman need not repair to a menstrual hut during her period and will continue to work alongside her husband in sago processing and gardening (unless she experiences discomfort) and to sleep adjacent to him in the longhouse. The fact that menstrual blood is accorded no special status is also reflected in linguistic usage. The generic term for "blood" is *heare,* which includes tree sap and analogous substances that flow through living things. Menstrual blood is simply termed *udia heare* or "woman's blood." It is distinguished from circulatory blood only by location.

Since the maternal contribution to a teenage boy's physical and spiritual constitution is minimal, no reconfiguration is effected in male initiation. This has already been accomplished by this time. There are thus no female substances that must be purged or extracted from boys in the course of initiation in order for them to attain manhood. (This contrasts with the removal of female substance through penis and/or nose bleeding and induced vomiting as is practiced in the eastern Highlands; see Langness 1974; Feil 1987:172.) Likewise, the death of a female-engendered boy and his rebirth as a man with an altered and masculinized spiritual constitution is unnecessary since an *ausulubo* derived from male *Sigisato* spirits is already in place, as is the nascent *hame* strengthened by the father's and inseminator's transmission of life force. (This contrasts with the Walbiri and other Australian tribes; see Meggitt 1962:294; Hiatt 1971; Feil op. cit.) In the Etoro case, bringing the development of the male physical and spiritual constitution to completion only requires reversal of the depleting effects of the womb on male growth by augmenting the male contribution. However, this process has occurred progressively over time through insemination initiated at about the age of 10 (or as early as the age of 2 if the Etoro follow the Gebusi practice described earlier). Male nurturance and men's contribution to the growth of healthy flesh and blood through the provision of game also commence at weaning. Moreover, a boy will have moved to the men's section of the longhouse by the age of 5 so that psychological separation from his mother and incorporation into a more male-oriented world is long since completed (cf. Sørum 1982).

In these respects, there is no marked transition that takes place at initiation. Schieffelin (1982:195) argues that the somewhat similar Kaluli institution lacks the central feature of a rite de passage: the objective of "separating a youth or youngster (both socially and psychologically) from his former childhood status and admitting him (sometimes in graded steps) into a new social status or stage in the life cycle." He concludes that the Kaluli *Bau a* ceremonial hunting lodge ought not to be categorized as an initiation. While Schieffelin's argument has stimulated my perception of distinctive "missing features" in Etoro initiation, the latter does entail dramatic changes in life-cycle position (addressed below) that I believe justify inclusion within this general category.

One of the main thrusts of Etoro initiation is thus to dramatize and put the finishing touches on a male creation of manhood that has been in process for an extended period. The extensive hunting and trapping emphasize the male contribution to the growth of healthy flesh, blood, and skin. However, the significant transition this embodies is that the bachelors and the neophytes procure this game themselves. It is consequently their dependence on their fathers and other senior men that is reconfigured. Similarly, concerted insemination completes the augmentation of the *hame,* or breath soul. Here too, junior-senior relations are rearranged in that a youth's insemination by the man nominated by his father is supplanted by generalized insemination of the neophytes by the recently matured bachelors. I would thus propose, contra Schieffelin, that there is a very significant transition. The final completion of manhood is an act of self-creation by the unmarried young men, as a group, which reorders their prior dependence on their fathers and other senior men and asserts a measure of independence.[11] Self-sufficiency is dramatized by the lodge members' hunting, trapping, sago processing, gardening, and the construction of the lodge itself. The bachelors and neophytes provide for all their own needs. Having done so, they return to society prepared to assume the role of providers toward others. In other words, the initiation lodge is a liminal period of self-sufficiency that divides dependent childhood from the responsibilities of adulthood. Most importantly, the neophytes complete a period of maturation during which they are recipients of life force (*hame*). Henceforth they will give rather than receive semen. Thus they will assume the responsibility of maturing the next group of initiates (about five years hence) and subsequently reproducing the next generation of children (after marriage), with these responsibilities progressively draining their life force. This generous and self-sacrificing role in the transmission of life force is the essence of the manhood they have achieved. The transition effected is thus the most dramatic of all transitions, namely the transition from life (receiving semen) to death (losing semen). While the initiates are not reborn, they now attain the much more elevated state of being causal agents in the perpetuation of life itself.

At the end of the seclusion period, a *kosa* ceremony is held to celebrate the attainment of manhood, the emergence of the lodge members (the bachelor mentors and initiates), and their reintegration into society. The latter entails renewed participation in the ritual life of the community, communal gardening, and longhouse residence. About five months later there is a second ceremony at which the initiates' heads are anointed with tree oil by an older man, typically a mother's brother (or member of the latter's lineage). This rite marks the final transition to manhood and entitles a man to enter into marriage. Although lack of participation in a seclusion lodge may not have precluded marriage in traditional (pre-1964) times, it is the case that the one permanent bachelor among the Etoro failed to fulfill his role as inseminator during his term as a bachelor mentor in a late-1950s initiation. It is said that he proved to be impotent in the generalized insemination expected of the bachelor mentors, eventually withdrew from the lodge, and will never marry (although he may not be impotent in heterosexual contexts). Serving as an inseminator is therefore viewed as a prerequisite to marriage, although this responsibility can be fulfilled outside the context of the seclusion lodge.[12]

This is consistent with the fact that insemination is one component of an exchange in which a man transmits life force to a youth and then receives the latter's true or classificatory sister in marriage. Male life force is thus exchanged for female reproductive capacity, so that neither party to the transaction is indebted to the other. The Kamula provide an instructive contrast here. The primary inseminator of a Kamula boy should ideally be his future wife's father or wife's elder brother (Wood 1982:80). Thus both life force and a wife are supplied by the same party, and the recipient is doubly indebted. This underwrites a young man's obligation to perform labor for his wife's father or elder brother (ibid.:106). In contrast, Etoro affinal relations between wife's brother and sister's husband are characterized by equivalence, and a man assiduously avoids assisting his prospective wife's father in felling trees (as noted in chap. 2).

The completion of the initiate's maturation and his attainment of manhood are publicly enunciated by the final ritual act: his head is anointed with oil by his mother's brother. This is a central symbolic moment in which virtually all significant components of the social and cosmological system are referenced. The role of the mother's brother as ritual agent is explicable in relation to the reproductive exchanges of the previous generation. An initiate's mother's brother will ideally have been inseminated by the initiate's father (since the ideal designated inseminator of any ego is his sister's husband). The mother's brother thus represents (1) the maternal contribution to reproduction (i.e., the initial component of flesh, blood, and skin derived from the initiate's mother, which the mother's brother shares with her and the initiate); (2) the paternal contribution (i.e., the life force and semen derived from the initiate's father, which the mother's brother also shares with both men); (3) the exchange of male life force for female reproductive capacity (in his role as wife-giver and semen-receiver); and (4) the union of male and female substance that engendered the young man he anoints.

At the most general level, the tree oil represents substance transmitted from one generation to the next. More specifically, the tree oil connotes female substance in that it is *heare,* an analogue of blood. However, the tree oil is obtained by men in trade from the neighboring Onabasulu (where it is collected by men as well). It thus represents a generically female substance that is produced, obtained, controlled, and applied by men. Likewise, the mother's brother is a male representative of the maternal contribution. Both the mother's brother who serves as ritual agent and the tree oil he applies thus represent a feminine, maternal contribution to the initiate's physical constitution that is, at a deeper level, heavily masculinized and entirely under male control. The tree oil is thus an analogue of the maternal physical components of flesh, blood, and skin that have been progressively supplanted by the game animals that men procure as a result of the beneficence of the male *Sigisato* spirits. Moreover, it is the initiate's hair—derived from the father's semen—that is anointed so that the paternal and male-controlled maternal substances are brought into conjunction. Although the initiate's mother's brother himself obtains the tree oil through trade, the initiate gives him the shell valuables that are exchanged for the oil. The completion of maturation as an act of self-creation is thus also referenced in that the initiates, through their intensive hunting and trapping at the seclusion lodge, supply themselves with the final infusion of growth-producing game and are likewise the ultimate source of the tree oil. More precisely, the shell valuables an initiate gives to his mother's brother constitute a prestation. The tree oil with which the initiate is anointed thus completes a compulsory exchange that is equivalent, leaving neither party indebted to the other as a consequence of the transaction. This parity replicates the egalitarian consequences of the initial exchange of male life force for female reproductive capacity that this exchange of shell valuables (semen) for tree oil (*heare*) symbolically recreates. Moreover, manhood is not bestowed but achieved (cf. Schieffelin 1982:195–96). In all, three contributions to the completed physical and spiritual constitution of the initiate are referenced: the paternal contribution, the initiate's contribution, and the maternal contribution that has been progressively overshadowed by masculine accretions, first by senior men's provision of game and finally by the initiate's self-provisioning. The male *Sigisato* spirits that yield up the game are also indirectly referenced.

The initiate now embodies, in his completed physical and spiritual constitution, all the relational components that constitute the social system. He is linked to his father and agnates by a shared bone and hair substance, and to his mother's brother by shared blood, flesh, and skin. However, insofar as this has been largely overshadowed by game supplied by men and male *Sigisato* spirits, this substance connection is now overlaid and largely replaced by an exchange relationship. The initiate has given his mother's brother shell valuables and received tree oil. In the next generation, the mother's brother's son will inseminate the initiate's son and marry the latter's sister, in accordance with father's sister's son's daughter's marriage (see fig. 3.1). Shell valuables will then flow in the opposite direction, as bridewealth.

The key point here is the reconfiguration of a matrilateral substance relationship as an exchange relationship, through the exchange of shell valuables (representing bridewealth and semen) for tree oil (representing female reproductive capacity under male control). The feminine maternal component

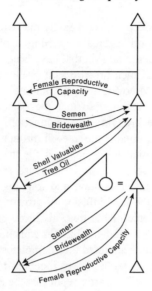

Fig. 3.1. The exchange of person-constituting substances

has thus been transformed into that which is exchanged and links social groups by exchange.[13] The initiate represents his lineage, whose bone and hair substance he embodies; the mother's brother represents his lineage as wife-givers, the providers of female reproductive capacity that will be reciprocated by the initiate (or his lineage). Thus the ritual agent may be a man of mother's brother's lineage other than mother's nuclear sibling, i.e., a man related to the initiate by exchange but not by substance. The men of mother's lineage do not all share the same maternal flesh and blood by which ego is linked to his mother's brother, since these men are the sons of many different mothers, respectively. The relational insufficiency of maternal substance creates structural (or connective) limitations in the construction of a broader social order that are transcended by the reconfiguration of maternal substance relations as exchange relations.

The initiate is also linked to matrilateral siblings, men whose mothers were of his mother's lineage. With these men he shares the same "mother's brothers," men of a lineage that is a common source of mothers and a common destination of daughters. These matrilateral sibling relations, which are of central structural importance in establishing brother relations between lineages (Kelly 1977:93–119), are referenced at the emergence ceremony by the anointing of individuals so related by their common "mother's brother." The relational insufficiency of maternal substance is equally apparent with respect to these critical linkages. As with their brothers, the women of mother's lineage (mother's "sisters") do not share a common maternal flesh and blood, since they are the daughters of different women. Thus matrilateral "siblings," whose mothers were of the same lineage, are not linked by any shared substance. They are linked only by shared exchange relations with a patrilineage that is a common source of mothers and a common destination of daughters.

Unlike paternal substance, maternal substance has no capacity to underwrite broader social relationships and is potentially divisive. Maternal flesh and blood link ego only to individuals, not groups, establishing a connection to true mother's brother, mother's sister, and the latter's children. As Meyer Fortes (1959) emphasized, these ties of complementary filiation provide a scheme of individuation that differentiates and divides the men of a patriline (unless agnates marry true sisters). In contrast, exchange relations link whole lineages as affines (wife-givers and wife-takers), and coexchange links whole lineages as "brothers" (matrilateral "siblings"). The reconfiguration of relations based on shared maternal substance as exchange relations is thus the basis upon which the social world—as the Etoro construct it—rests.

The progressive masculinization of maternal substance is not only the first step in the reconfiguration noted above but also contributes to the construction of a broader social order in another way as well. While the initial components of maternal flesh, blood, and skin link an individual to only a few close kin, the game that ensures the growth of these components is predominantly derived from adult men as a group. Game is shared out to all members of the community by those who procure it. The game ego consumes as a child is thus provided by the adult men (and occasionally women) of all the communities in which he (or she) has resided. A connection to maternal kin that is very limited in scope is thus progressively overshadowed by accretions that link ego to all men senior to him, and to the collectivity of male *Sigisato* spirits that offer up the game. The potential divisiveness of substance-based ties of matrifiliation is thus transcended in this way as well. (See n. 10 in relation to these points.)

Broader social ties are also forged by participation in the seclusion lodge. Etoro patrilineages are quite small, containing an average of only about six males over the age of 16 (Kelly 1977:90), and an individual draws on relations with men of other lineages in nearly every aspect of social life (e.g., accumulation of bridewealth, witchcraft compensation, homicide compensation, support in conflict). The longhouse community also includes men of about four different lineages. Homosexual relations are regulated by kinship in the same way as marriage, and the generalized insemination of the initiates by the bachelors (and some older men whose duty as inseminators is not yet fulfilled) thus facilitates social bonding between individuals of different lineages who are not closely related in other ways. In the most recent initiation, bachelors and neophytes from seven of the eleven longhouse communities and a few young men from the neighboring Onabasulu tribe participated. Thus, Tylor's functionalist dictum ("marry out or be killed out") admits of an alternative additional strategy he did not envision, confirming the view that there are functional alternatives for everything. Moreover, while generalized heterosexual relations might be expected to disrupt marriage and be counterproductive in this respect, generalized homosexual relations establish male bonding both directly (rather than through the medium of affinity) and effectively. As noted earlier, the generalized insemination that takes place also emphasizes the spiritual community of all males, who ultimately share a common pool of life force. The construction of broader social ties is thus a theme that pervades all aspects of male initiation.

It is important to recollect that the mother's brother, as ritual agent of the anointing, personally embodies the paternal semen and maternal flesh that constituted the initiate at birth (or he is an analogue of the true mother's brother who does). The maternal and paternal substances are symbolically brought into conjunction when the tree oil is applied to the initiate's hair. The complementarity of male and female contributions to reproduction is thus symbolically articulated. The initial maternal contribution is never purged or excised, despite the fact that it is progressively overshadowed by male contributions to the growth of flesh and blood, and the *relations* between men that are based upon it are reconfigured in terms of exchange. While these alterations are instrumental to the construction of a broader social order, the complementarity of male and female in a socially constituted reproductive union brought about by marital exchange is also instrumental, and this too is celebrated (cf. Sørum 1982:60). Given the absence of a purging of maternal substance, or a spiritual death and rebirth that alter the initiate's spiritual constitution, the mother-son relation remains unchanged. The mother therefore need not acknowledge any revised relationship at the emergence ceremonies. Moreover, no hostility, antagonism, or opposition toward women is expressed, since female substance poses no threat to male well-being. The most dramatic and violent expressions of antagonism occur in those ethnographic cases where inimical maternal substance and feminine influences are purged (see, for example, Read 1965:133–37). Etoro initiation contrasts markedly in that the solidarity of men is based upon the male substance they share, rather than a common antithesis to female substance. The homosexual bonding of the Etoro seclusion lodge is not constructed by invoking shared opposition to women. Thus the maternal contribution to reproduction is positively acknowledged (rather than being expunged and rejected), with this acknowledgment taking place in the context of a ritual dramatization of male-female complementarity. This is consistent with the Etoro conception of the social order as encompassing both same-sex solidarity and gender complementarity, a conception that is instantiated in the design of the longhouse as discussed in chapter 1.

It is also important to note that the emergence ceremony does not celebrate the creation of a permanent male association from which women are excluded. On the contrary, it celebrates the termination of a liminal (and relatively brief) self-sufficient, male-exclusive period that prepares the initiates for marriage, social responsibility, and full participation in a communal life that is grounded in the complementarity and joint effort of men and women. This contrasts with the initiation ceremonies of the Baktaman and other groups of the Mountain Ok region, in which men are inducted into a male cult that may include a succession of progressively higher grades attained throughout their life cycle (with each grade distinguished by its secret knowledge) (Barth 1975; Poole 1976, 1981a, 1982; Jorgensen 1983). Such features lend permanence to what is, in the Etoro case, a transitory liminal phase. The "higher stage" that Etoro initiates attain with manhood is full participation in the communal longhouse, not in a male cult house. Moreover, they complete a preparation for marriage, heterosexual relations, and conjugal domesticity. Thus the initiation complex serves to order the relationship between same-sex solidarity and gender complementarity that are the twin bases of day-to-day social life within the longhouse community (as well as establishing the foundation for lineage-level sibling and exchange relations by the transformation of maternal substance).

While the anointing ceremony celebrates a male appropriation of the reproductive processes by which the initiate's physical and spiritual constitution is brought to the completion of manhood, this appropriation is carried out in the service of creating a broader social world that encompasses male-female complementarity as well as sibling and exchange relations between lineages. The emergence ceremonies contain no symbolic statements of gender opposition, overt male domination, or female subjugation to male authority. Moreover, the doctrine of life-force transmission does not serve as an ideological basis for the exploitation of women but rather underwrites the assumption of economic responsibility by newly matured men. The retarded growth, short-windedness, and lack of vitality that prevent a boy from doing a man's work have been remedied, and the graduates of the seclusion lodge will now shoulder more than half the burden of subsistence food production in accordance with the division of labor detailed in chapter 2. As noted earlier, generosity and self-sacrifice are the essence of the manhood they have achieved, and these are enacted in the sharing of the foods men procure.

The emergence ceremony marks a change in the life-cycle position (or culturally defined age) of prior groups of initiates, since life stages are defined by a man's role in the transmission of life force. The relevant male groups are listed below as a guide to discussion of this point.

Male Group	Approximate Chronological Age	Role in Life-Force Transmission	Sexual Orientation	Typical Marital Status	Number of Non-tabooed Native Taxa	Linguistic Category
Pre-initiates	10–16	recipient	homosexual	—	63	*manasa*
Eligible for initiation	17–21	recipient	homosexual	betrothed	78	*manisa*
Bachelors	22–26	donor	homosexual	betrothed	78	*tono* ("man")
Recently married men	27–31	double donor	bisexual	married	80	*tono*
Older married men	32–45	donor	hetero-sexual	married	81	*tono*
Men with grown children	46–60	donor	hetero-sexual	married	81	*tono*
Elderly men	61 +	completed	usually celibate	often widowed	83	*tole*

The newly anointed initiates (aged 17 to 21) have now become bachelors eligible to marry. However, they are betrothed (through arrangements made some years earlier) to girls at least ten years younger who have not yet reached marriageable age (see Kelly 1977:169–71 regarding the age differential between spouses). The bachelor mentors (aged about 22 to 26), who resided at the seclusion lodge with the initiates and organized the gardening, hunting, trapping, and ritual aspects of the seclusion, are now in a position to celebrate their previously arranged marriages. As their marriages take place (over the next few years), they will enter the bisexual stage of the male life cycle, as double donors of life force, because the maturation of their respective wife's brothers (who are also roughly ten years junior) is typically not yet complete. Most of the boys who are protégés of these men will constitute the next group of initiates about five years hence.

The recently married men (aged about 27 to 31), who served as principal inseminators of the newly emerged initiates from about age 10 until they entered the seclusion lodge for five months at age 17 to 21, will now become exclusively heterosexual insofar as their protégé's maturation is finally complete. They enter the class of older married men (aged 32 to 45) who typically have young children. (A woman usually bears her first child at age 20, when her husband will be 30 or more.) The marriage of a man's protégé (or designated inseminee) will typically take place when he is a member of this age group (32 to 45). Likewise, the fathers of the newly emerged initiates will mark the attainment of manhood by their sons. This normally occurs sometime after age 46. It is also at about this age that established mediums withdraw from active participation in séances in favor of the successors they have trained. A prospective medium must acquire a spirit wife and complete his initial training before he marries his human wife so that active mediums are all between the ages of 20 and 46. It may be that the maturation of the medium's spirit son marks the close of his career (the impetus to this early retirement being one of the questions I failed to think of while in the field). At this same life stage, beginning roughly at age 46, a man becomes eligible to be accorded the status of *tafidilo*. The social positions of spirit medium and *tafidilo* are thus in complementary distribution.

In his early to middle 60s, a man will typically cease hunting, and it is said that "he no longer goes to the forest." His participation in other subsistence activities likewise tapers off. If the man had been a *tafidilo*, he will typically retire from performance of the functions associated with this status, although he may still be referred to by this term. Men who are widowed after the age of 50 rarely remarry (Kelly 1977:303), this undoubtedly being largely attributable to increased concern with life-force depletion among older men. Similarly, a man is expected to embrace celibacy after his wife is past childbearing age. The latter tends to occur when a man is about 60, so elderly men (*tole*) are typically celibate. The statement that a man "no longer goes to the forest" has this meaning as well, because heterosexual relations are confined to the forest.[14]

The male life cycle is partitioned into a series of life stages that are defined by a man's position within the encompassing system of life-force transmission. Although a man participates actively in initiation only twice, as a neophyte (*manisa*) and as a *tono fetei* (literally "man grown") or bachelor, his life stage is also altered by the progression of his protégé and his son through these stages. The transitions between these stages are, in most cases, marked by a change in sexual orientation, in the behavioral sense of this term (including the change from homosexual recipient of life force to homosexual donor). In most instances, there are other markers as well. A pre-initiate's head is shaved, except for a topknot. A *manisa* (eligible for initiation) ceases to shave his head and wears a leg band, just below the knee, indicating he is betrothed. A bachelor adopts a hairstyle in which the hair above the forehead is shaved to accommodate a headband. Older men do not shave any portion of their hair. Traditionally, they wore greased dreadlocks (before this was discouraged by patrol officers on ostensibly hygienic grounds). Elderly men's hair turns gray. Hair, which is the only visible manifestation of male substance, thus provides a primary marker of successive life stages. The most significant transition, from recipient to donor of life force, is marked by the taking of a new name. Food taboos also change at certain of these transition points. When a boy becomes a *manisa* (eligible for initiation), the number of native taxa he may consume increases from 63 to 78 (see Kelly 1977:42–44), with the added items including a number of forest mammals that are the object of the initiation lodge members' hunting and trapping. When a man marries, the available taxa increase to 80, when his first child is born to 81 (adding eels), and when he becomes a *tole* all 83 may be eaten. Linguistic categories do not distinguish among active initiated men (aged 22 to 60), all of whom are simply "men" (*tono*). Nevertheless, these "men" are further subdivided by the other markers noted here. Only the dividing line between mediums and *tafidilos,* at about age 46, is unaccompanied by these distinctions of attire and food taboos, since not all men on either side of this line occupy these respective social positions. There are also no insignia that identify the occupants of these positions.

Each man thus passes through a series of life stages defined directly or indirectly by his present or past role in the transmission of life force. It is important to note that men at the same life stage do not constitute a coactive group subsequent to their participation in the seclusion lodge, nor do they form part of a named category. Moreover, individuals may reach a particular life stage at a wider range of chronological ages than I have indicated in the preceding discussion. Although the Etoro take cognizance of the relative age of individuals based on birth order, and employ the term "age-mate" (*esama*) for those born in the same season of a given year, cohorts based on chronological age are, of course, a completely foreign concept. However, the phrase "men aged 32 to 45" is more convenient in exposition than "eel-eating heterosexuals with greased dreadlocks" and makes the relative order of such unnamed categories immediately apparent. Nevertheless, it should be kept in mind that this shorthand refers to a cultural reality of life stages defined by a collection of attributes.

The transition from young girl (*townisa*) to woman (*udia*) is also publicly noted and accompanied by a change of attire (but not of name). This occurs at the time a girl's breasts become rounded (at about age 16 to 17), when she is classed as an *udia totora* or "full-breasted woman" and dons a woman's skirt. These changes are marked by a modest evening celebration at the longhouse (that I had an opportunity to observe). The young woman sings quite beautiful songs of her own composition for about an hour, while the longhouse community shares a meal of leaf-wrapped packets of sago and greens prepared by her parents. The young woman will have largely processed the sago herself, with her parents' assistance. The ceremony thus celebrates the attainment of productive and reproductive maturity. Each girl's coming of age is celebrated individually. She is the center of attention and the object of readily apparent parental pride. At the *kosa* ceremony, the male performers also sing songs of their own composition and are the center of attention, as soloists. This transition to womanhood is the only occasion when women do likewise. While the *kosa* performer's songs are sad and induce tearful remembrance of deceased relatives, the young woman's songs might be described as joyful, celebrating life. Other than the singing and the communal sharing of sago (which is normally consumed by the work group that produced it), the event is like a typical evening at the longhouse. People chat in the communal section for a time and then retire to their sleeping platforms in the rear of the house. Although a girl would typically have already been married before this event, she would not commence sexual relations with her husband until her maturation is publicly acknowledged. She may also move to another longhouse with her husband and reside apart from her parents after this celebration, although this residential separation often does not occur until many years later, and may not occur until the woman's parents' demise.

Unless a woman is widowed, her public persona remains unchanged throughout the remainder of her life. When her breasts become flat she will be classified as an *udia seli* (rather than *udia totora*), but this transition to a postreproductive stage is not socially marked (except in that a woman who is beyond childbearing age and also a widow may consume previously tabooed bush hen eggs). The transitions in the female's life cycle that are accompanied by changes in food taboos are those from child to *townisa* (aged 12 to 17) and from the latter to mature woman (*udia*). The number of native taxa that may be consumed increases from 63 (child) to 67 (*townisa*) to 70 (*udia*). In addition, widows and the male and female children of deceased men are the most heavily restricted categories with respect to food taboos (see Kelly 1977:42–45). These restrictions are not specifically age related and will thus be discussed further along. The main point to be noted here is that females beyond childhood are divided into only three life-cycle stages: young girl (*townisa*), woman of reproductive age (*udia totora*), and postreproductive woman (*udia seli*). As in the case of men, the distinctions are informed by a concern with reproduction. However, the distinctions among women are more tied to physical characteristics, and the more complex male system of life-force transmission entails a greater number of distinctions.

Logically, one might suppose that a woman would be perceived to be depleted by menstruation, childbearing, and breast-feeding, with menopause providing a definitive index of this underlying process. The Kamula cosmology encompasses this type of gender parallelism, which focuses on female loss of menstrual blood (through both menstruation and childbearing) as well as male loss of semen (Wood 1982:79–90). The Kamula cosmology of female depletion underwrites a son's indebtedness to his mother, which is manifested in his obligation to supply her with game in exchange for the sago she provides (as discussed in chap. 1). Etoro cosmology differs in that it entirely lacks any male acknowledgment of female depletion. Leading questions along these lines are uniformly answered by the respondent replying that men have no knowledge of such things.

Etoro men therefore are not indebted to their mothers in the same way that they are to their fathers. This is quite clearly expressed in food taboos. When a man dies, his surviving children are prohibited from consuming 59 of a total of 83 native taxa of game animals (as opposed to the 30 prohibited to the children of living men). These taboos remain in force until a girl reaches the age of 12 and a boy reaches the age of 17. They are informed by the concept that a deceased man's children embody his life force, now utterly depleted. (The surviving widow, as the agent of his depletion, is prohibited from consuming 65 taxa until she remarries, generally within two to three years.)[15] In contrast, a woman's death does not lead to the imposition of any additional food taboos on her surviving children or spouse. The restrictions consequent upon male death are consistent with the cosmology of life-force transmission in that a greater proportion of a man's life force is transmitted to sons than daughters, and the former remain under the taboos for a longer period as a result.[16] Moreover, it is evident that a concept of female depletion is not expressed in food taboos. Therefore, if Etoro women privately espouse a concept of depletion that remains unknown to me (for reasons explained earlier), it does not enter into relations among men, or between men and women (e.g., son and mother), but could only be relevant to relations among women themselves. If a daughter assumes no taboos on her mother's death, then parallel public manifestations of such an ideology in relations among women are also absent. Moreover, the ritual at which a girl's attainment of womanhood is publicly acknowledged contains no ritual reference to life-force or substance transmission, suggesting that maturation occurs naturally without extraordinary infusions of supplements or additives. This would be in keeping with the concept that females, born of females, are not depleted by the period of time they spend in the womb. Nevertheless, the process by which a girl becomes capable of reproduction and subsequently, at menopause, ceases to have this capacity remains unexplained. The doctrine that game provides for the growth of blood and flesh does not account for the transitions. Men consider the source of female maturation to be women's legitimate secret, just as the insemination complex is men's legitimate secret. However, the men's secret has many ramifications in public social life and in the interaction of men and women, while the women's secret does not. Parallelism in the Etoro case does not extend beyond men's belief that women have knowledge of the processes underlying the transitions in a woman's life cycle that men should not seek to learn, just as women should not inquire into the male mysteries.[17]

Women are present at the emergence ceremony and perform the opening dances in the clearing in front of the longhouse (as they do before all *kosa*). As with reproduction, their main ceremonial contribution is to the initial part of the proceedings.[18] What a mother witnesses on this occasion is her brother anointing her son's hair with *heare,* a symbol of female substance. The manhood he has attained is a prelude to marriage, conjugal domesticity, male-female complementarity, and assumption of the full responsibilities of an adult man in the division of labor. Do women's understandings of this ritual selectively focus on these aspects of it that are most pertinent to their lives and social relations, omitting or downplaying the aspects that pertain to the male mysteries they are not supposed to know? It is difficult to imagine that it could be otherwise if one credits the concept of the actor's point of view. Surely a woman sees her brother predominantly in terms of her own relationship to him, rather than as the person inseminated by her husband. Although a woman knows that she was betrothed and given in marriage by her lineage as part of an exchange of women and is probably aware that her son privately gave a shell valuable to her brother before going into seclusion, it is difficult to imagine that she does not focus on the tree oil as a symbol of her contribution to her now-mature son's physical constitution while downplaying or failing to notice that it symbolizes the exchange in which her reproductive capacity was transferred. It thus seems safe to conclude that the anointing ritual does not mean exactly the same thing to men and women. Consideration of the socially differentiated actor's point of view (rather than the undifferentiated native point of view) strongly suggests this.

This raises the question of the extent to which women fully appreciate that the anointing ceremony celebrates a male appropriation of the reproductive process by which the initiate's physical and spiritual constitution is brought to completion. The more prominent aspects of the ceremony encourage women to focus on the maternal contribution. Moreover, women are not supposed to know the male secret so they clearly are not called upon to acknowledge, ratify, or endorse the specific content and full ramifications of it. An important myth (discussed further along in the chapter) suggests that women see the male appropriation of reproduction as a flattering but failed attempt at emulation. The important question of divergent male and female interpretations of common cultural property (myth and ritual) and the issue of false consciousness will be further considered in conjunction with discussion of this myth.

The general point being made here concerning actor-centered interpretations can be extended to other groups of actors in distinctive structural positions as well. It seems plausible that same-sex solidarity, casting off dependence, and the assertion of a self-created status as a man among men are the aspects of initiation that are most prominent to the initiates themselves. Likewise, elder men can take pride in the flowering of manhood they have engendered by the transfer of life force. The emergence ceremony thus has a something-for-everyone quality that makes it meaningful—in somewhat different ways—to a socially differentiated constituency. While the ritual's capacity to play to different audiences entails a measure of heterodoxy at one level, it also entrenches a hegemonic ideology at another. This stems from the partial nature of the selective interpretations made available. The hegemonic ideology, expressed in the overall logic of the ritual, encompasses and recontextualizes these partial interpretations.

MORALLY EVALUATED SOCIAL DIFFERENTIATION

Thus far I have been concerned to describe and analyze the cultural construction of social differentiation. Consideration of Etoro doctrines concerning the physical and spiritual constitution of the person, and successive transformations of these constitutional components, elucidates the nature of culturally configured social differences. Although male and female are minimally different in spiritual constitution insofar as they possess sexually dimorphic *ausulubos,* the more profound differences between them arise from their different roles in reproduction and in the transmission of *hame* or life force to others. Men transmit life force while women do not. Moreover, the birth of males from females retards masculine development and thus necessitates counteractive measures. Age or life-cycle position is likewise delineated with respect to a sequence of roles in reproduction of the succeeding generation (for both males and females). The witch differs radically in spiritual constitution (in possessing a *tohorora*) and plays a subversive role in the intergenerational transmission of life force. A medium's *ausulubo* has a special capacity to enter the spirit world. Through the assistance of his spirit wife and spirit child, a medium can forestall and sometimes reverse the witch's damage to a victim's *ausulubo* and *hame*. The social positions of both the medium and *tafidilo* are also life-cycle-related, although they are not delineated by substance transmission or reproductive role. *Tafidilos* are men of an age-group whose contributions to reproduction and the maturation of the succeeding generation are very substantial and nearly complete (but not all men of this age-group are *tafidilos*). Moreover, *tafidilos* are men who have never been accused of witchcraft, i.e., the self-serving diversion of life force. Thus nearly all social differences are delineated by spiritual constitution (male, female, young, old, witch, nonwitch, medium) and by role in reproduction and in the transmission, extraction, or restoration of life force (the above listed with the age and gender categories further subdivided by the gradations that differentiate senior men, bachelors, married women of reproductive age, widows, etc.).

This cultural scheme of social differentiation is not ontologically value neutral; social differences are simultaneously delineated and valorized. A comprehensive and systematic system of inequality is constructed on a cosmological foundation. Senior men who are not witches are intrinsically and profoundly generous and self-sacrificing in the transmission of life force. Witches are profoundly selfish and self-aggrandizing. Mediums seek to cure, thwart, and counteract acts of witchcraft, to single out the perpetrators, and to mediate relations with powerful spirits on which people depend for growth-producing sustenance. Moral worthiness and denigration are inseparable aspects of these differentiated social categories that define the central actors in a struggle between good and evil that turns on the perpetuation of life. Women and young men are not actors in this drama and are accorded neither moral worthiness nor denigration.

The moral superiority associated with generosity accrues to senior men, while the prestige associated with public-spirited counteraction against witchcraft and maintenance of relations with the supernatural accrues to mediums. Stigma, which is the negative reciprocal of prestige, is assigned to the witch. Again, women and young men are accorded neither. Although the birth of males from females retards male maturation, this constitutes an inevitable feature of reproduction that is simply part of the nature of things. There is no explicit doctrine that assigns a negative value to women's role in reproduction as a result of this. It merely sets the stage for men's heroic efforts to compensate for an unavoidable setback. In this respect, Etoro cosmology does not stigmatize or negatively value women but rather fails to assign supernatural significance to their role in reproduction and the perpetuation of life. The female contribution lacks the supernatural qualities of the male contribution, and the women's role therefore has only mundane rather than cosmic significance. Essentially, women are upstaged but not disvalued by this aspect of the cosmology (but are stigmatized by the association of feminity and witchcraft discussed further along). Young men are the special beneficiaries of life-force transmission and are thus laden with the responsibility to undergo depletion, in turn, in order to reproduce the succeeding generation. In other words, young men are assigned responsibility rather than prestige or stigma.

These are the explicit inequalities generated by Etoro cosmology. However, there is a second set of implicit inequalities that is generated by the metaphoric relation between the two modes of interaction through which the transmission of life force is effected, namely witchcraft and sexual relations. While the radical difference between witch and nonwitch crosscuts all other principles of social differentiation in the first instance, this metaphoric conjunction brings these crosscutting schemes of inequality into alignment. This aspect of the systematicity and coherence of the Etoro cultural formulation of inequality remains to be elucidated.

In earlier discussion, I have attempted to establish and document the point that an array of Etoro beliefs concerning sexual relations may be interrelated through a general equation whereby receiving semen : life, growth, and vitality :: losing semen : weakness, senescence, and death. This formulation also constitutes the specific ideational content of a more general and fundamental conceptual orientation of Etoro cosmology, viz., the concept that the total system is closed and bounded such that accretion at one node necessarily entails a corresponding depletion at another (and vice versa). This general concept is also expressed in the domain of witchcraft belief, as is evident from material adduced earlier. A witch consumes portions of the *ausulubo* and *hame* of his victim and thus grows unusually large and vigorous while the victim is weakened and enfeebled by the resultant illness. The *hame* of the victim is depleted (as evidenced by respiratory distress), while that of the witch is augmented such that he or she begets children of exceptional size. After the victim's demise, the witch is thought to return to the burial platform by night to fatten himself or herself on the flesh of the corpse. An executed witch (and external enemies killed in warfare) are subject to cannibalism, although other members of the Etoro tribe are not. The flesh of the witch is consumed just as the witch consumes the flesh of his or her deceased victims. (However, no spiritual elements or personal attributes are transferred in cannibalism, and this view is understandable insofar as the soul of a witch is inherently evil and his or her characteristics totally undesirable.)[19]

There is a further correspondence between these two domains of belief that follows from the structurally analogous position of witchcraft and sexual relations as alternative modes through which life force is transmitted. This brings the two sets of beliefs into an immediate relation such that each is partially defined with reference to the other. This is evident when the equation noted above is reformulated at a more general level, viz., augmentation of the *hame* : life, growth, and vitality :: depletion of the *hame* : weakness, senescence, and death. Homosexual relations (from the standpoint of the youth), acts of witchcraft (from the perspective of the witch), and conception (vis-à-vis the child) are all interchangeable in terms of augmenting the *hame* and are equally productive of life, growth, and vitality for the youth, witch, and child respectively. Similarly, homosexual and heterosexual relations (for an adult man) and acts of witchcraft (from the perspective of the victim) are interchangeable with respect to depletion of the *hame* and the effects that follow from this. There is, moreover, a threefold identification of youth, witch, and woman as *agents* of depletion in addition to the identification of child, youth, and witch as *beneficiaries* thereof. The logical derivatives of these identities are the oppositional equations:

child : father :: witch : victim

protégé : inseminator :: witch : victim
(youth)

woman : man :: witch : victim
(wife) (husband)

All these invidious comparisons are applicable to Etoro thought and behavior in some degree, although each is elaborated in a somewhat different way and is thus modified in its final ramifications. This elaboration takes the form of internal differentiation by contrasts (and further similarities) among the four terms which are here identified (i.e., child, youth, woman, and witch).

A witch is the epitome of maliciousness and antisocial selfishness, in that a witch feeds on the souls and bodies of others out of spite and with full intent to cause harm; a witch sates his or her gluttony as well as hate, and grows large and vigorous at others' expense. A woman, on the other hand, does not augment her *hame* through heterosexual relations. The loss of life force a man suffers in this context contributes to the conception and early growth of his children. A woman is thus an agent of depletion but not a beneficiary, and, conversely, a child is beneficiary but not agent. Neither manifests the intentional maliciousness of the witch, and the diminution of a man's *hame* is here viewed as part of the essential tragedy of human existence—that senescence and death are preconditions for the perpetuation of life through birth.

However, excessive copulation and sexual relations that are not productive of offspring deplete a man to no end. A woman who encourages, entices, or insistently requires her husband to engage in needless copulation—from which he alone will suffer—thereby approaches the purely negative role of witch. She sates her sexual appetite selfishly, knowingly causing harm, and perhaps with malicious intent. (This connotation applies with double force to a woman who consorts with an immature youth, whose growth and development will be permanently arrested by loss of semen.) The identification of woman and witch thereby refers in only a restricted sense to an inherent quality of womanhood, while being fully applicable to the potential characteristics of aggressive and demanding femininity and unregulated feminine sexuality. The association thus contributes to a constraining delineation of the female role and is not merely a static negative characterization.

Witchcraft also has its primeval origin in the epitome of unregulated sexuality—the act of incest. Moreover, the myth that recounts the event emphasizes the responsibility of the female for releasing this agent of death upon mankind.

> At a longhouse community of the distant past there lived a brother and sister (of about age 8 and 10). One day they went to the forest together and copulated secretly there. The girl became pregnant and grew large with the child. "What have you been doing?" an elder man asked her. But she didn't answer; she turned her head aside and said nothing. In due course, she gave birth to a boy. Secretly, she suckled it at her breast. The elders did not know of this at first, but one day a man came upon her as she was nursing the child. As he drew near, she tried unsuccessfully to conceal the baby from him.
>
> They had become witches, these three, and the elders decided they must be killed. The men caught the brother and sister and struck them, and they cried out in pain as they died. Then, for the first time, the men heard the (now characteristic) whistle of the witch from the other side of the longhouse. "Tua, tua," shrilled the witch-child as he slipped away. "Now we have witches and men will die," an old man lamented. "Before today there were none, but these two became witches and henceforth we will die."

According to Etoro exegesis, the precocious siblings were transformed into witches by their incestuous conjunction itself, and the first witch-child (or *kagomano*) was the fruit of their union. Thus incest begat witchcraft and introduced sickness and death into the world. Before this time men were immortal.[20] The evil of unregulated sexuality (in its most extreme form) is thus ontologically prior to the evil of witchcraft and the origin of (premature) death.

It is important to note that the agent of death is "of woman born." The girl refuses to confess her evil act when queried by her elders and later conceals the child from them. Worst of all, she suckles the witch-child rather than submitting it to infanticide (as would be expected under the circumstances). By not only bringing death into the world but nurturing it at her breast, she thus transfers to women the ultimate responsibility for mankind's lost immortality. The paradoxical concept that women give birth to death, which is manifested in this myth, goes beyond the failure to assign supernatural significance to the female role in reproduction and the perpetuation of life (noted earlier) by engendering a stigmatizing association between femininity, witchcraft, and death. Moreover, the stringent food taboos applicable to widows (but not widowers) constitute a covarying debility legitimated by the connection between the female reproductive role and male death. Female reproduction that lacks the critical male contribution (i.e., *hame*) produces a stillborn child, while female reproduction incorporating this contribution produces a dead (or depleted) husband.

The full force of the latent association of femininity with witchcraft is inapplicable to a woman during the period she is actively bearing children, since her role as depletor is essential to reproduction of the next generation. However, this association casts a pall over all sexually active pre- and post-reproductive females and, especially, barren women. Young women generally commence sexual relations with their husbands when their breast development signals maturation at about age 16 (and following the puberty rite described earlier). However, young women do not bear their first child until they are 20. If a woman does not produce a child at this time or soon thereafter, the potential interpretation that this may be due to barrenness comes to the fore. The episode of conjugal conflict between Tuni and Wadome described in chapter 2 illustrates the emergence of such an interpretation. In light of the deeper cosmological significance of childlessness, one can readily appreciate the feelings of purposeless depletion and unfulfilled reciprocity in the conjugal division of labor that informed Tuni's action as well as the extreme sensitivity to an imputation of barrenness that sparked Wadome's reaction. A woman in this position is double-bound because efforts to increase the frequency of intercourse with her husband or to attempt to become pregnant by another man entail the aggressive and unregulated sexuality that invokes an association with witchcraft. Moreover, the woman's opportunity to become pregnant may be further decreased if her husband takes a second wife in order to have the children he desires and consequently reduces the frequency of intercourse with his putatively barren first wife. (Tuni was already beginning to seek support for this course of action among his agnates.) Childlessness thus tends to initiate a culturally programmed scenario in which a woman's actions galvanize and substantiate a latent association between femininity and witchcraft that is a product of the metaphoric relation between witchcraft and sexual relations in Etoro cosmology.

A postreproductive woman (over age 50) who has already borne children does not confront this same dilemma. However, she would be expected to engage sparingly in sexual relations and to eventually become celibate. Failure to conform to these expectations entails the selfish depletion of a man (or men) to no purpose and parallels witchcraft.

A widow who seeks to control her marital destiny in remarriage by soliciting the sexual attentions of a bachelor or married man shares the predicament of the childless woman in that this sexually aggressive posture may conjure up an association with witchcraft if the approach is not deftly executed, or if a number of men are importuned. At a more general level, widows provide continual validation of Etoro cosmology in that they perfectly embody the association between aggressive female sexuality and male death through depletion. A widow's deceased husband provides vivid documentation of the consequences of excessive copulation, while the widow's behavior clearly reveals her propensity to engage in this. The reason why the woman's husband died young is unmistakable, given the interpretive context provided by Etoro cosmology.

The widow and children of a deceased man have both contributed to his demise (as agent and beneficiary of his depletion) and are subject to additional food restrictions as a result. As was noted earlier, these correspond to the differential male contribution to the growth of male and female children, in that a boy is relieved of these taboos at age 17 (when he becomes a *manisa*) and a girl at age 12 (when she becomes a *townisa*). The taboos to which a widow is subject remain in force until she remarries, or indefinitely if she does not (with the exception of the taboo on bush hen eggs, which is removed when a widow passes childbearing age). This contributes to the desirability of remarriage (as does the appeal of securing assured access to male labor, discussed in chap. 2, as well as the cultural and emotional significance of the conjugal relationship).

These restrictions on food consumption are significant in that they follow from the joint responsibility of widow and child for a husband/father's death and also impose disabilities consequent upon this responsibility. To be "eaten" is a euphemism for sexual intercourse (of either variety), and a man is indeed spiritually consumed by it. It is therefore appropriate that the consumption of those who have partaken of him be restricted after his demise.

The position of the uninitiated youth differs from that of a woman or child in that he is both agent and beneficiary of his inseminator's depletion. However, frequent homosexual intercourse within the context of this relationship is not negatively regarded since a youth grows in size, strength, and prowess in direct proportion to his consumption of life force (and is also thought to require a heavy dosage in order to attain full maturity). Here again we encounter the tragic necessities of human existence. The full association of youth with witch turns on unregulated sexuality in this instance as well but concerns inappropriate liaisons (and not excess within sanctioned relationships). It is the youth who consorts with others of his age class—and enhances his own growth and vitality at their expense—who replicates the behavior of the witch. The immature young men from whom the culprit draws life force will suffer arrested or retarded development at the least and may well die young as a result. The youth who garners this additional life force manifests precocious, preternatural maturation and will not only reach puberty at the early age of 13 or 14 but will also possess a fairly well developed beard shortly thereafter (more specifically, the beard of a man in his early to middle 20s). Any individual who possesses this trait (i.e., early beardedness) is thought to have taken advantage of other immature young men and is included within the cultural category *sa:go* which designates such transgressors. *Sa:gos* are not only like witches but are universally deemed to *be* witches and especially vicious ones at that. As in the case of women, the association of uninitiated youth with witch is fully applicable only with respect to a potential characteristic and thus serves to regulate and bound sexual behavior.

The category *sa:go* is a particularly important one inasmuch as it represents an intersection of the ideologies of witchcraft and sexual relations. A *sa:go* is deemed a witch as a consequence of his sexual transgressions. While all *sa:gos* are thought to be witches, the converse does not hold, and the category thus contributes in a unique way to the cultural specification of the defining qualities of the witch. A *sa:go* is the more despicable of the two. His essential depravity turns on the fact that he intervenes in and perverts the normal transmission of life force prescribed by the "natural" order of the system, expropriating for himself that which would otherwise provide for the growth and maturation of others. Such behavior is not only evil (by virtue of its harmful effects upon the depleted victim) but also subversive; it is a crime against both "nature" and human society.

A witch (other than a *sa:go*) also intervenes in natural process by appropriating life force that would otherwise be bestowed upon the next generation, but acquires only a portion of this as his victims have typically reproduced themselves to some extent. He foreshortens the life span of individuals who would otherwise expire from sexual depletion at an advanced age but does not so severely threaten the perpetuation of life itself as does the *sa:go*. The *sa:go* embodies and most fully expresses the full range of dimensions that comprises the Etoro conception of evil.

While woman bears the ultimate responsibility for mankind's lost immortality, the *sa:go* brought about the death of the first *Sigisato* and effected the separation of these beneficent spirits from a shared existence with mankind in the everyday world. This created the conditions of diminished spiritual protection that allow witchcraft to often succeed. This too is established in myth.

There was a young man who lived alone at his bush house. Alone, he went down to an expansive river to get water. Going down to the river he saw the water swirling, the rushing water creating a foamy froth. He took some of the foam and carried it back to his house. He placed it in his bush house and went to sleep.

In the morning he awakens and sees—mother! mother![21]—that the foam has formed huge teeth, long and sharp, and fishlike scales. It continues to change before his eyes, now taking on a doglike shape. "What's happening here?" he wondered. It continued to grow larger and larger, and he sees that it has become a crocodile with huge sharp teeth.

The crocodile went off into the forest. Later he returned to the house carrying a dead cassowary. The man also saw—mother!—that he carried a huge dead wild pig. The crocodile stopped close by the house and ate his catch. He continued to grow until he was as big around as a patrol box.

The next morning they spied a large raiding party approaching the house. The crocodile went out from the house in one direction and the man, carrying his bow, in another. They fought the raiding party. The crocodile slashed at the men's throats with his teeth. Men were lying scattered here and there on the ground, their throats slashed. The whole raiding party lay dead, save one, a *sa:go*. "Just wait until tomorrow, then we'll get you," he said. The young man and the crocodile put their slain enemies in a rock cavern. Then they slept.

They awakened to the war cries of another large raiding party, already just outside the house. The young man and the crocodile fought and fought until all the members of the raiding party were dead except the *sa:go*. "Just wait until tomorrow, we'll get you then," he said.

They slept. In the morning they set out through the forest and traveled until they came to a big lake. The crocodile slipped into the water to hide, while the young man changed himself into a bat and flew up to the treetops. He waited silently in the treetops until he saw the *sa:go*, accompanied by many older men, coming to kill the crocodile. They tracked the crocodile to the water's edge. One of them went down into the water to get him. From his treetop perch the man saw a huge pool of blood rise to the surface and float there, together with dismembered body parts. One by one they went into the lake to kill the crocodile, but each was dismembered in turn. The remaining men began to dig a ditch leading out of the lake. They dug and dug and dug until all the water emptied out from the lake. Then they went into the lakebed and killed the crocodile.

Alone, the young man in the treetops wept and wept. He wept and lamented as the raiding party carried the crocodile off to be eaten, chorusing victory cries as they went. The young man followed secretly behind, weeping. They had gone a long way when he saw—mother!—a huge longhouse. They entered with a chorus of war cries. Alone,[22] the young man turned himself into a termite. When he had become a termite, he picked up some ashes and entered the house, taking up a position on a ceiling beam. He began to drill a hole in the beam. He drilled deeper and deeper until he had penetrated the beam. Below him, the slayer of the crocodile was cutting it up. As he was cutting, the termite dropped ashes through the hole. Startled and blinded by the ashes in his eyes, the man slashed out wildly with his knife, killing all the men standing near him. Another man came forward from the men's quarters of the longhouse. "You have done this all wrong, I will do it," he said. And he commenced to butcher the crocodile. But again the termite dropped ashes through the hole into this man's eyes, and like his predecessor he slashed out wildly, killing all those about him. Again and again this was repeated until all the men except the *sa:go* lay dead.

Then the women arrived at the house, and one of them began to cut up the crocodile. As she cut, the termite again dropped ashes into her eyes. Startled, she slashed out wildly, killing those around her. Again and again this was repeated until all the women were killed. The *sa:go* came out of the men's quarters. "How am I going to eat all this by myself?" he said. "How can anyone my size eat all of this?" So saying he came out into the common room where the crocodile lay and then returned to the men's section from whence he had come. Seeing this, the termite came down from his beam and changed himself back into a man. He took a killing stick from its place against the wall and with this he slew the *sa:go*. Then he took an arrow and dipped it into the blood of the crocodile. He shot the arrow up into the sky. He saw the arrow rise until— mother!—like this it disappeared from view.

The young man returned to his own house. He slept there many nights. Then he went out and climbed a tall *morobe* tree. He climbed into the topmost branches, and there he came upon a house. He saw—mother!—another young man! "Age-mate! vi! vi! vi!" he greeted him. The second young man had been formed from the crocodile's blood. He had become the first *Sigisato*. This *Sigisato*'s name was *Marapea*. He took a wife and had many *Sigisato* children.

The crocodile (and *Sigisato* to be) comes into being like Aphrodite, sprung from foam upon the water. The foam is a symbol of semen, which is independently generative. The crocodile behaves as if he were an agnate of the man who mediates his "birth" and growth (attributable to the consumption of game animals), hunting the same territory and assisting this man in combat. Their relationship as coresidents of a secluded hunting lodge also resembles the relationship between co-initiates. Though massively outnumbered by raiding parties, they fight valiantly and successfully, killing all but the *sa:go* (whose comparative longevity is attributable to the appropriation of life force).

The *sa:go* relentlessly mounts repeated raids and finally succeeds, by guile, in killing the crocodile. The crocodile's "age-mate," who is revealed to be a spirit medium by his capacity to transform himself into a particular bat (*utagete*), weeps profusely as if grieving for a deceased kinsman. (That behavior betokens relationships is a stock device of Etoro mythology.) This expression of grief and the heartfelt emotional bond it signifies are central to the story because they contrast with the utter callousness of the *sa:go*. When the *sa:go's* entire community lies dead,[23] he can only think of himself, wondering aloud how he can eat the entire crocodile single-handedly. He feels nothing for his coresidents, many of whom would necessarily be his closest kin. Seeing what has happened, he merely turns and walks away. It is difficult to convey the Etoro sense of the odiousness of such a lack of regard for one's fellows, and their antipathy to the mental picture of the *sa:go* about to selfishly and self-centeredly gorge himself with unshared food while surrounded by the untended corpses of his coresident kinsmen. He is justly killed with a heavy, sharp-edged, black palm "broadsword" employed in witchcraft executions and pig killings. The crocodile's "age-mate" thus exacts the vengeance that betokens a close agnatic relationship. By the spirit medium's action of shooting the blood-drenched arrow skyward, the crocodile is reborn—from man alone—as a spirit entity, the first *Sigisato*. The spirit medium then reestablishes his relationship with his *Sigisato* "age-mate." Etoro exegesis establishes that the *Sigisato*'s descendants are linked to the agnatic descendants of the spirit medium and to subsequent mediums of that lineage, whom they assist in war and in curing and thwarting witchcraft in continuation of the original joint effort in combating the *sa:go* witch. However, the *sa:go* nevertheless succeeded in bringing about the death of the *Sigisato* (crocodile) and removing him from man's side where he provided complete and total protection. Thus the *sa:go* created the conditions that enable witchcraft to often succeed and, like the girl in the preceding myth, the *sa:go* bears a measure of responsibility for the afflictions of sickness and death. While the girl's incest epitomizes the dire consequences of unregulated sexuality, her nurturance of the resultant witch-child is an unthinking, nonmalicious act that is intelligible in terms of the mother-child bond. In contrast, the *sa:go* embodies a sociopathic lack of emotional bonds to others and a concomitant unmitigated selfishness that is consciously malicious.

The metaphoric relationship between witchcraft and sexual relations plays an important role in valorizing socially differentiated categories. Witchcraft and sexual relations occupy analogous structural positions within a larger conceptual system—a system in which life and death are complementary and reciprocal aspects of the transmission of life force. The analogic relation engenders a semantic interplay between the two constellations of beliefs in which witchcraft and sexual intercourse are ideologically grounded. The semantic dimensions of each set of beliefs are enriched and expanded by their juxtaposition; the cultural meaning of witchcraft is informed by the idiom of sexual relations (and vice versa). Moreover, this juxtaposition establishes a metaphoric relation through which the attributes of actors in one domain are projected upon their counterparts in the other, such that social positions are also invested with added dimensions of meaning. More specifically, the analogic correspondence between acts of witchcraft and acts of sexual relations connotes a like relation between the characteristics of the (respective) actors. At the same time, both the actors and their interaction are delineated—in the domain of sexual relations—by social roles. The social positions of wife, protégé, and (to a lesser extent) child thereby acquire a penumbra of negative attributes (derived from the characteristics of the witch) that sharply demarcates the boundaries of acceptable behavior, particularly in the sexual sphere. Behavior that exceeds these bounds is not merely erroneous, ungrammatical, or transgressive; it replicates the behavior of the witch and is categorically "evil." The strongest negative sanction—the witchcraft accusation—may be marshalled against those who violate such norms. The extensive social disabilities that accrue to an accused witch are detailed in the following chapter. It is instructive here to contrast the respective cultural evaluations of a husband and wife who engage in excessive sexual relations. He is, at worst, foolhardy in his beneficent generosity with the gift of life force while his wife—party to the selfsame acts—is thought to be a witch.

These attributions of differential moral quality to male and female behavior are a direct product of a specific structural arrangement within the larger belief system, namely the metaphoric relation between witchcraft and sexual relations. This metaphoric relation completes the Etoro cultural construction of inequality by bringing the crosscutting witch/nonwitch distinction into relationship with the scheme of social differentiation based on gender and life-cycle position (i.e., cultural "age"). Relations of inequality between adult male (on one hand) and adult female, young man, and child (on the other) are fully delineated by the relationship of these categories to the encompassing system of life-force transmission and by the metaphoric relations between the idioms of witchcraft and sexual relations within this system.

Moral worthiness is an intrinsic attribute of senior men by virtue of their beneficent role in the intergenerational transmission of life force. This characteristic stands in stark contrast to the self-aggrandizing moral depravity of the witch. Moreover, this opposition is central to the simultaneous construction and legitimation of inequality, since the senior man is as beneficent as the witch is malevolent.

The female role in reproduction is not assigned supernatural significance. By this critical omission, adult women are positioned as intermediaries in the intergenerational transmission of life force and are therefore agents of male depletion (rather than being subjects of a parallel female depletion). This construction denies any potentiality of intrinsic female generosity and therefore precludes attribution of the attendant moral superiority that accrues to senior men by virtue of their position in reproduction. At the same time, this construction positively establishes the potentiality for drawing a parallel between femininity and witchcraft. At best, a woman may attain a moderately positive moral evaluation as an effective intermediary in life-force transmission. At worst, a woman may approximate the stigmatized immoral character of the witch. While women are not explicitly denigrated nor accorded an invariant and intrinsic negative value by Etoro cosmology, that cosmology demarcates their potentialities as being largely confined within the neutral to negative range. Moreover, widowhood is negatively valued, and this is a social condition that many women experience at some period during their lifetime. While the trajectory of the male life cycle progresses toward the morally exalted status of senior man and (potentially) *tafidilo,* the trajectory of the female life cycle brings the potentiality of the problematic status of widowhood and the inevitability of a postreproductive period that is devoid of positive attributes. Thus, age enhances male but not female status, and the inequality that pertains to differential prestige and moral evaluation is amplified in the later stages of the life cycle (between the ages of 45 and 60).

Boys and young men who are the recipients of life force occupy a position within the culturally constructed system of inequality similar to that of women, in that their moral quality is confined within the neutral to negative range. At best, a young man may grow and mature in proportion to the life force he receives. At worst, he may engage in the morally despicable activities that characterize the *sa:go.* There is no potentiality for morally worthy generosity, although there is a potentiality for stigma. However, the position of a young man is radically transformed after the completion of initiation, when he becomes a donor in the intergenerational transmission of life force (at about age 22 to 26). The bachelors are virginal paragons of male strength and vitality and reservoirs of the supernatural *hame* that ensures the perpetuation of life. They occupy sleeping platforms in the extreme rear of the longhouse, high above the ground and proximate to the site of séances and the point of articulation with the spirit world. They possess a spiritual quality that senior men lack. Moreover, some of them will embark upon careers as spirit mediums (from which older men are excluded) that confer prestige second to none. Moreover, all these young men are accorded the moral standing that accompanies their newly attained position as self-sacrificing donors in the transmission of life force. They are charged with the sacred duty of maturing the next cohort of initiates and inseminating the brothers of their future wives. Their indebtedness to those who brought about their own maturation is discharged by fulfillment of these responsibilities toward their juniors. A measure of self-achievement of manhood is also ritually enunciated in the anointing ceremony described earlier, promoting the conception that each bachelor has become a man among men within the undifferentiated linguistic category *tono.* The degree of inequality between younger and older men within this category is thus attenuated. Moreover, the prestige that accrues to spirit mediums is restricted to younger men, and this counterbalances the prestige accorded to those who occupy the position of *tafidilo,* restricted to older men. *Kosa* performers are also typically young men. This complementary distribution of different forms of prestige among junior and senior initiated males is a strongly egalitarian feature of the Etoro sociocultural system that will be further elaborated in due course.

At the beginning of this chapter it was noted that cultural constructions of inequality evidence a marked systematicity and internal coherence. The ideological system as a whole provides answers to the questions posed by its internal logic, is regularly confirmed by individual experience in certain respects, and is often based on mystical elements that transcend experience (and are not subject to disconfirmation) in other respects. The Etoro cosmological system that comprehends reproduction, spiritual constitution, and life-cycle transformations clearly evidences these qualities. The mystical potency of semen is a core concept that is both nonfalsifiable and regularly confirmed by experience. Boys, who entirely lack semen, are inseminated and do indeed attain puberty thereafter. Although weak and short-winded prior to insemination, they progressively become stronger and develop endurance throughout the period during which they receive semen. Older men who have expended their life force do in fact become short-winded, and their strength diminishes.

The Etoro cosmological system also manifests another important self-validating feature. It engenders behavior that experientially confirms its underlying presuppositions. A childless woman, whose debilitating extractions of life force to no social purpose parallel the extractions of the witch, is led to pursue courses of action that serve to further validate the association between femininity and witchcraft. Senior men fulfill their inculcated self-image of generosity by the frequent distribution of game to community members so that their imputed intrinsic generosity is concretely manifested. All these features make the ideological system compellingly persuasive to social actors such that the legitimation of social inequality rests on a foundation of seemingly self-evident truth. Thus the elevated status of senior men appears—unquestionably—to be richly deserved.

GENDERED INTERPRETATIONS OF MYTHIC COMMENTARIES ON BASIC DOCTRINE

Etoro doctrines pertaining to the physical and spiritual constitution of the person and to the life-cycle processes of growth and maturation constitute a male appropriation of the reproduction of social persons. This appropriation provides the foundation upon which social inequality is formulated and legitimated. The mythological corpus includes a tale in which this appropriation is specifically addressed. This myth is of particular interest in that it is related in mixed company, in the communal section of the longhouse, and is equally appreciated by both genders.

Three women (*udia totora*) lived together with a young man (*aye negei*).[24] One day the young man went off into the forest. He turned himself into a wild taro. Then the women dug up the taro. They harvested the young man who had taken the form of a wild taro. "Take your wild taro and stick it in the ground over there," one said.

The three women turned themselves into wild red cucumbers.[25] Then the man picked them. The man cut off his little finger with his stone knife. Then he peeled another wild cucumber and cut off another finger. He peeled a third wild cucumber and cut off yet another finger and likewise with the fourth. The women who had transformed themselves into wild red cucumbers caused the man to cut off his fingers.

Then the women went to cut down a sago palm. They began to process the sago. This took place at *hauinimia* [named section of the forest] not far from here. They felled an *E:te* sago palm, and they processed the sago.

The young man went to look for the women but he couldn't find them. Then he went off alone to the forest. He was walking along when he noticed a fledgling *yawasagalo* bird. Alone, he took the bird. He took it and turned it into a baby. Then the man gave the baby his breast to suckle. He took the tube from the tip of a *sore* plant and put his nipple into the tube. Then he did the same for the other breast. Then he made himself a woman's skirt. He crooned to the baby, "*ee:, ee:.*" Then he went down to *hauinimia* and saw the women who had cut down a sago palm and begun to process it. As he came up to where they were, the three women exclaimed "My age-mate has a child in her net bag!" [i.e., has given birth]. And they exclaimed much over it. Then they approached closer to view the baby. Mother! The youngest woman comes up and sees—mother! mother!— the woman sees a huge erect penis that parts the man's grass skirt as it emerges. The three women abandoned their sago-working operation and fled. They ran saying, "Hea! that's a man down there!" The man turned away in disappointment and frustration. He swung the infant against the felled sago palm and killed it. When he had killed the infant he set off in pursuit of the women. He followed them, going on and on and on and on. The women slept along the trail. They slept one night. The man likewise slept along the trail. Then the next day the women continued on. They slept a second night along the way, as did the man. They went on and slept a third night on the run. The man also slept. They continued onward the fourth day. They crossed a huge river, the *Tinima* river that borders Petamini territory. They crossed it leaving the man behind on the other side. They see the man beginning to cross the river. Like this the water cuts the man as he tries to cross. The water cuts him again and again like a knife. Then the man was transformed into a black palm by the *Kesame* spirits [the spirits of the dead]. And that large black palm still stands there. That's what happened.

This myth can be interpreted differently by men and women, with these divergent interpretations keyed by identification with the perspective of the man or the three women, respectively. We may begin with the male point of

view. The myth asserts that man is entirely capable of the complete appropriation of female reproduction and nurturance. Man's transformative powers
readily enable him to create a child and suckle it. However, these powers
do not enable a man to become a woman. The child is perfect, but the gender
change is profoundly flawed. The man's essential maleness is ineradicable.
This essential and ineradicable maleness is elicited in relation to women.
Thus masculinity comes to the fore in complementary opposition to femininity. The flawed gender transformation is revealed by the erect penis. Disappointed at this revelation of the limitations of man's transformative powers,
the protagonist destroys the perfect child he has created, for man can take
life as well as create it. There is perhaps the suggestion that this side of the
male nature is evoked by femininity as well. In any event, it is evident that
essential, unalterable maleness has reasserted itself. Moreover, it is man the
life-taker who sets out after the fleeing women. At the river crossing, ineradicable gender differences once again come into play. The water through which
the women pass without incident cuts the man like a knife, and he is transformed into a tall black palm—a phallus. It is also from the exceptionally
hard wood of the black palm that bows and killing sticks are made.[26] Thus,
the protagonist has become a concretized phallus and instrument of death,
transformed by complementary opposition to the femininity he sought to
emulate. Man the transformer is himself transformed by contact with the
authentic femininity he tried to transformationally transgress. The gender
boundary is intractable, so that his efforts recoil upon him. Instead of becoming female he becomes an icon of masculinity. The *Kesame* spirits (who
reside in rivers and occupy the bodies of fish) take exception to this vain
attempt to infringe a fundamental ordering principle.[27] But there is also
another aspect to the transformation. The black palm, which is often left
uncut near longhouse sites, is frequented by the red bird of paradise, the
corporeal abode of a medium's spirit wife (the daughter of *Kesame* spirits
born in the afterlife). The black palm is thus a point of connection with the
supernatural as well as a symbol of the phallus and of man's instruments of
death. The connection with the supernatural that is the source of man's
transformative powers is thus an equally essential attribute of masculinity.
The iconic phallus has mystical properties.

The first part of the myth also addresses gender differences. In this
instance, they pertain to sexuality. A woman may "harvest" a man's penis
in intercourse without suffering any ill effects whatsoever. But when a man
"peels" a woman's vagina, he loses his flesh and blood (i.e., his substance).
It is this asymmetrical vulnerability that is man's Achilles' heel. And in the
end, the protagonist—for all his life-creating and life-taking powers—is done
in by this vulnerability. The river cuts him like the knife with which the
women caused him to amputate his fingers when he "peeled" them. Symboli-

cally, he dies of depletion. The moral of this tale is thus that man cannot become that which is antithetical to his nature and that the gender boundary is intractable even to man's considerable powers. Man must know his limitations. However, the capacity to appropriate female reproduction and nurturance are well within these boundaries. The effort to become a woman is flawed because the identification with women this entails is contrary to appropriation. Appropriation creates a problem of blurred genders that the myth addresses and resolves.[28]

From the female point of view, the protagonist in this tale is something of an inept buffoon. Everything he attempts turns out badly, starting with his peeling of the wild cucumbers, during which he cuts off his fingers. It is noteworthy that he repeats this mishap no less than four times in succession. If there are intrinsic dangers here, the man is clearly slow to recognize them and desist. Next, the young man goes to search for the women but cannot find them. Again he appears inept, as muddy Etoro trails retain tracks that are easy to follow, and the sounds of sago processing can be heard some way off. The women, meanwhile, are entirely competent and self-sufficient. They have felled a sago palm by themselves and are processing it without any difficulty, just as they harvested the taro without a mishap. The man's attempts to transform himself into a woman with a child are flattering but somewhat ludicrous. In reality, the child is actually a bird (in nature if not in appearance), the breasts are makeshift, and the reproductive organs are unaltered. As the youngest (and therefore most comely) of the three women draws near, the superficial facade of transvestism is revealed as such. A man is, after all, merely a man, and the essence of masculinity is typified by the erect penis. The superficial masquerade (entailing no significant transformations) is a flop. The women now flee from the young man, whose true intentions and proclivities have become readily apparent. The man then kills the bird-child, negating the concept of male nurturance and renouncing his unsuccessful efforts to emulate women's intrinsic capacity to bring forth life. The man's efforts to catch the women are also a failure as they outdistance him repeatedly over four successive days. But, as in the earlier episode of four finger-loppings, he dully persists, driven on by lust. On the fourth day, the women make a successful crossing of a major river. This is of a piece with all their endeavors throughout. The hapless man who has failed at all else fails here as well. The river cuts him as he earlier cut himself and, symbolically, these wounds are equally self-inflicted, a product of his foolhardy lust. Finally, he who attempted transformation is transformed, becoming a metonymic phallus, a reduction to essence. As in the earlier episode, man is reduced to this single, defining attribute and shorn of the pretense that he is more. The moral of the story is thus that man's pretensions to emulate femininity and the creative achievement of womanhood in reproduction are superficial puffery without substance. Man is what he is and no more. And while he ineptly carries out these pretentious antics, women competently go about their business.[29]

This myth contains a number of ambiguities that are readily open to alternative interpretations. Is the killing of the child a demonstration of man's power to take life as well as create it, or a renunciation? Does the man pursue the women in anger or in lust? Although the loss of the fingers may be caused by the women, the man's persistence can be taken to make at least three-fourths of the loss self-inflicted. The reading on this point also keys the interpretation of the cause of the man's ultimate fate. Was he done in by the depleting forces of femininity, by his own foolhardy desires, or by the *Kesame* spirits? The myth includes multiple levels of causality that provision different interpretations. The black palm is likewise interpretable as either an expansive or reductive symbol, the mystical phallus that embodies male supernatural potency or male consciousness writ small. The evident humor evoked by the mental picture of the erect penis parting the grass skirt is also juxtaposed to quite serious matters of life and death by a rapid shift to a startling infanticide. Perceiving the shifting tone of the story as essentially humorous—or not—also promotes divergent readings. In short, the myth is a masterpiece of multidimensional ambiguities that positively invites alternative interpretations. These are clearly keyed to the actor's point of view, in that the story unfolds quite differently depending upon whether one adopts the perspective of the man or the three women.

This myth is particularly significant in that it places male efforts to appropriate reproduction squarely in public view, while at the same time encouraging gender-specific interpretations of this as accomplished fact or failed farce. I would argue that this male appropriation—which is the foundation of inequality—does not exist only in men's minds, as a male point of view, because the basic cosmological doctrines that underwrite it are pervasively manifested in the public domain in the form of food taboos, in the spatial restriction of widows to the periphery of the longhouse common room, in women's avoidance of stepping over food, firewood, and men's possessions, in the differential elaboration of male and female rites of passage, and so forth. Both men and women live in a conceptual world shaped by a male-centered cosmology, which is therefore entirely hegemonic. It may also be proposed that this is contested by alternative female interpretations of myths that are common cultural property. However, this female point of view does exist only in women's minds, in that it does not reciprocally shape the conceptual world in which men and women live and is not manifested in the public domain. This is partly due to the fact that Etoro women do not publicly articulate an alternative female-centered cosmology, but rather adhere to a negative critique of what they interpretively perceive as male pretension. In other words, they contest the hegemonic androcentric ideology only in a negative sense, thus conceding its hegemony. Insofar as this ideology does, in fact, pervasively shape social life (and resonate with it), the female view that male efforts to appropriate reproduction are a failed farce represents a disjunctive imagined reality. The female perspective lacks the potentiality to be institutionalized because it takes the form of a negative critique. It can thus readily be encompassed within the cultural repertoire, as an amusing satire or "roast" of the archetypal male hero. This is facilitated by the fact that the archetypal hero (the *aye negei*) is an unmarried young man, i.e., a junior male. The myth itself is unproblematic for men and is retold by them (the translation being based on a recorded male narration).

Etoro metaphysical formulations—pertaining to the fundamental causes and processes of being and becoming—delineate the physical and spiritual components of the person, successive transformations of these constitutional components over the life course, and the positive and negative contributions of specified human and spiritual agents to the life-cycle processes of procreation, growth, maturation, senescence, and death. Social categories are thereby simultaneously delineated and valorized, instituting a morally evaluated scheme of social differentiation. Social inequality is thus fabricated as a moral hierarchy or hierarchy of virtue.

The central ideational content of the foundational metaphysic is monolithic, insofar as socially differentiated actors (such as men and women) do not have divergent views concerning the nature of reality or the fundamental causes and processes of being and becoming. However, socially differentiated actors have different perspectives or points of view that may eventuate in divergent interpretations of mythic commentaries on basic doctrine. Both of the interpretations discussed in the preceding pages are grounded in acceptance of the fundamental doctrine that sexual relations deplete men but not women, and this also entails tacit acceptance of the underlying premises that inform this doctrine. The female interpretation of this myth proposes that deleterious male depletion is largely a product of male lust, thus attributing prime responsibility for the consequences of a tragic condition of human existence to the men who are the victims of it. This interpretation of the myth does not deconstruct or qualitatively alter the moral hierarchy that confers intrinsic virtue upon men (but not women) for their self-sacrificing contributions to the perpetuation of life. Male lust remains, at worst, foolhardy and self-destructive rather than evil or subversive. It is deleterious only to a man himself, not to others. The female interpretation thus promotes a conception of woman's role in procreation as neutral rather than negative. Similarly, by shifting the responsibility for male depletion to males, the female interpretation seeks to disavow responsibility for the ultimate consequence of that depletion, i.e., death. This weakens the implicit symbolic association of femininity and witchcraft and thus also works to promote a conception of women's role in life-cycle processes as neutral rather than negative. It is important to recall that this association is implicit rather than doctrinal. That men are depleted by their contributions to procreation is explicitly stated by informants, while the notion that a woman is analogous to a witch is never so stated but only logically implied. There is thus scope to indirectly refute the implication. Women can consequently seek both to define themselves as morally neutral, rather than negative, and to encourage men to see them in this light. They can also celebrate the fact that only women give birth. However, there is no scope within the framework of the existing doctrine of male spiritual depletion (which the female interpretation accepts) to redefine the nature of procreation in such a way as to imbue giving birth with a comparable measure of virtue. (A doctrine of parallel female depletion would, however, contribute to a redefinition along these lines.) In this sense, the moral hierarchy remains unchallenged by the perspective and interpretive point of view of female actors. They can, at best, attain a position of moral neutrality at the conceptual midpoint of this hierarchy, between intrinsically virtuous male perpetuators of life and the evil witches who selfishly appropriate the central ingredient of it.

The myth that recounts the origin of witchcraft is also susceptible to gendered interpretations. While unregulated sexuality is the uncontested root cause of lost immortality, the issue of the allocation of responsibility can be viewed in several ways. A female perspective that takes male lust as a point of departure would shift the burden of responsibility for initiating a joint act of incest onto the male. Grounding evil in unregulated sexuality, which is a general theme of Etoro doctrine, intrinsically provisions the potentiality for alternative interpretations of the gender responsible for this. While women can perceive men to be driven by lust, men can perceive women as sexually predatory, as epitomized by the sexual advances widows make toward the virginal bachelors. The prevalence of ongoing affairs between widows and bachelors within a typical longhouse community provides community members of both genders with a life experience that can be grist for either mill. Thus, a male perspective that takes the sexually predatory nature of women as a point of departure would shift the burden for initiating the mythic joint act of incest onto the female. This interpretation, according responsibility for the origin of witchcraft to women, receives additional support from the mythic facts that the girl is older than the boy, does not reveal how she became pregnant when questioned, fails to submit the witch-child to infanticide at birth, attempts to conceal it, and nurtures it at her breast. However, a myth can condition but cannot compel a specific interpretation. Women can thus view this train of events—culminating in the origin of sickness and death—as the unwitting consequence of maternal nurturance, the ultimately tragic results of which could not have been known to the protagonist. Similarly, the myth of the male mother (which is probably female authored) cannot compel a single interpretation, even if the female interpretation may be judged to be stronger on impartial hermeneutic grounds internal to the text, since these two interpretations are each conditioned by the gendered perspective of the cultural interpreter who is neither impartial nor bound by the canons of hermeneutics.

The myth that recounts the origin of witchcraft therefore does not compel women to accept ultimate responsibility for this, but at the same time allows men to draw this inference if they so choose. (The third alternative is to focus on the act of incest itself as the root cause.) It is important to note that the myth does not conclude by stating "therefore women are ultimately responsible for mankind's lost immortality." This conclusion is part of an interpretation, not part of the text. Men and women may thus conceptually position women at different points within the morally neutral to negative range. Moreover, both may apply the ideologically available moral principles to the classification of individual women, such as the widow whose unself-regulated sexuality led to her expulsion from the community (i.e., the widow discovered consorting with a bachelor she favored in the men's section of the longhouse and additionally suspected, due to a past history of adultery, of also making advances to one or more married men).

The myth of the male appropriation of reproduction is the first of a trilogy concerning the three women. In the second myth, the women are living in the region west of the *Tinima* river, where they are visited, in succession, by several young men from the Etoro area they previously fled.

> Two young men (*aye negei*) lived together. They remained together for many seasons. Then one of them said, "I am going visiting." He went alone. He went on and on and on until he came to a river, which he crossed. He continued on and on and on until he came to another river, which he also crossed. This was the *Tinima* river. He continued on alone until he came upon a clearing in the forest. He stopped at the edge of the clearing and decorated himself (for a formal visit)[30] before proceeding. Continuing on, he arrived at the house. There were no men there; the women lived there alone. Mother! The women gave him cooked bananas. They gave him cooked taro. They gave him cooked sago. He ate with them. When they had eaten—mother!—he heard much howling in the forest beyond the clearing. Like this (in the manner of husbands chorusing on return from a hunt) they came, a large pack of dogs. They carried pigs they had killed. They carried cassowaries they had killed and yet more cassowaries. They brought forest mammals they had killed. The women proceeded to cook the animals. As they did so, the dogs sniffed the women's genitals and then mated with them. Like this (as the women were bent over cooking) they mated with them. Then they returned to the forest from whence they had come. The women

finished cooking the pigs and cassowaries and offered some to the young man. After they had eaten they slept.

When they awoke in the morning the dogs were still gone. The three women said, "We are going to dig taro." They each announced this in turn. The young man went together with the youngest to dig taro. They proceeded to the garden. The young woman dug and dug and dug and dug for taro. Then she cut a piece of sugarcane and gave it to the young man to eat. He seated himself on a fallen log while he ate it. The young woman then began to excavate a very large taro. As she dug, her arm went further and further and further into the ground until it was no longer visible. At the same time her skirt was progressively drawn up higher and higher and higher, until it was above her hips. But the young man turned and sat with his back to her as she progressed to dig in this way. She finished and brought the taro over to him, giving him some. Together they carried it back to the house. Mother! That day they cooked a lot of taro. They cooked sweet potatoes as well. While they were eating, they heard the pack of dogs howling as they approached from the forest beyond the clearing. They came howling as before. They brought pig and cassowary and birds and forest mammals they had killed, many of them. The women heated stones to cook the game. When it was cooked, they gave some to the young man. They ate and then slept till morning.

The young man departed. He took with him some of the food he had been given that he had put aside. He carried some forest mammal, pork, taro, and sweet potato as he proceeded back to his house. He went on and on and on, coming to the *Tinima* river, which he crossed. He continued on and on and on until he reached his house. He greeted his age-mate, saying, "I have brought you some pork." He gave a share to his age-mate, but the latter only sulked and wouldn't partake of it. The age-mate said, "I too am an *aye negei,* I will follow in your footsteps." He went off to the forest and later returned. The first young man said, "If you do go, be sure not to watch the women digging taro." "I know," the second replied.

The second young man goes forth in the same manner as the first [repetition omitted], arrives at the house, is offered sweet potato and sugarcane and begins to eat with the women. He notices that their chests are all scratched up from extensive mating with the dogs (their dog husbands whose advances they desire). Once again, in the midst of the meal, the howling pack of dogs is heard approaching. They arrive with a large quantity of game, (but this time) the women put the game aside. The young man exclaimed, "You act such! You are no good! Who is going to eat all this food?" Then the women cooked the game, but when it was cooked the young man said, "The dogs who brought this to you will bite me. I won't eat any; this is all no good." So they didn't give him any of the meat, not any of all that meat. Then they ate and slept till morning.

When they awoke, one of the women said to the young man, "I'm going to dig taro, come along with me." They went together to dig taro. Mother! They set out for the garden. Upon arriving, the woman gave the young man some sugarcane, and he seated himself on a fallen log as he ate it. The woman proceeded to dig taro (in the same manner as before). As she dug deeper and deeper and deeper, her arm disappeared from view and her skirt was drawn up above her hips. As she was digging, the young man said to himself, "I am looking at that woman," and (thus becoming aroused) he copulated with her. Later they returned to the house. "What have you been up to out there?" the other two women asked. "Go; go away from here," they said to the young man. "I won't go; I don't want to leave this house," he replied. So he stayed, and they gave him cooked sweet potatoes and cooked taro of several kinds. They all ate together. But as they were eating, the women suddenly exclaimed, "The dogs are coming! Run from here, young man; they will kill you! Run away before the dogs kill you!" So away he ran. But as he fled, panting from the exertion, he ran directly upon the returning pack of dogs. The dogs killed the young man and ate him raw. Then they proceeded on to the house. Now the first young man lives on, alone.

This myth is, in many respects, a response to the prior myth. Like several other Etoro myths, the central theme is the causal relationship between heterosexuality and death. The first of a pair of age-mates rejects heterosexuality and lives, while the second succumbs to temptation and is killed. Although death is not attributable to depletion, which only takes effect over time, the end result is the same, i.e., heterosexuality for a young man leads to an early demise. Within this general framework of a culturally well-recognized theme, the myth unmistakably asserts the male view of the sexually predatory nature of women. Capitalizing on the denouement of the first myth of the trilogy, which leaves the three women beyond the *Tinima* river by themselves, the sequel conjures up a vision of an approximation of female autonomy. Unable to do without masculine contributions to existence, the three women become the consorts of a pack of dogs that supplies them with game. The women are given to excessive intercourse with their dog husbands (or husband analogues), and this is most inappropriately conducted in public, at a habitation, and during meals. Many proprieties related to the spatial regulation of sexuality are violated, suggesting that women do not behave commendably when left to their own devices in a social world of their own construction. That the women are driven by lust is established in the ensuing scene in the garden. A brazen and tasteless effort to seduce the first male visitor is enacted, employing an approach that has proved successful with the dogs. This is then repeated with the second visitor, leaving no doubt that the propensity to lust is characterological and not specific to a relationship. This follows not long after the young woman mated with her dog "husbands" and is not only excessive and adulterous in intent, but also inappropriate as to location since copulation takes place in a garden. Three additional counts of unregulated sexuality are thus attributed to the female protagonist. Moreover, it is made clear that the women are well aware of the potentially lethal consequences, since they tell the second young man, who succumbs to these advances, to flee for his life. In all these ways, the myth strives to make the point that women, not men, are driven by lust and are sexually predatory by nature. An effort is thus made to establish female responsibility for male sexual depletion. This squarely addresses the issue raised in the prior myth.

It may additionally be noted that the second young man is a flawed *aye negei* who behaves inappropriately from the start. He does not accept the pork his age-mate graciously offers to share with him, rudely upbraids his female hosts for initially failing to offer him meat, and then refuses it when they do. His flawed character foreshadows his subsequent failure to reject inappropriate sexual advances. However, the fact that efforts are made to seduce this thoroughly unappealing young man is consistent with the interpretive theme of indiscriminate female lust.

This myth lacks the ambiguities that characterized the initial myth of the three women and does not so readily lend itself to an alternative, gynocentric interpretation. The difference is attributable to the fact that this myth monolithically articulates the orthodoxy of the hegemonic androcentric ideology, while the first myth constructs a counterhegemonic female perspective that necessarily includes aspects of the hegemonic ideology it satirizes. Nevertheless, the myth provides openings for a less unfavorable interpretation of femininity. The women are not as hospitable to the second visitor, suggesting a measure of discrimination consistent with a courtship interpretation, as opposed to one entailing indiscriminate promiscuity. In other words, the women can be seen to seek proper human husbands, being prepared to employ their sexuality as a means to this end. This proposes that they are not enthralled at being the wives of dogs. Moreover, only one of the women invites the second visitor to accompany her on her trip to the garden, while all three invited the first young man. Thus two of the women implicitly reject the second visitor, presupposing that they are not driven by lust to the extent that any man will serve as well as the next. These same two women also express disapproval of the tryst in the garden (the occurrence of which they deduce) and tell the second visitor to depart at once. Thus, they uphold morality in this respect. These behavioral differences on the part of the three women are conducive to the conclusion that women in general are not characterologically driven by lust. Only some women fit this mold, while others employ their sexuality as a means to matrimonial ends. This attenuates but does not obviate female responsibility for male sexual depletion. However, the interpretation that is more favorable to women works to locate them closer to the morally neutral position. As in the case of the first myth, these two interpretations are keyed by identification with the perspective of the male or female protagonists, respectively. From the perspective of the male experiences in the myth, women uniformly appear to be lust-driven and want only one thing. From the perspective of the varied female behaviors, women are discriminating in accordance with a matrimonial hidden agenda.

The first myth of the three women is very probably female authored, while the second is very probably male authored. Although authorship cannot be directly traced, this conclusion is plausible on grounds pertaining to the characteristics of the mythic constructions in each case. As a set, the two myths thus appear to constitute a gendered repartee within the framework of an ongoing debate concerning male versus female responsibility for male sexual depletion. The larger issue is the moral quality of women. While this is contested, the intrinsic virtue that accrues to men as a result of their contributions to the perpetuation of life is conceded, since the doctrine that sexual relations deplete men but not women is an underlying premise of the debate.

In the final myth of the trilogy, feminine morality is achieved through proper courtship and marriage. The establishment of conjugal and affinal relations implicitly resolves the problem of unregulated sexuality and unites the divided genders who are earlier at cross-purposes. The characters are two young men and three women, as in the second myth, but the story unfolds as if this second episode had not occurred. In other words, the third myth provides an alternative conclusion and thus circumvents the difficulty of character development that is not ideally conducive to a utopian conclusion. The women of the second myth are too tainted to be the heroines of such a drama and are replaced by analogues. Although this appears as a disjunction from the perspective of ethnocentric conceptions of a trilogy, the Etoro represent the following myth as the conclusion to the tale of the three women.

Two young men (*aye negei*) lived together. They were living together when one of them decided to go visiting alone. Alone, he set off, traveling on and on and on and on and on until he came to a wide trail. He continued along this, going on and on and on until he arrived at a sheer cliff. The trail led straight to the face of the cliff. Alone, he looked about, searching for the continuation of the trail. But he saw none. Then he noticed—mother!—a thin vine hanging down the face of the cliff. As he was inspecting it, an *awini* (marsupial) descended and then went back up the vine, revealing the trail. The young man proceeded to climb. He climbed up and up and up and up and up until he reached the top of the cliff. Upon reaching the top he saw—mother!—a garden. An old man was residing there. The young man had brought some pork with him. He gave some to the old man and began to set out again. But the old man said, "Night will catch you along the trail; if you like we two can spend the night together here" [proposing, by use of the dual pronoun, a homosexual tryst]. "I'll not sleep here," the young man replied, "I'm going on to my own house." Alone, he proceeded, going on and on and on. As night began to fall, he set about to construct a small bush house. When he had finished building it, he put his things inside and retired for the night. He cut off some of the pork, cooked and ate it, and then went to sleep. He slept till morning.

Upon arising, he continued a little further and then commenced to clear a site for a longhouse. Alone, he cleared the site and then cut corner posts for the house. He cut forked poles. He cut horizontal beams. He cut ridge poles. He cut thatch-supporting roof poles. Then he carried all these to the cleared site. Having done so, he returned to his bush house. He cut off some pork, cooked and ate it, put the rest aside, and then slept. In the morning he went back to the house site he had cleared and saw—mother!—the house was framed. The corner posts, beams, ridge poles, and thatch poles were all in place. Alone, he set off to get sago leaves for thatch. He assembled two piles and carried them to the house site. In the afternoon, he returned to his bush house. There he chopped firewood, heated stones, and steam-cooked some pork. He hung the rest of his store of pork in a tree and went to sleep. After he awakened, in the predawn hours, he retrieved the pork. Counting the packages he discovered some of the cooked portion was missing. After putting the remainder back in the tree, he went back to sleep. In the morning, he returned to the house site and saw—mother!—that the balance of the thatch needed for the house was assembled there. Alone, he looped string around the thatch poles and proceeded to thatch the roof. When he had done enough for a day, he returned to his bush house. He cooked and ate some pork, stashed the remainder in a tree, and went to sleep. He awoke in the predawn hours and again discovered that someone had taken some of his pork. He went back to sleep and slept till morning. Upon arising, he went to the longhouse site. Mother! Both sides of the roof were completely thatched. Alone, he proceeded to cut upright and horizontal wall poles. Then he cut a tree for siding, split it into siding boards, and assembled these materials at the site. On the way back to his bush house, he cut firewood. Upon returning, he cooked and ate some pork and went to sleep. He slept till morning. Upon arising, he once again discovered some pork was missing. He went to the house site and discovered the walls had been put up. He began to construct the sleeping platforms. He returned to his bush house, and [repetition omitted] everything transpired as before. In the morning he discovered missing pork and also found completed sleeping platforms in both the men's and women's sections. Collecting his things, he moved into the new longhouse.

The next day, the young man transformed himself into a biting fly. So transformed, he took up a position atop the pork which he had hung on the outside wall of the house. He waited there to see who had been taking his pork. Mother! He is laying in wait. During the night he sees, approaching, one woman, then a second, then a third. The young man thought to himself, "Good! What attractive women!" He seized the youngest with his hands. The young woman turned herself into a stone. Still he carried her. She became a piece of firewood, but still he carried her. She became a chunk of clay, but still he held tight. She became a vine, but still he did not lose his grip. The other two women said, "You are truly strong, you really held on to her." Then the three women departed.

The young man slept. Upon awakening (in daylight) he could see—mother!—

the women's footprints. He followed them. As he did so, he saw blood on the
ground and tears as well. He followed the trail of blood and tears. He went on
and on and on until he came to the base of a large *pigilo* tree. It was huge.
Mother! He sees that the tracks lead up into the tree. As he paused there, he saw
a large *habumi* marsupial descend and then retrace its steps. Following this lead,
the young man climbed the tree. He climbed up and up. High in the upper
branches, he sees blood and tears on a limb. He follows it out and comes to a
wapai tree leaning horizontally against the limb and forming a bridge. He proceeds along the trunk of this until he reaches the base. Mother! At the base of the
wapai tree there is a trail lined with planted *ilogo* (cordyline). As he follows this
trail—mother!—as he goes along silently he sees—mother!—some women approaching. First comes the mother, leading the way. Behind her is a young
woman, and another young woman and then, finally (he is elated to behold) the
youngest—the one he had held. He sees she has cut off the last joint of one of
her little fingers and one of her little toes because she pined for him and so longed
to marry him (hence the trail of blood and tears). As she drew near, the young
woman said, "You are truly strong." But he remained silent. He accompanied
them along the trail, continuing until a longhouse came into view. Mother! Such
a huge longhouse. Two of the young women and their mother went on into the
bush. The youngest—who had cut off her finger, like this, with a knife, because
she wanted the young man to be her husband—continued on to the house with
the young man. She went into the women's section. He hid himself in the wood
crib in the communal section. He is hiding there later in the afternoon when he
hears people approaching. He can see many men coming (from his hiding place),
drawing nearer and nearer. Mother! He sees they are carrying a pig they had
killed. A large pig with tusks! They brought a cassowary they had killed as well.
They began to make a fire to heat stones to steam-cook the meat (in an earth
oven). When it was cooked, they distributed it. The youngest woman brought
the young man some cooked sweet potato. She gave him cooked bananas as well.
She gave him some pork she had saved for him. He ate silently, remaining
hidden. When he had eaten, he slept.

In the morning, the old woman—his prospective wife's mother—said, "Today I will tell my 'sons' that you came and are here." Everyone had left for the
bush (the forest interspersed with gardens and sago stands). But the old woman,
her daughter, and the young man remained at the longhouse. In the afternoon,
the men returned, bringing many pigs they had killed. They cooked the pigs and
distributed the pork. The old woman gave him a portion. She asked for an extra
portion, saying "A man has came to marry the youngest of the women; he is
here now." Then she said to the young man, "You who are hidden, come out
into the common room." He emerged into the central passageway and was
greeted, "Brother-in-law, *vi! vi! vi!*" as each shook his hand in turn. Then one
of the girl's brothers said, "The marriage payment will be this many pigs [count-
ing]: 34 once, 34 twice, 34 thrice, 34 fourfold, 34 fivefold in all, but no cowrie
strings or pearl shells."

So the young man set out for his house. When he arrived he began to call his pigs. As he called, they began to come in from the forest. Seeing that 34 had emerged, he hobbled them. He continued calling and hobbling his pigs in batches of 34 until he had assembled the five sets. Alone, he led the pigs along the trail, going on and on and on until he came to the *pigilo* tree. He climbed it, and the pigs followed after. They continued on until they reached the house. Entering the central passageway, he said, "My brothers-in-law, you set the marriage payment [woman *su*], and here it is." "Where will we put all these pigs!" they replied, "It is completed." So the young man married the woman and lived there with her brothers. That's how it came to pass.

This myth differs from the second myth (and many others in the Etoro corpus) in that it lacks a contrastive structure whereby two age-mates elect different courses of action that lead to distinctive consequences. The first *aye negei*'s sojourn leads directly to a felicitous conclusion, and his age-mate's presence as a character is notational. However, there is an internal contrast in the myth in that the hero rejects a potential homosexual relationship and pursues a course of action leading to heterosexual wedlock. The proffered homosexual relationship with an older man is quite inappropriate because the protagonist is mature and consequently should be the inseminator of a wife's (or prospective wife's) younger brother rather than being an older man's inseminee. In the end, the hero does indeed acquire wife's brothers, creating the conditions for culturally appropriate sexual relations, both heterosexual and homosexual. In short, this myth turns on the rejection of inappropriate sexual relations and unregulated sexuality in favor of proper arrangements. Unlike the first myth, the hero is not confused about his gender identity and does not try to establish relations with women by becoming one. In this tale, men are men and women are women, setting the stage for a relationship based on complementarity (as explained below). Although women take the initiative in establishing this relationship, as in the second myth, they do so in an appropriate rather than inappropriate manner. The flawed relations between the genders that characterized the first two stories are thus set right.

The hero of this tale is a self-sufficient bachelor. In contrast to the imperfect attempt at female autonomy that characterized the preceding story, the hero is capable of an autonomous existence without a surrogate animal spouse or sexual partner. He demonstrates his capacity to live on his own by proceeding to construct his own longhouse by himself. But he receives unsolicited assistance from the three women, who take the initiative in seeking to establish a relationship. More precisely, they initiate an exchange relationship in which they perform labor and receive pork in return. They help themselves to the pork, but the hero tacitly accepts this arrangement. The way in which the women initiate this relationship contrasts markedly with the female advances in the preceding myth. The women do not lavishly feed the sojourning *aye negei* and subsequently solicit sex. Instead they proffer contributions to production and take food in return. More precisely, the proposition implicitly made to the self-sufficient bachelor is one entailing participation in a gendered division of labor and in the conjugal exchange of work and food this entails. In the protracted middle portion of the tale, the hero and the three women work productively together to complete the construction of a longhouse and, at the same time, share food (although not in each other's company). It is only after the task is completed that the hero seeks to discover with whom he has been working and sharing pork.

The hero transforms himself into a fly in order to lie in wait undetected. According to exegesis, this capacity for transformation reveals that he is a spirit medium. The young woman he captures seeks to escape through transformation, becoming a series of objects in succession. She is thus revealed to be a spirit woman (destined to become his spirit wife). It thus emerges that the women are from *selesaya,* the treetop spirit world (as explained in exegesis). The marsupials, who are spirit helpers, guide the hero there over the hidden trail as he proceeds to follow the track of blood and tears. His relations with animals are appropriate, in contrast to the second myth. The chase is reminiscent of the first myth, but in this instance the hero successfully overtakes the three women.

The heroine amputates the last joint of one finger and one toe and weeps because she pines for the hero and longs to marry him. This finger loss harkens back to the initial scene of the first myth and brings the sequence of events full circle. In that prior text, the women cause the man to cut off his fingers when he "peels" them. Sexual relations lead to male depletion (while the responsibility for initiating these relations is contested). However, this time the heroine rather than the hero experiences the loss. But it is not a consequence of sexual relations and is self-induced. The man does not cause the young woman to inadvertently cut off her fingertips; rather she does so as an intentional act in order to signal her interest in marriage.[31] This female initiative also contrasts with the advances made by the antiheroine of the second myth, who solicits sexual relations that lead to the early death of the second *aye negei* (who fails to reject the solicitation). One of the basic messages conveyed by this amputation is thus that it is appropriate for a girl to pine for a man she favors in order to induce him to offer for her. This interest in marriage is appropriately signaled by self-sacrifice, rather than by a seduction that depletes a prospective husband. Moreover, blood is emblematic of the female contribution to reproduction, and offering reproductive substance connotes the male-female complementarity of reproduction rather than the antinomy of sexual depletion (i.e., the complementarity of blood and semen as sources of the corporeal constituents of the person, flesh and bone). In other words, the heroine proffers her childbearing potential (as well as her contributions to production). She seeks marriage rather than sex.

The heroine's mother acts as a facilitator in initially announcing the hero's marriage proposal to the heroine's brothers. The marriage is subsequently arranged by the prospective groom and his prospective wife's brothers. The self-sufficient bachelor accumulates the substantial bridewealth requested on his own and concludes the transaction. Through proper marriage, he thus acquires not only a wife but many wife's brothers as well.

Marriage unites the genders that are at cross-purposes in the earlier myths and establishes a framework within which the problems of unregulated female and male sexuality can be resolved. Unlike the two earlier tales, this one does not end in male death. It ends in marriage (regulated sexuality), implicitly proposing that this obviates the problem of a premature male demise. The issue of responsibility for male sexual depletion raised by the prior myths is not directly resolved, since neither sexual relations nor male depletion takes place. There is thus the suggestion that this issue recedes into the background in the context of duly constituted marital reproduction. Moreover, the female contribution to reproduction is foregrounded, so that females as well as males are seen to play a role in the perpetuation of life across generations. Each contributes equally to the physical constitution of the person. The unequal aspect of male and female contributions that pertains to spiritual constitution (and is linked to male spiritual depletion) is not broached in this myth. Thus, the aspect of reproduction conducive to a sense of gender complementarity is emphasized and associationally linked to marriage. In contrast to the first myth, the hero does not attempt reproduction on his own, but rather seeks a wife. The necessity of a female contribution to reproduction is acknowledged. In addition the protagonists all behave commendably, and the character of neither gender is satirized or impugned. Thus, divergent male and female interpretations are not stimulated. Both men and women are in agreement that marriage unites the otherwise divided genders and constitutes a fundamental ordering principle of utopian social life. Marriage itself is made in heaven, i.e., in *selesaya*. Moreover, the spirit wife is established as a model for the behavior of earthly women (cf. Cantrell n.d.). However, a medium's spirit wife cures and combats witchcraft and thus occupies an elevated position in the moral hierarchy that is unavailable to her counterparts in the real world, who are unable to transcend a morally neutral position. In addition, the spirit wife constitutes a model subject to male-exclusive formulation, since only male mediums possess spirit wives who communicate through them (as discussed further in chap. 5).

Elucidation of the cultural construction of inequality as a moral hierarchy (i.e., as morally evaluated social differentiation) provides a basis for

returning to several issues that arose in the context of the general inquiry into
the relationship between economy and inequality conducted in chapter 2.
One of the central points that emerged from the consideration of economic
organization is that the division of labor entails two central aspects. The first
pertains to the assignment of individuals to tasks on the basis of principles
of categorization formulated in terms of gender and life-cycle position (i.e.,
cultural age). The second aspect pertains to the cultural valuation of activity,
i.e., to the division of value accorded to labor. While the division of labor
embodies a form of social differentiation, social differentiation is not generated out of the labor process—or economic process more generally—but
rather imposed upon them. From the standpoint of actual economic activity,
differences between the genders are blurred (due to an absence of task exclusivity). However, from a cosmological standpoint, the genders are clearly
defined as discrete. This is to say that a cosmologically formulated scheme
of social differentiation is transposed onto economic process. Moreover, it
is a morally evaluated scheme of social differentiation in which social inequalities are inscribed at the outset.

The division of value accorded to labor and the products of labor is
derived from the same cosmological source as the scheme of morally evaluated social differentiation. This division of value is central to the production
of social inequality. While the division of types of work, and the exchange
of one form of labor for another, are not, in and of themselves, a source of
inequality, inequality is engendered by differential valuations. The game that
is predominantly procured by men promotes growth, while the starch staples
predominantly produced by women only sate hunger. Male products thus
have a prestige-producing potential that female products lack. Although the
producer holds rights to distribute and/or exchange the products of his or her
own labor, the identity of the "producer" is intrinsically ambiguous in a
system of male-female coproduction in which the labor of both genders is
intermingled in many final products. The cosmological system provides the
basis for an arbitrary definition of the "producer" as the individual who
completes the process of production. Distributional control over joint products (such as pigs) that possess a potential for deployment in prestige-
enhancing distributions and system-constituting exchanges is thus arbitrarily
assigned to men. It is not control over the means of production but rather
control over the cultural definition of producer and over the cultural valuation
of products that is critical. In short, the cosmological system is central to the
production of inequality in instituting a morally evaluated scheme of social
differentiation that is inscribed in economic process, in assigning differential
prestige value to the products of labor, and in supplying the basis for according distributional rights over these products.

The specification of the cosmological system carried out in the present chapter thus supplies answers to questions that initially arose out of a comprehensive examination of the economic processes of production, distribution, and consumption, carried out with a view to identifying economic sources of inequality. But, at the same time, these answers raise further questions. If the source of social inequality is essentially ideological, in what sense is that ideology hegemonic? Are the critical valuations that provide the basis of moral hierarchy shared or contested? In the final section of this chapter, I have attempted to answer these questions. The hegemonic ideology is institutionalized and shapes the social world in which the lives of all socially differentiated categories of persons are played out. The central doctrines of Etoro metaphysics are not contested but rather constitute the underlying premise of what is contested, namely the extent to which females are responsible for male sexual and spiritual depletion. While the basis of the moral superiority of males is thus conceded, the question of whether women are morally neutral or negative is subject to divergent gendered interpretations (which can alternatively be resolved by assigning specific women to different points within this range).

Central questions that remain to be addressed concern the source, nature, and mechanisms of control over the cosmological formulations that underwrite the hegemonic ideology. These aspects of control pertain to the locus of vested authority with respect to doctrine. It may be noted, in anticipation of future discussion, that the requisite spiritual authority is in the hands of the elite that occupies the apex of the moral hierarchy, i.e., spirit mediums. The role of spirit mediums in the formulation of witchcraft accusations is addressed in the next chapter, and the shamanic career is analyzed in chapter 5. This will lay the groundwork for consideration of this elite's control over the cosmological foundations of social inequality in the concluding chapter. However, the main focus of chapter 4 concerns the overall process of the allocation of stigma (the negative reciprocal of prestige), in the form of witchcraft accusations. While the fabrication of a moral hierarchy that constitutes the basis of social inequality has been delineated, the question of the extent to which the distribution of prestige, stigma, privilege, and debility covaries with morally evaluated social differentiation remains to be addressed. This question is a central theme of the next three chapters.

CHAPTER 4

Stigma: Witchcraft and Inequality

While the cosmologically grounded moral hierarchy of ascribed virtue constitutes the main focus of chapter 3, this chapter and the next are directed to
elucidation of the prestige/stigma hierarchy based on achieved distinction.
The prestigious social statuses of spirit medium and *tafidilo* are examined in
chapter 5, while the stigmatized social status of the witch is the subject of the
present chapter.

The Etoro say that an individual has "made himself (or herself) a witch"
(*mugwabe hamosa*). It is the malice and ill will in a person's heart that
nourish the seed of witchcraft, fostering the development of the *tohorora*.
The individual thus bears ultimate responsibility for attainment of the capacity and inclination to perform supernatural acts of witchcraft that cause illness
and death. Such acts are also elective. A witch chooses to deploy these
supernatural powers only at certain times and against selected individuals;
his or her *ausulubo* carries out premeditated acts of witchcraft under conscious direction. A witch is thus fully accountable for the deaths he or she
brings about. This is reflected both in the concept of liability for compensation and in the requirement that a witch foreswear future acts of witchcraft
as a precondition for reintegration into the community (as witch and victim
are coresidents in two-thirds of the cases). The social status of witch is thus
achieved through elective social action in terms of both the development and
deployment of the capacity to cause illness and death. Possession of a
tohorora—and the supernatural powers this entails—constitutes a form of
distinction, although in a negative register. The stigma of witchcraft is thus
the negative reciprocal of the prestige accorded mediums and *tafidilos*. Moreover, the virtue of self-abnegating generosity in contributing to the perpetuation of life across generations (through donations of life force and the
distribution of growth-including game) is counterposed to the morally despicable vice of subverting the intergenerational process of life-force transmission through self-serving appropriation. The senior *tafidilo* and adolescent
sa:go are thus opposites, as are the death-dealing witch and the spirit medium
who seeks to cure, thwart, and combat witchcraft, and to definitively identify

the perpetrators so that they may be brought to account through compensation or retributive execution. The prestige system is thus more accurately characterized as a prestige/stigma hierarchy, and the stigmatized statuses of witch and *sa:go* are integral to its constitution.

Prestige is defined as the esteem accorded to the attainment of virtues that are achieved through elective social action. Although prestige is earned, it is a reputational quality that is bestowed upon an individual by the members of society. Selected individuals are thus assigned the prestigious status of *tafidilo* on the basis of achieved distinction. The term *tafidilo* is a nominalized form of the verb "to be first," and the status thus marks off the apex of the continuum phenomenon of comparative distinction in ordinal terms. Selected individuals are likewise assigned the stigmatized status of witch by the members of society on the basis of achieved distinction in the realm of morally despicable vice. Although the conventions of the anthropological literature tend to represent individuals as attaining a prestigious status and being ascribed a stigmatized status, the elements of individually achieved distinction and societal assignment are equally present in both instances. However, the relative emphasis on these two components differs in that no one aspires to attain a stigmatized status. Although the members of society who bestow the stigmatized status of witch upon an individual regard it as earned and richly deserved, it is not so regarded by the recipient, to whom it appears mistakenly and unjustly imposed. In contrast, the societal and actor's points of view (of the bestowers and recipient) are isomorphic with respect to the earned achievement of prestige. Nevertheless, it is the societal perspective that is determinative, since both prestige and stigma exist only insofar as they are socially acknowledged and culturally constituted. Employing the actor's point of view to delineate the characteristics of a system would confound levels of analysis. The stigmatized status of witch is therefore appropriately regarded as achieved. Stigma thus constitutes the negative reciprocal of prestige (and vice versa) within a conceptually unified system.

A witchcraft accusation recruits an individual to membership in the morally denigrated category of witch and simultaneously accords a stigmatized status that entails marked disabilities. The accused's life is placed in jeopardy, and a transfer of wealth from accused to accuser is coercively required. Relations with kinsmen may become strained as a result of the accused drawing them into unwanted social conflict with other members of the community. A witch is frequently induced to migrate to another longhouse community, where he or she is both less favorably situated in terms of kin support and very vulnerable to a second accusation. The stigma associated with an accusation also undermines the virtue and moral worthiness of those who aspire to the prestigious statuses of medium and *tafidilo*. An accused adolescent is precluded from becoming a medium, and a man in his

30s who is subject to an authenticated accusation (i.e., one ratified by the spirit medium who has jurisdiction in the case) is likewise precluded from attaining *tafidilo* status when he reaches the appropriate age (of about 45). An accusation against an established medium has the potential to undercut his spiritual authority and impair his capacity to function effectively, prompting early retirement from the position of senior resident medium of the community. An accusation against a member of a *tafidilo*'s family involves him in conflict that impairs his capacity to effectively coordinate community enterprises. An accusation against a *tafidilo*'s wife or child also typically leads to migration and the temporary or permanent loss of the central prerogative of *tafidilo* status, namely an acknowledged leadership role in the community. A witchcraft accusation thus disrupts and may effectively end the career of a spirit medium or *tafidilo*.

Witchcraft accusations constitute an arena of power with respect to social inequality in that they consign individuals to a markedly disadvantaged social category, and to a stigmatized status that negates prospective prestige attainment and has the capacity to strip away privilege, and redistribute prestigious status among individuals within a community, by dislodging established mediums and *tafidilos*. Stigma and debility thus go hand in hand. This chapter focuses on the central questions raised by these potent negative consequences of witchcraft accusations and the arena of power they engender: who exerts influence or control over the complex process through which such accusations are formulated, and how are accusations distributed among socially differentiated categories of individuals? The extent to which the distribution of accusations conforms to and ratifies the cosmologically grounded system of inequality (or moral hierarchy) analyzed in the preceding chapter is also at issue. Are stigma and debility allocated to the morally unworthy so that the moral hierarchy and prestige/stigma hierarchy are concordant? More specifically, is the implicit association of femininity and witchcraft realized in a disproportionate frequency of accusations? And does the intrinsic self-abnegating generosity of senior men substantially shield them so that they are infrequently accused? Alternatively, is the fundamentally egalitarian concept of a singular, socially undifferentiated agent of supernatural attack expressed in an equally undifferentiated pattern of accusations? The social praxis of accusations is equally capable of accentuating or leveling social inequalities. It is here that two divergent cultural visions of Etoro society clash and the contest between egalitarian and inegalitarian social forces is joined.

To address the issue of control over the machinery of witchcraft accusations, and thus come to an understanding of their distribution among socially differentiated categories of persons, it is first necessary to describe how witchcraft is believed to operate and to elucidate the complex sequence of events that is involved in an act of witchcraft and in the determination of the perpetrator's identity. The branching diagram presented in figure 4.1 provides a guide to the main outlines of this account.

The sequence of events begins with an initial attack by a witch that produces illness. The victim may then request that a medium undertake a cure. If the request is denied (due to the advanced state of the supernatural attack) or if the witch persists (rendering the treatment ineffective), death ensues. The complex process of determining the identity of the witch is then initiated. Certain aspects of this process provide scope for public opinion to nominate suspects, and *tafidilos* can potentially play an influential role in shaping widely shared suspicions. In addition, the resident spirit medium initiates a spirit inquest that unfolds during the course of a series of nightly séances. The medium's *Kesame* spirits undertake to track the witch, and they provide cryptic information, as their detective work progresses, that may also nominate certain suspects. However, the final selection of two prime suspects, whose guilt or innocence is oracularly determined, is in the hands of the victim's next of kin. The selection is informed by the deathbed testimony of the deceased and preliminary oracles that are privately consulted. However, the choice is also influenced by public opinion and the séances that both play upon and are informed by it. The definitive oracle is then publicly consulted by the principal next of kin (i.e., a deceased man's brother or a deceased woman's husband or son). All those who have come to the mortuary gathering are in attendance and participate in interpreting the results, which are typically contested by the incriminated party. In a séance later that night, the spirits of the senior resident medium authenticate the outcome and render a final verdict.

The process of determining the identity of the witch (or witches) responsible for a death thus entails a complex interplay between sources of information and suspicion derived from the next of kin, the resident spirit medium and public opinion, with the latter influenced by *tafidilos,* séances conducted by the medium, and the close and more distant kin of the victim. One of the principal objectives of the account previewed here is to provide a detailed description of this process that elucidates the subtle interplay of influences involved. This lays the groundwork for consideration of the extent to which the respective interests of the principal next of kin, mediums, *tafidilos,* and the community at large are exerted and realized. Adherence to due process and the degree to which a potential suspect is effectively tried by his or her peers in a court of community opinion can also be assessed, as against the potential alternatives of victimization of competitors or personal enemies by the elite or the deceased's next of kin. Consideration of this arena of power will also elucidate important aspects of the social positions of the senior resident medium and leading *tafidilo,* who constitute the community's elite,

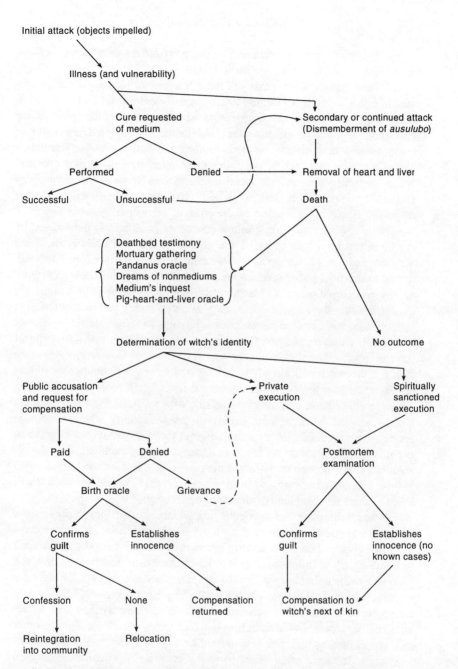

Fig. 4.1. The sequence of events in an act of witchcraft, in determination of the alleged witch's identity and guilt or innocence, and in resolution through execution or compensation

and will likewise reveal a measure of the prerogatives that accrue to those who enjoy these prestigious statuses.

Determination of the identity of the witch responsible for a death eventuates in either a public accusation and request for compensation or an execution. The latter may or may not be expressly authorized by the spirits of the entranced medium at the time the final verdict is rendered. Payment of compensation may also be refused, creating the potentiality for retributive execution. The factors that condition these alternative outcomes are analyzed, including the intricate social pressures conducive to the payment of requested compensation (insofar as such payment entails a tacit admission of guilt). However, resolution of the issue of compensation does not mark the end of a witchcraft case. Guilt or innocence is ultimately determined by the birth oracle, which turns on the gender of the next child born to the accused and his or her spouse. The establishment of innocence through appeal to this final oracle reverses the prior guilty verdict and leads to a return of any compensation paid. Alternatively, confirmation of guilt definitively establishes that the accused possesses a *tohorora* and is indeed a witch. Not infrequently this outcome necessitates a promise to foreswear future acts of witchcraft, as a precondition for reintegration into the normal social life of the community, and this implicitly entails confession. However, more often than not the witch will already have migrated to another community so that reintegration into the community where the witchcraft took place is not an issue. In either case, confirmed possession of a *tohorora* makes the witch a leading suspect when a death occurs in the community where he or she resides. The accumulation of multiple accusations is strongly conducive to eventual execution, and very few thrice-named witches avoid this fate. Available data make it possible to assess the potentiality that a once-named witch will be exonerated as opposed to the likelihood that a single accusation will lead to others that eventually culminate in execution.

Witch killings are of particular importance in that they represent the most extreme debility associated with the stigma of witchcraft. Five executions that occurred during or shortly before the fieldwork period are examined in some detail in order to elucidate the characteristic features of both the process and the individuals subject to this fate. Executed witches are typically estranged from their closest kin, to whom they have become a liability as a consequence of successive accusations. One of the five witches was in fact killed by her closest living adult kinsman (her father's brother), and two other men were killed by their first cousin (mother's brother's son). The individuals who are killed have often migrated to the community where the execution takes place within a year prior to the event. Their virtually complete lack of support from both kin and coresidents is evident from the fact that the execution does not generate any subsequent conflict. Postmortem examination of the witch's heart invariably establishes the presence of a *tohorora* and thus legitimates the execution. Compensation is always paid to the deceased witch's next of kin and is accepted without any rancor.

It is particularly noteworthy that execution typically occurs after all the components of the lengthy process of establishing the suspect's guilt have been completed (excepting the birth oracle). It is a deliberate rather than spontaneous or precipitous act. More often than not, execution is legitimated by spiritual authorization. A spirit medium will thus have played an identifiable role in the course of events leading to this conclusion. Consideration of the moral basis for execution amplifies the point that stigma is grounded in a system of moral evaluation that provides the underpinnings of social hierarchy. An understanding of the processes involved in the formulation and resolution of witchcraft accusations informs the subsequent analysis of the distribution of both accusations and executions. Distribution is a product of the internal logic of social practice, and this largely dictates the extent to which it conforms to the contours of moral hierarchy.

ACTS OF WITCHCRAFT

The defining characteristic of the *mugwabe* (witch) is the possession of a *tohorora;* this is both the cause of this distinctive state of being and the source of the supernatural powers that enable a witch to perform acts of witchcraft. The force or power that emanates from the *tohorora* can be released and directed through the witch's eyes so as to topple a tree upon an intended victim or induce a fatal fall during the crossing of a flood-swollen torrent. Only fatal accidents are attributed to witchcraft because it is believed that witches seek only to kill their intended victims (and consume their life force) and do not trifle in lesser misfortunes. Similarly, witches are believed to be responsible only for serious, life-threatening illnesses that are induced as a facilitating prelude to the same ultimate objective. In other words, a witch always seeks to kill his or her victim by conscious, premeditated supernatural attack that is entirely controlled and directed. Within the Etoro system of belief, there is no scope for a witch to beg off by claiming that unintentional harm was inadvertently caused by lack of complete control over the supernatural power that emanates from the *tohorora*. An act of witchcraft is always believed to be entirely malicious.

In the standardized narrative account of a witchcraft-induced illness, it is said that the witch "stared" at the victim from a concealed position and caused pebbles, splinters, or other small foreign objects to become lodged in the victim's *ausulubo* or spirit body. These objects are believed to be thrown or impelled by supernatural force. It is strongly believed that an individual cannot see a witch and survive, so that the identity of the witch responsible for an illness cannot be known to the victim at this point (although it can become known at the moment of death as explained further along). An individual who is ill also does not know if the illness is due to witchcraft or to natural causes (*orai memana* or "nothing" sickness). In the latter case, healing is inevitable without counteraction, since death (other than homicide) can only be a result of witchcraft.[1] To seek the intervention of a medium is thus to concede to oneself that an illness is life-threatening. Supernatural healing is applicable only to situations where a relentless witch seeks one's death, and such healing is therefore not requested lightly or frequently.

When a medium is asked to cure someone, he relates this to fellow community members and proposes to convoke a séance that night or the following night. Séances take place about once every six to ten days and are therefore regular rather than extraordinary events. However, only about 10 percent of these séances include inquiry into or treatment of illness, and curing only occupies one segment of those séances of which it forms a part (cf. Knauft 1985a:308)

A medium cannot undertake a séance, or effect a cure, without the assistance of a chorus of at least five or six individuals. The chorus echoes the entranced medium's sotto voce pronouncements in song. This coparticipation is necessary to mobilize the spirits, and a séance is thus a collective endeavor. The supporting chorus is invariably made up of the young men of the community, with the bachelors forming the core of this group. When a member of the community is seriously ill, kinsmen and coresidents are more than willing to lend their voices to the curing effort as a manifestation of their concern. The chorus may then swell to ten or more enthusiastic singers.

Séances are normally conducted at the back of the men's section of the longhouse (see fig. 1.1), although they are occasionally held at garden houses. The spirit medium sits cross-legged facing a small fireplace, while the chorus is arrayed in a semicircle opposite him. The medium takes a number of deep draws on his cylindrical bamboo pipe and then assumes a hunched-over position, remaining motionless. His *ausulubo* leaves his body and travels to one of the spirit worlds so that he may become the vessel of one of his spirits. The medium's spirit wife is the first to appear, followed later in the séance by the spirit child and finally by the medium's *Sigisato*. The spirit wife enters the medium's body through the spiritual orifice of his armpit and moves up into his collarbone. This is signaled by wheezing and whistling sounds and the resumption of bodily movement. The spirit that occupies the medium's body then speaks through him in a voice different from his own. The distinctive tonal quality serves to identify the particular spirit within him. The chorus repeats and amplifies these sotto voce communications in melodious song that can be heard by all within the longhouse (including the women, who can hear but not see the performance from the communal section or women's section of the dwelling). The audience members periodically react to the performance by shouting, "Truly!" or "That's no lie!" in response to various pronouncements, or exclaim "I'm fearful!" or "Mother!" as warnings of the activities of witches are issued. Audience members also joke and chat among themselves and occasionally take naps during the nightlong séance (which should ideally last from about 10:00 P.M. to dawn). A medium thus has a continuous reading of the audience members' degree of engagement and a sense of their reception of his spirit's revelations.[2]

The interchange that takes place at a séance is between the audience and the spirits. The medium is not present, since his *ausulubo* (and consciousness) have left his body to visit various spirit worlds (cf. Knauft 1985a). The spirits directly address specific audience members on occasion, telling an individual to set a cassowary snare in a particular place or warning that a litter of pigs will soon become feral if not captured and brought to the longhouse. Individuals may also put questions to a spirit, asking the whereabouts of a lost pig or inquiring after the welfare of a recently deceased relative (who resides in the riverine spirit world of the *Kesames,* together with a medium's spirit wife and spirit child). Once I asked if my parents in America were well. The spirit said at first that he could not see their faraway land, but then a few moments later returned to the issue and related that an airplane that had flown over a few days earlier was sent by my parents to check on my welfare. This inquiry and response were entirely consistent with the characteristic tone of audience-spirit interactions (cf. Sørum 1980:284).

CURING WITCHCRAFT-INDUCED ILLNESS

An individual who is ill likewise queries a spirit. He or she asks if the illness is due to witchcraft or is merely a "nothing" sickness (or a relative puts this question on his or her behalf). If the spirit replies that it is the latter, no cure is required since the illness is bound to pass of its own accord. However, the spirit may add that he (or she) will watch over the person to protect them from any supernatural attack that may occur, for witches are thought to be prone to beset the weak and vulnerable. *Sigisato* spirits, who are "strong," generally undertake to protect a person in this way. The spirit wife and spirit child, who are "afraid" of witches, may undertake to watch over a person but are thought to be incapable of combating a witch. The most they can do is place their hand over a person's heart to passively protect it, while a *Sigisato* may kill a witch.

The *ausulubo* or spirit body of a person is on the same "plane of existence" as the *Sigisato* and *Kesame* spirits, so that the latter may be seen in dreams (but not in a waking state).[3] Likewise, these spirits see the patient's *ausulubo* as if his or her corporeal flesh were transparent. The presence of foreign objects or the absence of limbs or organs is thus readily apparent. If the patient has been the victim of an initial witchcraft attack, the stones, splinters, or other foreign objects that the witch has impelled into the victim's *ausulubo* are likewise easily plucked and removed by the spirits. The observable actions of the entranced medium during curing are somewhat variable between practitioners and may also differ from one patient to the next. However, it is not necessary for the medium to engage in any physical contact with the patient, and the latter may be in another part of the longhouse (e.g., the women's section) for a cure to be effected. The invisible spirit simply removes the readily apparent foreign objects from the patient's *ausulubo* and deposits them at the medium's spiritual orifice. In other words, the entranced medium runs his hand up his side and under his armpit, producing a stone, splinter, bit of plant stalk, or other similar foreign object. Alternatively, the patient may be close to the medium. The medium then places his hand on the afflicted area (usually the chest) and subsequently produces the foreign object from his mouth (suggesting that the spirit works from inside, rather than outside, the medium in these cases). The exact mechanisms of curing are not known to laymen, and mediums themselves can always take refuge in the fact that they were not present at the time in deflecting the anthropologist's questions.

A patient may also be treated with *"Kesame* water." This is obtained by a *Kesame* spirit (e.g., the medium's spirit wife or spirit child) from the rivers that run through the sky world of the *Sigisatos*. Since the *Sigisatos* are immortal, their rivers are not inhabited by spirits of the dead. Thus while the rivers of the everyday world are the abode of the spirits of the dead and the offspring of their afterlife (both comprising the collective *Kesames*), the rivers of the sky world contain an oppositional water of life. This *Kesame* water is applied by the spirit wife or spirit child (but not a *Sigisato*) to cure a feverish patient, who is "cooled" by it.

A witch's initial attack, entailing the introduction of foreign objects into the victim's *ausulubo,* is only a means of producing illness and vulnerability so that the witch can subsequently consume the victim's spirit body and life force. A witch (or rather his or her *ausulubo*) is thought to come on successive nights to remove, carry off, and eat the limbs of the victim's *ausulubo,* one by one. Finally, the witch rips out the heart and liver from the victim's *ausulubo* and consumes them, bringing about the final demise. The *hame* or life force that animates the victim's spirit body is incorporated by the witch when the limbs and organs of the *ausulubo* are consumed (as explained earlier).

The fact that illness and death are the results of two separate (but usually sequential) acts of witchcraft is a particularly important doctrine in several respects. Illness is not a *cause* of death, in Etoro thinking, since death results from a specific type of supernatural attack (different from the one that causes illness). The cure of an illness therefore does not necessarily preclude the subsequent death of the patient. (The word "cure" is nevertheless more accurate than "treatment," since the cause of illness is removed.) The witch may well persist in attempting to secure the life force of a targeted victim and once again introduce foreign objects into the latter's *ausulubo*. Or the witch may simply proceed to remove the limbs and organs from a recovering individual who is still somewhat weak and vulnerable. When a second medium is asked to cure an illness already treated somewhat earlier by another practitioner, his spirit may say that his predecessor's spirit failed to extract all the objects introduced in a single act of witchcraft. However, the spirit of a medium who treats a patient twice in succession will say that a second supernatural attack has occurred. (Competition between mediums will be discussed more fully in the next chapter.)

Since a cure does not in and of itself preclude the death of the patient, the most critical element in spiritual intervention is the continuing protection that a *Sigisato*, spirit wife, or spirit child can provide. This was discussed earlier. This continuing spiritual protection is also the grounds for evaluating the efficacy of different mediums. Although all spirits are equally capable of removing foreign objects from a patient's *ausulubo*, some are said to be lax in watching over and protecting the patient from renewed supernatural attack. A medium whose spirits acquire such a reputation is not sought after for curing, and he will ultimately lose the support he requires to mobilize a chorus in order to conduct séances of all kinds. This provides for a measure of attrition among young men who undergo apprenticeship with the intention of becoming mediums (as is discussed in the next chapter).

The identity of the witch responsible for an illness is never publicly revealed at the time of the initial cure. It was explained to me that the spirits typically do not see the witch introduce foreign objects into the victim, since this occurred before spiritual attention was directed to the sick individual. People say that if the spirits knew the identity of the witch, they would reveal it, so that the failure to do so is a sure sign that they lack this knowledge. Thus an illness provides no occasion for a confrontation between victim and witch. Although secondary cures are relatively uncommon, these do logically provide the potentiality for identifying a persistent witch, since a spirit is presumably watching over the patient following the initial cure. A *Kesame* spirit might witness a secondary attack but, lacking "strength," would be unable to prevent it (although capable of saving the victim's life by covering his or her heart and liver). Nevertheless, no witch was publicly named in the few double cures that took place while I was in the field. I do not know of any instances when the witch responsible for an illness was named. Thus available data indicate that witchcraft accusations are only lodged in the event of a death. Suspicions regarding the identity of a witch responsible for an illness are not publicly voiced even to close kin, so far as I know. However, an individual who has been cured acquires spiritually authenticated knowledge that he or she has been the victim of supernatural attack, and one would expect that such an individual thinks about possible perpetrators. This speculation may come into play later if the victim eventually dies, because the deathbed statement of the deceased figures prominently in the determination of the responsible witch's identity. However, the main point to be noted here is that the victim of a supernaturally induced illness cannot have certain knowledge of the witch's identity and studiously avoids making his or her suspicions known to others.

Nearly all cures are completely efficacious in that the patient recovers. Likewise, nearly all the persons who die were not supernaturally cured beforehand. This is due to the fact that the spirits decline to cure most serious illnesses on the grounds that the witchcraft attack has progressed to the point where a cure is no longer possible and death is inevitable. When the sick individual petitions a spirit in the course of a séance convoked for this purpose, the spirit relates that the main limbs of the *ausulubo* have already been consumed by the witch and hence cannot be recovered. In most instances, the heart and liver of the *ausulubo* are also said to have been removed but not yet consumed by the witch. The spirit then explicitly forecasts the imminent death of the bewitched (which will occur as soon as the vital organs are consumed). This dramatic pronouncement is a crushing psychological blow to the seriously ill petitioner and may perhaps hasten his or her demise.[4] In any event, seven persons whose death was forecast in this manner while I was in the field died within three days. In another twelve cases in which events prior to the death were well known to me, no séance was convoked because the individual died within several days of the onset of illness and no medium was available during this interval (e.g., the coresident medium or the potential patient was at a garden house, or the medium himself was also ill at the time). In one case, an individual who was cured subsequently died, with this being attributed to a secondary attack by the witch.[5] My data thus indicate that mediums are very selective in undertaking curing, declining some cases on the grounds that the illness is not due to witchcraft and others on the grounds that the illness has progressed to an incurable stage. This selectivity allows experienced mediums to achieve a very high rate of success. The mediums Nogobe and Kayago, who were connected with the Kaburusato longhouse community, performed four successful cures there during a fifteen-month period and declined at least two other requests on the grounds that the illness was not due to witchcraft.[6] Both of these individuals recovered on their own accord as foretold. One individual died shortly after taking ill, without requesting a cure. Community members thus expressed considerable confidence in the capability of these mediums as healers (although individuals differed as to which of the two was regarded as superior in this respect).

DETERMINATION OF THE WITCH'S IDENTITY FOLLOWING A DEATH

One of the fundamental tenets of Etoro doctrine is that "if you see a witch, you will die." The central idea expressed in this oft-repeated phrase is that only a doomed individual has certain knowledge of the identity of the witch responsible for an illness. This belief turns on the notion that the victim of a fatal sequence of supernatural attacks occupies a space between life and death in which consciousness is located in the *ausulubo*, even though the victim is in a waking state. The victim's consciousness and perception are thus on the plane of existence where the fatal acts of witchcraft are taking place. Death occurs when the witch removes and eats the heart and liver of the *ausulubo*, and the victim witnesses this act. The dying victim thus has the capacity to name the witch responsible for his or her demise in his or her last words. Individuals are reported to waken from delirium in the middle of the night, say "X has taken my liver!" and expire. Others proclaim that they are being choked or burned with a firebrand in an apparent visualization of their symptoms as an act of witchcraft. In addition to the victim's identification of the witch in his or her last words, the victim is sometimes said to have "known from the start" that it was X. For example, the victim may be reported to have said on return from sago processing that so-and-so had bewitched him or her, to collapse no sooner than these words were uttered, and then to expire later that night or the following night. The critical doctrinal point here is that the victim of fatal acts of witchcraft is believed to have certain knowledge of the identity of the perpetrator and to be capable of communicating this information to others.

A dying person is invariably attended by others, and these individuals thus become the repositories of this vital information. In a sample of seventeen cases for which data pertaining to this point are available, one to four persons were said to have heard the deceased identify the witch, with two being the median number. In 65 percent (11/17) of these cases, two or more individuals shared this knowledge. The two individuals most commonly in attendance are a male victim's wife and brother and a female victim's husband and child (son or daughter). The other individuals present include a male victim's affines, close agnates (e.g., father's brother's son), and matrilateral siblings (e.g., mother's sister's son) and a female victim's classificatory daughters (e.g., husband's brother's daughter). The kin represented generally parallel the patterns of coresidence that obtain in Etoro longhouse communities (see Kelly 1977:145–60).[7] If a person dies in the sexually segregated sleeping quarters of the longhouse, same-sex kin may be the only auditors of the deceased's last words. Males and females are also represented among the auditory witnesses in proportion to the ratio of male to female deaths in this sample.

The close kin who have heard the deceased name the witch responsible for his or her death do not publicly reveal this information until it has been confirmed by oracles and ratified by spirit pronouncements. A public accusation is only made in the context of a request for compensation. Such a request is legitimated by the presentation of comprehensive evidence that is primarily derived from oracles and spirit pronouncements as well as the deathbed testimony. Confronting an alleged witch with the deathbed testimony alone would surely lead to a refusal to pay compensation on the grounds that the evidence was incomplete and insufficient. Such premature public action would be pointless. A death is thus followed by a socially dramatic interlude during which speculation and rumor are rife while authentic knowledge remains publicly unrevealed. At the same time, this interlude creates a space in which various influences derived from mediums and public opinion can play upon the final outcome.

Within a day or two, the deceased's body is moved from the longhouse to a burial platform in the clearing in front of the longhouse or in an adjacent garden. Individuals from neighboring communities come to commiserate with the surviving next of kin and pay their respects to the deceased. Each day there is a substantial gathering, and each night there is a séance. Like many Melanesian peoples, the Etoro believe that the corpse may indicate the identity of the witch by bodily movement or the release of gases or fluids of decomposition at the moment when the guilty party stands before the burial platform to (falsely) grieve and pay his or her respects (compare Knauft 1985a). The mortuary gathering (*guano*) continues until the bones show through the flesh, and the corpse may well give off such signs at some point during the extensive decomposition that takes place. Other indications may be provided by the routine steam cooking of banana-leaf-wrapped packets of sago that are prepared each afternoon by all those present. If one of these packets is found to be "raw," this is taken to signal the identity of the witch. However, this may be said to be the person who placed and subsequently retrieved the packet, or the person who cut the firewood or the one who sealed the steam pit with leaves. Moreover, what is judged to be slightly undercooked by one person may be judged to be "raw" by another. The state of the food thus provides a vehicle for individuals to voice their suspicions concerning the identity of the witch. Corpse movement provides a similar vehicle, since a large number of people are likely to be in the immediate vicinity when this occurs. Both of these potential indices of guilt give laymen (as opposed to mediums) direct access to the process by which accusations are formulated. Thus a witch can sometimes be nominated by public acclamation before the case is considered by mediums.

While the mortuary gathering is in progress, the next of kin privately consult the pandanus oracle at some secluded location. Two slabs of pandanus are placed in a steam oven with the invocation, "If X is the witch responsible for so-and-so's death, let this pandanus be raw; if Y . . . , let this [second] one be raw." This invocation is addressed to the *Sigisato* spirits, who are believed to determine the outcome. The individuals present are often the same persons who heard the deceased's deathbed testimony. The invocation is performed by the person who will publicly lodge the witchcraft accusation (in due course) and distribute the compensation received. This is generally a deceased man's brother and a deceased woman's husband or son (hereafter referred to as the principal next of kin).

The two names put before the oracle are the name of the person identified by the deceased and the name of a second individual selected by the next of kin. The second suspect is typically someone who has previously been publicly accused of witchcraft. In most instances, the two suspects are also individuals who were in close proximity to the deceased at the time of the onset of serious illness, although this could include an individual encountered along the trail during a harvesting or foraging expedition.

After the requisite time has elapsed, the pandanus is removed and tasted. If a piece is raw, it is said that it pricks the tongue or even that it makes the tongue bleed. (This sensation is probably due to the presence of sliverlike crystals of oxalic acid that are normally broken down by more complete cooking.) There are always several people present, typically including both males and females. They all taste the pandanus and confirm the outcome. If both slabs of pandanus are fully cooked, the oracular consultation is believed to have been improperly performed and is redone, employing the names of the same two suspects. An outcome in which one or both slabs are raw is taken to be valid. In the latter case, the result is interpreted as indicating that two witches collaborated in bringing about the death. The pandanus oracle thus invariably confirms the guilt of one or both of the individuals whose names are placed before it. The innocence of a suspect is only taken to be established when the pandanus identified with that individual's name is fully cooked while another slab of pandanus, steamed in the same earth oven, is not.

Since the pandanus oracle is performed privately, no one other than those individuals actually present are in a position to know the manner in which the oracle was employed (re: retests) or the extent to which a reported outcome conforms to what actually transpired. The pandanus oracle therefore does not figure prominently in accusations. However, it serves as a pretest for a second oracular consultation that is performed in public by the principal next of kin of the deceased victim. Toward the conclusion of the mortuary gathering, a pig heart and pig liver, each enclosed in a leaf-wrapped packet of sago flour, are steam cooked in an earth oven to the names of two prime suspects. The same form of invocation employed with respect to the panda-nus oracle is repeated, and the *Sigisato* spirits are likewise responsible for determining the outcome. The primary significance of the prior pandanus oracle is thus that it serves as a basis for establishing the identity of the two suspects whose names are placed before this more definitive pig-organ or-acle. However, other events transpire before this second oracle is consulted, and these should be discussed in order to convey the sequential flow of action through which an accusation unfolds.

Within a day or two after a death, people begin to speculate upon the identity of the witch in open group conversation. A person may say that he or she heard from an unidentified party close to the case that the deceased named X in his or her last words or that the pandanus oracle revealed that Y was responsible. The pandanus oracle may also be performed by anyone inclined to do so and the results introduced into public discussion. The events of the first days of the mortuary gathering are related insofar as these may provide indications of the identity of the guilty party stemming from corpse movement or undercooked packets of sago. The failure of a particular person to come to the *guano* may also be taken to be significant, since absence may betoken the fear that one's guilt will be revealed. Any known (i.e., previ-ously accused) witches who were in close proximity to the victim at the time of the onset of illness are likely to be mentioned as suspects. I have not heard the names of individuals who have never previously been accused of witch-craft mentioned in these public conversations, although suspicions concern-ing such persons may be broached in more private contexts.

Past séances are also a source of information. For example, in early February 1969, one of Nogobe's spirits warned that a particular witch, Nomaya, was active in the vicinity of Kaburusato longhouse at night. No-maya, who had been accused of causing three deaths in the past four years, had recently moved from the Ingiribisato longhouse community to Sarado, within shouting distance of Kaburusato. Not long after this warning was issued, a group of people from Kaburusato who were out late at night captur-ing frogs heard sounds of cracking twigs. They fled back to the longhouse in much agitation, fearing witchcraft. It was speculated that Nomaya was the lurking witch, as Nogobe's spirits had forewarned. Five months later, when three individuals from Sarado drowned in a tragic accident, the name of Nomaya immediately came to the fore.

Although this case was extraordinary in many respects, it provides an instructive illustration of the role of open community discussion in shaping public opinion. It was said that Wasagaya had taken a sweet potato from Nomaya's garden and cooked it thoroughly but, strangely enough, it remained raw and he vomited after eating a bite. Other people's food was said to have remained uncannily raw when Nomaya cut the firewood with which it had been cooked. These events were related on the same day the bodies of the three were recovered. (They had gone out in the middle of the night to capture a litter of pigs and bring them back to the longhouse for domestication [see Kelly 1988]. While crossing a large river, three of four people in the party were swept away by a flash flood caused by heavy rain on the high peaks of Mt. Sisa.)

On the following morning, Ibo reported that he had seen Nomaya in a dream. Ibo was walking up the trail to Nomaya's garden house and saw Nomaya gnawing on something. When Nomaya noticed Ibo approaching, he tried to conceal what he was eating, but not quickly enough, for Ibo saw clearly it was a raw human heart dripping with blood. This exceptionally vivid testimony was all the more compelling in that it came from a respected *tafidilo*. Although laymen are incapable of seeing acts of witchcraft (which are visible only to *Kesame* and *Sigisato* spirits), they can see persuasive circumstantial evidence pertaining to acts of witchcraft when they enter the *ausulubo* plane of existence in dreams. While Ibo's dream was therefore not entirely equivalent to the indictment of an entranced medium's spirit, in that it lacked the supernatural authority of a spirit pronouncement, it was nevertheless utterly damning. The dream was widely retold and solidified the groundswell of public opinion that seems to have begun with Wasagaya's story of vomiting the sweet potato from Nomaya's garden. Wasagaya (aged 16) was the younger brother of one of the young men who drowned. He was also the only member of the party of four who survived.[8] (However, it should be noted that in this case, as in other sudden accidental deaths, the victims uttered no last words identifying the witch.)

By the afternoon of this second day after the bodies were recovered, everyone was convinced that Nomaya was responsible, and many said outright that he should be killed. The brother of one of the victims announced his intention to carry out the execution. Public opinion was thus entirely formed before the séances connected with the mortuary gathering had progressed beyond the point of recruiting the spirits to track the witch. In a more typical case, there would be a greater degree of interplay between tentative public opinion and the information related in séances.

During a mortuary gathering, séances take place every night for a week or more. The medium or mediums of the community in which the death occurred play a leading role and make the final pronouncement, but mediums from other communities may also take part. In the first séance, the assistance of the senior resident medium's *Kesame* spirits (i.e., spirit wife and spirit son) is solicited. They invariably agree and proceed to search for the tracks of the witch that will lead them to this guilty party's garden house or sago stand (etc.), revealing his or her identity. Although the *ausulubo* of a witch is invisible to laymen, it has mass and therefore cracks twigs underfoot and likewise leaves footprints. The medium's *Kesame* spirits will not have witnessed the fatal acts of witchcraft (else they would have prevented them), but they can return to the scene of the crime and pick up the trail of the perpetrator. The witch's *ausulubo*'s trail must of necessity lead to the place where his or her physical body was sleeping. The medium's *Kesame* spirits may also locate other *Kesame* spirits (not linked to any medium) who did witness the acts of witchcraft. Thus, the medium's spirit wife and spirit son play the role of supernatural detectives, operating on the *ausulubo* plane of existence where the witchcraft took place, and ultimately are able to reconstruct what transpired in considerable detail.[9]

However, this takes time. The first information to be reported in the séances that are conducted during the *guano* thus concerns the characteristics of the footprints and the direction in which they seem to lead. But this information is conveyed in a vague and cryptic form. A trail that passes a waterfall (or whatever) could be any one of a dozen trails known to the audience and many persons may have a broad foot, splayed toes, or a high arch. Moreover, there may be many twists and turns in the witch's trail before a final destination is reached a number of nights later. The early séances thus provide information that requires very substantial interpretive contributions by those who seek to draw specific meanings from it (cf. Knauft 1985a). A medium may thus present the audience with an opportunity to interpretively construct an account in response to a suggestive word-picture that is the equivalent of a Rorschach inkblot. The medium may then embroider upon the emergent interpretation supplied by the audience in subsequent séances. Although the degree to which a medium plays an active role in shaping the interpretation that points to a particular individual's guilt is variable from case to case, there is typically substantial interplay between the medium and the audience. (The cases in which a medium played a more definitive role in the formulation of an accusation and the potential scope of a medium's influence will be discussed further along.)

The typical situation that obtains several days after a death is thus one in which there are myriad sources of information. But these bits of information are either vague and open to multiple interpretations or derived from secondhand reports that are potentially erroneous. The sources include the cryptic information derived from early séances, the indications deducible from corpse movement, allegedly undercooked food, and lack of attendance at the *guano,* and secondhand reports of the deathbed testimony and the results of the pandanus oracle. The information derived from the séances is usually just as pliable as the other sources and provides no clear-cut interpretive keys (although prior séances may have prefigured perceptions). It is thus through open discussion that a dominant interpretation begins to take shape and gather adherents. In this context, an outspoken person may weigh in heavily with a particular point of view (as the preceding discussion illustrates). This might be anyone, male or female, young or old who holds strong views regarding the case. However, the next of kin speak with special authority based on more definitive knowledge (that may be leaked or intimated indirectly before it is publicly revealed) and the opinions of a *tafidilo* are influential by definition (else he would not be accorded this status). The question of who controls the machinery that governs the formulation of witchcraft accusations thus turns on the issue of who shapes public opinion in the open discussions that take place after a death has occurred. However, before addressing this more comprehensively, it will be useful to complete the account of events leading up to a public accusation.

As the *guano* continues, the séances provide progressively more definitive information, although no specific names are revealed before the pig-heart-and-liver oracle is employed. The tempo of the proceedings is dictated by the medium's spirits, who first instruct the next of kin to consult the pandanus oracle (on the first or second night) and subsequently instruct them to consult the pig-organ oracle (on the fourth to as late as the ninth night, but usually the fourth to sixth). This variability in timing is interpretable as the medium's guiding of the proceedings so that they progress in accord with the development of public opinion.[10]

A pig is thus slaughtered, and the heart and liver are each encased in sago wrapped with banana leaves. These two packets are then placed in an earth oven, to the accompaniment of the invocation addressed to the *Sigisato* spirits: "If X is the witch responsible for so-and-so's death, let this heart be raw; if Y . . . , let this liver be raw." As with the pandanus oracle, this is done by the individual who will lodge the public accusation and request compensation (or, alternatively, execute the witch), typically a deceased man's brother or a deceased woman's husband or son. This individual then covers the earth oven with banana leaves so as to steam cook the contents. The pig that supplied the oracular organs is cooked in the earth oven at the same time (although the sides of pork are not encased in sago flour). The meat is parceled out among all who are present at the gathering, and sharing in consumption of the oracular pig entails tacit acceptance of the outcome of the proceedings (Kelly 1988:126).

The two prime suspects are the individuals whose guilt has already been indicated by the pandanus oracle. One of these is also presumed to be the individual named by the deceased. However, neither the identity of the person indicted by the deathbed testimony nor the results of the pandanus oracle have been publicly announced by an authoritative source, so this is implicit rather than explicit. At the time a public accusation is lodged, it will be said that all the evidence consistently pointed to the same guilty party (or parties), but there is no way to know if this is indeed the case.

The pig-organ oracle is distinctively different from these other sources of evidence precisely because it *is* performed publicly. There is no question as to what names were submitted. However, the results are not unambiguous, since the organs are almost never entirely raw or fully cooked. Large numbers of persons from many communities are generally present, including near and distant kin of the deceased and the two prime suspects and their supporters. These suspects seek by their presence to demonstrate their confidence in complete exoneration. They also come to see the results and to register their interpretation of them. As might be expected, they generally perceive the organs to be adequately cooked, while others do not. What transpires then is that public opinion dictates a prevailing interpretation of the outcome: adequately cooked (*nesi*) or "raw" (*kahe*), i.e., undercooked, with respect to each organ. At the séance that takes place that night, this predominant view will be ratified by a *Sigisato* spirit speaking through an entranced medium. Since the *Sigisato* spirits determine the outcome, their pronouncement cannot legitimately be disputed by the alleged witch, even though he or she may have insisted that the organ was *nesi* at the time the packet was unwrapped. Ambiguity has become certainty.

However, the intervening ambiguity, and the empowerment of public opinion this entails, protects a suspect from an accusation that is not well supported by community members. Thus, when a twice-accused witch's mother died, this notorious witch (Tame) was unable to lodge an effective retaliatory accusation against the man (Hariako) who had most recently accused him of witchcraft. Tame was reduced to performing the pig-organ oracle in private in order to control the interpretation of the outcome, but the results consequently lacked credibility or public backing. The spirits of a medium related to Tame as mother's brother purportedly authenticated the guilt of the accused, but this medium resided at a longhouse community of the neighboring Petamini tribe and therefore did not have proper jurisdiction in the case (i.e., was not the resident medium of the deceased's community). The spirits of the appropriate medium (Nogobe) completely exonerated Hariako. Moreover, Tame's own father, Nawa—who was the husband of the deceased woman and therefore equally entitled to serve as a principal in the case—contradicted Tame with respect to the deathbed testimony. Nawa said publicly that his wife died without ever naming a witch, while Tame maintained that she explicitly named Hariako. This case shows how utterly ineffectual the self-interested engineering of an accusation can be. The main point, however, is that the machinery by which an effective accusation is formulated is very responsive to public opinion. The outcome of a credible pig-organ oracle requires collective substantiation by those present, the medium who has jurisdiction is constrained by the views of his constituency, and the individuals who were in a position to hear the deathbed testimony must be in complete agreement. These constraints will be explored in more detail further along.

At the séance held the night after the pig-organ oracle is performed, the medium's *Kesame* spirits come and confirm that the individual they have tracked is indeed the guilty party indicated by the oracle. Subsequently, the medium's *Sigisato* comes to verify the oracular outcome per se. This is the first time during the *guano* séances that the *Sigisato* appears, and the two sources of spiritual authority are thus shown to be in complete agreement as to the identity of the witch responsible for the death. This spiritual consensus provides a model for social consensus. This is amplified by the testimony of the spirits of other mediums. If there is a second medium who resides at the longhouse of the deceased, his *Kesame* and *Sigisato* spirits will now enter his body in sequence and confirm the guilt of the designated witch. When two mediums coreside, they are typically related as spiritual mentor and protégé, and the second medium to enter trance will be the latter. Next, other mediums of neighboring communities that are in attendance at the *guano* may take their turn. These, too, may be related to the resident medium by the lines of transmission of spiritual knowledge. (These relations will be discussed in the next chapter.) An impressive weight of spiritual authority is thus marshaled in support of the verdict.

If the deceased's next of kin who serves as principal in the inquest desires to execute the witch rather than seek compensation, he should request the permission of the *Sigisato* spirits. This request may be put to the senior resident medium's *Sigisato* spirit during the final séance of the *guano*. The petitioner says, "We want to kill this person because he (she) is a witch who has killed many people." The *Sigisato* may then say, "I give you this man (woman) to kill." Or he may decline to grant this permission. In the case of the three drownings attributed to Nomaya, this request was made and permission granted by the *Sigisato*. Nomaya's guilt in these cases brought the total number of deaths attributed to his witchcraft to six in a four-year period, demonstrating his irredeemable recidivism.

The pig-organ oracle admits of several possible outcomes. If both the heart and liver are judged to be adequately cooked (*nesi*), it is generally presumed that the oracle was improperly performed. This question is put to the resident medium's *Sigisato* spirit. In Nomaya's case, in which this occurred, the spirit confirmed that procedural errors were made. The pig slaughtered to obtain the organs was said to have been too small. The *Sigisato* thus instructed that a large pig be slaughtered and the oracle performed once again. This time the oracle indicated Nomaya's guilt at the same time that a second suspect was exonerated. The credibility of the oracle is enhanced by its capacity to discriminate in this manner; one person is proven to be innocent at the same time another person's guilt is established. This is the typical verdict of a properly performed oracle. However, there is also the possibility that both the heart and liver will be deemed to be "raw" (*kahe*). In this case the two suspects are adjudged to have been coconspirators. It is believed that one ate the heart of the victim and the other ate the liver, so that both are guilty in equal measure. In the thirty-five deaths in the sample that eventuated in witchcraft accusations, the guilt of two coconspiring witches was oracularly determined in six cases (or 17 percent of the total). In three cases, the coconspirators were a pair of men, and in three cases a man and woman. Thus the theme of male-female cooperative endeavor extends into the realm of witchcraft. Male-female cooperative complementarity is also manifest in the relations between spirits (e.g., *Kesame* spirit wife and spirit son) and in the relation between humans and spirits (e.g., medium and spirit wife).

The deaths (other than witch executions) that do not eventuate in a witchcraft accusation are attributable to unusual conditions arising from epidemic mortality. In the typical situation, the community in which these deaths occurred is significantly depleted by such mortality. The persons who have died include the senior resident medium and many of the next of kin who might be expected to press for an inquest and forward the formulation of an accusation. A relatively inexperienced medium, or one of another community, is then left with an extraordinary caseload. He takes up these cases one by one, acting first upon those of important persons and proceeding to those for which there is an insistent next of kin. As the accusations unfold, executions are carried out, and some accused persons flee without paying compensation and take refuge with kinsmen living among the Petamini tribe. The remaining cases are never subject to spiritual inquiry or final oracular determination of the guilty witch's identity and thus result in no public accusations. However, the surviving next of kin (who are often not close kin) believe that an already-named witch is responsible for their own kinsman or kinswoman's death as well. Inasmuch as the suspected witch is either dead or has fled, there is little point in pursuing the case to a formal conclusion.

This description applies to the communities of Katiefi and Haifi in 1969. In the epidemic in January of that year, twelve individuals in these two neighboring communities died in the space of two weeks (out of a total combined population of sixty-five persons). The Haifi longhouse was abandoned, and most of the former residents moved to Katiefi. Piawe, the senior medium who had served both communities, was among those who died in this epidemic. It thus fell to Piawe's protégé, Wato, to conduct a spiritual inquiry into ten adult deaths. Wato, who was in his early 20s, had only acted as Piawe's second up until this time and had never conducted a witchcraft inquest on his own. He processed seven cases in the next several months but took no further action in the following four months. Three cases thus resulted in no formal determination of the witch responsible for the death. A very similar pattern obtained at Hilisato where the senior resident medium also died, leaving two novice protégés in their early 20s to assume his duties. Two of five adult deaths were never addressed. In all, one adult male death and four adult female deaths in these three communities did not eventuate in witchcraft accusations, while six adult male and four adult female deaths did. There is a definite tendency to consider the deaths of important senior men before others. Each of the two novice mediums took up the case of his deceased mentor before considering other deaths that occurred at about the same time. Overall, 88.5 percent (23/26) of adult male deaths and 61.1 percent (11/18) of adult female deaths due to illness or accident led to a public accusation during the four-year period from mid-1965 to July 31, 1969. (See n. 5 for a discussion of this sample.) The total for both adult male and adult female deaths combined is 75.5 percent (34/44). When the deaths that occur within a community are spread out over time, they are more likely to result in public witchcraft accusations. Child deaths also may occasionally eventuate in an accusation under these circumstances. Epidemic mortality thus reduces both the proportion of illness deaths that result in an accusation and the proportion of such deaths that eventually lead to an execution (cf. Knauft 1985a). Increased illness deaths and the resultant dilution of homicides as a proportion of total deaths also decrease the homicide rate, although this rate is nevertheless quite high (see n. 11).

THE RESOLUTION OF WITCHCRAFT ACCUSATIONS

Once the identity of the witch responsible for a particular death has been oracularly determined and confirmed by a medium's spirits, there are two possible courses of action the principal next of kin may take. He (always a male) may lodge a public accusation and request for compensation, or he may elect blood vengeance. Etoro thinking with regard to these alternatives takes the posited emotional state of the next of kin as the point of departure. It is presumed that this central actor is filled with grief and anger and that vengeance offers an emotionally satisfying resolution of these feelings. Compensation is thus envisioned as acting directly upon the next of kin's emotional state. The transfer of compensation conveys the accused witch's empathy and commiseration with the grief and sorrow of the next of kin, which he (and others) have publicly expressed in weeping at the burial platform of the deceased. The payment of compensation is thus taken to indicate the remorse of an accused witch, who also tacitly admits his or her guilt (at least provisionally, as explained below). In other words, the emotional state of an accused witch who agrees to pay compensation is also posited, and the meaning of compensation resides in this imputed dialogue of emotions between accuser and accused. By further extension of this same cultural logic, the next of kin acknowledges the remorseful and empathetic gesture of the accused by accepting the promise of compensation and subsequently redistributing this to those who share his grief when it is received. It is likewise posited that the next of kin's anger is assuaged by the accused witch's empathetic response to his loss. The desire for vengeance is thus extinguished. There is no notion that a compensation payment is equivalent in value to a life, or that it funds a bridewealth payment and thus provides a mechanism for the replacement of a loss to the social group (e.g., lineage). The meaning of the transaction is grounded in a currency of emotions rather than one of person-equivalent stocks of valuables.

The rejection of a request for compensation is also informed by the meanings elucidated above. The alleged witch is held to be remorseless and lacking in sympathy for the emotional suffering of the deceased's next of kin. Moreover, the request for compensation is construed as a generous offer, compared to the alternative of retribution, and this has been refused. On both these grounds the next of kin's anger is considered to be justly inflamed. While the alternative of killing the witch is regarded as justifiable at the onset, it takes on added dimensions of legitimacy once compensation is refused. The remorseless witch appears all the more cruel, malicious, selfish, self-centered, and antisocial. This is, of course, entirely consistent with the generic character traits of a witch (attributable to the mutation of the soul represented by the *tohorora*) and lends additional weight to the already-substantial evidence of guilt. Moreover, an alleged witch who denies that he or she is indeed a witch, in conjunction with a refusal to pay compensation, cannot promise to exert control over the inherent propensity to harm others that derives from the *tohorora*. The expression of remorse through the payment of compensation lays the groundwork for the foreswearance of future acts of witchcraft, while the refusal to pay compensation betokens the continuation of evildoing. The remorseless and unrepentant witch is deemed likely to kill again and again. Execution at this juncture thus constitutes a public service to fellow tribesmen in addition to providing individual emotional satisfaction through vengeance. At the same time, the alleged witch's social support beyond the range of immediate kin will have been substantially undercut by the imputations that accompany a refusal to pay compensation. In short, the alleged witch will be seen to have acted in precisely the way that onlookers would expect a spiritually deformed, antisocial individualist to act. The propensity to harm others by unseen supernatural means is transposed upon the plane of social relations, where a callous disregard for others is plain to see.

The main point I seek to make here is not that witches are often killed after refusal to pay compensation (as this rarely occurs), but rather that an accused witch is placed in such a position that meeting a request for compensation is preferable to refusal to do so despite the tacit admission of guilt this entails. The only publicly acceptable grounds for refusal to pay compensation are that the accusation is not properly authenticated or that the alleged witch was not in sufficiently close proximity to the victim to have carried out the purported acts of witchcraft. (These will be further elucidated in due course.) The accused witch's heartfelt conviction that he or she is entirely innocent is not acceptable grounds, and refusal to provide compensation on this basis will lead to an erosion of support among those from whom support might otherwise be expected (due to the negative connotations explained above). However, an accused witch can profess innocence at the same time that compensation is paid or promised. The birth oracle, which will subsequently provide a final and irrevocable determination of the guilt or innocence of the accused, provides scope for this course of action.

If the next child born to an accused man and his wife (or an accused woman and her husband) is of the *same* sex as the individual he (or she) is alleged to have killed by witchcraft, the guilt of the accused is confirmed. But if this child is of the sex *opposite* that of the victim, complete innocence is established (irrespective of prior oracular determinations and spirit indictments). The *Sigisato* spirits determine the sex of a child by implanting a male or female *ausulubo* in the fetus, and the outcome of the birth oracle is thus directly attributable to the purposeful action of these spirits. More specifically, the *Sigisato* associated with the child's (and father's) patrilineage is the source of the gendered *ausulubo*. Thus, while an accused person will have been indicted by the statements and oracular outcomes governed by the resident spirit medium's *Sigisato* spirit, the final arbiter of guilt or innocence is a *Sigisato* spirit of the accused's own lineage. This is significant in that it makes the reversal of an earlier spirit indictment intelligible. However, the more important point is that the accused has every reason to have complete confidence in the veracity of his (or her) own lineage spirits and the integrity of the oracle. There is no doubt as to the identity of the witch under oracular consideration, the result is publicly revealed, and the outcome is totally unambiguous. Sexual characteristics are an "empirical fact" and not a matter of interpretation (unlike the question of whether a pig heart is or is not adequately cooked).

The birth oracle precludes any legitimate grounds for refusing to provide requested compensation (when an accusation is properly authenticated), because compensation paid at this time will be returned in the event that the birth oracle subsequently proves the accused innocent. This amplifies the negative connotations attached to the refusal to pay compensation. In Etoro thinking, a person who is convinced of his innocence should pay compensation in recognition of the next of kin's emotional suffering, while stating his confidence in complete exoneration through the birth oracle. The kin and supporters of the accused often promote acquiescence to compensation, and offer to contribute to it, both to avoid the potentiality of armed conflict and because this course of action is clearly in the best interest of the accused. Payment of compensation precludes execution, allows the accused to appear in a comparatively favorable light, and provides scope for future exoneration that is genuinely expected. The greatest concern of those close to the alleged witch (e.g., parents, spouse, and/or siblings) is that he or she will be repeatedly accused, so that execution becomes inevitable. They thus hope that the present accusation can be resolved through compensation in a way that is conducive to deflecting subsequent accusations.

To the deceased victim's next of kin, the payment of compensation conveys a tacit acknowledgment of guilt, irrespective of any protestations of innocence. This is part of what makes compensation "work," in that the principal next of kin receives emotional satisfaction from a transaction that conveys remorse for acknowledged wrongdoing and a gesture of making amends. Moreover, he and his supporters are persuaded in their own minds that the guilt of the accused will assuredly be confirmed by the birth oracle. At the same time, the accused and his or her supporters are confident of eventual exoneration and can easily disregard any tacit acknowledgment of guilt, seeing the compensation as expressing sympathy and serving instrumental ends. This divergence of interpretations allows an inherently conflictual and potentially explosive situation to be neatly resolved. However, it is difficult for the accused not to be stung by the allegation of witchcraft (with all the appalling character defects it conveys) and thus to feel hostility rather than empathy toward his or her accuser. In other words, it is difficult for the alleged witch not to act in an incriminating fashion and thus play the role in which he or she is now cast in a way that confirms the label (and possession of a *tohorora*) in the eyes of fellow tribesmen. In such cases, exoneration by the birth oracle may not preclude subsequent accusations.

Although the birth oracle offers the possibility of exoneration, this is not equally available to all categories of persons. Young women, who marry early, are advantaged compared to young men. A man will normally be in his 30s before his first child is born and may thus have accumulated several witchcraft accusations before he has an opportunity to be cleared. If an individual has been accused of causing both a male and female death before his (or her) first child is born, there is no possibility of unambiguous exoneration. Childless couples, unremarried widows and widowers, and women beyond their reproductive years are also disadvantaged, as are men whose wives are beyond the childbearing period. However, since men are generally ten to fourteen years older than their wives (Kelly 1977:170), and women may bear children in their late 40s, there are few men in this position. The effect of delayed marriage thus works to the disadvantage of young men and the advantage of older men. Conversely, young women are advantaged while older women are disadvantaged. An accused witch is considered guilty until proven innocent, so that one has nothing to lose and a great deal to gain from the birth oracle. The differential availability of potential exoneration thus institutionalizes inequalities among social categories of persons differentiated by age, sex, and marital status. This and other related aspects of the witch-craft complex will be explored more fully after the full sequence of events (diagrammatically presented in fig. 4.1) has been described.

In the 42 instances when an individual was named as the witch (or one of two coconspiring witches) responsible for a death, compensation was paid in 17 cases (40.5 percent) and the witch was killed in 8 (19.0 percent).[11] In 9 cases (21.4 percent), compensation was refused. In 4 other instances (9.5 percent), the witch fled to a neighboring tribe. In 3 cases (7.1 percent), compensation was not requested, and 1 case (2.4 percent) was pending when I departed.

The four cases of flight all involved the same individual, a boy of 14 who was named as the witch responsible for four deaths that occurred during the epidemic of January 1969. Harogo's father and father's brother had been killed as witches only sixteen months earlier, and his sister (aged 4) and father's brother's son (aged 3) were abandoned without food or water and left to die when they contracted influenza during the January epidemic. Both were said to be *kagomano* or witch-children, as was Harogo. There was thus little doubt as to what fate awaited Harogo had he not fled. Nor was it at all certain that he would elude retribution over the long term.

REFUSAL TO PAY COMPENSATION

The witchcraft accusation was not properly authenticated or was otherwise flawed in nearly all the instances when compensation was refused. In two cases, the resident medium's spirits specifically exonerated the suspect, and the evidence against the accused consisted only of the reported deathbed testimony and the purported results of privately performed oracles. In both instances a family member contradicted the accuser with regard to the evidence. As was discussed earlier, Tame's father (Nawa) denied that his deceased wife had named Hariako as the witch responsible for her death as Tame maintained. When Tsmari (a *tafidilo*) accused Kayari of killing his wife Waime by witchcraft, Tsmari's son Maka privately told others that the pig heart cooked to Kayari's name (in private) had not been raw. The spirits of the resident medium (Wato) subsequently affirmed this as well.

Compensation is nearly always refused when the accused was not within about a quarter of a mile of the deceased person just prior to the onset of illness and around the time of death. Although the *ausulubo* of a witch can in theory operate over greater distances according to Etoro beliefs, the accused invariably cites lack of proximity to the scene of the bewitchment as his primary grounds for refusing to pay compensation. Thus when Kayago (a medium) and his brother (Waua) were accused of causing Habwili's death in a community a mile-and-a-half away, they denied any responsibility on these grounds. While Wato's spirits confirmed Kayago's and Waua's guilt at the Katiefi longhouse, Kayago's spirits proclaimed that he and his brother were entirely innocent in séances conducted at Turusato. However, this did not by any means settle the issue of whether or not to pay compensation. The critical question to be decided was whether the men of Turusato would actively support Kayago and Waua if they refused to pay. This question was addressed in an open community discussion that I witnessed. An account of this discussion and the events leading up to it will elucidate a number of important features pertaining to the resolution of witchcraft accusations. However, it is first necessary to explain the coercive manner in which compensation is requested when an unrelated person of another community is accused of witchcraft.

The accuser and his supporters come to the longhouse of the individual to be accused, fully armed and with their faces painted in the colors of anger (black with red markings). Someone with kin or affinal ties to the accuser's community will usually have given warning of this impending visit so they are not unexpected. The armed party is met by the accused and his equally well armed supporters in the clearing in front of the longhouse. When a woman is accused, her brother and/or husband respond to the accusation on her behalf. The accuser then states his case, reciting the evidence of guilt derived from the deathbed testimony, pig-organ oracle, and spirit statements and closing with the request for compensation. In intercommunity accusations such as this, the evidence is often disputed. The accused may say that reliable sources have told him the deceased died without naming a witch, that the pig heart or liver was likewise reliably reported to have been *nesi,* and that the spirits are mistaken (or even that they have lied). The accused closes his refutation by stating that he will not pay compensation. When this refusal is voiced, the accuser and his supporters vent their anger and articulate the threat of execution that lies behind their demand by shooting arrows into the ground just in front of the accused. The accused and his supporters assert their determination not to pay compensation by responding in kind and shooting arrows into the ground in front of the accuser's party. This exchange takes place at the point-blank range of only twenty-five to thirty feet so that, on the one hand, the level of accuracy is high and, on the other hand, there is scant chance of dodging a misplaced arrow. Not uncommonly, someone is wounded by an arrow bouncing off the hard-packed clay in front of the longhouse. One of the deaths in the sample (Hasuan) was due to an infection from a thigh wound caused by an arrow that was inadvertently misfired too high.[12] However, despite these woundings, I know of no instance when the confrontation escalated. I believe that the point-blank range at which this exchange takes place is an effective deterrent, since anyone who shoots to kill would undoubtedly be killed in turn by a volley of many arrows fired in response. (The two parties usually number about six to twelve bowmen each.) Thus the accuser and his party retire after emphatically telling the accused man (or woman's husband and brother) that he or she is marked for death unless the compensation is forthcoming.

If the alleged witch is subsequently killed, this will take place at a sago stand or garden when the individual is accompanied by few or no defenders. There are no instances of this in the sample of forty-two witchcraft cases, but one woman was killed in this way while I was in the field (see n. 11), and I know of another instance a generation earlier. Women are clearly more vulnerable to this type of execution because they are unarmed. Moreover, a woman is not in a position to pay compensation on her own behalf. When a woman is accused of witchcraft, half the compensation is provided by her father or brother and half by her husband. A woman is jurally a minor in these situations since she lacks both the capacity to pay compensation and the capacity to participate in or marshal the show of force necessary to refuse (as well as the capacity to protect herself from the potential consequences of refusal). Her life is quite literally in the hands of her father, brother, and husband. This constitutes another institutionalized inequity of the witchcraft complex. However, a woman's vulnerability to execution is taken into account by her husband and brother, in that compensation is rarely refused when this would put her at risk. While seven of twenty-eight (25 percent) of the men accused of witchcraft refused to provide compensation, this occurred in only two of fourteen (14.3 percent) of the accusations against women. In one of these cases, an affinal relation between the accuser and the woman's husband precluded any risk. In the second case the woman was potentially at risk, especially since compensation was still not paid after she bore a child confirming her guilt.[13] However, no attempt was made on her life while I was in the field (covering fifteen months after her guilt was confirmed). The inequities of the witchcraft complex that put women in a disadvantaged position do not lead to a disproportionate rate of female executions since care is generally taken not to put women at risk. However, the intrinsic disabilities of a woman's position clearly enhance her dependence upon her father, brother, and husband, since she must look to these men to protect her and to resolve witchcraft accusations against her in a way that does not endanger her life. This point will be elaborated in due course.

If an authenticated accusation lodged by someone outside the community is to be met with a refusal to pay compensation, the accused witch will require firm support from his or her kinsmen and coresidents. They will need to back the accused with their armed presence in addition to easily given expressions of verbal support. It would therefore be folly to consider such a refusal without being assured of the requisite support. A community discussion is held to consider the options. Potential supporters may take the position that they are too few in number relative to the party expected to accompany the accuser. They may also say that an amicable settlement through compensation is preferable for the reasons explained earlier. They then argue that their coresident is surely innocent, but the birth oracle will eventually confirm this and the compensation will subsequently be returned. They may express their willingness to contribute to compensation. Individuals who are affinally related to the men of the party expected to come to request compensation are especially likely to take this position, since they do not want to face off against their wife's brothers or sister's husband. On the other hand, there is a strong obligation to back coresidents in armed conflicts with outsiders (see Kelly 1977:212). A man cannot sit out the confrontation and expect his coresidents to support him in the future. Since there are likely to be close kin and affines of the accused who are quite prepared to risk refusal of compensation, a public discussion is necessary to establish an agreed-upon course of action.

Word of the impending accusation against Kayago and Waua first reached Turusato in early February, about a month after Habwili's death. While Mogoya of Turusato was at Katiefi exchanging sides of pork with the medium Wato (his wife's brother), Wato told Mogoya that the deathbed testimony, oracles, and his own spirit's pronouncements indicated Kayago's and Waua's guilt. He also specified the items of compensation requested (four pearl shells, one ax, one pig, and nine cowrie strings). Mogoya related this information on his return. That night Kayago conducted a séance. Kayago's *Kesame* spirits proclaimed that he and Waua were entirely innocent. This implied that the compensation should be refused, but no decisions were made at that time.

A week later Mogoya traveled to Katiefi with his wife, Yagwa, who visited her kin while he harvested pandanus he had previously planted in that vicinity. Yagwa related that Kayago's spirits had exonerated him (and Waua) and that there was no movement toward accumulating compensation. When Mogoya returned to the house, the men of Katiefi were angrily planning an armed confrontation to demand compensation after having agreed on this course of action in community discussion. Wato confronted Mogoya, reiterated the request, threatened to kill Kayago and Waua, and drew his bow on Mogoya to express his anger. This conveyed the point that this affinal relationship would not deter him. Mogoya hurried back to Turusato to report this while Yagwa remained at Katiefi. It was said that she would come later to forewarn Turusato of the impending arrival of the Katiefi men and their allies.

That night another séance was conducted at Turusato, and Kayago's *Kesame* spirits predicted some (undesignated) individuals would be wounded in the forthcoming confrontation. The next day Mogoya consulted the pandanus oracle on the question of whether Kayago and Waua would be killed by Wato and his supporters. The pandanus oracle revealed that Waua would not be killed but Kayago would. This dialogue of spiritual insights preceded the community discussion. In effect, Kayago predicted (through his spirits) that he would receive strong support from his coresidents in refusing compensation, even though it would be a rugged confrontation in which wounds would be incurred. Mogoya, who favored payment, picked up on the theme of the likely casualties and predicted (through the pandanus oracle) that Kayago himself would be killed. This clearly suggested that refusing compensation was not worth the evident risks.

The community discussion regarding compensation occurred later that day. Illawe, who was Kayago's wife's brother, went to Turusato from the neighboring community of Kaburusato to learn of the latest developments and offer support; I accompanied him. (See fig. 4.2 regarding the genealogical relations among the participants in the discussion named below).

Mogoya did not directly advocate paying the compensation in so many words, but he argued for this indirectly by playing up the extent of the threat. He said Wato was lining up supporters at Haifi and in the neighboring Petamini communities of Sedado and Modoa. He named nineteen men he expected to come, this being an exceptionally large number. The *tafidilo* Ahoa questioned this estimate. Ahoa, who was Kayago's and Waua's sister's husband, strongly and explicitly advocated refusal to pay compensation. He portrayed the request as sheer extortion, given the obvious innocence of the two men (who were far removed from the scene of the bewitchment). Since the men of Turusato were all kin and affines of Kayago and Waua who would be expected to contribute to any compensation that was paid, this portrayal suggested that they were all being affronted by extortion and should resist. Ahoa was far more emphatic and outspoken than anyone else present. Tagili obliquely and tentatively supported Mogoya's position but spoke haltingly, was interrupted by Ahoa, and desisted. (Tagili, aged 26, was married to Kayago's father's brother's daughter, but Wato was his mother's brother's son.) Two of Kayago and Waua's agnates (Osiama and Araradado) and one

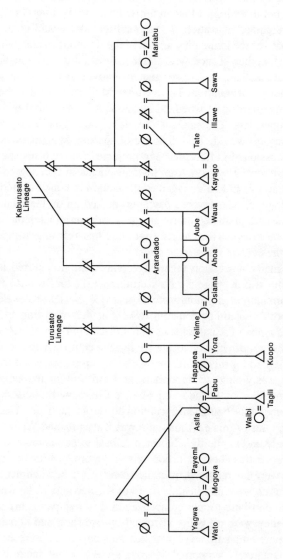

Fig. 4.2. Genealogical relations among Turusato men considering the issue of compensation

affine (Kuopo) indicated their active support for Ahoa's position by saying, "Truly." Neither Mogoya nor Tagili sought to restate and amplify his views (as Ahoa had), so it was understood that they had acceded to the course of action that Ahoa articulately advocated and others supported. Both Kayago and Waua absented themselves from the discussion, going off into the adjacent garden just out of earshot to smoke while awaiting the outcome. The women of the community were present but largely remained silent. However, Kayago's wife Tate spoke to amplify Ahoa's point that her husband and Waua were clearly innocent, noting their whereabouts at the time Habwili sickened and died. Yora and Mariabu, who were both semiretired *tafidilos* in their late 50s, did not enter into the discussion. Nor did Mogoya's older brother Pabu, whose recently deceased wife was Wato's father's sister. Their silence was taken to indicate assent (according to Illawe), since otherwise they would have raised objections to Ahoa's position. The refusal of compensation was the only course of action explicitly advocated, and assent was signaled by the failure to question the wisdom of this, once it had been put forward, and by the failure to argue for an alternative. Thus, it was decided to refuse compensation and the talk turned to recruiting outside support. Illawe said he would go back to Kaburusato to get his bow and arrows and then return, bringing his older brother Sawa and possibly others with him.[14]

Although a few supporters gathered at Turusato, they dispersed after several days when the expected confrontation failed to take place. A few weeks later, when the ranks of Kayago's and Waua's supporters were depleted by a trip to the patrol post (to carry in my supplies), Wato, Habwili's son, and a few supporters arrived unexpectedly at Turusato to demand the compensation. This was refused. However, none of the half-dozen men on either side was injured during the exchange of arrows (shot into the ground as explained earlier). Death threats were made but were not carried out during the remaining five months I was in the field. By the time of my departure, nothing further was expected to happen until Kayago's wife gave birth to a child, providing a definitive index of his guilt or innocence. Kayago (age 29) was recently married, and his wife Tate (age 17) would be expected to bear a child in three or four years. Waua (age 31) was betrothed to a girl of 12 and would not father his first child for eight or nine years. However, it was expected that the claim to compensation would be reasserted at these later dates if the birth oracle subsequently indicated that either one or both of these two men were guilty. A decision as to whether or not to pay the compensation would then be made once again at that time.

The positions taken by individuals in the public discussion concerning the decision on compensation are almost entirely predictable in terms of affinal relations. Ahoa and Mogoya, whose views diverged, are half-brothers. However, Ahoa was the sister's husband of the accused and

Mogoya was sister's husband of the accuser (see fig. 4.2). It is entirely typical that witchcraft accusations engender affinal alignments that segregate agnates (see Kelly 1977:76–77).

This case is informative with respect to the role of spirit mediums. Wato's actions illustrate the activist end of the spectrum of possibilities. Habwili's next of kin was his son Kayupa (married and in his late 20s). Wato was Habwili's father's father's brother's son's son. However, Wato not only named the two witches (through his spirits), but also served as principal accuser, conveying the original request for compensation and attempting to line up participants for the armed party that came to demand that it be paid. Wato, who was only 21 and unmarried, had just succeeded to the position of senior medium at the community of Katiefi following Piawe's death less than a month earlier. He had come to Katiefi only a few weeks before with the remnants of the disbanded community of Haifi. Habwili had been a *tafidilo* at Haifi, and this was the first accusation in which Wato served as the senior resident medium. Thus one may speculate that he was touchy about the disregard for his spiritual authority that the refusal of compensation implied and anxious that his coresidents back the accusation and demand for compensation with an armed show of force.[15] However, there are other instances in which a medium played a very active role in the resolution of an accusation, so Wato's activism is not reducible to special circumstances.

In contrast, Kayago was entirely passive in the domain of this-worldly social practice. While his spirits made pronouncements and predictions that were obviously in accordance with his interests and predilections, he did nothing *in person* to advance these. Thus he did not directly solicit or appeal for support, as he well might have, but left his coresidents to decide this in his absence. From the standpoint of Etoro belief, he was also absent from the séances at which his spirit proclaimed him innocent.

Events at Turusato illustrate the point that mediums do not have a monopoly on spiritual knowledge. While Kayago predicted through his spirits that he would receive the support that he desired in refusing compensation, Mogoya had recourse to the pandanus oracle to generate spiritual knowledge conducive to a decision to pay the compensation. We also saw earlier that Ibo related a dream that was the analogue of a spirit pronouncement, indicting Nomaya prior to any definitive pronouncement by a medium. This is relevant to an overall assessment of the role of mediums, which will be developed in due course.

The relatively few cases in which compensation was not requested all involved close relationships between the principal next of kin and potential compensators. When Hamone died, his son's wife Waime was named. However, Hamone's son was both the principal next of kin due to receive compensation and the individual required (together with Waime's brother) to pay it. While compensation was out of the question, the marriage ended in divorce within a year. The accusation against Waime reflected poor relations between her and her husband's closest kinsmen. When Yebe died, the principal next of kin was his wife's son by her previous marriage, Selagu. Tumame was named. However, she was the wife of Selagu's foster father's brother and the sister of his future wife's father (i.e., father of his betrothed). When Siari died, his father's brother's son's daughter Nawadia was named. The individuals responsible in the event of compensation were thus Siari's surviving brother's close agnate (father's brother's son) and classificatory daughter's husband. All these cases (entailing no request for compensation) involved accusation against women because it is in such instances that close kin or affines may stand as both principal next of kin and potential compensators.[16]

The three cases in which compensation was not requested document the point that specific accusations may well be contrary to the interests of the principal next of kin (and formal accuser). In all these instances, it appears that the deceased's deathbed testimony eventuated in an accusation that was socially disruptive for the surviving next of kin. The accusation was nevertheless lodged due to belief in the authenticity of the testimony and regard for the deceased's last words.

WITCH EXECUTIONS

The cases resolved by execution of the witch rather than a request for compensation remain to be discussed. The impending execution of Nomaya (described earlier) is prototypical of the spiritually sanctioned execution. Nomaya (age 34) had previously been accused of causing three deaths and now stood accused of causing three more. All the appropriate oracles had been performed, and the spirits of several mediums had confirmed his guilt. These mediums included not only the resident medium of the community where the deaths occurred (Nasu) but also the medium of Nomaya's natal community, from which Nomaya had recently moved. The latter medium, Wabiaka, came to the *guano* and ratified the findings of his colleague, Nasu (as did Nogobe). Wabiaka was Nomaya's father's brother's son. Nomaya was estranged from his closest kin, who were weary of being repeatedly called upon to support him and contribute to compensation on his behalf. Their relations with others had been impaired as a result of being drawn into conflicts stemming from accusations against Nomaya. Thus, he was the only man who permanently lived apart from his true brothers, one of whom was the leading *tafidilo* of his natal community. He also had no close kin or affines at Sarado, where he had taken up residence.[17] There was considerable public sentiment favoring his execution. At the concluding séance of the mortuary gathering, the next of kin of the deceased asked the *Sigisato* spirit of the entranced resident medium for permission to execute Nomaya, and this was granted. Those present greeted this with exclamations of approval. (See n. 35 regarding the general tenor of Nomaya's social relations.) He was a marked man who would not be taken in by any community and thus had no recourse but to await the inevitable conclusion, alone, at his garden house.

The execution of Udali was similar in many respects. Udali was first accused of witchcraft when she was a recently married young woman of 17, in late 1967. She was living with her parents and husband at Katiefi. Her father was the spirit medium Piawe. The woman she was alleged to have killed by witchcraft was Siebulu (aged 51 to 55), her father's lineage brother's wife (i.e., her classificatory mother). (See fig. 4.3 regarding the genealogical relationships among the individuals discussed here.) Siebulu died during the night without having previously been ill. She reportedly muttered in her sleep that Udali was choking her and then expired. Waime, Siebulu's daughter, was the only auditor of this deathbed testimony. The accusation against Udali was thus initiated by her lineage sister. Udali's guilt was oracularly confirmed by Tiebora, the brother's son of Siebulu's deceased husband. There was never a spirit pronouncement as Piawe was the senior resident medium. However, Piawe and Udali's husband Kulubido promptly paid the requested compensation to Ahoaba, the brother of Siebulu's deceased husband.

This initial accusation against Udali had significant political consequences in that it prompted Piawe's migration from Katiefi to the neighboring community of Haifi. Piawe thus relinquished his position as senior resident medium of Katiefi to Abenamoga, who was Piawe's (deceased) sister's husband but not Piawe's protégé. Abenamoga, who was also married to the daughter of the leading *tafidilo* of Katiefi (Kusuame), had only moved there about a year and a half earlier. The coresidence of two mediums who are not related as mentor and protégé is an unstable arrangement that occurs infrequently and is invariably of brief duration (as discussed in chap. 5). The beneficiaries of Piawe's departure included the *tafidilo* Kusuame, as well as Abenamoga, because Piawe (then aged 45) was in the process of retiring from spirit mediumship and assuming *tafidilo* status. Kusuame (then aged 63 or 64) was the oldest Etoro man accorded *tafidilo* status. He would have initially shared the prerogatives of community leadership with, and been succeeded by, Piawe. Piawe's departure thus had the effect of maintaining and prolonging Kusuame's position as leading (and sole) *tafidilo* of Katiefi and additionally secured the ascension of his daughter's husband to the position of senior resident medium. Although Abenamoga benefited from Piawe's departure by securing this position somewhat earlier than would otherwise

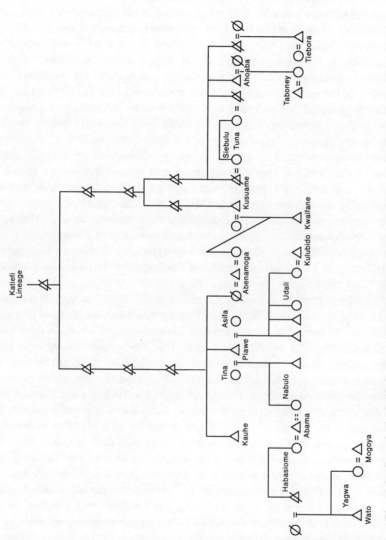

Fig. 4.3. Genealogical relations among selected residents of Katiefi and Haifi involved in the witchcraft accusations against Udali

have been the case, there is no evidence that he played a role in the accusation. Compensation was paid on the basis of the deathbed testimony, confirmed only by the pandanus oracle, and there were no spirit pronouncements by either Piawe or Abenamoga. Moreover, Udali was Abenamoga's (deceased) wife's brother's daughter. There is also no evidence connecting Kusuame to the formulation of the accusation, although it was publicly put forward by his father's brother's son Ahoaba and the latter's son Tiebora and involved a very distant female agnate (Ahoaba's and Kusuame's father's father's father's brother's son's son's son's daughter). The deathbed testimony of the widow Siebulu (who was a member of the production team and hearth group of her deceased husband's brother, Ahoaba) precipitated the accusation. Moreover, there is substantial evidence of ill feeling between Udali and the wives and daughters of her distant agnates, four of whom were instrumental in the formulation of this and subsequent accusations against her. Udali was not appropriately deferential toward kinswomen fifteen or more years her senior. She assumed a grating air of self-importance that was evidently derived from her sense of being the (eldest) child of a very influential spirit medium who had recently attained *tafidilo* status as well. This sense of self-importance was highly inconsistent with respect for seniors, as well as the egalitarian ethos of social relations. (Mediums themselves are typically self-effacing in demeanor; a medium represents himself as only the vessel of important spirits.)

Although the witchcraft accusation against Udali had significant political consequences, there is thus no evidence that it was the result of machinations on the part of the beneficiaries in this instance. (However, in other cases such machinations can be established.) Had Abenamoga sought to amplify the consequences of the accusation, he could have done so through the pronouncements of his spirits, but this did not occur. The consensus view that Udali was indeed the witch responsible for Siebulu's death could have been discreetly promoted by Kusuame, but Udali's unpopularity with the women of the community made this unnecessary as many were prepared to speak against her. Udali's poor social relations with these women constituted the principal cause of the witchcraft accusation against her. However, the frictions in these social relations are attributable to a division between distantly related lineage segments of Katiefi and the ramifications of status inequality between the elite (mediums and *tafidilos*) and nonelite. While Piawe was both a medium and *tafidilo,* Ahoaba (who put forward the accusation) had been passed over for *tafidilo* status. At age 53, he was well beyond the point at which it is typically accorded (circa age 45). Both of these structural factors of lineage division and status inequality pertained most directly to relations among men but were played out in the relations between the women associated with them (as wives and daughters).

While Piawe's influence was significantly diminished, he continued to be the senior medium of Haifi, to which he moved. He had already acted in this capacity for about a year, following the death of Haifi's senior medium Sanimako. The ramifications of status inequality that played a role in this accusation against his daughter therefore did not lead to "leveling" but to a rearrangement of positions among the elite. Although witchcraft accusations constitute an arena of social practice in which all adult members of the society participate, the consequences of practice are encompassed by the hierarchical structure in place. The intrinsically egalitarian nature of such social practice and the leveling potential of witchcraft accusations therefore do not engender egalitarian society, or constitute a social force conducive to this, but only play a role in succession to the influential positions of senior medium and leading *tafidilo* on the part of those already at the apex of the prestige/stigma hierarchy (i.e., mediums and *tafidilos* generally).

While discussion of the political dimensions of witchcraft accusations is largely reserved for chapter 5, these will be introduced when they are an aspect of an accusation that is being considered from another perspective. We thus return to the main theme of the present account, i.e., the sequence of events leading to Udali's execution and the characteristics of cases that eventuate in this conclusion.

Udali was considered to have confessed her guilt and foresworn future acts of witchcraft. Passive confessions like this one are not uncommon. Udali was explicitly asked by Ahoaba if she had eaten Siebulu's heart and liver. She remained silent, eyes downcast, and "did not deny it." This is taken as a confession. She was then asked if she would foreswear future acts of witchcraft and reportedly nodded almost imperceptibly in assent. Udali could alternatively have asserted her innocence and proclaimed her confidence that the birth oracle would confirm this.

Not long after this, Udali and her husband Kulubido moved to Kaburusato, while her father Piawe and his two wives and other unmarried children moved to Haifi. This relocation followed an established pattern as 78.3 percent (18/23) of the accusations involving a coresident witch and victim lead to the departure of the alleged witch (excluding cases resolved by execution).[18] Only a few months later, Kulubido was accused of coconspiring with Tame to cause the death of Hau (a *tafidilo* at Kaburusato). Compensation was requested and paid. Then in July 1968, Kulubido was killed by Pabu (of Turusato) as the witch responsible for Pabu's wife's death (as will be discussed shortly). Udali then moved to Haifi to live with her parents.

During the epidemic of January 1969, there were many deaths at Haifi. Habwili died on the first of the month and then Piawe, Asifa, Waime, Tuna, and Habasiome all died within a ten-day period (January 13 through 22). The initial report reaching Kaburusato was that Udali was named by each and every one of these last five individuals in their deathbed statements. This included Udali's mother, Asifa, and her father, Piawe. This information was supplied by Udali's lineage brother, Kwaifane, who was Kusuame's son. He was residing nearby at Katiefi, but had been at Haifi for Habwili's mortuary gathering when the subsequent deaths occurred. Later, it was said that he had been misinformed, and that only Tuna and Habasiome had named Udali. Nevertheless, the report was indicative of a widespread propensity to attribute the many deaths that had occurred to Udali's witchcraft. The situation was similar to that which obtained prior to the multiple accusations against Nomaya. Although bewitching one's parents was unprecedented, people at Kaburusato were prepared to believe that Udali had done so. She was well known at Kaburusato, where she had recently resided (during the early stages of the fieldwork period).

Tuna was Siebulu's sister and, like the latter, was Udali's father's lineage brother's wife (and classificatory mother) of a distantly related lineage segment. Habasiome was not related to Udali in any direct way, but was a woman of a lineage related to Udali's lineage by matrilateral siblingship (and being in the parental generation was thus a classificatory father's sister). Habasiome was the wife of Abama, whom she had married leviratically after Sanimako's death. Abama was also betrothed to Udali's half sister, Nabulo (aged 14), so Udali was additionally related to Habasiome as the latter's future co-wife's half sister. Habasiome and Udali were coresiding at Haifi, while Tuna had come there from Katiefi for Habwili's mortuary gathering. Habasiome told her husband, Abama, that Udali had bewitched her the first day she sickened. She and Tuna both died three days later, after Wato's spirits proclaimed them incurable. In her last words, Habasiome again named Udali, relating this to her sister's daughter, Yagwa (also Wato's sister). Tuna also named Udali in her last words, relating this to her brother's daughter, Taboney, Udali's lineage sister.

The pig-organ oracle was consulted by Udali's father's brother, Kauhe, with respect to each of these deaths. In each case, Udali's guilt was established. This was then confirmed by Wato's *Sigisato* spirit, who also authorized Udali's execution. This was a general authorization, not one issued in response to a specific request put to Wato's spirit by a member of the audience. That same night Kauhe slit Udali's throat while she slept. It was said that he took it upon himself to carry out the general warrant for execution. He was Udali's closest male kinsman (with the exception of her younger brothers under the age of nine). Like Nomaya, Udali was estranged from her closest agnatic kin at this point and also had no other community to which she might readily go. Her father, mother, and husband were all dead, and Kauhe was the person to whom she would have looked for support, protection, and the payment of compensation on her behalf. The fact that three women of her mother's generation with whom she had lived had accused her of witchcraft in their deathbed testimony was indicative of her relations with older women (as was the credibility of the rumor that her own mother had named her). Two of her elder lineage sisters had also forwarded these accusations by relating this testimony. Estrangement from her lineage brothers as well was indicated by the incriminating rumors that Kwaifane related at Kaburusato.

After the execution, Udali's heart was cut out and impaled on a stake in front of the longhouse. This postmortem examination confirmed her guilt for all to behold. Many individuals from Kaburusato who traveled to Katiefi to inspect it attested that they saw the frogs and worms that are the seeds of witchcraft in the auricles and ventricles, respectively. (I do not know of any cases in which a postmortem examination of a witch's heart failed to confirm his or her guilt.) Udali's body was not consumed, as it would have been traditionally, so that intact skeletal remains could be shown to the Australian patrol officer in the event that someone relayed news of the execution to the patrol post. After the earlier execution of Kulubido, individuals from the neighboring Onanafi tribe had attempted to extort "compensation" from the Etoro at Kaburusato and Turusato (based on extremely distant if not fabricated kin ties to Kulubido) under the threat that they would act as informers. The Etoro refused the "compensation" and vowed to carry out a raid against the community of the Onanafi men who requested it if the threat were enacted. This counterthreat proved effective, and neither case ever came to the attention of the authorities.

After a witchcraft execution, compensation is paid to the witch's next of kin. I do not know of any cases in which this was not done.[19] As executioner, Kauhe was responsible for accumulating the compensation while, as next of kin, he would also be due to receive and redistribute it. However, this did not nullify the necessity for compensation since there were kin of Udali whose grief and loss needed to be addressed. Even though Udali was estranged from her kin and no one disputed the appropriateness of her execution, there was still sadness afterward as kinspersons remembered their relationship to her as a child before she had "made herself a witch." Kauhe contributed nearly 20 percent of the total value of the compensation in cowrie-string equivalents (see table 6.4), and another 45 percent was contributed by four of his five coresident agnates. Most of the remainder was contributed by Kauhe's matrilateral siblings, a cross-cousin, and a mother's brother who all resided elsewhere. The compensation was given to Wato, who was related to Udali as a classificatory matrilateral sibling but who, more significantly, was the shamanic protégé of her father, Piawe. (It is important to keep in mind that from the Etoro viewpoint it was not Wato himself but a *Sigisato* spirit who authorized Udali's execution.) I did not learn exactly who received shares of the compensation, but it was primarily distributed to Udali's kin within and outside the community. Within the Katiefi community, which now included the remnants of Haifi as well as the survivors of an equally decimated Katiefi, the transaction was instrumental in laying the groundwork for the recreation of community in the aftermath of deaths, witchcraft accusations, and retribution.

As was noted earlier, Wato was responsible for conducting spirit inquests into the deaths of ten persons who died at Katiefi and Haifi in January 1969. Two deaths were attributed to Udali, and three to Harogo, who fled to take up residence with relatives among the Petamini tribe in order to elude execution. (Harogo was named in the deaths of Udali's parents, Piawe and Asifa, and in the death of the *tafidilo* Kusuame.) One external accusation was lodged against Kayago and Waua in conjunction with Habwili's death. Tsmari accused his coresident Kayari of bewitching Waime (Tsmari's wife), but Wato's spirits exonerated Kayari. Nevertheless, Kayari moved to Kaburusato with his wife, two widows of his deceased elder brother, and four of the latter's children.[20] Three remaining cases were never subject to spiritual inquiry, although it was widely presumed that either Udali or Harogo was responsible for these deaths. Thus all but one of the ten deaths were directly or indirectly attributed to witches within the compass of the two neighboring communities that were now merged. This was not atypical as most accusations are internal (see n. 18).

Udali's husband Kulubido was executed about six months before she met the same fate. The Etoro often say that "only a witch will marry a witch," and accusations against a husband or wife can potentially cast suspicion on a spouse. In the case of Udali and Kulubido, the process was synergistic. Earlier accusations against Kulubido contributed to the initial accusation against Udali, and the latter contributed to Kulubido's prominence as a suspect in subsequent cases. This led to two closely spaced accusations against Kulubido when the couple lived at Kaburusato (as discussed below) that likewise further enhanced Udali's reputation as a witch when she moved to Haifi after his execution. The Etoro also believe that a witch couple will not submit the witch-children (*kagomano*) they beget to infanticide, so that the offspring of such a couple are also suspect. Although Kulubido and Udali were childless, this belief contributed to the four accusations against Harogo and the deaths of the children Aheo and Taniginiame (as explained further along). It is thus not a rarity that more than one family member may be subject to execution. Fear that the surviving witch will retaliate through witchcraft plays a role in this. As a consequence of these beliefs, an accusation against a man's wife is potentially damaging to his reputation, as well as embroiling him in conflict. Migration following an accusation against a family member also leads to a loss of position as occurred in the cases of the medium Piawe and the *tafidilo* Tsmari (discussed in n. 15).

Kulubido (aged 36) was natally of the neighboring Petamini tribe. It was said that he had been accused of witchcraft at the Petamini community of Sedado before moving to Katiefi to live with his wife Udali and her parents, but no details regarding the number of prior accusations are available. After Udali was accused of bewitching Siebulu, they moved to Kaburusato. He was Tsmari's half sister's son and was related to a number of other men at Kaburusato as a classificatory sister's son or father's sister's son. In November 1967, within two months of his arrival, he was accused of coconspiring with Tame (aged 19) to bring about Hau's death by witchcraft. It is probable that his name was placed before oracles as a second suspect due to his known past history of witchcraft. His guilt (and Tame's) was then confirmed by the spirits of Kayago and Nogobe (Kayago's protégé). Compensation was jointly paid by Kulubido and Tame's father Nawa. Kulubido continued to reside at Kaburusato, probably because he and his wife had no other more-desirable residential options at this time. Moreover, the main animus that arose in connection with the death of the *tafidilo* Hau was directed at Tame (as will be described further along). In contrast, there were no evident hard feelings directed at Kulubido during this early period of my residence at Kaburusato (late April to July 1968). Although Tame's witchcraft was frequently mentioned to me, the fact that Kulubido was also accused of causing Hau's death did not come to light at this time. In notes dating from this period, I described him as "a cranky and ill-tempered individual who seems to have no friends." I recorded his complaints that others did not do their share of the work building the new longhouse. But I have no record of complaints against him, despite the fact that he stood out as a loner.

Pabu's wife Taifa died in late April 1968, at the neighboring community of Turusato. Taifa reportedly told her husband Pabu and son Tagili that she had been bewitched by Kulubido when she encountered him on a trail returning from her garden. She reiterated this before she died two nights later. Kulubido's guilt was later confirmed by the pig-organ oracle and Kayago's spirits. However, no public accusation was ever lodged since Pabu decided that he would kill Kulubido rather than request compensation. He did not ask the permission of the *Sigisato* spirits, nor was a generalized death warrant proclaimed in the context of confirming Kulubido's guilt. Moreover, there was no public sentiment favoring execution at Turusato. Pabu's decision was thus an individual matter. The next of kin is not constrained to seek compensation rather than retribution but is free to choose between these alternatives. Moreover, a spirit injunction to "kill all witches" is a standard refrain of every séance, so that execution is spiritually licensed by this blanket authorization even though a specific request should nevertheless be made (and can, in theory, be denied). After the execution, Kayago's *Sigisato* expressed approval.

Although Pabu's intentions were known to Turusato residents, no specific warnings reached Kulubido at Kaburusato. However, there was a séance conducted by Kayago at Kaburusato in late June at which his *Sigisato* spirit made a dire prophecy: "One man of Kaburusato—I see him [i.e., know his identity] but you do not see him—mark my words well for he will die within one moon." This was retroactively said to have foretold Kulubido's death, but my informants maintained that no one at Kaburusato knew that he was the individual marked for death at the time this prediction was issued. Indeed, a death due to witchcraft rather than homicide was anticipated at that time.

On about July 15, two and one-half months after Taifa's death, Pabu invited Kulubido to his garden house to share some game. Later that night, while Kulubido was sleeping, Pabu slit his throat. No one else was present at the garden house during Kulubido's visit, and Pabu acted entirely on his own. At a *kosa* ceremony at the Petamini community of Sedado five days later, Pabu said "I am truly strong (*keloi*), I alone killed Kulubido." Pabu was glowing with the elation of fulfilled vengeance (see plate 3), as he had been very deeply attached to his wife.[21] By this time, Kulubido's guilt had been confirmed by postmortem examination of his heart, and Kayago's *Sigisato* spirit (who had obliquely foretold Kulubido's death a few weeks before) proclaimed his enthusiastic approval of the execution. Pabu later paid an especially large compensation to Tsmari, Kulubido's mother's brother (see table 6.4). Many of the men of Turusato and Kaburusato contributed to this. It was largely redistributed to Kulubido's affines at Haifi and Katiefi, with a portion reaching Kulubido's "brothers" at the Petamini community of Sedado.

The fact that Pabu came to Kulubido's natal community of Sedado for the *kosa* ceremony a few days after killing him was an act of boldness. However, as in the other witch executions, Kulubido was estranged from his agnatic kin. None had contributed to the compensation he accumulated (with Tame) at the time of Hau's death. His "brothers" were therefore quite content to accept compensation for his execution and eschew vengeance, as was Tsmari. Pabu remained on good terms with Tsmari.

About eight months after killing Kulubido, Pabu accused Kayari and the latter's deceased brother's wife, Esopa, of being witches who were additionally responsible for Taifa's death. He demanded compensation. This was uniformly regarded as sheer extortion. Pabu's son Tagili, who had heard Taifa's last words (with Pabu), denied that she had named anyone but

Kulubido. He and others also said the pig heart and liver cooked to Kayari's and Esopa's names by Pabu were *nesi*. Kayago's *Kesame* spirits said Pabu lied and fully exonerated Kayari and Esopa. Despite general support for Kayari (who was now residing at Kaburusato), he paid the compensation demanded. He acknowledged that he did this only because he feared Pabu, who had clearly established his willingness to take vengeance.

There had been ill feeling between Pabu and Kayari for more than twenty years because Pabu had run off with the wife of Kayari's elder brother Kanamabe. They had lived among the Huli for twelve years, returning only after Kanamabe's death. This woman was Asifa, whose death occasioned Kulubido's execution and the accusation against Kayari and Esopa. There was thus a degree of logic in Pabu's thinking that Kayari had a personal motive for bewitching Taifa. Moreover, Kayari had previously been accused of witchcraft. I believe that Kayari was the individual Pabu himself truly wished to accuse, although all the evidence pointed to Kulubido. The case thus illustrates the point that the principal next of kin is not readily able to channel a legitimate accusation against a personal enemy. This would require the complicity of others who heard the deathbed testimony as well as that of the resident medium. It is consequently very difficult to use a witchcraft accusation in the service of a personal vendetta. Thus Pabu did not succeed in damaging Kayari by this accusation, but rather undercut his own social standing. Although Pabu recouped the valuables he had expended in putting together the compensation for Kulubido's execution, those who contributed to Kayari's compensation payment to him resented his illegitimate demand. These included Kayago and Pabu's brother's son, Kuopo. In my view, the potential costs of alienating the spirit medium Kayago and others were much greater than anything Pabu gained. This is to say that the accusation was prompted by Pabu's inability to overcome his grief over his wife's death and is not intelligible in terms of a calculating self-interest. Emotion, not rational calculation, was at work. It is also noteworthy that Pabu was not regarded as a *tafidilo* although he was a senior man of the eligible age group.

Two of the remaining witch executions that occurred during the four-year sample period were carried out in retribution for a single death. These executions are of particular interest because they illustrate the extent to which a medium himself can take decisive action, rather than remaining substantially removed from the unfolding of a witchcraft accusation, through pronouncements made by his spirits, while the medium himself (i.e., his *ausulubo*) is in distant spirit worlds. In late 1967, the *tafidilo* Sia of the Hilisato longhouse community became ill and died four days later. At some point during the illness he named Samabe of Haifi as the witch responsible, relating this to his father's brother's son Saba. Saba conveyed this information to the spirit medium Nagubi. On the second and third nights of the illness, séances were held in which Nagubi's *Kesame* spirits proclaimed that Sia was beyond curing and would die. When Sia did die on the fourth night, Nagubi went forthwith to a garden house where Samabe and his brother Sayaga were staying and slit their throats while they slept. Nagubi carried this out entirely on his own, without consulting Sia's brother Wabulu or Sia's father's brother's son Saba. His spirits subsequently revealed in a séance that they had witnessed the fatal acts of witchcraft performed by both Samabe and Sayaga and had conveyed this information to Nagubi at that time. The spirits also provided ex post facto authorization for the execution. Saba reportedly approved of the execution when he learned of it, despite the fact that Sayaga was his half sister's husband (see fig. 4.4). Sayaga and Samabe were also Nagubi's close kin, namely his father's sister's sons. The exchange relationship between Sia's lineage (Sarado) and Sayaga's and Samabe's lineage (Haifi) was substantially unbalanced in that the former line had given four women and only received one in return. The direction of the accusation thus followed an established pattern in which members of lineages that are substantially delinquent in providing wives in exchange for those received are subject to witchcraft accusations (see Kelly 1977:126). Although Nagubi's lineage (Hilisato) had an equivalent exchange relationship with Haifi, Nagubi himself would have had a direct claim upon Sayaga's daughter, Taniginiame, his father's sister's son's daughter. His actions suggest that he did not anticipate this union. It thus seems likely that dissatisfactions concerning the degree of reciprocity in the exchange of women were an underlying cause of the evident ill feeling and hostility directed against individuals who were closely related by past and present marriages. In addition, there was undoubtedly a prior history of negative relations between Nagubi and his cross-cousins that was more prominent in prompting his actions, but I lack the data necessary to address this point. The case is informative with respect to the role of mediums despite the fact that the data are insufficient to elucidate Nagubi's motives.

After the witch killing Nagubi paid compensation to Habwili, the elder brother of Samabe and Sayaga, who redistributed this to the deceased men's kin, including a number of agnates of Haifi lineage. As in all the other cases of witch execution, this completely resolved the matter and there were no further repercussions.

Although Samabe had not previously been accused of witchcraft, he was said to be a *sa:go* (a category of precocious male witches described in chap. 3). He was only about 14 or 15 years of age. His brother Sayaga (aged 30 to 35) was said to have previously been accused of witchcraft although I lack details on this point. However, Sayaga and his wife Mifa were the parents of Harogo and Taniginiame, who were both said to be *kagomano* or witch-children who were not subject to infanticide because both their parents

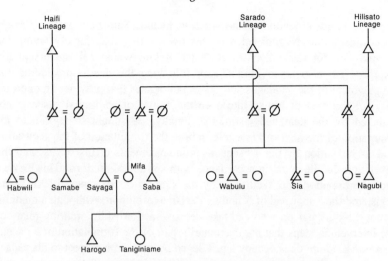

Fig. 4.4. Genealogical relations among individuals involved
in the execution of Sayaga and Samabe

were witches as well. Mifa died in the epidemic of January 1969, Taniginiame was left to perish as a *kagomano*,[22] and Harogo was accused of being responsible for four deaths. This constitutes the second set of accusations and executions involving several members of the same family (noted earlier). The first accusation against Harogo stemmed from the deathbed testimony of Nagubi, who also died in this epidemic. This accusation was quickly authenticated and made public by Arubia, Nagubi's protégé, whereupon Harogo fled. Wato's spirits subsequently identified Harogo as the witch responsible for three additional deaths in his natal community. It is of interest here that Wato did not introduce the names of Saba, Wabulu, or Nagubi's protégé, Arubia, as suspects in any of the many spiritual inquests he conducted in early 1969 but instead followed Nagubi's lead in the multiple indictments against his own agnate Harogo. This was not at all atypical, as reciprocal accusations are very uncommon and once-named witches tend to be named again.

In the typical witchcraft accusation, the resident medium's spirits authenticate the guilt of a suspect whose name has been put forward by the deathbed testimony of the deceased, and the results of the pandanus oracle, and then substantiated by the public pig-organ oracle. Nagubi's execution of Sayaga and Samabe shows the extent to which a medium can actively take control of the formulation of an accusation and its resolution. Sia reportedly named only Samabe in his deathbed statement, while Nagubi expanded this preliminary identification of the witch to include Samabe's brother Sayaga as coconspirator. Nagubi acted on his own, rather than merely laying the groundwork for the actions of the next of kin, whose role he essentially usurped. He also acted immediately following the death, precluding the employment of the pandanus and pig-organ oracles that provides an opportunity for the next of kin to introduce the names of additional suspects not indicted by the deathbed testimony. Finally, he sought to legitimate his usurpation of the next of kin's role in both the formulation of the accusation and its resolution by the subsequent pronouncements of his spirits, and the revelation that he acted in accordance with spiritual directions. This ex post facto legitimation was facilitated by the support of Sia's next of kin, who registered their approval of Nagubi's decisive resolution. Although a medium is not the only person who can take decisive action while omitting many of the intervening steps that are customarily part of the formulation of an accusation, a medium does occupy a privileged position with respect to his capacity to spiritually legitimate his actions. While it is rare that a medium will exploit this privileged position, Nagubi's actions in this case demonstrate the potentiality.

The remaining witchcraft execution that occurred during the sample period entailed nonpayment of compensation. Yo (aged 44) was killed by a Petamini man (Tuamo) in retribution for a death she was alleged to have caused. The details of the accusation, including the gender of the witchcraft victim, are unknown as the accusation originated outside the tribe. (This case is thus part of the sample of deaths but not of the sample of witchcraft accusations, see n. 11.) Yo had previously been accused of coconspiring with Nomaya to cause the death of Saniko at the Ingiribisato longhouse community. There may have been earlier accusations against her as well. In the case of Saniko's death, compensation was paid on Yo's behalf by her husband Fagu and her brother Kauhe (while Nomaya refused to pay the half for which he was responsible as coconspirator). Despite the fact that compensation was paid, Yo was said to fear that she would be reaccused and killed. She therefore joined her brother, Kauhe, at the Petamini community of Sedado (neighboring Katiefi) where he was then residing. Her three children accompanied her. Her husband and his first wife and four children remained at Ingiribisato. Their failure to accommodate her desire to relocate after the accusation is indicative of problems in the co-wife and conjugal relationships.

While at Sedado, Yo was again accused of witchcraft. She and her brother Kauhe then moved to Katiefi (the neighboring longhouse of their natal lineage). The compensation was not paid on this occasion because Yo's husband, Fagu, from whom she was separated, balked at providing the half that was his responsibility. Tuamo then sought retribution. He ambushed

Yo and shot her in the hip with an arrow while she was working in a garden. However, he was then driven off, before he had a chance to dispatch her, by Kauhe and others who came to her defense. Yo then returned to Ingiribisato, to increase the distance between herself and Tuamo to a day's walk. She died there four months later from the wound. Not long thereafter (in November 1968) Tuamo came to Ingiribisato to deliver the homicide compensation payment of two pigs, two pearl shells, and a large (but not precisely recalled) number of cowrie strings. The case came to light when part of the pork was redistributed to kin and affines at Kaburusato. As was noted earlier, compensation is usually paid on a woman's behalf because of female vulnerability to retribution. This did not occur in this instance because Yo was estranged from her husband, and her brothers Kauhe and Piawe were not on good terms with him as a result. They considered her husband Fagu to be partly responsible for her death and did not travel to Ingiribisato to receive their share of the compensation from him. This was relayed to them through others. This was the only case where execution occurred after non-payment of compensation, rather than in lieu of a request for compensation. The case illustrates the extent to which a woman is dependent upon her husband and brother when she is accused of witchcraft.

Witchcraft executions are generally not spontaneous but deliberate, even though the emotional motives of grief and anger that are attributed to the next of kin by the Etoro do appear to very accurately characterize the psychological state of the aggrieved. Pabu bided his time for two-and-one-half months before luring Kulubido to his garden house to kill him. Udali was killed thirteen days after she was first named by Tʉna and Habasiome in their deathbed testimony and twenty days after she was initially believed to have caused five deaths, including those of her own parents. In these cases, and in the case of the impending execution of Nomaya, the full sequence of events that enters into the formulation of a fully authenticated accusation was played out in its entirety, and no precipitous actions were taken. While the execution of Sayaga and Samabe differed in this respect, it is evident that executions characteristically entail "due process" in the form of the publicly performed pig-organ oracle and a measured and protracted spirit inquest that is conducted by a medium so as to be responsive to community sentiment. Moreover, both the execution of Udali and the impending execution of Nomaya were explicitly authorized by the resident medium's spirits before any action was taken. The outcomes were community-inspired, rather than being individualistic acts of vengeance. Pabu's execution of Kulubido differed in that there was no community sentiment pushing for this outcome, and no explicit spiritual authorization was sought or given. However, Kayago's *Sigisato* spirit's foretelling of Kulubido's death clearly entailed an implicit legitimation of Pabu's intended course of action. Even Nagubi's ex post facto spiritual authorization of his actions shows the significance of spiritual legitimation. This form of legitimation clearly represents witchcraft executions as acts that transcend the mere playing out of individual grief and anger. The killing of a witch in just retribution is thus conceived as quite opposite in character from the individualistic witch's consumption of his or her victim's life force, which is perceived to be motivated by malice, greed, and selfishness.

The public display of the executed witch's heart, which invariably confirms the presence of a glowing *tohorora* and the seed of witchcraft, serves to further legitimate and justify the action that has been taken to fellow tribesmen. In all these respects, there is a strong emphasis on the theme that social justice has been done. Moreover, I do not think I would be reading unwarranted meanings into this dramatic public display of the executed witch's heart to say that there is also a sense of the triumph of good over evil. The ranks of the agents of death have been visibly depleted, and anyone who has lost a relative to witchcraft can share in the satisfaction of just retribution. The witch's heart has been ripped out, just as the witch ripped out the heart of his or her victim causing the victim's demise. The justice of *lex talionis* has been realized.[23] At another level, the witch's heart impaled on a stake is a depersonalized icon of evil rendered powerless. The *tohorora* is also separated from the *ausulubo* by this act of excision, so that the witch's soul goes to the afterlife purified of evil. The execution of a witch and display of the excised heart thus doubly defeat death by destroying its agent and banishing the underlying cause of death from the afterworld to secure immortality for humankind. Witch killing is a morally uplifting religious act carried out at the behest of the *Sigisato* spirits.

Available data clearly indicate that the ultimate fate of a once-accused witch is eventual execution in most instances, provided that the initial accusation is properly authenticated. In other words, a once-named witch will tend to be named again and again and ultimately killed, whether he or she moves to another community or remains in the community where the first accusation occurred. This ultimate fate is consistent with a central doctrine of Etoro ideology pertaining to witchcraft: witches are a distinctly separate category of human beings that are inherently predisposed to kill others by supernatural means in order to consume their victims' life force. Witches are spiritually deformed by the possession of a *tohorora* and can at most only strive to control and repress their intrinsically evil predispositions for a period of time. Thus the *Sigisato* spirits regularly counsel séance audiences to kill all witches before they are killed by them. A policy of extermination is the logical derivative of the Etoro conceptualization of witches as a category of irredeemably evil persons. Indeed, it is only in death that the *tohorora* is separated from the witch's *hame* and *ausulubo* so that the witch's soul goes to the afterlife as a *Kesame* spirit purified of evil. Thus execution *is* redemption. This doctrine is conducive to the acceptance of execution by the witch's next of kin, and also plays a role in those cases where the next of kin himself kills the witch (as in Kauhe's execution of Udali). The postmortem examination and display of the witch's heart always confirm the presence of a *tohorora,* and I know of only one case where the deceased witch's kin sought to take vengeance for his or her death rather than accepting compensation (see n. 19).

Before presenting the data that document the ultimate fate of a witch, it will be useful to describe the social relations between an accused witch and the members of the community in which the accusation took place, including the mechanisms for the witch's reintegration into this community when he or she does not move to another. Tame of Kaburusato provides an illustrative example.

Tame was first accused of witchcraft in September or October of 1967, when he was about 19 years of age. His age-mate (and distant agnate), Wayoro, had slipped while crossing a flood-swollen torrent and had drowned. Wayoro was with Tame, two other unmarried young men (Hariako and Selagu), and Tame's father, Nawa. Araradado's *Kesame* named Tame as the witch responsible for this death, and Hariako and Selagu both maintained that they had seen Tame staring intently at the rock that turned beneath Wayoro's foot, causing him to fall. Tame stoutly denied his guilt and refused to pay compensation. This did not put him at any significant risk of execution because Wayoro's father, Mariabu, who requested the compensation, was an agnate (and also a matrilateral sibling of Tame's father, Nawa). However, there was considerable resentment over the unpaid compensation. No one other than Nawa supported Tame's decision. Indeed, it is noteworthy that the medium Araradado who indicted Tame was his closest agnatic kinsman outside his immediate family. (Nawa and Araradado were father's brother's sons whose mothers were also sisters; see fig. 4.5.)

A few months later Hariako's brother Hau sickened and died. Hau had been processing sago with Tame and Kulubido. He became ill and returned to the longhouse. On his arrival, he told Hariako, his wife Suagua, and his agnate Tuni that he had been bewitched by Tame. That night Nogobe's *Kesame* pronounced him incurable, and he died the following day. The names of both Tame and Kulubido were placed before the pig-organ oracle, which indicated both had bewitched Hau. Kayago and Nogobe's spirits subsequently confirmed this. (Nogobe is the protégé of Kayago who is the protégé of Araradado.) Tame responded belligerently to this accusation, denied his guilt and once again said he would not pay compensation. This led to an altercation which ended in Tame's being tied to a housepost and threatened with execution. Hariako and others were being actively dissuaded from

Constructing Inequality

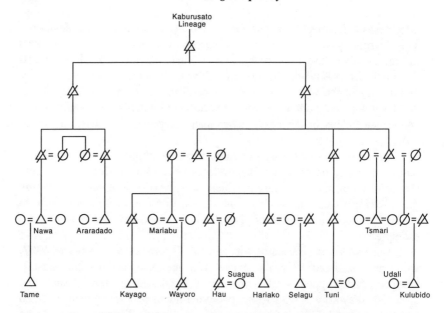

Fig. 4.5. Genealogical relations among individuals involved
in the witchcraft accusations against Tame

killing Tame on the spot when Nawa managed to cut him loose. Nawa and
Tame repaired to their garden house a half-mile away, where they continued
to reside in a state of semiostracism for about a year. When Tame came to
the longhouse at Kaburusato not long after my arrival, he was verbally
taunted and pelted with dirt clods by the boys of the community. Although
the compensation had been paid not long after Tame was threatened, his
earlier belligerent denials of guilt undercut the implicit expression of remorse
that compensation is meant to convey. There was thus a great deal of residual
animosity toward Tame, and I was often told the story of how he killed
Wayoro and Hau by witchcraft.

As time passed, Tame came to the longhouse more often and encountered no further acts of outright antagonism. There were also some friendly
overtures from his close kin, particularly his "mother's brothers" Sawa and
Illawe (who were Tame's mother's co-wife's brothers). However, there were
also slights. On one occasion when Illawe was delousing Tame's hair,
Illawe's father's brother, Kayari, said, "It is right that you should delouse
him, for you are his *nebabo* (mother's brother), but don't look in his eyes."
The clear implication was that even his close kin were not safe from his
witchcraft.

The acceptance of Tame's presence at the longhouse was facilitated by an indirect confession and expression of repentance. Although Tame did not personally acknowledge his guilt and express his remorse, his father Nawa did this on his behalf. Nawa publicly stated that Tame had acknowledged his witchcraft, regretted causing the deaths of his agnates Wayoro and Hau, and foreswore future acts of witchcraft. Although the payment of compensation is taken to convey an acknowledgment of guilt and an expression of remorse, an affirmation of this accompanied by a promise to control one's innate propensity to kill others by witchcraft is generally a precondition for any significant reintegration into the community. However, an individual cannot promise not to commit further acts of witchcraft without acknowledging that he or she is indeed a witch (i.e., possesses a *tohorora*). The communication is rather like admitting that one is an inveterate psychopathic killer who on the one hand acknowledges an unalterable propensity to murder and on the other hand promises to keep this under control. Moreover, confession undercuts the potentiality to claim that one is not a witch if the birth oracle subsequently indicates innocence. People would be free to conclude that the confessed witch is indeed a witch although wrongly accused in that particular case. The need to acknowledge guilt in order to lay the groundwork for reestablishing superficially normal social relations is thus at odds with the hope of exoneration through the birth oracle. The accused witch is thus perfectly double-bound. Taking up residence at another community provides the most favorable resolution of this predicament because the alleged witch may then continue to profess innocence and confidence in exoneration. The new community does not contain the next of kin of the deceased to whom one must express remorse (and thereby acknowledge guilt). This is why the accused witch relocated in nearly 80 percent of the cases. However, a younger person like Tame, whose parents are still alive, will often remain in the community where the accusation was lodged. Older individuals, like Kulubido and Udali, may have already exhausted their residential options and likewise remain in place. Confession, repentance, and the foreswearing of future acts of witchcraft are then virtually obligatory. In the normal course of events, these are elicited from the witch by direct questioning, as in Udali's case (described earlier).

Members of the community are generally prepared to regard a witchcraft accusation as settled once compensation is paid. Resumption of superficially normal social relations by the accused witch is readily attainable if the compensation is graciously paid and accompanied by expressions of remorse and the promise to foreswear future acts of witchcraft. The deceased victim's next of kin implicitly accept these expressions of remorse and regret in accepting compensation. A basis for reintegration into the community is thus established. This normally goes more smoothly than it did for Tame, who never did pay compensation for Wayoro's death and resisted paying compensation for Hau's as well. Moreover, the transparently concocted accusation he lodged against Hariako following his mother's death in the January 1969 epidemic rekindled ill feeling against him. But in other cases the process of reintegration was less troubled. It might even be said that a past accusation was essentially regarded as water under the bridge.

However, a previously accused witch is always vulnerable to being accused again whenever a death occurs in the community in which he or she resides, so that letting bygones be bygones with respect to one act of witch-craft does not preclude a subsequent accusation. A person who possesses a *tohorora* is forever a witch and consequently predisposed to kill others and consume their life force. Such a person is thus automatically a suspect in any local death other than that of a close kinsperson. A known witch's name will very frequently be placed before the oracles as a second suspect, together with the name of the person nominated by the deathbed testimony. Since a double negative outcome is attributed to procedural errors, there is a substantial chance that guilt will be oracularly established. If the possible outcomes of (1) guilty for suspect A and innocent for B, (2) guilty for B and innocent for A, and (3) guilty for both A and B were all equally likely, then any suspect whose name is put before an oracle would have a two out of three chance of being found guilty. This is an oracle that intrinsically tends to confirm the operator's suspicions. Thus a once-named witch tends to be accused again and again. The only significant exception to this pattern entails improperly authenticated or otherwise flawed accusations, such as the accusations against Hariako (by Tame), Kayari (by Tsmari), Kayari and Esopa (by Pabu), and Kayago and Waua (by Wato), all discussed earlier. Since these individuals were believed to be innocent by the members of the communities in which they resided, there is no reason to expect that any of them would come to mind as a suspect when a death occurred within these respective communities. The capacity of a senior resident medium to fail to authenticate the results of oracles and to exonerate an accused individual thus exerts a significant influence on the life course of coresidents.

The question of successive accusations can be elucidated by subdividing the sample (described in n. 5) into the prefieldwork and fieldwork periods. In all, eighteen individuals were accused of witchcraft (for a total of twenty-two accusations) between mid-1965 and May 1, 1968. Two of these individuals were executed during this period. Four other accused witches moved to Petamini communities, so that subsequent accusations against them probably would not have come to my attention. Three more died of illness or accident during the fieldwork period and thus were not exposed to potential accusations after most of the mortality occurred, during the January epidemic. This reduces the list of previously accused witches potentially subject to (knowable) reaccusation during the fifteen-month fieldwork period to nine individuals. Of these, six were accused again and three were not. The latter included Tame, Nawadia, and Tumame. However, the three communities in which these individuals resided all experienced few illness deaths during the fieldwork period. Only Taifa died at Turusato where Tumame resided, and only Tame's mother died of illness at Kaburusato. No one died at Kasayasato where Nawadia lived. Thus, these individuals were subject to almost no situations in which they ran a significant risk of being named. Moreover, Nawadia was in fact widely believed to have bewitched Tame's mother. She was not accused because Tame lodged an unauthenticated accusation against Hariako instead. The residents of Kaburusato who uniformly rejected this accusation against their coresident openly voiced their suspicions regarding Nawadia's probable responsibility for this death. The *tafidilo* Ibo, who is Hariako's sister's husband, was particularly outspoken in forwarding this supposition.

These data suggest that it would only be a matter of time before Tame (aged 20) and Nawadia (aged 24) attracted a third accusation. Tumame's prospects were more positive. Tumame was an older woman (aged 50 to 55), and the frequency of accusations declines after the age of 40. She had only been named once during the four-year sample period, and if there were any earlier accusations against her these had been forgotten. Moreover, the fact that she had been bypassed when Taifa died boded well for the future. It is of interest that Tumame passively confessed in the same manner as Udali (described earlier), and also moved with her husband from Kaburusato to Turusato after the accusation (just as Udali moved from Katiefi to Kaburusato). She had been accused of bewitching Yebe, one of her husband's agnates. Her husband was the *tafidilo* Mariabu who was displaced by this change of residence (as discussed in chap. 5).

Of the six individuals accused during both the prefieldwork and fieldwork periods, four were either executed or marked for execution (Udali, Kulubido, Nomaya, and Yo), while only two survived (Heanome and Nasu). Nomaya (aged 34) was named as the witch responsible for six deaths (with the last three being a simultaneous multiple accusation), Udali (aged 19) was thrice accused, and Kulubido (aged 36) is known to have been accused twice, with earlier accusations within his natal tribe also alleged. The past history of Yo (aged 44) is not well known to me, but she was accused at least twice.

The two reaccused witches that survived had each been named only twice. Heanome (aged 21) fled to her natal community to seek the protection of her father and brothers immediately after the death of her husband's brother Maua, either having gotten wind of his deathbed testimony or assuming that he would accuse her. Her own husband had died the day before, and the data presented here clearly indicate that she correctly assessed the danger she was in. Although witchcraft between spouses is unprecedented, rumors initially attributed her husband's death to her as well. Her situation was thus much the same as Udali's, except that there was a safe refuge to which she could flee.

Nasu (aged 37), who is a spirit medium, remained at Sarado following the second accusation against him. (The first accusation had been lodged when he resided in another community.) However, with Maua's death he became the senior resident medium, with his protégé Ibasia also coresiding. This virtually precluded any well-authenticated internal accusations against him. As was the case with Kayago, the accusation against Nasu during the fieldwork period was instigated by a medium outside the community and was therefore both less damaging and not indicative of internal loss of support. When Susa died at the neighboring community of Hilisato, his wife's brother Arubia was the auditor of Susa's last words (with others) and, in addition, had just begun to assume the position of senior resident medium (succeeding his mentor Nagubi). The activist role of Arubia, who acted as principal accuser, therefore closely parallels the activist role of Wato, who also named a medium of another community in one of his first independent pronouncements. There is a further parallel in that Nasu initially refused to pay compensation, as did Kayago. However, the birth oracle confirmed Nasu's guilt about seven months later, and he then provided the requested compensation. Even so, Nasu did not appear to be significantly at risk of execution in future, despite two prior accusations, due to the fact that he was not vulnerable to internal accusations as a consequence of his position as senior resident medium. On the other hand, the birth oracle's confirmation that he was, in fact, a witch clearly damaged his position as a spiritual authority. Evidence of this will be discussed further along.

In all, a close examination of the question of the ultimate fate of a once-accused witch bears out the point made at the onset. If the initial accusation is properly authenticated, it is highly probable that the witch will be accused again when deaths of individuals who are not close kin occur within the community in which he or she resides. This process then repeats. Eventual execution is the very likely end result, especially if the first accusation occurs when the alleged witch is less than 25 years of age. Thus, of the nine witches accused during the prefieldwork period, four were reaccused and executed while three others would appear to be significantly at risk in future (Nawadia, Tame, and Heanome). If this assessment is accurate, execution would eventually claim 78 percent of these individuals.

Consideration of the witches accused during the prefieldwork period who died of natural causes is also consistent with the general conclusions advanced here. Kusuame was the subject of a single unauthenticated accusation. Tahopi drowned at the early age of 27 and did not have an opportunity to attract additional accusations. Waime did live to the age of 39 after being accused three times in all, but the first accusation against her did not occur until she was 35. However, Waime is the only person other than Harogo who was accused of witchcraft three times and was not eventually executed. If she had not died in the epidemic there is little doubt that she would have been held responsible for some of the deaths that occurred and faced a high risk of execution.

During the fieldwork period, there were nine accusations against six witches accused during the preceding period and twelve accusations against eight individuals that had not been accused in the preceding two-and-three-fourths years. Six of the latter accusations, involving five persons, were not authenticated by the resident spirit medium who had proper jurisdiction (i.e., those against Hariako, Esopa, and Kayari twice) or were flawed due to the lack of proximity between the deceased and the alleged witch (i.e., those against Kayago and Waua). It was not likely that these individuals would be accused again, unless the birth oracle confirmed their guilt. The possible exception would be Kayari, who was said to have been accused before 1965. The other three individuals (Harogo, Hagabu, and Hagua) were all likely to be accused again in accordance with the pattern identified here. At the end of the fieldwork period, there were thus six individuals who would be prime suspects in the event of any local deaths (these three plus Tame, Nawadia, and Heanome), just as there were nine prime suspects at the onset of this

These prime suspects are the persons whose names are likely to be placed before the oracles in addition to that of the individual specified by the deathbed testimony. They essentially form a category of scapegoats, since they may be accused irrespective of the character of their social relationship with the deceased, provided they are not close kin. Being induced to change residence as a result of prior accusations, they are also likely to live in communities where they have few close kinsmen. Kulubido and Nomaya are cases in point. Both were very recent arrivals in the communities where they were accused, and there was no evidence of any prior conflicts or bad feelings between them and the persons they were alleged to have bewitched. The witches in the scapegoat category have no motive other than an incessant hungering after the life force of others that automatically follows from the possession of a *tohorora*. Conversely, a witch accused for the first time generally has a plausible relational motive, since there is no a priori supposition that such an individual possesses a *tohorora*. He or she will likely be nominated by the deathbed testimony. The Etoro expression that a person has "made himself or herself a witch" captures this distinction, in that it is the malice and ill will in an individual's heart that nourish the growth of a *tohorora* from the seed of witchcraft. This malice and ill will are usually relationally expressed. The career of a witch thus entails a transition from an initial, relationally motivated accusation to subsequent, characterologically motivated accusations once the possession of a *tohorora* is established.

By the same token, there are essentially two types of accusations. In all, half (21/42) of the accusations in the sample involved scapegoats who had previously been accused.

There are several exceptions to this typical career trajectory of a witch. These arise from the fact that there are two grounds for establishing an a priori supposition of possession of a *tohorora* when an individual has not previously been accused. A person may be alleged to be a *kagomano* (witch-child from birth) or a *sa:go*. An individual classified in one of these ways is in the same position as a previously accused witch. Harogo, who was said to be a *kagomano*, was thus subject to the simultaneous multiple accusations that are usually reserved for established witches the very first time he was accused. Harogo was only 14 or 15 years of age, as was Samabe, who was said to be a *sa:go*. The latter was killed the first time he was accused, this also being a fate generally reserved for established witches accused several times in succession. There is little doubt that Harogo also would have been killed had he not fled. Only a young male is susceptible to being classified as a *sa:go*, and male children are also statistically more likely to be labeled *kagomano*. They are consequently at greater risk of being included within the scapegoat category susceptible to substantial likelihood of eventual execution. In all, four of the six individuals executed during the four-year sample period were males. Similarly, the six individuals identified as those who would be prime suspects in the event of any local death at the close of the fieldwork period include four males and two females. Since these are the individuals who have a great likelihood of being executed, the sex distribution of executed witches can be expected to be reduplicated over an expanded time period.

The birth oracle holds out the possibility that a properly authenticated accusation can be reversed, so that an exonerated individual avoids becoming known as an established witch and thus escapes being considered as a prime suspect in all local deaths. But in practice, such oracular reprieves are rare. This is due to the fact that an accused witch often attracts multiple accusations before he or she has an opportunity to become the parent of a newborn. In all, the sample includes twenty-seven witches (accused a total of forty-two times). Of these, nine were never-married males and one additional man was widowed. Since men marry late and their young wives do not have their first child until some years later (at 20), it would be many years until the birth oracle could come into play with respect to these individuals. By then they would be likely to have been subject to multiple accusations, so that the child oracle could not effectively clear them (as explained further below). The sample also includes two widows of reproductive age who would likely remarry after the completion of mourning but were not in a position to have immediate recourse to the child oracle. Two other accused female witches were beyond childbearing age, as was the wife of one alleged male witch. This leaves eleven individuals who would be in a position to be subject to the child oracle and thus have an effective opportunity to be exonerated. But of these, five were executed before this could occur. Three other men had not yet fathered their first child but would be expected to do so soon.

The birth oracle had therefore only come into play with respect to three accused witches in the sample. Nasu's wife gave birth to a male child after he had twice been accused of bewitching males, so his guilt was unambiguously confirmed. Nawadia likewise gave birth to a male child after having twice been accused of bewitching males. Waime had been accused of causing one male and two female deaths in a four-year period before giving birth to a male child. This child was taken to confirm that she was indeed a witch, since the first accusation entailed a male death. However, a dispute arose when her husband, Tsmari, demanded that the compensation he had paid for her most recent accusation be returned on the grounds that she had been cleared. (See n. 15 for an account of this dispute.) This points up the ambiguities that arise after multiple accusations involving persons of both sexes. In such instances an accused witch cannot be unambiguously exonerated in the eyes of fellow tribesmen and therefore does not cease to be a prime suspect when deaths occur in future. Thus the ten unmarried male witches are likely to accumulate multiple accusations before fathering a child and have only a very scant chance of exoneration. The sample does include two widows likely to remarry shortly and three men who should soon become fathers. But of these, Heanome has already been accused of two male deaths and Kayari of two female deaths so that several children apiece would be required to completely clear them. Kayari has more to lose than to gain by the outcome of the child oracle, because both the accusations against him were unauthenticated.

Interestingly, the three individuals who have a clear chance of complete exoneration were all subject to unauthenticated accusations and are all believed to be innocent, namely Esopa, Kayago, and Hariako. It thus appears that the birth oracle would actually operate so as to sometimes exonerate those believed to be innocent and to nearly always confirm the guilt of those believed to be true witches. This is because the latter are subject to multiple accusations, so that exoneration is a practical impossibility, while those seen to be innocent and falsely accused are not likely to be accused again before the birth oracle comes into play. This constitutes yet another aspect of legitimacy that the system as a whole attains, even though exoneration must be infrequent. There are no cases of exoneration in the sample (due in part to the relatively short time period this encompasses), and there are only one or two instances in prospect. On the other hand, the three confirmations of guilt that occurred were expected and were eminently believable.

Thus far the account presented in this chapter has focused on the complex, variable and temporally drawn-out sequence of events that is involved in the formulation of witchcraft accusations and their eventual resolution. The dynamics of this process elucidate the influence that the principal next of kin, public opinion, spirit mediums, and *tafidilos* exert upon the assignment of stigma. An understanding of these processual dynamics and structurally situated influences also informs the analysis of the distribution of accusations by age and gender that will be taken up momentarily. However, the political consequences of accusations, which are discussed in more detail in chapter 5, should also be noted here so that they may be kept in mind.

The sample includes three accusations against spirit mediums (Nasu twice, Kayago once), an accusation against the daughter of a spirit medium (Piawe's daughter Udali), and closely spaced accusations against the spirit medium Taipa's coresident mother (Imasala), brother (Warope), and a second brother's wife (Nawadia). The five accusations that involved a coresident witch and victim all led to the migration of the spirit medium to another community (Piawe, Taipa, and Nasu, following the first accusation against him). Other spirit mediums benefited from these departures in each instance, and in two cases (Taipa and Nasu) the beneficiaries authenticated the accusations that prompted relocation. In the two accusations that did not involve a coresident witch and victim, a medium of one community was the principal accuser of a medium of another community in addition to authenticating the accusation (i.e., Wato's accusation against Kayago and his brother Waua and Arubia's against Nasu). There is thus ample evidence that witchcraft accusations play a role in competition between mediums.

In addition, the sample includes two accusations against the (respective) wives of the *tafidilos* Tsmari and Mariabu. Both of these accusations prompted relocation to another community and a consequent loss of position and influence. The migration of Piawe, who was a *tafidilo* as well as a medium, can be included in this set of cases as well. In addition, the *tafidilo* Kusuame was himself accused of witchcraft but did not relocate. Interestingly, three of these four accusations were never authenticated by any medium (the exception being the accusation against Mariabu's wife). Mediums thus tend—through inaction—to ameliorate rather than accentuate the consequences of accusations against *tafidilos* and members of *tafidilos'* families. Although the accusations against Piawe's daughter Udali and Tsmari's wife Waime were not authenticated, both *tafidilos* paid compensation on the basis of the deathbed testimony. Kusuame did not pay compensation (the accusation having been made by an individual other than the next of kin, who himself denied its validity; see n. 16). Compensation was not requested in the case involving Mariabu's wife Tumame since her brother (the *tafidilo* Ibo), who would have been responsible for providing half of it, was the principal next of kin's (i.e., Selagu's) prospective wife's father. An individual does not request compensation from the man to whom he will pay bridewealth, since the bridewealth would then be indirectly funded by a witchcraft accusation.

It is also noteworthy that *tafidilos* are never the principal accusers of other *tafidilos* or members of another *tafidilo*'s family. There is no concrete evidence of competition between *tafidilos,* while competition between mediums is transparent. Thus, while Kusuame benefited from Piawe's departure following the initial accusation against Udali, he played no discernible role in the formulation of this accusation. Ibo became the leading (and sole) *tafidilo* of Kaburusato following the emigration of Tsmari and Mariabu, but he likewise played no role in the accusations against these men's wives. Moreover, Mariabu's wife Tumame is Ibo's sister, and it is implausible that he would have played any part in forwarding an accusation against her. (An accusation against a *tafidilo*'s or medium's sibling is not as consequential as one against a wife or child because it does not generally prompt a change of residence by the *tafidilo* or medium. If the sibling moves to another community, the *tafidilo* or medium who remains is not drawn into conflict with coresidents by any subsequent accusations.)

Conflict between mediums and *tafidilos* is also uncommon. Although the spirit medium Kayago did authenticate the accusation against Mariabu's wife, Kayago moved to the Turusato community where Mariabu took up residence less than a year later and the two men remained on good terms. There are thus no grounds for supposing that Kayago sought to induce Mariabu to leave the community in which Kayago was a practicing medium. Kayago also played a role in the *tafidilo* Tsmari's departure from Kaburusato. When Kayago's mother named Tsmari's wife Waime as the witch responsible for her death, Kayago was unavoidably cast in the role of principal next of kin, and he requested and received compensation from Tsmari. When conflict later arose over the return of this compensation, Kayago accommodated Tsmari's request out of his own resources when those to whom the compensation had been redistributed refused to refund it. Kayago's actions indicate that he sought to ameliorate this conflict. Nevertheless, there is circumstantial evidence that Tsmari subsequently played a role in formulating the flawed and improbable accusation against Kayago and his brother Waua (see n. 15). However, there is no evidence that *tafidilos* were involved in the other accusations against mediums or members of their families.

The relations between the senior resident medium and leading *tafidilo* of a community are typically mutually supportive, rather than competitive or conflictual, so that they jointly constitute a power elite rather than the components of a system of checks and balances. Working in tandem, a senior resident medium and leading *tafidilo* are able to determine the course and outcome of most of the significant events that occur within a community. This is exemplified by the *tafidilo* Ahoa's staunch support for Kayago's refusal of witchcraft compensation when Kayago (his wife's brother) was accused. Ahoa strongly advocated the refusal although this was contrary to the position of his own half brother Mogoya. In contrast, relations between coresident mediums are inherently competitive. Cooperative relations in which intrinsic competition is suppressed very rarely obtain unless coresident mediums are related as mentor and protégé, and competition may also occur between the latter. These aspects of relations between and among members of the elite will be elaborated in chapter 5. However, the eleven politically significant accusations noted here are also relevant to certain features of the overall distribution of accusations by age and gender addressed in the following pages. (The individuals accused in these eleven cases may usefully be listed here, as they serve to label these cases for future reference. They are Kayago, Waua, Udali, Imasala, Warope, Nawadia, Waime, Tumame, Kusuame, and Nasu, who was twice accused.)

THE DISTRIBUTION OF WITCHCRAFT ACCUSATIONS BY AGE AND GENDER

Having described and analyzed the sequence of events that enters into the formulation of a witchcraft accusation and its eventual resolution (as sketched in fig. 4.1), we are now in a position to address the questions posed at the beginning of this chapter regarding witchcraft accusations and inequality. In addition, the extent of the disability imposed by a witchcraft accusation should by now be quite clear. The accused witch not only suffers the psychological distress of being placed in a reviled category but also must draw upon the support of his or her kin in a way that strains these relations. Since accusations are generally within the community, nonimmediate kin are pulled both ways, and the accused witch's relations with them may never be the same again. The witch typically moves to another community, being separated from some kin with whom he or she formerly resided and being less favorably situated in terms of support. The accused witch is also very susceptible to additional accusations that definitely place his or her life in jeopardy. In sum, there is every prospect of a short and unhappy life. Assignment to the stigmatized category of witch thus entails many palpable disadvantages, so that social differentiation in terms of the witch/nonwitch distinction and inequality in the form of concrete disadvantages go hand in hand.

But to whom are these inequities applicable? The distribution of accusations shown in table 4.1 clearly reveals that individuals of either gender over the age of 40 are rarely accused and that males are accused twice as often as females (28 accusations to 14).[24] There are a number of reasons for the preponderance of accusations against males. The most important of these is that there is a strong tendency toward same-sex accusations on the part of males, so that a male witch is four times more likely to be accused than a female witch when a male dies (28 accusations to 7). But when a female dies, a male or female witch is equally likely to be named (7 accusations to 7). The fact that the tendency toward same-sex accusations does not carry over to the female side is due to a substantial degree of male control over the formulation of accusations. Males predominate in the employment of oracular procedures at which they can introduce the names of second suspects in addition to the individual specified by the deathbed testimony. And the spirit pronouncements that authenticate an accusation are made by male mediums. Thus the tendency of women to name female witches on their deathbed is counterbalanced by the tendency of the deceased woman's husband or son to introduce the names of male suspects into the oracular proceedings (as will be documented further along). In addition, there are more male deaths because males comprise a larger proportion of the adult population and also do not live as long as females (see nn. 5 and 7). The median age of thirty-two males who died during the four-year sample period was 38 while the median age of twenty-two females who died during the same period was 48. An imbalance in the age structure favoring males within younger age-groups is thus progressively balanced out by heavier male mortality at later ages, when deaths are much more likely to eventuate in witchcraft accusations. Moreover, 88.5 percent of adult male deaths but only 61.1 percent of adult female deaths due to illness or accident eventuate in an accusation. This is also due to male control over the formulation of accusations which is here evident in the tendency to consider cases involving male deaths before those involving female deaths following periods of heavy epidemic mortality (as explained earlier). The female deaths then do not lead to a formal accusation although they are informally attributed to individuals already accused. The preponder-

TABLE 4.1

The Distribution of Witchcraft Accusations by Age and Sex,
Mid-1965 to July 31, 1969

Age Cohort of Witch	Male Victim/ Male Witch	Male Victim/ Female Witch	Female Victim/ Female Witch	Female Victim/ Male Witch	Total Accusations of Males	Total Accusations of Females	Total Accusations
41–70	1	1	1		1	2	3
31–40	10	2	3	4	14	5	19
21–30	3	4		2	5	4	9
14–20	7		3	1	8	3	11
Total	21	7	7	7	28	14	42

ance of male mortality and the fact that a larger proportion of male deaths result in accusations thus combine with the tendency of male witches to be named for male deaths, so that twice as many males as females are accused of witchcraft. The distribution of executions also parallels the distribution of accusations in that twice as many males (four) as females (two) were killed.

The distribution of witchcraft accusations by age and sex can be more accurately specified by comparing the percentage of total accusations directed against individuals within each sexually differentiated age-group with the percentage of all individuals in the population included within each of these age/sex categories.[25] If individuals were accused in accordance with their proportional representation in the population, the ratio of frequency of accusations to demographic representation would be 1.0 (e.g., 10 percent of total accusations accorded to 10 percent of the population yields 10 divided by 10 or 1.0). A ratio of .5 indicates that the incidence of accusations is only half of the demographically expected value, while a ratio of 2.0 indicates twice as many accusations as would be attributable to proportional representation in the population alone. These ratios are analytically significant because they take into account the fact that there are fewer women than men to accuse as well as fewer accusations against women. The relevant data are presented in table 4.2. These data show that witchcraft accusations are still disproportionately directed against males, although the magnitude of the imbalance evident in table 4.1 is reduced by taking proportional representation in the population into account in table 4.2. The ratio for males as a group is 1.18 while that for females is .78.

Table 4.2 differs from table 4.1 in that it includes younger age-groups not subject to specific witchcraft accusations. However, since two children were left to perish on the grounds that they were *kagomano* (witch-children), I have also expanded the category of accusations to encompass these attributions of witchcraft as well.[26] This reflects the fact that children are at some risk of being placed within the socially differentiated category of witch, although they are never accused of being responsible for specific deaths. However, children of either gender (other than newborns) are rarely labeled *kagomano* as reflected in the low ratios shown in the table. (See n. 26 regarding infanticide of *kagomano* newborns).

The proportional distribution of the witchcraft accusations that are directed against males is in accord with cultural valuations of the phases that characterize the male life cycle in some respects but not others. The generous and beneficent role of senior men—who have depleted themselves through the transmission of precious life force to their protégés and children and a class of initiates—stands in conceptual opposition to the selfish and malicious role of the witch. It is thus expectable that men over the age of 40 who occupy a position at the apex of the moral hierarchy are very rarely accused of witchcraft. (It is also noteworthy that the single accusation that did occur was both flawed and unauthenticated; see n. 16.) This virtual immunity from accusations is applicable not only to *tafidilos* but to all senior men. Given the analogic equation, protégé : inseminator :: witch : victim, it is likewise expectable that adolescent males (aged 14 to 20) would be disproportionately accused. The most despicable evil agent, the *sa:go,* is also a precocious adolescent who is a greedy double recipient of life force (from both mentor and age-mate). The most radical transition in the male life cycle occurs after the completion of initiation (at no later than age 21), when a young man becomes a donor in the intergenerational transmission of life force, charged with the duty to mature both his protégé and the next class of initiates, as a bachelor mentor. The virginal bachelors who are reservoirs of precious life force and paragons of male strength and vitality constitute three-fourths of

TABLE 4.2

The Proportional Distribution of Witchcraft Attributions by Age and Sex,
Mid-1965 to July 31, 1969

Age/Sex Category	Individuals in Population		Attributions of Witchcraft		Attributions as a Percentage of Cohort Population	Ratio: Percentage of Attributions Divided by Percentage of Individuals in Population
	Number	Percentage	Number	Percentage		
Males, aged						
41–70	31	11.2	1	2.3	3.2	.21
31–40	27	9.8	14	31.8	51.9	3.24
21–30	31	11.2	5	11.4	16.1	1.02
14–20	18	6.5	8	18.2	44.3	2.80
0–13	48	17.4	1	2.3	2.1	.13
Total Males	155	56.1	29	66.0	18.7	1.18
Females, aged						
61–70	4	1.4	0	0	0	0
51–60	13	4.7	2	4.5	15.4	.96
31–50	32	11.6	5	11.4	15.6	.98
21–30	25	9.1	4	9.1	16.0	1.00
16–20	9	3.3	3	6.8	33.3	2.06
0–15	38	13.8	1	2.3	2.6	.17
Total Females	121	43.9	15	34.1	12.4	.78
Total Males and Females	276	100.0	44	100.1	15.9	1.00

the 21- to 30 age-group, with recently married men making up the remainder. That the incidence of accusations declines from nearly triple the proportionate rate for adolescents to a level very close to the proportionate rate for bachelors is thus expectable as well. However, the fact that accusations then skyrocket to the most disproportionate level during the ages 31 to 40 is surprising from a cosmological standpoint. A perfect fit between the cosmologically grounded moral hierarchy and the assignment of stigma in practice would entail a continual decline in the proportionate rate of accusations directed against this age-group (to a ratio below 1.0). In this event, the incidence of accusations would be expectably high among recipients of life force and decline gradually among each successive cohort of donors to almost nothing among older men who have been depleted by their generosity. This could be accomplished if ten of the fourteen accusations against men aged 31 to 40 were directed against sexually active, nonreproductive females instead. In other words, men in this age-group draw the accusations that might be expected, on ideological grounds, to be directed against these women. This would also shift the balance of accusations between the genders so that women, rather than men, were disproportionately accused. I will return to the question of why this cosmologically expected outcome does not occur after discussing the pattern of female accusations.

The female age categories employed in table 4.2 are grouped and subdivided so as to reflect ideologically significant transitions in the female life cycle. The category of females aged 16 to 20 comprises young women who are married and also engaged in sexual relations with their husbands but who have not yet borne a child.[27] That these prereproductive young women are subject to twice the proportionate rate of witchcraft accusations (2.06) is expectable. The ratio then declines to 1.00 among women aged 21 to 30, in accordance with the transition to the childbearing period. The ratio also remains at nearly the same level (.98) during the later reproductive years (ages 31 to 50) as well (although disproportionately high and low ratios are applicable to the first and second decades of this age grouping, as is discussed further along). This neutral ratio applicable to women in the *udia totora* category, aged 21 to 50, is entirely consistent with the neutral position of women of reproductive age in the moral hierarchy. The category of females 51 to 60 includes postreproductive women (*udia seli*) who are still sexually active, while women aged 61 to 70 are invariably celibate. It is not surprising that women in the latter group are not accused of witchcraft. However, the ratio of .96 for sexually active, postreproductive women is unexpectedly low given the fact that these women are in the same structural position in relation to the system of life-force transmission as prereproductive women. The analogic equation, (nonreproductive) wife : husband :: witch : victim is equally applicable to both. A perfect fit between cosmologically grounded moral hierarchy and practice would thus entail a higher incidence of accusations directed against both these categories of women. If such a fit were to obtain, the excess accusations directed against males ages 31 to 40 would be allocated among these two groups of women (with a few additional accusations directed against adolescent males aged 14 to 20 as well). Culturally valorized social differentiation that accords qualities of moral unworthiness to adolescent males and sexually active, nonreproductive females would then covary with the stigma and manifest disadvantages that are attendant upon assignment to the category of witch. But as it is, this outcome is only partially realized.

The disjunction evident here follows the contours of the definitional distinctions introduced at the beginning of chapter 3. Social differentiation in terms of cultural age and gender is inextricably interwoven with differential moral evaluations that are embedded in the cosmological system that comprehends reproduction, spiritual constitution of the person, and life-force transmission. Moreover, differential moral standing is intrinsic to the disposition of cultural value embedded in delineations of moral worthiness. But concrete (rather than symbolic) advantages and disabilities are not invariably distributed in accordance with the resultant moral hierarchy. In other words, the disjunction is in the relationship between moral standing and privilege. Thus, men aged 31 to 40 are accorded moral worthiness by virtue of their generosity as donors in the transmission of life force but they do not secure the privilege of a low incidence of witchcraft accusations. Sexually active, postreproductive women aged 51 to 60 are subject to the metaphoric association of femininity with witchcraft, but this symbolic moral debility is not accompanied by a disproportionate rate of witchcraft accusations. The disjunction between moral standing and privilege evident here parallels that noted earlier with respect to prestige and privilege. The prestige derived from generosity in food distribution is not accompanied by privileged consumption. The same disjunction appears in a number of contexts. It is characteristic not only of the Etoro sociocultural system but of comparatively egalitarian systems in general.

While the distribution of witchcraft accusations deviates from expectations derived from culturally valorized social differentiation in certain critical respects, it also displays a noteworthy pattern in its own right. In other words, practice has its own pattern and logic in addition to being only partially reflective of these ideological conceptions. The distinctive feature of this pattern is that age is much more significant than gender in the distribution of witchcraft attributions. Both male and female children are rarely labeled *kagomano*. Adolescent males and females who have just entered into the system of life-force transmission and reproduction (respectively) but are not full adults (and reproducers) are disproportionately subject to accusations. Young men and women (aged 21 to 30) who have become life-force donors and child producers are not disproportionately accused. This parallelism indicates that the dominant pattern is age determined but largely gender neutral. A recalculation of the ratios for women aged 31 to 70 in accordance with age categories that match those relevant to the male life cycle (and disregard a different pattern of transitions in the female life cycle) also leads to results consistent with this general conclusion. Women aged 31 to 40 are subject to a disproportionate rate of accusations (indicated by a ratio of 1.75). This parallels the situation for males of the same age category (although the magnitude of the disproportionate rate of accusations is not as great in the case of the women). Finally, the incidence of accusations directed against women aged 41 to 70 is disproportionately low (at a ratio of .40) as it is for men over the age of 40, although not quite as low as the latter (at a ratio of .21). The age-specific incidence of accusations is thus similar for males and females, but the peaks that occur during the sexually active, prereproductive period (age 14 to 20 for males, 16 to 20 for females) and at ages 31 to 40 for both genders are higher for males than for females, while the diminution after age 40 also proceeds to a lower level for males than for females. In other words, the female pattern replicates the male pattern at lower amplitude as illustrated in figure 4.6. The fact that the ratio of frequency of accusations to demographic representation is 1.18 for males as a group and .78 for females as a group is only mildly inconsistent with the conclusion that the overall pattern is relatively gender neutral. Men are subject to a disproportionate frequency of accusations, but not by a wide margin.

The disproportionately high rate of accusations directed against men aged 31 to 40 remains to be addressed. As was noted earlier, this is unexpected from the standpoint of the ideology of life-force transmission and inconsistent with the moral hierarchy derived from this. In addition, the greatest difference in amplitude between males and females in the proportionate incidence of accusations over the life cycle occurs at this point (see fig. 4.6). This pattern is intelligible when one considers the consequences of these accusations. They have the effect of disqualifying a significant number of men from subsequently attaining *tafidilo* status when they reach their early 40s and enter the male age-group that is virtually immune from accusations. Men who are accused of witchcraft when they are in their 30s acquire a stigmatized reputational status in the prestige/stigma hierarchy just at the point in their lives when they need to manifest virtue as a prerequisite for being acknowledged as *tafidilos*. In all 29.6 percent (8/27) of the men aged 31 to 40 were subject to one or more accusations during the sample period, and this is nearly equivalent to three-fourths of the percentage of men aged 45 to 60 who are not accorded *tafidilo* status (i.e., 42.1 percent). Moreover, accusers (as opposed to the victims of witchcraft) are characteristically men

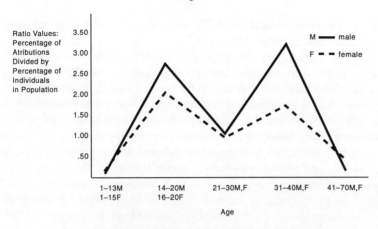

Fig. 4.6. The proportional distribution of witchcraft accusations
for equivalent-aged males and females over the life cycle

whose median age (28 years) is only a little younger than the median age of
men in the 31 to 40 age-group (33 years). The disproportionately high incidence of accusations directed against men in their 30s thus represents status
competition both among mediums and among men who are in the process of
establishing their credentials for attainment of *tafidilo* status. Both of the
spirit mediums accused of witchcraft were in the 31 to 40 age-group at the
time the three accusations against them took place. Moreover, none of the
men of this age-group who have been subject to an authenticated accusation
that is not reversed by the child oracle have any realistic chance of becoming
a *tafidilo*. Thus while the disproportionately high incidence of accusations
against men aged 31 to 40 is inconsistent with the moral hierarchy, it is
instrumental to the allocation of individuals to positions in the prestige/stigma
hierarchy. Status competition also accounts for the disproportionate frequency of accusations against men as a group. Control over the machinery
through which accusations are formulated is largely in the hands of males,
who tend to accuse each other.

I will return to the disproportionately high incidence of accusations
against women aged 31 to 40 further along in this section, in conjunction
with consideration of accusations against unremarried widows and women
who have at some point experienced a divorce. However, it may be noted in
advance that segregating these two categories of women reduces the proportional frequency of accusations for the remaining women in this age-group
to .70. The only women subject to an incidence of accusations that exceeds
their proportional representation in the population are sexually active, non-

reproductive females aged 16 to 20, divorcées (irrespective of subsequent remarriage), and unremarried widows.

At the beginning of chapter 3, it was noted that the Etoro ideology of witchcraft encompasses two divergent conceptions. On the one hand, the Etoro espouse a unitary concept of the witch (defined by possession of a *tohorora*) that is undifferentiated with respect to age and gender and thus conceptually egalitarian. On the other hand, the larger cosmological system that encompasses witchcraft as one mode of transmission of life force creates metaphoric associations between witchcraft and social categories differentiated by age and gender, establishing implicit, symbolically formulated inequalities. The proportional distribution of witchcraft accusations partakes of both of these divergent cultural visions in being largely gender neutral (and gender egalitarian) but markedly discriminatory with respect to age.[28] However, the causal factors responsible for this are intelligible in terms of a logic of practice, entailing status competition that is grounded in an interplay of factors pertaining to control over the formulation of accusations. We are now in a position to explore the relevant aspects of practice in detail in order to substantiate this.

The principal next of kin who is centrally involved in determining the identity of the witch responsible for a death is always a male, and this ensures a substantial degree of male control over the formulation of accusations. However, this control is by no means complete because very considerable credence is lent to the deathbed testimony, whether this comes from a male or a female. As was noted earlier, women are also represented among the auditors of the deathbed testimony in proportion to the percentage of female deaths. There are thus no gender inequalities with respect to either the weight given to the deathbed testimony or the custodianship of this transmitted knowledge. Women also freely enter into both private and public discussion in which suspicions are voiced, rumors regarding the deathbed statement and outcome of the pandanus oracle are circulated, and the events that transpired at the mortuary gathering are interpreted in an incriminating fashion.[29] Women are very much part of the public whose opinion comes into play during the period when an accusation is formulated. As noted earlier, any outspoken individual who has strong feelings about the case can play a substantial role in shaping the dominant interpretation that develops through these discussions. Women who are among the next of kin also participate in consultation of the pandanus oracle. However, women are not involved in the final stages of the formulation of an accusation, involving the publicly performed pig-organ oracle and the spirit pronouncements of an entranced medium.

This shift from female involvement in the private consultation of the pandanus oracle to noninvolvement in the public consultation of the pig-organ oracle is directly attributable to the potentiality for a confrontation between the accuser and the accused. The performer of the pig-organ oracle will voice his interpretation of the outcome publicly, and the person who is incriminated will be in the audience to dispute it. The performer needs to be in a position to back his assertion that the oracle was properly performed with threats of recourse to violence if this becomes necessary, and must likewise be in a position to counter any threats made by the incriminated individual. The same considerations apply when a formal accusation and request for compensation are lodged following the spirit pronouncements. A man and male supporters always state the case to an accused man (or woman's husband or brother) and his supporters because both the request and the potential refusal are backed by threats of violence. This is why an accused woman is jurally a minor, for whom decisions are taken by men. A woman cannot act as performer of the pig-organ oracle or as formal accuser because she is not in a position to use force or respond to the use of force. Although women may influence the early stages of the formulation of an accusation, a man ultimately places two names before the pig-organ oracle, and a male medium ultimately authenticates or fails to authenticate the outcome. This constitutes the basis of substantial male control. As in other domains of the Etoro sociocultural system, this turns on completion of a process in which women are involved in the earlier stages.

Both the male next of kin who acts as principal in the case and the presiding medium are usually between the ages of 20 and 40. All active mediums are in the 20-to-45 age-range. Of the known pronouncements made with respect to cases in the sample, 68 percent (17/25) were issued by mediums under the age of 31, and all but one were issued by mediums under the age of 41. The principal next of kin is most typically a deceased woman's son and a deceased man's younger brother. In 83 percent (29/35) of the cases this man was below the age of 41, with the median age for all accusers being 28.

The key components of the machinery through which accusations are formulated are thus in the hands of younger men below age 41, many of whom are unmarried, rather than elder senior males. These individuals evidence a strong tendency to preside over the development of accusations directed against contemporaries. In all, 93 percent (39/42) of the accused individuals in the sample were also below the age of 41. In contrast, the deceased victims of witchcraft tend to be older, with 60 percent (21/35) being over 40. The accused witch is thus more likely to be a contemporary of the accuser than of the victim.

The identification of the specific witch responsible for a given death is a direct consequence of the names placed before oracles. As was noted earlier, the oracles intrinsically tend to confirm rather than disconfirm the operator's suspicions because double negatives are regarded as due to procedural errors and are discounted. The name of the person indicted by the deathbed testimony is invariably placed before the pandanus oracle and, given the tendency toward confirmation, will very likely be placed before the pig-organ oracle as well. There are at least some cases in which the deceased fails to indict a suspect. However, this is rare due to the typical conditions of death. Usually a medium will have pronounced a sick person incurably ill from witchcraft prior to the person's demise. The victim then has certain knowledge that he or she has been bewitched, firmly believes that the witch will now be visible, and knows that an indictment is anticipated by his or her next of kin. I believe that a deathbed statement is invariably made unless the sick person is comatose. There is thus little scope for the operator of the oracles to supply two names due to the absence of a deathbed statement, although this may occur occasionally in illness deaths. In the comparatively small number of deaths due to accidents (e.g., drowning) the operator would routinely supply both names.

There is also little scope to substitute a different name for that provided by the deceased because there are generally several auditors of the deathbed testimony. Moreover, the next of kin place considerable faith in the last words of the deceased. However, the operator always selects the name of the second suspect considered by the pandanus oracle and potentially selects a third name if either of the first two names is conclusively proven innocent. The tendency of the oracle to confirm suspicion, combined with the likelihood of unconscious manipulation, makes conclusive proof of innocence unlikely. An outcome in which two slabs of pandanus steam-cooked in the same pit are both "raw" is all that is required to substantiate the appropriateness of the two preliminary names as candidates for the pig-organ oracle. Moreover, no one but the next of kin ever has direct knowledge of the results of the pandanus oracle, so that the operator may readily persuade himself that unanticipated outcomes were due to procedural errors and employ retests. There is consequently great likelihood that expected results are obtained and suspicions confirmed. There is certainly a potentiality that the suspect nominated by the deathbed testimony may be deselected. However, accusations that are problematic for the next of kin and entail no potentiality for requesting compensation due to the relationship between next of kin and accused do emerge, indicating that deselection did not occur in instances where it would have been in the interest of the operator in these respects. This suggests that the name of the suspect indicted by the deathbed testimony is generally placed before the pig-organ oracle. Nevertheless, somewhat more than half the names placed before this public oracle will be supplied by the next of kin. This is clearly germane to the fact that accuser and accused tend to be contemporaries and to the disproportionate incidence of accusations against males as well.

The individual indicted by the deathbed testimony may be someone who has never previously been accused but is believed by the victim to bear him (or her) ill will. Malice provides a basis for the supposition that this person possesses a *tohorora*. Alternatively, the person indicted may be a previously accused witch who is thought to be motivated only by the compulsion to consume the life force of others. The second suspect is extremely likely to be of the latter type. Public opinion invariably focuses suspicion on known witches, and I have never heard the names of individuals who have not previously been accused put forward in public discussion.

It is important to recall that most accusations are within the community, and public discussion is therefore not disinterested. Everyone is anxious to assign guilt to an individual outside their own circle of close kin and supporters, and known witches are suspects everyone can agree upon. They frequently have few local supporters due to change of residence following an earlier accusation. Moreover, the effect of public opinion weighs heavily upon the selection of the second suspect, since the next of kin of the deceased is invariably influenced by this. Public opinion also influences mediums, who may then provide cryptic indications of the guilt of a popular suspect that are picked up by the next of kin. However, the trajectory of the sequence of séances following a death is ordered in a way that makes it difficult for the spirit medium to strongly influence the selection of names placed before the pandanus oracle, because the medium's spirits will usually have done no more than agree to track the witch before this oracle is performed. Nevertheless, a medium's spirits could report finding footprints that would be consistent with the guilt of the popular suspect, lending further weight to this selection. The medium's influence at this stage may be greater if he is a close kinsman of the deceased and was among the auditors of the deathbed testimony, or if he is close to the principal next of kin and in direct consultation with him. However, the most significant influence upon the formulation of an accusation that accrues specifically to mediums, irrespective of their relationship with the principal next of kin, resides in the medium's capacity to fail to authenticate and thereby undermine an accusation. This comes at a later stage. The more general point here is that the employment of oracles empowers the principal next of kin with the capacity to take the initiative in the formulation of an accusation. The medium's role is thereby reduced to one of passing judgment upon, and amplifying, oracular indictments.

Tafidilos, who are invariably outspoken in public discussion, are more influential than mediums in promoting the selection of a specific suspect. One of the characteristics attributed to *tafidilos* is that "people listen when they talk," so their views clearly carry weight in the shaping of public opinion. In one instance there is reason to suspect that a *tafidilo* successfully channeled an accusation toward individuals who had not previously been accused, but against whom he had personal animosity (see n. 15). However, in this case, the *tafidilo* either performed the pandanus oracle himself (as sister's husband of the deceased) or was in close consultation with the individual who did so (the deceased's son). The influence that a *tafidilo* may have, irrespective of his relation with the principal next of kin, resides in directing suspicion toward one known witch rather than another.

While many influences come into play in nominating a second suspect, they are generally conducive to the selection of a previously accused witch. There is only very limited scope for the principal next of kin to effectively channel the selection toward a personal enemy who did not have a troubled relationship with the deceased, unless that individual is a known witch. Moreover, transparently concocted accusations, such as Tame's retaliatory accusation of Hariako and Pabu's accusation of Kayari and Esopa, typically fail to receive authentication from the resident spirit medium who has jurisdiction in the case.

On the other hand, spirit mediums themselves are clearly in a privileged position with respect to the authentication of accusations that impinge upon their own personal interests. When a spirit medium is the principal next of kin, or closely associated with him, there is consequently scope for playing a role in the development of an accusation and subsequently authenticating it. There is also a potential for the formulation of an accusation against an individual who is neither a known witch nor a probable suspect on interpersonal grounds. Moreover, mediums can be linked to most of the eleven politically significant accusations that affected the careers of other mediums and *tafidilos*. There is a considerable degree of overlap between the set of cases in which a medium played a role in the development of an accusation and the set of cases in which accusations had politically significant consequences. When the father of the novice medium Nogobe died, Nogobe placed the medium Nasu's name before the oracles and Abenamoga authenticated the accusation. When the wife's brother of the medium Arubia died, Arubia was among the auditors of the deathbed testimony, was in close consultation with the performers of the pandanus oracle, authenticated the accusation against Nasu, and was an active participant in the request for compensation. When Nogobe's father's second wife died, Nogobe was in a position to influence his "brother's" designation of suspects. Those accused as coconspirators were the mother (Imasala) and brother (Warope) of the medium Taipa. Nogobe's mentor Kayago provided authentication. The medium Wato both authenticated and played an active role in forwarding the accusation against the medium Kayago and his brother Waua. This accusation was probably fomented by the *tafidilo* Tsmari in retaliation for Kayago's earlier role as principal next of kin in the accusation against Tsmari's wife. However, both Wato and Nasu are agnates of the principal next of kin who performed the oracles. Finally, the medium Nagubi usurped the role of the next of kin when he took it upon himself to execute Sayaga and Samabe. His spirits subsequently confirmed their guilt as well.

These 8 accusations represent 19 percent of the sample (of 42 cases). However, they have a significant effect on patterns evident in the sample as a whole. Seven of the eight individuals accused are males and five of these men are in the 31-to-40 age-group. Accusations in which mediums exerted a direct influence or played a leading role thus account for half of the 10 "extra" accusations against men aged 31 to 40 that produce the markedly elevated disproportionate rate of accusations against members of this cohort. This striking feature of the data can thus be very directly linked to status competition. It is also noteworthy that 6 of these 8 accusations (or 75 percent) were against individuals who had not previously been accused, while only 44 percent (15/34) of the remaining accusations in the sample were against such individuals. The one woman accused (Imasala) also accounts for 1 of only 2 accusations against women in the 51-to-60 age-group.

Mediums were instrumentally involved in all but 1 of the 8 politically significant accusations against mediums and members of their families (the exception being the initial accusation against Piawe's daughter Udali). The 7 cases include those mentioned above (excluding the execution of Samabe and Sayaga) plus the initial accusation against the medium Taipa's brother's wife (Nawadia). In this case, Araradado (Kayago's mentor) authenticated an accusation in which the alleged victim was a boy of about two years of age. This is the only accusation in the sample resulting from a child's death, and Taipa himself had earlier declined to conduct a spirit inquest, since child deaths are not thought to be due to witchcraft. The accusation was 1 of 3 against Taipa's mother, brother, and a second brother's wife that led to his departure from Turusato, creating a vacancy filled by the mediums Kayago and Araradado. (This sequence of events is examined in detail in chap. 5.) A medium was also involved as next of kin in 1 of the 2 politically significant accusations against *tafidilos* or their wives (excepting the case of Piawe's daughter, included among those pertaining to mediums). As mentioned above, Kayago played this role when his mother named the wife of the *tafidilo* Tsmari in her deathbed testimony. In 8 of the 11 politically significant accusations, mediums played a role apart from their standard one of authenticating an accusation developed by others in accordance with customary procedure. Mediums authenticated 8 of these accusations as well. Although available data suggest that the deathbed testimony was instrumental to several of these accusations, and that they would have eventuated irrespective of medium involvement, there is clearly a discernible statistical tendency for medium involvement to result in politically significant accusations.

The general observation that the deathbed testimony and employment of oracles empower the next of kin to take the initiative in formulating an accusation continues to be valid. However, this provides scope for status competition that is particularly evident when the next of kin is himself a spirit medium. It is also the case that a spirit medium's usual role is limited to passing judgment upon oracular indictments. However, being closely related to the deceased or next of kin enables a spirit medium to influence or determine the names placed before oracles as well as authenticating the outcome of them. Finally, the targets of self-interested accusations that are implausible in terms of the accused's relation to the deceased are regularly exonerated by spirit mediums. However, spirit mediums do not exonerate those they themselves believe to be guilty. Although the overall system of procedures through which an accusation is formulated contains many elements of due process that impede the expression of self-interest, this system lacks any mechanism for precluding a spirit medium who is the principal next of kin (or closely related to him) from nominating suspects whose guilt is then authenticated by the same spirit medium or a close associate. The overall system thus fails to inhibit the expression of self-interest on the part of spirit mediums while suppressing comparable expressions of self-interest by others. *Tafidilos* do not enjoy a comparable advantage. Authentication of accusations put forward by *tafidilos* is not guaranteed, as evidenced by Wato's disconfirmation of Tsmari's accusation of Kayari.

It is important to emphasize that there are many constraints on the expression of personal animosities and personal interests. If these elements are apparent in the names placed before the pig-organ oracle the audience may well interpret the results as clearing the suspect or argue that the oracle was improperly performed. This can be circumvented by performing this oracle privately. However, this is a sure sign that the results were rigged, and they are then next to worthless. Apart from status competition among mediums, the main personal interest that can be realized through a witchcraft accusation lies in bringing grief to a personal enemy. However, the principal next of kin and those in a position to directly influence him are constrained by the knowledge that this can rarely be effectively accomplished unless the personal enemy is a known witch or was also a personal enemy of the deceased. Material interests are only marginally involved in the formulation of an accusation because one can collect compensation from a wide variety of persons. The prospects for successfully collecting compensation are somewhat reduced if the accused is a member of another longhouse community, but there is no evidence that calculating the odds of receiving compensation is a consideration in selecting the second suspect. It is important to keep in mind the emotional state of the principal next of kin, who is engulfed in grief and anger that preclude an attitude of calculating rationality. However, he may easily conflate anger against those who have harmed him and his kin with the purported malice of a suspected witch toward the deceased. A grudge can be unconsciously translated into suspicion of witchcraft.

The only personal interest that regularly comes into play lies in deflecting accusations from one's own close kin and supporters. The principal next of kin, mediums, *tafidilos,* and the members of the community who constitute public opinion all share this interest, although the parties they seek to protect are not the same. But there are very good prospects that they will find common ground in promoting the selection of a previously accused witch as a suspect to be oracularly evaluated. Divergent private interests are thus melded into a community interest in scapegoating. The second suspect is thus almost certain to be a known witch. This is substantiated by the fact that half the accusations in the sample (21/42) were directed against previously accused witches. There were seven improperly authenticated or otherwise flawed accusations that can be attributed to the expression of private interests, five of which were against individuals not previously accused.[30] The bulk of the remaining sixteen accusations (38.1 percent) of individuals not previously accused appear to have originated from the deathbed testimony of the deceased. In many of these instances, a troubled relationship between the deceased and the accused can be established (while in others I lack sufficient background knowledge to address this issue). Some of these accusations were directed against individuals labeled as *sa:go* or *kagomano* who were held in disrepute by many members of the community in addition to the deceased.

The sources of the names placed before the pig-organ oracle provide the key to the age distribution of the accusations in the sample. The previously accused individuals who constitute some of the first and nearly all of the second suspects are virtually all below the age of 41. This follows from the fact that an accused witch is likely to be accused again and again and then executed within a relatively short period of time, so that almost none of the potential scapegoats survive beyond the age of 40. The specific individuals within the scapegoat category (discussed earlier) are all below this age.

When an accusation reflects the private interests of the accuser, the target will be someone with whom he has been in conflict, and this is most likely to be a male and often a contemporary. The seven flawed accusations that entail the intrusion of private interest stemmed from two male and three female deaths, but six of the seven individuals accused were male (and the one female was named as a coconspirator with her deceased husband's brother, with whom she gardened). The interests of the accuser are disproportionately likely to play a role in cases of female deaths. Introduction of the names of male second suspects by male next of kin counteracts a strong tendency for female victims to name female witches in the deathbed testimony, contributing to the disproportionate incidence of accusations against males. All but one of these seven accusations were also against individuals below the age of 41. But the one that was not provides the only instance in which an elder senior male was named. Kusuame (aged 61 to 65), who was the sole *tafidilo* at Katiefi, was accused of causing the death of the retired medium Sanimako. However, this accusation was lodged by a member of Sanimako's longhouse community who was not the principal next of kin (see n. 16). Like most of the private-interest accusations, this entailed an attempt to get back at someone who had played a role in a previous accusation against the accuser or his immediate kin.

The remaining source of names placed before the pig-organ oracle is the deathbed testimony. This might be expected to provide the greatest scope for naming contemporaries, over the age of 40, with whom the victim had a troubled relationship. Sometimes this does occur (as will be detailed below), but the potentiality is largely counteracted by the fact that persons over 40 who have not previously been accused are very implausible suspects. If a person possessed a *tohorora,* he or she would be driven by the compulsion to consume the life force of others and would commit acts of witchcraft that would be discovered by oracles and mediums. In other words, it is considered implausible that an individual could conceal an irrepressibly evil nature for some twenty years. Moreover, those whose evil nature is revealed when they are younger frequently do not survive beyond the age of 40. There is thus an a priori assumption that an individual over 40 who has not previously been accused does not possess a *tohorora* and cannot then be guilty of acts of witchcraft. Moreover, any individual who does in fact manage to avoid being accused of witchcraft for twenty or more years is indeed likely to be an unselfish, good-hearted, easygoing, community-spirited person who has good relations with his or her coresidents. Such individuals do not come to mind when a mortally ill victim visualizes the witch responsible for his or her condition. An elder is thus much more likely to suspect a junior than a contemporary. However, there are a few exceptions. Two women aged 51 to 60 were named as witches by a woman and a man of the same cohort in their respective deathbed statements and were subsequently accused, even though neither had previously been accused. Both of these accusations were politically significant. When Pilime died, she reportedly named her contemporary Imasala as the witch responsible. Imasala and her son Warope were subsequently indicted by the oracles, and the accusation was authenticated. They are the mother and brother of the medium Taipa. Available data suggest that the deathbed testimony was accurately reported (insofar as there were several auditors), but it is probable that the medium Nogobe influenced the selection of Warope as the second suspect whose name was placed before the oracles. The second case involved Tumame, the wife of the *tafidilo* Mariabu and sister of the *tafidilo* Ibo. She was named by one of her husband's agnates.

It is clear that this accusation originated from the deathbed testimony since it placed the principal next of kin in a very awkward position. Compensation was not requested because Tumame's husband (Mariabu) and brother (Ibo) were the "father" and prospective wife's father of the principal next of kin (the stepson of the deceased). This was an accusation that created unwanted difficulties for the young man who lodged it, and it is evident that he did so only because he felt compelled to follow through on the deathbed testimony out of regard for his deceased stepfather's last words. While some accusations reflect the personal interests of the accuser, others are clearly not in the interest of the accuser. Most are neutral in this respect.

Extensive male control over the formulation of witchcraft accusations clearly does not eventuate in the victimization of women. The implicit association of femininity with witchcraft that is established through metaphoric association is not realized in a disproportionate frequency of accusations.[31] Instead, men largely impose the disabilities that accompany assignment to this stigmatized category upon each other. This constitutes another instance of the general phenomenon whereby moral standing and prestige do not covary with privilege and prerogative, but in a negative register. Symbolically constructed moral unworthiness grounded in the association of femininity with witchcraft is not reflected in the assignment of stigma and disability in the form of public accusations. However, women are still disadvantaged by the symbolic association of femininity with witchcraft because this narrows the range of acceptable behavior to which they need to conform in order to avoid suspicion of witchcraft.

Women are also disadvantaged by the witchcraft complex in that they are reduced to the status of jural minors with respect to matters of compensation. They are not in a position to contest accusations against them or to refuse to pay compensation. Decisions regarding the response to an accusation are made on their behalf by their fathers, brothers, and husbands. At the same time, this embeds a significant degree of female dependence upon men related to them in these ways. This dwarfs a woman's dependence on males to cut trees so that she may garden, in that a witchcraft accusation is a life-threatening situation in which a woman is very vulnerable to retributive execution if compensation is not paid. And she cannot readily look to other men, not closely related to her, as alternative protectors. In other words, the social substitutability of one man for another that provides a potential attenuation of dependence grounded in the sexual division of labor is significantly reduced in this context.[32] This undoubtedly conditions a young girl to heed the wishes of her father and brother in the marriage arrangements they make for her. It creates an important reason for a woman to need a husband, and one that contributes to the desirability of the married state both for young girls and mature widows. A woman is also likely to see her own interests as closely identified with those of her father, brother, and husband. Finally, male control over the transfer of valuables in witchcraft and homicide compensation sets a precedent for male control over the transfer of valuables in bridewealth payments, also regarded as compensatory (cf. Whitehead 1986). The complex of beliefs and practices relating to witchcraft is thus a central locus of gender inequality in that it generates female dependence and male control that extend into other domains of social life. Although women are not victimized by male control over the formulation of accusations, they are led by perception of their vulnerability to concede the legitimacy of male control in this and other areas.

It is also important to recognize that the execution of male and female witches does not convey entirely equivalent messages to the males and females who witness them, or hear vivid accounts, because the genders differ in their sense of their own vulnerability to this fate. While the tribal audience of an execution is dramatically reminded of the importance of having the solid support of close kin and positive social relations with coresidents, men know that they are capable of defending themselves and of marshaling reciprocal support from other men to whose aid they can come in a like manner in comparable situations. In this respect, the threat of violence is conducive to reciprocal egalitarian relations among men. But female members of the audience are only reminded of their vulnerability and dependence. The execution of Udali by her own father's brother, to whom she would have looked for protection and support after her father's and husband's deaths, must certainly have conveyed a potent message to other women concerning the importance of their relations to close male kinsmen (also see n. 32). But these same women would not have seen Udali as a victim of male domination, since all the witchcraft accusations against her originated from the deathbed testimony of senior female kin (two classificatory mothers and a father's sister) and were forwarded by her elder "sisters." No women in her community or in others questioned the legitimacy of her execution or doubted that she was indeed an evil witch deserving of this fate. Kauhe was the executor of female-dominated public opinion in this instance (and this public opinion was at work over an interval of several weeks before he acted). The key point is that the execution of female witches contributes to female dependence upon men without calling into question the legitimacy of this dependence or of male control more generally. Women's feelings of dependence are immersed in positive, kinship-based affect entirely lacking any sense of "oppression." In other words, women feel that they are cared for, not oppressed, by their close male kin. The second point is that the distribution of executions, which disfavors males by a ratio of two to one, is not as significant as the different meanings that executions convey to male and female members of the tribal community that constitute the audience for these dramatic events.

Men perceive the need to intensify reciprocal, egalitarian relations (cf. Knauft 1985a).

The social category that exercises the greatest degree of direct control over the formulation of accusations is unmarried young men (i.e., "junior males"), in that more than half (19/35) of the principal next of kin are in this category. Another fifth (7/35) are recently married young men who have not yet fathered a child. Uninitiated adolescent males are jural minors with respect to matters of witchcraft compensation, in that a father or elder brother will be the principal contributor and solicitor of contributions in the event that compensation is paid following an accusation. However, the position of adolescent males is quite different from that of women because they are often prepared to respond to the threat of violent retribution that underwrites a request for compensation and may insist that a father or elder brother not make a payment on their behalf. Decisions are not made for such adolescent males, with the possible exception of the very youngest of those accused (aged 14). Adolescents as young as 15 may also act as the principal next of kin in formulating an accusation (as in Wasagaya's accusation against Nomaya following his brother's drowning). Thus, neither adolescent males nor older unmarried young men are rendered dependent by the complex of beliefs and practices pertaining to the formulation of witchcraft accusations and their resolution. Moreover, these two social categories are not excluded from exercising the measure of control over accusations that accrues to the principal next of kin, but indeed play this role more often than older men.

Adolescent males are subject to symbolically constructed moral unworthiness through cultural formulation of the *sa:go* category, since they are the only individuals who are susceptible to being classified as such. The *sa:go* is the epitome of evil and the most stigmatized social category in the entire scheme of social differentiation. This stigma also entails the maximum disability with respect to witchcraft accusations because classification as a *sa:go* provides grounds for establishing a priori supposition of the possession of a *tohorora*. An individual so classified is thus in the same position as a previously accused witch whose guilt has been confirmed by the child oracle. A *sa:go* is within the scapegoat category and runs a significant risk of execution the first time he is accused of witchcraft. While a woman is metaphorically "like a witch" in terms of her role in the system of life-force transmission, a *sa:go is* a witch, even if he has never been accused of being the agent responsible for a specific death. Here stigma and disability go hand in hand. Unlike women (as a group), adolescent males are subject to a disproportionate frequency of accusations and a disproportionate risk of execution.

The distinctively different aspects of inequality that have been identified through this contrastive analysis of women and adolescent males are systematically applied to the full range of socially differentiated categories of persons in table 4.3. This shows that there is a fairly close association between moral evaluations derived from the cosmology of life-force transmission, on one hand, and a range of prerogatives and disabilities pertaining to the complex of witchcraft-related practices, on the other. This generalization is particularly applicable to jural capacities (as adult or minor and as potential principal next of kin). In other words, moral worthiness and full jural capacity go hand in hand, as do moral unworthiness and the absence of full jural capacity. (The only exception to a one-to-one relation pertains to morally unworthy adolescent junior males who sometimes act as principal next of kin and may sometimes dispute an accusation but lack the valuables and relations to potential contributors that would enable them to pay compensation on their own behalf.) In contrast, there is a much less predictable relationship between moral evaluations and susceptibility to a disproportionate frequency of witchcraft accusations. The reasons for this and the points of disjunction have already been established.

Two social categories are advantaged in every respect, namely elder senior males and the virginal bachelors who are junior males but are repositories of the life force through which reproduction is achieved. This shows that neither age nor marital status is critical to attainment of a socially advantaged station (contra the central importance Collier 1988 accords to marriage as instrumental to male prestige and prerogative). Moreover, while only elder senior males can be *tafidilos,* they cannot be mediums. Likewise, initiated (but unmarried) junior males can be mediums but not *tafidilos.* There is thus a consistent pattern of dual advantage for these two categories of males. This is apparent in the *kosa* ceremony as well, where the prestigious roles of dancers and burners are generally accorded to bachelors and elders, respectively.

The only category of person that is disadvantaged in every respect is sexually active married women who have not yet borne a child. This includes all young women aged 16 to 20 but may extend to older women as well. This pattern of systematic disability is also consistent with a wide range of material presented earlier, including the conjugal strife between Tuni and Wadome and the modest support Wadome received from other women of Kaburusato. Although not represented in the table, separate analytic categories of junior and senior females would be warranted. Senior females freely enter into public discussion, while junior females generally do not. Senior females may also play the prestigious role of burners in the *kosa* ceremony on occasion. A distinction between junior and senior females would also be in keeping with the earlier observation that age overrides gender in the proportional distribution of witchcraft accusations.

It is noteworthy that marriage does not lead to either enhanced moral evaluation or to positive changes in the distribution of prerogatives and disabilities, for either males or females, in this particular domain. The critical point of transition for both genders turns on joining the ranks of reproducers. Males make this transition when they become life-force donors (following initiation) and females when they bear a child. Widowhood is significant for females because it typically (if not invariably) relocates them within the category of nonchildbearing women, at least temporarily. Widower status is not significant for men because they will continue to be life-force donors in homosexual relations (if of the appropriate age). Widows are subject to a disproportionate frequency of witchcraft accusations (as documented below), while widowers are not.

There is a direct association between divorce and witchcraft accusations with respect to women because witchcraft is the only grounds on which a man can initiate a jural divorce with return of bridewealth. (A woman can initiate a de facto divorce by taking up residence with another man without specific grounds; see Kelly 1977:255–64.) In addition, jural divorce is a possibility only if a woman has not borne a child by the union. A jurally divorced woman is thus both a witch and a nonreproductive depletor, by definition. Of the 14 witchcraft accusations against women, 5 were against women who were either jurally divorced as a result of the accusation (1 case) or had previously been jurally divorced but were now remarried (4 cases). Another 5 of the 14 accusations of female witchcraft (or 35.7 percent) involved unremarried widows. This is greater than the percentage of unremarried widows in the ever-married female population as a whole (i.e., 22.0 percent) so that the ratio of frequency of accusations to demographic representation is 1.63.[33] Only 4 women who were neither unremarried widows nor divorcées were accused of witchcraft during the sample period. Thus, if these two categories of women are segregated from the sample presented earlier in table 4.2, the proportionate frequency of accusations against women of various age-groups would be very substantially reduced. The disproportionately high ratio of 1.75 for all women aged 31 to 40 would decline to a disproportionately low ratio of .70 for women aged 31 to 40 who were neither unremarried widows nor divorcées. The ratio of .40 for all women 41 to 70 would likewise decline to a ratio of .28 for women in this age-group who were neither unremarried widows nor divorcées. This is to say that the only women subject to a disproportionately high incidence of accusations are sexually active, nonreproductive females aged 16 to 20, divorcées (irrespective of whether they remarry), and unremarried widows.

The marital experience of the women accused of witchcraft is shown in table 4.4. In all, 71.4 percent (10/14) of the accusations of female witchcraft were directed against women who were either widows at the time or had at some point experienced a divorce (including the instance in which the woman was about to be divorced in conjunction with the accusation). A widow has

TABLE 4.3

The Domain of Witchcraft: Covariations between Social Differentiation, Moral Evaluation, and Prerogatives and Disabilities

Socially Differentiated Categories		Distinctive Cultural Features		Moral Evaluation		Prerogatives and Disabilities				
Larger groupings	Subdivisions	Role in Lifeforce Transmission	Supernaturally Significant Reproductive Role + = present	Intrinsic Generosity and Self-Sacrifice + = present	Symbolic Association with the Selfish Witch − = present	Control over Accusations as Potential Principal + = present	Jural Adult + or Jural Minor −	Independent Agent + or Socially Dependent −	Narrowed Range of Acceptable Behavior − = present	Disproportionately Low (+) or High (−) Frequency of Witchcraft Accusations
Senior males	Elders >45	donor	+	+	+	+	+	+	+	+
	Ever-married men <45	donor	+	+	+	+	+	+	+	−
Junior males	Never-married initiated males >20	donor	+	+	+	+	+	+	+	+
	Uninitiated adolescent males 14–20	beneficiary	−	−	−	±	±	±	−	−

Women	Postreproductive Females 51–70	depletor	−	−	−	−	−	−	−	−	+
	Mature reproductive females 21–50	agent	−	−	+	−	−	−	−	−	+
	Married prereproductive females 16–20	depletor	−	−	−	−	−	−	−	−	−
Children	Girls 1–15	beneficiary	−	−	−	−	−	−	+	+	+
	Boys 1–13	beneficiary	−	−	−	−	−	−	+	+	+

by definition depleted her husband (as discussed earlier with respect to food taboos), and a jurally divorced woman is likewise a depletor because only a woman who has not borne a child can be jurally divorced. In the case of a woman who has previously experienced a divorce, this association could potentially be retrospective because she may have since remarried and given birth. But neither Nawadia nor Waime had produced any children during the period when they accumulated five accusations. They were thus prototypical representatives of the morally unworthy category of married, sexually active, nonreproductive women. Moreover, 10 of the 14 accusations of female witchcraft were directed against women who had not by then produced a child (see table 4.4). Thus the preponderant majority (71.4 percent) of accusations of female witchcraft were lodged against "junior females," i.e., sexually active women who had not joined the ranks of reproducers by bearing a child. This amplifies the point that this social category is maximally disadvantaged and likewise underscores the analytic utility of making a distinction between junior and senior females.[34] It is also apparent that the cosmology of life-force transmission has a direct bearing on the distribution of those witchcraft accusations directed against women. The metaphoric association of femininity and witchcraft that is engendered by this cosmology is quintessentially applicable to women who engage in sexual relations without producing children, and such women account for most of the accusations of female witchcraft. At the same time, it is also important to recall that these accusations are typically attributable to the deathbed testimony of a woman.

The complex of witchcraft beliefs and practices not only generates female dependence and male control but also shapes female interests so that they coincide with or complement male interests. As was noted earlier,

TABLE 4.4

Marital and Childbearing Experience of Women Accused of Witchcraft
during the Sample Period

Woman	Age Cohort at the Time Accused	Marital History	Number of Children at the Time Accused	Number of Witchcraft Accusations
Imasala	56–60	widowed	4	1
Tumame	51–55	married	4	1
Esopa	36–40	widowed	2	1
Yo	36–40	married but separated	2	1
Waime	31–40	twice divorced, thrice married	0	3
Nawadia	21–25	twice divorced, thrice married	0	2
Heanome	21–25	married, then widowed	0	2
Udali	16–20	married, then widowed	0	3

female vulnerability to retributive execution makes a woman dependent upon the father and brother who arrange her marriage as well as the husband she weds. When a woman is accused of witchcraft, her husband is responsible for half the compensation, and her father and/or brother are responsible for the other half. This divided liability for a woman's witchcraft thus maintains these two sets of dependencies. Since these men are a woman's critical sources of support, she is likely to see her own interests as closely identified with theirs. Thus, when a woman acts in terms of her own self-interest she will seek to marry, agree to marry the man selected by her father or older brother and cleave to him. She will likewise seek to bear children in fulfillment of her component of the division of labor and thereby avoid the possibility of divorce. Jural divorce and remarriage are entirely contrary to her interests, because they can be provoked only at the expense of being labeled a witch. The Etoro frequently espouse the view that "only a witch will marry a witch," so that the prospects of achieving a more favorable union by jural divorce and remarriage are slim. A woman can establish a de facto divorce only by engaging in immoral adultery and at the additional expense of alienating her father and brother as well as other close male kin. This, too, is contrary to her interests.

This is well illustrated by the case of Kabano. She was initially married to the medium Nagubi but left him a few years later for the medium Abenamoga, becoming the latter's second wife. Kabano's father and father's brothers were upset at the disruption of both planned marital exchanges and their affinal relationship with Nagubi, but they were not in a position to send Kabano back to Nagubi because she had already taken up residence with Abenamoga rather than returning to them (her agnates). Abenamoga paid a bridewealth four-and-one-half times greater (in total value) than that originally paid by Nagubi a few years earlier so that Nagubi's bridewealth payment could be returned with plenty to spare.

Fourteen years later Abenamoga died, widowing Kabano. Within six months, the notorious thrice-named witch Nomaya sought to make arrangements to marry her. Kabano was much opposed to this proposed union and told Abenamoga's younger half brother Yakea that she had much affection for him and wanted to be his wife. But Yakea did not want to risk disruption of his soon-to-be-realized betrothal in order to marry a woman ten years his senior. Yakea was also persuaded to go along with the union between Nomaya and Kabano by a number of kinsmen and affines who recognized its potential to fruitfully redefine lineage sibling and exchange relations. (These considerations are detailed in Kelly 1977:252–54.) Among the individuals who favored the union for these reasons were Kabano's father's brothers (her father now being deceased). Kabano went to Sesimato (a Petamini long-house) to seek refuge with her agnates who resided there, hoping she could remain with them as a widow rather than marrying Nomaya. This would normally be a potential option. However, Kabano was now making claims on relationships to her father's brothers that she herself had previously discounted. They consequently returned her to Yakea so that he might exercise his right (as Kabano's deceased husband's brother) to marry her to Nomaya. The union took place in November 1968, a year after Abenamoga's death.[35]

Kabano was now in an undesirable position in several respects. Although already in her early 30s, she was childless. Moreover, being married to a witch implied that she too was a witch, although she had not been accused. Kabano's de facto divorce of Nagubi was therefore not in her self-interest over the longer term, given the eventual high cost of alienating her close male kin so that she could not draw on their support and protection when Nomaya sought to marry her. The key point here is that the penalties and disabilities that shape a woman's self-interest are virtually all linked, in one way or another, to the domain of witchcraft. This amplifies the conclusion that this domain is a central locus for the production of inequalities based on gender (and age) that extend into other domains of social life. However, the domain of witchcraft is itself an integral component of the prestige/stigma system that is also the source of inequalities pertaining to statuses that transcend those based on age and gender, i.e., the statuses of spirit medium and *tafidilo*.

CHAPTER 5

Prestige: Mediums
and Tafidilos

The statuses of spirit medium and *tafidilo* surmount the pinnacle of the prestige/stigma hierarchy, while the contrastive social categories of witch and *sa:go* anchor the base. The principal objectives of this chapter are to elucidate the means by which individuals achieve each of these prestigious statuses, the progression from novice or aspirant to eventual retiree, and the roles of established mediums and *tafidilos* in the social life of the community. In the course of addressing these topics, I will also be concerned to examine relations among mediums, among *tafidilos*, and between mediums and *tafidilos*. The main features of these interrelations were previewed in chapter 4. The senior resident medium and leading *tafidilo* of each respective longhouse community collectively constitute the social elite of Etoro society, and the present chapter also investigates the extent to which they enjoy privileges, prerogatives, and other culturally pertinent advantages.

BECOMING A MEDIUM

An individual is designated as a future medium by a spirit, who communicates her elective affinity for the candidate through an established medium. In effect, a medium thus nominates a potential apprentice. The nominee must be an initiated young man who is eligible to marry but has not yet wed, because a spirit wife will only come to a bachelor (although a spirit medium may subsequently take a human wife as well). The medium designate will thus be in his late teens to middle 20s (or possibly somewhat older), but the most typical age is 19 or 20. During the fieldwork period, two of five eligible bachelors living at Kaburusato learned that the spirits had chosen them. Sawa (aged 26) undertook training with his sister's husband Kayago, who had nominated him, but he did not complete it. He married a few months later and thus became ineligible. Sawa's younger brother, Illawe (aged 20) was nominated by Nogobe, Kayago's protégé, who related that a *Sigisato* spirit of Illawe's lineage awaited him. However, Illawe did not undertake training during the ensuing seven months (prior to my departure), and it appeared unlikely that he would do so.

These data clearly indicate that the number of young men offered the opportunity to become mediums is greater than the number who complete apprenticeship. Since 40 percent (4/10) of the young men aged 21 to 25 (in the eight-community sample) have become novice mediums, and one other young man this age is known to have been nominated, the position must therefore be open to more than half the male population. There is then attrition among novice mediums who are not successful at curing and at directing spiritually inspired fish-poisoning expeditions and consequently fail to gain the confidence of community members. As a result, mediums comprise only 14.5 percent (8/55) of all men in the sample aged 26 to 45 (i.e., those in the four succeeding cohorts). This attrition occurs within three to five years, so that a novice medium will either have become established or have ceased to practice by about age 26. Mediums ultimately constitute a select group, comprising 14.6 percent of the initiated male population over the age of 20 and 18.5 percent (12/65) of men aged 21 to 45.

This selectivity is achieved by a winnowing-out process that first eliminates those who lack the motivation to respond to the opportunity and then eliminates those who fail to master the craft. Only young men who have been named as a witch or are thought to be a *kagomano* or *sa:go* are positively excluded. Others who show no signs of either interest or capability do not receive the call. However, I believe that any young man (other than a witch) who made his interest known would have an excellent chance of being nominated and of receiving training. Available data contain no evidence of exclusivity at the point of entry into the shamanic profession. But making the transition from novice to established medium is far from assured. This requires intelligence, mastery of the craft, community support, and the capacity to survive a competitive jostling for position among the mediums residing in the community. This competition is a natural outgrowth of a system that is quite open at the entry level but in fact has the capacity to absorb only a limited number of established practitioners. A longhouse community can accommodate no more than two fully established mediums over the long term, and they will very likely be related as mentor and protégé. Other configurations are unstable. These points will be developed and documented in due course.[1]

The age differential between mentors and protégés is shown in table 5.1, together with the genealogical and lineage relations between them.[2] A medium cannot begin to train an apprentice until he himself becomes established and acquires the full repertoire of spirits, normally at about age 24 to 26. However, he may then nominate a potential apprentice only a few years junior. Since a medium ceases to practice at about age 45, and a potential

TABLE 5.1

Mentor and Protégé: Age Differential, Genealogical Relation, and Lineage Relation

Protégé or Nominee*	Protégé's Current Age	Mentor	Mentor's Current Age	Age Difference. Protégé is:	Genealogical Relation. Mentor Is Protégé's:	Lineage Relation. Protégé's Lineage Is Related to Mentor's as:		
						Own Lineage	Brother Lineage	Exchange Lineage
Sanimako	deceased	Tofono	deceased	-2	WZH		X	
Tofono	deceased	Mugu	deceased	?	FZS			X
Piawe	46	Mugu	deceased	?	F	X		
Hoamo	44	?	?	?	?			
Araradado	41	Tofono	deceased	-7	WFFBSS			X
Nagubi	40	Arugwei	deceased	?	FFFBSS	X		
Taipa	38	Piawe	46	-8	FZS			X
Nasu	37	Tofono	deceased	-11	FBDH			X
Maua	36	Waroa	deceased	?	FBS	X		
Kayago	30	Araradado	41	-11	FFFBSS	X		
Wabiaka	30	Hoamo	43	-13	FBDH			X
Nogobe	26	Kayago	30	-4	FZDH		X	
Sawa*	26	Kayago	30	-4	ZH			X
Arubia	23	Nagubi	40	-17	FBWB			X
Hewa	23	Nagubi	40	-17	FBWB			X
Ibasia	22	Nasu	37	-15	FBDHFBS			X
Wato	21	Piawe	46	-25	FBSWZS		X	
Illawe*	20	Nogobe	26	-6	FFFBSDS			X
Median	30		40	-11	Total	4	3	10

apprentice must be initiated, the age differential cannot exceed about 25 years. The median age differential of 11 years is quite close to the 11.5-year midpoint of this potential range (of 2 to 25 years in age difference).

The data presented in table 5.1 show that the transmission of shamanic knowledge is not restricted by kin or lineage relations and does not conform to any narrowly confined pattern. Established mediums nominate as protégés kinsmen both close and distant, who are related in a wide variety of ways. Shamanic knowledge is also transmitted both within and between lineages. Transmission between lineages, which predominates, may entail individuals who are of brother lines or, more frequently, exchange lines. Although bilateral exchange generally occurs between intermarrying lineages, and there are consequently multiple genealogical relations between individuals of these lines, there is nevertheless a tendency for the mentor's lineage to have recently received women from the protégé's lineage (7 of 10 cases). The mentor, who is then a classificatory sister's husband of his protégé, could potentially be the protégé's inseminator as well. Such a relationship would be consistent with the doctrine that an inseminee acquires the talents and capabilities of his inseminator (as discussed in chap. 3). It is probable that an established medium will nominate his inseminee, but the latter may not take up the apprenticeship or may later fail to establish himself, so that shamanic mentor and protégé would be related as inseminator and inseminee in only a small proportion of the cases. The same restrictions limit familial transmission of shamanic knowledge; only one medium was trained by his father (see n. 1).

The significant point here is that it is very difficult to transmit mediumship to a closely related person. Unlike the developed Big Man systems of the Highlands, in which an extant Big Man may provide his son with the initial advantage of several wives and an established network (see Strathern 1971a:195–210), an Etoro medium has no capacity to advantageously position a son (or inseminee). Nepotism is unfeasible because success as a practitioner requires talent and motivation that are not widely distributed. There is nothing instrumental to success that can be transmitted to facilitate this. Access to the position of spirit medium is thus unrestricted in two respects. It is open to nearly all young men (except witches) who have any inclination to pursue it, and no enabling kin relation of any one particular type is required in order to secure training.

This has the further ramification that mediums are not the recipients of marital or material benefits from prospective apprentices who seek to be nominated and trained. Although a father could probably ensure that his son would be nominated by betrothing his daughter to a medium (who would then be his son's designated inseminator), doing so would be entirely unnecessary in order to achieve this goal. In the only case in which the mentor was the protégé's sister's husband, the marriage had been arranged before the mentor became a medium (so that it was not apparent that he would attain this position), and the apprentice (Sawa) never completed his training. Thus while shamanic knowledge tends to be transmitted along the same channels in which male substance is transmitted—from "fathers" (senior agnates) to "sons" (junior agnates) and from wife-receivers (potential inseminators) to wife-givers (potential inseminees)—the parties to the transaction are only analogically rather than substantively related as donor and recipient of semen. By the same token, a medium is under no specific obligation to train any particular person. Finally, no payment of any kind is made to the mentor for the training received. A protégé owes a debt of loyalty to his mentor, but this debt cannot be discharged through material gifts.

The absence of narrowly specified lines of transmission of shamanic knowledge creates a situation whereby an established medium may draw apprentices from a virtually unlimited pool. There is consequently a potential for considerable variation among mediums in their degree of success in attracting novices for training and in turning out practitioners who survive the winnowing-out process and go on to become established mediums who train others. Thus 8 of the 14 practicing mediums (in the eight-community sample) are the shamanic descendants of Mugu, 3 are descendants of Arugwei, 2 are descendants of an unknown individual, and 1 was trained by Waroa (see figure 5.1).[3] Mediums are the custodians of cosmological doctrine in that their séances reveal the nature of the spirit worlds of the *Kesames* and *Sigisatos* and the mode of operation of witches. Mediums also establish interpretive and procedural precedents in their handling of witchcraft cases and in curing. The success of Mugu and his shamanic descendants in reproduction has thus established an interpretive and doctrinal legacy that prevails in the communities of Katiefi, Haifi, Turusato, and Kaburusato, where these 8 practicing mediums reside and hold séances. Although there is enormous scope for innovation in shamanic performance (see Schieffelin 1985b), the fact that the majority of practicing mediums are the intellectual descendants of a single man who died only about ten years earlier engenders a counterbalancing tendency toward a widely shared doctrinal and interpretive tradition.

RELATIONS BETWEEN MEDIUMS

Mediums form part of a network that is partly based upon but also transcends whatever kin relations may obtain between them. The dyadic relationship between mentor and protégé is typically a very strong bond. The two men tend to coreside and to practice their profession within a framework of cooperation and mutual support based on their relation of spiritual filiation. However, the relationship is also intrinsically hierarchical and occasionally sours

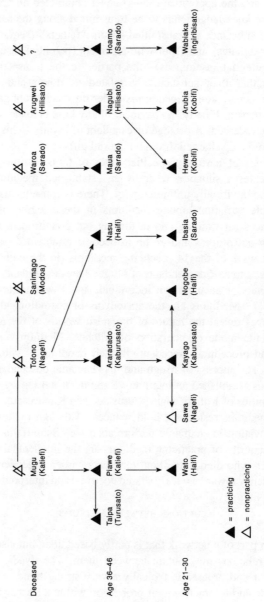

Fig. 5.1. Patterns of transmission of shamanic knowledge between lineages

(as will be detailed further along). The protégé initially acts as a second and ratifies his mentor's pronouncements. However, the mentor must eventually allow his protégé to succeed him if the latter is to become fully established in his own right (and if they are to continue to coreside). This clearly provides one impetus to retirement. It is also difficult for two mediums who are not related as mentor and protégé to cooperate effectively in rendering supernatural services to the same community, since there is no clear-cut basis for one to take precedence over the other in conducting inquests into the identity of the witch responsible for a death. It is therefore not easy for a protégé to move elsewhere without invading an established medium's domain.

These dynamics shape the interrelations between mediums. This can be illustrated by the evolving relations of cooperation and competition that obtained among the three mediums who resided at Kaburusato at one time or another during the period from 1957 to 1969. In about 1957, the Kaburusato lineage fissioned, and one of the emergent lines moved to a separate part of the lineage territory to construct their own longhouse (later abandoning this longhouse and moving as a group to the Petamini community of Sesimato). The resident spirit medium (Kago) was a member of this offshoot segment, and the original longhouse community was thus left without a medium.[4] Araradado then moved there and assumed this position. Araradado was a protégé of Tofono and had previously coresided with him at a longhouse community on Nagefi lineage territory. He was a member of the Kaburusato lineage segment that predominated at the Kaburusato longhouse community and thus rejoined his agnates. In about 1960, Araradado trained Kayago. The two men enjoyed a close cooperative relationship throughout the decade and characteristically performed séances jointly. Until late 1966, Araradado conducted spiritual inquests and identified the witches responsible for deaths, with Kayago seconding these pronouncements. After this time Kayago assumed the role of senior resident medium, with his own protégé Nogobe serving as his second. Nogobe, who was then 24 to 25, had initially been trained by Kayago a few years earlier. However, the period during which all three men coresided at Kaburusato was brief. Both Kayago and Nogobe split their residence between Kaburusato and the neighboring longhouse community of Turusato in 1967, and in 1968 Kayago and Araradado moved to Turusato while Nogobe remained at Kaburusato. The course of events that led to these relocations, and to Nogobe's succession to the position of sole resident medium at Kaburusato, requires some explanation.

The departure of Taipa, the resident medium of Turusato, set the stage for Kayago's and Araradado's assumption of his position. This was precipitated by several witchcraft accusations. Pilime died in early 1967 and named her contemporary Imasala as the witch responsible for her death. Imasala was Taipa's mother (see fig. 5.2). Kayago was then residing part-time at

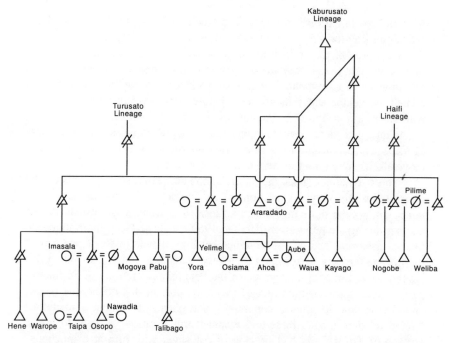

Fig. 5.2. Genealogical relations among selected residents of Turusato in early 1967

Turusato (and gardening with his half sister and half brother, who were married to Ahoa and his sister, respectively). Kayago conducted the spirit inquest into Pilime's death and confirmed Imasala's guilt, together with that of her son, Warope, oracularly identified as coconspirator (though not named in the deathbed testimony). The oracles were performed by Pilime's son, Weliba, who is Nogobe's father's brother's son. Weliba thus introduced Warope's name into the proceedings. (Nogobe was also residing at Turusato with Kayago at this time.) As a result of this accusation, Taipa subsequently moved to the Petamini community of Sesimato with his brother Warope and mother Imasala (after his current garden was harvested). At about the same time, Taipa's half brother Osopo moved to Kasayasato with his wife Nawadia, who had been named as the witch responsible for Talibago's death several months earlier (in late 1966). Talibago, who was somewhat less than two years old, had not named a witch when he died. Moreover, the pig-organ oracle was not performed. This accusation was thus based solely on a spirit inquest conducted by Araradado at Pabu's request (Pabu being Talibago's father). Araradado presided because Taipa declined to conduct an inquest to determine the identity of the witch, having declared the death not to be due to witchcraft. This is the typical finding when a child this age dies.

The net result of these three accusations against Taipa's mother, brother, and another brother's wife was to prompt relocations that pared down the agnatic core of the community to four brothers and a sister who were closely tied by sister exchange to Kayago and his brothers (Waua and Osiama). The community not only lacked a medium, but also included none of Taipa's siblings and supporters. In effect, the Turusato lineage emerged in a de facto state of fission as a result of witchcraft accusations that divided relatively distant agnates (see fig. 5.2). This would not have occurred if the four brothers who remained at the longhouse community had not favored this outcome and pressed for a witchcraft accusation in a situation of child death in which inaction would be the typical outcome. The fact that Pabu used Taipa's conventional pronouncement as grounds for bringing in an outside medium is indicative of underlying dissatisfaction with Taipa's spiritual leadership. The departure of Taipa and his siblings therefore cannot be attributed to the independent machinations of Araradado, Kayago, and Nogobe. However, Araradado provided the indictment against Nawadia that Pabu clearly desired, and Kayago followed up with the subsequent indictments of Imasala and Warope within a few months. The auditors of Pilime's deathbed testimony included not only Weliba but also Hene, who is Taipa's father's brother's son and is not closely related to Weliba and Nogobe. There is consequently no reason to doubt that the deathbed statement was accurately reported. The placement of Warope's name before the oracles could have been influenced by Nogobe, but this only amplified the consequences of the accusation without changing its structural character or the impetus to relocation it provided. Thus, neither Kayago nor Nogobe can be said to have determined the outcome of the accusations that prompted Taipa's departure. However, all three mediums did further an existent tendency toward fission that created an opening for a resident spirit medium at Turusato and thereby resolved a problem of overcrowding and of succession at Kaburusato.

The events that led to Araradado's and Kayago's relocation at Turusato were also intertwined with witchcraft accusations at Kaburusato. Kebo, Yebe, and Hau all died at Kaburusato later in 1967, with Waime, Tumame, Tame, and Kulubido being named as the witches responsible. Kebo, who was Kayago's mother, named Tsmari's wife Waime, and compensation was paid on the basis of this deathbed testimony without any spirit pronouncements being issued. Tsmari, who was a *tafidilo*, moved to Haifi as a result. Yebe named Tumame, one of two wives of his half brother, the *tafidilo* Mariabu. Kayago confirmed the deathbed testimony and oracular outcome, even though Mariabu was his father's brother and the two were on good terms and indeed remained so. Nogobe ratified this confirmation. Mariabu and his family then moved to Turusato where his daughter lived with her husband (Pabu's son Tagili).[5] Araradado, who was a close friend and ally of the *tafidilo* Mariabu (his FFBSS), moved to Turusato as well so they might continue to coreside (this being the reason Araradado himself gave). Shortly thereafter, Kayago joined them (and his brothers, sister, and sister's husband) as well. However, in the interim he confirmed that Tame and Kulubido were responsible for Hau's death, with Nogobe ratifying this. This led Tame and his father Nawa and their family to move to their garden house.[6]

Kayago thus became the senior resident medium at Turusato, while continuing to coreside with his close companion and mentor Araradado. Araradado essentially stepped down insofar as he no longer took the lead in conducting witchcraft inquests. Nevertheless Kayago and Araradado continued to perform séances jointly on many occasions, as they had in the past, and both engaged in curing. However, only Kayago organized spiritually motivated fish-poisoning expeditions. It is thus evident that Araradado was in transition toward retirement as a spirit medium, gradually allowing his protégé to take precedence in the most significant components of the position. If he followed the typical trajectory, he would next restrict his activities to curing alone, responding only to the requests of his contemporaries who had faith in his capabilities based on past experience. At this time (near the end of the fieldwork period), he was 42 years of age and was thus following the typical pattern that leads to retirement from mediumship by about age 45. However, we should not overlook the fact that Araradado's protégé and protégé's protégé were established as senior resident mediums in two major longhouse communities and that he had considerable personal influence with both. Moreover, he might yet become recognized as a *tafidilo* following his retirement from spirit mediumship.

It should be noted that Kayago was exceptionally well positioned at Turusato in that he was the *tafidilo* Ahoa's wife's brother and a classificatory affine of all four senior men who formed the agnatic core of the community. His own brothers Waua and Osiama resided there (the latter married to Ahoa's sister), as well as his mentor Araradado and his father's brother, Mariabu, a *tafidilo*. Ahoa's elder half brother Yora was 59 years of age and was progressively relinquishing the functions associated with his former status as leading *tafidilo* to Ahoa. There was thus every prospect that a solid cooperative political alliance between Kayago and Ahoa would guide the social life of the community for years to come. This stable arrangement would, in turn, very likely attract others to the community so that it would grow in size.

Meanwhile, Nogobe became the sole resident medium at Kaburusato and was beginning to nominate protégés of his own (i.e., Illawe). With the departure of the *tafidilos* Tsmari and Mariabu, Ibo had become the sole *tafidilo* as well. However, Nogobe was not well positioned at Kaburusato because he was not closely related to any of the married men of Kaburusato lineage other than Kayago (his father's sister's daughter's husband and thus a matrilateral sibling; see fig. 5.3). Nogobe's father had executed Nawa's mother as a witch following refusal of compensation fifteen years earlier,[7] so there was a predisposition to an underlying antipathy in Nogobe's relations with Nawa and Tame. This antipathy was shared with the close agnates and affines of Hau and Wayoro, the two men Tame was accused of killing through his witchcraft. Moreover, Nogobe had exonerated Hau's brother Hariako when Tame accused Hariako of witchcraft on the occasion of Tame's mother's death. The *tafidilo* Ibo was Hariako's sister's husband. Nogobe's relations with the married men of the community were thus largely grounded in a shared antipathy to Nawa and Tame and in mutual support relating to witchcraft accusations that were exchanged between two lineage segments related as distant agnates (Tame and Hariako being related as FFFBSSS). But over the longer term, there was no solid kinship-based support upon which Nogobe could rely.

There was thus a plan to eventually recreate the Nagefi longhouse community that had been disbanded in 1965. The core male coresidents were to be Nogobe, his father's brothers' sons Selagu and Weliba, of Haifi lineage, and their cross-cousins Sawa and Illawe and the latter's father's brother, Kayari, of Nagefi lineage (see fig. 5.3). All of these young men had co-resided at the former Nagefi longhouse from birth until their teens or early 20. However, this future plan awaited the marriages of Nogobe, Selagu, and Illawe. In the meantime, all of these young men resided at Kaburusato (with the exception of Weliba, who moved to Sarado in 1969 so that his young wife [aged 17] could coreside with her parents). They constituted nearly the entirety of the chorus when Nogobe conducted séances and a like proportion of the work group when he organized fish-poisoning expeditions. Thus Nogobe's position at Kaburusato was one in which he was most closely related to the unmarried and recently married young men, with all of these except his age-mate Hariako being nonagnates residing there only temporarily. Through his friendship with Hariako he received the support of Ibo (Hariako's sister's husband) and Yeluma (Hariako's half brother), but he was largely disconnected from Tuni and not on good terms with Nawa. These four plus Kayari were the older married men of the community.

In 1968–69, Kayago visited Kaburusato on a regular basis and performed about a dozen séances there, primarily in the early part of this period. Occasionally he was accompanied by Araradado, who also took part in a few séances. The relationship between Kayago and Nogobe was initially cordial, cooperative, and mutually supportive but progressively evidenced developing tension centering on issues of mentor precedence versus peer equality. Professional jealousy emerged and was competitively expressed. A sequential account of some of the prominent aspects of this deteriorating mentor-protégé

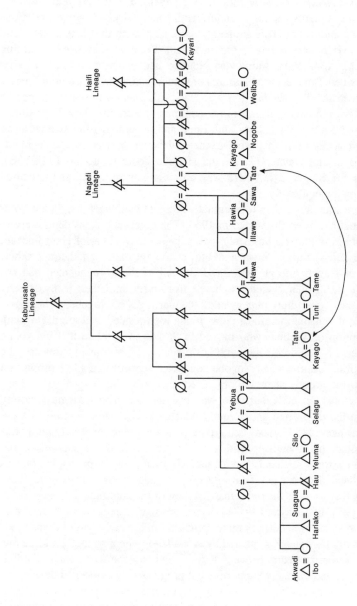

Fig. 5.3. Genealogical relations among selected residents of Kaburusato, April 1968

relationship will provide insights into the relations between mediums and community members as well as between mediums themselves. While Araradado's stepping down in favor of Kayago exemplifies the closing phase of a medium's career, Nogobe's first year as sole resident medium at Kaburusato illustrates the early phase that entails gaining the confidence of community members.

During the first seven months that I resided at Kaburusato, Nogobe and Kayago were on good terms. They held a number of joint séances on the occasions when Kayago visited Kaburusato (where he had many kinsmen). In June, they jointly conducted a highly successful fish-poisoning expedition, in accordance with the instructions of Kayago's *Kesame* spirit wife. Kayago took precedence in instigating the expedition, selecting the (spiritually designated) site, and directing the operation. Nogobe acted as his second and assistant. However, there was no evidence that this preexisting arrangement was problematic at this time.

In October, Ibo's wife Akwadi developed a protracted illness and sent word to Kayago at Turusato requesting that he cure her. He came and conducted a séance jointly with Nogobe in which both of their *Kesame* spirits were said to have cooperatively extracted a splinter from Akwadi's *ausulubo*. However, she remained ill. A few weeks later she once again sent word to Kayago, who came and, acting with Nogobe in the same manner as before, removed a second splinter. While relations between the two mediums still appeared to be untroubled, I believe that Nogobe was disappointed that Akwadi had not relied on his own curing abilities rather than calling on Kayago. It was evident that she specifically sought Kayago's services and that Nogobe's coparticipation was superfluous. Two spirits are not necessary to perform a cure. Had she felt Nogobe's spirit was efficacious, she would not have needed to call on Kayago at all. While Kayago made every effort to include Nogobe as an equal participant, Akwadi clearly did not accept him as Kayago's equal or accord him the prerogatives of resident medium by seeking to be cured by him. The event of this cure thus made Nogobe painfully aware of his continuing juniority and his lack of acceptance as Kayago's successor on the part of older community members. His age-mate and cross-cousin Sawa had requested that Nogobe cure him, but older individuals continued to look to Kayago as they had in the recent past.

In late November 1968, a séance was held to celebrate Weliba's capture of a cassowary,[8] and a number of affinally related Turusato residents were invited to share in the feast and celebration. It was initially said that all three mediums would take part in the anticipated séance, but Kayago later declined to participate and also remained in the communal section of the longhouse with his wife and others rather than joining the immediate audience in the men's section. The two performing mediums sat facing the chorus with

Nogobe on Araradado's left. Both Araradado and Nogobe became entranced at the outset of the séance, but Araradado's spirit spoke through him during the first segment and Nogobe's during the second and so on in alteration for several hours. The atmosphere was jovial and celebratory with considerable audience commentary on the mediums' pronouncements. Individuals exclaimed, "That's no lie," "Truly," and "I'm afraid/astonished" at various points, and there were also comments that elicited general laughter. Nogobe progressively engaged in longer segments, compared to Araradado, and perhaps did not sense that the audience was looking for the séance to be concluded at about midnight. In any event, during a pause in his performance, Kayago's wife Tate called from the communal section, "the cassowary is cooked, tell the *Kesame* spirit to depart." The séance then wound down and concluded shortly thereafter, as it became apparent that the chorus members were eager to get on with the feast.

It appeared that through overeagerness to perform in his role, Nogobe had gone on longer than the audience wished. While an early end to the séance was not unusual in this context, Nogobe undoubtedly hoped that his performance would generate sufficient audience interest to justify its continuation for a longer period. He evidently saw his truncated performance as indicative of his less-than-complete acceptance. Under the circumstances, he could not have appreciated Tate's blunt suggestion that he conclude. It might be read as patronizing, suggesting that he was not in touch with his audience, and perhaps also dismissive. I believe that in some way Nogobe also took Tate's remark as reflecting Kayago's view of him as still a professional junior, requiring guidance and direction, rather than a peer. In any event, the deterioration in their relationship was very noticeable from this point onward.

Two nights later there was another séance in which Araradado and Nogobe jointly participated, with Kayago again failing to take part. This séance may have been staged in order to provide an opportunity to assuage any offense to Nogobe's spirits, as community members should be eager to hear what the spirits have to say and welcome interaction with them. In addition, I believe that Nogobe wished to recontextualize some earlier predictions that he had made that had not been entirely borne out. He had an agenda, and the truncated séance of two nights earlier had precluded completion of it.

This agenda turned on Nogobe's desire to become the government-appointed "boss man" of Kaburusato. Nogobe had put himself forward for this position by greeting the patrol officer personally and showing him around as he inspected the longhouse to see if it was being kept free of refuse as he had instructed. The kiap had jokingly referred to him as boss man, grasping Nogobe's intent. However, Nogobe only picked up the form of address and not the sarcastic tone. Nogobe later queried the government interpreter, Hari, who reportedly told him the kiap did intend to appoint him to this position (although it is doubtful that Hari was this definite). Nogobe then proclaimed himself acting boss man on this basis and proceeded to direct trail-clearing operations in response to the kiap's complaint that the trails were not being kept wide enough to accommodate his carriers.[9] The young men of Kaburusato followed Nogobe's initiative in this effort.

Before a séance that took place in mid-November, just prior to a trading expedition to Huli territory and Komo patrol post, Nogobe pumped me for information about when he would receive the lap-lap that constituted the official boss man's dress and insignia of office. It was clear that he sought to make a prediction in the séance scheduled to take place that evening. This probing took the form of making a number of statements about the subject and trying to get me to verify one of them. He said the kiap would give him the uniform at Komo. I said I didn't know. Somewhat later he returned to the subject and said he would receive it at Kaburusato. Again, I said I didn't know. However, realizing what he wanted at this point I told him something that was germane (and not yet known to the Etoro), so that he would not be led to make a false prediction. When the trading party arrived at Komo, they would find the present kiap had departed and a new kiap had assumed the position in his place. This information was meant to indicate to Nogobe that he was unlikely to be appointed boss man anytime soon.

That night Nogobe's *Sigisato* spirit prophesied that the kiap who had visited recently would no longer be at Komo, and that a new kiap would present Nogobe with the boss man's uniform when he visited Kaburusato in future. It was also prophesied that many shoats would be procured in trade with the Huli near Komo. This latter prediction turned out to be correct. However, the information I had provided was only partially accurate, and the prediction based upon it therefore partially false. Both the prior kiap and his successor were at Komo, so that the former had not in fact departed. This was the errant prophecy that Nogobe wished to recontextualize. Moreover, he wanted to make further prophecies about bestowal of the boss man's insignia of office, following up on his *Sigisato* spirit's earlier predictions.[10] He had not been able to do this in the earlier truncated séance. The protracted séance two nights later thus provided an occasion for Nogobe to return to these issues.[11]

Although Kayago did not take part in this second séance, he conducted a séance of his own the next night (Araradado having already returned to Turusato). Nogobe spent the early part of this séance at my house and was clearly disgruntled. When I asked him if he were going to participate, he made a face, and when I later pressed him as to why he remained at my house, he made a disparaging remark about Kayago's séance being "no good" (*nefate*). He later went to the longhouse when I retired, but he slept in the communal section, ignoring the séance in progress. He thus reciprocated Kayago's nonparticipation in his séance the night before. This marked a complete transformation of their relationship, in that previously they had always participated jointly in any séances held when Kayago was present at Kaburusato. Although I do not know all the specifics of their falling out, the main outlines were clear enough. Kayago was not entirely relinquishing his position as senior medium to Nogobe, even though Kayago was no longer a resident of the community. This blocked Nogobe's succession to this position, undercut his efforts to gain complete acceptance from the older members of the community, perpetuated his juniority, and rendered him less than Kayago's peer. While Kayago's failure to participate in the first two séances (with Nogobe and Araradado) might potentially be interpreted as a gesture indicating that he was giving over his former position to his protégé, the fact that Kayago held a séance of his own the following night nullifies this potential interpretation. Kayago clearly continued to cultivate his local following and retain at least some aspects of his former position in the community.

Open competition between Kayago and Nogobe surfaced shortly thereafter and continued throughout the next five months. The first manifestation of this was in fish poisoning. Nogobe's spirit wife called for a fish-poisoning expedition, specifying the location and day and foretelling success, all in the usual manner. Nogobe then directed the endeavor the following day, designating the placement of the dams and breakwaters and determining the sequence of their construction (see Kelly 1977:38–40). The project appeared to be overly ambitious in scale in relation to the size of the work party and took from 8:00 A.M. to 4:30 P.M. to complete. Only Sawa, Illawe, Selagu, and his younger brother Igioto (aged 14) had been successfully recruited for the project. Selagu's mother and two sisters (Yebua, Asigila, and Saffara) also helped somewhat by gathering moss to plug holes between the rocks that formed the dam. In addition to being undermanned, the project did not go smoothly. The location and order of placement of the dams and breakwaters left something to be desired. When one part of a dam was completed, the water level was raised so that a previously constructed section was too low and required additional work that did not entirely correct the problem. In notes made that afternoon, I wrote, "this operation appears to me to be much less professionally carried out than the previous expedition Kayago directed." In retrospect, I am sure I was not the only one to think of this comparison (although I did not grasp the developing competition between Kayago and Nogobe at that time).

When the site was finally sealed off and the water level began to drop within it, Nogobe inspected the enclosed area for signs of fish. He was anxious

Center left, top picture, the spirit medium Nogobe leads by example in constructing dams for a fish-poisoning operation carried out at the direction of his spirits. *Lower picture,* Nogobe, being a bachelor, finds it necessary to do the female as well as male components of the work of processing sago that he intends to deploy in trade with the Huli to procure a shoat.

The *tafidilo* Ahoa draws his bow *(top picture)* to express his anger at my uninvited attendance at a *kosa* ceremony early in my fieldwork. After we had subsequently become friends, Ahoa accompanied me while I carried out measurements of a garden, where he posed for the photograph below.

Pabu *(upper picture)* attended the *kosa* ceremony at Sedado only five days after he had executed Kulubido (natally of Sedado) as the witch responsible for the death of his beloved wife. He was elated at the fulfillment of vengeance. He wears the charcoal-darkened black face of anger and the black cassowary-feather headdress typically donned by a warrior before a predawn raid. The *kosa* ceremony celebrated Nogobe's betrothal to Keke, the second girl from the right in the lower picture. It would be at least eight years until they wed.

Nogobe performs the *kosa*. The streamers accentuate his graceful dancing as he sings sad songs he has composed to commemorate the members of the host community who have passed away in recent years.

Kauhe performs the *kosa*. The dance movements are sometimes likened to the mating dance of the red bird of paradise, the corporeal abode of a medium's spirit wife and of other spirit women.

Hariako performs the *kosa* while an elderly *tafidilo* of the host community weeps as he recollects the deceased relative being commemorated in song. Those moved to tears in this way burn the dancers on the back with a torch, but the knife Hariako carries in his right hand enjoins the potential burner to exercise appropriate restraint in carrying out the burning and thus enhances the dramatic tension of this ritual expression of grief.

to see what the catch might be when the poison was deployed after the site had more completely drained. Seeing no signs of fish, he became despondent and lay on a large boulder with his head buried in his arms. His kinsmen and age-mates comforted him. He then disheartedly proceeded to the poisoning. However, the women left with Igioto before this began, and I was also encouraged to leave (and did) as it was said to be about to rain (although it was not). The catch was later reported by Illawe to be only a single fish.

One of the first fish-poisoning expeditions that Nogobe directed on his own was thus markedly unsuccessful in terms of the extensive labor expenditure involved.[12] The yield would have been less than a half-ounce per man-hour as opposed to eleven ounces per man-hour in the earlier expedition directed by Kayago. That night a séance was held to determine why Nogobe's spirit wife had led the participants into this unproductive endeavor that failed to meet with the prophesied success. The spirit wife related that the fish poison had been brought to the site before it was sealed off and the *abaso* had smelled it and fled. This preserved the reliability and credibility of Nogobe's *Kesame* but implicitly acknowledged that Nogobe's secular direction of the project was flawed. The message was that the spirit could be counted upon to make accurate predictions (in that there *had* been many fish at the specified site), and that Nogobe himself would in future avoid the procedural error he had made on this occasion.

It is important to note that curing hinges on the same aspect of mediumship that is involved in fish poisoning, namely the medium's ability to secure the complete cooperation of his spirits. A spirit wife who fails to provide information that eventuates in a favorable result in fish poisoning may also fail to watch over and protect a cured patient from subsequent witchcraft attacks. The spirits are considered to be entirely capable of providing accurate information and continuing protection; this is unquestioned. But the spirits may be lax in following up on cures or may fail to keep a medium posted about the movements of the fish. This variable turns on the medium's relationship with his spirit wife and spirit son rather than their intrinsic capabilities. Lack of success in fish poisoning and curing thus calls into question the medium's ability to mediate essential relations with the supernatural. Nogobe therefore sought an explanation that placed the blame on his secular direction of the project and did not call into question the reliability of his spirit wife or his capacity to secure her cooperation and effective assistance.

The following day Kayago undertook a small fish-poisoning operation not far from Kaburusato with Ahoa (his sister's husband). The catch was only a single *abaso* in this case as well, but the labor expenditure was only about 5 man-hours (versus 45.5 for Nogobe's expedition), so the yield was considered acceptable although on the low side. The fact that Kayago chose to engage in fish poisoning at this time might well have remained unknown to the residents of Kaburusato had he selected a site nearer Turusato. One can only assume Kayago desired that the expedition and results become known at Kaburusato so that invidious comparisons could be made, as indeed they were. Moreover, it seems that Kayago set out to show up Nogobe by conducting a fish-poisoning operation the day after he learned of Nogobe's lack of success. The small scale of the operation insured that it could not involve the magnitude of wasted effort that Nogobe's had engendered. Under these circumstances, there was no risk that Kayago could come off as poorly, and there was considerable opportunity for a comparatively favorable result. Although the results were acceptable, they fell short of complete success, and Kayago also deemed it necessary to conduct a séance to inquire into the reasons for this. It was revealed that he had incautiously followed the instructions of an unattached *Kesame* spirit (not his own spirit wife) in site selection and timing. She was lax and unreliable in that she had failed to inform Kayago that the fish had, in fact, mostly moved to another point in the river by morning. This recontextualization was easily accomplished since spirits are only identifiable by slight differences in the way they are voiced by the medium. People might then say, in retrospect, that it indeed had not sounded like the voice of Kayago's spirit wife. The reputation of the latter thus remained entirely intact (and Kayago had risked nothing in this respect). Moreover, one might certainly expect that he would not listen to this unreliable spirit woman again.

In January, further competition was manifested in the realm of curing. Tuni became ill during the epidemic, and his respiratory condition persisted. He sent word to Turusato to request that Kayago cure him. Kayago came to Kaburusato and conducted a séance, but his spirits related that Tuni's illness was not due to witchcraft and would pass of its own accord. Although Nogobe's services were not requested (and he had absented himself from this séance), he nevertheless addressed Tuni's condition in a later séance. Nogobe's *Sigisato* related that Tuni was in fact threatened by witchcraft attack but that he (the *Sigisato*) would watch over him and protect him. There was an oblique suggestion that Kayago's spirit had not been aware of a lurking witch who sought to introduce (or perhaps already had introduced) foreign objects into Tuni's *ausulubo*. In other words, Tuni was encouraged to seek a cure from Nogobe's solicitous and watchful *Sigisato*. That would have enabled Nogobe to remove causes of illness that Kayago's lax spirit had allowed to be introduced by not being on the lookout for witchcraft. However, Tuni improved and did not take up this invitation.

In late April, Araradado sent word to Kaburusato requesting that Nogobe come to Turusato to cure him. He had not previously sought or received Kayago's services (i.e., Nogobe was his first resort). This request was a tribute from a highly respected medium, and it gave Nogobe's reputation as a healer a very considerable boost. One can only surmise that this was exactly what Araradado hoped to achieve. It also had the effect of rectifying the underlying problem in the competitive relationship between Kayago and Nogobe. In a single masterful stroke, Araradado publicly anointed Nogobe as Kayago's peer and equal. This alleviated Nogobe's need to try to competitively equal Kayago's success in curing and fish poisoning in order to establish himself as the latter's successor at Kaburusato. I believe that Kayago, on his part, was inclined to follow the implicit suggestion of his respected mentor that he disengage from his former relationship to the Kaburusato community, leaving that field to Nogobe. In any event, there were no further competitive incidents. By the time I left the field, Nogobe finally appeared secure as resident medium at Kaburusato and Kayago had not performed any séances there in many months.

With the issue of succession now resolved, it was not unlikely that the two men would reestablish their formerly close relationship. Each would then be likely to take part in the séances conducted by the other during the course of mortuary gatherings, seconding and lending additional spiritual authority to each other's authentication of witchcraft accusations. Such relationships interconnect the mediums of different communities in a loose network.

The distribution of mediums and *tafidilos* among the 8 of 11 communities that make up the sample is shown in table 5.2. Six of the 8 communities have at least one medium in residence. One of the 2 communities that lacks a medium is the very small community of Kasayasato, which called upon Kayago when curing and the authentication of witchcraft accusations were required. The other is Katiefi, where Piawe had formerly resided before he moved to the nearby community of Haifi. Piawe continued to visit Katiefi and perform séances there on a regular basis in 1968. His relocation was prompted by the first witchcraft accusation against his daughter Udali, which had taken place at Katiefi not long before he moved. It was facilitated by the fact that the deceased former medium of Haifi (Sanimako) either had not trained a protégé or had trained one who predeceased him. Piawe had already been conducting séances at Haifi before he moved there.[13] When the communities of Haifi and Katiefi combined after the January 1969 epidemic (in which Piawe died), his protégé Wato became the resident medium. Thus the only community that lacked a resident medium throughout the fieldwork period was Kasayasato, which was too small to provide a viable base of operation for a medium. Only three young men resided there, not enough to form a séance chorus. A medium would also hope to establish himself in a community likely to endure over time, while Kasayasato was likely to disband before long, with its residents moving to other communities.

When two or three mediums reside at the same longhouse, they are

TABLE 5.2

The Distribution of Mediums and *Tafidilos* by Age and Community, May 1, 1968

Males, Aged	Longhouse Community								Cohort Total	Mediums		Tafidilos	
	Turusato	Kaburu-sato	Sarado	Ingiri-bisato	Haifi	Katiefi	Hilisato	Kasaya-sato		Number of Mediums	Percentage of Cohort	Number of Tafidilos	Percentage of Cohort
66–70				1			1		1		0		0
61–65	2**			1		2*	1		4		0	1	25.0
56–60	1				2**		1	1	6		0	4	66.7
51–55				3*	1*§	1	1*		6		0	2	33.0
46–50		2*	1*	1	1		2**		7	1	14.3	5	71.4
41–45	2§	2	4§§	3§			1		7	2	28.6		0
36–40	2*	2	4§§§	5	1	1	1§		10	3	30.0	1	10.0
31–35	2	2				2	3	2	17		0		0
26–30	5§	2§	2	4§	1§	4	2	1	21	3	14.3		0
21–25	2	2	1§	3	1§	1	2§§		10	4	40.0		0
Total males	14	10	8	21	7	11	14	4	89	13	14.6	13	14.6
Number of mediums	2	1	3	2	2	0	3	0					
Number of tafidilos	3	1	1	1	3	1	3	0					

* = *tafidilo*
§ = medium

nearly always related as mentor and protégé(s). This configuration prevailed at Turusato (Araradado/Kayago), Ingiribisato (Hoamo/Wabiaka), Haifi (Piawe/Wato), and Hilisato (Nagubi/Arubia and Hewa). Sarado presents only a partial exception as two of the three resident mediums are related as mentor and protégé (i.e., Nasu/Ibasia). However, Maua was not Nasu's mentor. Maua had been senior resident medium at Sarado for a number of years prior to his death in January 1969, while Nasu was a recent arrival. Nasu had moved to Sarado in early 1966 after he had been accused of witchcraft at the Nagefi longhouse (which also disbanded at that time, following three closely spaced deaths). Nasu was a protégé of Tofono but did not accompany him after the breakup of Nagefi (see n. 16). Although he was not Maua's protégé, he was a close kinsman (mother's sister's son) of Maua and his brother Ailoe. The protégé Nasu trained shortly after his arrival was the son of the *tafidilo* Tuaya. Nasu was thus fairly closely connected to three of the other five married men of the community (he himself being the sixth). The fact that Maua had no protégé also facilitated Nasu's incorporation into the community as a practicing medium. When Maua died, Nasu became the senior resident medium. He authenticated the accusation against Heanome, whom Maua had named in his deathbed statement. However, Nasu himself had been accused of witchcraft a few months before this, and the subsequent confirmation of his guilt by the birth oracle undercut his position as a spiritual authority. This will be discussed further along. The central point to be noted here is that coresiding mediums are nearly always related as mentor and protégé.[14] After Maua's death, Sarado conformed to this markedly predominant pattern as well. Although mediums do change residence, they tend to move to a community that lacks a resident medium. Moreover, mentor and protégé may relocate as a pair.

The mentor-protégé relationship provides a basis for cooperation in conducting joint séances. It also provides the grounds for precedence in organizing fish poisoning and in authenticating witchcraft accusations so that competition between coresiding mediums can potentially be avoided. Cooperation and precedence are much more difficult to arrange when mediums are not so related. The intrinsic potentiality for competition under these circumstances accounts for the comparative infrequency and short duration of coresidence involving mediums not related as mentor and protégé.

THE SHAMANIC CAREER

A medium's career can be divided into three distinct stages: novice apprentice, journeyman, and semiretired senior figure. A young man is first nominated by the revelation of an established medium's spirit that a female *Kesame* spirit has an elective affinity for him and desires to become his wife.

The nominee must then undergo training. This entails an extensive sequence of séances in which only he and his mentor participate. His spirit wife-to-be first comes to him in a dream to give him spirit tobacco. After smoking this, he is able to meet his spirit wife on the *ausulubo* plane of existence in trance as well as in dreams. The main object of these meetings is to have sexual intercourse with her, consummating their union and begetting a spirit child. It is the spirit wife who is said to educate the medium in the course of their interactions and the term for spirit medium is *Kesame taua*, one who knows a *Kesame*. In other words, the mentor is believed to serve as a guide to self-revelatory, experiential development of relations with the spirit world. However, I have no additional data regarding what transpires during the private training séances and therefore cannot assess the nature and extent of the guidance and training provided. These private sessions are said to go on nightly for seventeen days. Sawa's training was discontinued after five nights because he failed to develop a relationship with his prospective spirit wife or consummate their union.

Following this intensive induction, the medium-in-training becomes a novice apprentice. He will conduct séances jointly with his mentor, with his participation initially limited to comparatively short segments. Only his spirit wife will speak through him. After the requisite nine months, a novice medium's spirit child is born, but is preverbal. Although precocious, the spirit child will not play an active role for several years. The first spirit child is always a son. Older mediums may have several spirit children, but sons still predominate, and daughters are quite rare. A novice medium may also take a second spirit wife. This is essentially a prophecy of polygyny in real life, as there are thought to be parallels between the medium's life course in the supernatural and secular domains. (The rates of polygyny for mediums and *tafidilos* will be presented in due course.)

Several years later, the novice medium acquires a *Sigisato* spirit who reveals his elective affinity for the practitioner in a dream. This spiritual acquisition is delayed because a *Sigisato* cannot be received until the spirit son "makes a trail." In other words, the spirit son must occupy the medium's body and speak through him before the *Sigisato* may do so. But the spirit son must first acquire language, which takes several years. The *Sigisato* is always a male spirit and is always connected with the medium's lineage. The *Sigisato's* wife and children are unknown and have no interactions with séance audiences. However, a *Sigisato's* agnatic sibling relations are known, and the *Sigisatos* of two mediums of the same lineage are said to be brothers. They are never reported to be father and son, even if the two mediums are so related or are of successive generations (e.g., Araradado and Kayago). A medium's relation to his own *Sigisato* is also configured as a relation between agnatic age-mates and is siblinglike (as in the *Sigisato* origin myth related in chap. 3).

After a medium is established, *Sigisatos* connected with other lineages may also speak through him when there are a number of men of that lineage in the audience. A *Sigisato*'s beneficent aid is directed toward members of the lineage with which he is associated through co-ownership of territory (see Kelly 1977:89–90). Thus, the *Sigisato* of the deceased Nagefi medium Tofono spoke through Nogobe to Nagefi men living at Kaburusato. However, the *Sigisatos* of the living Kaburusato mediums Araradado and Kayago did not likewise speak through Nogobe to Kaburusato lineage members at the longhouse of the same name. A variety of *Kesame* spirits other than a medium's spirit wife and spirit child may also speak through him. However, this multiplicity of spirit voices awaits attainment of journeyman status.

About three years or more are required before a novice medium can acquire a *Sigisato* spirit. Since only a *Sigisato* can pass judgment upon the outcome of a pig-organ oracle, a novice medium cannot authenticate a witchcraft accusation. However, his spirit wife can track a witch and thus ratify the findings of his mentor's spirits with respect to the witch's identity. Only a *Sigisato* spirit can authorize an execution, so a novice medium is precluded from making this potent pronouncement as well. In addition, a *Kesame* spirit will come only to the longhouse while a *Sigisato* spirit (associated with the forest) can also enter an entranced medium at a garden dwelling or hunting lodge. A novice medium therefore cannot make house calls to engage in curing and would be unable to conduct séances at the seclusion lodge where initiation takes place. This longhouse restriction has the effect of preventing a novice from conducting séances that are not held under the auspices of his mentor.

In all other respects, a novice medium has the capabilities of a journeyman. The possession of a spirit wife enables him to engage in curing (at the longhouse) and in organizing fish-poisoning expeditions. A novice medium can also conduct or jointly participate in what might be termed the generic séance. This involves foretelling the seasonal cycle, which takes the form of predicting the imminent ripening of various collectibles and making prophecies of success in procuring seasonally available game (such as flying foxes and cassowaries) that become vulnerable to hunting or snaring when certain forest fruits ripen. It may also be predicted that shoats born in the forest will become feral if not brought to the longhouse soon. Warnings of witchcraft are invariably issued, and predictions of illness striking an undesignated community member are often made. The success of trading expeditions and other ventures may be foretold. Queries from the audience are fielded regarding the whereabouts of lost pigs and the welfare of recently deceased relatives now residing among the *Kesames*. Finally, considerable portions of the generic séance are devoted to entertaining tales of the exploits of the *Kesames* in the spirit world. Many of the communications noted above are asides interjected by the spirit wife or spirit son in the course of these exploits (cf. Knauft 1985a:295–310). For example, they may happen upon a lurking witch that threatens the community as in Nogobe's spirits' warnings about Nomaya. Prophecies may also relate directly to anticipated events, as in Kayago's prediction that wounds would be sustained in an expected demand for compensation and Nogobe's prediction that the kiap would bestow the boss man's accoutrements upon him. However, this does not imply that the future is ordained. Rather, the spirits are able to discern the intentions of social actors and thus forecast what they are inclined to do. This capacity evidently stems from their ability to carry out eavesdropping at any point in the social universe, while remaining unseen. By the same token, they cannot be everywhere at once and thus miss a great deal. Hence, they typically do not witness the acts of witchcraft that cause illness and cannot identify the witch responsible.

A medium ceases to be a novice when he acquires a full complement of spirits. However, he may remain an apprentice beyond this time if he only holds séances jointly with his mentor and takes no independent action. Journeyman status is marked by single-handed curing, the direction of fish-poisoning expeditions, and primary authentication of witchcraft accusations. If an apprentice medium's mentor dies, he may advance to journeyman status at an early age, rapidly acquiring a *Sigisato* if he previously lacked one. Wato thus made this transition at age 22, following Piawe's death. Otherwise, attainment of journeyman status is likely to be delayed. Kayago did not begin to authenticate witchcraft accusations independently until he was 28, and Nogobe's first independent pronouncement (exonerating Hariako) was made when he was 27. Arubia's first authentication was made somewhat earlier, at age 24. A medium would not undertake to train a protégé until he had acquired a full complement of spirits and had also achieved most (if not all) the components of journeyman status.

A medium enters the third stage of his career, as a semiretired senior figure, when he begins to relinquish primacy in authenticating witchcraft accusations to his protégé. A mentor will likely relinquish the direction of fish poisoning somewhat earlier. But while stepping aside in these respects, he will continue to be active in curing and conducting generic séances until he retires completely at about age 45. Araradado entered semiretired status at age 39 and Nagubi at age 40. Piawe and Tofono were still practicing when they died at age 46, while Sanimako was not practicing when he died at age 43. A senior medium's active career may be extended if his protégé and designated successor either predeceases him or has moved to another community. This occurred in the cases of both Piawe and Tofono.

A medium's reputation also has a bearing on the length of his career. Tofono was not only widely renowned but was also connected by kinship and/or mentorship to nearly all western Etoro mediums. He was the mentor of Sanimako, Araradado, and Nasu. He collaborated with both Kago and Abenamoga in authenticating recorded witchcraft accusations (and Abenamoga was probably also one of his protégés; see n. 3). Kayago was the husband of his brother's daughter, Tate, whom Tofono had reared after his brother's death and whose marriage he had arranged. Wabiaka was married to his daughter Tabiemi. Nogobe was Tofono's sister's husband's son, and Araradado was married to Tofono's classificatory daughter. Hoamo was the father's brother of one of Tofono's wives, Nagubi was the father's "brother" of another, and Piawe was his father's sister's son's son (see fig. 5.4). Tofono was thus a nodal figure in the network of interrelations among practicing mediums that is based on relations of kinship and mentorship. Although he died shortly before the inception of my fieldwork, he was reputed to have conducted séances in a wide range of communities. Among the mediums practicing in 1968–69, Kayago had the widest range of activity in this respect. He conducted séances and carried out curing and the primary authentication of witchcraft accusations at Kaburusato, Turusato, and Kasayasato. He also participated in mortuary gathering séances at Sarado and Ingiribisato, seconding the findings of other mediums. Piawe had also been active at both Katiefi and Haifi when he was somewhat younger, and had conducted séances at Turusato with his protégé Taipa before Taipa moved away. Hoamo conducted séances at Poboleifi as well as Ingiribisato. As far as I know, none of the other mediums performed outside of their community of residence other than participating in mortuary gathering séances at neighboring longhouses.

A medium's renown can also extend to an adjacent tribal group. The Petamini medium Tarume was famed for his curing and spiritual detection of witchcraft among the Etoro as well as within his natal tribe. When Ailoe died at Sarado during the January 1969 epidemic, Tarume was called in to authenticate the accusation against Hagua. This was done to enhance the credibility of a reciprocal accusation between two communities. The senior resident medium who was bypassed was Nasu, whose spiritual authority had been undercut by the witchcraft accusations against him. Since this case documents the point that an established medium can be undone by witchcraft accusations and also represents the only instance in which the jurisdictional prerogative of a senior resident medium was disregarded, it will be worthwhile to fill in the background in some detail.

Constructing Inequality

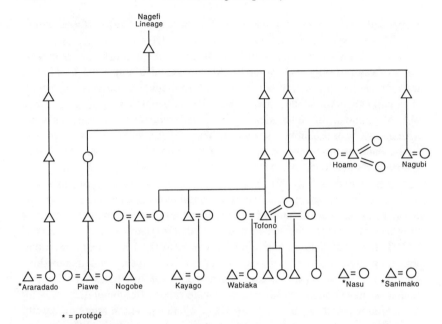

Fig. 5.4. Genealogical and mentorship relations between Tofono and other western Etoro mediums

In August 1968, Susa died at Hilisato and named the medium Nasu, of Sarado, as the witch responsible. Arubia, who was Susa's wife's brother, was one of the auditors of the deathbed testimony and also authenticated this accusation. This was his first such pronouncement. Five months later, Ailoe died at Sarado, naming Hagua of Hilisato. The naming of a Sarado witch by a Hilisato resident was thus reciprocated by the naming of a Hilisato witch by a Sarado resident. Nasu would normally have been called upon to authenticate this accusation as senior resident medium (following Maua's death). Nasu's brother Tahopi had also been the sole auditor of Ailoe's last words and served as the principal next of kin (both Nasu and Tahopi being Ailoe's mother's sister's sons). If Nasu were to authenticate the accusation, it would appear that it was merely retaliatory. Moreover, Nasu, who had a motive to retaliate (since he himself was the person accused earlier), controlled all the components of the accusation as presiding medium and brother to the custodian of the deathbed testimony and performer of the oracles. Hagua had been vociferous when compensation was demanded from Nasu, who had refused to pay at the time and had not yet paid when this counteraccusation was lodged. Hagua was also Arubia's "mother's brother" and close companion. In addition, the accusation was problematic because Hagua had not been at Sarado either when Ailoe sickened or when he died. He was supposed to have bewitched Ailoe initially when the latter was foraging in the forest between these two neighboring settlements. Finally, and certainly most importantly, Nasu's credibility as a spiritual authority was undercut by the fact that he had twice been accused of witchcraft. Hence, the renowned medium Tarume was called in to lend his considerable spiritual authority to the accusation. Tarume was a wife's "brother" of Tuaya, the sole *tafidilo* at Sarado, and Tuaya recruited him to act in Nasu's stead.

Tarume authenticated the accusation in the strongest possible manner; his *Kesame* spirit wife related that she had actually witnessed the acts of witchcraft (rather than merely tracking the witch). When compensation was demanded, the Hilisato men at first refused to provide it, as is typical in accusations against an individual not in close proximity to the victim. One man was shot in the ankle in the ensuing volley of arrows aimed at the ground in front of the refusers. About a week later, the Hilisato men delivered the compensation and the wounded individual also received a small compensation from Sarado. Two months later, Nasu's wife gave birth to a boy, confirming his guilt in Susa's death. Nasu then provided the previously refused compensation to Arubia at Hilisato. The birth oracle's confirmation of his guilt further undercut his spiritual authority.

The witchcraft case arising from Ailoe's death illustrates two important points. First, a medium's credibility in authenticating witchcraft accusations is substantially undermined by multiple witchcraft accusations against him. This reduced credibility provides a potential ground for refusal to pay compensation, undercutting a central objective for seeking authentication and rendering the medium ineffectual. In other words, a medium who is accused of witchcraft several times lacks effective spiritual authority, which is accorded (or withheld) by fellow tribesmen. It is to a significant degree a reputational quality. While Nasu could engage in curing and conduct generic séances, he was essentially reduced to the status of an apprentice because he could not effectively take the lead in authenticating accusations. Second, a renowned medium whose spiritual authority is widely respected can expand his activities into the community-delineated jurisdictions of other mediums. This multicommunity sphere of operation may even extend across tribal (ethnic) boundaries.[15] This represents the opposite end of the spectrum with respect to the enhancement of the reputational quality of spiritual authority. Among Etoro mediums, only Tofono appears to have approximated this level of renown in the recent past. As we have seen, Tofono was also a nodal figure in the network of relations between practicing mediums. This suggests that such connections may play a role in achieving the apex of spirit mediumship.

The Etoro articulate the view that an individual should not be both a practicing medium and a *tafidilo*. Although informants provided no reason other than "Etoro culture" (Etoro *mara*) as the basis for this separation of secular and spiritual authority, the consolidation of these two roles in a single individual was regarded as inappropriate and, in the abstract, repugnant. However, there are several exceptions to this general cultural dictum in practice. Tofono was said to have been a *tafidilo* as well as a practicing medium when he died in early 1968. This was attributed to an accident of demography. One of the *tafidilos* of the Nagefi longhouse community died, and the other moved to a different longhouse. Another senior man also died, leaving Tofono (then aged 43) as the only man in the community over the age of 35 at that time (late 1965). When Nagefi disbanded not long thereafter, both of the mediums who had coresided with Tofono (i.e., Nasu and Abenamoga) went elsewhere, while Tofono and most other former residents established a garden house settlement near Turusato. Tofono was therefore not in a position to retire from mediumship. He planned to direct the construction of a new Nagefi longhouse, which is a role consistent with *tafidilo* status. However, this plan did not come to fruition before he died several years later. I believe that in the normal course of events he would have relinquished his role as practicing medium to one of his protégés and assumed the status of *tafidilo*. As it was, he did not play the roles associated with *tafidilo* status at Turusato but only within the restricted domain of his small garden house settlement. He did conduct séances at the Turusato longhouse on occasion (infringing on Taipa's domain). When his associate (and probable protégé) Abenamoga died at Katiefi in late 1967, Tofono traveled there to conduct the spirit inquest and authenticate the accusation.[16] In so doing, he took precedence over Piawe, the former senior resident medium of Katiefi, who was then residing at the neighboring community of Haifi. (However, Piawe was moving toward retirement.) Thus, Tofono continued as a renowned practicing medium until his death (at age 46) but never actually performed the roles associated with *tafidilo* status within the context of a longhouse community, although he was accorded that status.

Piawe is the only other practicing medium who was said to be a *tafidilo* as well. This too was attributed to accidents of demography. Piawe had intended to relinquish his duties as medium to his sister's husband Abenamoga (at Katiefi) and his protégé Wato (at Haifi). But Abenamoga died while Wato still lacked the full complement of spirits. This led to a partial reversal of Piawe's semiretired status. However, he was not very active as a medium during this period (after he moved to Haifi in 1967). No authentications of witchcraft accusations are attributed to him. Although Piawe was said to be both a medium and *tafidilo* (and is double-listed in table 5.2), he was clearly in transition toward retirement from mediumship when he died (at age 46) in January 1969.

Consideration of the transition to *tafidilo* status illuminates the question of why mediums retire. Although the careers of highly respected mediums may extend into their middle 40s, it is precisely these illustrious mediums who tend to become *tafidilos* and thus relinquish mediumship. Tofono and Piawe are the two mediums who trained the largest number of successful protégés and both had a multicommunity sphere of operation. Other mediums, who are less renowned, tend to relinquish their position to a protégé at an earlier age due to successional dynamics. Araradado, Nagubi, and Hoamo are examples. Araradado stepped aside in favor of Kayago when he was 39, and Nagubi relinquished his position to Arubia at age 40. Hoamo (aged 43) had also been superceded by his protégé Wabiaka, although I cannot pin down the date at which this transition occurred. All three still continued to conduct séances and engage in curing but were no longer involved in the authentication of witchcraft accusations in 1968–69. Thus, when Susa died at Hilisato in August 1968, Arubia (rather than Nagubi) conducted the inquest that confirmed Nasu's guilt. Kayago's succession to Araradado's position was described at some length earlier.

The material presented thus far provides a basis for summarizing and further elaborating upon the central ingredients of successful mediumship. As was noted earlier, the position of novice apprentice is effectively open to nearly all initiated young men who show an interest, excluding only those who have been named as a witch or are thought to be a *sa:go* or *kagomano*. In addition, no enabling kin relation of any particular type is required in order to secure training from an established medium. Some intending novices fail to complete this training. The remainder move through a succession of grades as they successively acquire a *Kesame* spirit wife, spirit son, and *Sigisato*. A novice apprentice's progression toward mediumship at this stage can be materially assisted by a mentor who facilitates coparticipation in curing, fish poisoning, and the secondary authentication of witchcraft accusations. This enables the apprentice to begin to establish the reliability of his spirits and his ability to secure their full cooperation. Conversely, it is logical to conclude that a mentor could easily undermine his protégé's career at this point if their relationship sours. However, I know of no cases in which this occurred in the early stages of apprenticeship. Nevertheless, a supportive mentor is very probably the first requisite of successful entry into the shamanic profession.

As a medium begins to hold séances on his own, the requisites of a clientele and a following come into play. Successful mediumship requires that community members request cures and seek other supernatural services (such as locating lost pigs) both in order to provide justification for conducting séances and to generate contexts in which a medium's spirits can demonstrate their effectiveness. Intrinsic competition comes to the fore at this juncture because potential clients can select among available mediums in requesting cures. A sick individual who believes himself to be bewitched and fears death is inclined to select an established medium of proven curing ability. A protégé may thus find himself in competition with his mentor even if neither consciously desires this. This dynamic may then have repercussions with respect to their relationship. However, the potential community clientele may felicitously split along age and kinship lines such that the protégé is asked to cure his contemporaries and a few older individuals who are his close kin. This provides an opportunity for the protégé to build up the reputation of his spirits' efficacy. But success is not assured. The medium's first patients may fail to recover and thus seek secondary cures, possibly looking to an established medium at this point.

The novice medium Hewa was evidently failing to make the grade in this respect. When I asked my best informant, Illawe, to list the mediums whose spirits were effective at curing, he listed all practicing mediums except Hewa. He explicitly singled out Hewa's spirit for disparagement, saying that his *Kesame* spirit wife was "no good." Hewa was one of two protégés of Nagubi at Hilisato, the other being Arubia. The two were father's brother's sons and age-mates (born in the same year). Hilisato was the only community that contained two apprentices, and it appeared that intrinsic competition was at the base of community members' comparative evaluations of curing ability (picked up by Illawe). In any event, Hewa provides a probable example of attrition at this stage. By the end of the fieldwork period, he rarely conducted séances. Although a turnaround was perhaps possible, it did not appear very likely. Arubia, on the other hand, was quite successful in gaining the confidence of community members and graduated to the position of senior resident medium following Nagubi's death.

A medium requires a following as well as a clientele. A chorus composed of five or six young men is the sine qua non of a séance. Although a séance may last only from about 10:00 P.M. to midnight, this is considered something of a flop. Ideally, the séance should engage the interest of the chorus and audience so that it continues until at least the wee hours of the morning and, hopefully, until dawn. The dedication of the chorus is essential if this is to occur. They must remain awake themselves and sing with sufficient volume and exuberance to make it difficult for others to sleep (beyond short naps). It is important to recall that the medium's pronouncements are uttered in sotto voce and cannot readily be heard more than ten or fifteen feet away. The chorus amplifies these communications in song. A medium is thus utterly dependent upon his chorus. This means that he must have the support of the young men of the community, who will generally be his contemporaries in age. They will need to stay up all night about once a week if the aspiring medium is to enjoy a full measure of success.

A medium also requires the assistance of these same young men in order to engage in fish poisoning. They will likely constitute the entirety of the labor force in the early expeditions stimulated by his *Kesame* spirit's pronouncements and directed by him. As with curing, fish poisoning constitutes an arena in which success or failure can be comparatively evaluated. Although there are recontextualizations of the prophecy of success that can be employed to excuse poor results, the empirical outcomes are telling over the longer term. If considerable effort is repeatedly expended to no effect, it will become increasingly difficult to recruit a work party. As in any form of procuring fish, technical expertise and experience are of assistance, but there is an irreducible element of luck. An aspiring medium would probably do best to avoid grand enterprises that hold the potential for colossal failure. A good return on lesser efforts is sufficient to build a reputation with reduced risk of alienating one's following. This also provides an opportunity for chance to balance out over a period of time.

There is also a potentiality that an aspiring medium may be overeager in acceding to requests for cures. As was explained earlier, mediums achieve a very high rate of success by declining to cure individuals who appear likely to die. Overeagerness and ambition may make long shots appear tempting. Success would be impressive. But as with fish poisoning, a patient, conservative approach is likely to be more rewarding. The essential ingredient in contending with the chance factors involved in both curing and fish poisoning is intelligent management of the opportunities that arise (or are engendered). Successful mediums are quite clearly very bright and exceptionally perceptive in picking up the nuances of social life. These same qualities plus a measure of creativity also come into play in conducting engaging séances that capture an audience's interest and attention. Intelligence, perceptiveness, and a degree of poetic and story-telling creativity may thus be added to the list of requisites for success.

The third arena in which effectiveness can readily be evaluated pertains to prophecy. While this is less central than curing and fish poisoning, an aspiring medium can rapidly build up the reputation of his spirits by impressive prophecy. This is also a low-risk enterprise if the prophecies are sufficiently vague and opaque. After the fact, minor details come into focus such that the meaning of a vague prophecy becomes clear. Kayago's prediction that a Kaburusato resident would die within a month is a perfect example. Nogobe's somewhat self-serving prophecy that he would receive the boss man's accoutrements was evidently directed partly toward generating support that would bring this about, as well as to an impressive foretelling of the future. In addition, his efforts to pump me for information concerning where the visiting missionaries would sleep could have eventuated in a reputation-enhancing prophecy. The Etoro were anxious to know the intentions of missionaries and patrol officers. Nogobe's prophecies relating to these figures implied that his spirits could divine these intentions. In other words, these prophecies focused on an area of uncertainty that was of special concern to his audience.[17] He sought to establish himself as an individual who could mediate these troublesome and anxiety-provoking relations with an impinging colonial order. His efforts in this respect were undoubtedly related to the competition between himself and Kayago for jurisdiction over the Kaburusato community. I believe that he felt this was an area in which he could develop an edge, as Kayago was more oriented to the traditional social order. However, the significant point here is that Nogobe sought to build the reputation of his spirits' knowledgeability in this domain through prophecy. The spirits speak with authority because they have knowledge of both the *ausulubo* plane of existence and the spirit worlds that men and women lack. Prophecy is thus a revelation of knowledge that enhances the spiritual authority of a medium's familiars (and thus of the medium himself). A medium's access to relations with spirits establishes a base level of spiritual authority that is intrinsic to the social position. However, the degree of spiritual authority is variable among mediums and this variability is attributable to reputational qualities contingent upon a past record of success in curing, fish poisoning, and foretelling events. Community acceptance follows relatively automatically from success in these areas.

Although the importance of a following has been noted, the extent to which this constrains successful attainment of journeyman status remains to be addressed. Available data indicate that established mediums tend to be members of large lineages that are localized (in that they have a longhouse on their territory). These data are presented in table 5.3. Six of the 7 large western Etoro lineages (with 9 to 16 male members over the age of 15) are localized and also evidence a membership that includes one to three mediums. Kobifi is an exception with respect to localization but not with respect to mediums. Thus, all 7 large lineages have at least one medium. Of the 10 small lineages (with 1 to 4 male members), only 1 has a medium (Hilisato). But this exceptional small lineage is only 1 of 2 that are localized (the other being Kasayasato). Thus, small nonlocalized lineages invariably lack a medium (8 cases), while 1 of 2 localized small lineages possesses a medium. These data show that lineage size is a potent causal factor in accounting for the distribution of mediums in the population. Localization, which largely covaries with lineage size, is not sufficient in itself to engender mediumship among a lineage's membership (otherwise Kasayasato would possess a medium). However, localization increases the chances that a small lineage will possess a medium. In this sample, mediums constitute 20.0 percent (14/70) of all eligible males aged 21 to 46.[18] However, 24.5 percent (13/53) of the eligible males who are members of large lineages are mediums, while only 5.9 percent (1/17) of the eligible males of small lineages are mediums.

It is evident that lineage size acts as a significant constraint on the attainment of mediumship, in that a member of a small lineage has only a slight chance of becoming a medium. This is directly linked to an aspiring medium's need for a following in order to form a chorus and carry out the requisite labor involved in fish poisoning (cf. Knauft 1985a:235). A member of a large lineage has a greater number of close kinsmen he can enlist as

TABLE 5.3

The Distribution of Mediums among Localized and Nonlocalized
Western Etoro Lineages, May 1, 1968

	Living Mediums	Ever-Married Men	Young Men Aged 16–35	Total Men	Men Aged 21–46
Localized lineages					
Turusato	1	9	5	14	9
Sarado	3	8	2	10	7
Kaburusato	2	9	4	13	8
Ingiribisato	1	10	6	16	11
Haifi	3	5	4	9	7
Katiefi	1	6	3	9	5
Hilisato	1	1	2	3	2
Kasayasato	0	3	1	4	3
Total	12	51	27	78	52
Average	1.5	6.4	3.4	9.8	6.5
Nonlocalized lineages					
Nagefi	0	1	2	3	2
Alamafi	0	1	2	3	2
Salubisato	0	2	0	2	1
Kobifi	2	3	6	9	6
Hauasato	0	1	2	3	1
Somosato	0	1	0	1	1
Owaibifi	0	2	0	2	1
Somadabe	0	3	1	4	3
Kudulubisato	0	1	0	1	1
Total	2	15	13	28	18
Average	.22	1.7	1.4	3.1	2.0

followers. These include not only close agnates (brothers and father's brother's sons) but also cross-cousins and matrilateral siblings. A larger lineage also tends to have more father's sisters, mother's brothers, and mother's sisters than a small lineage. The role of close kinsmen is well illustrated by Nogobe's fish-poisoning expedition. The four young men who joined him in this enterprise were all either agnates or close kinsmen (as shown in fig. 5.3), while the six available men who did not take part were neither. Without this support, Nogobe would have been unable to advance his career.

There is one other factor that probably plays a role in the pattern noted. This has to do with the cosmological relationship between *Sigisato* spirits and lineage members. The assistance that a *Sigisato* provides is largely directed toward members of the lineage with which it is associated. Moreover, a medium's *Sigisato* spirit is always connected to his patrilineage, although he may receive other *Sigisato* spirits on occasion. There is a partial disjunction in the relationship of community members to their agnatic spirits when the resident medium is not of the same lineage. Although such a medium can be the vessel of the agnatic *Sigisatos* that individual coresidents wish to hear from and consult, this limits the medium's capacity to rely on his own spirit and thus build that spirit's reputation. A medium who coresides with a number of agnates during his apprenticeship can therefore most easily develop the spiritual authority of his *Sigisato*. There will always be many men of other lineages residing at the longhouse (Kelly 1977:176), but the presence of an agnatic contingent provides scope for this development of spiritual authority. A member of a small lineage who has few agnates would be at something of a disadvantage. I do not think this factor is nearly as important as the need for a following, but it probably plays some role.

While the position of novice apprentice is open to nearly all young men who show an interest, attainment of journeyman mediumship is largely confined to the members of larger lineages (containing nine or more male members over the age of 15). It should be recollected that Sawa and Illawe of the small Nagefi lineage were both nominated for mediumship, although Sawa failed to complete his training and Illawe was disinclined to undergo it. This shows that young men of small lineages do have the opportunity to become a novice apprentice but are less likely to exploit it or to successfully make the transition to journeyman status. Lineage size comes into play during the winnowing-out phase. However, the members of the large lineages constitute 75.7 percent (53/70) of the eligibly aged male population of all western Etoro lineages, so that the disadvantaged segment of the population is comparatively small. And at least some men of the disadvantaged quarter of the population do become mediums. Although the Etoro social system is not perfectly egalitarian among males in terms of absolutely equal opportunity to become a medium, it does not deviate greatly from this ideal type. Moreover, the principal form of disadvantage (among males) is attributable to demographic factors that are disconnected from other inequalities. The sons of mediums or *tafidilos* are not disproportionately likely to become mediums. However, disadvantage is closely linked to the inequities associated with the witch/nonwitch distinction. A *sa:go* or *kagomano* is ineligible for mediumship. A *kagomano* is by definition the child of a witch genitor (if not pater). Moreover, the only adolescent classified as a *sa:go* (Harogo) is the son of an executed witch (Sayaga). In addition, we have seen that witchcraft accusations directed against a medium or member of his family often lead to a change of residence that necessitates reestablishment of community acceptance elsewhere (e.g., the cases of Nasu, Taipa, and Piawe). An established medium's spiritual authority is also undermined by witchcraft accusations, so that he may be unable to effectively authenticate accusations. The taint of witchcraft thus carries distinct disadvantages at every step of a prospective or established medium's career.

Although a medium's primary spirit is a woman—his spirit wife—a woman cannot readily become a medium. The male medium's spirit wife bears a spirit child that resides among the *Kesames* on the *ausulubo* plane of existence. But if a woman were to acquire a spirit husband, the offspring of their union would be born into the mundane world and would lack the capabilities of a spirit child. Without a spirit child to "make a trail," a hypothetical female medium could not acquire a *Sigisato* spirit. Etoro beliefs are thus largely incompatible with female mediumship although there is a hypothetical possibility that a woman could acquire a spirit husband who might be the equivalent of a spirit wife and spirit son rolled into one. Although there were no female mediums among the Etoro, there was one among the Gebusi (Cantrell n.d.), and this raises the possibility that there may have been a few female mediums among the Etoro at certain times in the past or that they might arise in future.[19] It would not surprise me to encounter a female medium upon restudy because the Etoro lack rigid gender exclusion. Nevertheless, there were no female mediums in 1968–69, and there had not been any in the recent past. Access to mediumship is currently unavailable to women insofar as they are not nominated as potential apprentices by established mediums.

Complete male predominance in mediumship is critical to the hegemony of an androcentric cosmology and worldview. Myth, initiatory ritual, the *kosa* ceremony, and séances are the primary vehicles for the reproduction of socially constructed meanings. However, the *kosa* ceremony and male initiation follow a preset design, and the stock of existing myths to be retold is also fixed, although new myths that are borrowed from neighboring tribes (or said to be borrowed) are continually added to the repertoire. Only séances

are sufficiently labile to provide a regular forum for interpretively constructing the meaning of current events as well as representing and recreating a
worldview. Male mediums monopolize this forum while the exclusion of
women from mediumship deprives them of a comparable voice. The only
vehicle for the interpretative construction and systematic presentation of a
female point of view is myths that are authored or reworked by women. The
myth of the male mother discussed at the end of chapter 3 contains a commentary upon reproduction and the cosmology of life-force transmission that
expresses a female perspective (although not to the exclusion of a male
interpretative perspective). In the retelling of such a myth during an evening
gathering in the communal section of the longhouse, a female voice can be
heard by males and females of all ages. While this does provide some scope
for the public articulation of a female point of view, it is the only such
forum. Moreover, myth is understood as entertaining fiction, while séances
are perceived to express revealed truth, backed by spiritual authority. Thus,
men can create a cultural world while women can only offer a commentary
upon it.[20]

SHAMANIC RELIGION AND THE SOCIAL ORDER

A medium's repertoire of spirits and his relationship to them reduplicate the
central relationships of social life in the mundane world. Male-female conjugal complementarity is clearly the basic theme of a medium's relationship
with his spirit wife. This relationship is also the key to all others since it
engenders the spirit child who makes a trail for the *Sigisato*. The spirit wife
is the daughter of *Kesame* spirits. Although the latter include spirits of the
dead, the spirit wife herself is always born into the afterworld and is never
the spirit of a once-living person. She is of *ontangifi,* the river lineage. A
medium thus acquires an affinal relationship to the *Kesame* spirits through
his spirit wife. It is structurally significant that the spirits of the dead, who
might readily be configured as linked to the living by ancestry, are instead
linked by affinal relations (Kelly 1977:62). These relations are very close and
supportive ones in real life and lack the social distance and intrinsic asymmetry of ancestry. But while the affinal connection is important in establishing
the general tone of the interrelationship between men and *Kesame* spirits, a
medium's key relationship is with his spirit wife herself, not her brother.

The spirit wife comes to a man in a dream and initiates the relationship.
The union is thus a romantic one that is instigated by sexual attraction and
elective affinity (as is illustrated by the third myth of the trilogy presented in
chap. 3). In the mundane (as opposed to spirit) world, the spirit wife takes
the form of the beautiful red bird of paradise. These birds often alight on the
tall black palms that are left uncut at the sites where longhouses are con-

structed. The black palm is thus the point of articulation with the spirit world. As the first myth of the trilogy discussed in chapter 3 establishes, the black palm also symbolizes the phallus. Thus the spirit wife's original sexual attraction to her medium husband is symbolically reduplicated by the red bird of paradise's attraction to these black palms. In the Etoro sociocultural system, many important social relations entail a sexual component, and relations with the supernatural are no exception. The latter are thus intimate rather than distant relations. Moreover, they are relations of a kinship order. At a more general level, it is also evident that the phallus is the key that opens the door to relations with the supernatural. This perspective is central to the male interpretation of the myth of the male mother discussed in chapter 3. Connection with the supernatural is contingent upon possession of this essential attribute of masculinity, which has mystical properties. Women's relation to the supernatural is impaired, if not precluded, by their lack of the mystical phallus.[21]

The spirit wife is helpful, cooperative, loyal, trustworthy, and diligent. She is responsive to requests to locate lost pigs, track witches, cure bewitched individuals, and subsequently watch over them. She designates the times and places for fish poisoning because the fish are the primary corporeal abode of the spirits of the dead. The *Kesames* move to other points in the river or occupy the bodies of hornbills for the duration. The spirit wife's helpful cooperation makes this enterprise possible. The spirit wife is thus in many ways the ideal woman and ideal wife. In addition, the conjugal relationship is a model of gender complementarity that links opposites, a spirit woman and human man of radically different worlds. They cooperate together in fish poisoning to fulfill subsistence needs. The spirit wife is beautiful and sexually attractive but not sexually depleting. In addition, she is a mother who gives birth and maternally nurtures the couple's spirit child. She is a woman who has successfully fulfilled her reproductive role. Gender complementarity is again emphasized in her relationship with her spirit son. They cooperate in jointly tracking the witch responsible for a death.

Although the spirit wife provides a model for a woman's role as helpmate to her husband, this role and conjugal relations more generally are at the same time elevated in social significance by this representation. A spirit wife is the critical point of interconnection to the supernatural, a linkage upon which men are dependent. While having a real wife is not in any way a precondition for attainment of mediumship (and indeed precludes eligibility for apprenticeship), a spirit wife is represented as essential. Etoro cosmology thus represents women as more rather than less important than they are, in pragmatic terms, with respect to mediumship. A dependence upon a female component is constructed. Moreover, women are represented as significant in their own right, as actors, rather than merely as interstitial links. The symbolic message would be entirely different if the spirit wife's brother were the central figure in curing, witch tracking, and the like.

On the other hand, women are pragmatically excluded from the position of mediumship, while being encouraged to be good wives. There is thus a disjunction between the symbolic enshrinement of women as central figures in the supernatural world and the exclusion of women from the exercise of spiritual authority in the mundane world of social life. This neatly reverses the relations that obtain in the domain of life-force transmission, where women's role in reproduction is rendered supernaturally insignificant, and femininity is symbolically associated with witchcraft. While the moral worthiness of women is symbolically disvalued by the cosmology of life-force transmission, the moral worthiness of spirit women is symbolically established by the cosmology of mediumship (and of relations with the supernatural). Although the worthiness of real women is morally uplifted by association, they remain within the realm of social life where they can merely be compared to the spirit model but not attain spirituality.[22] In other words, what women are able to realize in practice is the role of the good wife, not the role of supernaturally significant actor.

A medium's spirit family, composed of himself, his spirit wife (or wives), and spirit children, also reduplicates a cultural emphasis on the familial hearth group that is accorded a spatial focus in the community section of the longhouse. The spirit son takes the form of a parrot (*caribe*) that is often seen in overflight at dusk. He is not functionally differentiated from the spirit wife and is also helpful, cooperative, loyal, trustworthy, and diligent. Although he may engage in curing, this is more frequently done by the spirit wife. The spirit son wanders more widely and is perhaps more often a source of information about lurking witches. However, the most prominent feature that arises from a comparison of the roles and activities of spirit wife and spirit son is the absence of a gendered division of labor. They both do very much the same things and are socially substitutable.

As was noted earlier, a medium's relationship to his *Sigisato* spirit is configured as a siblinglike relation between agnatic age-mates. The sky world of the *Sigisatos* is essentially an all-male world composed of groups of brothers. The immortal *Sigisatos* are not of woman born but derive from foam upon the water (i.e., semen). They are entirely constituted by masculinity. Although *Sigisatos* are believed to have wives, the existence of those wives is merely notational. This is consistent with the fact that *Sigisatos* are organized in lineage formations, since males are the prominent actors in those contexts in which lineage membership plays a role (such as the arrangement of marriages). In acquiring a *Sigisato* spirit, a medium thus joins the all-male world of the *Sigisatos*. This corresponds to the male domain spatially constituted by the men's section of the longhouse.

A medium's repertoire of spirit relations thus resonates with the spatially formulated groupings manifested in longhouse design, viewed from a male perspective. His *Kesame* spirit family is an analogue of the families whose hearths are located in the communal section, while his relations with adult male *Sigisato* spirits are an analogue of the male-exclusive relations conducted in the men's section of the longhouse. The conjugal relation, which crosscuts gender segregation and thus provides the central integrative principle of Etoro community organization, is prominently represented by a medium's relationship to his spirit wife.

While the spirit wife is instrumental to a medium's acquisition of the full ensemble of spirit relations, she is important only in the initial stages of the development of these relations. This corresponds to women's initial role in the reproduction of social persons, in pig rearing, and in performing the opening dances of the *kosa* following male emergence from initiatory seclusion. Moreover, the supernatural realm of the *Sigisatos* is entirely distinct from the realm of the *Kesame* wife and *Kesame* spirit son. The two are respectively associated with the polar opposites of sky and water and of night and day.[23] The high-to-low relation of the *Sigisato* to *Kesame* realms corresponds to the elevation of the men's section above ground level while the communal section of the longhouse is connected to and largely rests upon the ground. The male-exclusive world of the *Sigisatos* is not only spatially higher but also dominant. The *Sigisato* spirits are "strong" and can drive off or kill a witch, while the *Kesames* can only passively protect a victim's vital organs by covering them with their hands. Moreover, the *Sigisato* spirits have the final say in determining the identity of a witch by providing a definitive reading of oracles whose outcome they also determine. This includes the birth oracle that provides the final determination of the guilt or innocence of the accused. Here too the female spirit's contribution is initial, and the male spirit's contribution is final and definitive. The link between the realm of *Sigisatos* and the male-exclusive section of the longhouse thus provides a basis for the former to serve as an analogic model for the latter, instantiating the symbolic domination of men in the final instance. Men predominate in a social world that importantly includes women because men prevail in the final phases of all significant processes and because they have the last word.

The relations between men and women, and between gender-exclusive groups and conjugal complementarity, are thus played out in every medium's relationships to two distinct spirit worlds in a way that provides a model for orchestrating these relations in social life, within the longhouse community. At the same time, age-mate relations and relations of siblingship, descent, filiation, conjugality, and affinity all play a role in the organization of these spirit worlds and the modes of interconnection that link men (i.e., male mediums) to them. The nodal figure in all these relationships is the spirit medium who is husband, sister's husband, father, "brother," and age-mate to various spirits. He is also a participant in both the male-exclusive world of *Sigisatos* and the gender-integrated world of *Kesames*.

The prominence of mediums in relations with the spirits is all the more marked due to the absence of *tafidilos* in these spirit worlds. Since a medium's *Sigisato* spirit is an age-mate, senior men are generally not present in the spirit world revealed through séances. Moreover, a medium's union with a *Kesame* spirit wife eventuates through romantic courtship and is never troubled by an intrinsic absence of reciprocity in the bestowal of women. The beneficent and generous *Kesames* are a continual source of wives but never receive wives in return. Moreover, they are not compensated with shell valuables for the emotional loss represented by the marriage of their daughters. The lack of female mediums precludes an exchange of women (or persons) between humans and *Kesame* spirits. By the same token, the brother-sister relationship and the sister's husband–wife's brother relationship are much less prominent in relations with the spirit world than they are in real life. Woman as wife thus takes precedence over woman as sister. A medium's connection to the spirits therefore provides a selective idealized model of certain socially significant relations rather than a comprehensive reflective model of the social order.

The most notable feature of this utopian vision of social life is the absence of certain asymmetrical relations, that are inegalitarian in character, and the reversal of key relations of dependence. Thus while a this-worldly wife depends upon her husband both to cut trees in order to facilitate her gardening efforts and to protect her from the consequences of witchcraft accusations, the spirit wife is independent in both these respects. It is the medium husband who is dependent upon his spirit wife in order to engage in the subsistence task of fish poisoning, and he is equally dependent in requiring her assistance in dealing with witchcraft. He can do nothing without her. A similar reversal is apparent in a medium's relation to his spirit son. The spirit medium thus anchors dependency-reversed conjugal and paternal relations. *Tafidilos* and senior men generally are absent from the scene, and the relationship to wife's father and wife's brother to whom one owes women in reciprocity is markedly effaced. Finally, the spirit medium, as nodal ego, has no relationship to a spirit medium since the spirit world clearly requires no such figures. The medium himself is absent from the séances in which his spirits speak through him and does not appear as a dramatis persona in the séances in which the adventures of the spirit people are related. The central actors in these scenes are women, children, and to a lesser extent, young men (the *Sigisato* age-mate). The spirit wife dominates the bulk of the séance. Thus while social organizationally significant relations enter into the construction of man's relation to the spirit world of the *Kesames*, the latter does not mirror the social order but instead constitutes a reversal of it in important respects. Likewise, a séance entails a performance in which a potent woman speaks through the inert body of a male.

However, the structure of the séance insures that this reversal of the social order will be undone. The *Sigisato* spirit always appears last, after the spirit wife and spirit child have departed the medium's body (in sequence). A male-exclusive world thus supercedes the reversed spirit world of the *Kesames,* and a powerful male spirit speaks. He quite literally has the last word. Since the *Sigisatos* are immortals and do not die, they attain a different version of equality. They are all age-mates and brothers, lacking any significant social differentiation by age, generation, or filial status. This spirit world thus reverses rather than mirrors the social order as well. However, it also sequentially supplants an egalitarian vision based on gender complementarity with an egalitarian vision based on a lack of social differentiation among men.

Etoro religion thus enshrines two incommensurate utopian visions of equality and proposes that an alternation between them resolves the intrinsic contradictions. Social life entails a comparable alternation as the gender complementarity of daily work organized by the sexual division of labor and the integration of shared meals gives way, in the evening, to same-sex sociality. Men withdraw to the men's section to socialize among themselves, to engage in intimate homosexual relations, to conduct séances, and to sleep. It is likewise after dark that the world of *Sigisato* spirits takes shape. These spirits depart the bodies of cassowaries that they have occupied in their daily foraging for fruits and nuts on lineage lands and return to their longhouses in the sky to interact, in human form, as men among men. The animality of the food quest thus gives way to the realization of humanity in male sociality. It is also noteworthy that the *Sigisato* spirits enforce gender segregation in their domains in that the word for woman cannot be uttered in the upland forest where men seek to hunt and trap the *Sigisato*'s "pigs." The *Sigisatos* also punish women who blaspheme and who bring lowland things, associated with the riverine world of the *Kesames,* to upland places.

The egalitarian utopian worlds of the *Kesames* and *Sigisatos* are free of witchcraft and thus free of sickness and death. A witch goes to the afterworld of the *Kesames* without the *tohorora* that predisposes him (or her) to evil and enables the perpetration of supernatural harm. The immortals of the *Sigisato* world likewise lack witchcraft as the absence of witchcraft is the prime requisite of immortality. Utopia can never be attained in a this-worldly life pervaded by witchcraft, although men can strive to achieve it by the systematic elimination of all witches as the *Sigisatos* routinely counsel. Etoro religion thus proposes that witchcraft is the root cause of inequality. It is what prevents the this-worldly realization of utopian equality.

It can be concluded that Etoro religion is, in certain respects, the opiate of women, children, and junior males. However, this is achieved by enshrining utopian visions of equality that also have quite opposite effects. Equality is idealized as the ultimate goal of human aspirations.

TAFIDILOS

The term *tafidilo* is a nominalized form of the verb "to be first." The eldest of a group of same-sex siblings is designated as *tafidilo,* as is the first person in a line of individuals walking single file along a forest trail. The social status of *tafidilo* likewise entails seniority and being in the forefront of collective social action within the longhouse community. The core meanings of the term are best captured by translating it as "active respected elder." A *tafidilo* who subsequently withdraws from active participation in the collective activities of the longhouse community due to age and infirmity may continue to be regarded as a *tafidilo* for a period of several years but eventually will no longer be regarded as such. The eldest men (*tole*), who "no longer go to the forest," have ceased to hunt, and are thus no longer engaged in the prestige-enhancing distribution of game, cease to be considered *tafidilos*. Most men become *tole* in their early 60s, though a few remain vigorous longer. The active elders thus largely comprise men aged 46 to 60 whose sons and/or inseminees have been initiated (or men who are age-mates of men at this life stage). This largely corresponds to the age-group of the most productive hunters (see Dwyer 1983). More than half (11/19 or 57.9 percent) of the men in this age-group are regarded as *tafidilos,* while only one younger and one older man are accorded this status (see table 5.2). This shows that age is strongly correlated with *tafidilo* status and that this acknowledged social standing is not narrowly restricted to a select group among those who are appropriately aged.

On the other hand, *tafidilo* status is not automatically ascribed to all active elders on the basis of age or life-cycle position, but is achieved through the accumulation of prestige and avoidance of stigma. *Tafidilos* are senior men who have attained prestige through generosity in the distribution of growth-inducing game to community members over the years and have not been subject to an authenticated witchcraft accusation. The category *tafidilo* is thus an acknowledged social standing in the prestige/stigma hierarchy that serves as a prerequisite for assuming a leadership role in a longhouse community. The social status and leadership position often go hand in hand but are distinct insofar as some acknowledged *tafidilos* are either aspiring or semi-retired community leaders.

Senior men who do not command sufficient respect to take the lead in community affairs are not accorded *tafidilo* status. Although this often stems from a witchcraft accusation, those who are excluded have other characteristics as well. Among the Kaburusato and Turusato men I knew well, two of five of the relevant age were excluded, namely Nawa and Pabu. Nawa was alienated from other community members as a result of repeated witchcraft accusations against his son Tame. He resided at his garden house and never distributed game at the longhouse. Pabu was an inveterate rule-breaker who had "stolen" his matrilateral sibling's wife and who extorted witchcraft compensation from Kayari through an illegitimate and unauthenticated accusation after already having executed the legitimately accused individual. He was thus seen as a self-serving person, exemplifying the antithesis of generosity. Neither of these men was well regarded, and both would be incapable of effectively leading by example. The three other men of these two communities aged 46 to 60 were Ibo, Mariabu, and Yora, all of whom were well respected and thus readily able to effectively coordinate community enterprises. The proportion of *tafidilos* to non-*tafidilos* in these two communities is essentially the same as that of the larger sample, and Nawa and Pabu exemplify the characteristics of appropriately aged individuals who are excluded from *tafidilo* status.

However it is also important to recall that there were a total of 14 attributions of witchcraft directed against the 27 men in the 31-to-40 age cohort (see table 4.2). Eight of these men, or 29.6 percent of the cohort population, were subject to one or more accusations. It is thus evident that a number of men are disqualified from *tafidilo* status in the decade before they become eligible, as a result of witchcraft accusations. The percentage of men aged 31 to 40 who are accused is nearly three-fourths of the percentage of men aged 46 to 60 who are non-*tafidilos*. Since men over the age of 40 are almost never subject to a witchcraft accusation, individuals such as Nawa and Pabu (who are 49 and 50, respectively) do not appear on the roster of recently accused witches. However, given their personal characteristics it is very likely that they were among those accused during the period ten to twenty years earlier when they were members of the age cohort subject to the highest incidence of accusations. In other words, "respected" elders are essentially those elders who were not accused of witchcraft earlier in their lives. These same individuals earn prestige through generosity in the distribution of game while men previously accused of witchcraft are unable to effectively participate in the system of prestige attainment (as explained further along).

A *tafidilo* is thus an active respected elder who generally leads by example and plays a significant role in collective community activities. As community leader, his responsibilities include: (1) selecting the sites for communal gardens and new longhouses; (2) setting the dates for *kosa* ceremonies, male initiation, and the coordinated pig killings associated with affinal exchange; (3) supervising the construction of longhouses and male initiation lodges; (4) supervising preparations for ceremonies; and (5) leading raiding parties in dawn attacks on the longhouse communities of other tribes and being in the forefront of battle in both internal and external armed conflicts. It is said that "people listen when he talks," and a *tafidilo* thus has a leading voice in the discussions through which community members reach consensus about important matters. One of the most noteworthy of these discussions arises when a community member has been accused of witchcraft by an outsider and the coresident kinsmen of the accused must decide whether to pay compensation or face down the party of armed men that will come to request it. We have seen that the *tafidilo* Ahoa was forthright and outspoken in advocating refusal of compensation when Kayago and Waua were accused of witchcraft. Ibo was equally outspoken in community discussions regarding the probable identity of the witches responsible for recent deaths.[24]

A *tafidilo* will likewise take the lead in advocating construction of a new longhouse and proposing that the community host a *kosa* ceremony. A decision is then reached through community discussion. However, the concrete proposal and well-defined position of the *tafidilo* significantly shape these discussions in that participants are in a position of responding to an advocated course of action. In other words, a *tafidilo* does not open discussion by saying, "What do people think we should do about this?" but rather by saying, "We should do the following, and these are the reasons why." He then responds to any differing interpretations of the situation that would be conducive to an alternative course of action. Given this structuring of the discussion, he is likely to speak in response to each questioning individual and thus will hold the floor the majority of the time. There is often a continuous voice vote with regard to the views expressed and the points being made, as individuals interject comments into the ongoing discussion, saying, "Truly," or "That's no lie," or occasionally making a disparaging remark or joke at the speaker's expense. Those who support the position advocated by a *tafidilo* affirm this by their interjections and generally do not otherwise speak to the issues. Discussion thus tends to be relatively brief as a limited number of differing interpretations and objections are aired and typically laid to rest. A *tafidilo* will know in advance that there is considerable support for the course of action he proposes, so that his views invariably prevail (in all observed instances).

In many cases, the nature of the decision being made allows scope for individuals to pursue alternatives on their own, declining to participate in an inconveniently located communal garden or moving elsewhere when a new longhouse is to be built too far from the sago stands, pandanus groves, and hunting territory they wish to exploit. Community members can readily vote with their feet, and this insures that a *tafidilo* will advocate a popular course of action to which nearly everyone can be won over. If a senior man cannot effectively develop a consensus concerning the collective enterprises of the community, the community will shrink in size (or dissolve) and he will not be regarded as a *tafidilo*. Sagobe, the senior man of the smallest longhouse community (Kasayasato), is a case in point. In this instance, witchcraft accusations against a family member also worked against Sagobe's efforts to attract coresidents. His notorious, twice-accused daughter Nawadia had returned to Kasayasato (with her husband, Osopa) to live with him, and this both prompted departures and reduced the appeal of this longhouse as a potential residence. However, the main point to be noted in this context is that a *tafidilo* is constrained to promote an inclusive consensus that will hold the community together and must be an effective leader in this regard. This is expected of him. I have thus designated a range of decisions as the *tafidilo*'s "responsibility"—even though these decisions are made by consensus—since coresidents look to a *tafidilo* to propose a course of action in these areas.

A longhouse discussion that took place at Kaburusato concerning an alleged pig theft provides an interesting illustration of the tenor of these comparatively infrequent community events. Ibo had been unable to locate one of his pigs despite several days of searching the area in which it usually foraged. In the course of this search, Ibo's dog, which accompanied him, located the rank head, forelegs, and entrails of a pig that had been stashed in the hollow trunk of a tree. Ibo thus assumed that someone had killed his pig, eaten most of it, and attempted to conceal the unconsumed remains where they would not be found. The members of the community were gathered in the communal section of the longhouse for the late afternoon meal when Ibo began to relate these events. When he got to the part of the story entailing the discovery, he rose to his feet, produced the incriminating forelegs from leaf-wrapped packages in his net bag, and dramatically brandished them aloft for all to see. The image of the culprit clandestinely eating stolen and unshared pork was vividly portrayed in contemptuous tones. This was the archetypal antisocial act in that sharing meat is the prime symbol of unity and encompassing social communion. The theft was thus an affront to the community, not merely to Ibo, in that community members would otherwise have shared in eating this pig (or one given in return for it). This point was implicitly but very effectively made by the fact that everyone was, at that very moment, eating a wild pig that Ibo had shot and brought to the longhouse that day. Ibo thus encouraged his audience to share his righteous indignation as they shared the pork he provided. In notes recorded later that evening, I remarked upon the masterful rhetoric of the juxtapositions Ibo constructed between unshared and shared pork, rottenness and succulence, selfishness and generosity, theft and gift, antisocial individualism and the communitarian ethic. All this seemed designed to create a polarity between the guilty party and the community, laying the groundwork for strong support of the indictment that was to follow.

Pig theft is a serious offense that requires compensation if guilt can be established. It may also lead to reciprocal theft from a suspect. One inter-community armed conflict (that will be described further along) began in just this way. With war an outside possibility, Ibo's disclosure raised issues that clearly required community consideration. Everyone thus took a keen interest in the discussion that ensued.

The key issue was the identity of the antisocial thief or thieves, and this in some ways paralleled the determination of the identity of the witch respon-sible for a death. Pig theft was, moreover, the sort of greedy and self-serving act that is characteristic of a witch (who also consumes the flesh as well as the *ausulubo* of his victim, returning to the burial platform by night to privately feed off the corpse). When the animated expressions of surprise and condemnation that followed Ibo's dramatic production of the incriminating evidence had subsided, he went on to address the question of who might be responsible. While everyone else remained seated, he continued to stand, speaking in a clear, assured voice, and gesturing effectively with the pig foreleg he still held in one hand.

Ibo began by stating his suspicion that this had been done by someone who resided not far from the scene of the crime, implying that a resident of Kaburusato or a neighboring community was the culprit. Nawa immediately countered this with the suggestion that a dog might have killed the pig— perhaps Ibo's own dog who seemed to know where the remains were— supporting this with the observation that the forelegs were uncooked. Nawa undoubtedly surmised that Ibo was going to develop a case against his son Tame, the twice-accused witch and prime scapegoat for all occasions. Ibo, who had very probably given all relevant questions some thought beforehand, responded immediately that a dog could not have been responsible because the forelegs had been cleanly severed with a sharp implement, not chewed off. He reversed the foreleg he had been holding by the joint and, taking several steps, showed the cleanly butchered end to Nawa (thereby pointing the incriminating leg bone directly at him). Ibo added, somewhat caustically, that dogs do not conceal bones in hollow trees but bury them. I recall thinking at this point that Ibo had already gained ground in making the case that I too surmised he was developing, because Nawa's objections now appeared as the desperate casting about of a guilty person for some alternative explanation. Ibo's telling points received a number of supportive exclamations from the audience (the usual "truly" and "that's no lie").

The second alternative explanation was raised by Silo, Yeluma's wife. She was very probably led to speak by the fact that she was Tame's mother's sister (and Nawa's wife's sister) and thus supported Nawa's efforts to deflect the blame from Tame. Silo cogently pointed out that a trading party of Kosabi men (i.e., men from Mt. Bosavi) had passed through six days earlier, and this would have coincided with the time the pig was killed, judging from the current state of decomposition of the forelegs. The Kosabi groups had been traditional enemies of the Etoro and had only recently begun to travel through Etoro territory to trade with the Petamini. It was thus logical to suppose that they might well be guilty of this unconscionable act. This unstated background, known to all, lent credence to Silo's argument. Nawa enthusiastically voiced his support for his wife's sister as she made her points, adding depreciating remarks about the Kosabis. Yebua also affirmed the cogency of her friend Silo's argument and added that the trading party's route was in close proximity to the scene of the crime. These two women were married to men related as father's brother and brother's son and had coresided and gardened together for many years.

Ibo acknowledged that the timing might well correspond, but offered a very persuasive refutation. If a large party of men had killed the pig, they would have eaten it all, including the forelegs, head, and entrails. The deed must therefore have been done by one or two persons. The pig had not been very large (as evidenced by the size of the legs), and Ibo argued that two men might have gorged themselves on the meaty parts while concealing the head, forelegs, entrails, and other remnants he had discovered in the hollow tree trunk. Since a wild pig is brought back to the longhouse entire and everyone also knows when a domestic pig has been slaughtered and distributed, the culprits must have needed to avoid being seen with pork of inexplicable origin. Concealment of unconsumed parts of the animal clearly indicated that the large party of Kosabi men could not have been responsible. Even if they had not eaten all of the stolen animal, they would have no need to leave anything behind. They might readily have carried off unconsumed portions as they would not have had a problem of explaining their source to the Petamini, whose territory they would have reached after only a three or four hours' walk. The indictment of the trading party was thus implausible on several counts.

The arguments demonstrating this also supported Ibo's contention that the guilty party was from very nearby. It had to be someone who could not turn up at their longhouse of residence with incriminating pork. And it had to be someone who could be placed at the scene of the crime. Everyone knew that Nawa's garden house was a half mile from the place where the remains were found and that Nawa and Tame sometimes foraged in the area where the remains had been discovered. While this evidence was coincidental, the fact that Tame was a witch provided clear-cut grounds for presuming he would be capable of this antisocial act. Moreover, he had a motive for doing

Ibo an ill turn, since Ibo was Hariako's sister's husband and had minced no words in contesting Tame's recent witchcraft accusation against Hariako (following the death of Tame's mother, Waya). There was no explicit reference to this motive, but Ibo looked pointedly at Nawa when he asserted, in concluding, that it must have been two persons close at hand. There was no question as to whom he suspected, even though no names had been put forward at this juncture. Tame was not present, so Ibo directed his incriminating gestures toward Nawa. His suggestion that two men were responsible also included Nawa in the indictment he was developing.

No further alternatives to Ibo's interpretation were put forward. Only a few individuals other than those noted above spoke beyond giving exclamations of support. Yeluma carried on a mumbled monologue that was inaudible and was entirely ignored. As Silo's husband and Ibo's wife's brother, he was in the middle and seemingly desired to do something that could later be recontextualized as support for both. In any event, he succeeded in appearing to have a position without making it clear what it was. Tuni spoke a number of times in the clear, assured voice of a mature man. However, he had nothing relevant to add to the discussion. He pointed out no fewer than four separate times that the pig everyone was eating was not the missing pig, since the one being consumed had been delivered to the longhouse intact, forelegs, head, and all. No one was confused on this point, and the reiteration of this non sequitur appeared to be motivated by Tuni's feeling that, as a mature married man, he should enter into this important discussion. All the participants who went beyond saying "truly" were the older members of the community. The *tafidilo* Ibo was 47, Nawa was 49, Silo 34, Yebua 55, Yeluma 39, and Tuni 34. The only comparably aged individuals who did not speak were Yebua's co-widow Pegome and Ibo's wife Akwadi. The younger men (Hariako, Selagu, Nogobe, Sawa, and Illawe) voiced support for Ibo but did not speak. However, it is not unusual for those who support a position to indicate this without directly holding the floor. Younger men did speak in other public discussions, although they were more likely than others to be interrupted and they rarely spoke with assurance.

When it was clear that there were no further contending interpretations to be put forward, Ibo commenced to summarize the evidence for his position. No one now contested the key point that a local party was responsible. Instead, individuals began to present personal alibis. As those present cleared themselves, and supported each other in this, the field of suspects was narrowed to Tame. Someone recalled that he had gone off alone very early one morning, in the rain, and had not returned until quite late in the day. Tame was at Komo patrol post getting my mail and thus not present to account for his whereabouts. Nawa could not have said anything that would place Tame without indicating that he and his son were together. Since this would only confirm Ibo's suspicion, he remained silent. The indictment was thus generated by the community as a whole, through a process of elimination that left Tame outside all shared alibis. As in witchcraft scapegoating, everyone shared an interest in identifying a readily agreed upon guilty party other than themselves or their close kin. Ibo said almost nothing during this phase of the discussion. He only agreed that Tame was indeed the prime suspect after others first put forward his name. Ibo had cautiously avoided mentioning any names himself in his earlier statements, although it was quite clear that he suspected Tame and Nawa.

At this point Ibo turned to me and asked me to oracularly determine the guilt or innocence of the prime suspects. He said I should write down the name of his pig on three separate pieces of paper. I should then add the name of one suspect to each of these. These names were to be Tame, Nawa, and a third person selected by myself. Having done this I was then to reveal which one(s) of these suspects were indeed guilty. He did not indicate how I was supposed to determine this, but it seemed no manipulation of the pieces of paper would be required. Taken totally by surprise by this request, I could think of nothing better to say than that this would lead to indeterminate results. Much to Ibo's disappointment, I also suggested that perhaps it was the Kosabi men after all, adding feebly that they might have just eaten when they came upon the pig. Ibo then reiterated his main arguments, enumerating the number of men in the trading party, invoking the small size of the pig, and stating how easily it could have been consumed by a group this size even if they were not hungry. He ended by reasserting that they could also quite readily have carried any leftovers with them as they continued on their way. I had no answers to these arguments and could only nod in assent.

The discussion was now at an impasse because I had given a response that was the equivalent of the results of an improperly performed oracle (in which both items are *nesi*). At the same time, I held out no prospects that repetition (the customary recourse) would resolve the issue, having declared the newly invented paper oracle to be intrinsically incapable of providing definitive results. The discussion thus ended on this inconclusive note as Ibo suggested no other means to confirm the guilt of the suspects and did not press for compensation as I had earlier guessed he would. This would have been the culturally expectable conclusion. However, he may have planned to put the question of Nawa and Tame's guilt to Nogobe's or Kayago's *Kesame* spirit at the next séance before making a formal request.

The next day Ibo found his missing pig. I was quite relieved, as I feared he would feel I had crossed him, and he was a good friend. He had been the first to include me in the social life of the community, inviting me to share in a cassowary he had trapped early in my stay. Given his position as *tafidilo*, this had made my acceptance by others much quicker and easier. However, my response now appeared almost too perfect, since "none of the above" was revealed to have been the only correct oracular outcome. Since the named pig was alive and well, no one was guilty, and repetitions of the oracle would correctly indicate this every time. Like the spirit medium in whose role I had been placed, I appeared to have extraordinary knowledge.[25]

Community members now made an effort to locate and account for all their own pigs. It was thereby discovered that the stolen animal was Illawe's. He did not suspect Nawa, his sister's husband, or Tame, his sister's co-wife's son. Instead, he thought the guilty party was his age-mate Maka, Tsmari's son. He asked his cross-cousin Weliba, who was traveling to Petofi, to consult the renowned Petamini medium Tarume regarding Maka's guilt. Nothing further transpired. Soon thereafter, I became caught up in the developing witchcraft accusation against Nomaya and thus never asked whether this inquiry was indeed made and what the results were if it was. However, Illawe did not raise the question of compensation in public discussion during the month I remained in the field.

This community discussion exemplifies the general format and tone of such events. It shows the considerable advantages that accrue to a *tafidilo* who has a well-developed position that he has considered in advance. He will very likely have worked out answers to the questions and alternative interpretations that are likely to arise. As the initiator of discussion, he is well prepared while others are not. He will thus have a number of cogent arguments to put forward. As a result, the *tafidilo* is comfortably self-assured and appears knowledgeable, wise, and judicious. Others are likely to put forward arguments based on first thoughts that he can readily refute. The opposition thus appears feeble, as the initial exchange with Nawa illustrates. Not all *tafidilos* possess Ibo's rhetorical abilities. However, the structuring of the discussion in relation to a *tafidilo*'s considered position ensures that any *tafidilo* will very likely appear to be a wise and judicious leader nonetheless.

Only the presentation of counterarguments constitutes dissent from a *tafidilo*'s stated position. Silence conveys assent, which may or may not be unenthusiastic. Verbal affirmations signify active support and agreement. A *tafidilo*'s position thus has a special standing in the discussion in that it prevails unless overturned. Moreover, silence constitutes tacit agreement with the *tafidilo*'s position, but this does not apply to counterarguments, which require active support indicating that the views represented are widely shared. In other words, it is assumed that a *tafidilo* speaks for the majority of those present, while other speakers are not granted this presumption.

Anyone may speak in these discussions, although younger individuals are the least likely to do so and may be interrupted. However, mature women who speak receive a hearing no different from that accorded to their male counterparts. Cogent arguments are given careful consideration irrespective of the gender of the speaker. It is noteworthy that mediums are less rather than more likely than others to participate actively in community discussion. A medium's spirits may be called upon in a séance to address issues that initially arose in community discussion. It is thus important that the medium himself appear impartial. If a medium took a strong public position on a question, the credibility of his spirits' statements would be impaired. Although it is the *Kesame* spirits and not the medium himself who passes judgment, they are his wife and son. Thus Nogobe said nothing.

Although Ibo's request that I use slips of paper to oracularly determine the guilt of the prime suspects was entirely novel, recourse to oracles is not. It may be recalled that Mogoya consulted the pandanus oracle early in the day that a community discussion concerning payment of compensation was anticipated (regarding the witchcraft accusation against Kayago and Waua). Anyone may consult the pandanus oracle and introduce the results into community discussion. However, a *tafidilo* may be in a better position than others to employ oracles when he initiates a discussion that has not been anticipated. In the community discussion described in the preceding pages, it would have been premature to employ oracles beforehand as this would have indicated that Ibo had irrevocably settled on the prime suspects. In contrast, Ibo only made general arguments and left it to community members to specify names. At that point, recourse to oracles or spirit statements became appropriate. The timing of recourse to oracles is thus variable, although they are often brought to bear on issues considered in public discussions.

Most of the community activities that entail coordination and consensus occur quite infrequently. An initiation lodge was traditionally constructed only once every 5 or so years (and also served a group of communities). A new longhouse is constructed about every 4 years. A community hosts a *kosa* ceremony about once every 2 years. The coordinated pig slaughter associated with (one form of) affinal exchange occurs at about 18-month intervals. The men of Kaburusato took part in a raid against a Kaluli longhouse in the 1940s but were not involved in any extratribal armed conflicts between that time and 1968. In the 15 years prior to fieldwork, there were two four-day armed conflicts with the neighboring Sarado community but none with any other longhouses. A community decision on payment of compensation to an external accuser occurred in only three instances in 15 months among eight communities, indicating that such decisions are required only once every 3 years in any given community (and this assumes continuous epidemic mortality). If the annual incidence of each of these decisions is calculated, a community might be expected to make only two collective decisions a year.[26] A *tafidilo* thus takes responsibility for proposing a course of action to be considered in public community discussion quite infrequently. *Tafidilos* consequently are not visibly prominent in community affairs. Moreover, some decisions are so noncontroversial as to be made almost unnoticed. When Sawa was planning to marry, Ahoa suggested that Turusato and Kaburusato jointly host a *kosa* ceremony to celebrate the union. Ibo readily agreed, and since hosting a ceremony under these circumstances was entirely customary, there was no actual discussion. Had I not asked how the two communities had come to be cohosts, I would have been unaware that *tafidilos* had played any role.[27]

The one decision that occurs more frequently than those listed above entails the least comprehensive coordination. New communal gardens are initiated about once a year (see Kelly 1977:47–49). While the whole community must work together in constructing a new longhouse or increasing production to provision a ceremony, communal gardening is not all-inclusive. Any man may propose to cut a garden at a particular site, invite others to join him, and commence at a mutually convenient time to begin to fence an area commensurate with the needs of the group recruited. *Tafidilos* are not the only men who initiate gardens, but they are always among those who do. *Tafidilos* also make an effort to accommodate widows who have not been invited to join in other gardens and to recruit a bachelor to cut trees for each of these women so as to create a balanced division of labor (as discussed in chap. 2).

The Etoro have a well-developed concept of the supervisory role. This role is designated by the term *ei sano*, literally translatable as "name-speaker." The *ei sano* allocates tasks among the participants in a collective enterprise. When a new longhouse is being constructed, the *ei sano* will say, "Sania, you cut house posts; Maka, you gather cane lashings," assigning various tasks to individuals by name. The supervisory role of *ei sano* is always assumed by a *tafidilo*. However, there are only three circumstances in which such supervision is required, namely construction, preparation for *kosa* ceremonies, and predawn raids on the longhouses of extratribal enemies. All three of these activities require coordination of a division of labor that goes beyond the scope of the routinized sexual division of labor. Longhouse construction is carried out by men, but there is no customary division of labor that allocates the diverse tasks among them. The *ei sano* thus directs this allocation during the initial phase of construction, when building materials are gathered. To a large extent, individuals perceive what is in short supply to complete the tasks at hand as the construction proceeds. Someone will offer to go to the forest to get what is needed. However, if no one has volunteered, the *ei sano* will tell one of the participants in the construction project to leave off what he has been doing and get needed building materials. If there is an on-site job that needs to be done, the *ei sano* (and *tafidilo*) will generally lead by example. Generally speaking, the *ei sano* makes an effort to minimize his supervisory role and avoids giving direct instructions as much as he can.

When I first arrived at Kaburusato, I contracted with Tsmari to build a house for me in exchange for a substantial quantity of steel axes and bush knives. This went quite slowly as Tsmari was no longer the resident *tafidilo* of the community and had difficulty recruiting a work party for a project no one welcomed.[28] Three weeks later, Tsmari learned that the Komo patrol officer would visit in a week. Tsmari was concerned that he would be held responsible for the delays and tried to speed up the construction. When he told everyone to work more quickly, they did so in a mocking way, dashing about in an exaggerated fashion amidst much laughter and joking at his expense. It was evident that he had overstepped the bounds of the supervisory role. Although this was a nontraditional situation and Tsmari lacked the degree of local support that a *tafidilo* typically would have, the incident was nevertheless instructive. An *ei sano* ideally provides a low-key facilitative coordination but does not engender a sense that individuals are working at his direction. When my house burned down nine months later, it was rebuilt by Ahoa, on his own initiative and with no prior agreement concerning payment.[29] That project went more quickly and required less explicit supervisory direction because the individuals involved identified with the goal of the project this time around and also had a high regard for Ahoa. He was the youngest *tafidilo* (being only 40 years of age) and the only charismatic leader among the thirteen *tafidilos* I knew. He had boundless energy and an infectious enthusiasm for communal enterprises.

The *tafidilo* who serves as *ei sano* in the construction of a longhouse assumes the task of hoisting the central ridgepoles into position, an act which is both a feat of strength and a symbolic deed. Individuals sometimes describe their residence in terms of "living with" the *tafidilo* who has played an important role in engendering the community as a collectively functioning social, economic, and ceremonial unit living together under one roof. The longhouse itself is a monument to cooperative effort, coordinated by the *tafidilo* who supervised its construction.

Hosting a *kosa* ceremony entails the accumulation of sufficient food to feed about 150 to 200 people who are assembled from about two in the afternoon until the following dawn. If two communities are cohosts, as is typical, each would need to provide about as much food as their entire community would consume over three days. The extent of surplus production is therefore modest. The fare provided is also exceptionally plain, consisting of large quantities of sago and starchy bananas and more limited quantities of sweet potatoes and/or taro. Greens are served at wedding celebrations (Kelly 1977:220) but not at other ceremonies. Meat, nuts, grubs, and marita pandanus sauce are not served. If wedding pork or forest mammals given in affinal exchange are presented to individuals, these are eaten later, after the event. The quantities involved also would not be sufficient to share among this many people. Provisioning a *kosa* ceremony largely entails drawing on existing resources. The bananas provided would have been planted a year earlier, and ceremonies are not planned this far in advance. The relatively small quantities of tubers required can also be harvested from current gardens. In both these cases, host communities draw on existing stocks of starch staples they might otherwise use for their own consumption. The organization of food production for a *kosa* ceremony thus entails little more than a coordinated effort to harvest bananas and produce a modest surplus of sago.

The *ei sano* who supervises preparations for the ceremony begins by inquiring about his coresidents' stocks of ripening bananas. Community members report on what they can supply in about a month to six weeks. The quantity of sago that will be required is then determined. After some discussion, a tentative date is set that will allow for the necessary sago processing and banana harvesting. The *ei sano* (and *tafidilo*) then consults with his counterpart in the other host community. They review the number of bunches of bananas and standard-sized bundles of sago flour their coresidents have committed themselves to provide, reconcile the tentative dates by which this is to be accomplished, and settle upon a mutually agreeable timetable, usually about a month hence. Each *ei sano* then knots a string with one knot for each day until the ceremony. One knot is untied each evening to mark the passage of a day. Formal invitations are now issued. Young men go painted[30] to neighboring communities to advise them of the planned date and provide them with duplicates of the knotted string. The recipients will have already heard that a ceremony is in the offing.

The host communities now set about sago production. As the date of the ceremony draws near, there is nightly discussion concerning the progress being made. Although it should be a relatively simple matter to produce the modest surplus required, there is great anxiety about having enough food at the appointed time. About 160 person-hours would be required to produce 310 pounds of sago flour so that each of 200 guests would be provisioned with an ample 2,000-calorie portion. This would entail 121.6 woman-hours and 38.4 man-hours. However, the labor force of the two cohost communities is available for this task. Twenty-one women who resided at Turusato and Kaburusato were available to process sago for the *kosa* celebrating Sawa and Hawia's marriage. Thus, each woman would need to contribute only 5.8 hours of labor to produce the quantity required to feed the guests. The male contribution entails a lesser amount of sago-processing labor plus the banana harvesting and provision of banana-leaf "plates," long bamboo tubes of drinking water, and firewood. The hours of labor required would be somewhat less but of the same order as the women's contribution. Thus both men and women should easily be able to complete the necessary work over the course of a week while continuing their normal subsistence tasks (requiring less than 21 hours a week for men and less than 17 hours a week for women). Despite this, there is much talk about how hard everyone is working and how little time there is to complete the preparations. I believe this is largely due to the fact that this is the only firm deadline in Etoro day-to-day life, and it is consequently experienced as an oppressive time pressure. Virtually all components of subsistence can be undertaken at any time of the year, so that tomorrow is as good as today, and procrastination is standard procedure. But in this context, a commitment to a specific date has been made to half the tribe. It can in fact be revised, but this requires consultation with the cohost community, delivery of a new set of knotted strings to all the guest long-houses, evaluation of whether the stockpiled bananas will become spoiled, and so on. As supervisor, the *ei sano* is more responsible than others for meeting the timetable. He consequently frets about whatever remains unaccomplished. He and his wife also lead by example in stockpiling a disproportionate share of the requisite sago and donating all the sufficiently ripe bananas they have on hand. It may well be that all the talk about the amount of labor being expended stems from the *ei sano*'s emphasis on the example he is setting and from each individual's desire to make it known that he or she is conscientiously doing his or her share. In the end, the timetable is almost always met, and there is a large quantity of food left over after the guests have departed.

A *tafidilo* does not supervise affinal exchange of pork but only attempts to coordinate the timing of individual exchanges so that pork is widely available in all the communities involved and can thus be festively shared by all coresidents. Individuals declare their intention to slaughter a pig at a community discussion, and a date mutually agreeable to participating pig owners is set. The *tafidilo*'s main role is to then meet with his counterparts in other communities in order to reconcile the tentative dates and knot strings to coordinate the timetable. The event often does not come off as planned because the free-ranging pigs cannot be located or captured at the agreed-upon time. Thus while nine men of Kaburusato and Turusato pledged a total of 13 pigs, only 5 were actually slaughtered on schedule for the one affinal exchange that took place while I was in the field. One was successfully delivered ten days late, 6 eluded their owners at the appointed time, and 1 other pig was captured but subsequently escaped. These 7 pigs were never delivered. It is possible that some of their owners did not make every effort to locate and capture them, perhaps being content to express their good intentions. The *tafidilo* who coordinates the exchange may not be among the participants. However, it is his responsibility to coordinate intercommunity events, since multicommunity group discussion to set a timetable is unfeasible. (See Kelly 1977:222–28 for a detailed description of the affinal exchange mentioned above.)

Intertribal warfare also entails a collective effort by men of different communities, coordination of timing for a raid, and some allocation of specialized roles among participants. One *tafidilo* is the acknowledged leader of the entire raiding party. It was said that Ahoa would have played this role if the western Etoro communities had raided the Onanafi community whose members had threatened to reveal Kulubido's execution to the patrol officer unless they received "compensation." This selection of one *tafidilo* is based on recognized leadership ability. The *tafidilo* Harepa of Hilisato led the large-scale raid on the Kaluli in the 1940s. He was not closely related to either of the two Etoro men of Tifanifi killed in the earlier Kaluli raid that prompted retaliation, nor were these men members of his longhouse community. The brothers of these two victims, one of whom was also a *tafidilo*, were active in recruiting participants from a large number of longhouse communities and took responsibility for compensation, but Harepa directed the raid itself. He set the date of departure and specified the place where the raiding party (of over one hundred men) would spend the night before the predawn attack. He is also said to have designated two men to serve as scouts, dispatched to watch the targeted longhouse throughout the night. Various contingents were likewise directed to take up positions on different sides of the longhouse. The *tafidilo* gives the signal for the longhouse to be set on fire by coordinated groups of men moving in from different directions after the component contingents are deployed. The warriors then shout war cries in unison and twang their bowstrings in order to terrify the inhabitants and create disarray among them by communicating the extent to which they are outnumbered. After this, the members of the raiding party act on their own without subsequent direction. The main coordination of the raid thus has to do with synchronizing individual effort so as to achieve complete surprise. The need to maintain silence obviously precludes on-site discussion as to who will do what and when, putting a premium on reliance on a single leader to give the signal when everyone is in his assigned position.

In this raid on the Kaluli, everything went as planned, and none of the adult inhabitants of the longhouse escaped. However, the raiding party lost two men when members of other Kaluli longhouses came to the assistance of the house under attack. The men of the Tifanifi community who organized the raid were largely responsible for covering the withdrawal. They also were responsible for compensating the kinsmen of extratribal allies who were killed. The raiding party included men drawn from 13 Etoro, 3 Petamini, and 2 Onanafi longhouses. One Petamini man was killed, and his brother was thus compensated.[31] The men of Tifanifi also paid the equivalent of five homicide compensations to their Kaluli enemies in a peace settlement arranged through an influential Onanafi man (Tadua) who had ties to both sides. Although this compensation did not equalize the disparity between Kaluli and Etoro casualties, the two sides were said to be in a state of equivalence, and no further raids took place. The central point here is that the *tafidilo* Harepa served only as the supervisor (*ei sano*) of the raid. He was not involved in the recruitment of allies by the brothers of the Tifanifi men killed in the earlier Kaluli raid or in the payment of compensation and the negotiation of peace with the Kaluli. The *tafidilo* of Tifanifi was largely responsible for coordinating these aspects of the war.

Tafidilos are also prominent in intratribal conflicts between Etoro communities. This is well illustrated by accounts of a brief engagement between Kaburusato and Sarado in 1963 that stemmed from reciprocal pig theft. Taipa stole one of Ailoe's pigs, and Ailoe stole one of Nawa's pigs in retaliation. The individuals who urged recourse to arms at Kaburusato were the injured party Nawa and the *tafidilos* Mariabu and Ibo. Kaburusato's desire to fight was yodeled to Sarado, and it was arranged by this means of communication that they would meet at a pair of abandoned gardens on opposite sides of a small river that delineated the border between their respective lineage territories. Each side recruited kinsmen from other longhouses so that men from seven different communities took part. The total number of combatants on both sides reportedly numbered seventy to eighty men between the ages of 18 and 60. The prearranged location precluded anything other than a duel between archers, and no clubs or killing sticks were brought to the battlefield. The exchange of arrows largely took place at a range of about 100 feet.

In all, eight wounds were sustained by seven individuals. The injured parties whose pigs were stolen were clearly among the most active participants, as Ailoe was wounded once and Nawa twice. However, four of the five remaining wounds were sustained by *tafidilos*. Three of the archers who found their mark were also *tafidilos,* and another was the initiator of the pig thefts, Taipa. *Tafidilos* and principals in the dispute were thus in the forefront of the battle. In all, *tafidilos* comprised 42 percent of the most active participants, who inflicted or received wounds, while *tafidilos* represented less than 14 percent of the men who took part. This is particularly noteworthy in light of the fact that these *tafidilos* were all in their early 40s to late 50s at this time. Ibo, then 42, shot the *tafidilo* Wabulu (his mother's brother's son) who was about the same age. Mariabu, who both inflicted and received wounds, was then 55. The *tafidilo* Alua, who was wounded by Mariabu, was 58.[32] It seems evident that these two senior men placed themselves in the forefront of the battle in fulfillment of expectations arising from their role as leading *tafidilo* of their respective communities. They were also active in resolution of the conflict, which lasted four days. They shouted across the river that they had had enough of shooting at their kinsmen. Later that afternoon, after the combatants had retired, Alua (of Sarado) went to Kaburusato. He was accompanied by two influential individuals with ties to both sides who had elected not to participate in the fighting, the *tafidilo* Kukubia and the renowned medium Tofono. After consultation with Mariabu and Ibo, it was arranged that each of the two men who lost a pig would be compensated by the thief (and his supporters). The injured parties both agreed to this. The two payments were identical. No compensation was paid for wounds, in accordance with customary procedure. None of the wounds was serious, and the individuals who received them all recovered. There were no lingering animosities. On the contrary, the event was recalled as one in which all the participants acquitted themselves as befits men and an exciting time was had by all.

Every longhouse, with the exception of Kasayasato, has at least one resident *tafidilo* and may contain as many as three (see table 5.2). Kasayasato, which also lacks a medium, is too small to host ceremonies or to provide a chorus in order to conduct séances. Since it does not serve as a ritual center, it is not regarded as a full-fledged longhouse community in all respects. The senior man of the community is not regarded as a *tafidilo* because he has not engendered a collectively functioning ceremonial (as well as social and economic) unit.

As was noted earlier, more than half of the men aged 46 to 60 are regarded as *tafidilos*. Only one unusually vigorous older man (Kusuame, aged 64) and one younger man of exceptional leadership ability (Ahoa, aged 40) are *tafidilos*. Several other current *tafidilos* were first accorded this status when they were in their early 40s (e.g., Ibo and Wabulu). Several former *tafidilos* are no longer regarded as such due to age and transition to *tole* status (e.g., Alua). A man may thus expect to attain the status of *tafidilo* when he reaches his middle 40s, provided that he is well regarded by his coresidents so that he can effectively coordinate community enterprises and lead by example. One principal correlate of exclusion is involvement in witchcraft cases as the father or husband of an accused witch or, very rarely, as the subject of an accusation. Men over the age of 40 are very infrequently accused of witchcraft. However, these same senior men are responsible for payment of compensation when their sons, daughters, wives, or sisters are accused and thus have maximum exposure to involvement in witchcraft cases as a close supporter of a witch. Since most witchcraft accusations are internal to the community, such involvement often leads to divisiveness and to a senior man's alienation from coresidents. The social consequences of Nawa's support for his son Tame in two internal accusations perfectly illustrates this process. Nawa would be incapable of functioning as a facilitator of cooperative enterprises. This is exemplified by the fact that no one outside his immediate family and his closest kin and affinal relatives would join in the gardens he initiated. His coresidents did not want to be in close proximity to Tame on a regular basis. Sagobe faced the same problem at Kasayasato due to the repeated accusations against his daughter, Nawadia.

A witchcraft accusation against a family member can also undercut the position of an established *tafidilo* and provide an impetus to a change of residence. Thus, Mariabu moved from Kaburusato to Turusato after his wife Tumame was accused of witchcraft. Although he continued to be regarded as a *tafidilo*, he did not function in the capacities associated with this status because these responsibilities were divided between the aging *tafidilo* Yora and his successor, Ahoa. It is unlikely that Mariabu would ever recover his former position as community leader because he was 60 years of age (in 1968) and approaching *tole* status. Tsmari also moved from Kaburusato to Haifi after his second wife Waime was accused of witchcraft. He played a minor role there until the *tafidilos* Habwili and Piawe both died in the epidemic of January 1969. Kusuame also died at Katiefi at the same time so that Tsmari became the sole *tafidilo* of the combined community that took shape after the epidemic. Waime also died in the epidemic, and Tsmari therefore was not involved as a close supporter of the accused in any of the many witchcraft accusations that eventuated. It thus appeared that he would be able to function effectively as a community leader during his remaining active years. He was then 58, although in good health and still vigorous.

When a community contains several *tafidilos* who have been long-term residents, they will often divide the responsibilities of the position. Turusato provides an illustrative example. Yora, the senior *tafidilo*, was 59 years of age, in poor health, and nearing the time when he would retire from active involvement in community enterprises. Ahoa, his younger half brother, was 40. Yora continued to select sites for communal gardens as he was the most knowledgeable concerning the past productivity of formerly cultivated lands that had now reverted to forest. He also initiated new gardens. Ahoa followed Yora's lead in this area of endeavor and did not seek to initiate any other large gardens that would compete for participants. Both men spoke to the issue of whether to build a new longhouse, as some residents desired. These two *tafidilos* agreed that it was better to wait a year and then build closer to an area of anticipated land and sago exploitation that Yora had in mind. However, it was said that Ahoa would supervise the construction when the house was actually built. Ahoa took the lead in suggesting that Turusato cohost a *kosa* ceremony on the occasion of Sawa and Hawia's marriage. He coordinated the community's contribution to the stocks of sago and bananas accumulated to feed the guests. Yora would not have been able to make the substantial contribution expected of a *tafidilo* as easily because he was a widower. Ahoa also took the lead in arguing for the refusal of compensation when Kayago and Waua were accused of witchcraft. He would be foremost among those who would meet and face down the accusers on their arrival (and subsequently was). Yora was no longer agile enough to desire to play this role and deferred to Ahoa in this community discussion. The accommodation worked out between these two coresident *tafidilos* played to their respective strengths. The man best suited to the requirements of the situation at hand took the lead. This arrangement typically provides a basis for a smooth transition in community leadership, since a senior *tafidilo* who is no longer vigorous will normally defer to his more junior counterpart with respect to the more physically demanding responsibilities of the position. I detected no evidence of competition between *tafidilos* comparable to that between mediums. However, the high frequency of witchcraft accusations against men in the 31-to-40 age-group suggests competition at an earlier stage.

Many men of average talents and abilities become *tafidilos* and adequately fulfill the relatively undemanding supervisory functions and responsibilities of this position. However, there are additional qualities that the Etoro say a *tafidilo* should ideally possess: the ability to command respect, articulateness, physical strength and endurance, courage in battle, generosity, and a reputation as an enthusiastic worker in communal enterprises and as a conformist with regard to cultural rules and values. Many of these qualities are closely related to the various leadership roles a *tafidilo* assumes, so that this culturally formulated ideal type essentially expresses the idea that a *tafidilo* should be good at the things he is expected to do. For example a *tafidilo* needs to be articulate if people are to "listen when he talks," and he requires courage if he is to be in the forefront of armed conflict. These qualities are also ascribed to the status itself to some extent. A *tafidilo* commands respect by virtue of being a *tafidilo,* and there is likewise an intrinsic inclination to listen attentively to the course of action he proposes. The members of a longhouse community are thus predisposed to see their *tafidilo* as possessing these commendable qualities. This makes it possible for more than half of the senior men to measure up to this status and be accorded the admiration of coresidents. At the same time, prestige is intrinsically accorded to *tafidilos* insofar as they tend to be seen as paragons of virtue in the many respects noted above. The same qualities a man manifests in order to achieve this social status are ascribed to the holders of it, so that emergent virtue is concretized.

Tafidilos do manifest most of these desired qualities in practice. For example, available data indicate that all the *tafidilos* of Sarado and Kaburusato except Tsmari were in the forefront of battle in the armed conflict between these two communities. These individuals were clearly more active participants than others (excepting the two men whose pigs were stolen), and they displayed the courage attributed to them. Ibo was an impressive public speaker and masterful rhetorician, while Ahoa was quite articulate and dominated discussion by force of personality. Tsmari, Mariabu, and Yora were all quite articulate as well. All these men commanded respect in their own communities, although Tsmari was no longer highly regarded at Kaburusato. This was due to the dispute over return of the compensation he paid when his wife Waime was accused of bewitching Kebo. It is noteworthy that even Tsmari's son Ayage opposed him in this dispute, so that he was completely isolated and without support (see n. 15 of chap. 4). He thus appeared as an individual attempting to manipulate the rules of compensation through reliance on a dubious technicality. Moreover, he appeared to lack the culturally expected empathy toward Kebo's bereaved next of kin. This shows how a *tafidilo*'s position can be undercut by a witchcraft accusation against a family member.

Yora, Mariabu, and Tsmari were all 58 to 60 years of age, and the first two men traveled to other communities for *kosa* ceremonies and mortuary gatherings less than they had when they were younger. They had begun to withdraw from these aspects of social life, and their influence outside their own communities was thus on the wane. However, Ibo and Ahoa were very active in this respect. Ahoa in particular was known for his leadership ability in a wider sphere. Thus it was said that he would play the role Harepa had played in the past in leading raiding parties (composed of men from different communities) against external enemies, should the occasion arise.

Both Ibo and Ahoa were men of above-average size and physical strength who were known for their capacity for work. Both did more than their share of the labor in felling trees and constructing fences in communal gardens. They characteristically worked energetically, took fewer breaks, and continued after others had ceased for the day. Their efforts in construction were of a piece. Ibo put on an impressive display of physical strength during the construction of my house by shinning up one of the center posts with one end of a 45-foot ridgepole on his shoulders and hoisting this into position with one hand. A group of men using forked poles could have done this quite easily. This feat was accomplished to the accompaniment of cheers and general adulation. Ahoa performed a similar feat of strength on another occasion when he undertook to elevate one corner of the house whose post had settled deeper than the others. Yora reputedly performed similar feats of strength when he was younger, while Mariabu and Tsmari were dogged workers, although they were comparatively smaller men.

Senior men in their early 40s to middle 50s hunt an average of 1.67 hours longer per hunting day and are an average of 4.4 times more successful in terms of game procured per hour than are young men aged 16 to 25 (Dwyer 1983). This early-40s-to-middle-50s age-group largely overlaps with that of active *tafidilos*. Although data are inadequate to establish that *tafidilos* invariably hunt more often or more proficiently than other men of the same age, it is evident that they will be among the main providers of game within the community. In the community for which adequate data are available, the contrast between *tafidilo* and eligibly aged non-*tafidilo* is striking. Ibo provided 56 percent of the game consumed at Kaburusato, although I believe he was probably exceptional among *tafidilos* in the extent to which his distributions overshadowed those of other men of the community. Nevertheless, Ibo was the preeminent game provider while the non-*tafidilo* Nawa never distributed game at the longhouse.

This pattern may have obtained elsewhere as well. Tsmari returned to his lineage lands near Kaburusato to hunt quite frequently, so that I was aware of the considerable time he devoted to this activity (although I did not often see the results since he brought his bag to Haifi to share with co-residents). Ahoa operated one of the more extensive sets of traplines at Turusato. It is thus quite likely that Tsmari and Ahoa were major providers of game in their respective communities, although probably not to the same extent as Ibo. This is consistent with the cultural view that *tafidilos* should be generous. Moreover, the available evidence suggests that they are quite generous in sharing game. Although Ibo may have been exceptional among *tafidilos,* it can definitely be established that his reputation for generosity was grounded in actual practice rather than selective perceptions attributable to his status. Generosity was not merely ascribed but continuously manifested.

While senior men as a group are proficient hunters who put in long hours, *tafidilos* very probably share a greater proportion of their catch with coresidents than non-*tafidilos,* so that their generosity is further amplified. An individual like Nawa who is estranged from his coresidents spends a large proportion of his time at his garden dwelling, and is thus less engaged in reciprocal food sharing than others, if not entirely disengaged, as Nawa was. Thus the *tafidilo*/non-*tafidilo* distinction appears to correspond to actual differences in generosity both because the senior men not accorded this status are, for the same reasons, disinclined to share food and because *tafidilos* make an effort to fulfill cultural expectations.

Tafidilos are reputed to maintain large gardens which they draw on to provision ceremonies and to give produce to individuals whose family stocks have run low due to illness. Since family plots within communal gardens were not separately measured, I cannot evaluate this indication that *tafidilos* would be expected to cultivate more land per capita than others. I suspect that this would not be uniformly true of all *tafidilos,* although it may be true of some. However, it is noteworthy that Dwyer's data showing that senior men as a group hunt longer hours match my own data indicating that they also work longer hours in tree felling and fencing. The latter data would be consistent with the maintenance of large gardens. On the other hand, *tafidilos* would not need to put much additional land into production in order to contribute a disproportionate share of bananas to the provisioning of a *kosa* ceremony every other year. There is much greater scope for generosity in sharing game than in sharing garden produce. The former might be done quite frequently, while suitable occasions for the latter arise only at long intervals.

The preceding discussion shows that individual *tafidilos* do manifest most of the cultural values that are credited to them. This is attributable to three factors. First, men who obviously lack these qualities are not recognized as *tafidilos*. Second, certain qualities, such as "commands respect," are essentially ascribed to the status itself. Third, *tafidilos* are stimulated by cultural expectations and make a substantial effort to fulfill them.

While senior men as a group are intrinsically generous by virtue of their position in the system of life-force transmission, *tafidilos* are also generous in practice in providing a disproportionate share of the game that is believed to provide for growth and maturation. *Tafidilos* are the prime beneficiaries of the cultural construction of prestige but at the same time make substantial efforts to fulfill the high expectations that accompany this. They do so both in their efforts, as younger men, to lay the groundwork for eventual recognition as a *tafidilo* and in their efforts to display the requisite qualities when the position is attained. Although closed to women,[33] this major component of the prestige system works to bring out the best in men as the Etoro define this. Senior men are not accorded prestige simply by virtue of being senior men, but as a result of their conformity to culturally valued ideals. Appropriately aged men who are not recognized as *tafidilos* do not reap the ideological benefits of the intrinsic generosity attributable to their life-force position. On the contrary, they provide the contrast that highlights the prestigious qualities and accomplishments of *tafidilos*.

In summary, the category *tafidilo* is an acknowledged social standing—achieved through the accumulation of prestige and the avoidance of stigma—that constitutes a prerequisite for assuming a leadership role in a longhouse community. The social standing and the social position are clearly distinguishable since there are acknowledged *tafidilos* who do not perform any of the functions associated with the leadership role (i.e., Mariabu of Turusato and Tsmari of Haifi, during the period prior to the deaths of Habwili and Piawe). Conversely, Sagobea, who is the senior man of Kasayasato, does perform many of these functions but is not regarded as a *tafidilo*. An individual is a *tafidilo* only if members of the longhouse community and larger society label him as such, and the social standing is thus essentially reputational.

Although seniority is strongly correlated with *tafidilo* status, it is neither necessary nor sufficient for the attainment of this social standing. A number of senior men are excluded, and some younger men are acknowledged to be *tafidilos*. Ibo, Ahoa, and Wabulu were all initially regarded as *tafidilos* in their late 30s to early 40s, well before any of their children were fully grown or their inseminees had attained maturity. It is thus evident that *tafidilo* status is not simply ascribed by age or life-cycle position but is achieved. The fact that this social standing is attained by the majority of senior men does not alter its achieved basis but rather indicates that the accumulation of the requisite prestige is not difficult. Most senior men are capable of being proficient hunters and trappers since the necessary skills are largely a product of experience. Attaining distinction through the frequent distribution of growth-inducing game to members of the longhouse community over many years is therefore primarily a matter of effort. It entails a choice to devote additional hours to hunting and trapping and also a choice to regularly bring the game procured to the longhouse rather than distributing it at a garden house.

The fact that the attainment of prestige through generosity does not require exceptional talents or abilities does not diminish the significance of comparative distinction relative to less generous younger men and peers. There are very substantial differences between individuals in the effort expended (documented in Dwyer 1983:168–71), and even more striking differences in the actual frequency of distribution separate skilled and energetic seniors from unambitious peers and desultory juniors. Moreover, a man who achieves notable distinction in this respect at an earlier age may be accorded *tafidilo* status in his late 30s or early 40s. In the instances for which empirical documentation is available, the individuals who distributed the greatest quantity of game to community members were regarded as *tafidilos* or held an equivalent status. At Bobole, where the position of deacon of the church had become an analogue of *tafidilo* status by 1979, the two most productive hunters (of thirty-one total) were both deacons (i.e., Maga and Siagoba, see Dwyer 1990:128; Dwyer 1983:168–71). Maga is in the age category characteristic of *tafidilos,* while Siagoba is in Dwyer's middle-30s-to-early-40s age class (ibid.).

It is also important to note that *tafidilos* who no longer hunt and trap cease to be regarded as such, as exemplified by Alua. While these men's established past contributions of life force and growth-inducing game are undiminished by the passage of time, they are not currently in a position to distribute game to coresidents. Thus they no longer manifest comparative distinction in this respect. The social standing of *tafidilo* is accorded on the basis of prestige and must be maintained on the same basis. A reputation that is not reaffirmed dims and is eclipsed.

All these data are conducive to the conclusion that prestige-enhancing generosity is central to the achievement of *tafidilo* status. Moreover, prominence in game distribution is indexical with respect to most of the qualities a *tafidilo* should ideally possess. An individual who achieves distinction in this regard is, by definition, generous and hardworking, and likewise my definition possesses continued vigor and endurance at middle age, conforms to key cultural values, and commands respect. Insofar as prestige is defined as the esteem accorded to distinction in the attainment of virtues achieved through elective social action, the social standing of *tafidilo* is clearly prestige-based rather than ascribed by age. This is particularly evident at the point of attainment of this status (and especially when this occurs comparatively early). Subsequently, a *tafidilo* appears to possess all the requisite qualities by definition, since many of them are artifacts of functioning as a community leader and assumption of this position is automatic if residence remains unchanged. As noted earlier, a *tafidilo* commands respect by virtue of being a *tafidilo* and acknowledged community leader. By the same token, people "listen when he talks." Moreover, the qualities instrumental to achievement of this social status are also ascribed to it, and virtue manifested through past achievement is thus concretized. Performance of the modest · functions and responsibilities of community leader requires only average talents and abilities rather than exceptional qualities, so that more than half of the senior men can readily serve as effective community leaders and display the requisite virtues.

It is important to recall that a prestige system is more accurately characterized as a prestige/stigma system and that stigma largely negates prestige. Moreover, there is no true intermediate position whereby an individual could manifest balanced qualities of each. A man who is the subject of an authenticated witchcraft accusation is by definition selfish, possesses vigor and endurance as a result of having appropriated the *hame* of others, is lacking in a community-spirited nature, does not conform to central cultural values, and does not command respect. A witchcraft accusation is indexical of all the qualities that contrast with those a *tafidilo* should ideally possess. An accused witch is thus essentially debarred from effective participation in the system of prestige attainment. Acts of generosity in the distribution of game are discordant with the recipient's perceptions of the donor's intrinsically selfish nature, tend not to be remembered over time, and thus do not contribute to cumulative reputation building. Given the reputational quality of *tafidilo* status, the stigma of an authenticated witchcraft accusation constitutes an insurmountable obstacle. Thus witchcraft accusations are not an external factor with respect to the prestige system but an integral component of a prestige/stigma system, based on contrastive characteristics of manifest virtue and vice, that engenders oppositional classifications.

An acknowledged *tafidilo* whose wife, son, or daughter is accused of witchcraft also experiences a marked setback because this almost invariably leads to a change of residence (as exemplified by the cases of Tsmari and

Mariabu). Such a *tafidilo* loses the position of community leader at the longhouse he leaves and does not immediately accede to a leadership position at the community he joins, since the latter position is already occupied. Moreover, he will not possess an established reputation for generosity among his coresidents since he has not distributed game to them. However, he need only do what he has done in the past in order to earn prestige locally and renew his social standing. With the passage of time, the senior *tafidilo* of the community will either retire or die, typically being replaced by a younger man who shared community leadership with him. The immigrant *tafidilo* may then share community leadership as junior partner to the latter, if the immigrant *tafidilo* is still vigorous and no further witchcraft accusations against family members have occurred. If he outlives other qualified senior men, as Tsmari did, he may attain the position of leading *tafidilo* of his new community by default. However it is evident that a witchcraft accusation against a family member constitutes a setback, since it produces a disjunction between the prestige associated with this social standing and the prerogative that *tafidilo* status normally confers, i.e., a leadership role in the community. In other respects, the prestige that is instrumental to the attainment of *tafidilo* status is at the same time the reward that accrues to those who achieve this social standing. There are no notable material advantages or special privileges that accrue to *tafidilos* other than the prerogative of community leadership (entailing the functions detailed earlier). However prestige itself is a very significant form of culturally pertinent advantage in its own right and should not be discounted.

The preceding discussion reveals that all *tafidilos* are not equivalent in the extent to which they enjoy the prerogative of a community leadership role. There is only one leading *tafidilo* in a longhouse community. Other resident *tafidilos* are either junior partners who are next in line to succeed to such a position, semiretired former occupants of this leading position, or immigrants attempting to reestablish their credentials. Thus while the eight-community sample in table 5.2 includes 13 *tafidilos* (representing 14.6 percent of the initiated male population over the age of 20), only 7 of these are leading *tafidilos* of their community (since the senior man of Kasayasato is not regarded as a *tafidilo*). This elite represents 7.9 percent of the adult male population over the age of 20 and 36.8 percent of the men in the eligible age category (46 to 60). A very similar pattern obtains with respect to spirit mediums. Although the sample in table 5.2 includes 13 mediums (likewise representing 14.6 percent of the male population over age 20), only 5 of these held the position of senior medium in a longhouse community in May 1968 (since two communities lacked resident spirit mediums and Nogobe of Kaburusato was not a senior medium at that time). The spirit medium elite thus represents 5.6 percent of the adult male population. Overall, 28.1 percent

(25/89) of adult men over age 20 have a prestige status in the prestige/stigma hierarchy, while 13.4 percent (12/89) are senior mediums or leading *tafidilos* who constitute the elite of Etoro society. This elite constitutes 7.4 percent (12/163) of the male and female population over age 20 and 4.3 percent (12/276) of the total population.

However, it is also important to recall that 40 percent (4/10) of the men aged 21 to 25 are novice spirit mediums, and 58 percent (11/19) of those aged 46 to 60 are *tafidilos*. A substantial majority of men who live until their late 40s have a prestige status at one or more points in their lifetime, and nearly all of these men who have such a status eventually attain a position of community leadership. Viewed over the male life cycle, the prestige system is quite open (although it is entirely closed from a female perspective). But at any particular point in time, there is a quite restricted male elite that plays an important role in shaping the course of events within each longhouse community. Moreover, there is an extremely select group of exceptional individuals who are members of this restricted male elite throughout most of their adult lives, becoming senior mediums in their middle to late 20s and going on to attain *tafidilo* status in their middle to late 40s, while at the same time retaining influence over several protégés who have become the senior mediums of their respective communities. Tofono best illustrates the realization of this potentiality. The Etoro social system can thus be characterized as both egalitarian among males in certain significant respects and as highly stratified in other respects.

As noted earlier, 29.6 percent of the men aged 31 to 40 were subject to a witchcraft accusation during the sample period. In all, 15.7 percent (14/89) of all initiated men over the age of 20 were accused (as were 9.5 percent of all women over age 20). However the higher figure is more representative of the proportion of men whose reputation is tarnished by a witchcraft accusation at the point in their lives when they need to manifest virtue as a prerequisite for attainment of *tafidilo* status. Thus the roughly 30 percent of men who have a stigmatized reputational status in the prestige/stigma hierarchy is approximately equivalent to the percentage who have a prestige status (i.e., 28.1 percent). Most of the men who make up the remainder of the male population will eventually achieve *tafidilo* status if they live to the eligible age. The preceding discussion suggests that all male nonwitches who make an effort to achieve this social standing will succeed.

PRIVILEGE AND PREROGATIVE

Although prestige accrues to mediums and *tafidilos,* the question of whether this prestige entails special privileges, marital advantages, or material benefits remains to be considered. It has already been established that *tafidilos* put in more hours in hunting and gardening than other men and that mediums likewise expend considerable efforts in conducting séances that frequently last all night an average of once a week. However, neither enjoys privileges in terms of consumption or reduced labor in other areas. Thus mediums and *tafidilos* perform all the tasks that ordinary men perform while taking on the added responsibilities of their respective positions.

While *tafidilos* are not materially compensated for their efforts, mediums do receive gifts from individuals they have cured. Although there is no specific customary payment for such services, the patient does incur an obligation to provide a token of his or her gratitude. This is usually discharged by giving smoked game or a small pig to the healer. Occasionally, a mature pig may be given. There is thus a potentiality that mediums could accumulate greater numbers of pigs than others. However, this is not realized in practice. A survey of pig ownership indicates that age accounts for observable differences among men in the per capita holdings of family groups (Kelly 1988:143–49). The family groups of men aged 21 to 30 own 1.65 pigs per capita, those of men aged 31 to 40 own 2.22 pigs per capita, and those of men aged 41 to 60 own only .59 pigs per capita (these figures being the average of initial and final pig censuses during a 14-week sample period). The holdings of both mediums and *tafidilos* included in this sample are entirely typical of the age-groups to which these men belong. Neither mediums nor *tafidilos* own more pigs than other men of the same age cohorts who lack these social distinctions. Like other senior men, *tafidilos* own few pigs and do not make an effort to acquire more through trade (ibid.: 148). The deployment of pigs is not a significant source of prestige. Moreover, wealth in pigs is disconnected from social status in the Etoro system. Mediums and *tafidilos* do not require more pigs than others to attain their respective positions and do not accumulate pigs as a material benefit of their elevated social standing.

Male marital experience is also strongly conditioned by age as is shown in table 5.4. In 1968, men typically did not marry until age 26 to 30. Earlier marriage was rare, and 41.7 percent (5/12) of the men aged 31 to 35 were still bachelors. (See Kelly 1977:169–70 for a discussion of demographically induced changes in age of first marriage.) In addition, all married men aged 21 to 30 had just one wife. At age 31 to 40, 2 of 22 men (or 9.1 percent) had acquired a second wife. In one instance, this was due to the death of a brother and the acquisition of a second wife through the levirate. Abama, who was then 31 years of age, took Habasiome, aged 53, as his second wife. She was one of several women beyond childbearing age who had never borne a child. She did not marry a single man both because she was a nonreproductive woman and because all potential leviratic spouses were married. More importantly, she wished to remain with her deceased husband's brother and initi-

TABLE 5.4

Male Marital Experience by Age Cohort, May 1, 1968

Age Cohort	Never-Married Men	Ever-Married Men with				Ever-Married Men	Previous marital experience of wives			Total Men	Total Wives
		No Wife	One Wife	Two Wives	Three Wives		None	Widow	Divorcée		
66–70			1			1	1			1	1
61–65		2	2			4	2			4	2
56–60		2	2	2		6	4	1	1	6	6
51–55			6			6	4	1	1	6	6
46–50		1	3	3		7	9			7	9
41–45			5	1	1	7	9	1		7	10
36–40			10			10	9	1		10	10
31–35	5	1	9	2		12	10	3		17	13
26–30	11		10			10	7	1	2	21	10
21–25	9		1			1	1			10	1
Total	25	6	49	8	1	64	56	8	4	89	68

ated the union herself. Of the widows in a larger sample who remarried, 47 percent wed bachelors, 17.6 percent wed widowers, and 5.9 percent wed divorced men (Kelly 1977:302). The 29.4 percent of widows that wed married men were typically older women, like Habasiome. The fact that widows who are potential child producers predominantly wed single men shows that these women are not monopolized by senior married men. Unmarried men are also the husbands younger widows typically desire. As noted in chapter 2, Etoro women display a marked preference for the married state. Habasiome exemplifies this point as she would not have needed to remarry. She was not being sought as a spouse by anyone, nor was she urged to remarry by her deceased husband's brothers.

Mogoya (aged 35) is the other man in this age-group who took a second wife. His first wife, Yagwa, had not yet borne a child although she was 27 years of age. She was presumed to be sterile. Taking a second wife under these circumstances is standard procedure. Every man is considered to be entitled to a wife who bears children, so that a man in this position is essentially regarded as an unmarried man in terms of the legitimacy of his claim to a wife vis-à-vis those of other men. Such claims are based on need as well as reciprocity in the exchange of women.

Only 3 men in the 31-to-40 age-group had lost a wife due to death or divorce. Two of the 3 had remarried by May 1, 1968, while the third, Nomaya, remarried during the fieldwork period (see n. 34 to chap. 4). As of the sample date, 33 ever-married men aged 21 to 40 were married to 34 women, closely approximating a one-to-one ratio (i.e., 1.03 wives per man).

The prime years for polygyny are between the ages of 41 and 50. There are several reasons for this. First, a man's first wife is typically 10 years younger than her husband and thus very likely to still be living when he is 50. Moreover, men below the age of 50 generally remarry if their wife dies. At the same time, a second wife may be obtained during this period. In all, the 14 men in this age-group included 1 unremarried widower, 8 monogamists, and 5 polygynists married to a total of 19 women or 1.36 per man. Although older widows who are beyond, or close to being beyond, reproductive age typically wed married men, only one of the five second wives of these men was a widow. Asifa became the third wife of the spirit medium Hoamo largely on her own initiative. She was 17 years older than Hoamo and her remarriage was very similar to that of Habasiome. Hoamo is the only man with three wives in the sample.

Nawa, who was another of these five polygynists, acquired Susa as a second wife while he was in his late 30s. Susa was a partially crippled woman who had been severely injured by a felled tree as a child and had a deformed spinal column as a result. She also had not yet borne a child by 1969 although she was then 28 years of age.

The *tafidilo* Wabulu married two young women close in age at about the same time if not simultaneously. These women were the last two living persons of the Tifanifi lineage and were related as father's brother's daughter to each other. They had grown up together and having no living close kin (including mother's brothers as well as patrikin) did not want to be separated. They consequently sought to be co-wives to Wabulu, who had initially been betrothed to the elder of the pair (aged 32 and 29 in 1968). Wabulu thus became a polygynist long before he became a *tafidilo* and under circumstances entirely unrelated to that status.

Both Osiama and the medium Piawe also possessed two wives who had not previously been married (i.e., were neither widowed nor divorced), who were close in age, and who had both produced children. However, unlike Wabulu their pairs of wives were not lineage sisters. Osiama arranged to marry a Petamini woman and also exchanged sisters with Ahoa while Piawe's polygyny was in fulfillment of shamanic prophecy. The medium Hoamo's second wife was likewise acquired on this basis. (As noted earlier, Hoamo's third wife, who was many years his senior, was a leviratically acquired widow who was in her middle 40s when they wed and who had settled on Hoamo of her own accord.)

As is evident from the foregoing discussion, polygyny is typically a result of special circumstances, because the Etoro hold to the view that an individual ought not to have two of anything so long as a kinsman does not have one. A first wife's barrenness provides grounds for legitimating polygyny. The acquisition of a second wife who is not expected to bear any additional children, or who is crippled, is a counterpart of the same extenuating circumstances. Acquiring a second wife who is not an Etoro woman may be considered quasi-acceptable on the grounds that she does not form part of the pool of women readily available to one's kin. Finally, the shamanic prophecy of polygyny legitimates the acquisition of a second wife. This provides mediums with a definite prerogative unavailable to others. The extent to which this eventuates in a disproportionate rate of polygyny will be considered below.

The incidence of polygyny declines among men aged 51 to 60 as wives are lost through death but are not replaced. Men this age very rarely remarry. Of the 12 men in this cohort, 5 have lost a wife at some point during their lifetime. Two of the five lost wives earlier and remarried, one polygynist was reduced to monogamy, and two more recently widowed men have not remarried. Two polygynists remained such, so that the 12 men in this cohort are married to a total of 12 women. The ratio of ever-married men to wives thus returns to the parity that obtained among men aged 21 to 40.

After age 60, the processes noted above intensify. Men's wives die but they do not remarry. In all, the 5 men in this age-group lost 4 wives, so that all 5 are either monogamists (3) or widowers (2). The ratio of wives to ever-married men declines to .6. The polygynists in this cohort include the *tafidilos* Tsmari and Mariabu. The circumstances of Mariabu's polygyny are quite similar to Wabulu's. The husband of his first wife's sister died, and this woman (Akwadi) came to live with her sister (Tumame) and Mariabu as a widow with young children. The two sisters desired to perpetuate this arrangement and jointly proposed polygyny to Mariabu.

It is important to note that a man's first wife must agree to accept a polygynous arrangement in order for this to come about. A first wife who does not accept the arrangement may simply take up with another man, engendering a de facto divorce, or create domestic havoc and discord, impelling the second wife to leave. Ibo's wife (also named Akwadi) iced out a widow who was obviously flirtatious and was signaling interest in an extra-marital liaison with Ibo leading to wedlock. Akwadi said publicly she did not want a co-wife. When I asked Ibo about his views on the matter, he said he would not take a second wife against Akwadi's wishes. Theirs was a romantic union, as they had eloped when Akwadi was already betrothed to another man. Ibo assiduously engaged in trade and accumulated his entire bridewealth on his own, since no one would contribute to legitimation of his irregular union that violated the principles of arranged marriage. However, their marriage was accepted after bridewealth was paid and their first child was born.[34] At the time the widow in question came forward, Ibo and Akwadi were still very attached to each other, and Ibo was quite content to accede to Akwadi's wishes. He expressed no regrets. The more general point to be noted here is that special considerations are required to legitimate polygyny in the eyes of both the second wife-giver and the extant wife.

Tsmari is the only man who acquired a second wife while he was a *tafidilo*. He married Waime who was twice divorced and twice accused of witchcraft, and who had not previously borne a child although she was 37 at the time. She was not being sought as a spouse. She also took the initiative in instigating an adulterous liaison with Tsmari with a view to wedlock. I do not know why Tsmari's first wife (Nagayemi) agreed to have her as a co-wife. However, Tsmari was a forceful person, and Nagayemi was rather the opposite. In addition, polygyny reduces a woman's workload by about 25 percent (while increasing a man's by about 50 percent). Whatever the reasons, Nagayemi appeared quite content with the arrangement. However, Tsmari's marriage to Waime was the cause of his downfall as a *tafidilo* at Kaburusato. Waime was accused of witchcraft on the occasion of the first death that took place at Kaburusato after she had taken up residence there. This led to a change of residence, a subsequent dispute with his agnates over return of compensation, and a falling out between Tsmari and his son, who failed to support Tsmari in this dispute. Tsmari thus ceased to be a respected *tafidilo* at Kaburusato. The case thus illustrates the pitfalls of polygyny when this is achieved by acquiring a second wife who is available because she is an undesirable spouse.

The entire sample includes 58 currently married men with a total of 68 wives, or 1.17 wives per married man. Nine men, or 15.5 percent are polygynous. If widowers and divorced men are included in these calculations, there are only 1.06 wives per ever-married man, and the proportion of polygynous men drops to 14.1 percent. Polygyny is facilitated by a late age of first marriage for men and an early age of first marriage for women, as is well known. However, equally important in the Etoro case is the fact that men widowed after the age of 50 do not remarry. This is a direct product of the ideology of sexual depletion, which increasingly becomes a concern among older men. The wives that might go to older widowers are consequently available to younger men, and this ideology thus has egalitarian consequences in this respect. Older widows who might otherwise wed widowers of close to the same age thus become the second wives of younger men, often some years their junior. If widowers did remarry, the rate of polygyny would contract markedly (other things being equal), since there would be fewer women available to be second wives. More specifically, the remarriage of the six widowers in the sample would entail a reduction of the number of polygynists from nine to three, or 4.7 percent of currently married men (assuming the age of first marriage for men remained the same).

While both men aged 20 to 35 and those aged 51 to 70 have less than one wife per man, only men aged 41 to 50 have a disproportionate share of the marriageable women. The remarriage of older widows and divorcées contributes to this. An unmarried young man does not seek to wed a woman who is already past childbearing (or nearly so) as his first wife. Widowers over 50 rarely remarry, so the older previously married women tend to go to married men aged 41 to 50 or younger. Moreover, the women themselves often initiate these unions. Many polygynists therefore arrive at this state by marrying women no one else seeks to wed. This would clearly apply to four of the nine polygynists (Nawa, Abama, Tsmari, and Hoamo, with respect to his third wife). Two others are engaged in sororal polygyny instigated by their wives (i.e., Wabulu and Mariabu). This is significant in that it is commonly assumed that polygyny by older men entails monopolization of potential spouses, achieved both through coercive control over women and at younger men's expense. On the contrary, the majority of Etoro cases of polygyny are instigated by women, and most of these also entail a man's marriage to a second wife who is not being sought by anyone. As was explained in chapter 2, polygyny is not economically advantageous for men since it increases a man's workload while there is no prestige-enhancing use to which the additional female labor can be put. It should also be kept in mind that the ideology of male sexual depletion reduces the appeal that polygyny may have in other societies. Taboos also narrowly restrict the frequency of heterosexual intercourse.[35]

There are, however, a few instances in which a man married two young never-married women on his own initiative. Mogoya's second marriage, due to the barrenness of his first wife, did not entail monopolization as he was considered to be entitled to a childbearing woman. Leaving this case aside, there were three instances, two of which involved spirit mediums (Piawe and Hoamo). Spirit mediums are thus the only men who are considered to be legitimately entitled to more than one childbearing wife from among the pool of women who might otherwise go to unmarried men. This is the only exception to an otherwise egalitarian ideology that is grounded in the assumption that the essentials of life should be shared. One should not possess scarce items in multiple when others lack them. However, mediums are intrinsically polygynous since they are wedded to both a spirit wife and one in the flesh. The spirit wife is always accommodating in accepting a co-wife. The acquisition of a second spirit wife foretells and legitimates mundane polygyny as well, although there is no explicit doctrine that explains why this should be either necessary or desirable.

The current marital status of *tafidilos,* mediums, and ordinary men is shown in table 5.5.[36] The data presented in this table show that mediums are not significantly more likely to be polygynists than other men their age despite their distinctive prerogative. Moreover, mediums tend to marry somewhat later than other men. Among men aged 21 to 35 who are not mediums, 51.2 percent (21/41) are ever-married, while only 28.6 percent (2/7) of mediums in this age-group are ever-married. The delay is probably due to the fact that a medium must establish a relationship with his spirit wife before he weds. Neither of the two polygynists in the 21-to-35 age-group is a medium. Among currently married ordinary men aged 21 to 45, 9.4 percent (3/32) are polygynous. Comparatively, one of seven or 14.2 percent of the currently married mediums in this age-group is polygynous. This slight difference is partly due to the fact that fewer mediums than ordinary men are currently married, so that this segment of the sample is small and one instance of polygyny produces a higher percentage. Moreover, all four of the ever-married mediums outside the eight-community sample have only one wife (i.e., Taipa, Kago, Hesi, and Bagaloa). The percentage of polygynous mediums in this expanded sample is 9.1 percent, almost identical to the figure for ordinary men (which would not be significantly altered by recalculation in terms of an expanded sample). The one *tafidilo* in this age-group (Ahoa) is also monogamous. The marital experience of men aged 21 to 45 is thus essentially undifferentiated with respect to social status.

This conclusion is not equally applicable to the 46-to-60 age-group, in

TABLE 5.5

Current Marital Status of *Tafidilos*, Mediums, and Ordinary Men, May 1, 1968

| Age Cohort | Never-Married Men | | | Ever-Married Men with | | | | | | | | | Total |
| | | | | No Wife | | | One Wife | | | Two or Three Wives | | | |
	T	M	O	T	M	O	T	M	O	T	M	O	
66–70									1				1
61–65						2	1		1				4
56–60				1		1	1		1	2			6
51–55							2		4				6
46–50				1			2		1	2		1	7
41–45								1	4		1	1	7
36–40							1	3	6				10
31–35			5			1			9			2	17
26–30		1	10					2	8				21
21–25		4	5						1				10
Total	0	5	20	2	0	4	7	6	36	4	1	4	89

T = *tafidilos*.
M = mediums.
O = ordinary men.

which *tafidilos* predominate. Only 12.5 percent (1/8) of ordinary men in this age-group are polygynous, while 36.4 percent (4/11) of *tafidilos* have two wives (counting Piawe as a *tafidilo*). The main factor responsible for this is that older previously married women who take the initiative in their own remarriage select *tafidilos* or men who subsequently become *tafidilos* (i.e., Tsmari and Mariabu). The same features that would prevent a man from being recognized as a *tafidilo* would also make him less appealing as a prospective husband. *Tafidilos* are not advantaged as a result of control over the marital destiny of older, previously married women but because they constitute a category from which less desirable potential husbands are excluded.

Two of the three widowers in this age-group are *tafidilos* (i.e., Faya and Yora). This shows quite clearly that it is not necessary to have a wife in order to be regarded as a *tafidilo*. Although a widower is at something of a disadvantage in providing a disproportionate share of the sago and bananas to provision ceremonies, he can circumvent this by forming part of a work group in which he is paired with a widow. Alternatively, a widowed *tafidilo* can leave this aspect of the position to other *tafidilos* in the community without suffering any diminution in social standing. When there is more than one *tafidilo* in a community, it is necessary that they alternate in the role of *ei sano* in any event. Neither mediums nor *tafidilos* are dependent upon wives in order to attain or function in these positions.

The total sample of 89 men includes 10 who have been accused of witchcraft. All but 1 (the *tafidilo* Kusuame) are between the ages of 21 and 40. The proportion of ever-married men in this age group is essentially the same for accused individuals (44.4 percent or 4/9) as for nonaccused (42.9 percent or 21/49). There is thus no evidence that a witchcraft accusation precludes or delays marriage, although there is a tendency for a witch to be restricted to a less desirable pool of women if he is accused prior to betrothal or remarries after being widowed. This is illustrated by the case of Nomaya, which additionally shows that even a thrice-accused witch held to be responsible for his first wife's death is able to remarry (see n. 35 to chap. 4). Neither of the 2 polygynists in this age-group has been accused of witchcraft. This is expectable since an older widow who takes the initiative in her own remarriage would be unlikely to direct her efforts toward bringing about a union with an accused man, unless the accusation was unauthenticated. If an accusation is unauthenticated and no further accusations are made, the initial episode is likely to be forgotten and the man's marital experience will not differ from that of other men. If there are repeated accusations, eventual execution is likely before the individual reaches the prime age for polygyny (41 to 50). While a man's life trajectory will often be significantly affected by a witchcraft accusation, this is not reflected in his marital experience. An accused individual will marry at about the same age as other men and, if he survives, will have a marital history not dissimilar from other men (i.e., if widowed will remarry, etc.).

Age is by far the most significant factor in male marital experience, in that most of the differences among men are attributable to this factor. The marital experience of men aged 21 to 45 predominantly entails a transition from bachelorhood to monogamous marriage that is almost entirely undifferentiated with respect to social status. The only exception to this is that individuals accused of witchcraft are not among the very small fraction of men who are polygynists (generally as a result of special circumstances). Among senior men aged 45 to 60, social differentiation with respect to *tafidilo* status does account for differential rates of polygyny among men. However, the tendency for a substantial number of men to make a transition from monogamy to polygyny is attributable to age-related factors, and *tafidilo* status is itself strongly age determined. In other words, *tafidilos* are frequently polygynous because they are within the only age-group characterized by a substantial rate of polygyny and, secondarily, as a consequence of their differential social status (or of the same criteria that lead them to be differentiated). The marital experience of mediums is also strongly conditioned by age. Although there is a translation of the prestige of mediumship into the prerogative of polygyny, the prerogative is not realized in practice. This is because mediums are predominantly outside the age-group characterized by a substantial incidence of polygyny and are unable to overcome age-determined factors conducive to monogamy. Two older mediums (Hoamo and Piawe) are polygynists, but they would soon cease to be mediums so these two statuses tend not to coincide. This is because the same age-related factor that facilitates polygyny leads to retirement from mediumship.

In summary, the principal advantages of *tafidilo* status are the prestige intrinsically associated with it and the prerogative of community leadership. *Tafidilos* are esteemed, are prominent in the organization of community enterprises, and play an important role in shaping the course of significant events within the community. *Tafidilos* are in a position to influence decisions to pay or refuse witchcraft compensation, to take up arms against a neighboring community, or to conduct a retaliatory raid against a neighboring tribe. *Tafidilos* are likewise in a position to influence the process of determining the identity of the witch responsible for a death by publicly nominating a suspect. They are thus prominent in all decision-making processes pertaining to social conflict. However, they by no means control these processes, as evidenced by the fact that the wives and children of *tafidilos* are also subject to witchcraft accusations (as exemplified by the cases of Tsmari, Mariabu, and Piawe). In collective enterprises, a *tafidilo* serves as *ei sano*.

Tafidilos are also prominent among those who enact the important ritual role of publicly weeping and burning the dancers in a *kosa* ceremony hosted by their community. Unlike other older men, a *tafidilo* may also make a cameo appearance as a dancer when his community is among those who are the invited guests at such a ceremony. Comparative frequency in the performance of both of these roles may be regarded as a ritual prerogative of *tafidilo* status, although neither is restricted to *tafidilos*. These roles are aspects of the general social prominence of a *tafidilo* in his capacity as community leader.

In other respects, *tafidilos* are not differentiated from other men of their age-group. There are no insignia that distinguish them from others, and they enjoy no spatial prerogatives within the longhouse. They are likewise undifferentiated in terms of consumption (governed by universally applicable food taboos). They perform the same tasks as others, although they devote more hours to hunting and gardening than do other men. They are economically undifferentiated with respect to pig ownership. However, they are much more likely than other men of the same age-group to contribute shell valuables to the marriage payments of young men (as detailed in the following chapter). This parallels the generosity of *tafidilos* in distributing growth-inducing game to coresidents. Moreover, the shell valuables are the symbolic equivalents of semen. *Tafidilos* are economically differentiated in terms of their prominence in distribution by virtue of their prototypical generosity. They are generous donors of semen, game, and bridewealth valuables.

Tafidilos are more likely than other men to be polygynous, but polygyny does not constitute a means to an end of securing any culturally pertinent advantages. Moreover, it is noteworthy that the three *tafidilos* whose wife or child were accused of witchcraft constitute three of the four *tafidilos* with two wives. None of the seven monogamous and two widowed *tafidilos* experienced an accusation directed at a wife or child. Thus polygyny is very strongly correlated with temporary or permanent loss of the central prerogative of *tafidilo* status, namely the prerogative of community leadership. None of the seven leading *tafidilos* of longhouse communities were polygynous at either the beginning or end of the fieldwork period since Tsmari had been reduced to monogamy by Waime's death when he regained this position. Polygyny is thus a positive disadvantage rather than an advantage. Although it is unclear why this should be the case, the empirical correlation is very striking.

It is particularly noteworthy that *tafidilo* status does not confer any advantages with respect to witchcraft accusations. All men over the age of 40 are virtually immune from such accusation, even though these men include non-*tafidilos*, many of whom were very likely subject to an accusation when younger. The advantage thus pertains to age rather than *tafidilo* status.

Moreover, the one accusation against an older man (which was unauthenticated) was in fact directed against the *tafidilo* Kusuame. In addition, the wives and children of *tafidilos* are neither more nor less likely to be accused of witchcraft than the wives and children of non-*tafidilos* of the same age-group. Overall, the preceding summary substantiates the central point that all privileges, prerogatives, and advantages that accrue to *tafidilos* are closely linked to the role of community leader.

The situation with respect to spirit mediums is much the same. The principal advantages of spirit mediumship are the prestige intrinsically associated with this status and the prerogatives connected with serving as the senior medium of a community. Senior mediums play an important role in determining the identity of the witch responsible for a death, authenticating accusations, and legitimating executions. They are thus instrumental to the processes by which stigma is assigned to some individuals, but not others, and they also legitimate lethal violence directed against a proportion of the former. Through prophecy, they can influence the same collective decisions pertaining to social conflict that are more directly influenced by *tafidilos*. However, a senior spirit medium can authenticate or dispel a witchcraft accusation that has the capacity either to preclude attainment of *tafidilo* status or to induce an extant *tafidilo* to migrate to another community, vacating his local leadership position. A senior medium can also derail the career of a novice medium or peer in the same manner. In these respects, the position of senior medium is potentially more powerful than that of leading *tafidilo*. Moreover, a medium possesses spiritual authority that enables him to interpret and shape the cosmological doctrines that are central to the delineation of the hierarchy of virtue. This point will be elucidated in the conclusions.

Spirit mediums enjoy the ritual prerogative of conducting séances as an integral component of their social position. However, they are not otherwise socially prominent and generally tend to remain in the background, often refraining from speaking during community discussions. (Nogobe's efforts to secure the position of "boss man" constitute an exception to this more general pattern.) Spirit mediums play a distinctive role in the organization of fish poisoning but are otherwise economically undifferentiated from other individuals of the same age with respect to production, distribution, and consumption, as well as ownership of pigs and the deployment of shell valuables. They are likewise not distinguished from others in terms of insignia or spatial prerogatives. Although potentially entitled by the spiritual authority of prophecy to more than one wife, they are not empirically more likely than other men to be polygynous.

Spirit mediums are only somewhat less likely to be accused of witchcraft than others of the same age. The absence of a significant advantage is largely due to competition between mediums. While 23 percent (11/48) of nonmediums aged 21 to 40 were accused of witchcraft during the sample period, 20 percent (2/10) of the mediums in these age cohorts were also accused. However there is a greater disparity with respect to wives. None of the wives of spirit mediums was accused during the sample period, while five wives of nonmediums in this 21-to-40 age-group were accused. (The children of spirit mediums are generally too young to be at risk, although the daughter of Piawe, the oldest medium, was accused.) Spirit mediums thus have only slightly better prospects than others for achieving *tafidilo* status when they reach the appropriate age, insofar as they are only a little less likely to be stigmatized by a witchcraft accusation in the preceding decade. However, they are the only individuals who can potentially be members of the influential elite throughout most of their adult lives.

It is notable that prestige and influence are the principal advantages that accrue to the social elite of Etoro society. Neither spirit mediums nor *tafidilos* enjoy material benefits. The egalitarian cultural dictum that no one should own two of something that another individual lacks, and the enshrinement of generosity as the preeminent virtue, precludes any translation of prestige and influence into material advantage. Moreover, individuals who combine the two prestigious statuses of spirit medium and *tafidilo* are generally unable to maintain the preeminence this entails. Piawe was undone by witchcraft accusations against his daughter Udali, and Tofono by witchcraft accusations that led to the dissolution of the community over which he presided. Both men's careers were in decline when they died shortly thereafter. Polygynous *tafidilos* are also very likely to experience a comedown. Egalitarian values and the leveling effects of witchcraft accusations impose constraints that place an upper limit on the degree of preeminence and prerogative that can be attained in the Etoro sociocultural system.

CHAPTER 6

The Production and Circulation of Wealth

Analysis of the distribution of prestige, privilege, and culturally pertinent advantage—and their negative counterparts (stigma, debility, and disadvantage)—is one of the central themes that runs through chapters 4, 5, and 6. We have seen that the assignment of stigma largely conforms to the contours of the Etoro scheme of morally evaluated social differentiation that delineates age and gender categories. The social categories subject to a disproportionately high incidence of accusations are primarily those in the lower ranges of the moral hierarchy, i.e., uninitiated adolescent males, prereproductive married females, unremarried widows, and divorcées. Similarly, the social category that is subject to a disproportionately low incidence of accusations is the one at the apex of the moral hierarchy, i.e., elder senior men. The latter are virtually immune from the stigma of witchcraft. Moreover, married women of reproductive age are subject to a proportionate rate of accusations consistent with their neutral position in the moral hierarchy. The disproportionately high incidence of accusations against men aged 31 to 40 constitutes the principal disparity in the relation between moral hierarchy and the assignment of stigma (although postreproductive married women are accused somewhat less frequently than would be expected on these grounds). There is likewise a considerable degree of consistency between moral standing and prestige. Only those social categories in the higher ranges of the moral hierarchy are eligible for the prestigious statuses of spirit medium and *tafidilo* (although not all individuals within these age-gender categories attain them). It can thus be concluded that the prestige/stigma hierarchy is essentially prefigured by the moral hierarchy. In other words, categorical evaluations of moral worthiness and unworthiness (that provide the foundation of social inequality) largely dictate an individual's prospects for attaining prestige and also influence an individual's vulnerability to the assignment of stigma.

Stigma and debility go hand in hand, insofar as individuals subject to authenticated witchcraft accusations have strong prospects for short and unhappy lives. Prestige and privilege likewise go hand in hand, insofar as mediums and *tafidilos* generally succeed, in due course, to the positions of senior resident medium and leading *tafidilo* and subsequently enjoy the prerogatives intrinsic to these positions. The distribution of privilege and debility is thus predictable in terms of the prestige/stigma hierarchy, which is in turn informed by the moral hierarchy (that is grounded in the cosmology of life-force transmission). The constitution of social inequality is thus largely explicable in terms of this chain of causal relationships, or more precisely, this chain of predominant influences. In other words, what predominantly shapes the distribution of privilege and debility is the prestige/stigma hierarchy (and so on down this chain of relationships).

Privilege and prerogative differ from other culturally pertinent forms of advantage in that they are legitimated. Privilege and prerogative thus go hand in hand with prestige because the attainment of a prestigious status constitutes the legitimating basis of privilege and prerogative. Whether or not other advantages also accrue to those who hold prestigious statuses and occupy the privileged positions of senior resident medium and leading *tafidilo* remains to be systematically considered, although pertinent data have been presented in earlier chapters. We have seen that mediums as a group are not significantly more likely to be polygynous than other men of the same age. Although *tafidilos* as a group are advantaged in terms of polygyny, leading *tafidilos* are not so advantaged and are typically monogamous. In addition, we have seen that mediums and *tafidilos* do not do less work than others but rather more. *Tafidilos* hunt longer hours and maintain larger gardens than other men. Spirit mediums devote considerable energy to conducting weekly séances while maintaining the same level of subsistence-related labor as others. Neither spirit mediums nor *tafidilos* enjoy privileged consumption. This is equally true of those at the apex of the moral hierarchy. Although the distribution of game animals is governed by taboos that are largely congruent with position in the moral hierarchy, these are offset by the prohibition on the consumption of domesticated pork, so that overall consumption of animal protein is essentially equalized. The data considered thus far are consequently conducive to the preliminary conclusion that prestige is not translated into material advantage. The Etoro system of social inequality does not evidence either material privileges (i.e., legitimated advantages of a material nature) or other material advantages that are manifested in the realm of the subsistence economy (analyzed in chap. 2). However, the production, circulation, and distribution of wealth remain to be analyzed with respect to the issue of social inequality. The present chapter is directed to this objective. The requisite analysis constitutes a necessary precursor to arriving at any definitive conclusions regarding both the relationship between economy and inequality and the relationship between prestige and advantage (of both types).

Shell valuables are the form of wealth that is the central focus of analysis in this chapter. These are acquired through external trade and are deployed internally in social payments, e.g., marriage and compensation payments. Shell valuables are accumulable and also readily convertible into all imported commodities (e.g., salt, axes, tobacco, and pigs). However, the principal significance of these valuables resides in their role as the components of system-constituting social payments, since this conveys the potentiality for control over the formulation of central social relationships. It should also be noted that the Etoro socioeconomic system lacks other phenomena that are sometimes included under that general (and somewhat imprecise) rubric of "wealth," e.g., prestige goods and productive property (in the strict sense of the term). Items that confer prestige simply by virtue of their possession are absent, and shell valuables do not have this character. There is also no form of individually owned productive property that intrinsically generates accumulable wealth, or whose ownership is instrumental to wealth generation.

The production and circulation of wealth have been prominent ingredients of theories of social inequality since Engels's (1884) publication of *The Origin of the Family, Private Property and the State.* Engels' ([1884] 1942:5) proposed that

> the lower the development of labor and the more limited the amount of its products, and consequently the more limited also the wealth of the society, the more the social order is found to be dominated by kinship. However, within this structure of society based on kinship groups, the productivity of labor increasingly develops, and with it private property and exchange, differences in wealth, the possibility of utilizing the labor power of others, and hence the basis of class antagonisms . . . [leading to the development of the state].

Wealth is thus instrumental to the evolution of social inequality. Fried (1967:74) follows Engels in employing the paucity of wealth as a prime criterion for his category of egalitarian societies. These societies eschew the possession of surpluses and duplicates and generally lack valuables (or tokens possessing exchange value). In societies where wealth in the form of valuables does circulate, such weath is invariably viewed as integral to the generation or amplification of relations of inequality. In Sahlins's (1963) formulation of the ideal-typical "Big Man" system, contributing to a young man's bridewealth payment is seen as generating social relations of indebtedness that engender political support, recruiting the recipient to the donor's following or faction. Godelier (1982:32) directly links the emergence of Big Men to the exchange of women for wealth (rather than other women), such that "the accumulation of wealth becomes a direct condition for the reproduction of kin relations."

Goody (1973:5) has also pointed out that bridewealth enhances a young man's dependence upon his father (or "fathers") and reinforces paternal authority, even when the payment appears to be principally geared to the furtherance of an egalitarian distribution of wives. The view that more pervasive inequalities are generated by senior men's control of bridewealth has been developed by Meillassoux (1964, 1972, 1973a, 1973b) and elaborated by Collier and Rosaldo (1981) and Collier (1988). Collier and Rosaldo (1981:288) provide a succinct statement of this theoretical perspective on social inequality:

> In bridewealth societies, where marriages are validated through the exchange of goods the young and poor have difficulty acquiring, young men work for those who provide their marriage payments, and relations between husbands and wives are shaped by men's need to acquire the goods that enable them to participate in others' marriages, and thus to acquire rights in the labor and products of the young.

In this formulation, bridewealth requirements shape the relations of production both between junior and senior males and between husband and wife. More generally, the marriage process is seen as the source of key dependencies that are central to the production of inequality. Although these current anthropological theories of inequality differ significantly from Engels's earlier views, it is noteworthy that wealth is invariably cast as an instrumental component of more developed systems of social inequality. The foregoing examples illustrate the general thrust of anthropological thinking in this respect: equality and the circulation of wealth in social payments are inherently antithetical. When transactions in valuables are integral to a social system, unequal accumulation and/or relations of dependence and indebtedness are not far to seek. The most egalitarian societies, or those manifesting the most restricted forms of inequality, are invariably the societies in which the circulation of wealth is most attenuated. Moreover, elaboration of the circulation of wealth goes hand in hand with the evolution of inequality. In the more recent formulations, the development of bridewealth constitutes a watershed in this evolutionary process (as is particularly well illustrated by Godelier's statement, cited above). These theoretical positions inform the general inquiry into the Etoro production and circulation of wealth that follows. The data presented also provide a necessary background to the evaluation of Collier's (1988) brideservice model that is taken up in the concluding chapter.

Analysis of the circulation of wealth may usefully begin with specification of the relevant accumulable valuables and consideration of the process by which wealth is "created" or initially introduced into the social system. Bridewealth, compensation payments, ceremonial payments, and inheritance will then be examined. These are the transactions through which wealth circulates, and they hold the potentiality for altering the initial distribution of wealth that follows from the circumstances of its creation.

The items that are included in social payments are mother-of-pearl shell ornaments and strings of cowrie shells—in substantial numbers—plus no more than one pig and one axe. The pig never survives the occasion of its transfer; it is always cooked and distributed among the recipient's kin for immediate (or near-term) consumption. Pigs therefore are not part of a "circulating pool of resources" (Goody 1973:5). Axes (formerly stone, currently steel) are a marginal component of this pool, since they constitute only a small, limited, and nonobligatory part of some social payments. The principal valuables are thus the mother-of-pearl shell ornaments and cowrie strings that must be included in all payments. These are tokens that possess convertible exchange value but have no use value except as bodily adornment (Ernst 1978:190). They constitute part of a circulating pool of resources that is deployed in social payments, and they represent an accumulable form of wealth. It is the initial acquisition, circulation, and distribution of these tokens that we seek to chart.

Mother-of-pearl shell ornaments and strings of cowrie shells are acquired through trade with two neighboring tribes, the Huli to the north and the Onabasulu to the east. The Huli were the main source of shell valuables (and steel axes) in 1968–69, although this represented a recent (post-1953) development attributable to the Australian colonial administration's interjection of very substantial quantities of mother-of-pearl shell into the traditional economies of the central and southern Highlands (see Kelly 1977:11–15; Ernst 1978:190–93). Before about 1953, the valuables transferred in bridewealth and compensation payments were cowrie strings, dog's-teeth ornaments (headbands/necklaces), stone axes, and pigs. Both the dog's teeth and stone tools were obtained from the Bedamini, western neighbors of the Etoro. Mother-of-pearl shell ornaments were not included in social payments and were either absent from the Etoro area or used exclusively for adornment by a few individuals. These shell ornaments are thus a recent substitution for dog's-teeth ornaments.

This change in the principal valuables deployed in social transactions also entailed a change in the relative importance of the Huli as a source of supply. Before the early 1950s, the Etoro obtained dog's-teeth ornaments and stone axes from the Bedamini in exchange for salt and cowrie strings, derived from the Huli and Onabasulu. In 1968–69, the Etoro obtained all valuables (i.e., mother-of-pearl shell ornaments, cowrie strings, and steel axes) from the Huli, with the Onabasulu representing a secondary source of supply. The main point here is simply that the trade system through which valuables were obtained was transformed in the early 1950s as an indirect consequence of

Australian administrative activity.[1] The effect of this transformation on the circulation of wealth will need to be considered at several points in the discussion that follows, although the main conclusion is that the principal features of wealth distribution were not altered.

The initial acquisition of valuables—and their mode of entry into the Etoro social system—remained essentially unchanged despite these changes in both the items involved and the sources of supply. Under both traditional and contact-altered conditions, the necessity of accumulating a substantial quantity of valuables for inclusion in a bridewealth payment provided the overwhelmingly predominant stimulus to the active acquisition of these exchange items. Trading expeditions that traveled to Huli, Onabasulu, and Bedamini communities to obtain valuables were carried out almost entirely by unmarried young men (aged 20 to 30 years). These same bachelors were also the segment of the male population most active in concluding exchanges with trading parties entering Etoro territory. Thus wealth was largely "created" by unmarried young men, entering the social system through their efforts and being held by them in the first instance. However, this newly created wealth was also slated to be deployed in the bridewealth payment that stimulated its acquisition, and thus to be redistributed to the kinsmen of some bride's father or brother. A potentiality for reordering the distribution of wealth was thus built in. The extent and nature of the redistributive process will be considered shortly. However, it will be useful to answer two antecedent questions first, namely: (1) how did unmarried young men acquire the items they exchanged for shell valuables? and (2) why was this acquisition through trade necessary if a circulating pool of wealth was already in place and available, through the contributions of kinsmen, to fund bridewealth payments?

Etoro trade is quite complex. This is largely due to the fact that the Etoro both act as middlemen in the movement of goods between higher and lower altitude ecological zones and also engage in extensive exchange with the Onabasulu, who play the same middleman role (see Kelly 1977:11–15; Ernst 1978; Ernst 1984:79–93). In practice, this means that many trade items are both imported and exported, and may well be imported even though they are locally manufactured (see table 6.1). Moreover, there are a large number of items that figure in this trade, and they tend to be rather widely exchangeable against each other.[2] The important consequence of these features of the regional trade system is that substantial shell wealth can be accumulated with minimal initial capital. Thus Ernst (1984:84) notes that an Onabasulu man could theoretically begin with nothing but sago (the starch staple) and eventually convert it into shell valuables through a series of transactions. Although the acquisition of shell valuables is much simpler than this in practice, the general point is nevertheless quite significant. A young man is not dependent on anyone to provide him with the wherewithal to engage in regional trade. He might readily manufacture bows and arrows; obtain hornbill beaks, feathers, and cassowary-bone knives through hunting and trapping; grow tobacco and produce the foot-long cylindrical rolls employed in trade; process sago; capture juvenile cassowaries; or rear pigs by the nonintensive methods characteristic of the Etoro (see Kelly 1988).

It is notable that none of these wealth-generating activities require female labor inputs of any significance. While women normally do three-fourths of the work in sago processing, young men may process sago on their own when they plan to use it in trade. Pigs are infrequently fed and probably receive less than 5 percent of the coproduced sweet potato crop (Kelly 1988:119). This can be supplied from the produce of bachelor gardens. Tobacco is grown in gardens maintained exclusively by men.[3] The remaining activities listed above fall on the male side of the division of labor and entail no male-female cooperative effort. Young men therefore are not dependent on either their father's capital or their mother's (or sister's) labor in order to

TABLE 6.1

A Synopsis of Etoro Trade Transactions, 1968–69

Item	Locally Manufactured	Imported from			Exported to		
		Bedamini	Onabasulu	Huli	Bedamini	Onabasulu	Huli
Sago flour	+						+
Net bags	+						+
String	+						+
Juvenile cassowaries	+						+
Mature pigs	+						+
Shoats	+			+			
Bows	+	+	+			+	+
Arrows	+	+	+			+	+
Feathers	+	+	+			+	+
Hornbill beaks	+	+	+			+	+
Cassowary-bone knives	+	+	+			+	+
Tree oil			+				+
Tobacco	+	+	+	+	+	+	+
Cowrie strings			+	+	+	+	+
Mother-of-pearl shell ornaments			+	+	+	+	
Salt			+	+	+	+	
Steel axes			+	+	+	+	
Matches			+	+	+	+	
Razor blades			+	+	+	+	

engage in trade and accumulate wealth.[4] Indeed, young men take pride in accumulating a substantial portion of their own bridewealth and in the connotations of adult status that this entails. This attitude provides part of the answer to the second question posed at the beginning of this discussion, viz., the question of why young men need to acquire shell valuables for bridewealth if a large circulating pool is already on hand and readily available to them.

This conundrum is nicely illustrated by a sister exchange that took place in 1968–69. Wabiaka of Ingirabisato lineage married Sawa's father's brother's daughter Tabieme, and Sawa of Nagefi lineage married Wabiaka's father's brother's son's daughter Hawia (see fig. 6.1). Sawa received a bridewealth payment of one pig, four mother-of-pearl shells, and 11 cowrie strings at the time of the ceremony celebrating his "sister's" union. He redistributed all of this, keeping not a single item for himself (although the retention of one major valuable—a mother-of-pearl shell ornament—would be typical). About six months later, Sawa's marriage to Hawia was celebrated, and he transferred a bridewealth of one pig, six mother-of-pearl shells, and 31 cowrie strings to Hawia's father, Mari. Of this total payment, Sawa personally provided one pig, two mother-of pearl shells, and 12 cowrie strings. The remainder of the payment was accumulated through contributions from kin.

Although a number of questions might be raised, the key one for our purposes is the question of why Sawa needed to acquire shell valuables in trade to put toward his bridewealth payment.[5] One might expect that a direct, restricted exchange of women would entail equivalent marriage payments (if any such payments were indeed required). In this event, Sawa might have drawn contributions from all those individuals to whom he redistributed portions of his "sister's" bridewealth. He then would not have had to engage in any trade at all. In short, his bridewealth would simply be provided from the circulating pool of wealth already in place and readily available from his kinsmen.

This sequence of events was precisely what Sawa sought to avoid. He set Tabieme's bridewealth well below the going rate, kept none of it, and made up most of the difference between what he received and gave in bridewealth through diligent trade. In all, Hawia's bridewealth exceeded Tabieme's by two mother-of-pearl shells and 20 cowrie strings, while Sawa's personal contribution was two mother-of-pearl shells and 12 cowrie strings. The correspondence would be even closer if Hawia's father had not insisted on adding 4 cowrie strings to the previously agreed-upon amount just a few days before the union was to be celebrated. These valuables were easy to come by, however, as there were many kinsmen willing to contribute. This would also be entirely expectable if, as should now be evident, the circulating

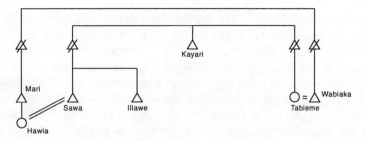

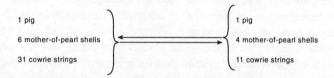

Fig. 6.1. "Sister" exchange between Sawa and Wabiaka

pool of wealth has an inherent tendency to increase. Indeed, this feature makes it necessary to explain why bridewealth contributions are not over-subscribed by kinsmen eager to generously deploy the valuables in their possession.

The circulating pool of wealth amassed by the Etoro tends to increase over time as a result of the trade carried out by young men seeking to compile a substantial contribution to their own bridewealth payment. A prospective groom normally provides about half of the marriage payment in terms of total value (computed by converting pigs and mother-of-pearl shell ornaments into cowrie-string equivalents at the external exchange rate of 3.5 to 1). Although the composition of bridewealth changed in the early 1950s and the amount required nearly doubled (in total value) between circa 1953 and 1968, the 50 percent contribution of the prospective groom remained unchanged throughout this period (Kelly 1977:215).

The proportion is relatively invariant because every young man takes pride in providing it. Moreover, the trading expeditions, carried out by a group of age-mates, are in part a rite of passage. After emergence from seclusion at the hunting lodge, the newly initiated bachelors embark upon a trading expedition in order to procure the mother-of-pearl shell ornaments that they subsequently present to their respective mother's brothers. These shell valuables are a symbolic analogue of semen, of which the initiated bachelors are now donors. They also constitute a prestation, employed by the recipient mother's brother to procure the tree oil with which he subsequently anoints the initiate (as described in chap. 3). Obtaining these shell valuables on their own is a critical element of the newly initiated bachelors' enunciation of their self-sufficiency and independence from seniors. After the ceremony that marks the completion of initiation, the bachelors go on additional trading expeditions to procure the valuables that make up half of their bridewealth payment. Men of all ages enjoy relating their youthful exploits during trading expeditions to strange and far-flung places. They often claim to have traveled farther, or in different directions, than their predecessors (compare Ernst 1984:91).[6] It would consequently be unthinkable for a young man to fail to acquire shell valuables in trade, even if his sister's bridewealth payment was fully adequate to fund his own. The trade and the acquisition of shell valuables are an integral part of the transition to adult male status effected by initiation and consolidated through marriage. The valuables acquired also enable a young man to contribute to the social payments of others and thus engender a transactional network that is drawn on for generalized social support. This network normally includes affines and close kin of all types plus age-mates that are somewhat more distantly related by kinship (Kelly 1977:217).

Other things being equal, each Etoro generation would thus add 50 percent to the circulating pool of wealth. During the period from the early 1950s to 1968–69, this potentiality was realized, and the increase was absorbed by bridewealth inflation. In earlier times, this tendency for Etoro holdings of shell valuables to increase was counterbalanced by expenditure for Highlands-produced salt (which was consumed) and by the relatively high rate of breakage of stone tools. Substantial numbers of cowrie strings were required to obtain a stone axe/adze, and this wealth was essentially spent when the tool was no longer serviceable. New wealth would have to be created to purchase replacement axe/adzes and to fund salt consumption. The indirect effect of young men's trade to acquire bridewealth would thus be to maintain (rather than increase) the circulating pool of wealth by offsetting the unavoidable expense of stone axe and salt imports for internal use.[7] Under these conditions, Etoro bridewealth would not be subject to continual inflation, shell valuables would not be as readily available, and there would be no expectable tendency for bridewealth contributions to be oversubscribed.[8] However, unmarried young men would still be the generators and initial holders of new wealth, and there is no discernible reason to expect that the circulation of wealth would have differed greatly in these earlier times. In short, I believe the patterns under consideration are traditional and are not a product of postcontact developments that made shell valuables more widely available. Moreover, increased availability would not reduce the magnitude of social inequalities in this instance, unlike that of the

New Guinea Highlands (see Golson 1982:133), due to the differences between the Etoro social system and the social systems of the pertinent Highland societies.[9]

Having established that wealth enters the social system predominantly
through unmarried young men's trade, we may now proceed to trace the
subsequent internal circulation of it. Although young men engage in trade in
order to amass a large share of their own bridewealth payment, the valuables
acquired are often initially deployed as contributions to the bridewealth and
compensation payments of others, especially the bridewealth payments of
age-mates. This is evident in the data presented in table 6.2, showing the age
distribution of contributors to three 1968–69 bridewealth payments.[10] On
average, prospective grooms contributed 51.3 percent of the total value, and
other young men below the age of 31 contributed an additional 25.3 percent.
Men aged 31 to 40 (excluding one groom) contributed 16.2 percent of total
value, and men aged 41 to 60 contributed the remaining 7.2 percent. Contributions to bridewealth payments (in terms of percentage of total value) are
thus inversely proportional to age, and the slope of the decline accompanying
increased age is quite steep.

Although this accurately reflects the extent to which bridewealth contributions are derived from young men, it does not take the proportional representation of different age-groups (in the total population) into account and
therefore does not accurately depict the level of participation of men of
various ages relative to their numbers. This is analyzed in table 6.3, which
excludes the groom's unavoidable contribution and employs a ratio value
analogous to that employed to measure the proportional distribution of witchcraft accusations in chapter 4. These data show that men (other than the
groom) aged 16 to 20 and 21 to 30 make disproportionately large contributions to bridewealth. Non-*tafidilos* aged 31 to 40 make contributions somewhat less than commensurate with their proportional representation in the
population, and non-*tafidilos* aged 41 to 60 contribute only one-fifth as much
as would be expected on the basis of their numbers. In other words, men are
active contributors to the bridewealth payments of others from their late teens
through their 20s, taper off in their 30s, and infrequently contribute after age
40 unless they become *tafidilos*. Those who do become *tafidilos* not only
maintain but in fact exceed the level of participation of young men (relative
to their proportional representation in the population). This does not mean
that *tafidilos* play a major role in funding bridewealth payments. Their contributions make up only 10.6 percent of the total value of all contributions (see

table 6.2) and are dwarfed by the contributions of the groom and his age-mates. However, *tafidilos* are often seen to contribute to bridewealth and thus manifest generosity in this way, even though the extent of their contribution is not great. *Tafidilos* comprise a larger percentage of donors than of total value contributed (see table 6.2) because they tend to make a token contribution. In many instances, this consists of a single cowrie string. However this is frequently an unsolicited contribution to the bridewealth of a bachelor who is not a close kinsman and consequently betokens generosity beyond its modest value. The conspicuous generosity of *tafidilos* also contrasts strikingly with the infrequent contributions of non-*tafidilos* of the same age. (The contributions of spirit mediums are entirely typical of men of their age-group and consequently are not segregated in any of the tables presented in this chapter.)

On the basis of marital status rather than age, the percentage of total value contributed would be: groom 51.3 percent, other unmarried men 24.7 percent, *tafidilos* 10.6 percent, and other married men 13.2 percent. (Only a little more than half of Etoro men aged 26 to 35 are married; see Kelly 1977:169–70, 304.) In all, 76 percent of the total value of these bridewealth payments was provided by bachelors, with *tafidilos* providing nearly half the

TABLE 6.2

Contributors to Bridewealth Payments: Age Distribution
(value of contributions in cowrie-string equivalents)

	Hariako's Bridewealth		Sawa's Bridewealth		Weliba's Bridewealth		Total for Age Subset		Percentage of Total	
Donors	No.	Value	No.	Value	No.	Value	No.	Value	Donors	Value
Males, aged:										
16–20	—	—	1	7	1	2	2	9	5.7	6.8
21–25	2*	17	2	3	1	1	5	21	14.3	15.8
26–30	2	3	6*	32	5	6	13	41	37.1	30.9
31–35	1	4.5	2	3	2*	31.5	5	39	14.3	29.4
36–40	1	1	2ᵗ	7.5	1	4.5	4	13	11.4	9.8
41–45	—	—	—	—	—	—	—	—	—	—
46–50	—	—	2ᵗᵗ	2	—	—	2	2	5.7	1.5
51–55	—	—	1	1	2ᵗ	3	3	4	8.6	3.0
56–60	—	—	—	—	1ᵗ	3.5	1	3.5	2.9	2.6
Total	6	25.5	16	55.5	13	51.5	35	132.5	100	99.8
Grooms	1	15	1	22.5	1	30.5	3	68	8.6	51.3
Tafidilos	—	—	3	8.5	2	5.5	5	14	14.3	10.6

* = groom of this age category (the groom's contribution is included in the total and also listed separately under groom).
ᵗ = *tafidilo* of this age category (the *tafidilo*'s contribution is included in the total and also listed separately under *tafidilo*)

remainder. Ever-married men who are not *tafidilos* comprise 54.7 percent (52/95) of the total population of men aged 16 to 60 but provide only 27.1 percent of the total value contributed (excluding the groom's contribution), yielding a ratio of .50. The comparable ratio for bachelors as a group is 1.57. (Bachelors constitute 32.6 percent (31/95) of the population and provide 51.2 percent of the total value apart from the groom's contribution.)

All contributors to bridewealth payments are, of course, kinsmen. In kinship terms, the age bias toward youth evident in these figures thus reflects a young man's somewhat stronger dependence upon "brothers" (including mother's sister's sons) as opposed to "fathers." (See Kelly 1977:217 regarding the percentage contributions of various kin categories.) Although close kin of both generations generally do contribute, the more distant kinsmen that provide valuables tend to be either age-mates or *tafidilos*. Individuals within these two classes of contributors are especially likely to volunteer to give shell valuables without any request having been made. It is this practice that creates the potential for a bridewealth payment to be oversubscribed. It is attributable to the fact that generosity is a virtue.

TABLE 6.3

The Proportional Distribution of Contributions to Bridewealth by Age and *Tafidilo* Status (excluding the groom's contribution)

Contributors	Individuals in Population		Percentage of Total Value Contributed	Ratio: Percentage of Total Value Contributed Divided by Percentage of Individuals in Population
	Number	*Percent*		
All males, aged				
16–20	11	11.6	14.0	1.21
21–30	31	32.6	38.0	1.17
31–40	27	28.4	33.3	1.17
41–60	26	27.4	14.7	.54
Total	95	100.0	100.0	1.00
Tafidilos vs. non-*tafidilos*				
Non-*tafidilos* 31–40	26	27.4	21.7	.79
Non-*tafidilos* 41–60	15	15.7	3.1	.20
Tafidilos 36–60	12	12.6	21.7	1.72

THE ACCUMULATION OF COMPENSATION PAYMENTS

The pooling of valuables for compensation payments differs from bride-wealth accumulation in that the particular individual responsible for making the payment contributes a much smaller share (i.e., 16.7 percent of total value) than a groom contributes to his own bridewealth. This is readily understandable, since there is no issue of demonstrating graduation to adult status in these situations. A man who needs to assemble a compensation payment for causing death through witchcraft, or for executing a witch, thus commits whatever shell valuables he has at hand and seeks the assistance of his kinsmen in getting together the additional amount required. The accumulator of compensation may be young or old (median age 36 to 40), whereas the prospective groom accumulating bridewealth for his first marriage is invariably relatively young (median age 26 to 30). One might therefore expect that contributors to compensation payments would be more equally distributed across age cohorts. However this expectation is largely un-fulfilled; young men still contribute disproportionately to compensation payments (see table 6.4). On average, young men below the age of 31 contributed 51.7 percent of the total value of compensation payments (compared to 53.5 percent of the total value of bridewealth payments).[11] Men aged 31 to 40 contributed 34.2 percent of the compensation (versus 40.5 percent of the bridewealth), and men aged 41 to 60, including *tafidilos,* contributed 14.1 percent of the compensation (versus 7.1 percent of the bridewealth). Although the elder senior males (aged 41 to 60) contribute more to compensation payments than to bridewealth, they are nevertheless a relatively minor factor.

The proportional distribution of contributions to compensation payments (shown in table 6.5) is similar in many respects to the proportional distribution of contributions to bridewealth.[12] In both cases, men aged 41 to 60 contribute only about half as much to social payments as their numbers would lead one to expect, while men aged 21 to 40 provide disproportionately large contributions that make up the shortfall. However the youngest contributors (aged 16 to 20) donate less to compensation than to bridewealth. Neverthe-less the most striking difference is in the contrast between *tafidilos* and non-*tafidilos*. While *tafidilos* make disproportionately large contributions to bridewealth, they generally do not contribute to witchcraft compensation at all (and are not represented among the contributors to any of the three such payments included in table 6.4). *Tafidilos* seek to avoid being identified with the accused witch and his supporters. *Tafidilos* do contribute to homicide compensation paid when a witch is executed or an individual is killed in a dispute involving a refusal of compensation (e.g., Hasuan's homicide com-pensation). They are among the contributors to two of three such payments

TABLE 6.4

Contributors to 1968–69 Compensation Payments: Age Distribution (value of contributions in cowrie-string equivalents)

Donors	Hau's Witchcraft Compensation		Udali's Homicide Compensation		Hasuan's Homicide Compensation		Susa's Witchcraft Compensation		Taifi's Witchcraft Compensation		Kulubido's Homicide Compensation		Total for Age Subsets		Percentage of Total	
	No.	Value	No.	Value	No.	Value	No.	Value	No.	Value	No.	Value	No.	Value	No.	Value
Males, aged																
11–15	—	—	1	3.5	—	—	—	—	—	—	—	—	1	3.5	1.6	1.5
16–20	1*	3.5	1	2	—	—	1	3.5	1	3.5	—	—	4	12.5	6.3	5.5
21–25	—	—	1	1	—	—	2	2	2	3	2	7.5	7	13.5	10.9	5.9
26–30	6	23.5	4*	16	3*	13	2	11.5	3	8	4	16	22	88	34.4	38.8
31–35	1	1	2	8.5	2[t]	5.5	1	1	1	5.5	3	14.5	10	36	15.6	15.9
36–40	2*	10	2	5.5	2	5.5	2*	5.5	1*	6.5	2[t]	8.5	11	41.5	17.2	18.3
41–45	1	3	—	—	1	4.5	—	—	—	—	1	2	3	9.5	4.7	4.2
46–50	1	4	—	—	—	—	—	—	1	1	—	—	2	5	3.1	2.2
51–55	1	2	1	2	—	—	—	—	—	—	1*	10	3	14	4.7	6.2
56–60	—	—	—	—	1	3.5	—	—	—	—	—	—	1	3.5	1.6	1.5
Total	13	47	12	38.5	9	32	8	23.5	9	27.5	13	58.5	64	227	100.1	100
Accumulators	2	7	1	7.5	1	5	1	2	1	6.5	1	10	7	38	10.9	16.7
Tafidilos	—	—	—	—	1	2	—	—	—	—	1	6.5	2	8.5	3.1	3.7

* = accumulator of this age category.
[t] = *tafidilo* of this age category.

included in table 6.4. However, their general disinclination to contribute to payments linked to social conflict, if this is avoidable, reduces their contribution to all compensations to less than a third of what would be expected based on their proportional representation in the population. In contrast, non-*tafidilos* in the same age cohort (36 to 60) make disproportionately small contributions to bridewealth and disproportionately large contributions to compensation payments. This remains the case even when the contributions of compensation accumulators (four of whom are in the 36-to-60 age-group) are excluded. Non-*tafidilos* tend to be involved in the conflicts from which *tafidilos* seek to dissociate themselves.

THE REDISTRIBUTION OF BRIDEWEALTH AND COMPENSATION PAYMENTS

Men aged 16 to 40 contribute 94 percent of the total value of bridewealth payments and 85.9 percent of the total value of compensation payments. The question of whether or not they share in the redistribution of these social payments to the same extent that they donate to them remains to be addressed. The organization of these transactions clearly contains the possibility that the total cycle of accumulation and redistribution may systematically favor certain age-groups. For example, the total cycle would systematically

TABLE 6.5

The Proportional Distribution of Contributions to Compensation Payments by Age and *Tafidilo* Status (compensator included; one donor 11–15 omitted)

Contributors	Individuals in Population		Percentage of Total Value Contributed	Ratio: Percentage of Total Contributed Divided by Percentage of Individuals in Population
	Number	Percentage		
All males, aged				
16–20	11	11.6	5.6	.48
21–30	31	32.6	45.4	1.39
31–40	27	28.4	34.7	1.22
41–60	26	27.4	14.3	.52
Total	95	100.0	100.0	1.00
Tafidilos vs. non-*tafidilos*				
Non-*tafidilos*				
36–60	24	25.3	29.1	1.15
Tafidilos				
36–60	12	12.6	3.8	.30

transfer wealth in shell valuables from younger to older men if the latter were more heavily represented among recipients in redistributions than among contributors.

The recipient of a social payment (e.g., the bride's father/brother or the deceased's husband/brother) redistributes much of it among kinsmen who have previously contributed to his own social payments or who would be expected to contribute in future. However, the expectable reciprocity is distinctly generalized rather than precise. An individual donates to the social payments of kinsmen and age-mates in accordance with his resources and their needs and expects the recipient to do likewise, so that balance may be achieved over the long term if needs are balanced. A "brother" who contributed several cowrie strings to ego's bridewealth might well receive somewhat more or less when ego had the occasion to redistribute a social payment. Similarly, a recipient in a particular redistribution may not donate at all to the redistributor's next accumulation of a social payment. For example, nearly half (7/15) of the individuals who received a share of Sawa's "sister's" bridewealth payment did not contribute to Sawa's own bridewealth payment only six months later (in the sister exchange discussed earlier). Moreover, six of the fifteen contributors to Sawa's bridewealth had received nothing from him in two prior redistributions he had made in the past year (i.e., his sister's bridewealth redistribution and the redistribution of his deceased father's brother's witchcraft compensation).[13]

This strikingly illustrates the point that the Etoro treat surpluses of shell valuables in much the same way that they treat surpluses of game. An individual who possesses shell valuables that he does not require for his own immediate use is likely to retain only a few and donate the others to whoever may need them at the time, despite the fact that shell valuables are both readily accumulable and also readily convertible into commodities (e.g., salt, axes, pigs, tobacco, or Western trade goods). In other words, wealth in the form of shell valuables is largely disbursed in accordance with the egalitarian principle of "from each according to his ability, to each according to his need." As in the distribution of game, generosity is a virtue, and hoarding is unseemly and morally reprehensible. Those who received valuables when Sawa redistributed his "sister's" bridewealth thus were likely to give them to others who needed them at the time rather than to retain them so as to be able to contribute to Sawa's own bridewealth payment in the foreseeable future. Moreover, Sawa's bridewealth accumulation was oversubscribed (i.e., more contributions were volunteered than were required to meet the amount requested by his prospective wife's father), so that a point was reached at which he had no demonstrable need, disobligating potential donors.

The fact that generalized reciprocity prevails and there is no one-to-one

relationship between recipients of redistributed social payments and contributors to the redistributor's subsequent accumulation of a like payment creates
considerable scope for a systematic redistribution of wealth entailing transfers from young to old, male to female, ordinary individuals to *tafidilos,* or
vice versa. A strictly equivalent reciprocity would preclude this because
donors would be "repaid." Available data indicate relatively small shifts, but
the cumulative effects of these are significant. One of the more interesting
of these entails the transfer of shell valuables to women in the redistribution
of social payments (see table 6.6).

It may be recalled that women contribute very little to the generation of
wealth, in the form of shell valuables, through trade. The bulk of the trade
is of a middleman variety involving the import and export of items that have
not been locally produced. When local production is entailed, it tends to
involve male labor exclusively. There are only a few exceptions to this
general pattern, and these involve string, net bags, sago, and mature pigs.
String and net bags are manufactured by Etoro women. They are also made
by women of all neighboring tribes, and are consequently not a very valuable
or frequently traded item. In the only transaction that came to my attention,
a young man asked his "mother" (father's brother's wife), to whom he had
often given pork and game, for a net bag so that he could obtain some salt
from a Huli trading party passing through the community. She obliged. Sago,
which is produced more through female than male labor, is commonly traded
to the Huli for recently weaned shoats. If the animal survived to maturity it
would be deployed by a male in some social transaction, but consumed
predominantly by females. Men of all ages may engage in this trade although
young men (aged 21 to 30) are the most active (Kelly 1988:144). These
young men, who are typically unmarried, sometimes process the sago deployed in this trade on their own. Moreover, black palm bows can also be
exchanged for shoats, so that sago is not essential to their acquisition. It is
noteworthy that net bags and sago, which are products of female (or mostly
female) labor, are traded for consumables, i.e., salt and pigs, in which
women will share.

Mature pigs are the only item exchanged for shell valuables (rather than
consumables) that is produced with some female labor contribution. However, such transactions are very infrequent, and only one instance came to
light (as part of a late-1950s bridewealth accumulation). This is due to the
fact that mother-of-pearl shell ornaments, exchangeable for one mature pig,
can readily be obtained from the Huli for juvenile cassowaries, tree oil, or
three to four cowrie strings, or from the Onabasulu for cassowary-bone
implements (Kelly 1977:217; Ernst 1984:82). (These are only observed transactions; other exchanges are also possible.) Moreover, the female labor contribution to pig husbandry is not great since pigs are regularly fed (jointly

TABLE 6.6

Recipients in the Redistribution of Social Payments: Age/Sex Distribution
(value of payments in cowrie-string equivalents)

Recipients	Hau's Witchcraft Compensation Distribution		Maua's Witchcraft Compensation Distribution		Ailoe's Witchcraft Compensation Distribution		Tofono's Witchcraft Compensation Distribution		Tabieme's Bridewealth Payment Distribution		Pileme's Witchcraft Compensation Distribution		Hasuan's Death Compensation Distribution		Tate's Bridewealth Payment Distribution		Totals for Age/Sex Subset		Percentage of Total	
	No.	Value	No.	Value	No.	Value	No.	Value	No.	Value	No.	Value	No.	Value	No.	Value	No.	Value	Recipients	Value
Males, aged																				
11–15	—	—	—	—	—	—	—	—	1	1	—	—	—	—	1	1	2	2	1.7	.9
16–20	—	—	1	2	2	7	2	4.5	1	3.5	—	—	—	—	2	2	7	17	6	7.3
21–25	2*	10.5	3*	5.5	1	2	—	—	1	1	—	—	3	5.5	1	1	9	22	7.7	9.5
26–30	5	18	1	1	3*	6.5	6*	11	6*	11	1	1	2	5.5	4	6.5	30	65	25.6	28
31–35	2	3	1	5	—	—	2	2	1	2	1*	3.5	2	3.5	1	1	9	15	7.7	6.5
36–40	4	10	3t	5	2	7	1	1	4t	10	3t	3	2	6.5	2t	2	21	44.5	18	19.1
41–45	1	2	—	—	—	—	—	—	—	—	2	6.5	2*	4.5	1	1	6	14	5.1	6
46–50	2	5.5	1	3.5	1t	2	—	—	—	—	1t	1	2t	2	—	—	7	14	6	6
51–55	1t	2	1	1	1	1	1	1	1	1	1	1	—	—	2*t	2	8	9	6.8	3.9
56–60	1	4	—	—	—	—	—	—	—	—	—	—	—	—	1t	1	2	5	1.7	2.2
Females	2	5.5	2	5.5	2	4	3	3	—	—	3	3	2	2	2	2	16	25	13.7	10.8
Total	20	60.5	12	23.5	12	29.5	15	22.5	15	28.5	12	19	14	29.5	17	19.5	117	232.5	100	100.2
Distributors	1	7	1	3.5	1	2	1	3.5	1	0	1	3.5	1	3.5	1	1	8	24	6.8	10.3
Tafidilos	1	2	1	2	1	2	—	—	1	1	2	2	1	1	3	3	10	13	8.5	5.6

* = distributor of this age category.
t = tafidilos of this age category.

produced) sweet potatoes only during the first three to six months after weaning, when they are small and consume relatively little (Kelly 1988:116–19). Although women tend these small pigs, the men do most of the work in keeping track of and occasionally feeding pigs during the year or two when the pigs forage unattended in the bush. Moreover, a pig exported in exchange for shell valuables would have been reared by a bachelor, so that an even greater proportion of the labor expenditure would be male. In sum, only those shell valuables received in exchange for mature pigs are traceable to a production process involving female labor, and the amount of labor involved is slight. Moreover, available data indicate that less than 1 percent of shell valuables are acquired in this way.

The main point of the preceding discussion is to precisely document the fact that shell valuables are obtained almost entirely through male effort. It is important to clearly establish this, because the generation of wealth in a number of recently studied New Guinea societies has been described in terms of male appropriation of the products of female labor (Modjeska 1982; Josephides 1985). From the vantage point of current neo-Marxian theoretical perspectives, it would seem that women appropriate the products of male labor in the Etoro case, insofar as they receive about 11 percent of the total value of the shell valuables given out when social payments are redistributed.

Women always receive a share of the compensation paid when someone dies (i.e., death compensation for homicide and witchcraft compensation for all other deaths, except those of small children, that are not the direct result of humanly inflicted bodily injury). These recipients are generally (10 of 14 cases) female agnates of the deceased (a man or woman's Z, BD, or FZ) or the daughter of a female cognate (e.g., a man's ZD). A deceased man's wife and daughter may also receive valuables on these occasions (2 of 14 cases of female recipients of compensation distribution in table 6.6). However, they would typically receive a share of the inheritance rather than the compensation (as explained more fully in a later section). Women do not normally share in bridewealth distribution, but the distributor of such a payment may give an item or two to his own wife, or a closely related "brother's" wife (both of the 2 instances of female recipients in bridewealth distribution in table 6.6). This occasionally occurs in the case of witchcraft and death compensations as well (1 of the 14 instances noted above). Some of these shell valuables may later be turned over to the husband and donated, by him, to some social payment. This would be particularly applicable when the female recipient is the distributor's wife (2 of 16 instances in all). However, available data indicate that the bulk of the shell ornaments received by women are retained and worn as bodily adornment (in accordance with their use value, rather than their more prominent exchange value). Shell ornaments may also be given to a daughter to wear. Women do not require valuables for the purpose of making social payments because they do not make marriage payments and because the compensation for death caused by a woman's witchcraft is paid by her brother and husband. Kinswomen are not solicited for contributions to social payments and do not volunteer them. Wives may return valuables to their husbands who originally gave them to the wife in the context of acting as a redistributor. Exceptions to this general pattern are rare. The shell valuables given to women thus generally do not return to the circulating pool of valuables except through inheritance; they are bequeathed to husbands and sons as well as daughters.

The full range of net gains and losses resulting from the total cycle of accumulation and redistribution is shown in table 6.7.[14] In general, those age-groups that contribute the most to bridewealth and compensation payments also receive the most when these are redistributed, and those age-groups that contribute the least likewise receive the least. The rank order of male age-groups of contributors and of recipients is the same. However, there is nevertheless a net transfer of 17.5 percent of the total value of these social payments. This constitutes a redistribution of wealth. More than half of this net transfer (10.8 of the 17.5 percent) is due to the fact that women do not contribute to social payments but receive in their redistribution. The remaining 6.7 percent of total value redistributed is gained (as well as lost) by men.

The overall pattern of gains and losses for men follows a life-cycle trajectory. Adolescent males (aged 16 to 20), who are as yet minor participants, experience a very modest net gain. Young men (predominantly bachelors) aged 21 to 30 experience substantial losses. These losses continue at a somewhat higher level among men 31 to 40. This continual drain is reversed among men 41 to 60, but the gains experienced are only 29 percent of the prior losses, so that former holdings of shell valuables are not recouped. The earlier losses are taken on substantial holdings, while the gains are registered as a smaller percentage of significantly diminished holdings, so that these remain at a low level. Interestingly, it is not *tafidilos* but non-*tafidilos* that are the prime beneficiary of this modest reversal of fortune among older men. This is due to the fact that non-*tafidilos* engage in accumulation and do not contribute as much to bridewealth as they could. In other words, they do not redeploy all the shell valuables they receive in redistribution, whereas *tafidilos* do. These data are thus consistent with the virtuous antiaccumulative generosity of *tafidilos*.

Taken together, these data suggest that the pool of wealth a young man acquires through trade is progressively diminished over the course of his lifetime. This wealth in shell valuables is extensively contributed to the social payments of others and to funding the young man's own bridewealth. On average, the amounts received from redistributions tend to be less than that contributed on other occasions, so that the initial pool of trade-accumulated wealth gradually shrinks over time and is not replenished.[15] This is particularly true with respect to bridewealth, since a young man provides half of his own but would normally retain only 10 percent of that received on the occasion of his sister's marriage. The difference operationalizes a fairly broad network of kin relations and provides a fund of social credit upon which a young man can draw throughout his lifetime (see n. 13).

This is rather the opposite of the formulations noted in the introduction, since the unreciprocated donations and shares of redistribution that are outstanding at any point in time tend, on average, to leave older men indebted to the generosity of younger men rather than the reverse. However, these imbalances, which shift back and forth from one party to the other over time, do not carry any connotations of inequality in social status. They are imbalances within a framework of generalized reciprocity, operating between kinsmen, in which exact calculations of equivalence are inappropriate. Young men simply give more because they have more to give. The main thrust of the circulation of wealth in social payments is to put male kin of all ages on a relatively even footing as coparticipants and thus to foster equality.

TABLE 6.7

Net Gains and Losses in the Accumulation and Redistribution of Social Payments by Age, Gender, and *Tafidilo* Status (including the groom's contribution)

Contributors and Recipients	Bridewealth: Percentage of Total Value Contributed	Compensation: Percentage of Total Value Contributed	All Contributions: Weighted Average Percentage of Total Value Contributed	Redistribution: Percentage of Total Value Received	Net Gain/ Loss in Percentage of Total Value
All males, aged					
16–20	6.8	5.6	5.8	7.4	+1.6
21–30	46.7	45.4	45.6	37.8	−7.8
31–40	39.2	34.7	35.5	25.8	−9.7
41–60	7.1	14.3	13.1	18.2	+5.1
Females	0	0	0	10.8	+10.8
Total	99.8	100.0	100.0	100.0	±17.5
Tafidilos vs. non-tafidilos					
Non-tafidilos					
36–60	6.3	29.1	25.3	31.9	+6.6
Tafidilos					
36–60	10.6	3.8	4.9	5.6	+.7

Although young men receive their procreative capacity and life force from older men, the circulation of wealth constitutes an egalitarian counterweight to this spiritual imbalance. This conceptual equalizing of accounts is specifically articulated in the postinitiation ceremony described in chapter 3. The newly initiated bachelors receive "substance" (tree oil) from the senior generation, but the transaction through which this tree oil is obtained is funded by the shell valuables provided by the bachelors themselves. Although the newly initiated bachelors have received semen (and life force), they give shell valuables that are an analogue of semen in return. They thus emerge from initiation as men among men rather than as indebted juniors. The generosity of their inseminators in giving semen is matched by the young men's generosity in contributing to social payments in the ensuing years. The life force transferred from older to younger men can never be reciprocated in kind. However, the symbolic equation of shell valuables with semen engenders a total system in which reciprocity is attainable. Irreversible indebtedness is thus precluded insofar as imbalances are temporary rather than permanent and are contained within a framework of reciprocity.

The life-cycle pattern entailing the accumulation of shell valuables before marriage followed by gradual depletion thereafter almost perfectly mirrors the life-cycle pattern that obtains with respect to the transmission of life force. Men are depleted of shell valuables—which are symbolic analogues of semen—just as they are depleted of semen. The newly initiated bachelors are repositories of both accumulated life force and accumulated shell valuables. Marriage engenders a marked loss of both through heterosexual intercourse and payment of bridewealth. The loss of life force is greatest in magnitude when a man is a double donor (as both husband and inseminator) and subsequently decelerates when his inseminee completes initiation. The loss of shell valuables ceases at about the same age (middle to late 30s). The two patterns are not congruent beyond this point in the life cycle, but the parallels between the circulation of wealth and the circulation of life force are nevertheless quite striking. The symbolic equation of semen and shell valuables also elucidates the retention of the latter by women. Women receive but do not give shell valuables just as they receive but do not give semen (while men give and receive both). Women consequently fail to reciprocate and likewise fail to manifest the virtue of generosity while at the same time displaying the vice of accumulation. However, there are additional reasons why women do not contribute the shell valuables in their possession to social payments and thus fail to reciprocate.

Women receive shell valuables on the occasion of a death and in commemoration of the kin relationship between male and female agnates, prototypically that between brother and sister. This is an important relationship at many levels. A brother is a woman's protector and is responsible for accumulating half the compensation in the event that she is accused of witchcraft. A sister has a continuing obligation to assist in weeding her brother's garden throughout her life. Brother and sister often coreside and thus participate jointly in the same communal gardens and sago-processing operations (Kelly 1977:150–54). Ideally, they both have sexual relations with the same man (ibid.: 183).

It is noteworthy that it is this cross-sex sibling relationship, rather than the conjugal relation, that receives public social emphasis. Wives (and daughters) generally inherit a portion of a man's wealth in pigs and shell valuables. However, the distribution of inheritance is a private event that entails no public recognition of the relationships through which property is conveyed. It is thus woman in her role as sibling and female agnate that is accorded public recognition.[16] These are the aspects of a woman's social persona in which she is most nearly on an equal footing with a man. (For example, male and female agnates have equivalent rights to cultivate lineage lands.) Women also receive shell valuables at these public redistributions in the same way that men receive them; the recipients are not socially differentiated in any way. In other words, gender is not noticeably marked on these occasions, and social roles are not allocated or discriminated on the basis of gender (with the single exception that the agent of distribution is always male). Here, as in the case of young men, women's engagement in the circulation of wealth appears as an egalitarian counterweight to ideological disabilities formulated in the domain of life-force transmission.

However, there is another sense in which the presentation of shell valuables to women is not the same as the presentation of shell valuables to men, even though both receive them at the same redistribution of witchcraft (or homicide) compensation. A woman receives by virtue of her relationship to the deceased. A man receives partly in this connection and partly by virtue of his relationship to the distributor (the brother or son of the deceased if male, the husband if female). A man thus receives shell valuables as part of an ongoing social relationship in which reciprocity is appropriate, while a woman receives in commemoration of a relationship terminated by death in which reciprocity is an impossibility. There is thus a return in one case and not the other, and full engagement in the circulation of wealth in one case and not the other.

This aspect of the presentation of shell valuables to women does not obviate the egalitarian aspect noted earlier but rather overlays it. In one sense, the presentation of shell valuables to men and women alike is the same thing, means the same thing, and references the most egalitarian feature of male-female relations. In another equally valid sense, such presentations look like the same thing but mean differently. There is consequently a double message. This does not constitute two distinct levels of meaning that are read out by male and female actors respectively, but a double message, appreciated by both, connoting a certain ambiguity regarding the relation of women to men. This might be disambiguated to the effect that men and women are equal in some respects but not others, but I would suggest that it is a sense of ambiguity that is conveyed rather than anything as clear-cut as this.

Women thus receive shell valuables in a context that does not obligate them to reciprocate. However, they come to possess shell valuables that could potentially be contributed to social payments. Although such contributions are not solicited from them, women could volunteer them as men do on occasion. An opportunity to manifest generosity is thus missed. However, women have little to gain by attaining prestige through generosity, since they cannot achieve the prestigious status of *tafidilo*. Nevertheless, it remains the case that the prestige/stigma system provides universal metrics applicable to all members of the social system. The fact that women elect the vice of accumulation rather than the virtue of generosity when they possess the wherewithal to engage in the latter thus naturalizes the distribution of prestige. This recapitulates the situation that obtains with respect to the distribution of midsize game, discussed in chapter 2.

WITCHCRAFT COMPENSATION AND THE REDISTRIBUTION OF WEALTH

The circulation of wealth within the Etoro social system offers two logical possibilities for the development of distributional inequalities or covert extraction. The first of these, entailing the potential for systematic biases in pooling and redistribution, has been analyzed. The second possibility entails an uneven distribution in the making and receiving of social payments (e.g., making but not receiving witchcraft compensation). This remains to be examined. However, it is first necessary to more fully elucidate the nature and meaning of these social payments.

All social payments entailing the transfer of shell valuables are termed *su* by the Etoro (cf. Ernst 1978:187). Thus the bridewealth payment is "woman *su*," and witchcraft or homicide compensation is "death *su*." Compensation to a husband for commission of adultery with his wife is likewise termed *su*, as is compensation for personal injury or the accidental killing of a domesticated pig (in a deadfall trap set for game). The central feature of all *su* payments is that they engender no obligation to reciprocate in shell valuables but rather constitute the achievement of a balanced reciprocity that closes out a particular social transaction. Moreover, the attainment of this balance involves an equation of markedly unlike items: some aspect pertaining to a person on one side of the transaction and shell valuables on the other. Thus one accepts a death *su* of shell valuables in lieu of vengeance and in order to settle accounts and bring the matter to a close. The *su* would be seen by the Etoro as directed toward alleviating the feelings of the recipients and thereby curtailing the desire to take a life in return (cf. Lederman 1981). It is not a compensation for loss so much as it is compensation for grief. At the same time, the deceased's next of kin have an explicitly acknowledged customary right to kill the witch and thereby directly assuage their grief. If they accept the *su,* they forfeit the right to vengeance. Conversely, if they elect vengeance, they forfeit the right to *su* (but must themselves pay one if they do in fact kill the witch). *Su* may therefore be seen, in one sense, as the direct equivalent of a right and thus as entailing the substitution of shell valuables for rights pertaining to a person (cf. Modjeska 1982:55–56; Strathern 1982b; Godelier 1982:33). In another sense, strongly conveyed in the *kosa* ritual and closer to the more immediate understanding of the Etoro, *su* may be seen as compensation for feelings of grief.[17] In this respect, shell valuables are not being equated with rights pertaining to a person, and there is no principle of substitutability. Instead, the shell valuables are a palliative that assuages the grief of the recipients and represents an effort on the part of the givers to make amends (as discussed in chap. 4 with respect to witchcraft compensation).

Both of these meanings of *su* are expressed in Etoro discourse. They emerge in the bride's father's lament, a public display of grief that takes place not long after the father has distributed the wedding pig and the shell valuables that constitute the *udia su* (or bridewealth) to his kinsmen. The father weeps profusely for hours in an expression of grief wholly consistent with the fact that he has just received a *su* payment. But he specifically laments having accepted the *su* he has just recently redistributed and says he would return it all and have his daughter as she was before had his kinsmen not already eaten the pig, making this impossible. The context of this lament makes it clear that acceptance of the *su* by the father has altered his daughter's status and that the capacity to effect this status change rests entirely with the father. The idea that the marriage could be undone by returning the payment certainly implies that the payment is both necessary and sufficient. It is thus the *su* rather than the ceremony that renders the daughter married (while the consumption of the pig makes the *su* unreturnable).

The notion that a right pertaining to a person is equivalent to a *su* payment therefore seems to be present in the discourse, although it is present by implication and does not constitute the manifest content. It is the father's heartfelt grief that commands the attention of the Etoro present at this occasion. This palpable weeping gives considerable weight to the other meaning, viz., that the *su* compensates the father for the grief he feels when his daughter marries. *Su* payments are directly associated with weeping in the *kosa* ceremony (see n. 17), and death *su* is likewise given in conjunction with the mourning that takes place at funerals. The fact that Western culture also enjoins weeping at weddings and funerals makes Etoro sentiments readily intelligible at a basic level. Although the emotional outpouring on such occasions is conventional and predictable, it is nevertheless experienced by the actor as spontaneous and disconnected from cultural expectations. This is to say that the authenticity of such emotions is unimpeachable and one should not imagine that the Etoro father's weeping is any less heartfelt because it is conventional and stereotyped in form.

The shell valuables that are here termed "wealth" are thus a medium of exchange in external trade with nonkin and a medium of compensation (in the senses elucidated above) in transactions with kin and fellow tribesmen (cf. Ernst 1978).

The circulation of wealth through the pooling and redistribution of social payments that are essentially compensatory in nature presents two possibilities for the development of distributional inequities. One possibility, already discussed, is that the cycles of pooling and redistribution may entail biases favoring certain categories of individuals who systematically receive more than they give. The second possibility is that some individuals may make or receive social payments more often than others. Thus a man with several sisters could receive several bridewealth payments. A man whose mother, father, wife, brother, and child all died could receive witchcraft compensations for each death and yet might never pay such compensation himself. There is also one other *su* transaction that is amenable to the possibility of significant differences in the frequency of giving and receiving. The principal dancers who perform in the *kosa* ceremony must pay compensation to individuals who have been moved to tears by the beauty and pathos of their performance. Each of these three possibilities will be discussed in turn.

A man with several sisters (and no brothers) does indeed receive multiple bridewealth payments. However, he redistributes the component shell valuables to his kinsmen, keeping only a fraction for himself (about 10 percent of total value, on average). Another individual, who had no sisters, would have no marriage payments to redistribute but would nevertheless receive contributions to his own bridewealth payments from his kinsmen. These arrangements are conducive to an even distribution of wealth. The fact that payments are almost entirely redistributed precludes significant accumulation by a favorably situated recipient. The requirement that the needs of a kinsman must be met—irrespective of the present or prospective balance of receipts and donations—equalizes distribution, since those who have more to give must give more or give more often. The Etoro bridewealth system is thus essentially redistributive. It tends to equalize distribution of the shell valuables that constitute bridewealth simply by repeatedly serving as the occasion for parceling these out among kin, who then donate them largely in accordance with their capacity to do so (cf. Goody 1973).[18]

The redistributive propensities of the circulation of wealth in social payments are evident in the data presented thus far. Those persons with the most extensive holdings of shell valuables (i.e., younger men aged 21 to 40) experience a net loss, while those with the least extensive holdings (i.e., men aged 41 to 60, women, and adolescent males aged 16 to 20) experience a net gain. Moreover, the men aged 21 to 40 who realize a net loss receive in redistributions at a rate that is very close to proportional to their numerical representation in the population (the ratio of percentage of total value received divided by percentage of individuals in the population being 1.04). The men aged 16 to 20 and 41 to 60 who realize a net gain receive at a rate only two-thirds as great as would be expected on the basis of their representation in the population (i.e., a ratio of .66) due to the diversion of 10.8 percent of the total value redistributed to women. Thus, younger men aged 21 to 40 give in accordance with their capacity to do so (which is substantial) and receive shares that are equivalent to their numbers rather than equivalent to prior donations. This engenders a net loss for these men that funds the net gain realized by those with a lesser capacity to contribute to social payments.

There are some individuals who are repeatedly accused of witchcraft (and eventually executed) and others who are never accused. One might suppose that the compensation repeatedly paid by this select group of witches and their kin would leave them impoverished and engender marked inequalities in the distribution of wealth. However, there are a number of factors that quite effectively counterbalance this potential outcome. A type of compensation that is paid on the occasion of 40 percent of adult deaths[19] has a built-in tendency toward equalizing distribution of the specific compensation items involved, because everyone has many kinsmen who will die and everyone will consequently receive shares of such compensations. This equalizing tendency is amplified if the size of the payment does not vary in accordance with the social importance of the deceased, as is the case among the Etoro. Thus, valuables are repeatedly parceled out among men and (to a lesser extent) women on the basis of a qualification entirely unrelated to any feature of social differentiation, i.e., having a relative who has died (or, in the case of bridewealth, a kinswoman who has married). But while every man receives shares of witchcraft compensation at one time or another, only a delimited group of accused witches is required to assemble it. This might skew the distribution of wealth significantly were it not the case that many men have a kinsman or kinswoman who has been accused of witchcraft. About ten individuals normally contribute to the compensation payment made on behalf of an accused person (table 6.4), and this obligation is thus widely experienced. This ameliorates but does not entirely obviate the consequences that follow from the selectivity of witchcraft accusations. These remain to be more fully explored.

Witchcraft compensation is assembled and paid by adult men in the event that they themselves, or their wives, married sisters, unmarried daughters, or uninitiated sons are accused of witchcraft. In other words, all females and uninitiated males are jural minors with respect to witchcraft compensation. The liability for an adult woman's witchcraft is jointly shared by her husband and her brother (or father if her brother is a minor). The liability for an unmarried young adult's witchcraft rests with the father. Those who bear the burden of paying compensation are thus the men aged 21 to 60 who have holdings in shell valuables. It is especially important to note that the distribution of the burden of compensation among these men does not simply correspond to the frequency with which they themselves are accused of witchcraft, but to the frequency with which their wives, sisters, and children are accused as well. Although men over the age of 40 are very rarely accused of witchcraft, these same men tend to have the most extensive potential liability for the payment of compensations, because they have married sisters, wives (sometimes more than one), teenage sons, and daughters who are susceptible to witchcraft accusations. This offsets the tendency for somewhat younger men (with one wife or no wives and immune younger children) to be accused of witchcraft themselves, producing the net result shown in table 6.8.[20]

These data show that individuals of different age categories serve as compensators (or accumulators of compensation) roughly in proportion to their representation in the population, with one significant exception. Although males aged 16 to 20 evidence disproportionately low representation among compensators, this is due to the fact that four-fifths of them are jural minors. Taking this into account, the .22 ratio becomes 1.10, or roughly proportional. Only men aged 31 to 40 are disproportionately likely to serve as compensators. This is attributable to the fact that this age-group is also the most disproportionately accused of witchcraft (as noted in chap. 4). Nevertheless, it is evident that liability for compensation is much more evenly distributed among males of different age categories than is the incidence of accusation. Men aged 31 to 40 are more than 3 times more likely to be accused of witchcraft than would be expected based on their proportional representation in the population (ratio 3.24), but only 1.3 times more likely to be responsible for the accumulation of compensation.

Witches do not constitute as large a percentage of compensators as might be expected because witches are not compensators when a witch is killed and, more importantly, because nearly half (20/42) of all those accused of witchcraft are jural minors. The status of women and uninitiated males as jural minors plays a central role in diffusing the obligation to serve as the accumulator of compensation over the entire adult male population. Although men over the age of 40 are virtually immune from witchcraft accusations, they are not immune from liability for compensation. The advantage they hold with respect to the avoidance of stigma is thus not accompanied by a parallel material advantage of the same magnitude (although *tafidilos* are slightly advantaged as explained further along).

Witches comprise 36.8 percent of all compensators and are a little more than twice as likely to be responsible for accumulating compensation as would be expected based on their proportional representation in the population. The accumulator of witchcraft compensation provides about 17 percent of the total value, with the remainder being supplied by his kinsmen. This dilutes but does not obviate the material disadvantage associated with the stigma of witchcraft. A witch thus expends more valuables in compensation than others, but the loss is relatively small in magnitude.

Tafidilos constitute the only social category of males that is dispropor-tionately underrepresented among compensators (excepting males 16 to 20, who are largely jural minors). However, the extent of this under-representation is not great; *tafidilos* serve as compensators two-thirds as often as would be expected based on their proportional representation in the popu-lation. This is due to a combination of factors. Both *tafidilos* and non-*tafidilos* aged 41 to 60 are virtually immune from accusations, and many of the wives and sisters of both are also within the age-group of older women subject to a low incidence of accusations. The potential liability of both groups is somewhat reduced as a result. The small difference between *tafidilos* and

TABLE 6.8

The Proportional Distribution of Compensators by Age and Status

| | Compensation for | | Total for Age Subset | Percentage of Total | Ratio: Percent-age of Compen-sators Divided by Percentage of Individuals in Population |
	Witchcraft	Homicide			
Males, aged					
16–20	.5	—	.5	2.6	.22
21–30	4.0	2	6.0	31.6	.97
31–40	5.0	2	7.0	36.8	1.30
41–60	4.5	1	5.5	29.0	1.06
Total	14.0	5	19.0	100.0	1.00
Witches	7.0	—	7.0	36.8	2.19
Non-*tafidilos*					
41–60	3.0	—	3.0	15.8	1.01
Tafidilos					
41–60	1.5	—	1.5	7.9	.68

non-*tafidilos* in their proportional representation among compensators is due to a slight difference in the incidence of accusations against family members, particularly sons. The total sample (of 42 accusations) includes 5 accusations against the wife, sister, or minor child of a *tafidilo,* or .45 such accusations per *tafidilo* (for 11 men aged 41 to 60). The sample likewise includes 8 accusations against the wife, sister, or minor child of a non-*tafidilo* or .53 such accusations per man (for 15 non-*tafidilos* aged 41 to 60). The difference of .08 is not significant. Compensation was paid in 60 percent of the cases involving a *tafidilo*'s family member and in 50 percent of the cases involving a non-*tafidilo*'s family member. The compensation liability amounted to .136 per *tafidilo* and .166 per non-*tafidilo* because non-*tafidilos* were more frequently responsible for an entire compensation (due to an accusation against a minor son) as opposed to half a compensation (due to an accusation against a wife, sister, or married daughter). The extent of the advantage enjoyed by *tafidilos* over non-*tafidilos* of the same age is thus slight and is not due to a significant difference in the likelihood that a family member will be accused. Nevertheless, *tafidilos* are advantaged in comparison to all other social categories.

Although both the obligation to serve as the accumulator of compensation and the obligation to contribute are diffused over the entire adult male population, witchcraft compensation nevertheless serves as a vehicle for the redistribution of wealth. This redistribution, which is of modest proportions, involves a net transfer from witches to *tafidilos*. This stems from the fact that witches are disproportionately overrepresented among those liable for compensation, while *tafidilos* are disproportionately underrepresented. *Tafidilos* consequently supply the 17 percent of the total value of a witchcraft compensation that is the responsibility of the accumulator (or half of this in the case of an accusation against a wife, sister, or daughter) somewhat less frequently than others. As noted earlier, they also generally avoid contributing to the witchcraft compensations accumulated by others (in order to dissociate themselves from the supporters of the witch). *Tafidilos* consequently receive more in the redistribution of compensation payments than they contribute. They deploy these gains by contributing disproportionately to bridewealth payments, so that no net accumulation occurs (as established in table 6.7). In effect, the modest transfer of wealth from individuals assigned the stigmatized status of witch to individuals accorded the prestigious status of *tafidilo* thus serves to fund the prestige-enhancing generosity of the latter in contributing to bridewealth. *Tafidilos* therefore do not enjoy any material benefits pertaining to increased consumption, which could potentially be realized by converting their net gains in shell valuables to tobacco, salt, axes, or Western trade goods (rather than generously contributing to bridewealth). Surpluses of these would have to be shared in any event in a system where one cannot legitimately possess two of anything another individual lacks. But *tafidilos* do accumulate the one thing that is readily accumulable, namely prestige.

The redistributive transfer of wealth effected through the payment of witchcraft compensation impinges only upon witches and does not extend to their kin. Although some individuals are repeatedly accused of witchcraft, this does not have the effect of impoverishing their kin, who are obligated to contribute to compensation. As was noted in chapter 4, compensation is only paid with respect to 40.5 percent of all accusations, and thrice-accused witches are typically executed. The kin of an individual subject to repeated accusations would thus be likely to be a party to the nonpayment of compensation on one occasion, contribute to the payment of compensation on a second occasion, and then be the recipients of a homicide compensation paid when the recidivist witch was executed following the third accusation. Compensation payments for killing a witch are about one-third larger, on average, than a witchcraft compensation (see table 6.4). The kinsmen of a witch included in the scapegoat category would consequently tend to experience modest net gains rather than impoverishment over the long term.

The fact that some individuals are repeatedly accused of witchcraft while others are never accused therefore does *not* result in wealth being transferred from the kin of the former to the kin of the latter through the repeated payment of compensation, as one would intuitively suppose. From a distributionalist perspective, the total system of witchcraft and homicide compensation might be described as one in which extraction (from a witch's kin) is eventually counterbalanced by restitution. The main thrust is not essentially redistributive, as with the bridewealth system, but rather neutral. Moreover, this neutral result is achieved by offsetting a built-in tendency toward distributional inequality and is thus somewhat precarious. If the state government of Papua New Guinea were successful in its efforts to preclude witchcraft executions, the system would become purely extractive. In 1968–69, this had not yet occurred. Thus while there was much sorrow in being the close kinsman of a witch under traditional conditions, impoverishment was not an intrinsic component of the burden. It should also be kept in mind that the subject of successive witchcraft accusations does not share in the restitutive compensation received by his (or her) kinsmen, since it is only received after the subject witch has been killed. A repeatedly accused male witch does suffer economically, but that is also the least of his problems.

The concepts of extraction and redistribution employed in the preceding discussion are linked to notions of ownership, possession, and accumulation. While analysis from this vantage point is important in establishing the presence and extent of differentials in disposable wealth, this does not address or illuminate the key question of differential deployment. This is a separate issue inasmuch as differences in deployment are not contingent upon, and are not necessarily linked to, differential wealth resources. The contrast between *tafidilos* and non-*tafidilos* is instructive in this regard. Both *tafidilos* and non-*tafidilos* possess comparatively small holdings of shell valuables as a result of having expended those they accumulated through trade in their youth. Both jointly constitute the category of males aged 41 to 60, which realizes a small net gain in the total cycle of accumulation and redistribution of social payments. This is a result of having less to contribute than younger men do, on one hand, while receiving shares of redistributed social payments in amounts that more nearly approximate their proportional representation in the population, rather than their contributions, on the other hand. Both *tafidilos* and non-*tafidilos* thus have comparable quantities of shell valuables at their disposal. *Tafidilos* deploy a substantial portion of these shell valuables in contributions to bridewealth, rarely bypassing an opportunity to make an unsolicited token contribution to the marriage payment of a distant kinsman (as well as making normative contributions to the payments of closer kinsmen). Such contributions are generous by virtue of being beyond the range of expected kin obligation and by virtue of being offered in the absence of any request.

Tafidilos thus have little on hand to contribute to witchcraft compensations and are generally able to avoid making such contributions. In contrast, non-*tafidilos* contribute only to the bridewealth payments of closer kin and thereby conserve their resources in shell valuables, resulting in accumulation. They are consequently subject to requests for contributions to witchcraft compensation that they are not in a good position to refuse. Since the ratio of compensation payments to marriage payments was five to one during the fieldwork period (see n. 14), this passive practice of meeting requests for contributions resulted in five times as much being contributed to compensation payments as to bridewealth (see table 6.7). However the fulfillment of kin obligations in both of these contexts is normative such that non-*tafidilos* did not manifest any notable degree of generosity. The key difference between *tafidilos* and non-*tafidilos* is consequently in types of deployment rather than in the quantities of shell valuables at their disposal.

The *su* compensation paid by the main dancers in the *kosa* ceremony remains to be discussed. The Etoro *kosa* is a variant of a ritual form that is distributed throughout the region from the Strickland River to the Great Papuan Plateau. Knauft (1985b:323) provides a concise description of the main features of this widespread ritual form:

> The ritual is essentially an all-night dance and song fest at which persons from two or more longhouses aggregate. Upon the visitor's arrival, there is some initial display of anger, social distance, or provocation between visitors and those

from the hosting longhouse. . . . In all instances, however, persons who come to the event ultimately share a friendly experience. The gathering is a principal forum for hospitality, for socializing, and often for public (noncompetitive) food-giving, particularly between hosts and their visiting affines.

The primary aesthetic and symbolic focus of the ritual is the dancing of one or more men (usually visitors) and accompanying singing. The dance begins late in the evening and lasts until dawn, watched throughout the night by the assembled hosts and visitors. . . . At the ritual performance, the dancer appears as a figure of resplendent plumage and foliage, bouncing slowly and sensuously. His dance steps and postures are quite subdued, and he exhibits a generally downcast and somber demeanor. This demeanor is reflected in the dance songs, which are sorrowful depictions of persons alone at various places in the forest. The persona of the beautiful but melancholy dancer arouses a strong and distinct sense of pathos among the audience.

The Etoro variant of this shared form is similar to the Kaluli *gisaro*, described and analyzed in considerable detail by Schieffelin (1976) and Feld (1982), in that the dancers are burned with resin torches by members of the host community who have been moved to the tearful expression of deeply felt grief by the beauty and evocative pathos of the songs (see pls. 4–6). The dancers must then give a *su* to members of the guest community to compensate them for the grief the latter have been made to feel. It is this transaction in shell valuables with which we are concerned.

The *kosa* is grounded in an affinally configured host-guest relationship. The hosts include those who provide the food (sago and bananas), typically the members of the community where the event is staged plus at least one neighboring community. The guests provide the performance, with the dancers and singers generally drawn from more than one community as well. The affinal keynote of the host-guest relationship is provided by the highlighting of a single individual's affinal exchange, which takes place immediately after the opening hostilities (a general feature noted by Knauft, cited above). The hosts charge into the open area in front of the longhouse that separates them from the newly arrived guests, brandishing weapons and shouting war cries. They then withdraw, and the guests enact a similar display of mock hostility. Immediately after this, a man from the guest group presents seventeen smoked marsupials to an affine or cross-cousin,[21] and the hosts and guest intermingle, with each individual seeking out and heartily greeting his own kin and age-mates. The guests are then ushered into the longhouse, where large quantities of bananas and sago are served to them. After sharing this repast, the guests perform the *hia*, in which elaborately decorated pairs of men sing duets. A substantial number of men from the guest party perform over a period of six hours or so. This builds toward and is followed by the very beautiful and dramatic *kosa* performance which lasts from about 9:00 P.M. or 10:00 P.M. till dawn.

The *kosa* dancers are predominantly young unmarried men aged 20 to 35 and recently married men of the same age-group. Sometimes a *tafidilo* will make a brief cameo appearance, but men over 45 are not among the all-night performers. In contrast, the elders of the host community are particularly prominent among those who weep and burn the dancers.[22] Typically, the lineage of the dancer and the lineage of the burner will be related by past and/or current intermarriage (although wife's father is specifically debarred from burning daughter's husband). It would be quite inappropriate for an individual to be burned by a member of his own lineage (although an agnate could well be a resident of the host community). The Etoro also say that weeping and burning by a member of a brother lineage is "of no consequence" (*memana*) and engenders no obligation to provide compensation (*su*). The shell valuables that are given by the dancers to those that they have moved to profound grief thus pass between intermarrying lines. However, the recipients are often not the specific individuals that performed the weeping and burning, but young men who are agnates of the latter. These young men appear in the dancers' home community within an hour after the performers have returned (following the conclusion of the ceremony at dawn). They request a *su* of one to three cowrie strings and are given these valuables on the spot. The cowrie strings are usually provided by the dancer himself but may also be contributed by a close agnate, particularly a brother. There are generally 4 to 7 *kosa* performers, and a total of about 8 to 14 cowrie strings change hands (averaging 2 per dancer). Within a year or less, the guests will host a ceremony in their own community and this outflow of shell valuables will be reversed.[23]

The transfer of shell valuables in conjunction with the *kosa* ceremony has a definite potential to systematically reorder the distribution of wealth, but one that appears to be unrealized. If *su* payments were made directly from the dancers to those who burned them, they would pass almost entirely from junior males to elder senior males. When the host-guest roles were reversed, reciprocity could be achieved on a lineage-to-lineage basis without altering the consistent flow of valuables from juniors to seniors. However, the elders, particularly the *tafidilos* who are especially prominent in their prolonged and dramatic expressions of grief, do not themselves collect the compensation in most instances. The available quantitative data that can be brought to bear on this point are limited to the compensation payments connected with two *kosa* performances. However, these data indicate that four-fifths of the compensation goes to unmarried young men and recently married men (with no children), i.e., to individuals within the same age categories as the performers. Etoro "ceremonial exchange" of shell valuables thus entails a circulation of wealth among young men, consistent with the general pattern identified earlier.[24]

The young men who perform the *kosa* enact what is arguably the most prestigious ritual role in the Etoro sociocultural system (apart from that of entranced mediums) and are provided with an opportunity to appear as paragons of every virtue the Etoro cherish. Most notable among these virtues is the provision of compensation to assuage the grief one has caused another. The *kosa* performers generously and solicitously give a *su* to those whom they have made weep, while ignoring the second-degree burns they themselves have received from the latter. It is the emotional pain and not the physical injury that counts. This concept of *su* is clearly delineated and very strongly promoted by the *kosa*.[25] Inasmuch as all internal transactions in shell valuables are *su* payments, the general terms of the circulation of wealth are also delineated.

INHERITANCE

The conveyance of shell valuables in inheritance is the only transaction that remains to be examined. Relatively little is transmitted in inheritance and this is a direct consequence of general features noted earlier. We have seen that the pool of wealth a young man accumulates through trade tends to diminish over the course of his lifetime. This occurs as a consequence of expenditures for tools and consumables, through a disparity in the relation between contributions to social payments and shares of redistributions, and through expanded liability for witchcraft compensation that accompanies the developmental cycle of domestic groups. If a man's stock of shell valuables gradually diminishes with advancing age, there will clearly be little to pass along in inheritance. Moreover, the shell valuables a man has contributed to the social payments of others are given within a framework of generalized reciprocity, rather than with expectations of a precise return. There are consequently no grounds for regarding these as debts that can be called in after his death.

The deceased's estate would thus consist of whatever shell valuables, axes, pigs, and dogs he had on hand at the time of his demise (plus his holdings of sago palms, omitted from the present discussion; see Kelly 1977:140–41). This would normally include a couple of axes, one or two mother-of-pearl shell ornaments, and three to six strings of cowrie shells, this being the stock from which an individual would fund his own contribution to a social payment that he was personally responsible for making. In addition, an older man would typically be the senior owner of three to four pigs, co-owned with other family members (Kelly 1988:144). The pigs are passed on to these family members, especially a wife (or wives) and son(s). A wife typically inherits just one small pig, which she may jointly own with a young son. Larger pigs go to older sons and sometimes to a brother as well if there are several. Shell valuables are often inherited by the individual who is currently wearing them as bodily adornment. They are consequently distributed among a man's children and may also pass to a brother's son or sister's son. If a man has few shell valuables, they will likely go primarily to his son, with a daughter receiving at least one item. If he has more shell valuables, siblings' sons may also receive some. Either way, a son cannot expect to inherit more than one mother-of-pearl shell ornament and a few strings of cowrie shells from his father. He may also inherit a few shell valuables from his mother. In addition, a son will typically kill one or two pigs at the time of his father's death for oracular purposes and to provision the mortuary ceremony, offsetting any potential gains in pigs through inheritance. In sum, inheritance plays a very small role in the circulation of wealth. The holdings of shell valuables a young man possesses are largely amassed through trade, and inheritance provides only a minor contribution to this. Moreover, the shell valuables a son retains in redistributing the witchcraft compensation received following his father's death often exceed his direct inheritance.

Pigs do not form part of the circulating pool of resources deployed in social payments because they do not survive the occasion of their transfer. They have consequently not been included in the preceding discussion of the circulation of wealth. Nevertheless, the distribution of pigs is of interest, since they are deployed in bridewealth and compensation payments and in affinal exchange. Men aged 21 to 30, 31 to 40, and 41 to 60 own 1.65, 2.22, and .59 pigs per capita, respectively (based on the average of two pig censuses; see Kelly 1988:144). Elder senior men thus possess comparatively few pigs, just as they possess comparatively small quantities of shell valuables. They also make little effort to acquire pigs in trade. Neither spirit mediums nor *tafidilos* own more pigs than other men of the same age-groups, and a *tafidilo* may at times own no pigs at all (see Kelly 1988:145–49). Both pigs and shell valuables are disconnected from the attainment of the prestigious statuses of spirit medium and *tafidilo*. It is the generous distribution of growth-inducing game to coresidents that most notably distinguishes *tafidilos* from others, while making unsolicited token contributions to the bridewealth payments of distant kin is entirely secondary. *Tafidilos* also possess very small holdings of shell valuables and differ from others only in the mode of deployment they adopt. This parallels their predominant election of longhouse as opposed to garden house distribution of game. However, in the latter case, *tafidilos* also differ from others in the quantity of game they have at their disposal (as a result of assiduous hunting and trapping).

The Etoro thus differ markedly from Highlands societies in which the deployment of pigs and shell valuables is crucial to the attainment of the prestigious status of Big Man. The most far-ranging repercussion of this difference is that neither spirit mediums nor *tafidilos* are dependent upon the labor of others in order to achieve these prestigious statuses, while Big Men are so dependent. As a result, the prestige/stigma system and the economic system are interlocked in the Highlands and very nearly disarticulated among the Etoro, insofar as relations of production are not a source of inequality. While both subsistence food production and the circulation of wealth are integral to the generation of social inequality in the former social systems, they are, in many respects, a source of egalitarian counterweights to cosmologically formulated inequalities in the latter.

This contrast suggests that one of the key features of the evolution of social inequality turns on the development of an engagement between the prestige/stigma system and the economic system in which relations of production are instrumental to the attainment of prestige. This represents a watershed such that specific ethnographic cases that fall on different sides of this divide are not amenable to elucidation by the application of a monolithic theory of social inequality. However, taking the prestige/stigma system as the point of departure in analysis is equally productive in both types of societies, although this leads to different sets of interconnections in each case. Modjeska's (1982:86) orienting proposition that "pig production and the social relations of pig production, circulation and consumption [are] the important strategic points for understanding inequality in the Highlands" is applicable in that context because transactions in pigs are integral to the prestige system (see Kelly 1988:171–73). In the Etoro case, taking the prestige system as a point of departure leads most directly to consideration of the assignment of the stigmatized status of witch that precludes prestige attainment.

The central postulate of Meillassoux's theoretical framework is that control over matrimonial goods enables elders to control reproduction (in the broad sense) and thus engender both dependence on the part of junior males and their subjugation to the authority of the elders (Meillassoux 1964:217, cited in Terray 1972:166). As was noted in the introduction to this chapter, Collier and Rosaldo (1981:288) further extend this formulation in arguing that bridewealth requirements determine the relations of production between not only junior and senior males but also between husband and wife. Bridewealth requirements thus shape relations of production that in turn engender social inequality. It is evident that Etoro bridewealth requirements do not have any of these posited consequences. They engender neither dependence upon nor subjugation to the authority of elders, on the part of junior males, and they likewise do not impinge upon conjugal relations of production. The Etoro are thus classified by Collier (1988:258) as a brideservice society, even though bridewealth payments are made and bride service is absent. Although the label "brideservice societies" thus becomes somewhat misleading, I concur with this classification of the Etoro that places them in the same category as the erstwhile "egalitarian societies." The applicability of Collier's theoretical formulation to the Etoro is addressed at length in the next chapter.

It will be useful to briefly reconsider the main thrust of anthropological thinking with regard to wealth and inequality before turning to Collier's formulation. As noted in the introduction to this chapter, there is a pervasive perception that the sheer existence of accumulable forms of wealth breeds inequality. When transactions in valuables are integral to a social system, unequal accumulation and/or relations of dependence and indebtedness are inevitable. This presupposes that an egalitarian distribution of wealth is an impossibility. However, the Etoro approximate such a distribution. Some might contend that anything that is relatively equally distributed does not qualify as "wealth" (even if it is accumulable and serves as a medium of exchange). Such circular logic would certainly preserve the received wisdom adumbrated above, since any potentially disconfirming cases are disqualified by definition.

The Etoro case is of particular interest because wealth is not concentrated in the hands of the elders who are also accorded a prestigious status (as the adherents to Meillassoux's position would expect), but is rather concentrated in the hands of junior males who are ineligible for this status. Inequalities of prestige are thus undercut rather than amplified. Moreover, the circulation of wealth entails a strong tendency toward an egalitarian redistribution, since wealth flows, on balance, from those who possess the largest quantities to those who have the most restricted holdings. In short, the Etoro case shows that the sheer existence of wealth does not inevitably breed inequality and, more importantly, that an egalitarian circulation of wealth is not an impossibility. When transactions in valuables are not integral to the attainment of prestige, the presence of wealth within a social system has no inherent inegalitarian consequences.

CHAPTER 7

Theories of Inequality in Simple Societies

The general form and objectives of current theories of social inequality in premodern tribal societies have been most strongly influenced by the model provided by Marx's elegant and powerful account of social inequality in capitalist society. Like Marx, recent theorists seek to identify the central institutional locus for the production of social inequality, to trace inequality to its source, and to totalistically account for its varied manifestations (in any particular case) by linking them to this central locus of production. The locus of production is essentially a prime mover internal to the sociocultural system. This chapter is devoted to an examination of several prominent theories of social inequality in simple societies, both in general terms and in relation to the Etoro case documented in preceding chapters. The first half of the chapter is an extended critical evaluation of the most comprehensive extant model of social inequality in such societies, that developed by Collier and Rosaldo (1981) and Collier (1988). This model synthesizes a number of recent theoretical developments in the study of social inequality, so that evaluation of it affords an opportunity to address these as well. Moreover, the Etoro case has been specifically nominated as one to which the model can usefully be applied (Collier 1988:258). The second half of the chapter is largely devoted to developing an alternative theoretical understanding of social inequality in simple societies, to the formulation of a revised model, and to consideration of other recent theoretical works that contrast with Collier and Rosaldo in terms of the identity of the central locus for the production of inequality. The general form and explanatory objectives shared by these varied theoretical positions are also discussed in this context.

A CRITIQUE OF THE BRIDESERVICE MODEL

The analytic point of departure for the brideservice model developed by Collier and Rosaldo (1981) and restated in Collier's (1988) study is a posited asymmetry in the conjugal (husband-wife) relationship that stems from the authors' perception that marriage does not institute an equal exchange of male and female products.

> A focus on the sexual division of labor might suggest that marriage is equally beneficial to husband and wife, but a focus on the sexual division of obligations suggests the opposite. Because men are obliged to distribute their meat widely, a woman does not have to have a husband to gain access to male produce. She simply has to be a member of a social group. But because women are responsible for feeding their husbands and children, a man must have a wife if he hopes to eat regularly and without having to demean himself. The difference in obligations by sex, and its consequences for the meanings of marriage, are the twin insights underlying the brideservice model presented in this chapter. (Collier 1988:17)

In the earlier presentation of the model, Collier and Rosaldo (1981:282) emphasize the role of values in producing this asymmetry: "Men's game and women's gathered foods are not equivalents because they acquire their values from socially determined obligations that precede and underlie possibilities for exchange." This emphasis admits of the possibility that there is an exchange of male and female products between husband and wife but that the exchange is unequal. This is Josephides's (1985:105) understanding of Collier and Rosaldo's position as exemplified in the following paraphrase: "Male and female products are not equally exchanged because they are not equally valued; and this valuation is determined by social obligations preceding the exchange." In contrast, Collier's (1988:16) more recent version of the brideservice model emphasizes that "marriage does not involve a direct exchange or pooling of resources between husband and wife." The emphasis here is on the absence of exchange per se so that valuation of male and female products is no longer relevant to an assessment of equivalence.

It is my contention that the brideservice model is founded on a fundamental misconception of the conjugal relation that stems from a misreading of the exchanges that take place in the context of food distribution and from selective attention to only a portion of the data relevant to the economic relation between husband and wife. Although Collier (1988:258) has specifically designated the Etoro as one of the societies to which the brideservice model could be fruitfully applied, my objectives are not limited to demonstrating that this is not the case. I seek to employ the Etoro instance to exemplify a more general critique of the model, in the same way that Collier (1988) uses a single case to illustrate its general applicability. Reference will also be made to the cases that Collier and Rosaldo (1981) originally employed to illustrate their conception of the conjugal relation and to other Strickland-Bosavi tribes to which elements of the brideservice model have been applied (e.g., the Kamula). I will also be concerned to evaluate both of the somewhat divergent emphases noted above, i.e., that there is no direct exchange between husband and wife and that a lack of value equivalence renders the exchange of male and female products unequal. At issue are the nature of the conjugal relation in a certain class of societies and the more general contention that marriage is the primary locus of social inequality. Collier (1988:vii) provides a clear and succinct expression of this position in her preface.

> In societies without classes or estates, where kinship organizes people's rights and obligations, marriage, as the basis of kinship, organizes social inequality.

A division of labor by age and especially by gender is manifest, to some degree, in all premodern tribal societies. Men and women do not engage in an identical range of activities and/or do not perform common tasks to the same extent. Likewise, younger children do not perform the full complement of activities carried out by adults of the same sex. The division of labor therefore constitutes a primary locus of social differentiation embedded in economic process. Moreover, the discriminated classes of individuals not only perform different forms of labor but are often culturally envisioned as possessing distinctive capacities in this respect. Cultural conceptions of male and female persons are thus frequently delineated, in part, by a gendered division of labor. Cultural conceptions of age and the differential rates of maturation of males and females are also grounded in the attainment of capacities perceived to be intrinsic to adult gendered persons (so that a boy's first successful killing of a large game animal is noted as a signpost on the path to manhood). The social differentiation instituted by the division of labor is invariably a culturally constituted system of evaluated differences such that certain activities are prestigious while others are not and the products of different forms of labor are likewise of unequal value. Social inequality is thus engendered by the division of labor prior to any transactions in which the gendered products and services that eventuate from it are exchanged. However, male and female products do not "acquire their [nonequivalent] values from socially determined obligations that precede and underlie possibilities for exchange" (Collier and Rosaldo 1981:282) but from the culturally specific value system in place. The derivation of values from obligations is based on an external logic and leads to a misconstrual of the transactions in gendered products that eventuate from a gendered division of labor (as will be elaborated further along).

Although a gendered division of labor is ubiquitous in tribal societies, it is subject to variable forms and degrees of elaboration and may or may not be characterized by task exclusivity. In the Etoro case, both men and women engage, at least occasionally, in nearly all the tasks that subsistence food production entails. Thus women as well as men are seen to be capable of rearing pigs to maturity, checking and resetting traps, chasing game, and both climbing and felling trees, while men are likewise seen to be capable of processing sago and clearing, planting, and weeding gardens. Men and women are consequently envisioned as possessing similar rather than distinctive capabilities in many respects. A division of labor characterized by quantitatively rather than qualitatively different patterns of activity provides little scope for the grounding or elaboration of gender differences.

The Kamula illustrate the opposite end of the spectrum of possibilities in that hunting is ideologically conceived (at least by men) as an exclusively male activity requiring masculine capabilities that can potentially be obviated by female violation of menstrual taboos. Hunting is not only an activity that men perform but a component of a cultural conception of masculinity defined in opposition to femininity. Although women do hunt occasionally, this behavioral fact is not employed to forward a cultural definition of equivalence, but rather constitutes an exception to male conceptions of masculinity and one that men choose to ignore. The fact that men occasionally assist in some of the tasks involved in sago processing is likewise ignored in favor of the view that this activity is a distinctively female province.

The Kamula conception of a division of labor grounded in distinctive gendered capabilities establishes the necessity of an exchange of gendered products and explicitly denies the potentiality for self-sufficient economic autonomy. Marriage thus institutes a reciprocal exchange relation between husband and wife (although it is not the exclusive forum for an exchange of gendered products). This is evident from the fact that a young man is told the following cautionary tale at the time he marries:

> Ke! If you don't shoot pigs or wallabies your wife will kill your sons. There was a man who never went hunting—he would just sit in the longhouse all day. He wouldn't go hunting. His wife would go fishing every day and get plenty of fish but she never ate any cassowary or wallaby meat. She was very angry with her husband just sitting in the house and not hunting. So she killed her son and cut him up and put the flesh in her netbag. She pretended it was wallaby. She cooked the flesh and gave it to her husband as wallaby meat. While he was eating he saw his son's foot. And so our ancestors said: "If you don't hunt, your wife will kill your sons and feed them to you." (Wood 1982:55)

This tale clearly represents a man's failure to hunt as a violation of obligations vested in the conjugal relationship. It is the nonhunter's wife who suffers deprivation, is angered, and retaliates. Although Kamula hunters are obliged to share certain types of game (notably pig) widely, in accordance with the brideservice model, this does not render the conjugal relationship nonreciprocal. A Kamula wife is obligated to process sago to feed her husband (and family), and her husband is obligated to reciprocate by supplying her with meat as fulfillment of a direct exchange relationship. An exchange of sago for meat between the bride and groom is the central component of the ceremony that institutes a marriage (Wood 1982:98–99).

This contradicts Collier's (1988:16) assertion that "marriage does not involve a direct exchange or pooling of resources between husband and wife." The significant point is that such direct conjugal exchange is encompassed within a system that manifests the traits that provide the point of departure for the brideservice model: men are required to share game with group members while women are only responsible for feeding their families. It is evident that men are charged with a *dual* responsibility both to their family and to group members while women are charged with only a singular familial responsibility. This is true not only of the Kamula but of all the societies to which the brideservice model is said to be applicable (and evidence in support of this general pattern of dual male responsibility will be presented further along). It is in this respect that Collier has fundamentally misconstrued the conjugal relationship in these societies.

In denying that a direct exchange of products and services is a central component of the conjugal relationship, Collier lays the groundwork for her assertion (1988:17) "a woman does not have to have a husband to gain access to male produce. She simply has to be a member of a social group." This in turn leads Collier to the view that women in brideservice societies do not want or need husbands and are reluctant to marry (ibid.:23, 34).

Collier is partially correct in noting that a generalized distribution of game may provide an unmarried woman with access to some male products. However, it does not provide access to all male products since not all types of game are subject to groupwide distribution. Consequently, a woman does need a husband in order to gain access to the full range of foods. As in the case of the legendary Kamula wife whose husband failed to hunt, the lack of particular foods (cassowary and wallaby) may be experienced as a deprivation even though other foods are available. However, the critical point here is that the specific features of game distribution determine the extent to which unmarried women have access to the meat men procure through hunting. This will be elaborated in due course after the implications of the gendered division of labor have been more fully explored.

Although marriage in the Kamula case institutes a reciprocal exchange relationship between husband and wife, the exchange of gendered products (sago and game) may also take place between brother and sister and between mother and son. Insofar as the conjugal relation is not an exclusive forum for such exchanges, marriage is not a prerequisite for gaining access to the produce of the opposite gender (rendered unavailable as a consequence of the division of labor). Young women may consequently delay marriage, and widows may likewise elect not to remarry. This indicates that Kamula women do not need husbands, in accordance with Collier's observations regarding brideservice societies generally. However, this potentiality to forego or delay marriage does not stem from female access to male products irrespective of marital status, as Collier's model supposes, but is instead due to social substitutability in the exchange of gendered products.

Such social substitutability undercuts one of the basic tenets of Collier's model because it is not the case that "a man must have a wife if he hopes to eat regularly and without having to demean himself" (Collier 1988:17). The asymmetry in each gender's access to the products of the other that informs Collier's interpretation of marriage in brideservice societies is absent in the Kamula case. This important point is made by Wood (1982:344), who questions Collier and Rosaldo's (1981:281) suggestion that a man gains "privileged access" to the products of female labor upon marriage, whereas a married woman "appears to have no more privileged access to male products than her single sisters." Wood perceives the Kamula to be similar to the Mundurucu in that "males and females, as collectivities, depend upon each other for subsistence, but individual men and women do not so depend upon each other" (Murphy and Murphy 1980:188, cited in Wood 1982:345). Inasmuch as social substitutability in the exchange of gendered products is intrinsically symmetrical, there are no differences between males and females in access to the products of the other gender that would differentially impel men to marry. Moreover, a man has privileged access to the products of his mother's and sister's labor that is commensurate with his access to the products of his wife's labor (Wood 1982:345). As a result, bachelors are not compelled to marry in order to gain an otherwise unobtainable privileged access to the products of female labor (ibid.). The specific dynamic that Collier posits as setting the stage for a junior male's asymmetrical dependence on his wife's parents is thus absent in the Kamula case. Moreover, the social substitutability in the exchange of gendered products that renders the basic dynamic of the brideservice model inapplicable is not unique but is characteristic of a subcategory of simple societies. The Mundurucu, who constitute a second illustrative instance, are also one of the cultural groups that Collier nominates as a candidate for the application of her model (Collier 1988:258).

The Etoro division of labor enjoins coproduction by males and females so that very few items are the products of female or male labor exclusively. Most consumable products (to which individuals require access) are produced through the joint effort of males and females who each perform some of the component tasks required to bring production to completion. The organization of production entailed by the Etoro division of labor thus contrasts with that of the Kamula in that it does not eventuate in male-produced game and female-produced sago, necessitating an exchange of these products between the genders. In the Etoro case, sago is usually produced by men and women working as a team. While the game derived from hunting is predominantly male-produced, that derived from trapping is typically coproduced (insofar as both men and women check, empty, and reset traps). Both garden crops and domesticated pigs are likewise coproduced. This contrastive Etoro organization of production has a number of significant consequences with respect to marriage and relations between the genders. Males and females pool their labor and share rights to the consumption values created by their joint efforts. The right to distribute coproduced foods to individuals who did not participate in their production is assigned to the gender that completed the production process, but coproducers share consumption rights in like items subsequently received in reciprocation.

Males and females are thus characteristically coproducers and coconsumers who exchange labor rather than the products of gender-exclusive efforts. While the male and female members of a production team do envision their relationship as entailing an exchange of gendered products that each brought to completion, these products are not solely produced and therefore cannot alternatively be exchanged with some other person of the opposite gender, as among the Kamula. In other words, the "exchange" of gender-assigned products between Etoro males and females who make up a production team is compulsory. There is thus no social substitutability in the exchange of gendered products, although there is a potential for social substitutability in the formation of production teams. Marriage institutes a production team in that each party is obliged to fulfill his or her gender-specific tasks in coproduction with the other and cannot, within the terms of the conjugal relationship, elect to work with someone else *instead*. However, a married man or woman can engage in coproduction with others *in addition* to fulfilling his or her obligations to a spouse. This entails partial social substitutability in that a portion of a married individual's total subsistence labor is devoted to coproduction with someone other than a spouse. Thus a married man may fell trees for a widow included in his gardening group, and a married woman may help weed her brother's or parent's garden.

This social substitutability in gaining access to the labor of the opposite gender has the same consequences as social substitutability in gaining access to the products of the opposite gender through exchange. Thus among the Etoro, as among the Kamula, a man is not compelled to acquire a wife in order to be assured of eating regularly without engaging in demeaning labor. A bachelor can readily form a production team with an unremarried widow to whom he is related by kinship. In addition, a bachelor who elects to participate in an exclusive bachelor garden can call upon his sister to assist him with the task of weeding, even though she is married and gardening with her husband (compare Wood 1982:345). Collier misconstrues the nature of marriage in implicitly assuming that a man universally acquires *monopolistic* rights to his wife's labor and the products thereof. More typically, a woman's kin relationship to her parents and male siblings is only partially modified, so that she continues to be obligated to assist them to some extent. Indeed, these obligations may be integral to the custom of bride service when the bride continues to reside with her parents during the early years of the marriage. The parents not only gain the labor of a daughter's husband but also retain that of the daughter herself. The daughter's continuing labor obligation is grounded in her own kin relation to her parents and is not merely a by-product of her husband's affinal obligations. While Collier's characterization of married women in brideservice societies as being solely responsible for feeding their husbands and children is broadly applicable, such women may also continue to fulfill kin obligations to parents and siblings that entail providing labor assistance. In the Comanche case that Collier employs to illustrate the brideservice model, a man gives the "best part" of the game he procures "to his wife to take to her father" (Collier 1988:25). This mode of transmission can be interpreted as encompassing both a husband's obligation to his wife and a wife's continuing obligation to her parents. The specific nature of the transaction does not support Collier's representation of it as one that is exclusively between daughter's husband and wife's father.

The preceding discussion of the Etoro and Kamula illustrates the general point that marriage in simple societies does establish an exchange relationship between husband and wife. Indeed, fulfilling these exchange obligations is compulsory and integral to continuance of the conjugal relationship. However, spouses are not precluded from engaging in exchange with others. Thus, a man's obligation to distribute meat widely constitutes a form of exchange with other hunters. However, this does not mean that there is no direct exchange between spouses, as Collier supposes, but is indicative of a man's dual responsibility both to his family and to comembers of the local group. Women may likewise be obliged to provide labor assistance to kin outside the conjugal family in the context of reciprocal exchange relations. In the Etoro case, a woman's lifelong obligation to respond to a brother's request that she help in weeding his garden is part of a relationship that entails his continuing obligation to generate half the compensation payment in the event that she is accused of witchcraft. The cross-sex sibling relationship thus entails an exchange of services. A woman's obligation to her brother is additive and does not obviate her exchange relationship with her husband, just as a man's obligation to distribute meat widely does not obviate the exchange relationship with his wife. Both men and women have obligations to others outside the conjugal unit.

The preceding discussion also shows that an exchange relationship between males and females is instituted by the gendered division of labor. Moreover, the specific character of the division of labor shapes these exchange relations and delineates some of the principal contours of the conjugal relationship. The Kamula case illustrates a form of the division of labor characterized by a gender exclusive organization of major productive domains. This both lays the groundwork for and necessitates an exchange of gendered products between males and females. However, the division of labor does not itself stipulate the specific parties to such exchanges (and these may vary from case to case within this type). In the Kamula case, the parties to such exchanges need not be spouses, and the necessity to exchange with the opposite gender therefore provides no compelling economic inducement for either males or females to marry, stay married, or remarry, and positively facilitates the avoidance of conjugality. In addition, the gender-exclusive organization of major productive domains promotes same-sex bonding and camaraderie so that marriage unites individuals who largely move in separate worlds.

The Etoro case exemplifies a form of the division of labor characterized by male-female coproduction. This necessitates an exchange of labor between the genders and also promotes coconsumption by the male and female who make up a production team since their labor is intermingled in the final products of their joint effort. This is conducive to a comparatively long-term association between coproducers. (In contrast, a male-female exchange of the products of their separate labors does not intrinsically promote continued association after completion of the transaction.) The conjugal unit is particularly well suited to fulfilling the requirements of male-female coproduction because it provides each party with assured access to the labor of the opposite gender in a range of temporally integrated productive endeavors that constitute the subsistence economy. Although coproduction with an individual other than a spouse can be arranged, this particular form of the gendered division of labor does contain an economic inducement to marry in order to establish long-term assured access to the forms of labor provided by the opposite gender. This inducement weighs more heavily upon Etoro women than upon men insofar as the women do not consider themselves capable of performing the male task of forest clearance while the men consider themselves capable of the full range of tasks characteristically performed by women. Moreover, Etoro bachelors do not regard such labor as demeaning, as Collier supposes, but rather take pride in the display of self-sufficiency manifested by joining together in bachelor gardens.

A division of labor characterized by male-female coproduction also highlights the complementarity of male and female roles (in contrast to the potential oppositional properties of an exchange of the products of gender-exclusive labors). Within the context of the conjugal relationship, coproduction is conducive to an ethos emphasizing joint effort, shared endeavors, and common interests that contributes to conjugal solidarity. However, coproduction also creates the potentiality for one gender to deploy the products of joint conjugal labor in prestige-enhancing exchanges with other persons. In contrast, a gender-exclusive organization of productive domains precludes this form of appropriation of prestige values since both genders are transactors and the items distributed or exchanged embody only the labor of the transactor.

Having concluded that the division of labor in simple societies does not engender an exchange relation between husband and wife, Collier is led to focus her analytical attention elsewhere. She consequently fails to perceive that the division of labor is variable in form (as well as in content) and that these variations structure conjugal relationships in distinctive ways that have a direct bearing on the analysis of social inequality. The Etoro and Kamula illustrate two contrastive ideal types. However, there are many intermediate cases in which some products are coproduced and others are produced exclusively by each gender (as noted in chap. 1 with respect to the Strickland-Bosavi tribes as a group).

The brideservice model is based upon the contention that men are obligated to distribute game widely while women are only responsible for feeding their husband and children. I have argued that this represents a misreading of the data. Men have a dual responsibility, to their wives and families, on one hand, and to the larger residential group, on the other. This point can be further substantiated by consideration of the details of game distribution. These show that a man's dual obligations are sequentially discharged in distinct phases of the overall process.

Etoro conventions of game distribution vary in accordance with the size of the game animal and are also modified to some degree by whether the distribution takes place at the longhouse or at a garden house (compare Van Beek 1987:133–63).[1] The category of large game animals includes wild pigs and cassowaries; the category of small game animals includes mice, frogs, and other fauna of comparable or smaller size; and the category of medium-sized animals encompasses everything in between. Large game is always captured by men. The hunter or trapper is under a strong moral obligation to bring such game to the longhouse to be distributed among coresidents, so that there is only one legitimate context for distribution. The first stage of distribution begins with a subdivision of the animal into equivalent piles of meat, each of which contains portions of all the main components of the animal (e.g., flesh, fat, and organs). Each coresident male large-game procurer who is present at the longhouse at the time receives an equivalent share (cf. Dwyer 1990:121–39). The successful hunter's portion is the same as all the others except that he also retains some indivisible parts of the animal such as the head. This phase of the distribution is male-exclusive and is grounded in generalized reciprocity among the members of the community who comprise the "producers" of large game animals. Community member-ship rather than kin relation to the successful hunter thus guides this initial phase of distribution. The initial recipients of these equivalent shares are prototypically married men but also include bachelors who form a work group with a widow and are indistinguishable from married men in terms of game procurement.

The second phase of distribution takes place within the extended family group (and production team) that occupies one side of a hearth. Each man who received a pile of meat in the initial distribution shares this out among his wife and children and other attached individuals, such as an unmarried younger sibling or deceased brother's widow. Conjugal, parental, and sibling relations are thus the main focus of this second phase of game distribution (which occurs within production teams typically formed on the same basis). After the meal is underway, there is a third phase of sharing in which bite-sized morsels are given to others close at hand, especially members of the family occupying the opposite side of the hearth. These gifts and ex-changes thus largely take place between married siblings and affines (e.g., a man typically gives morsels to his brother, sister, sister's husband, wife's brother, niece, or nephew and a woman gives morsels to her brother, brother's wife, niece, or nephew). Bits of food may also be offered to extrafamilial kin and age-mates at adjacent hearths. While the second phase of distribution is governed by fulfillment of conjugal, parental, and sibling obligations, the third phase might best be described as affording an opportu-nity to express affection for a variety of coresident kin, affines, and age-mates.

The distribution of small game takes place within the family group. Husband and wife are about equally likely to have items to distribute and young children may also have something to contribute (e.g., the minnows caught by small boys). Children are typically favored in the distribution of these items because food taboos restrict their access to medium-sized ani-mals. Phase three distribution of morsels is more restricted than on other occasions since the quantity of food available is small.

The distribution of midsize animals is the most variable. Etoro food taboos are applicable to many midsize animals (while large and small game are subject to fewer restrictions). The potential consumers of any animal thus vary according to the taxa in question. The most heavily restricted individuals are widows, and deceased men's male and female children below the ages of 17 and 12, respectively. These are individuals who do not belong to a family group that contains a male producer who will redistribute game on other occasions, so that eventual fulfillment of generalized reciprocity cannot readily be envisioned. On the other hand, the individuals who are the main producers of midsize game are the least restricted. Moreover, restrictions decrease in accordance with increased productivity, so that married men can consume more taxa than unmarried young men (over 17), and the latter can consume more taxa than married women. Within this framework of food taboos, the operative guideline is that a portion given in primary distribution must be large enough for the recipient to subdivide it among the members of his extended family who are not prohibited from consuming it. A hunter thus assesses the potentiality to meet this requirement and decides whether to distribute his game among all resident hunters, in accordance with the pattern followed in large-game distribution, or to distribute only to some of these men. If the latter course of action is elected, the selection is made on a kinship basis that favors affines and siblings. In either case, secondary and tertiary distribution proceeds in routine fashion except that some members of the hearth group are likely to be prohibited from consuming a share. However, all but a few taxa can be shared with a spouse.

If an individual is currently residing at the longhouse rather than in a garden house, he should bring whatever midsize game he obtains to the longhouse to be distributed. However, an individual temporarily based at a garden house can legitimately share midsize game with those present at that dwelling. This will often include the affines and siblings who would be favored in a restricted longhouse distribution. In any event, the potential consumers will be sufficiently limited so that none need be excluded.

Both domesticated pig and the quantity of smoked forest mammals that are deployed in affinal gift exchange are given and subsequently shared out on a kinship basis (see Kelly 1977:220). The donor and recipient in the initial transaction are males, so that women receive meat from their husbands at a latter stage in the distributional process, as is the case in the game distributions already described. Domesticated pig that is not given in affinal exchange is distributed in essentially the same way as large game.

These data show that a man's obligation to share game widely is discharged in the first phase of distribution (of large and midsize game animals), while his obligation to his wife and children is discharged in the second phase (and in distribution of small game animals). A woman therefore does not receive game directly from a hunter, but from her husband. This has two critical consequences with respect to Collier's model. First, this mode of distribution clearly accommodates a direct exchange between husband and wife. A husband gives meat to his wife, and she gives starch staples to him. As often as not, the meat provided by the husband has not been produced by him, but has been given to him by another hunter to whom the husband has previously distributed game. However, the calculus of reciprocity applies only between direct recipients of game. The first phase of distribution thus entails reciprocity among game producers, while the second phase entails reciprocity between husband and wife. The wife therefore does not incur any obligation to provide starch staples (or sexual services) to the actual producer of the game. In effect, there are two separate spheres of exchange.

The second consequence of these data for Collier's model pertains to the asymmetry of male and female obligations. This asymmetry remains in that a man has a dual obligation while a woman's obligation is singular. However, Collier's (1988:17) deduction that "a woman does not have to have a husband to gain access to male produce" requires some modification. This statement is true in that an unmarried daughter will receive a share in secondary distribution from her father (or father's brother or elder brother if her father is deceased). A widow will likewise receive a share from the married man or bachelor to whose hearth group (and production team) she is attached, typically that of her deceased husband's brother. However, both a widow and the unmarried daughter of a deceased man are prohibited from consuming many taxa of game animals. These taboos are removed when a daughter reaches the traditional age of marriage and when a widow remarries. Although the transition is quantitatively less dramatic for other young women (with living fathers), married women can consume more taxa than single women so that access to meat increases with marriage. For a widow, remarriage greatly increases access to game animals (as edible taxa increase from 18 to 70).

Collier's first principle should thus be restated: a woman does not have to be married to gain access to a portion of male produce, but maximum access is only accorded to married women. Unmarried women thus incur relative deprivation, and there is consequently a significant economic inducement for them to marry (or remarry). This is enhanced by another feature of the distribution process. The first phase of distribution entails a division of the game into equivalent portions that are then given to other hunters. These portions therefore do not take into account the size of the hearth group that will receive shares of the meat during secondary distribution. If the group includes a widow or elder unmarried daughter, then everyone within it will receive less than they would if these women were married (and consequently members of another hearth group). A girl or widow who delays marriage therefore not only receives a smaller ration of whatever is being distributed, but also causes the close kin of her hearth group to receive reduced rations as well (unless the item falls under the food taboos noted above). An unmarried woman's knowledge that she is a burden to others may well provide a further inducement to marry.

The features of the Etoro game distribution system that restrict an unmarried woman's access to game are intelligible in terms of a basic principle applicable to all categories of persons. Those who contribute more in supplying game to the community are rewarded, through the system of food taboos, by superior access. Thus, women who contribute directly to the support of a primary producer of game through conjugal exchange gain enhanced access. Unremarried widows and elder unmarried daughters perform fewer hours of labor than married women in starch production when they are attached to a married man's hearth group (and production team) because the production of starch staples needed to provide a daily ration for the hunter is shared with the hunter's wife. The economic inducement to marry is thus at the same time an economic inducement to contribute as much labor to the provisioning of the community as the vast majority of mature women contribute (i.e., those who form part of a production team that includes only one adult male). A system founded on the principle of "from each according to his or her ability, to each according to his or her need" requires some inducement to ensure that the first half of the equation is fulfilled so that the second half can indeed be realized.

Many of the central features of Etoro game distribution are common to hunter-gatherers and hunter-horticulturalists more generally. In nearly all instances, the initial distribution of larger game entails a subdivision of the animal among individuals who are producers of such game, i.e., other hunters (see Testart 1987). Women generally do not receive until the second stage of distribution and are typically given meat by their husbands. In addition, smaller game animals are generally shared within family groups. These central features are present in the !Kung and Murngin cases cited by Collier and Rosaldo (1981:282) in the original formulation of the brideservice model. The Etoro therefore do not constitute a "not in my tribe" exception but rather illustrate general features of food distribution that show (1) dual male responsibility to both family and residential group and (2) a direct exchange of meat for starch staples between husbands and wives, since wives receive meat directly from their husbands rather than from other hunters.[2] This suggests that unmarried women are unfavorably situated with respect to the distribution process and that there is consequently an economic inducement for such women to marry (or remarry).

The Kamula constitute a partial exception to these generalizations in that the initial distribution of wild pig entails a subdivision into male and female shares (as described in chap. 2). The women then divide their share among themselves so that women do not receive pork directly from their husbands (although cooked portions are subsequently exchanged between husband and wife). It is not explained precisely how the women subdivide their share among themselves, but unmarried women do not appear to be unfavorably situated with respect to this type of distribution. However, the

Kamula are only a partial exception because the cautionary tale cited earlier makes it clear that a woman whose husband does not hunt will be deprived of cassowary and wallaby meat. This indicates that these animals are distributed in a different manner, evidently entailing provision directly from a husband (and thereby manifesting both direct exchange between spouses and dual male responsibility). In general, the ethnographic cases that deviate most markedly from the general features of game distribution outlined above are societies with uxorilocal residence patterns in which a man turns over his game to his wife who subsequently distributes it to other extended families. The Mundurucu (Murphy and Murphy 1980) and the Kayapó (Turner 1979) provide examples. But while these systems of game distribution differ, they nevertheless evidence direct exchange between husband and wife. Moreover, women gain direct access to male produce by marriage even though male produce is widely distributed. The fact that wives are the primary distributors of game also provides a different kind of economic inducement for women to marry.

The twin insights that underlie the brideservice model require substantial revision, necessitating revision of fundamental features of the model and undercutting its applicability as formulated. Although a woman only has to be a member of a social group in order to gain access to a portion of male produce, there are nevertheless a variety of inducements to marry. These include: (1) full access to male products and services, (2) avoidance of the social disapproval associated with being less fully productive than married women of the same age, (3) graduation to adult status, (4) acquisition of a *pater* or social father for whatever children she may bear (conferring upon them those aspects of social identity that derive from paternity), (5) paternal contributions to child rearing (cf. Collier 1988:35),[3] and (6) acquisition of the support a husband provides in situations of conflict stemming from allegations of supernatural attack. These inducements are commonplace in the societies to which the brideservice model might be applied.

In the Etoro case, and among hunter-horticulturalists generally, a woman typically needs a husband (or other male coproducer) in order to fell trees so that she can deploy her labor in swidden gardening. A division of labor entailing male-female coproduction provides an inducement to marry in order to establish assured access to the forms of labor provided by the opposite gender over the long term (and horticulture nearly always entails male-female coproduction). In an earlier critique of the applicability of the brideservice model to New Guinea societies, Whitehead (1987:255) also questions the validity of the postulated basic asymmetry between males and females in the need to marry. Women typically rely on male labor contributions in the production of starch staples in both horticulture and sago processing.

A woman who relied routinely upon the labor of a father or brother would certainly not starve; but she, like her bachelor counterpart, would be dependent upon the spouses of others for help that she would normally be expected to receive from a spouse of her own. In light of this state of affairs, the economic impulse toward marriage in New Guinea cannot be thought to arise solely in the hearts of young men. (Whitehead 1987:255)

Collier (1988:34) argues that "girls in brideservice societies want lovers, but not husbands; they want sex, not marriage." However sexually active girls soon become pregnant, engendering the inducements to marry associated with the acquisition of paternity that are included above. The Etoro data also indicate that widows employ sexuality in order to enhance the prospects of a union with a specific man, i.e., in an effort to gain some measure of control over their marital destiny. The material that Collier adduces to support her contention that women want sex rather than marriage is open to reinterpretation along these lines. Reports of young brides or brides-to-be running off with another man (Collier 1988:34) are more plausibly interpreted as an effort to control marital destiny than as reluctance to wed. Moreover, patterns of courtship that provide scope for sexual experimentation do not constitute evidence of a female reluctance to wed. When courtship takes this form, a girl's participation implies the opposite.

Collier's (1988:18) contention that divorce is typically "both easy and common" in brideservice societies also requires some qualification. What appears to be fairly common is that women elope with a man of their own choice rather than accepting an arranged union (see, for example, Elkin 1964:132). This pattern also indicates that women seek to exercise control over their marital destiny and does not lend support to Collier's view that women prefer an unmarried to a married state. The end result is always marriage. Moreover, marriages are generally very durable once established. Divorce rates calculated by standard measures tend, on average, to be much lower among societies that would fall into Collier's brideservice category than among those encompassed by her equal bridewealth category. Among the Etoro, 91.3 percent of women's first marriages are terminated by the death of one of the parties to the union, while only 8.7 percent are terminated by divorce (Kelly 1977:259). Mitchell (1967:23) provides a sample of the range of divorce rates in societies where bridewealth is predominantly derived from individuals other than the groom. The lowest divorce rate is 32.6 percent, and the median for 11 cases is 55.8 percent (calculated in the same manner as the Etoro figure of 8.7 percent, i.e., as the total number of marriages dissolved by divorce divided by the total number dissolved by both death and divorce). Although a systematic comparison is beyond the scope of this book, a preliminary survey indicates this would show (1) that women in brideservice societies are much more likely to avoid an arranged marriage by eloping with someone else and (2) the median divorce rate in bridewealth societies is at least twice and perhaps three times as great as that in brideservice societies.

When Collier argues that young women in brideservice societies want sex rather than marriage, she also takes the position that male "sexual services" are readily available outside of marriage (Collier 1988:16). This creates a logical inconsistency in Collier's formulation, since bachelors are portrayed as wanting wives, who will feed them, rather than lovers. While the sexual behavior of young women is attributed to interests derived from their structural position within a specific socioeconomic configuration, the sexual behavior of bachelors is not correspondingly explained in terms of these considerations. What then accounts for the bachelors' sexual availability? The answer seems to be that Collier implicitly adopts an essentialist position with respect to male sexuality: male sexual availability is a biological given that can be taken for granted and need not be explained.

The Etoro case provides an instructive counterexample as it clearly illustrates the point that male sexuality is culturally constructed. The idealization of premarital male virginity with respect to heterosexual relations described in earlier chapters restricts the sexual availability of bachelors even though this ideal is imperfectly realized among older bachelors (as in parallel cases where an idealized premarital female virginity is imperfectly realized). In other ethnographic instances, an extended period of male seclusion during or prior to male initiation also operates to effectively isolate bachelors and preclude involvement in sexual liaisons (cf. Whitehead 1987:244–45). This reinforces the earlier point that premarital sexual relations, when present, are characteristically a component of culturally constituted systems of courtship. Both young men and young women participate as part of a process leading to marriage. The sexual availability of bachelors is intelligible from this perspective without reliance on essentialist assumptions regarding male sexuality.

Collier's interpretation of the significance of marriage for men is centrally grounded in economic considerations. The acquisition of a wife allows a man "to eat regularly without demeaning himself" (Collier 1988:17). Insofar as a wife provides for her husband's needs, he is able "to become a political actor—an initiator of relationships through generosity" (Collier 1988:22). He can offer food and hospitality to others and "distribute meat widely without having to ask for anything in return" (ibid.). Marriage thus marks a major transition for a man and forms the axis of a central inequality between bachelors and married men.

The economic underpinnings of this argument are not borne out by the cases at hand. We have seen that in both of the two types of division of labor represented by the Etoro and Kamula, respectively, social substitutability enables bachelors to eat as well as married men, without demeaning themselves either by requests for food or by the performance of tasks regarded as unmanly. An Etoro bachelor can readily form a production team with a widow to effect an exchange of male for female labor, and a Kamula bachelor can engage in the exchange of gendered products with a mother, sister, or widowed kinswoman. Neither is impelled to marry in order to gain an otherwise-unobtainable privileged access to the foods derived from female labor. In addition, the performance of subsistence tasks normally carried out by women is not considered unmanly or demeaning in the Etoro case because masculinity is not defined in terms of gendered capabilities grounded in a task-exclusive division of labor. On the contrary, the self-sufficiency of bachelors is celebrated and is a central component of male initiation. The self-sufficiency that bachelors demonstrate during their residence at the seclusion lodge marks a transition from dependent childhood to responsible adulthood, so that each initiate emerges as a man among men. This critical transition in the male life cycle occurs at initiation rather than at marriage (which takes place some years later). The initiated bachelor's role in both reproduction and production is transformed: he becomes a donor rather than a recipient of life force and is also expected to expend the masculine energy he has acquired in contributing substantially to communal production by assisting his kinsmen in felling trees. Although young men hunt less often (and less productively) than senior men, their labor expenditure in subsistence is otherwise comparable.

Although the Etoro cosmological system that comprehends reproduction, the spiritual constitution of persons, and life-cycle transformations is a culturally specific formulation, the central features of Etoro male initiation noted above are similar in key respects to those Collier attributes to male initiation in brideservice societies generally.

> When these people [in brideservice societies] talk about male prowess, they appear to emphasize its acquisition. In male initiation rituals, youths *acquire* the qualities or marks that make them adult men. They are not portrayed as having to shed childish or feminine qualities. Nor are they portrayed as needing help from others to acquire male prowess. (Collier 1988:61, emphasis in original)

The Etoro are at variance with this characterization in that male maturation is brought about by the transmission of semen and life force and by the provision of growth-inducing game, all of these being provided by older men. However, this largely occurs prior to initiation, which entails termination of this earlier dependency. As noted in chapter 3, the final completion of manhood achieved during male seclusion is an act of self-creation by the unmarried young men (as a group) that reorders their prior dependence on their fathers and other senior men and asserts self-sufficiency and independence. In addition, the initiates are not purged of female substance or female qualities because they have already been masculinized; the maternal contribution to their physical and spiritual constitution is thus minimal at this point. The fact that the Etoro conform to Collier's characterization of male initiation in brideservice societies in these respects is significant because it shows that the Etoro are not a unique exception but rather a representative case to which the brideservice model should be applicable if valid. If initiation rather than marriage marks the critical transition in the male life cycle among the Etoro, and Etoro initiation conforms to Collier's general characterization, then this calls into question the explanatory priority accorded to marriage in other cases. If marked social inequality pertains to the relation between uninitiated boys and initiated men, then the initiatory complex and associated cosmology is itself a primary and independent locus for the production of inequality. This reduces the significance accorded to marriage as the central axis of inequality. At issue here is the central claim that marriage totalistically organizes inequality.

The Etoro male's life cycle is partitioned into a series of life stages that are defined by a man's position within the encompassing system of life-force transmission. In all, there are eight socially differentiated life stages (i.e., child, pre-initiate aged 10–16, young men aged 17–21 who are eligible for initiation, initiated bachelors aged 22–26, recently married men aged 27–31, older married men with children aged 32–45, men aged 46–60 with grown children, and elderly men over age 61). Marriage defines the point of transition into only one of these life stages and consequently accounts for only a fraction of the scheme of social differentiation among males. When one examines the covariation between socially differentiated categories, on one hand, and moral evaluation, prestige, disability, and prerogative, on the other hand, marriage does not emerge as a significant axis of social inequality. Initiation marks the first critical transition in a male's social position since it conveys eligibility for spirit mediumship as well as the transformation of a young man's role with respect to both production and reproduction (noted earlier). It also marks the point at which a young man begins to participate in trade and thus acquires valuables that are deployed in social transactions. The second critical transition occurs when a man becomes eligible to be a *tafidilo* (in his early to middle 40s) and enters a category virtually immune to witchcraft accusations. The middle category (in between uninitiated adolescent males and elders) includes both bachelors and married men, but these subclasses are not distinguished in terms of prestige, prerogatives, and disabilities in a way that distinctly favors married men. First, the bachelors have all the prerogatives of initiated men enumerated above. Second, they occupy a privileged place in the men's section of the longhouse and also enact the prestigious role of solo dancers in the *kosa* ceremony. Third, the sacred and virginal bachelors are repositories of male life force and vitality and represent the acme of the male life cycle in this respect. Fourth, they are the only males besides the senior men over 45 who are favored by a neutral or disproportionately low frequency of witchcraft accusations. In contrast, the principal advantages that accrue to married men center on the married state itself. In other words, marriage does not carry with it a bundle of subsidiary prerogatives that accrue to a man, by virtue of this transition in social status. Instead it represents a distinct comedown in several significant respects.

Why do men seek to marry? The first important point to note is that young men typically do not take any initiative whatsoever in bringing about their own marriages (cf. Whitehead 1987:254). A young man is betrothed to the sister (or "sister") of the pre-initiate he is charged with inseminating. After the betrothal is established, the prospective husband waits passively until his bride-to-be comes of age. It is frequently a long wait and, in the later stages, an older bachelor will almost invariably be subject to the temptation to succumb to the advances of a young widow. In this situation as well, the bachelor is characteristically a relatively passive responder and does not take the initiative. Moreover, a bachelor who forms a sexual liaison with a widow often does not seek to marry her but rather attempts to maintain his forthcoming arranged union with a younger girl (which will be broken off should he marry the widow). If discovery and public disapproval force a choice (as in Nogobe's case), the bachelor may well dissolve the sexual relation with the widow in order to preserve his betrothal. If the widow becomes pregnant (as in Hariako's case), the bachelor usually will be unable to avoid marrying her. However, Nogobe's case is especially instructive with respect to the issues at hand because it shows that the extension of bachelorhood is preferable to the married state. Nogobe's betrothed was only eight years old at the time his relation with the widow Iwame became an issue, so that his choice entailed remaining unmarried for another eight years (by which time he would be 32). The first part of the answer to the question posed above is thus that bachelors do not seek to marry, in the sense of taking any initiative, and that they are also in no rush to wed. The bachelor posited by Collier's model—one impelled into action leading to marriage by his desperate need for a status-enhancing wife—is clearly absent in this case.

However, bachelors do marry eventually, and there are a number of inducements to do so. These are similar to the inducements applicable to young women. They include: (1) the advantages of long-term assured access to the female labor required for coproduction, (2) full access to female labor, services, and products in areas outside of regular subsistence food production (including net bags, sago for trade utilization, etc.), (3) graduation to a status that is a precondition for later advancement to the prestigious position of *tafidilo,* (4) establishment of the precondition for having socially recognized offspring, (5) gaining maternal contributions to childbearing and child rearing, and (6) acquisition of affines who can be counted upon to provide support in situations of conflict. Although marriage does not constitute a major economic transition that enables a man to become a political actor in ways that were not previously open to him, it nevertheless offers many other advantages. The most important of these center upon having children. And children do eventually enable a man to enter into certain spheres of political action that are otherwise foreclosed, since a man will subsequently engage in arranging the marriages of his son and daughter and designating his son's inseminator. The role that senior men play in arranging marriages both contributes to and is facilitated by the passivity of the bachelors with regard to this arena of social practice (as will be elucidated further along).

The life cycle of Etoro females is partitioned into a number of life stages that are largely defined in terms of reproduction. A girl's attainment of reproductive and productive maturity is celebrated in a ceremony (described in chap. 3) that can be characterized as a puberty rite. This occurs when a girl's breasts have become rounded, at about age 16. Although a marriage ceremony typically has already occurred before this time, sexual relations with a husband are only initiated after maturation is publicly acknowledged. The puberty ceremony thus leads to establishment of a conjugal relation that is complete in all respects. The prior marriage ceremony precludes any possibility of premarital sexual relations because a girl already has a husband before she is sexually mature. As a consequence of this arrangement, the transition to adult status occurs at the time the conjugal relation is fully established rather than at the time the marriage is celebrated. There is thus a parallel between males and females in that transition to adult status is effected by a ceremony that marks the completion of maturation. Marriage occurs prior to this transition in the case of females and some years afterward in the case of males, and consequently is not the central organizing principle of intragender social differentiation in either case.

The female transition to adult status does not confer the same advantages that are enjoyed by adult (initiated) males. A woman does not become a full jural adult with respect to the domain of witchcraft accusations and the deployment of valuables in social payments, nor does she become eligible for spirit mediumship. In other respects, there are parallel changes. A woman is entitled to speak in public community discussions (although unlikely to do so until she is older) and takes on new ceremonial roles (as in performance of the opening dances of the *kosa* ceremony). Like her adult (initiated) male counterpart, she now contributes fully to subsistence food production and is a core member of a conjugally based hearth group and production team. And like her male counterpart, she has embarked on a new reproductive role. However, the initial consequences of this are decidedly negative as a young woman becomes a sexually active female who has not yet borne a child and thus is included in a category of persons subject to a disproportionately high frequency of witchcraft accusations. In contrast, young men who have just made the transition to adult status are favored by a reduced frequency of accusations. There are thus a number of gender inequalities that emerge at entry into adulthood. However, none of these is organized by marriage as Collier's formulation supposes. They are attributable to the cosmological system and to the fact that situations of conflict with a potentiality for violence have the effect of conferring jural prerogatives on males. If a woman did not marry, she would not elude any of these inequalities. Moreover, marriage confers a number of advantages described earlier in terms of the inducements to wed. Becoming unmarried, either as a result of divorce or widowhood entails a decline in a woman's status accompanied by social disabilities. Although the attendant inequalities are delineated in relation to marriage, it is unmarried rather than married women who are disadvantaged. This too is contrary to what Collier's formulation would lead one to expect.

The brideservice model is grounded in the proposition that marriage organizes inequality insofar as it confers burdens on women and privileges upon men. A woman is subject to additional work after marriage due to her responsibility for provisioning her husband, while a man reaps the benefits of this, and is enabled to join the ranks of political actors, but does not incur increased obligations and a concomitant increase in demands on his labor. This characterization of the differential consequences of marriage upon male and female labor expenditure is consistent with the ethnographic data on brideservice societies in certain respects. However, the asymmetry that Collier identifies turns on the differential age of marriage for males and females and the differential relation of age at marriage to the age of transition to an adult level of labor expenditure. Marriage per se does not engender this asymmetry, and it would not obtain if young men and women both married at the age at which they made a transition to full production.

The significance of the relation between differential age at marriage and transition to adult production levels can be illustrated by the Etoro case, although the point is applicable to brideservice societies generally. An unmarried girl does not contribute fully to subsistence food production. Her underproduction is made possible by the fact that her mother's labor provides the bulk of the starch staples that support the hearth group's game producer. However, an unmarried girl is not yet mature and so less is expected of her. At the time she becomes capable of an adult level of labor inputs, her maturity is publicly celebrated and she enters into a fully established conjugal relation. Marriage, in this operational sense, thus covaries with the attainment of full production. In contrast, a bachelor will have already assumed an adult level of labor inputs well before he marries. A newly married man does not experience significantly increased demands on his labor because his labor expenditure as an initiated bachelor is already comparable to that of a married man. The asymmetry that Collier points to thus turns on the differential age of marriage for males and females and the fact that marriage corresponds to the age of transition to an adult level of production for women but not for men. There is an inevitable transition from partial to full labor contributions for both genders, but this does not covary with the establishment of a conjugal relationship in both instances. If it did covary for males as well as females, this would lead to substantially reduced labor inputs on the part of bachelors. In other words, linking male maturation to initiation rather than to marriage has the effect of requiring initiated bachelors to assume adult responsibilities in production at a much earlier age than would otherwise be the case. This precludes a situation where bachelors would be subsidized by the labor of their fathers or elder brothers at a time when they were fully capable of an adult workload.

It is evident that these features of the Etoro case account for the asymmetry that Collier identifies as a general characteristic of brideservice societies. If a man does not incur any increased obligations at marriage that entail increased demands on his labor, then he must already be fulfilling his responsibility to distribute game widely. This in turn indicates that the transition to adult labor inputs occurs prior to marriage and, as a result, does not covary with it. If a woman experiences a significant increase in demands on her labor at marriage, then she must have been underproducing relative to the standard for adult females prior to this time. Her underproduction is subsidized by the labor of others, including both the labor of the hunters who provide the widely shared game she consumes and the labor of other women whose starch staple production supports male hunting efforts. Marriage covaries with the transition to an adult level of labor inputs that eliminates this subsidy.

The orienting proposition that marriage organizes inequality collapses analytically pertinent distinctions and lumps together a number of independently variable causal factors as a single variable assessed in terms of presence or absence (i.e., married versus unmarried). The asymmetry that Collier identifies is not engendered by marriage but by the differential age of marriage for males and females and the differential relation of age at marriage to age at transition to full production. The asymmetry will thus be found only in those ethnographic cases in which men assume an adult workload prior to marriage while women do not. Since marriage per se is not the causal factor that accounts for an unaltered workload for men and an increased workload for women, marriage does not organize the gender inequality identified as rooted in this economic disparity (and in the privileges and burdens derived from it). The guiding assumption that marriage is the preeminent locus for the production of inequality is thus once again called into question.

There is a potential economic inequality between the genders that arises with respect to the transition to an adult level of labor inputs. If females make this transition at an earlier age than males, then they will expend more labor over the course of a working lifetime than males, assuming equal labor inputs per gender per year. This can be most readily illustrated by an example. If females work 20 hours a week from age 16 to 60, and males work only 10 hours a week from age 16 through 19 and 20 hours a week from age 20 to 60, then the total hours worked by women over the course of a productive lifetime would be 4.7 percent (2,080/44,720) greater than the total worked by men. A differential age of transition to an adult level of labor inputs thus has the effect of increasing the total labor that women expend and constitutes a source of economic inequality (other things being equal).

In the Etoro case, females assume an adult workload earlier than males, but this does not offset the greater number of hours males work per week over a lifetime. A girl works half as many hours as an adult woman at age 13 and gradually progresses to a full workload by age 16. A boy works half as many hours as a man at age 15 and gradually progresses to a full workload at age 19. However, males work 20.5 percent more hours over the course of a lifetime despite the delayed transition to an adult level of labor inputs. In addition, males substantially outnumber females in the age structure of the population (Kelly 1977:29), so that males constitute 53.6 percent of the labor force even though females make the transition to an adult level of labor expenditure at an earlier age. If one were to calculate the amount of labor expended by males and females as groups, rather than as individuals, the results would show an even greater disproportion in the male labor contribution than that documented in chapter 2. Specifically, the male labor contribution would be increased from 55.8 percent (per person) to 59.3 percent (for males as a group).

These demographic factors are pertinent insofar as they suggest an explanation for the earlier age at which females make the transition to an adult level of labor inputs. There is a comparative shortage of adult female workers, and this adds to the workload of those that are available. Under these circumstances, adult women as a group benefit from the expansion of their ranks that is effected by recruiting girls into the labor force at a comparatively early age because the labor of these girls is directly substitutable for their own. Males characteristically outnumber females in premodern tribal societies so that the demographic factors conducive to this outcome are typically present. Moreover, girls usually accompany their mothers and are encouraged by them to contribute to the work at hand.

It is important to note that the proportional labor contributions of men and women that obtain among the Etoro are comparable to those found in a range of societies where hunting is a major component of subsistence food production. When measured in terms of output, female contributions to subsistence food production exceed male contributions in 79 percent of a sample of societies in which gathering is the primary subsistence technique and in 13 percent (2/16) of a sample of societies in which hunting is the primary technique (Schlegel and Barry 1986:144). However, labor inputs reveal a very different pattern because hunting is typically a much less efficient form of food production than gathering. Although the literature does not contain an assemblage of comparative data analogous to that noted above with respect to outputs, the preponderant majority of reported cases show that male labor inputs are either equal to or greater than female labor inputs.[4] In other words, men typically devote a greater number of hours to subsistence food production than women in brideservice societies. This is directly related to the prestige systems that are characteristic of these societies, as will be explained in the second half of the chapter.

The point of departure in the development of the brideservice model is an examination of the "social relations of the sexes in the process of production" (Collier and Rosaldo 1981:279). There is a basic asymmetry, an "imbalance in the nature and organization of obligations and the availability of public reward" (ibid.), that is grounded in productive relations. This asymmetry is seen to be organized by marriage, which "binds specific people together in a particular, hierarchical system of obligations, requiring that women provide services for husbands, young grooms enjoy privileges not available to bachelors, and husbands owe gifts and labor to wives' senior kin" (ibid.:285). Marriage thus engenders fundamental social inequalities between males and females, and between junior and senior males, thereby constituting a system of relations to which other aspects of inequality that obtain in brideservice societies can be related. Marriage is central to this formulation in that it is seen to obligate women to provision their husbands while obligating husbands to "distribute produce to senior in-laws, so as to win support and commitment from those who most influence their wives" (ibid.:285). The line of reasoning here could be more precisely specified by saying that marriage organizes distribution of the products of labor (through obligations) and that distribution impinges on the process of production in the sense of determining who produces for whom.

Production and distribution are not clearly distinguished in the model, and this obscures the fact that production is organized by a gendered division of labor that has a decisive effect on economic relations between males and females generally, including the parties to a conjugal relationship. The division of labor sets the stage for distribution by determining who produces what and with whom, and consequently delineates the holders of both products and distributional rights. In brideservice societies, the producer generally has distributional rights over the products of his or her own labor (Collier 1988:30). However, the identity of the "producer" is subject to culturally variable definitions, so that some individuals who contributed labor to the production process may fall outside this designation. The products available for distribution to others are also differentially valued by the specific cultural system in place. The division of labor therefore indirectly allocates distributional rights over prized and mundane products to different categories of persons.

The framework advocated here differs from that proposed by Collier and Rosaldo in directing greater attention to the processes of production that take place prior to distribution. Such scrutiny reveals the significance of the division of labor and of cosmological systems that define "producers" and differentially valorize their products and their labor. Inasmuch as the division of labor embodies a morally evaluated scheme of social differentiation, social inequality is already established prior to distribution and cannot be adequately accounted for by distributional obligations organized by marriage.

Collier and Rosaldo see women as disadvantaged with respect to the availability of public rewards as a consequence of their obligations to provision their husbands, while men are correspondingly advantaged by this provisioning. However, when one examines the prestige derived from generosity in the distribution of game, it is evident that women are disadvantaged by a division of labor ensuring that they are not the principal producers of distributable game and therefore have very limited access to the public rewards derived from game distribution. Conjugal obligations are not a decisive factor because single and widowed women—who have no such obligations—are in exactly the same disadvantaged position as married women. A cosmological system that accords special value to game and to hunting also impinges equally on married and unmarried women. This is equally true of a prestige system that enshrines generosity as a virtue. The consequences of this definition also take effect through the division of labor. In most hunting and gathering economies, hunting produces sporadic surpluses beyond the subsistence needs of the successful hunter and his family and thus provides the wherewithal for distribution to all group members. In contrast, gathering rarely yields windfalls, and a woman typically would be unable to generate a surplus of sufficient scale to distribute to all group members.[5] The division of labor thus severely limits a woman's capacity to display generosity in the distribution of her products. Conjugal obligations are not decisive in this instance as well, because the quantity of food an unmarried woman has available as a result of having no husband to provision will only feed one person and provides no scope for lavish generosity. Giving to some but not everyone carries the risk of generating resentment in some quarters at the same time one earns praise in others. A variety of factors thus conspire to overdetermine women's inferior access to public rewards, but conjugal obligations are not prominent among these and play a minor role at most.

In evaluating the availability of public rewards, Collier and Rosaldo do not focus on the contrast between single and married women but on that between bachelors and married men. They maintain that married men are subsidized by the provisions supplied by their wives and can thus focus their energies on prestige-enhancing activities. There are several difficulties with this line of reasoning. We have already seen that the brideservice model proposes that a man's workload is not increased by conjugal obligations and that this can only be the case if he has already assumed an adult level of labor inputs prior to marriage. If men's work consists of hunting, then a bachelor must hunt as much as a married man, and would consequently be expected to have as much to distribute, yet the latter is provisioned by a wife and the former is not. This constitutes a logical contradiction in the model as formulated. The Etoro and Kamula cases show that social substitutability in the exchange of labor, or of gendered products, enables bachelors to deploy their labor in much the same way as married men. Thus conjugal provisioning does not provide married men with superior access to the prestige derived from game distribution. Moreover, young married men are provisioned to the same extent as older married men but devote fewer hours to hunting, on average (and produce less game per hour) in the Etoro case. The presence or absence of a wife therefore does not account for these variations in the hunting efforts of married men of different ages.[6] Hunting success in terms of returns per hour improves with experience, and increased returns encourage men to progressively devote more hours to hunting as they gain experience with age. The cosmological system also imbues an older man with a self-image of self-sacrificing generosity that he seeks to fulfill through game distribution. While individuals do vary in the effort they devote to prestige-enhancing activities, these variations are not explained by marital status and therefore are not attributable to the presence or absence of wifely provisioning.

As was noted earlier, the brideservice model is grounded in the proposition that marriage organizes the distribution of the products of labor through conjugal and affinal obligations. Thus far, I have focused on a married woman's obligation to provision her husband with starch staples. Other aspects of distribution and the role of marriage in organizing them remain to be considered. Although Collier and Rosaldo see marriage as obligating women to feed their families, marriage does not appear to initiate a woman's obligation to feed her children since mothers do not withhold food from children born out of wedlock. In other words, this obligation is parental, not marital. The model does not propose that marriage obligates a man to provide food for his wife but rather focuses on a man's unchanged obligation to distribute game widely. However, insofar as a man has a dual obligation to both his family and the local group, this view requires modification. Marriage requires a man to share certain types of smaller game animals, and the portions of larger game animals he receives from other hunters, with his wife and children. If distributing large game to other hunters eventuates in equal returns at a later date, then conjugal obligations can be considered to be entirely symmetrical in terms of consumption values. A wife provides starch staples for her husband, and he reciprocally gives her meat. She benefits from his productive efforts to the same extent that he benefits from hers, in terms of consumption values, even though the meat he provides sometimes comes to him from other hunters to whom he has previously given shares of his bag.

The asymmetry in the exchange relationship between husband and wife turns on the fact that a husband's efforts generate prestige values and exchange values that he retains. A husband thus derives full benefit from his wife's labor, while she does not derive full benefit from his. Women's work and women's products have little potential to generate prestige values and exchange values, so that the asymmetry does not stem from an unequal exchange. A husband does not fail to reciprocate the consumption values he receives but only retains other values generated by his labor that are not equally generated by that of his wife. This analysis, which will be developed more fully in due course, is grounded in consideration of the role of the prestige system and the division of labor in defining the terms of exchange between males and females who exchange their labor or the products of their labor (including the parties to a conjugal relationship).

A man's obligation to distribute game widely is intrinsically extramarital and extends well beyond the scope of affinal relations as well. This obligation, which crucially shapes the distributional system, is neither directly nor indirectly organized by marriage. It is an ethnographically derived "given" in the brideservice model and takes on the character of a prime mover in that it generates the foundational asymmetry. Collier and Rosaldo recognize that the extrafamilial distribution of game enables men to gain prestige, but they do not develop the theoretical significance of this. This significance resides in the fact that the prestige system (and not marriage) organizes the initial distribution of the products of male labor. The central obligation of the distributional system originates in the prestige system. Moreover, the obligation to distribute meat widely is not commensurate with other obligations of a kinship order, because fulfillment of it generates prestige whereas fulfillment of kinship obligations is laudable but not prestigious. This is attributable to cultural conceptions that accord prestige to generosity, and to cultural definitions of generosity. This is well illustrated by the Etoro case in which generosity is defined in terms of (1) the creation of exchange value through sharing, (2) the realization of community through an encompassing distribution of exchange value, and (3) the concomitant generation of spiritual values that arise out of this realization of community. Under the terms of this cultural definition, provisioning a spouse and children does not qualify as generosity and therefore is not productive of prestige. The critical point here is that the asymmetry Collier and Rosaldo identify is grounded in the prestige system. The prestige system both organizes a man's distributional obligations and imbues them with a character that a woman's obligations lack. Although the requirement to distribute game widely is an obligation in one sense, it is clearly a prerogative in another. It affords an opportunity to earn prestige.

It is also important to recall that the obligation to distribute game widely is specifically linked to particular types of game (e.g., large game and midsize game procured in quantity). Strictly speaking, this obligation thus pertains to the game men routinely procure (in accordance with the division of labor) rather than to men per se. In the event that women procure the relevant types of game, they are expected to distribute these widely as well and are subject to negative evaluation if they fail to do so. This linkage of distributional obligation to types of game is a corollary of the prestige-based organization of large-game distribution. Moreover, this linkage ensures that the prestige system provides a universal metric of evaluation applicable to both men and women (i.e., generosity) and thus does not constitute a "*male* prestige system,*" although the division of labor ensures that men are in a favorable position to earn prestige while women are not. Women are not conceptually external to the prestige system but rather constitute a comparative counterpoint that highlights and naturalizes male prestige attainment. (See the critical evaluation of the concept of a "male prestige system" in chap. 2 for further discussion of the points summarized here.)

The concept of gendered obligations—of wife to family and husband to group—employed by Collier and Rosaldo (1981) and Collier (1988) is implicitly grounded in a flawed domestic domain/public domain distinction, and the concept of a "male prestige system" logically follows from this. This in turn implies that the cultural values that enshrine generosity as a virtue are gendered as well, leading to a false "two cultures" problem (since generosity is esteemed by both genders). The concept of gendered obligations also entails misplaced causality in that it obscures both the prestige-based organization of large-game distribution and the basic mechanism that eventuates in unequal rewards (in the form of the male attainment of prestige through generosity), namely the division of labor. Moreover, it is the substitution of (domain-based) gendered obligations for conjugal obligations and the gendered division of labor that leads to the conceptual tangles noted above. The concepts of conjugal obligation and a gendered division of labor lack the totalizing characteristics of the domestic domain/public domain distinction, and these concepts thus do not spawn the conceptual difficulties that eventuate in the "two cultures" dilemma. (See also Yanagisako and Collier's 1987:28–29 criticism of the domestic/public distinction.)

Obligations to senior in-laws remain to be discussed. In the brideservice model, marriage is seen to organize distribution of the products of labor not only by obligating women to provision their husbands but also by obligating men to distribute to the parents of their wives (or of their brides-to-be). Collier and Rosaldo (1981:285) argue that the latter pattern of distribution is motivated by a young man's pressing need for a wife in a context where eligible young women do not envision themselves as needing husbands.

> Marriage is cast, overwhelmingly, as a matter of a man's establishing claims to the moral commitment and daily services of some particular bride. Furthermore, men establish these claims, not by providing for wives and children, but, rather, by distributing produce to senior in-laws, so as to win support and commitment from those who most influence wives. (Collier and Rosaldo 1981:285)

As a result of this, parents-in-law gain "privileged access" to the products of hunting (ibid.:282) and

> a man's dependence on in-laws for help in controlling his bride combines with rules of meat distribution that consistently favor seniors to create a situation in which parents-in-law have first rights to the labor and products of young married men. (ibid.:285)

There are a number of difficulties with this formulation that pertain to the concepts of "privileged access" and "first rights." These arise out of (1) consideration of the relationship between a man's obligation to distribute meat widely and his obligation to distribute to parents-in-law, and (2) consideration of the consequences of reciprocity. If a successful hunter distributes game to all other coresident hunters in primary distribution, then a coresident father-in-law would receive a share in any event. Moreover, if the portions are equivalent, there is no potentiality for "privileged access." The Etoro fit these specifications with respect to large game animals. In the distribution of midsize game, affines and siblings are favored over other coresidents. However, the access of the former is no more privileged than that of the latter. Among the Kamula, a hunter gives his wife's parents "the flesh from the backside of any pig he shoots . . . and the flesh from between the legs of any cassowary shot." (Wood 1982:112) However, inasmuch as these large game animals are distributed to all coresidents, it is not clear what is "materially gained" by being affinally related to a successful hunter (ibid.:113). The specific portions allotted to the wife's parents are symbolically appropriate given their status as wife-givers. They are not the "best parts" (Collier 1988:25) but the symbolically appropriate ones. The concept of "privileged access" can thus be called into question on the grounds that the portions distributed to in-laws are neither larger nor better than those distributed to other coresidents.

Although this aspect of Kamula game distribution affirms affinal relations and distinguishes them from other kin relations, there is no reason to infer that it induces a girl's parents to bring their influence to bear upon her in order to deter her from leaving her husband. Moreover, a girl's parents would receive the same portions if she abandoned her husband for another man. Here, as elsewhere, social substitutability undercuts the argument. There is no scope for manipulation. Moreover, there is no evidence for either the manipulative motives attributed to husbands or the manipulability attributed to wife's parents.[7]

In the Etoro case, affinal exchange is reciprocal. Sides of domesticated pork or smoked forest mammals are given to wife's father, wife's brother, and other relatives by marriage but are subsequently reciprocated by the recipients. A hunter distributes midsize game to affines and siblings but likewise receives distributions from them on other occasions. A wife's father thus has no more privileged access to these products than a daughter's husband.

The evidence for maritally organized hierarchy would appear to be on firmer ground in those ethnographic cases in which a young man is obliged to perform labor for his in-laws before and/or after marriage. However, reciprocity casts such obligations in a somewhat different light. Among the Kamula,

> the relation between a DH and WF is often close—as one man put it in reference to his DH, "my *doko:* he is like my younger brother." Ideally, the WF and DH relationship implies close co-operation and co-residence. A DH may come to live around the fireplace that is adjacent to his wife's parents fireplace. A DH assists his WF in such things as house building, canoe making, gardening and hunting for his WF's minor feasts, e.g., when his WF requires pig meat to feed those who help pull his canoe out of the bush. While a WB may reciprocate his ZH's efforts in these activities, a WF does not always reciprocate to his DH depending on his age and general well-being. (Wood 1982:112)

These data suggest that the wife's father–daughter's husband relationship entails reciprocal obligations of mutual aid that are governed by the principle, "from each according to his ability, to each according to his need." Empirical asymmetries arise in the WF-DH relationship—but not the WB-ZH relationship—since senior affines are likely to have both greater needs for assistance and reduced capabilities. Senior affines may consequently gain material benefits from their daughter's marriage. However, a wife's father's affinal claim to a daughter's husband's labor is not more privileged than the reciprocal claim. Moreover, a daughter's husband who requires assistance that his wife's father is unable to provide may call upon his wife's brother, so that reciprocity between affines obtains in practice as well as in claims. This is at variance with the orienting proposition of the brideservice model, namely that marriage "binds specific people together in a particular, hierarchical system of obligations" (Collier and Rosaldo 1981:285), since the obligations arising from marriage are reciprocal rather than hierarchical.[8]

Among the Etoro, a young man typically coresides with his wife's parents after he takes up residence with his wife (following the puberty rite described earlier). The married couple will generally garden with the wife's parents. This benefits the latter in terms of labor expenditure if they have other children that are not yet old enough to assume an adult workload. The benefit accrues from the way in which cooperative labor is organized. The mother and daughter will jointly clear both garden plots while the father and son-in-law jointly fell trees and fence the garden. All will participate in weeding, with the women performing two-thirds of this work. Since the parents have additional dependents, their plot will be larger than that of the daughter and son-in-law. The daughter and son-in-law will thus have helped to prepare a larger area in exchange for help in clearing a smaller one. All such cooperative labor exchanges transfer labor from those with few or no children to those with several or more. An ideology emphasizing reciprocity, mutuality, cooperation, and joint effort thus eventuates in a somewhat unequal exchange of labor that yields material benefits for the parental generation. However, a son-in-law's labor is not diverted from the support of his wife as Collier and Rosaldo suppose. The diversion is from his own parents (and/or other senior kin that he would have assisted as a bachelor) to his wife's parents. The exchange of labor between husband and wife is not modified in the posited manner so that a wife produces for her husband while he produces for her parents. Thus, marital obligations do not organize either production or distribution into a hierarchical system and thereby engender social inequality. The labor transfer is attributable to the organization of cooperative labor (rather than marital obligations) and is equally applicable to young men both before and after marriage. It is also equally applicable to a recently married woman insofar as her labor expenditure would be reduced if she and her husband moved away so that she no longer helped her mother in this way. A young woman's labor expenditure is thus increased at marriage by the fact that she continues to assist her mother in addition to clearing and weeding an area that has been enlarged to provision one additional consumer (i.e., her husband). It is consequently misleading to attribute the increased workload to marriage alone. It would be more accurate to say that wife's father–daughter's husband coresidence after marriage entails the maintenance of a young woman's obligations to her family of orientation at the same time new obligations to her family of procreation are established.

The critical evaluation of the brideservice model undertaken here reveals a systemic problem of misplaced causality that takes two forms. First, inequalities that are attributed to marital obligations (pertaining to maritally defined statuses) can be shown to be due to other components of the sociocultural systems under consideration. The most pertinent of these are: (1) the division of labor; (2) the cosmological system that delineates a morally evaluated scheme of social differentiation, defines producers (who hold distributional rights) and differentially valorizes their products and their labor; (3) the prestige system that defines public reward; and (4) the system of conflict management that confers jural prerogatives on males through reliance on the potential or actual use of armed force to back claims to compensation or exact vengeance. Systematic comparisons of married and unmarried women and married and unmarried men show that privileges and disabilities generated in these four domains of the sociocultural systems under consideration do not covary with marital status.

This absence of covariation is connected to the second aspect of the problem of misplaced causality: inequalities pertain to statuses that are not defined by marriage, and marriage consequently does not produce all the consequences and effects attributed to it. In the Etoro case, the transition to adult manhood and womanhood is largely defined by initiation and puberty rites, rather than by marriage, and marital status consequently is not a central organizing principle of intragender social differentiation for either males or females. In brideservice societies generally, males make a transition to an adult level of labor expenditure prior to marriage, and social substitutability enables them to exchange their labor or the products of their labor with females within the framework established by the division of labor. Marriage and wifely provisioning do not have the posited consequences of conveying a bundle of subsidiary prerogatives pertaining to the alleviation of a demeaning economic position and the establishment of an entrée into the spheres of political action and prestige. A bachelor is already in a position to play a role in the politics of conflict management. Marriage is a precursor to playing a role in the politics of marriage negotiation and betrothal, but this comes into play later, when a man has daughters of betrothal age. Marriage does not enhance opportunities to earn prestige because prestige in brideservice societies is derived from activities that are predominantly or exclusively performed by males and that do not require direct female labor inputs. Thus, prestige is accorded on the basis of hunting success, generosity in distributing game, distinction in raiding and warfare, ritual performance, possession of sacred knowledge, and possession of spiritual powers (including those of spirit mediums). Stigma, the negative reciprocal of prestige, is imputed to individuals believed to be responsible for inducing sickness or death by supernatural means. A wife's labor cannot be harnessed to the attainment of these forms of prestige or to the avoidance of stigma. Social substitutability in the exchange of labor (or the products of labor) enables a bachelor to pursue the relevant prestige-enhancing activities to the same extent as a married man. Women have very limited opportunities to earn prestige, but this is not due to the fact that they lack wives to provision them.

The two forms of misplaced causality exemplified in this summary are largely two sides of the same coin: marriage does not produce all the inegalitarian effects and consequences attributed to it because these inequalities pertaining to age and gender are produced by other components of the sociocultural systems under consideration. Marital obligations are therefore not the principal locus for the production of social inequalities between males and females and between junior and senior males. The causal factors responsible originate in diverse domains and characteristically produce mutually reinforcing configurations of moral worth, prestige, privilege, stigma, and disability that overdetermine gender inequalities. However, inequalities between junior and senior males are often moderated by counterbalancing rather than mutually reinforcing configurations that emanate from these diverse domains. This, in brief, is the theory of the production of inequality that will be developed in the following section of this chapter. However, it will be useful to examine the potential inequalities connected with the marriage process before proceeding to the elucidation of this alternative formulation.

Brideservice societies differ from bridewealth societies in the manner in which marriage organizes relations of production.

> In bridewealth societies, where marriages are validated through exchanges of goods the young and poor have difficulty acquiring, young men work for those who provide their marriage payments, and relations between husbands and wives are shaped by men's need to acquire the goods that enable them to participate in others' marriages, and thus to acquire rights in the labor and products of the young. In such (bridewealth) societies, a wife's domestic services may be far less important to her husband than his rights to appropriate the products of her labor, to collect bridewealth for her daughters, and to demand compensation from her lovers. His bridewealth payments constitute a claim in the future, a stake in the outcome of activities in which a wife may or may not be engaged. By contrast, in the brideservice societies we are discussing, the only benefits a husband derives from marriage are the daily services of his wife. Because young

men create claims to women by performing services for in-laws, goods have no real value, in the sense that they cannot be converted into the kinship ties that structure productive obligations. And because goods have no transcontextual value, a husband can enjoy the privileges of his married status only so long as his wife acknowledges their bond. Finally, it is this dependence of husbands on wifely compliance that ensures husbands' performances of services for those most able to influence the behavior of wives. (Collier and Rosaldo 1981:288–89)

The crux of the typological distinction between brideservice and bridewealth societies does not turn on the presence or absence of marriage payments per se, but on the question of a young man's dependence upon elders in acquiring the requisite items. A marriage payment consisting of items a bachelor "can obtain on his own" is classified as brideservice since this is consistent with the organization of production characteristic of bride service rather than bridewealth societies (Collier and Rosaldo 1981:286). In bride-service societies, the acquisition of a wife may also entail sister exchange, inheritance of a wife from a polygynous older brother, and uxorilocal residence with the parents of an intended bride, as well as bride service per se (ibid.). The common feature that links these somewhat disparate modes of wife acquisition is a posited absence of dependence upon elders (of the bachelor's own social group) and the presence of a need to establish and maintain the support of wife's parents in order to sustain a conjugal relationship with a reluctant bride.

As noted earlier, the Etoro have been nominated by Collier as an ethnographic case to which the brideservice model might usefully be applied. The Etoro manifest the requisite characteristics in several respects. Although marriage payments are substantial rather than token, the groom typically contributes about half of the total value of these payments (calculated in cowrie-string equivalents), and other unmarried young men contribute another quarter (as established in chap. 6). Although the remaining quarter is derived from married kinsmen, the amount contributed by each is small. A prospective groom could readily accumulate his entire marriage payment by trade, and there is no dependence upon married men (generally defined as "senior males") or elders. Although a bachelor will often have gardened with the same kinsmen who contribute to this bridewealth, and thus assisted them in felling trees, contributions to bridewealth are not in any way contingent upon this, and relations of production are not organized by senior males' control over matrimonial goods. The valuables that constitute matrimonial goods are largely in the hands of young men, who acquire them in external trade.

Etoro marriage payments also differ from those characteristic of the typical bridewealth society in that they are not given in lieu of the obligation to provide a woman in exchange for one received. Women are exchanged for women, rather than for bridewealth, and marriage payments are designated by the same term (*su*) applied to other compensation payments.[9] The marriage payment compensates the wife's father for an emotional loss that cannot be erased by the fact that his son (or "son") receives a wife in exchange for the daughter given in marriage. Sister exchange is only perfectly equivalent from the standpoint of the brother who gives up a sister in exchange for a wife. Sister exchange with bridewealth enhances the equivalence by compensating each woman's father for emotional loss and therefore addressing a revision of the father-daughter relationship that occurs at marriage. It is the father rather than the mother who experiences an emotional loss, because the daughter's husband replaces the father rather than the mother within the context of the division of labor and in terms of a reordering of sentiments. The mother-daughter relationship is not altered by marriage in these ways and also does not entail residential separation for some years (as explained further below). It is thus logical that the father rather than the mother receives the compensatory marriage payment. (However, the same logic implies that the mother should receive compensation upon the marriage of her son, although no such payment is made.)

During the protracted betrothal period, a prospective groom periodically presents packages of cooked sago grubs or smoked forest mammals to his future wife's father. These are reciprocated in kind after an interval of several months, and the transactions are consistent with the reciprocal affinal exchanges that continue for the duration of the union. However, the prospective groom also gives unreciprocated gifts to his wife's parents at irregular intervals. These gifts are predominantly items derived from external trade (as are the bridewealth valuables subsequently transferred). The traditional gifts of salt, nonlocal tobacco, seed necklaces, stone tools, and barkcloth capes have been largely replaced by introduced trade goods such as glass beads, cloth, matches, salt, mirrors, and steel tools (Kelly 1977:213). These unreciprocated gifts are consistent with the expectations of the brideservice model in that they enunciate a young man's claim to a specific girl and affirm the girl's parents' acceptance of the forthcoming union by their acceptance of these gifts (see Collier 1988:26). In the Etoro case, as in many brideservice societies, these gifts reaffirm a prior betrothal arranged for the prospective groom by his father (and other senior male kinsmen) acting on his behalf. The significance of the betrothal gifts thus resides in the fact that a newly initiated young man who has attained jural adulthood actively affirms this earlier arrangement on his *own* behalf and thereby establishes a direct relationship with his future wife's parents.

The Etoro also conform to the brideservice model in that daughter's husband and wife's father typically coreside after the conjugal relation is established (following the puberty rite). This may be effected by the move-ment of either party to the longhouse community of the other and therefore does not invariably entail uxorilocality, although it has the same conse-quence. The coresidence also occurs after, rather than before, marriage. However, this practice is consistent with the main thrust of the brideservice model in that a man typically resides with his wife's parents during the early years of marriage when dissolution of the union is a possibility. Marriage is irrevocable after spouses have become parents (which typically occurs about four years after the conjugal relation is established). The principal effect of this pattern of coresidence is to ease a girl's transition into marriage. Her day-to-day social relations with her parents and unmarried siblings are un-altered, and she will continue to work together with her mother, share a sleeping platform with her mother or sister, and dine with her family at the same fireplace (although now on the opposite side). The son-in-law becomes part of his wife's parents' production team, and the labor contributions of both the daughter and son-in-law benefit the girl's parents if they have other children who have not yet assumed an adult workload (as explained earlier).

The Etoro lack the distinctive features of bridewealth societies that turn on the role marriage plays in the organization of production, and they could not appropriately be classified as a member of this typological category. The Etoro also manifest a number of the traits that characterize brideservice societies and clearly have a great deal in common with the other hunter-gatherer and hunter-horticulturalist societies included in this category. It is thus evident that the Etoro are appropriately classified as a brideservice society within the terms of this typology. However, the presence of the requisite traits is not associated with the posited internal dynamics pertaining to conjugal and affinal relations. I have argued that these problems are ge-neric to the brideservice model and are not limited to the Etoro case. The issue is consequently not one of classification but of the adequacy of the brideservice model in illuminating social inequalities within societies that manifest comparable forms of inequality between males and females and between junior and senior males.

It is this comparability in the forms and dimensions of inequality that justifies the formulation of a general model addressed to a delimited category of societies. I am thus in agreement with Collier and Rosaldo with respect to the utility and appropriateness of such an enterprise. I would define the category in different terms, although this would not significantly alter the societies included within it. I regard the distinctive characteristic of this class of comparable societies as a form of prestige system in which the attainment of prestige is dependent upon an individual's own efforts. There is conse-quently no prestige-enhancing use to which another individual's labor can be directly applied. The only benefits that can be gained from the labor of another person are a reduction in one's own workload and/or the capacity to focus one's efforts on prestige-enhancing activities (so that the division of labor through which such benefits can be realized is of central importance). That a producer characteristically has distributional rights over the products of his or her own labor is consistent with the linkage between the attainment of prestige and individual effort. These features circumscribe and give a distinctive character to the forms and dimensions of social inequality that obtain among the societies included within this category. The term "brideservice societies" has a number of drawbacks as a label for this category, but labels are not of great importance.

Having specified the nature of my disagreement with the brideservice model as one pertaining to the adequacy of the model rather than the boundaries of the category to which it applies, I now return to the issue of the relationship between traits and dynamics.

Although a recently married man clearly needs to establish amicable social relations with his wife's parents, this relationship lacks the asymmetrical and hierarchical qualities that Collier and Rosaldo (1981:279) attribute to it. While the daughter's husband helps the wife's father to fell trees in his portion of their garden, the wife's father reciprocally helps the daughter's husband in his. Each party favors the other in the distribution of midsize game. Neither the son-in-law nor the wife's parents can speak directly to the other, but this prohibition is reciprocal and is reciprocally relaxed after a relatively brief period. The nature of the transactions establishing the marriage is also conducive to an egalitarian relationship between daughter's husband and wife's father. Although a girl is betrothed and given in marriage by her father, he receives bridewealth as a counterbalancing compensation for his emotional loss. There is no outstanding obligation that indebts the daughter's husband other than his lineage's reciprocal obligation to provide a wife for a member of his father-in-law's lineage. A betrothal fulfilling this exchange obligation will typically be in place if the present union does not itself constitute the second half of a "sister" exchange (or analogous direct exchange between lineages). A daughter's husband is therefore not beholden to his wife's father (or wife's brother), and there is no asymmetry in this respect. In addition, the daughter's husband will have inseminated his wife's father's true or classificatory son, thereby incurring a loss of life force. The acquisition of the reproductive potential of a wife is thus counterbalanced by bringing about the reproductive maturation of her brother in an exchange of person-constituting substances and potentialities. This not only establishes the basis for a balanced relation between wife's brother and sister's husband but also establishes an analogue of a copaternal relation between wife's father and daughter's husband. The reciprocal character of affinal exchange is consistent with the balanced (nonasymmetrical) relations between both wife's brother and sister's husband and wife's father and daughter's husband.

These multifaceted exchanges of persons and substances have been analyzed by Lindenbaum (1984, 1987) in several insightful comparative articles that draw on Collier and Rosaldo's delineation of bridewealth and brideservice societies as ideal types (e.g., Lindenbaum 1984:360). Lindenbaum focuses on a contrast between New Guinea societies characterized by semen transactions and bridewealth transactions, respectively, and identifies insemination as a kind of bride service. In noting that the Arunta also fit this pattern, Lindenbaum (1984:345) concludes:

> In the eight-section sister-exchange marriage system of the Arunta, homosexual and heterosexual rights interweave, as they do among the Kimam and Etoro, where a man relinquishes access to his sister but acquires access to a brother-in-law when the sister is given or promised in marriage (Kelly 1976:52). Thus, life force (as semen) flows between same-sex and different-sex partners, linking individuals and groups in complex chains of mutual dependency and obligation. It might be said that semen is a kind of covenant that keeps the sister-exchange system intact, one that is tied to the problem of maintaining a balance of personnel in small-scale communities. The transmission of semen is in some ways the characteristic affinal offering of bride-service societies, a gift of one's own labor, except that the prestation here is an internal transformation of the labor of others, forming one part of the complex reciprocities whereby affines maintain egalitarian relationships.

The difficulty that arises from regarding the transmission of semen as a brideservice gift is anticipated by Lindenbaum in the qualification that the semen (and life force) is not actually a product of the donor's labor. In addition, the gift of semen that is conveyed by the insemination of a prospective wife's brother differs markedly from the game and the labor service that are the hallmarks of bride service in that the latter are given to a prospective wife's parents. It is these unreciprocated prestations of game and labor that are presumed to induce the wife's parents to exert influence on their daughter on behalf of the young man who seeks to marry her and maintain the union. The Etoro transaction that is most nearly an analogue of the unreciprocated brideservice gifts of game and labor given to wife's parents is the bridewealth payment itself (and the unreciprocated betrothal gifts that precede it). However, focusing on this particular analogy would tend to obviate the contrast between societies characterized by semen transactions and those characterized by bridewealth transactions. I would argue that the sets of societies being contrasted are more usefully distinguished by their prestige systems and by the utilization of prestige goods in the marriage transactions of the bridewealth societies of the New Guinea Highlands. As Lindenbaum (1984:349) perceptively notes, "the focus of interest here shifts from the women to the objects given in exchange." This shift is attributable to the fact that these objects play a role in the attainment of prestige.

In a subsequent formulation, Lindenbaum (1987) omits the problematic brideservice analogy and focuses on the interplay between hierarchy and equality that is interwoven into the exchange of women and semen:

> Since semen and sisters pass between affinal groups in both directions, but at different times, each group maintains a balance of services owed and services required. However, contrary to sister-exchange, an ideology concerning the exchange of equals, semen exchange is based on a well-defined dominance order. A man cannot give and receive semen at the same time, nor can the donor-recipient relations be reversed. The senior male gives, and the junior receives. An ideal marriage transaction involves two men who exchange sisters; the "atom of semenship," so to speak, requires three male partners linked in descending order (Lindenbaum 1987:231).

This interpretation radically alters the posited character of semen transactions. Whereas the semen-giver and wife-receiver was formerly portrayed as being in an inferior position to the wife-giver (wife's father)—for whom he performed a service—he is now portrayed as being in a superior position to the semen-receiver (wife's brother). The wife-giver/wife-receiver relation is now seen to balance out through sister exchange, while the semen-giver/semen-receiver relation does not. Although the relations between semen-giver and receiver are reversed by reciprocity at the lineage level, they are irreversible at the individual level. In effect, marital exchange is factored out as reciprocal, leaving an asymmetrical relation in the realm of semen transactions as the source of inequality. Thus, marriage does not organize inequality, in accordance with the tenets of the brideservice model. On the contrary, it is organized by semen transactions. Insemination becomes an unreciprocated gift that engenders inequality rather than a service performed by an individual rendered inferior by virtue of being a wife-receiver.

Lindenbaum's second interpretation illustrates the distortions that are introduced by attempting to assimilate the Etoro and other lowland New Guinea cases to the brideservice model, and the advance in understanding that can be made by focusing on the intrinsic characteristics of semen transactions rather than regarding them as a form of bride service. Lindenbaum's analysis is useful in pointing out that there is no precise equivalent of sister exchange within the realm of semen transactions, which manifest some of the characteristics of asymmetrical cross-cousin marriage. However, the relationship between a donor and recipient of semen is not hierarchical in tone or character as these formal properties might lead one to expect. The sister given as wife balances the transaction and engenders an equivalent reciprocal relation between a wife's brother and sister's husband, who are also semen-recipient and donor. Although a semen-recipient cannot reciprocate directly in kind, he can give female reproductive potential in exchange for the male reproductive potential received, thereby rendering the relationship symmetrical rather than hierarchical at the individual level. The semen-recipient can also reciprocate indirectly, at the lineage level, by inseminating a younger lineage brother or "son" of the donor (as explained further below). The fact that affinal exchange is entirely reciprocal constitutes a palpable Etoro representation of the wife's brother–sister's husband relationship as perfectly equivalent. For example, each gives the other an identical side of pork. There is also equivalence at the lineage level as each group provides both wives and semen to the other. Finally, it is important to recall that the wife's father–daughter's husband relation is balanced by the bride-for-bridewealth transaction discussed earlier. Moreover, the shell valuables that constitute the bridewealth payment given to a wife's father are a symbolic analogue of the semen transmitted to a wife's brother. The symbolic equation of semen with the shell valuables that constitute the marriage payment is entirely consistent with the interpretation that male reproductive potential is exchanged for female reproductive potential. The main thrust of the total system is thus to obviate all possible sources of relational inequality through counterbalancing transactions in female reproductive potential, male reproductive potential, and bridewealth, and through lineage level transactions in which all three are directly reciprocated.

The failure of semen transactions to generate the expectable asymmetries associated with unidirectional gifts is also attributable to the grounding of these transactions in the realm of moral hierarchy rather than the realm of material obligation. A recipient of semen and life force does not incur a specific obligation to the donor other than the obligation to provide female reproductive potential in exchange. However, the semen-giver attains an elevated moral standing through his generosity in giving the gift of life force. The wife he receives in exchange does not counterbalance this aspect of the transaction since she represents a second source of depletion. The generosity of the semen-giver and wife-receiver is thus enhanced by this doubling of his virtuous, self-sacrificing contribution to systemic reproduction and the perpetuation of life. Semen transactions do engender social inequality as Lindenbaum suggests, but this takes the form of asymmetries in moral standing rather than the unequal material obligations associated with bride service. The "dominance order" Lindenbaum identifies is the moral hierarchy. Thus, the elevated category of persons is owed nothing except acknowledgment of a superior moral standing in exchange for their generous unidirectional gifts that can never be directly repaid in kind. This moral standing is not translated into material prerogatives, unlike obligations to provide game, labor service, or payments in valuables. Moral worthiness also differs from obligation in that it is a sociocentric quality accorded by consensus rather than a property of dyadic relations. Thus, relational equivalence grounded in the exchange of male and female reproductive potential is overlaid by an asymmetry in moral standing that stems from the semen-giver's self-sacrificing contribution to the perpetuation of life, a sociocentric contribution that is redoubled rather than counterbalanced by the wife he receives in exchange at the relational level. The generosity of the life-force donor is a virtue worthy of general admiration.

Lineage-level reciprocities in the exchange of women and semen can be further elucidated by consideration of a model of such exchanges (fig. 7.1) that conforms to the Etoro preference for father's sister's son's daughter marriage and displays the patterns that emerge from the exchanges that occur between four descent groups. In the model, sibling bonds represent the relations between lineage brothers and sisters. In order to simplify the presentation and reduce the number of intersecting lines, I have abstracted the transactions that show the marriages and semen exchanges involving lineages B and C from the more inclusive model (presented in Kelly 1977:206). In the senior generation, the men B1 and C1 exchange sisters, B1 inseminates C1 and C1 inseminates B1's younger brother. In the following generation, B2 and C2 exchange daughters, give their sisters to A2 and D2 (respectively), and are inseminated by the latter. B2 and C2 themselves inseminate each other's sons, C3 and B3. The latter men of the third descending generation marry women of A and D and inseminate the brothers of these women (A4 and D4). In the fourth descending generation, the exchanges of the senior generation are reduplicated.

It is important to note that only true sister exchange is potentially incompatible with insemination of wife's actual brother by one of the parties to the exchange (due to the irreversibility of the donor-recipient relation). In the model, this is resolved by the second party inseminating the first's younger brother (rather than the elder brother who married his sister). This enables true sister exchange to be combined with insemination of wife's true brother, and the potential incompatibility then does not come into play. However, true sister exchange is quite rare, so this minor adjustment would only very infrequently be required. If a sister exchange entails at least one classificatory sister, each of the men can inseminate his wife's true brother as illustrated in figure 7.2. These models thus show that there is no incompatibility between the direct exchange of women and the irreversible transfer of semen from senior to junior males and from a man to his wife's true brother. All Etoro marriage and semen transmission preferences can be simultaneously realized. The insemination of wife's true brother can even be combined with

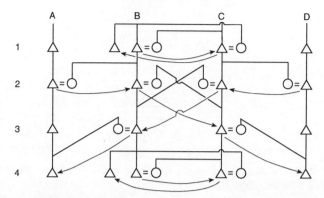

Fig. 7.1. A model of the exchange of women and semen under a regime of FZSD marriage

true sister exchange, provided that the older man of the exchanging pair has a younger brother. In practice, nearly all exchanges between lineages involve classificatory sisters (and daughters). Although the exchange of women and the transmission of semen are governed by different principles, relations between lineages nevertheless tend to be characterized by balanced reciprocity in both transactions. There are no structural impediments to the realization of this objective.

One of the difficulties with the brideservice model is that each marriage is conceptualized as an isolated event unrelated to other marriages. The dyadic relation between daughter's husband and wife's parents is thus analytically isolated without due consideration of this larger context. Although sister exchange is commonplace in brideservice societies, this is analytically relegated to the status of a mode of wife acquisition so that reciprocity in the exchange of women does not impinge on the analysis of relations between daughter's husband and wife's parents. The conceptualization of this relationship is radically altered by consideration of the entailments of reciprocal exchange. If the wife's parent's son is to marry the daughter's husband's sister, then the wife's parents have an interest in their daughter's marriage coming to fruition (and being maintained) that is unrelated to brideservice gifts. This interconnection provides a motive for the exertion of parental influence on a daughter that is much more plausible than the manipulation of their material self-interest through presentations of game in which they would share, in any event, as group members. The problem of the analytic isolation of the wife's parents–daughter's husband dyad is further amplified in the Etoro case because marriage takes place in a larger context that includes the transmission of semen as well as the reciprocal exchange of women between lineages. This provides both a prospective wife's father and

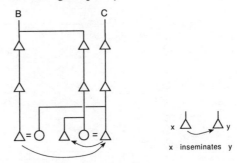

Fig. 7.2. The exchange of women and semen within the context of classificatory sister exchange

wife's brother with an additional interest in the realization of the daughter's (or sister's) betrothal.

Sister exchange and other forms of reciprocity in the exchange of women entail arranged marriage. However, arranged marriage is at variance with the central dynamic of the brideservice model, because a prospective daughter's husband does not secure a reluctant bride by inducing her parents to exert influence on his behalf. His father and/or other senior kinsmen provide whatever inducements are required at the time the betrothal is established. Whitehead (1987:245–67) addresses these issues in an earlier critique of the applicability of the brideservice model to New Guinea societies. She points out that the posited capacity of young men to bring about marriage through their own efforts is not borne out by the ethnographic data. In the coastal and riverine areas where sister exchange is prevalent,

> the young bachelor—who in Collier and Rosaldo's model should be going out to "make" his own marriage by hunting meat for his future in-laws, demonstrating violent prowess to would-be rivals, and seeking out [potential] mothers-in-law with whom to initiate exchange—is largely replaced by the young bachelor who, confined for long periods to cultic seclusion, passively awaits the day when adults of the community consider him sufficiently mature to take up residence with a bride designated for him in his childhood. (Whitehead 1987:254)

At issue here is the question of whether there is any evidence substantiating the presence of a structural actor manifesting the viewpoint posited by Collier and Rosaldo, or to whom such a viewpoint would make sense (ibid.). The central actor in the brideservice formulation is the bachelor driven by his desperate need for a hard-to-get wife. If acquiring a wife is assured without effort, the entire logic of the brideservice model is undercut, and none of the entailments of the bachelor's predicament follow.

The main thrust of Whitehead's criticism can be further elaborated. The brideservice model is grounded in a scheme of standardized perceptions and motivations that are attributed to a maturing girl, the young man who seeks to marry her (and retain her as a wife), and the prospective wife's parents. The girl purportedly perceives marriage as entailing onerous obligations (without commensurate rewards) and is motivated to avoid or delay marriage. Imputed perceptions focus on the economic disadvantages of marriage, and the resultant motives are informed by economic self-interest. Young girls become significant shapers of the cultural system since their disposition plays a key role in evoking the bachelors' standardized motivational pattern. Perceiving that girls are reluctant to wed and prone to abscond, young men seek to assuage their anxiety over acquiring and keeping a wife by currying favor with an intended bride's parents so that the latter will bring their influence to bear. The same motives also lead bachelors to cultivate a reputation that is intended to be offputting to rivals. For example, a Comanche bachelor is said to establish this by "demonstrating his capacity for violence by killing animals and enemies" (Collier 1988:39).[10] Bachelors are concerned to demonstrate their prowess in hunting and raiding in order to attract wives as well as discourage potential rivals from infringing on their claims to particular women (ibid.:36–37). A bachelor's motives are principally informed by his perception of the social and economic advantages of acquiring a wife as well as his perception of the intrinsic difficulty of achieving this. Thus, a Comanche bachelor's propensity to engage in prestige-enhancing raiding is seen as a means to the end of acquiring a wife rather than an independent strand of motivation.

The motives implicitly attributed to wife's parents are singularly economic. The parents are induced to exert influence upon their daughter, on the husband's behalf, by his performance of services. (Otherwise, there would be no logical reason for the husband to perform these services in order to achieve this result.) This implies that the wife's parents are easily manipulated through their material self-interest in the benefits they derive from the daughter's husband, and that their economic self-interest outweighs any empathy they might have toward their daughter's reluctance to wed.

Here, as elsewhere, the scheme of standardized motivations omits the relational motives that are so prominent in Etoro ethnomotivation, i.e., in their accounts of why a given actor has followed a certain course of action. Individuals certainly do not lack self-interest, but they perceive these interests to be realized through relationships that are a continuing source of varied forms of support and assistance over the long term. It is not feasible to extract a specific benefit from another person in a tit-for-tat transaction that occurs outside of the context of an ongoing relationship, as is possible within a framework of Western contractual relations. To be assured of access to desired forms of support and assistance, an individual thus has no recourse other than to invest in relationships. This gives rise to relational motivation. The recognition that reciprocity is central to the maintenance of vital social relations also blunts the individualistic pursuit of economic advantage. Self-interest cannot be discretely segregated from the interests of relationally connected others.[11] The significance of relational interests also connects with the point made earlier concerning sister exchange. A girl's parents envision her marriage as instituting a relationship within a context of extant and anticipated relationships, including their relation to their son and his relation to his future affines. The fact that marriages are arranged is also readily intelligible in terms of relational motivation. The larger context that is overlooked by the conceptualization of each marriage as an isolated event is a context governed by broader relational concerns.

In brideservice societies, the pursuit of prestige is the principal arena of individualistic interest because prestige itself is inalienable and therefore nontransactable. Being immune from the claims deriving from the relationships in which the social actor is enmeshed, prestige is subject to accumulation in a way that material goods are not. However, the self-seeking pursuit of prestige is harnessed to broader social interests insofar as prestige is attained by the generous distribution of game to others, by curing the sick, and by like contributions to the general welfare. As Andrew Strathern (1982a:39) notes with respect to an evaluation of the Highlands Big Man,

> the problem with "own interests" is that it cannot be defined at all outside the realm of culturally based cognition. If one's "own interests" include an aim of gaining prestige, and such prestige can only be gained effectively by securing the approbation of others, then "own interest" will lead to action which in fact coincides with the wishes of followers or at least a public; and in that case the straightforward opposition between individual interests and collective interests will not apply.

Consideration of the differences between prestige systems provides a basis for adding a corollary to this important point. The equation that encompasses individual and collective interests can be expanded to include the interests of other actors within a common collectivity. When the attainment of prestige is contingent upon the labor inputs of others, then both individual prestige interests and collective interests may be realized at the expense of certain members of the collectivity whose efforts are not commensurately rewarded in terms of prestige. Although individual and collective interests are not opposed, the allocation of prestige among those who contribute to the collectivity can be analytically segregated as a separate issue. The concept of opposed interests may then be relevant to relations between coparticipants in the production of prestige rather than the relationship between the individual and the group. However, this potentiality is moderated to the extent that prestige attainment is contingent upon individual effort.

The difficulty with the standardized motivational scheme that underwrites the brideservice model is not that it relies on individual self-interest but that these interests are conceptualized in narrow and simplistic terms that are predominantly economic. Relational interests are discounted, and prestige interests are reduced to maritally linked economic advantage. Although economic interests are relevant as one of several aspects of motivation, an excessive reliance on these engenders one-dimensional social actors that are analytically mismatched with the complexities of social life. This overly narrow conceptualization of actors' interests is a direct product of the manner in which these are deduced. Interests are assigned to actors "by the organization of production" (Collier 1988:209).

The brideservice model also entails a redistribution of the lines of force that are seen to shape the social systems under consideration. Young women are cast as culture-makers in that their reluctance to wed sets the stage for the enactment of strategies that shape the system. Bachelors are the central strategic actors whose courses of action eventuate in system-constituting practices. Senior males are advantageously positioned but are comparatively passive in that their actions do not have the system-shaping consequences attributed to elusive potential brides and desperate bachelors. In this sense, the model entails a reversal of the Levi-Straussian picture of senior males assigning passive brides to patient bachelors. The revisions proposed by the brideservice model raise interesting and important issues in that the seniors who constitute the privileged sector of society appear to effortlessly reproduce their advantaged position while young women's culture-making resistance to matrimony reproduces a disadvantaged position. Although the concept of unintended consequences can be employed to account for this paradoxical outcome, this has the paradoxical effect of absolving advantaged elites from a large measure of responsibility for societal inequality. According a culture-making role to women logically entails the assignment of some degree of responsibility for the reproduction of a gender-inegalitarian society. In contrast, the arrangement of marriages by senior males accords reproduction of central features of the social system to those who are advantaged by it, so that social inequality does not appear as an unintended consequence of practices undertaken to avoid inequality, but rather as the straightforward reproduction of advantage.

Available data provide a basis for assessing the motives of Etoro social actors engaged in the marriage process and evaluating the extent to which senior males are capable of exerting influence over this process. As was explained earlier, marriage is advantageous to both males and females, and many of the inducements to wed are complementary. However, initiated bachelors enjoy many advantages and are generally content to wait until the young girls to whom they are betrothed reach marriageable age. Men rarely marry before the age of 26, and a third of the men aged 31 to 35 remain unmarried (Kelly 1977:304). Although eligible widows of reproductive age are available, bachelors sometimes bypass the opportunity to marry such women in favor of waiting for a betrothed to come of age. This illustrates the absence of an urgency to wed. Both the comfortable status of bachelors and a measure of concern regarding the consequences of the sustained depletion of life force entailed by marriage provide motives for patience.

Virtually all marriages involving women other than widows are arranged by senior kinsmen of the parties to the union. Since all girls of marriageable age are married, the only alternative to arranged marriage open to bachelors (apart from marrying a widow) is absconding with another man's wife. Less than 1 percent of all marriages come into being in this way. This provides additional evidence of patience and passivity on the part of bachelors and is also indicative of the general absence of overt conflict over women. Nearly all overt conflict is motivated by witchcraft accusations that lead to revenge or demands for compensation.

It is of interest that male concepts of female attractiveness are based almost exclusively on age. All young women who are approaching reproductive maturity are considered highly attractive and desirable mates, and there is an absence of comparative evaluations expressing significant distinctions between them in terms of these qualities. The range extends from "youthfully attractive and eminently marriageable" to "truly youthfully attractive and eminently marriageable." Only women divorced as a result of alleged witchcraft are regarded as undesirable mates. However, never-married women are not differentiated in this respect, as none has been accused of witchcraft. Given this cultural perception of the nearly equivalent desirability of all young women, there is no reason for a bachelor to be dissatisfied with his betrothal on the grounds of strong personal preference for another woman. All the bachelors with whom I was acquainted were quite content with the arrangements made for them. The rare instances of absconding with a married woman all entailed female initiative.[12] Marriage to a widow rather than a betrothed is also typically a result of the widow's initiative.

Etoro girls are betrothed when they are about 5 years of age and grow up with the expectation of marrying a particular man. There is no evidence that they question these arrangements or are reluctant to wed. Every girl over the age of 16 has established a conjugal relation with a husband even though a girl can delay this event if she so chooses. Only 1.2 percent (2/168) of a large sample of women's first marriages have been dissolved on the woman's initiative, by establishing a de facto union with another man and bearing a child by him (see Kelly 1977:258–59). This form of the dissolution of marriage follows the pattern outlined by Collier (1988:27–28) in that a girl's parents generally do not make an effort to return her to her original husband. The girl's father typically returns the bridewealth instead, funding this out of the bridewealth paid by the second husband. The rejected husband is frequently provided with a lineage sister of the woman who left him (see n. 12).

The efforts made by the wife's father of an absconding bride are thus directed to restitution and to reestablishment of the original affinal relationship through substitution rather than to the coerced return of an unwilling bride. A long-term exchange relationship between the lineages that are parties to the original union provides an impetus to this course of action. The wife's father is motivated by concern that his daughter's dissolution of the original union may jeopardize the planned marriage of one of his "sons," who was to receive a bride in exchange, and he seeks to forestall this by aiding his daughter's former husband in securing a replacement. The dyadic relationship between wife's father and daughter's husband also provides a reason for the wife's father to be concerned about his former son-in-law's welfare insofar as the latter served as the inseminator of his son (or brother's son). Lindenbaum's (1984:344) formulation of the concept of "double affinity" is useful in this context since it brings out the continuity in this relationship that persists after the marriage is dissolved by divorce. Relational motivation is promoted by the multistranded nature of kin and affinal relations and by the fact that these are interwoven within a reticulated, closed system such that a disruption of one relationship impinges on others.

These aspects of relational motivation also have a bearing upon a girl's acceptance of the marriage arranged for her. She knows that the impending union is endorsed by her parents, brothers, and agnates, and that it is connected to other planned unions in which they have an interest. The nature of Etoro marital exchange and residence patterns is conducive to coresidence with "brothers" and "sisters" throughout a woman's life. Absconding with another man often entails a protracted period during which the couple takes refuge with a neighboring tribe until a child or children are born. A woman thus foregoes the typical postmarital coresidence with her parents and other close kin and instead resides with strangers. Even if this can be avoided, a woman who rejects her arranged union will generally have a significantly reduced opportunity to reside with close kin throughout her life as a consequence of her marriage not being part of duplicated exchanges. Her true and classificatory brothers and sisters are likely to move in different circles.

The social costs of female-initiated divorce also include the alienation of close kinsmen that a woman relies upon for support. The potential disruption of her relationship with her brother and other male agnates makes a young woman who selects her own spouse much more dependent upon her husband than would otherwise be the case. This is particularly well illustrated by Kabano's failure to avoid an undesirable remarriage to the notorious witch Nomaya (discussed in chap. 4). Kabano had alienated her father's brothers fourteen years earlier by leaving her first husband for another man and thereby disrupting planned marital exchanges and valued affinal relationships. The consequences of this came to light after her husband's death, when Nomaya sought to marry her. Kabano wanted to reside with her father's brothers as an unremarried widow, rather than marrying Nomaya. However, she was not welcomed and received no support from them since she was making claims on relationships she had previously discounted and petitioning individuals with whom she had had very little contact for an extended period of time. Lacking the support of a male kinsman who would fell trees and shred sago for her so that she might garden and process sago, she had little choice other than to marry Nomaya. The fear that a rejected Nomaya's displeasure might be expressed in deadly witchcraft directed against her also provided a compelling inducement. Cases such as this provide other women with palpable evidence of the disadvantageous consequences of rejecting an arranged marriage. Recognition of both the favorable life situation that surrounds arranged marriage and the disadvantages that go along with establishing a de facto union with another man are undoubtedly responsible for the very low incidence of female-initiated divorce.

It is important to note that a girl's mother and female kin specifically endorse her union. The unreciprocated betrothal gifts to wife's parents include the presentation of a barkcloth cape to a betrothed girl's mother. The mother's acceptance of this gift expresses an unequivocal ratification of the forthcoming union. At the marriage ceremony itself, there is a reciprocal exchange of garden products: two identical three-foot high mounds of sweet potatoes and taro, harvested and assembled by the bride's female kin and the groom's female kin, respectively (Kelly 1977:220). The shell valuables that constitute the bridewealth are displayed on top of the groom's mound of tubers. These valuables are presented by the groom to the bride's father (who often redistributes them at this time), and the sweet potatoes and taro are then simultaneously distributed to the groom's kin by the bride's female relatives and to the bride's kin by the groom's female relatives. These garden crops epitomize the complementarity and cooperative joint effort of males and females in coproduction. However, women hold distributional rights over these jointly produced starch staples, since they complete their production by harvesting and cleaning the tubers. At one level, the reciprocal distributions thus represent the marital union as an exchange of complementary male and female productive capacities that is endorsed by the female kin of the parties to the union. However, there is a second level of meaning as well.

Some women's names are the names for sweet potatoes and sweet potato varieties, and some men's names are the names for taro varieties. Given this gender symbolism, the women exchange male and female entities for male and female entities in a manner that structurally resembles sister exchange. However, this tuber exchange differs from conceptualizations of sister exchange as the exchange of women by men, since brother-sister pairs rather than sisters alone are exchanged. Moreover, the tubers are not resorted so that each is segregated from its "sibling" and matched with a nonsibling of the same gender, as would occur if one type of tuber remained in place and the other circulated. This transaction thus provides a symbolic representation of sibling pairs being exchanged by communities, suggesting that both brothers and sisters are equally exchanged and that the bond between them is unaltered by marriage. This is consistent with the fact that a brother and sister are ideally joined to the same man, one as inseminee and the other as spouse. This ideal entails the notion that brother and sister are exchanged as a unit. As noted above, each tuber is itself the product of male-female coproduction and an embodiment of gender complementarity in food production. The emphasis on production rather than reproduction in the tuber exchange carried out by the women is significant as a counterpoint to the transaction in bridewealth valuables.

The shell valuables that constitute the bridewealth payment are given by the groom to the bride's father and redistributed by the latter to other men, so that the transaction is entirely among males. The shell valuables are the symbolic equivalents of semen so that the marital union that occasions the transaction is represented as an exchange of male and female reproductive potentialities. At dawn, following a *kosa* ceremony, the bride holds out a piece of cooked marsupial meat that the groom snatches out of her hand as he runs by, continuing across the longhouse clearing into the forest. This represents a symbolic consummation of the union (see Kelly 1977:220), and the groom remains in heterosexual isolation in the forest for several hours or more. Having "copulated," he cannot share food or smoke with others for the remainder of the day. The piece of marsupial meat proffered by the bride thus represents the female reproductive potential received by the groom in exchange for male semen (i.e., bridewealth). The bride herself presents this to the groom, just as he personally presents the bridewealth. However, the bridewealth goes to the bereaved father of the bride rather than to the bride herself. The groom makes his exit at top speed in a state of virginal anxiety and acute embarrassment heightened by raucous female laughter that serves as a counterpoint to the wife's father's tears. In the interval between the presentation of bridewealth and the symbolic consummation of the union, many of the senior men present will also have wept profusely upon hearing the sad *kosa* songs sung by their junior affines. The songs are evocative of death and depletion. The *kosa* performers, who are predominantly bachelors, are burned by their senior classificatory affines and subsequently compensate the latter's sons and younger brothers with shell valuables in a sequence that conforms to the three-part "atom of semenship." It is important to recall that marriage payments and these payments to the junior kin of burners are both *su*, i.e., compensations for grief associated with loss.

The all-night, male-dominated ritual performance culminating in the presentation of shell valuables by the dancers to the sons and younger brothers of the burners contextualizes the marriage celebration and bridewealth presentation so that they appear as components of a male transactional domain. Within this overall context, the female exchange of tubers appears as a comparatively mundane transaction that plays a minor role in the proceedings and does not resonate with the main themes of the *kosa* or the unidirectional presentations of compensatory valuables associated with it. However, the female tuber exchange provides a counterpoint to the predominantly androcentric character of the event that is significant from the standpoint of the bride. In independently carrying out this exchange, the bride's and groom's kinswomen actively express their ratification of and support for the marriage. This conveys the message that the union is welcomed by the bride's husband's female kin as well as by her own "mothers," "sisters," and "father's sisters."

The marriage ceremony is similar to the ceremony celebrating the completion of male initiation in that it includes components that can be differentially emphasized by male and female actors who possess somewhat different points of view. Although marriage appears as a transaction between wife-givers and wife-receivers from the male perspective, it can be viewed from a female perspective as a merger of complementary productive capacities that entails the acquisition of male labor in exchange for female labor. Acquiring the labor of a husband/son-in-law is a prominent aspect of marriage when marriage is seen in terms of production, because the groom subsequently joins a preexisting production team composed of the bride and her parents. In this respect it is the groom, not the bride, who is transferred between units.

Marriage also entails the joining of male and female reproductive capacities. However, marriage involves wife acquisition when viewed from the standpoint of reproduction because a couple's children become members of their father's patriline. Women are exchanged by patrilines in order that these units can be socially reproduced. From a male perspective, familial and lineage reproduction are coterminous. From a female perspective, they are divergent because a woman's children do not belong to her lineage. This is conducive to separate conceptualizations of these two levels of reproduction. On one hand, a woman recognizes that her marriage is part of an exchange through which her lineage is reproduced. On the other hand, marriage is conceptualized as a merger of male and female productive and reproductive capacities through which familial reproduction is achieved. Although the children a woman bears are members of her husband's lineage, they nonetheless appear to her as preeminently her children and members of her family. From this standpoint marriage entails husband acquisition and family formation. The notion that she has been exchanged does not address or illuminate the aspects of marriage that are central to a woman's experience of it. It is consequently implausible that this is prominent in a female actor's point of view. The tuber exchange presents marriage in a way that makes sense from this female viewpoint. The bride's action in presenting a piece of cooked marsupial to her husband is also consistent with the interpretation that she views herself as actively engaging in an exchange, rather than passively being exchanged (cf. Strathern 1983). However, the groom does not merely accept the piece of meat, but snatches it. From his perspective, he has engaged in an exchange with the bride's father and brother, to whom he has given shell valuables and semen. The piece of meat, and what it symbolically represents, is his due. He consequently takes the meat and gives the bride nothing in return. However, when she later bears a child, he will provide her with large quantities of marsupials and other small forest mammals and thus provide direct reciprocation for the female reproductive capacity his wife gives to him at marriage.

There is no incompatibility between the male and female perspectives on marriage because both parties recognize that it entails conjugal complementarity as well as the exchange of women between patrilines and the exchange of cross-sex sibling sets between communities. However, these three aspects of matrimony have a different salience for male and female actors, and this is reflected in the respective roles they play in the ceremony celebrating the union.

Marriages are arranged by senior men on behalf of male and female children that are equally passive nonparticipants in these proceedings. In this respect, both males and females are "exchanged," as neither has any control over their marital destiny. The male prerogative of arranging marriages is ideologically grounded in patrilineality and cultural conceptions of substance transmission and maturation. Marriage is conceived as an exchange between lineages in that lineages constitute the relevant units to which a calculus of reciprocity is applied. Lineage members thus collectively hold rights to determine the marital destiny of sons and daughters in accordance with claims based on reciprocity arising from prior unions. The mother of a child who is to be betrothed does not share in these collective rights because she is not a member of the lineage that holds them. The betrothal of a girl also entails the designation of her brother's inseminator and this locates the process of simultaneously arranging marriage and insemination within a realm that is an exclusive male concern. Finally, the growth of both male and female children is brought about by the game provided by men. This further legitimizes male claims to distributional rights in accordance with the general principle by which such rights are allocated.

This is particularly significant with respect to daughters because there is no publicly articulated cultural theory of female substance transmission that provides an explanation of female reproductive maturation and thus no basis for assertion of a female claim to rights of distribution on the grounds that women complete the process of female maturation. As noted earlier, the female puberty rite entails no symbolic reference to such substance transmission. Male provisioning of growth-inducing game thus provides an ideological basis for the right to bestow daughters and reinforces lineage-based rights. Women consequently have no official voice in the arrangement of marriages. Although a girl's mother could potentially refuse to accept the barkcloth cape given to her by her daughter's prospective husband, and thereby withhold ratification of the planned union, I know of no instances in which this occurred. It is consequently not known whether this would be sufficient to derail an arranged marriage. A girl's mother would not in any event be in a position to designate a husband for her daughter, so that withholding approval is the extent of her official capacity to influence the process. However, a woman would have an opportunity to privately convey her views to her husband at the time her daughter's betrothal was being arranged. Since rejected proposals made by a young man's senior kinsmen are never made public, it is not possible to investigate the causes of rejection and assess the degree to which women informally influence the arrangement of marriages through disapproval of proposed matches.

A boy's betrothal is generally arranged when he is in his early teens, by his father and mother's brother. The mother's brother has a special interest in securing a bride for his sister's son, because the mother's brother's own son will ideally marry this sister's son's daughter under the terms of father's sister's son's daughter's marriage. The men whose daughters are the potential targets of proposals will likewise be true or classificatory sisters' sons of the boy's father, and the boy's father thus may well have played a role in the arrangement of the marriage that produced the daughter being sought. The mother's brother of the boy is also likely to be a matrilateral sibling of any man to whom a request is put (see Kelly 1977:176–77). The context in which a betrothal decision is made by a girl's father is thus dominated by relational motivation and claims based on fulfillment of reciprocity (in that a father is asked to promise his daughter to a man of his mother's lineage). The father of a 5-year-old girl will not normally be in a position to arrange his own son's marriage at this time, since boys are not betrothed until they are about 15 years of age. However, his agnates' need to secure wives for their sons is also a consideration, and the prospects for a classificatory sister exchange may well enter into the decision. The primary concern of the boy's father is to pose the request to an individual who will find it difficult to turn down. There is no basis other than kinship for evaluating the comparative desirability of 5-year-old girls as future wives. However, the girl's father can evaluate the desirability of a potential son-in-law as both a husband to his daughter and the designated inseminator of his son. A boy who had been accused of witchcraft would be an undesirable choice, since he would transmit the seed of witchcraft to the wife-giver's son. However, very few boys are accused of witchcraft before they are betrothed; such an accusation also cannot have been confirmed by the child oracle and thus could potentially be discounted. In other respects, boys of 15 are as undifferentiated as girls of 5 in terms of social status, and the characteristics they will eventually possess as mature young men are equally indeterminable.[13]

It is evident here that the Etoro case conforms much more closely to the Levi-Straussian model of senior males assigning passive brides to patient (and equally passive) bachelors than to the brideservice model that envisions reluctant brides, bachelors as strategic actors, and relatively passive seniors who take no initiative in the marriage process. Among the Etoro, senior males exclusively take the initiative in bringing about marriages (except in some cases of widow remarriage). A bachelor becomes an active participant in the proceedings when he begins to make betrothal gifts to his future wife's parents. A bride becomes an active participant when she initiates the symbolic consummation of the union and gives her reproductive potential to the groom (by giving him a piece of cooked marsupial). Both the groom and bride subscribe to arrangements made on their behalf by senior males. Although women are assigned husbands by senior males, they are not rendered "objects" as a result (Strathern 1983). Women are exchanged for women in person for person exchange. Women are not equated with the shell valuables given by the groom to the bride's father, since these are symbolic equivalents of semen. Moreover, these shell valuables are not "objects in the Western sense" (ibid.:164) but represent male reproductive potential exchanged for female reproductive potential. From a lineage perspective, a woman's reproductive potential is exchanged for semen that ensures the reproductive maturation of her brother so that he can reproduce the lineage through children born to the woman whose reproductive potential is secured in exchange for his sister. Both male and female reproductive capacity are exchanged in a transaction that entails the transfer of aspects of persons. From a community (rather than lineage) perspective, cross-sex sibling pairs are exchanged since the parties to a sister exchange generally coreside and brother-sister pairs thus move as units. From an individual perspective, a woman acquires a husband to the same extent that a man acquires a wife. Thus, while senior males arrange marriages, it is misleading to describe this as an "exchange of women" without adding a number of qualifications. It would be more accurate to say that senior males exchange the reproductive capacities of both male and female persons. The implicit distinction between "exchangers" and "exchanged" that is contained in this phrase is appropriate in the Etoro case, but the "exchanged" are not whole persons and are of both genders.

It is notable that a woman's status as a member of her natal lineage is not altered either jurally or in practice by marriage. Her right to exploit the resources of her lineage territory is unchanged. Over the course of a lifetime, she is likely to spend as many years residing on her own lineage territory as on that of her husband. Her relationship to her brother is unaltered. He will continue to be obligated to provide half the compensation in the event that she is accused of witchcraft (irrespective of her marital status), and she will likewise continue to be obligated to assist him in weeding his gardens if he calls upon her to do so. In more general terms, each will manifest a continuing interest in the welfare of the other.

Although a woman forms a coproduction team with her husband, he does not acquire monopolistic claims to her labor. Moreover, her labor obligations are to her husband alone, not to his lineage. If the union is dissolved by a husband's death, the surviving widow can take up residence in any community of her choice and participate in coproduction with any of a variety of kinsmen (although she typically remains with her deceased husband's brother). In other words, a woman's labor is not transferred to her husband's lineage by payment of bridewealth. The deceased husband's lineage is a successor to his exclusive claims to her reproductive potential, and the deceased husband's agnates can thus arrange a widow's remarriage and collect bridewealth (if the remarriage is nonleviratic). However, in practice, a widow is often able to influence her own marital destiny. Although a husband acquires a monopolistic claim on his wife with respect to heterosexual relations, a deceased husband's lineage is also not a successor to this claim. Thus, a deceased husband's agnates make no effort to exercise control over a widow's sexual behavior or to impede her capacity to form sexual liaisons of her choosing. In marriage, a woman thus enters into a relationship with her husband, not her husband's lineage. Her status as a member of her own lineage and as a sister is unaltered. The only aspect of her person that is "exchanged" is her reproductive capacity. Since a woman cannot reproduce for her own lineage in a patrilineal system, the assignment of her offspring to membership in another lineage does not actually constitute a change in her relationship to her natal lineage. The claims to a woman's reproductive potential that are assigned at marriage only pertain to the lineage identity of her offspring.

Lineages are residentially dispersed and do not form the basis of socio-economic groups to which members are physically recruited. The social reproduction of the lineage consequently does not entail the incorporation of either wives or sons as whole persons, as is the case with territorially based patri-virilocal descent groups that form corporate units (cf. Wood 1982:168). As a result, marriage is symmetrical for men and women, except in that the offspring belong to the husband's lineage (whose corporate estate consists of a territory and collective rights to determine the marital destiny of daughters and sons that derive from a lineage-based calculus of reciprocity in matrimonial exchange). A wife thus acquires claims to her husband's labor and to the heterosexual component of his sexuality that are identical to his claims upon her. The symmetry with respect to the latter claim is reflected in the fact that he requires her consent to take a second wife.

It is also important to note that the role senior males play in arranging marriages does not render junior males dependent but rather obviates any potential dependency arising out of matrimonial arrangements. A boy is typically betrothed when he is 15 to 17 years of age, before he has made a transition to a full adult workload. He does not begin to assist his senior kin in felling trees until he is about 19 years of age (following initiation), so that control over his matrimonial prospects does not provide a means of eliciting his labor contributions. There are no young men who are not betrothed, and there is no uncertainty regarding prospects for marriage that might be exploited. Moreover, the sexual relations and behavioral sexual orientation of a young man of this age are exclusively homosexual, and the depleting heterosexual relations that accompany eventual marriage are viewed more with trepidation than with eager anticipation. In other words, the designation of a future bride precedes any indigenous desire for matrimony on the part of the young man and also precedes the initiation that makes him both eligible and cognitively prepared for marriage.

Insofar as a marriage is arranged for him by his senior male kin, a young man has no direct relationship with his wife's father. The young man will reside at a different longhouse community from that of his future wife's parents until the conjugal relation is established (following both the marriage ceremony and his wife's puberty rite). The young man does not participate in communal gardens with his future wife's parents, cannot speak directly to them, and indeed cannot ever utter their names to others. The relationship is one of taboo and avoidance, except for the widely spaced occasions when betrothal gifts are presented. Even these gifts cannot be directly given to the future wife's parents but must be transmitted through a third party, typically the bachelor's future wife's brother. The bachelor's relation to the latter is close and familiar, since the boy is his designated inseminee. His relations with all his wife's "brothers" are likewise close and congenial. However, none of these young men will have played any role in the arrangement of his marriage.

By arranging marriages, senior males take the initiative in reproducing lineages as well as regenerating sibling and exchange relations between lineages. The distinction between "exchangers" and "exchanged" is thus accurate insofar as it conveys the notion that senior males control the configuration of interlineage relations through control over marriage. Men thus engender a structure of intergroup relations that imparts an added level of meaning to affinal exchange between individuals (as discussed in chap. 2). This appropriation of central aspects of the meaning of marriage is reduplicated in the marriage ceremony by celebrating the union through performance of a *kosa,* in which men are the central figures, and which culminates in transactions in shell valuables between men. The evocation of death and depletion is also pertinent to a male rather than female perspective on marriage. Senior males thus exert control over not only the process of marriage, but also the structure of intergroup relations, of which affinal relations are a part. They also control both the cosmological and the structural meanings of marriage, and of the elements of reproduction it entails.

The brideservice model has played an important role in the analysis of social inequality by specifying inequalities that obtain in societies whose egalitarian features had previously been the main focus of interest. The brideservice model also interrelates inequalities between males and females and between junior and senior males within a comprehensive framework and provides a clearly formulated theory of the production of these inequalities. The model thus has considerable heuristic value as a point of departure for the analysis of specific cases. However, the model has not been systematically employed in this way. Thus, while a number of authors (such as Whitehead, Josephides, and Lindenbaum, all cited earlier) have utilized selected aspects of the model, it has not been comprehensively evaluated against specific ethnographic cases. It consequently has not been determined whether any of the cases to which the model is said to be applicable conformed to the specifications contained within it. An extended evaluation of the model in terms of the Etoro case clearly indicates that the model is inapplicable as formulated (as does consideration of the contrastive Kamula case). However, this is not due to an absence of relevant traits or to misclassification of the Etoro case as one to which the model is applicable, but to the theoretical inadequacies of the model associated with the misplaced causality discussed earlier. Inequalities that are attributed to marital obligations are instead generated by other components of the sociocultural system, and inequalities pertain to statuses that are not defined by marriage. The critical evaluation of the brideservice model contained in the preceding section of this chapter has thus played an important role in laying the groundwork for the development of an alternative theory of the production of social inequality in brideservice societies. The remainder of this chapter is devoted to the development of this alternative theory.

RETHINKING SOCIAL INEQUALITY

One of the critical issues in the study of social inequality is the manner in which equality and inequality are conceived and defined and the consequent delineation of the phenomena to be explained. In many studies, social inequality is implicitly rather than explicitly defined, and divergent conceptualizations of the phenomenon have engendered theoretical disagreement in which the lines of argumentation are at cross-purposes and key issues have not been squarely joined (Ortner 1990; Mukhopadhyay and Higgens 1988; Flanagan 1989). It is consequently important to proceed from a set of explicit definitions and to make apparent the assumptions and theoretical predispositions that are embedded in them.

Following Fallers (1973) and Berreman (1981), social inequality can be minimally defined as social differentiation accompanied by differential moral evaluation. In other words, inequality is identifiably present when socially differentiated categories are subject to cultural evaluations of moral worthiness or denigration. This is a theoretically useful point of departure for several reasons. First, it lays the groundwork for an essential distinction between a moral hierarchy (in which moral worthiness is ascribed to age and gender categories) and a prestige hierarchy (encompassing achieved statuses that differentiate among members of certain age/gender categories). Often these two hierarchies are conflated. Second, it focuses analytic attention on the metaphysics of the cultural system through which social categories are defined and evaluated, and thus leads directly to specification of both the basis of moral standing and the bases of prestige and stigma. Taking moral evaluation rather than prestige itself as a point of departure has the advantage of ensuring that moral denigration and stigma are not omitted from consideration. Often they are in fact omitted. Thus, examination of social inequalities pertaining to the morally denigrated category of witch or sorcerer is almost entirely absent from the literature on the subject. This is particularly unfortunate in the case of "simple" or "egalitarian" or "brideservice" societies, because social differentiation is generally not limited to age and gender but also includes a distinction between individuals who engage in sickness-sending and those who do not, and an additional distinction between those capable of healing sickness and those who lack this capability. Shamanism is a

characteristic feature of nearly all the societies that have been grouped together under these various labels, and a category of sickness-senders is nearly
as pervasive. Moreover, the character, extent, and locus of inequality are
significantly altered by a failure to consider morally evaluated social differentiation pertaining to shamanism and sickness-sending. The significance of
such omissions with respect to theories of the locus of inequality is readily
apparent, since these social inequalities are not intrinsically linked to
marriage-delineated statutes or to the means and relations of production.
Consideration of these social inequalities thus entails theoretical reformulations.

The advantage of the point of departure advocated here is thus twofold.
It ensures that the full range of social differentiation is brought to light and
that stigma as well as prestige is considered in delineating social inequality.
Comprehensiveness is of particular importance because the components of a
scheme of social differentiation are systemically interrelated and defined in
relation to each other and because prestige is likewise conceptually intertwined
with stigma (as is evident, for example, in the case of purity and pollution).
Moreover, the assignment of stigma and debility constitutes an arena of
power that is not brought to light by a focus on the achievement of prestige.
While power is analytically disconnected from the conceptualization of a
"prestige system," the conceptualization of a prestige-stigma system provides
the nodes that readily facilitate its analytic incorporation. Inequalities of
power as well as prestige are thus encompassed within a conceptually integrated framework of analysis. Although the importance of examining gender
inequality within a broader framework of social inequality has been emphasized (Ortner and Whitehead 1981), the implementation of this has often
tended to take the form of interrelating gender inequalities with those that
obtain between junior and senior males within a framework that is broadened
but still less than comprehensive. This is partly due to the fact that broader
frameworks were advocated as a means to the end of attaining a better
understanding of gender inequality, which has remained the focal issue for
many writers. However, there do not appear to be any compelling grounds
for regarding gender inequality as a uniquely distinctive form of social inequality that is appropriately segregated from other inequalities, or that requires a
distinctive analytical and theoretical apparatus (cf. Strathern 1981). If gender
inequality is an integral component of a system of social inequality rather
than an isolatable domain, then this larger system is the appropriate object
of study, and the utilization of a comprehensive framework is essential.

The specification of social inequality logically entails a definition of
equality, since the latter constitutes the implicit benchmark against which
inequality is measured. If equality is not defined, the meaning of inequality
inevitably becomes fuzzy. When socially differentiated categories, groups,

or individuals are culturally evaluated as moral equivalents, the relationship between them can be described as an egalitarian relation (other things being equal). The relationship between moieties provides the clearest illustration of an egalitarian relation and can also serve as a model for evaluating egalitarian relations between individuals. The relationship between moieties is complementary and symmetrically reciprocal. Each provides spouses, ritual services, and so forth for the other. Role reversal and the exchange of exact equivalents are central to a complementarity that is egalitarian in character. Although one moiety may provide the "bosses" and the other the "workers" on a given social occasion, these roles are subsequently reversed on another occasion (see Meggitt 1972a). Temporary dominance is thus compatible with an egalitarian relationship, provided that role reversal ensures alternation.

Segmentation is another form of social differentiation that is egalitarian in character. Segments are formally defined as units that are equivalent in structure and function. Segments are also implicitly morally equivalent when they are equivalent subdivisions of a larger unity such as a clan. However, relations between segments that are not subdivisions of a whole can also be egalitarian if they are not subject to comparative moral evaluation. Equality obtains by default in the absence of acknowledged distinctions of moral worthiness, prestige, or stigma. In the Etoro case, relations between longhouse communities and between lineages are egalitarian by default, since there is no culturally elaborated scheme of comparative moral evaluation applicable to these socially differentiated units. Service (1978:4) defines band-level societies as egalitarian on similar grounds (see Flanagan 1989:246). Although the classification of whole societies as egalitarian on this basis is unwarranted, it is nevertheless useful to specify the egalitarian character of segmentary forms of social differentiation.

Equality and inequality are attributes that pertain to relationships between categories, social groups, and individuals. Structural relations between social groups provide the most clear-cut examples of egalitarian relations, as is evident from the preceding discussion. However, these egalitarian relations at the group level also predicate relations between individuals when the latter interact in their capacity as group members. The relations between individuals who exchange ritual services as members of opposite moieties are thus egalitarian in this respect. The relations between fellow clansmen who unite in complementary opposition to a coordinate group are also egalitarian. Although siblings can potentially be differentiated on the basis of age and gender, it is predominantly within the context of group membership that such differentiation is effaced. Thus, relations between social groups and between individuals as members of social groups are important sources of social equality within social systems. Indeed, it can be argued that social groups are the principal locus for the production of social equality. (For example, male and female lineage members have equivalent rights to garden on lineage territory in the Etoro case, and are equal in this respect.) Although it is important that the analysis of social equality and inequality not be confined to the group level, omitting this level from consideration is equally unwarranted and produces a distorted picture of both the extent of and potentiality for egalitarian relations within human society. In simple societies, social relations are frequently egalitarian in some respects and inegalitarian in others. A balanced account thus requires attention to both of these sides of the social equation.

The fact that equality and inequality are attributes of relationships has implications for the theoretical status of the concept of autonomy. Autonomy in the sense of independence from others precludes inequality by precluding relationship but lacks any of the positive features of an egalitarian relationship, e.g., symmetrically reciprocal complementarity. Autonomy cannot form the basis of egalitarian society since society intrinsically entails the transcendence of autonomy. It is consequently the relationships through which individuals interact that must form the grounds for a determination of the egalitarian or inegalitarian nature of a social system. Leacock's (1981:133–81) argument that Montagnais-Naskapi society was gender egalitarian because women were autonomous is thus logically flawed (see also Schlegel 1972). The considerations raised here bring out the importance of explicit definitions of equality and inequality.

Egalitarian relations between individuals take two basic forms that are reminiscent of Durkheim's distinction between mechanical and organic solidarity. In the first type, the inclusion of two (or more) individuals within a larger entity based on a commonality engenders an egalitarian relationship between them by defining them as equivalent in salient respects. Mechanical solidarity intrinsically contains egalitarian overtones and is always a central component of egalitarian ideology. It is this potentiality that makes social groups the central locus for the production of equality. In the second type of relationship, equality is predicated on exchange. However, the objects of exchange are culturally defined as equivalent and in the most clear-cut cases are identical (in contradistinction to Durkheim's vision of organic solidarity). The exchange of identical sides of pork between Etoro affines thus formulates the relationship between them as egalitarian (and also entails an enactment of equality in status). Social relations can of course be egalitarian in certain respects but not others, as noted above. However, the principal objective here is to clearly specify the grounds for designating a relationship, or aspects of a relationship, as egalitarian or inegalitarian.

While morally evaluated social differentiation constitutes the minimal basis for the specification of inegalitarian relations, such inequalities are subject to variable degrees of further elaboration that pertain to the distribution of prestige (or stigma), social privilege (or debility), and a potentially wide variety of other forms of culturally pertinent advantage. One of the theoretical presuppositions that is entailed in taking morally evaluated social differentiation as a point of departure is that significant social inequalities pertain to the distribution of culturally valued things among culturally recognized categories and between individuals engaged in ongoing social relations. (These "things" include intangibles such as deference.) Equality with respect to that which is of little or no value is not equality in any significant sense. One might think, for example, of equal access to junk mail. The same logic applies to inequalities in the distribution of nonvalued items. Similarly, equalities that obtain between etically defined groups or categories that are not culturally recognized by actors are not significant equalities. Although one might show that there are no significant differences in income between right- and left-handed persons, the argument that this constituted an egalitarian feature of the society in question would scarcely be compelling. Here, too, the same logic applies to inequalities that obtain between unrecognized groups or categories of individuals. Significant social inequalities are those that are felt or experienced by social actors within the sociocultural system in question. Workers need not manifest class consciousness to be aware that they are in a disadvantaged position and to experience social inequality. Contentment with a disadvantaged position grounded in acceptance of the cultural rationales through which it is legitimated does not reduce or eradicate social inequality, since this acceptance nevertheless entails recognition of social disabilities. It is also clear that the analysis of social inequality necessarily entails the employment of a theoretical apparatus external to the system under consideration in order to penetrate the mechanisms for the production of inequality, since these are generally not fully understood or articulated by social actors. These aspects of the analysis of social inequality are not at issue here. *What is at issue is delineation of the object of explanation.* The social inequalities that constitute the explicandum can only usefully be defined in terms of recognized differences in the distribution of culturally valued things among culturally recognized groups and categories and between individuals engaged in ongoing social relations. It is important to recall that social equality entails the foregrounding of salient similarities and the effacement of potentially recognizable differences between individuals. Equality can only be conceptual, and inequality should logically be defined in the same terms. *The range of differences that can be empirically discovered to obtain between individuals or groups is virtually infinite.* The sides of pork exchanged by Etoro affines could never be empirically identical in every respect, but can only be regarded as equivalent by the actors engaged in their exchange. An empirical or phenomenological approach cannot fail to discover limitless "inequality," but raises the question of the significance of what is being described and explained.

As noted earlier, consideration of the system of moral evaluation leads directly to the specification of the bases of moral standing and of prestige and stigma. Insofar as privilege is constituted as socially legitimated advantage, this approach also elucidates the principles through which such legitimation is effected and constitutes a useful entrée into consideration of the distribution of culturally pertinent advantage. However, the relationship between the system of moral evaluation and the prestige system requires some clarification. The system of moral evaluation can be defined as the component of the value system that delineates virtue and its opposites. Virtue has moral connotations that are linked to spiritual qualities and conceptions of good and evil, but also has connotations of superiority, merit, and distinction in areas that extend beyond moral and spiritual domains. Virtue in the first sense is illustrated by the opposition between the seven virtues and the seven deadly sins. Virtue in the second sense is illustrated by secondary meanings that include female chastity and the possession of manly strength and valor. The two connotations are additionally exemplified by the difference between virtuousness and virtuosity. Virtue also has the additional meaning of a power, as in the expression "by virtue of" (i.e., by the power or efficacy of). This is potentially applicable to both spiritual and secular distinction. The term virtue thus has the advantage of a range of meanings commensurate with the breadth of the phenomena being addressed in the analysis of other cultural systems.

Virtue can be either ascribed or achieved, although virtue in the second sense (virtuosity) is necessarily established through social action rather than being intrinsic to a state of being, and is thus achieved. In the terminology employed in this work, prestige is the esteem and general admiration accorded to virtue in this second sense (achieved distinction) and the prestige system delineates virtues established through elective social action.[14] The utility of the distinctions being employed here can be illustrated with respect to the status of generosity as a virtue in the Etoro system of moral evaluation. Senior men with mature children and inseminees are intrinsically generous insofar as their life force has contributed to the reproduction and maturation of their offspring and their juniors. They are virtuous by definition, are respected, and occupy the apex of the moral hierarchy (but are not accorded a place in the prestige/stigma hierarchy simply on the basis of normative life-force donations). In contrast, esteem is accorded to elective acts of generosity in which various individuals may engage to a greater or lesser extent (e.g., the provisioning of game distribution). Senior men are thus differentiated in terms of earned prestige although they are equivalent in terms of intrinsic generosity. It is consequently useful to designate generosity as a virtue, applicable to both of these contexts, while reserving the term prestige to refer to comparative distinction established through elective social action. The prestige-stigma system is thus a restricted component of a more encompassing system of moral evaluation in the usage employed in this work.

The systems of cultural values that shape and delineate social inequality are extremely varied so that what is a virtue in one system may be a vice in another. However, the criteria for delineating socially differentiated categories are much less diverse. Thus, age and gender constitute widespread criteria for social differentiation. The ways in which individuals are recruited to categories and virtue is assigned to individuals are likewise limited. The achieved/ascribed distinction has been employed to define basic variants. The utilization of these limited principles of categorization, recruitment, and assignment have served as the basis for typologies of systems of social inequality (Sahlins 1958; Fried 1967). A classification of societies that is based on these principles specifies clusters of societies that manifest comparable forms and dimensions of social inequality. Delineation of the features that generate these similarities then becomes a primary theoretical objective. This continues to be a productive framework for elucidating social inequality.[15] However, the characteristics of the class of societies that evidences the most limited forms of social inequality can usefully be amplified.[16]

In Sahlins's (1958:1–2) original formulation, the qualifications for status differentiation in the least stratified societies are age, sex, and personal characteristics. What remains unspecified in this and subsequent definitions (e.g., Fried 1967) is the nature of the system that governs the recognition of salient personal characteristics. It is evident that this is the prestige-stigma system (in the sense defined above). Moreover, the prestige systems of the societies that are grouped together in terms of the employment of principles of categorization based on age, gender, and personal characteristics are of a distinctive type. Prestige is accorded on the basis of distinction in culturally valued activities in which personal qualities that betoken virtue are manifested. These are consequently activities in which an individual's own skill and labor contribution are discernible and can be distinguished from the contributions of others. Thus, male prestige is typically derived from activities that are predominantly or exclusively performed by males and that do not require direct female labor inputs. Prestige is often accorded on the basis of hunting success, generosity in distributing game, distinction in raiding and warfare, ritual performance, possession of sacred knowledge, and possession of spiritual powers, while stigma is typically linked to sickness-sending and the violation of taboos. Female access to the performance of culturally valued activities is often limited. However, a substantial number of societies with minimal forms of social differentiation have both male and female shamans, and a few have female ritual leaders (see, for example, Poole 1981a). When prestige-producing activities are open to women, the same principles of allocation apply in that prestige is linked to the individual's own skill and labor. Thus female prestige derived from shamanism is diminished when the efficacy of female practitioners is defined as contingent upon male contributions (see, for example, Godelier 1986:120–21). This substantiates the centrality of the principle of individual effort. The general applicability of this principle is also evident from the fact that the prestige derived from hunting is significantly reduced or eliminated when hunting is collective.

Focusing on the prestige systems of simple societies opens several fruitful lines of inquiry into fundamental questions pertaining to social inequality. It is evident that these prestige systems entail restrictions on participation in the activities through which prestige is acquired and that this constitutes a basic source of social inequality. The effective mechanism through which access is restricted is, to a large extent, the division of labor or, more broadly, the division of activity. Individuals who are assigned to non-prestige-producing activities clearly have no opportunity to earn prestige. The division of labor is thus a central mechanism for the production of inequality.

This raises the question of what determines the contours of the division of labor. This can be resolved by recognizing that the division of labor entails two aspects: the assignment of individuals to tasks on the basis of age and gender, and the cultural valuation of activity, i.e., the division of value accorded to labor. The assignment of individuals to tasks is frequently based in part on enunciated concepts of natural ability attributed to age and gender categories. In other words, both males and females say that only men are capable of extensive tree cutting or other heavy labor, as in the Etoro case (also see Sillitoe 1985). However, these indigenous forms of essentialism only account for a portion of the division of activity and often fail to provide any basis for excluding women and uninitiated men from ritual performance and the acquisition of spiritual powers and sacred knowledge. Naturalistic essentialism is thus fleshed out by reliance on concepts of spiritual affinity. This frequently entails the formulation of a notion of spiritual affinity between men and animals that empowers male hunting ability. Totemism accompanied by male performance of rituals to ensure the reproduction of the animals instantiates the requisite linkage. There are, however, many cultural formulations other than this familiar Australian Aborigines variant that have the same effect. The assignment of individuals to tasks is thus ultimately based on the cosmological system. This system invariably includes features that are implicitly or explicitly conducive to restricting the access of women and uninitiated men to key prestige-producing activities. Moreover, the activities that are assigned to men on the basis of imputed natural (rather than supernatural) abilities are infrequently a source of prestige (e.g., tree felling).

The division of value accorded to labor is also grounded in the cosmological system. Game procurement takes on special significance because of its spiritual quality. This is well illustrated by Etoro fish poisoning (organized with reference to the affinity between Etoro mediums and the spirits of the dead, who occupy the bodies of the fish). Hunting in the high forest, which is the domain of the male *Sigisato* spirits, is a more subtle variant of the same phenomenon. In both instances, the products of the endeavor are rendered up by the spirits or procured through their good graces, so that the activity entails communion with the supernatural. In the Etoro case, generosity in the distribution of game also takes on a spiritual quality as a result (as explained in chap. 2).

Taking life in war typically releases spiritual entities and often entails ritual preparations, subsequent ritual cleansing, or ritual treatment of trophies (e.g., heads). Among the Keraki, the spiritual nature of taking life is strikingly illustrated by the invocation uttered as the fatal blow is struck: "*Tokujenjeni* [the bullroarer] is copulating with you" (Williams 1936:183). Raiding and warfare are typically ritualized in one or more of the ways noted above in the simple societies in which they are central to the prestige system as a salient domain in which distinction is measured. The spiritual quality of ritual performance and of the possession of sacred knowledge or spiritual power is self-evident. The prestige systems of the societies under consideration all evidence a striking similarity in that prestige-producing activities are characteristically activities that entail and evince spiritual qualities. The cosmological system establishes the spiritual quality of selected activities and is thus the source of the evaluations that imbue these activities with special value, rendering them prestigious (as will be further elaborated below).

The cosmological system thus delineates the division of labor in terms of both the categorical assignment of individuals to activities and the division of value accorded to those activities. The division of labor is the efficient cause of unequal access to prestige-producing activities and thereby generates the resultant social inequality. However, the latter is legitimate as well as shaped by the underlying cosmology. The cosmological system also constitutes the foundation for the larger system of moral evaluation (that defines virtue and its opposites) as well as the prestige system that forms a component of it. The connection between virtue in the moral or spiritual sense and virtue in the sense of superiority, merit, and distinction is evident from the preceding discussion. The notion of a spiritual affinity between men and animals that empowers male hunting ability also entails the concept of virtue as a power or efficacy.

The key aspect of the cosmological system that engenders these conditions is the metaphysical component that defines the fundamental nature of reality in terms of both the nature of being and the underlying causes and processes that order the cosmos. The Etoro cosmological system that comprehends reproduction, the spiritual constitution of persons, and life-cycle transformations entails a delineation of the fundamental nature of reality from which cultural evaluations logically follow. The compellingly persuasive and nonarbitrary character of value is a product of its metaphysical derivation. In other words, the cultural formulation of virtue and its opposites is grounded in delineation of the nature of reality, particularly the supernatural deep structure that accounts for its perceived surface manifestations. If death is caused by witchcraft, then witchcraft is intrinsically evil; the valuation is implicit in the description of the underlying cause of death (and the latter also establishes an essential foundation for the further elaboration of negative value). Stigma logically attaches to the practitioners of evil witchcraft, and combating the illness they induce is a virtue. If the perpetuation of life is contingent upon a transmission of life force that engenders conception, growth, and maturation at the expense of the donor's depletion, then such donations are the epitome of generosity and generosity is a virtue.

Recognition of the fact that metaphysics accounts for the basis of the cultural values that pertain to social inequality makes it possible to further elucidate the production of inequality. While the "cultural system," "meaning system," and "value system" constitute comparatively amorphous sources of social inequality that appear as the unmotivated residue of a past history in which all categories of persons participated, the source of Etoro conceptions of the fundamental nature of reality can be precisely specified.[17] Such conceptions are the product of a shamanic elite. Elucidation of the spiritual plane of existence that encompasses the causes and processes that order the cosmos (and constitute the deep structure that accounts for the surface manifestations of perceptual reality) is the express role of spirit mediums. Moreover, Etoro cosmology is not grounded in doctrine that is subject to the restrictions of an orthodoxy. The pronouncements of spirit mediums are revealed truth derived directly from the *Sigisato* and *Kesame* spirits and from sojourns in the spirit world (cf. Schieffelin 1985b:720). Spiritual authority thus resides in spirit mediums rather than in doctrine whose validity is rooted in the past (and restricted by conformity to past understandings). Etoro cosmology is consequently reproduced anew by each successive generation of spirit mediums. Although they doubtless retell much of what they learned from their mentors and predecessors, their source of knowledge is direct communication with the spirits. It is thus the acquisition of spirits rather than the mastery of traditional lore and doctrine that is the central qualification of spirit mediumship.

There is also clear evidence that spirit mediums can readily engage in cosmological innovation. When I related to a spirit medium that day and night were attributable to the rotation of the earth, which was round like the moon, aspects of this cosmological description were subsequently incorporated into séance pronouncements. Schieffelin (1977) provides a much more striking example of the same phenomena among the Kaluli. At a witchcraft inquest, a spirit speaking through an entranced medium graphically described a witch in the act of "saying grace" over the corpse of a victim before devouring it, thereby identifying witchcraft directly with Christianity (ibid.:169). Schieffelin's insight into the role of mediums as historical innovators can be applied to the development of the traditional cosmology as well as to its postcontact transformations.

Etoro male mediums construct cosmological realities from a male perspective and in ways that glorify masculinity and define virtue in masculine terms. It is unnecessary to credit these mediums with a cynical, self-conscious, and conspiratorial formulation of the underlying basis of gender inequality, since an androcentric actor's point of view is sufficient to account for the results. It is noteworthy in this respect that Etoro cosmology does not explicitly denigrate women or accord an intrinsic and invariant negative value to them. Women are upstaged rather than disvalued by a male appropriation of reproduction that fails to assign any supernatural significance to the female role in the perpetuation of life. Gender inequality is largely a product of omission rather than commission. The intent of the cosmological system can thus be deciphered as the elevation of males rather than the deprecation of females, and this is attributable to the androcentric point of view of its promulgators. The sacred quality of the virginal, recently initiated bachelors (who are repositories of the *hame* that ensures the perpetuation of life) is also consistent with this interpretation. Mediums begin their careers as members of this life-cycle group, are most active during the subsequent years, partially disengage in their late 30s or early 40s, and cease to practice by about age 45. The chorus on which a medium depends in order to stage a séance also consists of young men. The cosmology is not only constructed from a male point of view, but from the perspective of a recently initiated bachelor (as noted in chap. 3). The dominant perspective is consequently that of the life-cycle group that reproduces the cosmology. The character of the cosmology is thus attributable to the mode of its reproduction and to the social position of those engaged in this enterprise.[18]

The exclusion of women from the shamanic elite that eventuates in an exclusively male perspective remains to be explained. In the Etoro case this is institutionalized and the processes by which it developed cannot be directly discerned. It is reproduced by the cosmology in that spirit mediumship requires a spirit wife capable of giving birth to a spirit child who resides in the spirit world. Although a woman could, in theory, acquire a spirit husband, their child would be born into the mundane world, and thus could not provide the requisite connection to the spirit world. Male-exclusive mediumship is also effectively reproduced by a mode of recruitment in which existing mediums nominate potential protégés and serve as their mentors. No women are nominated.

A comparative study that encompassed systems that include both male and female practitioners would make it possible to elucidate the development of male control over the shamanic profession. Although this is beyond the scope of the present work, several points may be noted. Systems in which shamans are self-selected as a result of dream experience or illness tend to evidence practitioners of both genders, while systems in which shamans are nominated by established practitioners tend toward pronounced male predominance or exclusivity. Self-selection followed by apprenticeship constitutes an intermediate form in which females tend not to attain the higher levels of the profession and do not train and/or induct novices. These three types thus appear to constitute a developmental sequence that progresses from self-selection, to self-selection followed by apprenticeship, to nomination followed by apprenticeship. Coincident with this is a progression from gender-neutral to gender-stratified to male-exclusive shamanism. There is typically a statistical bias in favor of males in systems that are gender neutral in the sense of being open to both genders. Moreover, when shamanism goes into decline under contact conditions, female practitioners tend to disappear at an earlier phase. Such instances illustrate a historical progression from gender-neutral to male-exclusive shamanism in systems based on self-selection (and in which the mode of entry into the profession does not change over time). A preliminary comparison of societies characterized by the distinctive type of prestige system delineated earlier thus suggests that there is a definite tendency toward male predominance in the possession of spiritual powers (and spiritual authority) and a developmental trajectory that eventuates in male-exclusive shamanism.[19]

Competition between mediums may account for some aspects of the tendency toward male predominance in shamanic systems. Competition is intrinsic to Etoro spirit mediumship because a practitioner requires an audience, a supporting chorus, and a clientele composed of individuals who request cures and spirit inquests. The need for these services and the availability of choral support and audience interest are all limited. While the profession is comparatively open at the entry level, there are only a limited number of congregations that require a practitioner, and this generates competition. Competition is an intrinsic feature of most shamanic systems for the same reasons. Only those that require apprenticeship have an institutional capacity to limit entry into the profession. However, a tendency for established practitioners to recruit protégés undercuts realization of this potential to some extent.

It is evident that a female spirit medium would be at a disadvantage in the competition that occurs in the Etoro system. A competitor can be directly accused of witchcraft. A female practitioner would not be in a position to respond directly to the threat of force employed to extract compensation or exact vengeance. She would require male support that she would be unable to reciprocate in kind. A cooperative relationship with the leading *tafidilo* of the community is also conducive to securing and maintaining the position of resident medium. A female medium would also be at a disadvantage in establishing such an alliance because *tafidilos* are exclusively male and affinal relations between mediums and *tafidilos* provide an effective basis for establishing a close cooperative relationship. If there were female spirit mediums among the Etoro, the dynamics of competition between mediums would thus be conducive to their eventual elimination; they would be easier to dislodge and/or discredit than their male counterparts.

The development of a male-exclusive shamanic elite in the Etoro and comparable cases could be the product of a concerted, conspiratorial male effort to achieve this goal. Conspiracy invariably provides an economical explanation. However, unequal competition constitutes an alternative hypothesis: male predominance or exclusivity is the unintended consequence of disconnected episodes of individual competition in which female practitioners are at a disadvantage. The issue cannot be resolved on the basis of the data at hand, although it is implicitly raised by the logic of the argument being developed and therefore requires some discussion. This discussion also elucidates certain aspects of the reproduction of male exclusivity. Whatever the historical development of an Etoro male-exclusive shamanic elite may have entailed, it can be concluded that competition among mediums is an additional factor conducive to the maintenance of this pattern.

The ideology conveyed by spirit mediums is the hegemonic ideology by virtue of the fact that mediums possess unquestioned spiritual authority. There is no vantage point from which spiritually derived revealed truth can be effectively questioned. Mythmaking does provide a means of constructing commentaries upon ideological formulations, and both men and women can fabricate and relate stories that conform to the mythic genre. Ancestral authenticity is not a requisite, although myths invoke the past insofar as they begin with an analogue of "once upon a time." A myth that is appreciated, retold, and becomes part of the cultural repertoire is one that evidences qualities commensurate with those of enduring literature. The authorial source of a myth is unspecified and unimportant. The validity of the insights contained in myth is not vouched by spiritual or other authority but depends upon the extent to which they ring true to the listener.

The capacity of myth to independently construct rather than resonate with or elaborate upon cosmologically given realities is limited. A myth that questions one or two components of the hegemonic ideology can only do so through a critique that at the same time embraces the underlying premises of that ideology. This is illustrated by the myth of the male mother, discussed in chapter 3. Although the construction of events contained in this myth is conducive to the interpretation that male depletion is a product of male lust (and that responsibility for such depletion is thus attributable to males), this entails conceding the fundamental doctrine that sexual relations deplete men but not women. Moreover, a myth cannot compel a single interpretation, and this dilutes its ideological effect. Thus myth cannot effectively deconstruct a hegemonic ideology and, lacking authority, cannot instantiate an alternative. Moreover, a dialogue of gynocentric and androcentric myths and interpretations constitutes an inconclusive repartee. Although mythmaking provides women with a vehicle for the presentation of a divergent point of view, exclusion from positions of spiritual authority precludes access to cosmological formulation and to any effective impact upon the hegemonic ideology. There is only one Etoro metaphysic, and men and women do not have divergent views concerning the fundamental nature of reality.[20] Reality is culturally constructed but not through the equal participation of all members of a cultural group. The resultant constructs bear witness to this insofar as they manifest the unmistakable imprint of their male creators. Both men and women live in a social world shaped by an androcentric hegemonic ideology.

Privilege is constituted by the legitimation of a culturally pertinent advantage, and the cosmological system is the source of the requisite legitimation. Etoro food taboos, which constitute a hierarchical ordering of relative privilege (and debility) provide a clear example. The differential social categories and the number of native taxa that may be consumed by each are: widows (18), children of deceased men (24), children of living men (63), young women (67), mature women (70), unmarried young men (78), married men (81), and elderly men (83) (Kelly 1977:43). The debility that accrues to widows and the children of deceased men is a direct product of cosmological doctrine in that such individuals are the agents and beneficiaries, respectively, of the depletion that contributed to male death (and male death is the basis for assignment to these categories). The maximal privilege accorded to elderly men is likewise commensurate with their fully completed contributions to the perpetuation of life. Widows are not only the agents of accomplished male depletion but are also outside of the category of reproductive females by virtue of their unmarried state. The next three most restricted categories are all recipients of male life force who have not as yet contributed to reproduction. They are also ranked in order of their consumption of life force, so that young women who are approaching a maturation that occurs without infusions of *hame* are the least restricted of the three. *Townisa*, or young women between the ages of 12 and 17, can thus consume a greater number of taxa than boys of the same age, since the boys are still classified as children (*manasa*). This is consistent with the fact that these boys are being inseminated and are therefore consumers of greater quantities of life force than their same-aged female counterparts. The three most privileged categories are all life-force donors, and these are rank-ordered in terms of their contributions. Initiated bachelors are the inseminators of boys, married men are double donors who additionally contribute to the conception and early growth of children, and elderly men have completed their contributions to both aspects of reproduction and are depleted as a result. Mature married women who contribute to reproduction through childbearing are located at the conceptual midpoint of this scale, between consumers and donors of life force. The hierarchical ordering of privilege is thus a direct product of the cosmological system that comprehends reproduction, the spiritual constitution of persons, and life-cycle transformations. The delineation of socially differentiated categories, their moral evaluation, and the legitimation of the privileges and disabilities that accrue to each are all derived from the same source. Thus the system of food taboos mirrors the moral hierarchy.

If the social inequalities that constitute the explicandum are most usefully defined in terms of culturally recognized differences in the distribution of culturally valued things among socially differentiated and morally evaluated categories, then the Etoro system of food taboos is clearly of central importance inasmuch as it precisely corresponds to these specifications. The encompassing system of social inequality that is formulated in terms of food taboos provides both an apposite context in which to document and elucidate theoretical arguments that have been presented in the abstract and a particularly useful focal point for the consideration of a number of key issues.

The social inequalities that are enacted through the distribution of game in accordance with these food taboos are definitely experienced as such by social actors. Exclusion is all the more keenly felt in the context of an ethos that accords special value to an encompassing distribution of food to all community members. The ethic of generosity and sharing by equal division that is applicable to the distribution of domesticated pork and large game animals makes a restricted, discriminating distribution all the more poignant. These two modes of distribution thus constitute point and counterpoint, each highlighting the distinctive character of the other. While equality is vividly experienced through one mode, inequality is as vividly experienced through the other. Hierarchy is not smuggled in, subtly introduced, or soft-pedaled. However, there is no evidence that the palpable social inequalities manifested in restricted game distribution are either perceived as unfair and illegitimate or resented. No sulking, grumbling, or complaining was witnessed.

This raises the issue of the legitimation of social inequality and the related issue of the interconnection between differential rewards and differential contributions to the general welfare of the social group. The issues are related insofar as an ethnotheory of differential contributions typically serves as the basis for the legitimation of inequality. The Etoro case clearly conforms to this general pattern in that socially differentiated categories are ranked in accordance with their contributions to the perpetuation of life and assigned a commensurate measure of differential privilege in terms of access to game.

It is at this juncture that it becomes necessary to move outside the system of cultural definitions, since an explanation framed in cultural terms merely echoes the hegemonic ideology's rationalization of social inequality. This shift is facilitated by the distinction drawn earlier. Defining what is to be explained in cultural terms does not in any way require a commitment to explaining it exclusively in those same terms. One may consequently adopt a critical perspective. However, this entails a redefinition of the standards of evaluation insofar as the standards internal to the system are set aside. At the same time, the cultural construction of reality is replaced by the analyst's metaphysic. Ethnocentric value judgments necessarily inform the selection of the standards employed, and there is ample scope for the introduction of the analyst's political point of view as well. In the study of social inequality, this comes with the territory. The only antidote is to make these operations transparent to the readers so that they can make an informed judgment with regard to the explanations advanced and apply their own critical perspective to the data.

The Etoro system of food taboos is an indigenous solution to a classic social problem, namely the distribution of scarce resources. In the case of the midsize game to which these taboos predominantly apply, there is not enough to go around. There are essentially four major ways in which scarce resources can be allocated. The first is guided by the principle: from each according to his or her ability, to each according to his or her needs. The second possibility entails allocation in a manner commensurate with individual contributions to the production of resources or to the general welfare. The third entails differential distribution in accordance with a hierarchy that is established on grounds that are independent of, and do not necessarily covary with, abilities, contributions, and needs. A system guided by the realization of self-interest, in which each individual takes as much as he or she can get, constitutes the fourth possibility. It differs from the first three in that it does not take cognizance of the needs of others within a larger societal framework and is divorced from any concept of the general welfare.

The Etoro case can be assessed by evaluating the prevailing modes of distribution in relation to these four possibilities. For these purposes, it is useful to consider the restricted distribution of game that takes place in accordance with food taboos within a broader context that encompasses all forms of distribution of animal protein. Animal protein is the focus of the analysis because it constitutes the scarce resource. Starch staples are in ample supply, and their production can readily be adjusted to consumption needs.

As noted in chapter 2, the Etoro system of meat distribution does not entail privileged consumption measured in nutritional terms. This is due to the fact that large and small game are subject to few or no food taboos, and the allocation of domesticated pork counterbalances the distributional consequences of the taboos pertaining to midsize game. Moreover, the game animals that are subject to the most restricted distribution are predominantly those that are very infrequently taken. Although only 35 percent of the animal protein in the diet is available to widows, the taboos in force are only applicable to the two- to three-year mourning period prior to remarriage. A significant number of women never experience widowhood, and all widows of childbearing age remarry. A proportion of widows aged 46 to 60 also remarry, and widowhood is generally not protracted among women in this age-group as mortality is high (Kelly 1977:219–313). Moreover, formerly restricted items become available to unremarried widows past childbearing age, increasing available protein to 53.2 percent (Kelly 1977:45). Taking all these considerations into account, it is estimated that an average of 93 percent of the available animal protein in the diet is consumed annually by adult women over the course of a lifetime, while 82 percent is consumed by adult men.[21] The difference is principally attributable to three factors: (1) mature women other than widows can consume 97 percent of available animal protein; (2) men are prohibited from consuming domesticated pork half of the time (and such pork constitutes 34.4 percent of dietary protein by weight); and (3) taboos connected with widowhood are of shorter duration, over the course of an adult lifetime, than the periods of prohibited pork consumption that affect adult men. Girls aged 12 to 17 are also slightly favored over boys of the same age (75 percent to 73.8 percent), so that the pattern among adults with respect to gender is applicable to younger individuals as well. There are no differences among adult women in protein availability other than those pertaining to widowhood. There are also no significant differences between bachelors, married men, and elderly men, who can all consume 99.0 to 100 percent of the available protein in the diet when not subject to prohibited consumption of domesticated pork (Kelly 1977:45). Children require less and also receive less. Although the children of deceased men are disadvantaged, this is a temporary condition. Overall, the distribution of animal protein conforms quite closely to a model based on the principle of allocation in terms of nutritional needs. The deviations from this are small in magnitude and favor women.

It is thus evident that the system of food taboos encodes symbolic privilege rather than a materially advantageous form of privileged consumption. The hierarchy that is formulated on the basis of relative virtue is recognized through privileges that are essentially a form of deference. The animals that are specifically reserved for men are generally those that have spiritual properties (see n. 27 of chap. 2). The spiritual affinity between men and animals is thus the guiding principle behind the taboos that restrict consumption of these taxa to men. Here, too, virtue comes into play since spiritual affinity is a component of it. In effect, only the virtuous (i.e., men) are permitted to take communion but they gain no significant nutritional advantage as a result. The differential distribution of symbolic privilege thus conforms to a hierarchy of virtue grounded in the cosmological system rather than in the economic system. The hierarchy is not legitimated in terms of contributions to economic production and nutritional needs but in terms of contributions to the perpetuation of life.

It is important to note that the counterbalancing restrictions that affect the consumption patterns of men and women are of an entirely different moral character, although similar in certain other respects. Widows are disbarred from consuming a number of animals as a consequence of their responsibility for male death. Men are disbarred from consuming pork as a consequence of their responsibility for the death of a domestic pig. The former responsibility is on the order of a sin, while the latter is a secular lapse that does not impinge on male virtue. The widow's restrictions are a penance, while the husbandman's are a misfortune. Moreover, the husbandman renounces consumption as the primary caretaker of the domestic pig herd and thereby establishes distributional rights over the pigs that are coproduced by husband and wife. The husbandman's prohibition is also informed by the principle of generalized reciprocity. He does not share in the pork distributed by others, because the deceased pig represents a loss of that which he would have shared with others. The husbandman's assumption of responsibility that leads to disbarment from pork consumption is thus contextualized within a framework of generosity and is seen to increase the quantity available to others, most notably women (as discussed in chap. 2). In other words, the renunciation of domestic pork following the loss of a pig is on the order of a virtue and contrasts with the widow's penance in this respect as well. What the widow gives up compensates for the life force she has extracted; her restrictions are not seen as an indirect form of generosity but as payment due. Thus while women are slightly advantaged in terms of the consumption of animal protein by the net effect of the counterbalancing restrictions, they are clearly disadvantaged in the allocation of virtue and moral disability. In effect, men extract prestige value and distributional privileges from an equivalent exchange of restrictions.

It has been established that distribution of the scarce resource of animal protein is essentially governed by a needs principle (when measured in terms of external standards pertaining to nutrition). This is in accord with the first of the four types of allocation outlined earlier. In contrast, symbolic deference is allocated in accordance with a fixed hierarchy based on principles that are extraneous to needs. What remains to be examined is the relationship between distribution and contributions to production. This area of inquiry touches upon another classic dilemma of social life. If all are assured that they will receive in accordance with their needs, what ensures that they will produce in accordance with their abilities? In the Etoro system, the differential distribution of prestige provides the main stimulus, although there is a measure of material reward as well. An assiduous hunter such as Ibo will consume more meat than other men because he consumes part of all the game he procures. When a midsize game animal is insufficient to go around, only the producer, his family, and his siblings and affines will share in it, while others will not. Similarly, an assiduous pig husbandman will curtail the loss of his stock and promptly kill a pig when one inadvertently dies so as to quickly remove the prohibition on pork consumption. He will have sufficient mature pigs on hand to do so. He will consequently consume part of nearly all the pigs slaughtered, whereas a lax husbandman with little stock will infrequently receive a portion. In both cases, effort is materially rewarded to some degree, and production in accordance with ability is furthered. However, the increment gained through assiduousness is slight as a proportion of production since the producer's share constitutes only a small fraction of what is distributed. Thus, the prestige derived from generosity in the distribution of both domestic pork and game constitutes the principal reward and the main stimulus to production. Unlike the material rewards, the prestige gained is directly proportional to the results achieved. It is also important to note that prestige provides the central motive for bringing game back to the longhouse to be shared rather than consuming it privately in the forest. Private consumption entails a complete loss of the prestige values realized through distribution and also entails the risk of moral disapprobation.

The main producers of game, in the order of the increasing magnitude of their contributions, are mature married women, bachelors, and married men. The number of taxa that can be consumed by each increases in the same order, from 70 to 78 to 81, while the percentage of available protein increases from 97 to 99 percent. Rewards thus covary with contributions, with two exceptions. Widows may contribute as much as married women, but can consume far less, and elderly men who no longer hunt can consume all taxa. The significance of the relation between rewards and contributions is that a hunter is infrequently faced with the prospect of returning to the longhouse with an animal he or she is prohibited from consuming. Moreover, the game women procure during garden clearance is, with rare exceptions, the game they can consume. Male hunters likewise focus their efforts on types of game they can eat (cf. Van Beek 1987). Securing the prestige realized through distribution therefore does not entail giving up all of the consumption value, but only that which is in excess of the share a hunter would retain if it were distributed. This is a favorable trade-off from a male actor's point of view, since much is gained in comparison to both the marginal utility of what is relinquished and the risk of moral disapprobation that accompanies its appropriation. A female actor has less to gain because the prestige value that can be derived from distributing game procured during garden clearance to family members, siblings, and affines at a garden dwelling is comparatively restricted. In the case of a widow, the trade-off is particularly unfavorable, since the entire consumption value is more often at stake. The temptation to engage in private consumption is correspondingly much greater.

The system of food taboos is thus constituted so as to stimulate both production and sharing on the part of those who are the primary producers of the preponderant majority of nondomesticated animal protein. While men are motivated to hunt and share the proceeds by the prospects for prestige-enhancement, women are less motivated to hunt and are induced to share what they do procure more out of the avoidance of moral disapprobation than out of prestige aspirations. The degree of suspicion that private consumption has occurred corresponds to the level of temptation outlined above and is therefore greatest in the case of the most heavily restricted categories, especially widows and boys under the age of 17. It is probable that these suspicions are not entirely unfounded. In any event, men bring very substantial quantities of game to the longhouse to be shared with coresidents who are not members of their families, while widows and boys very infrequently do so. The failure to bring game that has been procured to the longhouse to be shared conforms to the type of distribution governed by material self-interest, in which each individual takes as much as he or she can get without consideration of the needs of others. The system is constituted so as to minimize this type of distribution, which would clearly be highly advantageous to the principal producers, i.e., men. Inequality in the distribution of prestige thus contributes to the general welfare in this respect. However, this is not to say that a system of prestige inequalities represents the only possible mechanism for inducing the primary producers of a scarce resource to share it with others.

The primary phase of large-game distribution entails parceling out equivalent portions to all resident male game producers who then subdivide their shares among coproducers of starch staples and dependent children in the secondary distribution. As noted earlier, the guiding principle of the primary distribution is generalized reciprocity. Those who receive are those who will provision like distributions on other occasions. The prohibition on consuming domesticated pork following the death of a pig is based on the same principle. A husbandman gains a place in the distribution through past or anticipated participation in generalized reciprocity and temporarily loses this place when the death of a pig negates his capacity to reciprocate. This principle of restricting primary distribution to producers clearly rewards those who contribute the most to the production of animal protein by according them distributional prerogatives, since domesticated pork and large game constitute 60 percent of the animal protein in the diet (Kelly 1977:34).

However, the "producer" is culturally defined as the individual who completed the process of production, so that women's contributions to the coproduction of pigs is not rewarded by distributional prerogatives, but only in terms of consumption. Distributional prerogatives are allocated among men in accordance with the second model, i.e., in a manner commensurate with individual male contributions to production. Women's lesser contributions are not commensurately recognized to a lesser degree but are instead defined out of existence by the stricture that delineates the identity of the producer. Here, as elsewhere, the cultural construction of reality plays an important role in generating inequality, and it is evident that these constructions are formulated from a male point of view. The principle that the person who completes a growth or maturation process is accorded distributional prerogatives is grounded in the cosmological system. However, the cosmological system does stimulate the most experienced and productive hunters to devote more time to hunting than any other category of persons so that they do not reduce their labor inputs as their efficiency increases, but just the reverse. Senior men hunt to fulfill a self-image of beneficent generosity as well as to earn prestige. In other words, the cosmological system and derivative prestige system induce those with the greatest productive capacity to employ this to the fullest extent and hence generate a surplus (relative to their individual needs) that is deployed in service of the general welfare. Ibo provides an illustrative case in point. But again it must be noted that this does not represent the only possible social mechanism for inducing this result.

Each instance of the primary distribution of domestic pork and large game is part of a series of transactions that take place within a context of generalized reciprocity. These transactions are formulated as a symmetrical exchange of equivalents, i.e., as the form of exchange that betokens an egalitarian relationship. Each game or pork producer gives to other producers and receives from them in a like manner on other occasions. Equivalents are exchanged, in the sense that individuals give and receive standardized portions of whatever is being distributed. The empirical differences between a standardized portion of one animal and a standardized portion of another are ignored.[22] Individuals who are not in a position to make like returns are excluded from the circle of transactors so as to preclude the inegalitarian consequences of a failure to reciprocate. Thus, only producers are transactors (i.e., distributors and recipients in primary distribution). The empirical fact that some individuals give more often than they receive does not create indebtedness because there is no point at which the books are closed and a tally of credits and debits calculated.

However, the difference between giving and not giving is registered as a difference in virtue and consequently in prestige. Generosity consists of sharing widely without the expectation of an immediate return. If such sharing is dictated by a moral imperative, then generosity is a virtue (by definition), and those who engage in it manifest superior virtue compared to those who do not. Presence versus absence constitutes a magnitude of difference too great to be glossed over, and this difference is encoded in the distinction between producers and nonproducers that defines the primary and secondary phases of distribution. Superior virtue is also manifested on each occasion when a primary distribution is sponsored by a successful hunter or husbandman. However, this alternates so that each man within the circle of producers evidences the superior virtue intrinsic to this category on some occasions.

While manifestations of superior virtue can alternate and thus be equivalently exchanged, virtue itself is integral to the person and is inalienable. Prestige is thus not only accumulable, but intrinsically cumulative because it cannot be given away and is subject to loss only through the negation of stigma. Prestige thus accrues with age among those within the circle of producers and is recognized in the rank ordering of bachelors, married men, and elderly men with respect to food taboos. Elderly men rank highest on the basis of accumulated prestige even though they may have ceased to hunt (and are also frequently widowers). The virtue associated with generosity as a life-force donor covaries with that derived from cumulative generosity as a sponsor of primary distributions. The two modes of generosity are also conceptually interrelated in that both meat and *hame* engender growth and maturation.

The game and pork that are produced and distributed manifest a potentiality for the realization of three distinct types of value, namely consumption value, exchange value, and prestige value. Exchange value in the sense employed here is the social value of engendering relationship through giving to others and receiving on like occasions. It is created by giving and remains unrealized in the event of private consumption. Exchange value accrues to those who possess distributional rights. These are accorded to the producer, culturally defined as the individual who completed the process of production. Prestige value resides in the potentiality to manifest the virtue of generosity through sponsoring a communitywide distribution. Unlike consumption value and exchange value, prestige value is not readily transferable. This is particularly significant with respect to the exchange of male and female products that is instituted by the division of labor.

The prestige value that is derived from generosity in provisioning an encompassing distribution to coresidents is exhaustively realized during the primary phase of distribution and accrues only to the producer who provided the large game or domestic pork. The standardized portions received by other producers do not contain any potential prestige value of this type that could be realized in secondary distribution. However, meat has the capacity to engender growth and maturation, and the standardized portions retain some residual prestige value in this respect, since contributing to growth and maturation is a virtue. The portions also possess consumption value and residual exchange value that is deployed when they are given to the comember(s) of the production team, prototypically the hunter's wife. Secondary distribution takes place within the context of a conjugal exchange of unlike products instituted by the division of labor. The wife holds distributional rights over starch staples whose production she completed. These possess consumption value and exchange value but little prestige value. This is due to the valuations that credit starch staples with the capacity to satisfy hunger rather than contributing to growth. They consequently make only a limited contribution to the perpetuation of life across generations. Provisioning others with starch staples is thus a virtue of quite modest proportions in comparison to the virtue of engendering growth. The realizable prestige value of starch staples is correspondingly attenuated.

The terms of conjugal exchange are dictated by what each party brings to the transaction. The exchange of consumption values is equivalent in that each receives foods needed for sustenance (although nonequivalent with respect to certain other aspects of consumption value, elucidated further along). Each party also deploys equivalent exchange value in giving to the other and engendering relationship. However, the nonexchangeable prestige values which accrue to the husband and wife as a result of provisioning the other are unequal so that the transaction constructs the superiority of male virtue. The wife receives a more valuable product in exchange for a less valuable one, and the terms of exchange are favorable to her in this respect. But virtue, which is the counterpart to this value, accrues to the giver. The exchange is thus nonequivalent and engenders asymmetry rather than equality. The source of this asymmetry is clearly attributable to differential prestige values that are derived from the cosmological system. If starch staples and meat were value equivalent, the exchange would be equivalent as well. The division of labor, in conjunction with the differential value accorded to the products of labor, allocates the cosmologically derived prestige values that husband and wife bring to conjugal exchange.

An analysis of conjugal (and other) exchanges in terms of consumption value, exchange value, and prestige value is useful in pinpointing the source of the inequality (or equality) that is engendered by these exchanges. The suppositions that inform this mode of analysis contrast with those evident in Collier's (1988:16) position that marriage does not entail conjugal exchange, and with Collier and Rosaldo's (1981:282) position that the values accorded to the products of male and female labor are determined by obligations (see also Josephides 1985:105). The analysis employed here also differs from one based on the labor theory of value. If a medical doctor and a plumber each perform an hour's worth of labor for the other, this exchange of services would be regarded as equivalent in terms of the labor theory of value. However, it is not equivalent when prestige value is taken into account, because contributing to the perpetuation of life through healing is a virtue and repairing the pipes in lavatories is not. The plumber receives a service of greater value in exchange for one of lesser value, but does not become more than equal as a result. The outcome is precisely the opposite, because prestige value is inalienable and accrues to the giver rather than the receiver. Consideration of prestige value thus isolates the source of inequality in this exchange, while labor value does not.

A parallel analysis can be applied to the exchange of male and female labor devoted to subsistence food production. Women get the better of this exchange in two respects. They receive scarce animal protein in exchange for comparatively abundant starch staples, and they expend fewer hours of labor in producing their product than men expend in producing theirs. Despite these material gains, the exchange does not render women more than equal to men in any significant sense. Although one could argue from a certain perspective that this exchange constitutes a female appropriation of male labor and of material rewards, this is more than offset by the prestige values that accrue to males. Focusing on material gains and failing to consider prestige value thus leads not only to a flawed analysis of exchanges between the genders but to the insupportable conclusion that Etoro men constitute an exploited group within a society characterized by female economic domination secured through unequal exchange.

It is evident here that the explicandum shifts in accordance with the metric used to evaluate exchange insofar as "inequality" is implicitly defined in terms of that by which it is measured. Employing consumption value, exchange value, and prestige value allows one to elucidate several dimensions of exchange transactions within a framework that defines social inequality in terms of recognized differences in the distribution of culturally valued things among culturally recognized groups and categories and between individuals engaged in ongoing social relations. Here, too, the metric used to evaluate exchange and the definition of inequality are aligned in that consideration of "culturally valued things" necessitates the development of concepts of prestige value and exchange value (that take distributional rights into account). However, independently establishing an appropriate definition of inequality through explicit consideration of the relevant issues is the point of departure, and development of the metrics necessary to evaluate it follows from that definition. This contrasts with the common practice of defining inequality implicitly, through selection of a metric used to measure a difference, so that the assumptions entailed in the definition are smuggled in rather than being set before the reader in a manner that renders them subject to the latter's critical judgment.

While exchange value and prestige value have been explicitly defined, consumption value remains to be considered. It is evident from the earlier discussion of food taboos that several diverse values are realized through the consumption of game animals and starch staples. The sustenance derived from these can be considered in terms of culturally defined values pertaining, for example, to the capacity of different foods to satisfy hunger or induce growth. In conjugal transactions, the exchange of growth-inducing for hunger-satisfying foods can be regarded as an exchange of complementary consumption values since both are needed for sustenance. The nonequivalent properties of the two foods are related to their respective prestige values, and these are most significant with respect to provisioning the subsequent generation. The prestige value of a transactable item pertains to the potentiality to manifest virtue through its deployment. However, food items may also potentially embody spiritual properties that derive from their cosmologically posited relationship to the supernatural. Consumption of them thus constitutes a form of communion that entails the recognition of virtuousness. Virtue is not produced through consumption (as it is in the deployment of items possessing prestige value) but is recognized and rewarded. Differential consumption of spiritually potent foods consequently entails the instantiation of inequalities with respect to moral evaluation. Consumption value thus encompasses not only a food's contribution to sustenance (evaluated in terms of either scientific or cultural properties) but also its spiritual properties. Both these types of properties are inherent in the item and are consequently transferable (in contrast to the inalienable character of prestige value).

Evaluation of the extent to which an exchange is equivalent in terms of consumption value thus requires consideration of spiritual as well as nutritional properties. Conjugal exchange is not equivalent with respect to spiritual properties because starch staples entirely lack such properties while some types of game and fish that are distributed to women (and children) possess them, most notably cassowary and catfish. Cassowaries are the corporeal abode of *Sigisato* spirits, and catfish are the corporeal abode of *Kesame* spirits. Both can be eaten by everyone except widows and the children of deceased men (see Kelly 1977:43). Wives thus receive spiritual consumption values that they do not (and cannot) reciprocate. While they obtain something of spiritual value in exchange for something of no spiritual value, this "gain" renders them indebted to their husbands and consequently engenders inequality. In addition, there are a few taxa of midsize game that only men can consume. As the producers of spiritually potent game, men realize superior status both through exclusive consumption of some and the exchange of others for nonequivalent starch staples.

In sum, men are very favorably positioned with respect to the deployment of exchange value, prestige value, and the spiritual component of consumption value while women are on a more equivalent footing only with respect to the aspect of consumption values pertaining to a food's contribution to sustenance. The production, distribution (including exchange), and consumption of subsistence foods engender inequality between men and women while at the same time producing substantial equality among men that derives from the exchange of equivalents and from alternation in the manifestation of virtue. Although men are equal in these respects, they are unequal in terms of moral standing and accumulated prestige. Moral standing covaries with age, while prestige is variably accumulated by individuals of each age class in accordance with virtuosity in hunting. Food taboos encode the former dimension of inequality, while the latter establishes certain individuals (such as Ibo) as paragons of virtue. The senior men who are prominent in this respect are invariably *tafidilos* (although not all *tafidilos* manifest this quality to the same extent as Ibo).

Inequality in the distribution of prestige underwrites an egalitarian distribution of the utilitarian component of consumption value, i.e., a distribution in accordance with need. Inequalities of prestige provide the requisite stimulus to production in accordance with ability on the part of the primary game producers. The prestige system organizes the production of animal protein in terms of individual effort and also organizes the distribution of the products of this labor. As was noted earlier, the central obligation to distribute game widely originates in the prestige system. Distribution of midsize game in accordance with food taboos also constitutes a distribution in terms of virtue. The division of labor assigns socially differentiated categories of persons to tasks that differ most significantly in their prestige-producing potential. Thus, the economy is one in which prestige is central to the organization of production, distribution, and consumption. Elucidation of the prestige system, and the cosmological system that informs it, is thus essential to the development of a comprehensive understanding of the economy and its role in the production of inequality.

A prestige-driven economy such as that of the Etoro tends to be characterized by a complementary distribution of prestige and material benefit. Men devote more hours of labor to subsistence food production than women because prestige is earned through individual effort and the division of labor puts men but not women in a position to earn prestige. Women obtain items of greater material value in exchange for items of lesser material value in that they receive scarce animal protein in exchange for amply available starch staples. Women also have superior access to animal protein over the course of a lifetime. When the system is evaluated in terms of these material benefits, women are thus seen to be in an advantaged position. However, an evaluation of the system in terms of the distribution of prestige is conducive to precisely the opposite conclusion. The same configuration is also applicable to the domain of witchcraft. Women are advantaged with respect to the proportional distribution of witchcraft accusations but are disadvantaged with respect to moral evaluations by the metaphysical association of femininity and witchcraft. The advantages are concrete, while the disadvantages are symbolic. The category of societies defined by the distinctive type of prestige system delineated earlier thus tends to be viewed as gender egalitarian when evaluated in terms of material benefits and concrete advantages but is seen to be markedly inegalitarian when evaluated in terms of prestige. Both these aspects of social inequality (or equality) are relevant to an overall assessment. The critical point is to recognize that a complementary distribution of prestige and material benefit is intrinsic to these systems insofar as prestige is often earned by providing material benefits to others (e.g., by distributing game widely).

Privilege and prerogative are constituted as socially legitimated advantage. In a society in which utilitarian consumption values are allocated in accordance with need, and the guiding principle of ownership is that one should not possess two of anything that another individual lacks, there is little scope for the development of legitimated material advantage. The main economic prerogatives thus take the form of distributional rights and privileged access both to prestige-producing activities and to the consumption of foods that possess spiritual properties. Insofar as the producer holds distributional rights over products engendered by his or her own efforts, the allocation of distributional prerogatives is contingent upon the division of labor and on the cultural definition of "producer" and of "efforts." The cosmological system that provisions the social construction of reality supplies the requisite definitions and at the same time legitimates the resultant prerogatives.

Men are thus accorded a variety of rights with respect to persons and things that are distributional in character, i.e., that entail the right to bestow. Children belong to their father's lineage, and the father designates his son's inseminator and his daughter's husband. Men hold exclusive or predominant distributional rights over virtually all things that contain a significant degree of exchange value or prestige value, i.e., those things that can be deployed to create or affirm social relations or to manifest virtue. Domesticated pigs, large game animals, and shell valuables are the most important items in this respect. Men likewise hold distributional rights over the foods that possess spiritual as well as utilitarian consumption value. Possession of these distributional rights enables men to earn prestige. Prestige is essentially its own reward when evaluated in strictly material terms insofar as it is not translated into material benefit. However, distributional rights also confer the capacity to shape the social relations that constitute the social system, and men occupy a privileged position in this respect as well. They also possess many other noneconomic prerogatives, including (in the case of a restricted group of men) spiritual authority and the forms of power derived from it.

Men enjoy spatial, ritual, marital, jural, and organizational prerogatives. The men's sleeping section of the longhouse is more spacious and comfortable than the women's quarters. The bachelors occupy the sleeping platforms that are high above the ground and adjacent to the rear veranda and to the men's fireplace that is the site of séances and constitutes the sacred center of the dwelling. In contrast, widows are restricted to the peripheral area along the outer walls of the communal section and cannot sit next to the fireplaces.

Spirit mediumship is an exclusively male profession and is effectively restricted to younger men (below age 45). Many mediums are bachelors. Bachelors predominantly constitute the chorus that echoes spirit pronouncements as well. The central performers in the *kosa* ceremony are the men who dance gracefully and sing beautiful melancholy songs of their own composition that move others to tears. Married women perform the welcoming dance in the clearing in front of the longhouse but do not sing. Betrothed girls line the two sides of the central aisle of the communal section of the longhouse along which the male performers dance. However, these young girls neither dance nor sing, but provide a background chant and rhythmic shaking of rattles. Bachelors are the predominant *kosa* performers, although recently married men sometimes play this prestigious role and *tafidilos* occasionally make a cameo appearance. The *kosa* singers are burned by those moved to tears, and senior men, especially *tafidilos,* typically enact this second prestigious role. However, senior women constitute about 10 percent of the burners.

A man may have several wives while a woman can only have one husband. Polygyny is a form of self-sacrificing generosity from the standpoint of life-force depletion. It is a socially legitimate prerogative only for spirit mediums insofar as they are the only men who are specifically entitled to a second wife. The general principle that an individual ought not to have two of something that another person lacks otherwise guides the allocation of marriageable women of reproductive age. Thus, many instances of polygyny are occasioned by sterility or involve a second wife who is beyond reproductive age or close enough to this point to be an unsuitable spouse for a bachelor (deemed to be entitled to a wife who will bear children). Other instances entail sororal polygyny established to accommodate the wishes of the first wife. The fact that a first wife's permission is a prerequisite for polygyny also diminishes its status as a male prerogative. However, polygyny is spiritually authorized in the case of spirit mediums so that this permission is compelled. It is noteworthy that spirit mediums have employed their privileged position as the conduits of revealed truth in order to construct a special privilege for themselves. Nevertheless, the privilege of polygyny is not realized in practice, insofar as mediums are not disproportionately represented among Etoro polygynists. Here, as elsewhere, privilege is essentially symbolic and is not translated into a concrete advantage. In other words, spirit mediums enjoy a privileged status that entitles them to more wives than other men, but mediums do not actually have a disproportionate share of the marriageable women.

It can be argued that spirit mediumship is the most prestigious status in the Etoro social system. Spirit mediums manifest the cardinal virtue of contributing to the perpetuation of life through their healing and by concomitantly combating the witchcraft that is the cause of death. At the same time, a spirit medium contributes to the perpetuation of life in all the same ways as other men so that his special contributions are additive. It is also the spirit medium's role as healer that is central to the social construction of males as life-givers. Elkin's (1964:300) insightful observations concerning the life-giving role of the Australian Aboriginal medicine man are equally applicable to the Etoro spirit medium and concisely make this point:

> An examination of these functions of the medicine-man shows that they are all life-giving in nature. He restores life by getting rid of sickness, or by recapturing the straying soul; he is the link with the unseen spirit world and the sky, from which life is obtained. . . .

The supreme virtue that constitutes the crux of the system of moral evaluation from which the cultural concept of prestige is derived is thus isomorphic with the primary virtue of the spirit mediums, who are the key formulators of this system (cf. Dahrendorf 1968; Collier 1988:199). By the same token, it is not surprising that men rather than women are defined as life-givers and that "Woman the Fertile, Woman the Mother and Source of All Life" (Collier and Rosaldo 1982:275–76) is entirely absent as a cultural construct. In Etoro cosmological doctrine, the unique contribution of female parturition is a stillborn infant, i.e., an infant without a soul and thus without life. Since the *hame* and *ausulubo* do not come from the mother, women are not life-givers but rather the progenitors of lifeless flesh that represents the antithesis of the life-giving role. In the absence of male *hame* and the *ausulubo* derived from the male *Sigisato* spirits, women are only capable of giving birth to death (i.e., lifeless flesh). This conception is developed in the myth that accounts for the origin of witchcraft and the concomitant origin of death (discussed in chap. 3).

Women are jural minors with regard to lodging and responding to witch-craft accusations and with respect to the associated issue of compensation. The decision to pay or refuse compensation is made on an accused woman's behalf by her brother (or father) and husband, because a woman is not in a position to respond to the potential use of force that underwrites the request for compensation. Men therefore possess jural prerogatives that women lack. There is no differentiation among men capable of using a bow and arrow with respect to these prerogatives.

Men possess organizational prerogatives in that only male *tafidilos* can select longhouse sites, set dates for ceremonies, and play the supervisory role of *ei sano* (or task designator) in longhouse construction and in preparations for ceremonies. Distributional rights confer organizational prerogatives on men in general in the sense that a game or pig distributor presides over the event of distribution. Such rights likewise confer the capacity to shape social relations. Although all men may serve as game distributors, only older men are in a position to bestow daughters or serve as *tafidilos*. Organizational prerogatives thus increase with age.

Senior men (over age 40) also enjoy nearly complete immunity from witchcraft accusations and are thus in an especially favorable position with respect to the most prominent disability conferred on members of the society (disability being the negative counterpart of prerogative). Women over the age of 60 are likewise immune from accusations. Women between the ages of 20 and 60 and bachelors aged 21 to 30 are all subject to a frequency of accusations that is nearly proportional to their representation in the popula-tion. The segments of the population that are most disadvantaged in this respect are sexually active prereproductive females (aged 16 to 20), male inseminees (aged 14 to 20), and mature men aged 31 to 40 (as established in chap. 4).

The prerogatives that are exclusively or predominantly enjoyed by men are unequally distributed among those of different age categories. However, this distribution is egalitarian in some respects and is sectorially bimodal in others, rather than being directly proportional to seniority as received wisdom would lead one to expect. All men possess the same jural prerogatives in conformity to an egalitarian model. While organizational prerogatives are concentrated in the hands of senior men whose children are of bestowable age, ritual prerogatives are concentrated in the hands of bachelors and re-cently married men. This distribution is largely constituted by, but also extends beyond, the juxtaposition of *tafidilos* and spirit mediums. Thus, bachelors are accorded spatial prerogatives while senior men enjoy privileged consumption of spiritually potent game animals. Each typically plays a prestigious role in the *kosa* ceremony. This countervailing distribution is conducive to the conclusion that the relation between junior and senior males entails a balance of both prestige and prerogatives rather than the straightforward superiority of senior males. The prestigious and privileged position of spirit mediums, on one hand, and *tafidilos* on the other, is particularly notable in this respect. Moreover, the former possess substantial spiritual authority while the latter exercise a modicum of secular authority, so that something of a balance of power also characterizes the relationship between these two categories of males differentiated by age. Neither is dominant. The relationship between mediums and *tafidilos* most nearly approximates that of contextually alternating superiority, described earlier with respect to moieties, and thus conforms to this distinctive mode of egalitarianism. The two roles are not symmetrically reversible, but they are typically sequential (in that a medium is supposed to relinquish his practice before assuming the position of *tafidilo*). Nevertheless, this configuration is barely confined within a conceptually egalitarian framework and clearly contains the seeds of hierarchy (as is more fully explained in ensuing discussion). This is significant in that it provides insights into the mysterious evolutionary process by which comparatively egalitarian societies give rise to incipiently hierarchical forms of organization that possess the potential for further evolutionary development in that direction.

The distribution of authority and influence remains to be considered. One of the distinctive characteristics of societies in which the attainment of prestige is dependent upon individual effort is that secular authority over other persons is very weakly developed. This is a direct covariant of prevailing social conditions in which there is no prestige-enhancing use to which another individual's labor can be directly applied. The development of authority over other persons goes hand in hand with the development of a prestige system in which the labor of others can be harnessed to an individual's attainment of prestige. Although documentation of this general proposition concerning the relation between prestige systems and authority systems is beyond the scope of the present work, the central point can be illustrated by a brief comparison between the Etoro and the Mae Enga (Meggitt 1965, 1977) of the New Guinea Highlands.

Among the Mae Enga, the male attainment of prestige is dependent upon participation in the *Te* exchange. This entails the deployment of pigs that are herded by sons (boys) and fed sweet potatoes whose production is contingent upon substantial quantities of female labor supplied by wives. Fathers exert authority over their sons insofar as failure to attend to the domestic pig herd may be punished by flogging, suspending over a fire, slicing the palm of the hand with a knife, or cutting off a boy's earlobes so that in the future he will heed his father's commands (Meggitt 1977:195). A wife is likewise subject to the authority of her husband. This is particularly well illustrated by the punishments for adultery (which poses the threat that a woman may abscond with another man so that her labor is lost). In the event of adultery, a husband may cut off his wife's nose or fingers, hamstring her, or insert hot stones in her vagina (Meggitt 1965:143). This extensive development of male authority is clearly related to the fact that the constitution of the prestige system requires men to exercise control over sons and wives upon whose labor they are dependent.

In the Etoro case, men are not dependent upon the labor of sons or wives in order to attain prestige and do not exercise any authority over them other than normative moral authority grounded in the obligations inherent in kin and conjugal relations and backed by public opinion. Although an unmarried son is expected to assist his father in tree felling in the communal garden in which his family participates, he is not compelled to do so and may take up residence with kinsmen in another community (see Kelly 1977:160 regarding father-son coresidence). Coercive paternal authority is not brought to bear if a son elects to do this. The only instance of physical violence between father and son that occurred during my fieldwork took place in the context of a dispute over the return of a witchcraft compensation (see n. 15 of chap. 4). Tsmari's son Ayage took the side of his coresidents rather than that of his father in this dispute. No one at all sided with Tsmari, and he felt betrayed by his son's disregard for the close kin relation that had led him to expect the latter's support. During the night following the dispute, when Ayage was sleeping, Tsmari struck him across the rib cage with the back of his axe, cracking several ribs. However, this incident entailed expressive violence rather than punishment in the service of paternal authority. Indeed, the absence of a concept of paternal authority informed Ayage's decision to side with his coresidents and afterward share a sleeping platform with his father without any thought that this entailed any risks. It was Tsmari's rather than Ayage's behavior that was atypical.

I know of no cases in which adultery resulted in physical violence between husband and wife. Adultery on the part of a young married woman who has not yet given birth to a child constitutes female-initiated divorce. As was explained earlier, the male corespondent typically pays bridewealth to the woman's kin, who then refund her husband's bridewealth payment. Often the husband is subsequently provided with a lineage sister as a replacement for the wife he has lost. One young man whose wife had taken up with another man in this way said, "If she doesn't like me, then so be it," and made no effort to alter the course of events leading to divorce by attempting to exert authority over his wife. In another instance, a sterile woman committed adultery with her husband's brother's son in the hope that she might become pregnant and thus forestall her husband's plan to take a second wife as a result of her sterility. She did not intend nor desire divorce. She was publicly shamed and chided by her husband, who lifted her skirt to expose her genitals in the course of a community discussion in which both parties were subject to moral condemnation, and the brother's son paid a compensation of one pearl shell to his aggrieved father's brother. The husband thus exerted only moral authority rather than coercive or punitive physical force. In a third case, a widow and bachelor who engaged in sexual relations in the men's section of the longhouse were both pummeled by their close kin. However, adultery was not an issue, and both physical and verbal abuse were employed by the men and women of the community to make it plain that they would not tolerate this outrageous behavior. It was not the sexual relationship but its public nature that was offensive. This incident involved Nogobe and Iwame. It is noteworthy that their sexual relationship was a continuation of an adulterous relation that predated Iwame's widowhood. She had been the second wife of Tofono, the most prominent man among the Etoro and one of only two senior men who continued as active spirit mediums after becoming *tafidilos* (see chap. 5). Tofono was said to have been fully aware that Iwame was unfaithful but to have entirely ignored it. His wife's adulterous behavior did not have any bearing whatsoever on his illustrious reputation but reflected only upon her own.

These cases document the point that coercive or punitive physical force is not employed in order to subjugate Etoro wives to their husbands' authority. It is also noteworthy that blasphemy and sacrilege on the part of a wife are believed to be punished by the *Sigisato* spirits (as discussed in chap. 2). A husband is not responsible for ensuring his wife's proper conduct in these respects. Although a husband is responsible for accumulating half the compensation in the event that his wife is accused of witchcraft, he is not charged with controlling her supernatural transgressions and does not share her guilt. A wife's behavior is construed as that of an independent agent rather than that of a woman under male authority.

Physical conflict between husband and wife is not uncommon in other societies with prestige systems based on individual accomplishments. However, this generally represents expressive violence rather than the exertion of male authority (and wives are sometimes reported to give as good as they get). Wife beating as a result of the discovery or suspicion of adultery expresses anger over violation of the terms of the relationship. Systematic punishment administered by a husband for the purpose of maintaining authority over his wife is characteristically absent. Moreover, marriage does not entail a transfer of authority, so that a woman's natal kin do not recognize and support her husband's legitimate right to discipline her through application of specified forms of acceptable punishments that are distinguished from other uses of physical force which are regarded as expressive. The hallmark of legitimated authority over persons is such specification of the appropriate sanctions by which it may be enforced.

In societies of the type under consideration, access to female labor and the products of female labor is secured through a conjugal exchange of labor effected in coproduction or through an exchange of the products of the husband's and wife's individual efforts. Since each party to the exchange requires what the other produces, coercively enforced authority over wives is unnecessary. Men also earn prestige through their own efforts and in many instances may do so as bachelors since the requisite activities do not require female labor inputs. Etoro spirit mediumship provides a pertinent illustrative example. Since neither wives nor children are essential to the attainment of prestige, a husband/father's authority over them is equally nonessential.

This configuration is consistent with the general proposition that concepts of secular authority over other persons are found in social systems in which males are dependent upon other persons, and that there is a one-to-one correspondence between the identity of the individuals on whom a man depends and the identity of those over whom he exercises such authority. Moreover, the pertinent relations of dependence originate in the prestige system. Dependence leads to the development of authority relations, provided that those who are dependent possess the coercive means to exert authority. However, possession of such means is necessary but not sufficient. Thus, authority relations do not develop in the absence of dependence. If male domination were an end in itself, rather than a means to the end of securing prestige, one would expect it to be equally developed in prestige systems of different types rather than to covary in accordance with the type of prestige system. Etoro men are as capable as Mae Enga men of imposing systematic punishment for adultery and thereby subjugating women to male authority. The underdevelopment of male domination in such cases thus substantiates the point that it is a means to an end rather than an end in itself.

Secular authority outside of the scope of kin relations is also extremely limited in the Etoro system. It is evident only on those infrequent occasions when a *tafidilo* supervises either preparations for a ceremony or the construction of a longhouse. The degree of authority is also quite attenuated (as described in chap. 4). The supervision of fish poisoning by a spirit medium entails a comparably attenuated exercise of secular authority. However, secular authority is directly derived from spiritual authority in this case.

While secular authority over other persons is minimal to nonexistent, spiritual authority is a well-developed component of the Etoro sociocultural system. Spiritual authority is derived from direct communication with the spirits, from oracles, and from dreams. Only mediums have access to direct communication with the spirits, while dreams and the employment of oracles are accessible to all initiated men. Although women participate with men in privately performing the pandanus oracle, I do not know of any instances in which women consulted this oracle on their own. Women do not perform the public pig-organ oracle because enunciation of the results may be contested by the individual whose responsibility for causing death through witchcraft is established. The operator of the oracle effectively lodges a public accusation and must be prepared to respond to the potential use of force on the part of the accused and the accused's kin. Publicly reporting dreams that constitute witchcraft indictments is governed by the same considerations. Moreover, the male *Sigisato* spirits who appear to lineage members in dreams do not appear to women. Thus, while a *Sigisato* spirit may inform a man of his wife's adultery in this way, these spirits do not perform the same services for women. Women's spiritually significant dream experience is thus limited to visitation from the *Kesame* spirits (i.e., ghosts and their progeny), and women's capacity to introduce information derived from these dreams into public discussion is severely curtailed by the considerations outlined above. Women thus have very attenuated access to spiritual authority and a very restricted capacity to employ it as well. It is the spirit wives of mediums rather than living women who possess such authority.

Mediums have very extensive spiritual authority but do not have a monopoly in this respect. Other men can obtain spiritual guidance directly from the pandanus oracle and introduce this into public discussion in contravention to the insights of a medium's spirits (see chap. 4). The reporting of a dream in which conclusive evidence of a witch's identity is revealed can preemptively co-opt the role of a spirit medium in delivering a spirit indictment. However, these infringements upon the legitimated spiritual authority of a medium are effectively available only to men who are confident that they have a measure of public support and consequently constitute only a limited check upon monopolistic control over authoritative information.

Spiritual authority is the primary vehicle for the social construction of reality, and this effectively shapes the public opinion that guides social action. This is particularly well illustrated by the sequence of events in a witchcraft case (discussed in detail in chap. 4), but the general pattern is equally applicable to other aspects of social life. In a witchcraft case, the authoritative information that enters into the construction of who did what to whom, as a consensually agreed-upon "reality," is derived from spiritual authority. The deathbed testimony, oracles, dreams, and the medium's inquest all enter into this construction. However, the medium's pronouncement is definitive in that it authenticates the other sources of information (and may, for example, declare an oracle to have been improperly performed). The shared "reality" that is constructed through reliance on spiritual authority defines the nature of a social situation to which customary procedures apply, so that social action follows in a predictable manner. However, there are several customary options open to the next of kin of the deceased so the outcome is not totally determined by control over the construction of reality (and the spirit medium's control is also less than complete). Despite these limitations, it is evident that spirit mediums occupy an extremely privileged position in shaping the course of events pertaining to witchcraft accusations.

Séances are held weekly and provide a regular forum in which a spirit medium can potentially shape perceptions concerning other aspects of social life as well. This is limited by the fact that the spirits do not concern themselves with everything, and spiritual authority therefore cannot be brought to bear upon many situations. For example, the spirits do not address the relative merits of alternative courses of action in arranging marriage. On the other hand, prophecy provides a vehicle for mediums to introduce opinions on a wide variety of topics. To foretell that a coresident's new litter of pigs will become wild if not soon brought to the longhouse is tantamount to issuing a directive. To forecast that a successful retaliatory raid will be carried out against a neighboring tribe is certainly likely to encourage men to organize and participate in one. To prophesy that a patrol officer will pistol-whip the residents of the community and arrest many on his next census patrol is conducive to extensive absenteeism when the patrol arrives. Spiritual authority thus provides spirit mediums with very substantial influence upon many aspects of social life (in addition to enabling them to shape the cosmological system as discussed earlier). The fact that this influence is very selectively brought to bear in practice does not diminish its magnitude. If a medium decides to employ the full force of his influence with respect to a particular issue, he can produce a very considerable effect upon the outcome. Moreover, the nature of the medium's influence is in some ways more potent than coercive physical force since it affects the thought processes that inform action while force may only induce superficial behavioral compliance. This is to say that the potency of the influence derived from spiritual authority should not be underrated on the basis of implicit comparison with concepts of power defined in terms of coercive force.

A *tafidilo* also has considerable influence in shaping public opinion. Much of this is structural rather than personal in that the position advanced by a *tafidilo* in community discussion prevails unless persuasive counterarguments are put forward that draw widespread support. It is presumed that a *tafidilo* speaks for the majority and in the name of the general welfare, so that silence conveys assent. Like a medium, a *tafidilo* can play an important role in the social construction of situational realities by, for example, authoritatively stating how many men are likely to lend their armed support to a demand for compensation or by establishing that the disappearance of a pig is due to theft. Engendering shared perceptions of a social situation is conducive to collective agreement concerning the course of action to be followed.

If a threat of recourse to vengeance by those demanding compensation is, in "reality," minimal, it can readily be confronted with little risk. *Tafidilos* are thus very effective in influencing the choices that are made between customary options, such as the decision to pay or refuse witchcraft compensation. The main constraint upon this influence is that members of the longhouse community can readily move to another longhouse if they become disaffected. It is here that personal (as opposed to structural) factors play a role. Although Ibo's remarkable proficiency as a hunter did not indebt his co-residents, or make them prone to agree with him for fear of receiving reduced shares of distributed game (since a standard portion is guaranteed), this proficiency did make Kaburusato an especially attractive community in which to reside.

The fact that influence is not consolidated in the hands of a single individual but is divided between the resident mediums and *tafidilos* of a longhouse community institutes potential checks and balances. However, the senior medium is typically the mentor of any others present in the community, and a protégé characteristically ratifies the pronouncements of his mentor. There is also typically only one leading *tafidilo* per community, while the other *tafidilos* in residence are semiretired. Moreover, if the senior medium and leading *tafidilo* are in concert, they constitute a formidable power elite rather than the components of a system of checks and balances. The medium Kayago and his sister's husband Ahoa, the leading *tafidilo* of Turusato, provide a case in point. Each of them was extremely likely to fully support the other on any issue that arose. Under these circumstances, their joint capacity to influence any decisions taken by the community approximated a capacity to dictate the outcome.

The key point to be noted here is that a virtual absence of secular authority over other persons does not constitute the social system as a power vacuum. If power is defined as the capacity to influence the course of events in social life, then it is present in substantial quantity in the Etoro social system. And it is very unequally distributed among community members. Moreover, there is a one-to-one correspondence between prestige and power in that power is concentrated in the hands of those who occupy the apex of the prestige hierarchy, namely mediums and *tafidilos*. From this vantage point, the Etoro social system is quite hierarchical and is dominated by a very elite group of males. In the two neighboring communities of Kaburusato and Turusato, whose internal workings I knew well, this elite consisted of Kayago, Ahoa, and Ibo, with Nogobe on the cusp of membership by the end of the fieldwork period. As the preceding chapters document, these three men played a very prominent role in virtually all the significant events whose outcome was capable of being shaped. There were no community decisions made in which the positions they advocated did not prevail. They also played a significant role in allocating the stigma and attendant disabilities of alleged witchcraft to others.

It is important to note that membership in the power elite is not restricted to elders or senior males since a spirit medium typically becomes the senior medium of a community by age 28, when he is still a bachelor. Kayago was only 30 years of age at the inception of the fieldwork period, while Ahoa was 40 and Ibo 47. Nogobe was only 27 when he became the senior medium of Kaburusato toward the end of the fieldwork period. The distinctive characteristics shared by these men that separated them from others were intelligence, skill, ambition in the attainment of prestige, and a willingness to expend the extra effort that the pursuit of this ambition entailed. Although a *tafidilo* need not possess exceptional intelligence, it is clear that the institution of spirit mediumship selects for precisely this trait. Although women are arbitrarily excluded, membership in the select power elite can be said to be restricted to the most capable men. In a system in which the attainment of prestige is based on individual effort, this is not surprising. Nevertheless, this conclusion is at variance with perspectives that emphasize the privileged structural and economic position of senior males who are analytically classed as an undifferentiated body to which individuals are mechanically recruited by age or marital status.

THE CENTRAL LOCUS FOR THE PRODUCTION OF INEQUALITY

The development of theories of social inequality has largely taken the form of efforts to specify the principal locus for the production of inequality in order to identify the central factors that generate it. The theoretical objective is to trace inequality to its source and thus to account for inequality in terms of the causal factors that produce it. The central impetus to this dominant genre of theoretical formulations is clearly derived from the writings of Marx. The direct heirs to this intellectual legacy take the position that all social inequalities are grounded in the dynamics of a particular mode of production and are either directly generated by this or built upon core relations of inequality that are so generated (see, for example, Wolf 1981:55). The brideservice model, and the formulations of Meillassoux (1972, 1973a, 1973b, 1981) from which the brideservice model is derived, are grounded in the insight that marriage organizes relations of production. The ultimate source of social inequality is thus pushed back one step further to a more fundamental generative locus. However, the structure of the theoretical formulation is much the same. Marriage organizes social inequality. Thus it might be said that all social inequalities are grounded in marital dynamics and are either directly generated by them or built upon core relations of social inequality that are so generated.

Others have argued in contradistinction that religion is the fount of social inequality (see, for example, Hiatt 1985, 1986). This, in turn, is countered by the argument that "it does not seem necessary to seek in religion, considered as an autonomous structure, the foundations of the generation hierarchy [in Australian Aboriginal society]: everything is already given in the kinship structure" (Testart 1989:9). Moreover, "inherent in kinship is a hierarchy," and "there is no need to seek the ultimate origins of inequality anywhere else" (ibid.:5). Here, too, the structure of the argument remains the same in that an effort is being made to identify an ultimate source of social inequality to which all its manifestations can be traced. Whitehead's (1987) argument is similarly structured. A male monopoly over intergroup violence enables men to control exchange and the creation of social bonds through exchange. This informs idioms of male fertility that are expressed in fertility cults and in an associated cosmology that provides the moral evaluations that underwrite gender inequality. Inequality is thus grounded in cosmologies that have their ultimate source in the male monopoly over intergroup violence. A wide variety of theories that have been put forward to account for social inequality in simple societies are thus very similar in form although widely divergent with respect to the particular generative locus of that inequality. All these authors strive to formulate a theory that is as parsimonious and reductive as Marx's theory of social inequality in capitalist societies, and that analogously traces inequality to a single source that constitutes an internal prime mover.

The present work was undertaken with a view to critically evaluating not only the specific theories described above, but also the more general explanatory objective to which they uniformly subscribe. Whether it is possible or useful to trace the source of social inequality to a single generative locus is thus taken to be an open question. This can be addressed by considering the extent to which the arguments developed herein concerning the centrality of the cosmologically derived system of moral evaluation are capable of accounting for the full range of phenomena to be explained. The most comprehensive extant model—that developed by Collier and Rosaldo (1981) and Collier (1988)—has already been critically evaluated, and I have argued that it is inadequate in this respect due to misplaced causality. At issue, then, is the question of whether the alternative formulation nominated to replace it can satisfy the same evaluative criteria. But at the same time, this necessarily raises the issue of whether the quest for a prime mover that totalistically organizes social inequality can be expected to ultimately yield up this intellectual analogue of the Holy Grail. In order to address this issue, it will be necessary to assemble the central arguments developed earlier as a causal chain or network, whose interrelations and scope can be scrutinized.

The Etoro cosmological system that comprehends reproduction, the spir-

itual constitution of persons, and life-cycle transformations is the central locus
for the production of inequality because it constitutes the source of morally
evaluated social differentiation. It constructs and defines not only age and
gender categories but also the categories of witch, spirit medium, and *tafidilo*.
It delineates intrinsic virtue and its opposites and differentially ascribes spiritual deformity, virtue, and the absence of virtue to these social categories as
integral components of the criteria through which they are formulated and
distinguished. Thus, senior men with mature children and inseminators constitute a category by virtue of their role in reproduction and their position in the
sequence of life-cycle transformations. As donors of life force, they are
intrinsically generous, and generosity is simultaneously defined as a virtue.

The cosmological system likewise stipulates the virtues achievable
through elective social action and consequently constructs the prestige system
as a system of comparative distinction measured in these terms. Spirit mediums, who manifest the cardinal virtue of generously contributing to the
perpetuation of life through both healing and combating death-dealing witchcraft, rank at the top of this scale of achieved virtue. They are followed by
tafidilos, a category comprising the inner circle of the intrinsically generous
senior men noted above. The elect consists of those senior men who have
eschewed self-interest and avoided the taint of association with stigmatic
witchcraft, and who have thus accumulated unnegated prestige through acts
of generosity in sponsoring encompassing distributions of large game over
the years.

The cosmologically derived system of moral evaluation is central to the
organization of production, distribution (including exchange), and consumption. Relations of production and the conditions of exchange are instituted
by a division of labor which is itself a scheme of morally evaluated social
differentiation informed by the same cosmological principles. These serve
as the basis for both the categorical assignment of individuals to activities
and the division of value accorded to those activities. Thus, only spirit
mediums can organize fish-poisoning expeditions, by virtue of the spiritual
permission required, and fish poisoning is simultaneously imbued with supernatural significance. Although hunting is not exclusively assigned to one
gender, setting cassowary snares requires the permission of male *Sigisato*
spirits, and the high forest that constitutes the most productive hunting locale
is the domain of these same spirits (and a place where the word for woman
cannot be uttered). Since fish and game are procured through the beneficence
of the spirits, both the activities themselves and the sharing of the take have
a spiritual quality. The inequalities rooted in the cosmology in these ways are
amplified by a spatial organization of male and female effort that ensures a
male predominance in game procurement, and by the conventions of game
distribution that eventuate in restricted sharing of the game women procure

during garden clearance. Men consequently predominate in the encompassing distribution of game to all community members that is the hallmark of
prestige-enhancing generosity. The cosmological system thus plays a major
role in shaping a division of labor that accords unequal access to prestige-
producing activities while at the same time delineating the specific virtues
that are prestigious (e.g., generosity).

Inasmuch as the gendered division of labor is a scheme of morally
evaluated social differentiation, inequality is inscribed in the relations of
production at the onset. And insofar as the cosmological system accords
differential value to male and female products, inequality is the inevitable
outcome of the exchange of those products instituted by the division of labor.
Male products possess superior prestige value that is realized by the giver.
Certain male products likewise possess spiritual consumption values that
female products lack and that consequently cannot be reciprocated. The
exchange of male for female products thus inevitably entails the male accumulation of prestige and the female accumulation of indebtedness (irrespective of whether or not the parties to the exchange are husband and wife).
Marriage recruits specific individuals to production teams and conjugal exchange relations, but marital obligations do not account for the values that
render these exchanges unequal.

That producers are accorded distributional rights over their products is
an artifact of a prestige system in which comparative distinction is measured
in terms of individualistic virtue. The cosmological system not only stipulates
the virtues that construct the prestige system, but also supplies the principle
that defines the producer as the individual who completed the maturation or
production of the item to be distributed. This supplements the allocation of
activity effected by the division of labor so as to ensure that men hold
distributional rights over all products that possess significant prestige value,
exchange value, and spiritual consumption value.

Received wisdom holds that the rule stipulating that producers are accorded distributional rights over the products of their own labor is the hallmark of an egalitarian economy. However, this deduction is contingent upon
a failure to consider (1) the differential value of these products; (2) the
division of labor that indirectly allocates distributional rights by assigning
social categories to production tasks; and (3) culturally variable definitions
of "producer" and "labor"—all of which are derived from the cosmological
system. Received wisdom also holds that the obligation to distribute game
widely provisions an egalitarian distribution in accordance with need. Although this conclusion is accurate, it is equally important to notice that
generosity in so distributing game is a virtue, that the obligation originates
in the prestige system, and that members of a delimited category of individuals who hold the requisite distributional rights accumulate prestige by

fulfilling this obligation. In other words, distribution is organized by the prestige system. This is additionally evident with respect to the distribution of midsize game (possessing differential spiritual consumption value) in accordance with food taboos.

It can thus be argued that the cosmologically derived system of moral evaluation—of which the prestige system is one component—is central to the organization of production, distribution (including exchange), and consumption. The cosmological system not only constitutes the source of morally evaluated social differentiation, but also shapes the relations of production, modes of distribution, and terms of exchange that generate further social inequalities pertaining to these socially differentiated categories.

Prestige and prerogative are constituted as socially legitimated advantages, and the cosmological system provides the requisite legitimation. Men therefore not only hold, but are morally entitled to hold, the distributional rights that confer the capacity to shape the social relations that constitute the system. Although achieved, the prestigious positions of spirit medium and *tafidilo* are male exclusive and in that respect a male prerogative. Ritual, organizational, and marital prerogatives are linked to these social positions (in a manner detailed earlier), as are spiritual authority and limited forms of secular authority. Men also enjoy privileged consumption of certain spiritually significant game animals (varying in accordance with life-cycle category), and bachelors enjoy specific spatial and ritual prerogatives. All of these legitimated advantages can be directly linked to the cosmologically derived system of moral evaluation. In addition, elder senior men (including *tafidilos*) enjoy the culturally pertinent (but not explicitly formulated) advantage of being virtually immune from witchcraft accusations and the stigma and disabilities associated with them. Spirit mediums are not immune and are not significantly less likely to be accused than other men of the same age, although members of their families are advantaged in this respect. The distribution of privilege, prerogative, and culturally pertinent advantage (other than material advantage) thus conforms very closely to the hierarchies of intrinsic and achieved virtue formulated by the cosmological system. There are no disconformities with respect to explicitly legitimated advantage although some deviation from the hierarchically expected distribution occurs with respect to witchcraft accusations. In all other respects enumerated here, virtue and advantage go hand in hand.

However, there is one set of prerogatives that are not directly linked to the cosmological system, namely the jural prerogatives of lodging and responding to witchcraft accusations and of demanding, receiving, and distributing compensation. These prerogatives also differ from others in that they are accorded to all males capable of employing a bow and arrow and are thus undifferentiated with respect to the hierarchies of virtue by which men are discriminated (in that uninitiated males can collect compensation, to cite one example). The jural system is thus organized in terms of a discrete logic, pertaining to the capacity to employ or respond to coercive physical force, that cannot be directly mapped onto the cosmologically derived system of moral evaluation. The discrete logic of the jural system stands as a potential exception to the argument that the cosmologically derived system of moral evaluation is the sole locus for the production of social inequality and is capable of totalistically accounting for the latter. However, the evidence adduced here nevertheless supports the claim that the system of moral evaluation is the central locus. I will return to this point further along.

The power to construct social reality, shape public opinion, and influence the course of events resides in the hands of a very elite group of established spirit mediums and leading *tafidilos* who occupy the apex of the hierarchy of achieved virtue. The capacity to reproduce and reshape the cosmological system that defines virtue is solely in the hands of spirit mediums. As was noted earlier, the supreme virtue that serves as the foundation for the system of moral evaluation from which the cultural concept of prestige is derived is isomorphic with the primary virtue of spirit mediums. It is also an intrinsic virtue of senior men and the virtue achieved in greater measure by the *tafidilos* among them. Spirit mediums typically become *tafidilos* after retiring from active practice and are thus assured a position at the apex of the prestige hierarchy throughout their lives. The cosmologically derived prestige system accounts for the distribution of power (in the senses noted above) inasmuch as there is a one-to-one relation between prestige and the capacity to influence the course of events. The cosmological system is the central locus for the production of social inequality as a result of the fact that those who control the production and reproduction of cosmological doctrine formulate that doctrine in a manner that accords moral superiority, prestige, privilege, prerogative, and power to the social positions they occupy and the social categories to which they belong. This is why the concept of a prime mover is indeed viable.

Social inequality is thus produced by an elite that is advantaged by it. This configuration resolves the paradox noted earlier with respect to Collier's (1988) attribution of a culture-making role to women who occupy a markedly disadvantaged position within the cultures they are deemed to have participated in shaping. In the Etoro case, women are excluded from any significant role in the formulation of cosmological doctrine that defines the fundamental nature of reality in terms of both the nature of being and the underlying causes and processes that order the cosmos. As nonparticipants in the cultural construction of this reality, the disadvantaged position women occupy with respect to the inequalities engendered by it is expectable rather than paradoxical. Although social practice in which everyone participates has the potential capacity to reshape selected aspects of a social system, practice does not impinge upon the metaphysics by which the "reality" of social action is constituted (although it may impinge on metaphysicians). Thus, while practice is intrinsically egalitarian in character, in that everyone participates in it, the ethnographic record displays ample evidence of a considerable degree of social inequality that does not covary with this. The prevalence of social inequality presupposes potent social forces conducive to this inegalitarian outcome. The argument advanced here is that this is attributable to the very considerable capacity of elites to reproduce an advantaged position. Moreover, control over metaphysics is the central mechanism through which this is accomplished in simple societies.

The cosmologically derived system of moral evaluation not only configures the aspects of the sociocultural system pertaining to inequality, but also shapes the self-image and motivation of social actors. Senior men are motivated to assiduously hunt and to generously distribute the game they procure in fulfillment of a self-image of beneficent generosity. Women and uninitiated young men lack a comparable self-image and also lack the associated motivation. It is thus not surprising that only two of thirty-one women at Bobolei were active hunters and that this pattern, by which women participate infrequently in the prestige-producing activities that are open to them, is pervasive (e.g., women are rarely the senior owners of pigs, and few women serve as burners in the *kosa* ceremony). Moreover, generosity is not only a virtue per se but an intrinsic virtue of senior men. The fact that women do not widely distribute the quantities of sago over which they hold distributional rights is thus partly attributable to a self-image that does not include intrinsic generosity. Moreover, sago is not an appropriate vehicle for prestige-enhancing generosity, since it sates hunger but does not contribute to growth and is not rendered up by the beneficence of the spirits. The cosmological system thus shapes the self-image of socially differentiated categories of actors engendering corresponding behavioral predispositions, as well as according differential value to the products of labor. In both these ways, it constructs impediments that are conducive to the realization of attenuated female generosity in practice. Practice thus largely ratifies morally evaluated social differentiation in the manner of a self-fulfilling prophecy.

In the account of the economy presented in chapter 2, it was pointed out that the Etoro division of labor is egalitarian in practice. Men welcome the inclusion and participation of women in hunting expeditions to the high forest (where the name for woman cannot be uttered) and in accompanying fish-poisoning expeditions and gathering moss (although all other tasks are an exclusive male responsibility). The general tenor of male-female relations in these contexts, and in gardening and sago processing, is one of cooperation, joint effort, and complementarity. Moreover, the division of labor is not task exclusive, so that women are seen to be capable of chasing game, climbing and felling trees, and repairing traps, while men are likewise seen to be capable of processing sago and clearing, planting, and weeding gardens. The day-to-day experience of social actors engaged in production therefore does not convey the notion that men and women are uniquely and distinctively different, but rather that they are potentially substitutable and thus equivalent in many respects. Although these observations continue to be valid, they have been implicitly recontextualized by subsequent elaboration of the inequalities embedded in the economy by cosmologically derived valuations of the division of labor. In short, the division of labor is markedly inegalitarian in concept, although at the same time egalitarian in practice. This shows that practice does not effectively revalue the division of value accorded to labor. When women hunt, hunting is not feminized. Both the spiritual affinity between men and (certain) animals and the growth-inducing properties of game remain unaltered. The association between the growth-inducing properties of game and semen ensures both the essential masculinity of hunting and the life-perpetuating character of masculinity. It is thus the huntress who is masculinized.[23] Similarly, sago processing is not masculinized when men undertake this task in its entirety. The hunger-satisfying properties of sago and the essentially feminine character of the activity remain unaltered, as does the limited contribution of femininity to the perpetuation of life. However, males who engage in sago production (principally in the context of the initiation lodge) are not feminized but are rather seen to have achieved self-sufficiency, autonomy, and independence. The consequences of practice are not symmetrical for the two genders in this respect. However, in both instances it is the actor rather than the gender system that is most susceptible to transformation through practice. The rigidity of gender as an attribute of persons is indeed effaced by egalitarian aspects of practice, but the cosmologically derived valuations of gender in which the moral superiority of masculinity is inscribed remain untouched. A blurring of the boundaries of gender categories through social substitutability therefore does not constitute a revaluation of those categories, such as that described by practice theorists in other instances (see Sahlins 1981; Ortner 1984).

The general features identified here are similar to those that obtain within a class structure characterized by individual upward and downward mobility. This individual mobility effaces the rigidity of class as an attribute of persons but does not alter the class structure as such. Indeed, it contributes to the reproduction of the latter. The egalitarian practice of mobility does constitute a counterweight to a rigid hierarchy grounded in the intrinsic attributes of persons but at the same time sustains and reproduces the inequality of a class-based system of evaluated social differentiation in which class is partially achieved rather than exhaustively ascribed. The same general logic can be applied to the gender-egalitarian practice of day-to-day work experience among the Etoro. It is an egalitarian counterweight that at the same time sustains more deeply embedded systemic inequalities. In this instance, practice is not systematically transformative. Moreover, it can be argued that it constitutes a form of mystification in that it makes gender categories appear mutable to social actors who misconstrue self-transformation as social transformation.

The role of coercive physical force as an independent source of social inequality remains to be considered. There are a number of authors who have invoked male aggression and/or a male monopoly over intergroup violence as the root cause of gender inequality (Mukhopadhyay and Higgins 1988; Divale and Harris 1976; Sanday 1981; Whitehead 1987). One of the principal difficulties with this argument as formulated is that it entails the unwarranted assumption that gender inequality is a distinctive form of social inequality that is appropriately segregated from other social inequalities. This assumption is the hallmark of all theoretical positions that are biologistic at the core, since biology ultimately provides the ground for marking off gender inequalities as distinctive. There is no other theoretical basis for artificially segregating gender inequality and extracting it from the more encompassing system of social inequality in which it is embedded in every ethnographic case. The specific difficulty that accrues to this segregationist theory of gender inequality is that neither male aggression nor the distinctive female reproductive role is capable of accounting for social inequality among men. Thus, the social deployment of coercive physical force that is held to biologically empower men empowers junior males rather than seniors or elders. The age-based inequalities specifically reverse this biological empowerment. It is senior or elder rather than junior males that occupy the advantaged position in the social hierarchy. If elders who might easily be dislodged by the superior fighting ability of young warriors are nevertheless able to maintain an advantaged position, then why should superior male fighting ability produce gender inequality? In short, there is no one-to-one relationship between capability in the use of physical force and social inequality, and the former therefore cannot be a primary determinant of gender inequality. It is neither necessary nor sufficient as a cause. Moreover, the refutation of this argument illustrates the intrinsic disabilities of segregationist theories of gender inequality.

The first step toward a reconceptualization of the role of coercive physical force in social inequality is the recognition that its deployment is socially constituted and morally legitimated. An accused witch can be killed because he or she has been authoritatively assigned to a category of spiritually deformed and morally despicable persons. In the Etoro case, both interpersonal and intracommunity violence that is disconnected from witchcraft accusations is quite rare. Thus, control over the machinery through which such accusations are generated confers substantial control over the deployment of coercive physical force. The cosmology of witchcraft dictates the rules of evidence that govern the development and authentication of an accusation. These rules of evidence empower three parties: the male next of kin of a deceased and the established spirit medium and leading *tafidilo* of the deceased's community. While the deathbed statement of the deceased nominates one individual whose name is put before oracles, the leading *tafidilo* is in a position to influence the next of kin's choice of a second name. Only a spirit medium can authenticate the results of the oracles. Moreover, a medium's spirit can say, "I give you this person to kill," and thus precipitate the employment of violence in lieu of a request for compensation. Although not all witch executions are authorized in advance by a medium, mediums clearly occupy a privileged position that confers a capacity to influence both the use of violence and the persons against whom it is directed. The fact that mediums are only accused by mediums of other communities, that accusations against *tafidilos* are rare and are never authenticated, and that mediums and *tafidilos* are never executed is consistent with this power elite's control over the machinery through which accusations are formulated and violence is channeled and directed. Moreover, women are not victimized by a disproportionately high rate of accusations or executions, nor are children or elderly males or females. All the categories of persons who are the most vulnerable to sheer physical force are the least likely to be subject to it. The victims of violence are culturally rather than biologically singled out. The "natural" advantage that the use of physical force confers on junior males is negated. Generally speaking, the characteristic form of male violence is one in which junior males largely kill each other under the direction of senior or elder males who occupy a superior position in the prestige hierarchy.

Establishment of the socially determined channeling of violence is conducive to the conclusion that violence is a vehicle or by-product rather than a cause (or prime mover) of social inequality, including gender inequality. Women are differentially subject to violence in different social systems, and the causes are located within those systems. This is well illustrated by the punishments for adultery that are applied to Mae Enga but not Etoro women. This point can be amplified by consideration of data concerning homicide among the neighboring Raipu Enga, whose prestige system is essentially identical to that of the Mae. Waddell (1972:223–24) reports that seventeen of twenty-one cases of individual crimes heard by the Wabag Supreme Court between May 1964 and October 1966 involved men charged with willful murder (or attempted murder) of their wives or of co-respondents in a marital dispute. All but one were monogamous and, from their statements, appear to have been men of low social standing, poor and sometimes old, whose wives were constantly threatening to desert them. (Waddell 1972:223)

In a prestige system in which male social standing is contingent upon control over female labor, force is frequently employed as a vehicle of control. When a man has been reduced to the status of "rubbish" in the eyes of other men by a wandering or recalcitrant wife, he directs his retaliation against the source of his downfall and resorts to a pyrrhic final act of control in order to assert his worth and, in some measure, reclaim his self-esteem. If forms of violence are a product of the prestige system, as this illustrative example suggests, then the fact that females reportedly resort to violence comparatively infrequently (Mukhopadhyay and Higgens 1988:469–70) is readily intelligible in nonbiologistic terms. Given the characteristically disadvantaged position that women occupy within prestige systems, they have little or nothing to gain by the use of violence as a means to an end.

In the Etoro case, witchcraft accusations are an arena of male status competition insofar as attainment and retention of the positions of *tafidilo* and spirit medium are undercut by accusations against an aspirant or members of his immediate family. Male control over the jural system is thus an adjunct to control over central aspects of this arena of status competition. Only men are entitled to lodge and respond to witchcraft accusations and to demand, receive, and distribute compensation. Uninitiated junior males are accorded the same jural prerogatives as other men because they are recruited by seniors to back demands for (and refusals of) compensation. In other words, the discordance between the jural system and the cosmologically derived hierarchies of virtue by which men are discriminated is intelligible in terms of junior males' exploitable capacity for violence. The latter are included, as men among men, in a context in which their inclusion serves the purposes of senior males.

This parallels the situation in modern nation-states in which racial and class-based discrimination is obviated in the domain of military service. In a pinch, ideological formulation of a female capacity to bear arms may also emerge in this context. It is evident here that allocation of the prerogative of participating in the deployment of socially legitimated violence is a by-product of an elite's reproduction of an advantaged position and is unrelated to imputed universal biological capabilities. Male aggression and/or a male monopoly on intergroup violence are ancillary by-products and means to an end, rather than prime movers with respect to social inequality in general and gender inequality in particular. Neither constitutes the primary locus for the production of social inequality, although both may contribute to it. In the

Etoro case, the jural system, and the socially constituted and morally legitimated deployment of coercive physical force it encompasses, are conducive to the identification of women's interests with those of their father, brother, and husband. As a result, women are asymmetrically dependent upon men.

The focal issue of the relationship between kinship and inequality can also be elucidated with respect to the theory of social inequality developed herein. As Collier and Yanagisako (1987:3) note, many recent analyses focus on "kinship as an aspect of broader systems of inequality." Collier (1988:vii) regards kinship as much more than merely an aspect of inequality, as is evident from her assertion that, "in societies without classes or estates, where kinship organizes people's rights and obligations, marriage, as the basis of kinship, organizes social inequality." Collier's position is paralleled by the widespread neo-Marxian conclusion that kinship is generative of social inequality insofar as it organizes relations of production. This is well illustrated by Modjeska's (1982:51) reflections:

> Like other anthropologists concerned with neo-Marxist problematics, I am led to conclude that production and its relations do not constitute an autonomous economic level dominating the totality of social relations, since relations of production are relations of kinship. To pursue the relations of production to their heart only to find structures of kinship is by now predictable, if disappointing.

The internal logic of these perspectives is pushed to its ultimate conclusion in Testart's (1989:5) assertion that "inherent in kinship is hierarchy. . . . There is no need to seek the ultimate origins of inequality anywhere else."

These related perspectives can only be evaluated in the context of a definition of kinship. Since neither Collier, Modjeska, nor Testart supplies an explicit definition, I will provide the one I consider most useful. Kinship relations are social relations predicated upon cultural conceptions that specify the processes by which an individual comes into being and develops into a complete (i.e., mature) social person. These processes encompass the acquisition and transformation of both spiritual and corporeal components of being. Sexual reproduction and the formulation of paternal and maternal contributions are an important component of, but are not coextensive with, the relevant processes. This is due to the ethnographic fact that a full complement of spiritual components is never derived exclusively from the parents. Moreover, the sexually transmitted ingredients of corporeal substance are frequently transmitted in other ways as well, as when a Gebusi father feeds semen to his son (Cantrell n.d.) or when ground-up ancestral bone is ingested (see Strathern 1973). Foods may also constitute essential ingredients in the spiritual or corporeal completion of personhood (ibid.). Finally, maturation frequently entails purging, replacing, adding, and/or supplementing spiritual and corporeal components of personhood. There is no analytic utility in artificially restricting the category of kin relations to relations predicated on some but not all of the constitutive processes of personhood because these processes are culturally formulated as components of an integrated system and the social relations they predicate are all of the same logical type, i.e., relations of shared substance or shared spirit. However, egocentric and sociocentric relations can usefully be distinguished as subsets, and the label "kin relations" is appropriately restricted to the former. Although aspects of kinship and aspects of religion are conceptually intertwined with respect to doctrines pertaining to spiritual constitution, kinship is analytically discriminable as a domain of social relations and can readily be marked off without deconstructing the interconnection. Defining kinship with reference to social relations rather than merely as a system of symbols obviates the twin Schneiderian predicaments whereby kinship (1) becomes undifferentiatable and (2) is "locked away" from social action (see Schneider 1980:119, 125).

I have argued that the Etoro cosmological system that comprehends reproduction, the spiritual constitution of persons, and life-cycle transformations is the central locus for the production of inequality because it constitutes the source of morally evaluated social differentiation pertaining to an ensemble of social categories (including those of witch, spirit medium, and *tafidilo* as well as life-cycle and gender categories). These same aspects of the cosmological system specify the processes by which an individual comes into being and develops into a complete social person, so that the locus for the production of kin relations and the locus for the production of inequality are one and the same. Thus, the masculine gender category is composed of individuals who share corporeal attributes (genitalia), substance (semen), and spirit (*hame* and *ausulubo*) that are qualitatively and quantitatively (with respect to *hame*) different from those that are shared by the feminine gender category. At the same time, kin relations are predicated on the shared bone substance component of paternal semen and shared aspects of flesh derived from maternal blood. Both gender and kinship are predicated on shared and differentiated substance and spirit. However, the critical evaluation of Collier's model presented earlier shows that it is not kinship—implicity defined as relations arising out of marriage—that "organizes social inequality." Moreover, the division of labor, rather than kinship, organizes relations of production (contra Modjeska). Marriage only recruits specific pairs of males and females to predetermined (and unequal) roles. The inequality that characterizes the relation between husband and wife is only a refraction of a more encompassing gender inequality and is not the source of the latter. Inequalities are realized and experienced in relations of kinship and marriage that bring particular men and women and specific senior and junior males into conjunction, but the "ultimate origins of inequality" (Testart 1989:5) are located in the cosmological system. Thus, being widowed or orphaned does not alleviate inequality. However, the fact that the same aspects of the cosmological system that generate inequality between social categories also generate kin relations facilitates misrecognition of the lines of causality and a displacement of the source of inequality onto the kin and marital relations in which it is experienced by individual actors.

HISTORY AS EPILOGUE

The Etoro cosmologically derived system of moral evaluation that constitutes the central locus for the production of inequality is continuously reproduced through the séances of spirit mediums and the recounting of myths. Insofar as cosmological doctrine is grounded in revealed truth rather than the received wisdom of a fixed body of knowledge, it is quite open to change. A séance audience expects the revelations of prophecy and is receptive to new knowledge. During the period from 1969 to 1979, such knowledge entered the system through successive Huli pastors of the Unevangelized Fields Mission based at Bobole, who usurped the traditional role of spirit mediums in this community (Dwyer 1990:19). Séances were no longer conducted, although the former spirit medium of the community continued to reside there. Cures were performed by singing hymns to exorcise the influence of the witch, now completely identified with Satan as one and the same (ibid.:20–21). Acceptance of this new cosmological order was pervasive. In 1979, all residents of the community except one man regularly attended services (ibid.). Polygyny was defined as a vice, and no new polygynous unions were contracted.

In 1979, only 10 years after the establishment of the community church, an important transition took place. The Huli pastor was succeeded by a young Etoro man who, a decade earlier, would undoubtedly have become a spirit medium. Efala, the new pastor, was a recently married man in his early 20s (ibid.:21). On Christmas Eve, Efala directed a pageant in which a version of the story of Adam and Eve that he had composed was enacted. Eve, played by the accomplished huntress Nowali, succumbed to the blandishments of the devil (witch) and induced her husband Adam (Maga) to share the fruit of the tree of knowledge.

> Through these scenes Eve and Adam wore European clothing and ate with metal knives and spoons from enamel plates. When God banished them from Eden they lost their fine clothing and other material possessions. They were sent forth from the church and beyond Eden dressed in only the traditional bark-string

> clothing of the Etolo [Etoro]. The play had told of a great loss in the distant past. For the players and audience, their participation in the congregation spoke of renewal. What once had been was concluded—people had erred and been punished—but what had been concluded could be reconnected: Christianity was the way back to Eden.
>
> But the end of the performance was true to the text. God and the Devil departed, as they had appeared, through the men's door of the church; Adam and Eve had left Eden through the women's door. Only the audience and the Cherubim remained. Fuago was the Cherubim, robed and standing guard at the entrance to Eden as Efala led the congregation in song. (ibid.:171)

The transformation of the cosmologically derived system of moral evaluation that was effected by the adoption of Christianity was gender egalitarian in certain respects. Men and women participated in the church congregation on a much more equal basis than they had participated in séances. Although the Huli pastor had instituted gender-segregated seating, this was abandoned in favor of seating by family groups after the Etoro gained control over the church through Efala's succession. The central partition that had formerly created a division between male and female seating areas was removed (ibid.:196). Men and women joined together in song and worship as equals. This new gender equality also carried over, to some extent, into the construction of a new longhouse at the neighboring community of Namosato in early 1980. The traditionally cramped quarters of the women's sleeping section were substantially expanded at the women's request (ibid.:217).

However, at a deeper level, traditional gender inequalities remained. The biblical role of Eve is perfectly congruent with the role of the primordial Etoro girl who engenders lost immortality by begetting and nurturing the first witch and thus bringing death into the world. Etoro and Christian myths convey essentially the same message in this respect. The casting of Nowali as Eve was probably attributable to her attainment of a measure of prestige through her hunting prowess. However, the role Nowali was privileged to play clearly carried a burden of stigma as she portrayed the archetypal woman who, in concert with the witch Satan, bears responsibility for the fall from a state of material well-being. The traditional association between femininity and witchcraft is thus reproduced. But more importantly, the structure of the prestige hierarchy remains unchanged. Senior men serve as deacons of the church, reduplicating the position of *tafidilo*. Moreover, the two most productive hunters—Maga and Siagoba—are both deacons. Similarly the young Etoro pastor is a perfect analogue of the traditional spirit medium. Efala employed the spiritual authority intrinsic to his position to promulgate a novel cosmological doctrine and socially construct a new reality readily accepted by his audience.[24] A structurally identical elite occupies the apex of the new prestige hierarchy and enjoys privileges, prerogatives, and the power to shape the social construction of reality and influence the course of events. Thus, while the cosmology that constitutes the central locus for the production of inequality has been radically transformed, the elite that locally controls the institutional structures through which it is interpretively transmitted, and thus effectively formulated, has perfectly reproduced its advantaged position. This was effected through processes of succession that were integral to reproduction of the traditional hierarchy. Established mediums retired and were replaced by younger men, and aging leading *tafidilos* were likewise eclipsed by more vigorous men in their middle 40s. The structure of succession to elite positions readily facilitated the replacement of older mediums and *tafidilos* by a pastor and deacons, despite the momentous nature of this change. Transformation at one level is reproduction at another (and vice versa). As Giddens (1976:16) has pointed out, the reproduction of society contains the potentiality for transformation and is "a skilled performance on the part of its members." However, the members of a society are both differentially positioned and differentially schooled in the requisite skills that they bring to this performance. Were this not the case, the potentiality for transformation that is inherent in societal reproduction would be expected to regularly eventuate in more egalitarian outcomes than those recorded in the ethnographic record.

It is unfortunate that recent Etoro history does not provide an uplifting utopian denouement to serve as the conclusion for this book. However, that history confirms theoretical insights pertaining to the production and reproduction of social inequality that have the potential to enrich our understanding of these phenomena. The knowledge gained can be shared equally by all those who read this book and may thus contribute to a redistribution of the skills that are brought to the task of reproducing (and transforming) the social institutions they inhabit.

Notes

INTRODUCTION

1. An early example of explicit recognition of this in ethnographic practice is Landtman's (1927) account of the Kiwai Papuans, subtitled "A Nature-Born Instance of Rousseau's Ideal Community." Landtman (1927:167–74) specifically addresses the extent to which the Kiwai conform to this ideal.

2. The emergent concern with gender inequality in the 1970s is clearly relatable to the development of feminism in the larger society. Although the feminist-inspired literature on gender inequalities has generally not sought to identify intellectual precursors (with the exception of Mead 1935), Lowie addressed a number of the basic issues in the 1920s and was undoubtedly influenced by the earlier feminism of that period (see Lowie 1947 [1920]:186–204, 297–338; Lowie 1924:205–21). The shift in the basic questions being asked that is noted here would appear less dramatic if Lowie's earlier contributions were reviewed, since he represents a potential (but unclaimed) ancestral figure.

3. These are rather similar to the bases of social differentiation postulated by Locke and Rousseau as engendering natural inequalities present in the "State of Nature" (Beteille 1981:62–64). Thus Locke allows that the subordination of wife to husband and of enslaved war captive to master have a foundation in Nature and that distinctions of age, virtue, and merit are likewise acknowledged. Rousseau perceives differences pertaining to age, bodily strength, health, and qualities of the mind or soul as providing the basis for natural inequality (ibid.). Social differentiation with respect to virtue, merit, bodily strength, health, and qualities of the mind or soul all fall within the category of individuating personal characteristics, while both Locke and Rousseau regard age distinctions as a basic source of natural inequality. Locke includes gender differences within this set of natural distinctions, while Rousseau does not explicitly do so.

4. The chapters summarized here contain citations referencing the sources of specific points of ethnographic data pertaining to the Strickland-Bosavi tribes. Such citations are thus omitted from the introduction. All data concerning the Kamula are derived from Wood (1982, 1987).

CHAPTER 1

1. It should be noted that the southern portion of the Strickland-Bosavi region encompassed several additional linguistically distinct cultural groups in precolonial

times that are not shown on map 1. These included the Doso to the west of the Kamula, and the Kopalasi to the east (Wood 1982:6–8). The latter were a component of the Kasua (Wood, personal communication). By 1976, these cultural groups were socially amalgamated with the Kamula and are therefore not depicted on map 1. See Wood (op. cit.) for a discussion of the earlier disposition of tribal territories in the southern portion of the Strickland-Bosavi Region.

2. The percentage of shared basic vocabulary between the Samo and Gebusi is reported by Knauft (1985a:11, 369–71) to be 70 percent. Shaw (1973) reported this percentage as 79 in 1971, but notes that this had increased to 90 in 1981 due to greater social interaction (Shaw 1986:52–54). These two tribes are somewhat more culturally distinct than 90 percent shared cognates suggests. Ernst (1984:33) regards the degree of linguistic relationship between the Etoro and Onabasulu as somewhat too high. Culturally, the Etoro and Bedamini are more similar to each other than the 67 percent shared basic vocabulary suggests. There is a dialect chain across Bedamini territory such that the Etoro dialect is mutually intelligible with that of their immediate western neighbors (whom the Etoro refer to as the Petamine), and the same situation obtains as one moves westward from one Bedamini regional grouping to another (see Kelly 1977:10–11; Wurm, Voorhoeve, and Laycock 1981). However, the Etoro regard the central Bedamini dialect as unintelligible (as is consistent with the 67 percent cognates between them reported by Shaw).

3. Shaw's (1986:53) data indicate that the Namumi are somewhat more closely related to the nonadjacent Etoro and Bedamini than they are to the neighboring Kasua. However, Franklin and Voorhoeve (1973:106–7) report a cognation percentage of only 15 to 18 percent between Fasu and Bedamini. Namumi, Fasu, and Some comprise the East Kutubuan subfamily. Despite these somewhat different findings regarding the degree of linguistic affinity along the eastern border of the Bosavi language family, these sources are in agreement with regard to the classification of Namumi and Fasu within the Kutubuan language family (Shaw 1986:56).

4. It may be noted here that Etoro and Bedamini longhouses are close to identical and that this cultural similarity accords well with the linguistic classification of these two tribes as members of the Papuan Plateau subfamily. However, the Onabasulu, which have also been tentatively classified within this subfamily, manifest a longhouse design essentially identical to that of the Kaluli and similar to that of the Kasua and Kamula, who make up the Bosavi watershed subfamily. Since the Onabasulu are linguistically intermediate, they might more appropriately be classified with the latter on cultural grounds. Shaw (1990:4) notes that he has taken cultural as well as linguistic factors into account in determining classificatory breaks along the continuum of related languages. Finally, the Samo and Gebusi longhouses are quite similar, except that the Samo dwelling includes a menstrual confinement section—a highly significant difference. This documents the point noted earlier (in n. 2) that these two tribes are culturally more distinct than 90 percent shared cognates would indicate, although they obviously belong in the same classificatory subunit. With the exception of the classification of the Onabasulu, Shaw's (1986) division of the Strickland-Bosavi language family into three subfamilies is consistent with the distribution of cultural

similarities and differences and fits these data better than the earlier classification of Wurm, Voorhoeve, and Laycock (1981).

5. Knauft (personal communication) reports that the women's section of Gebusi longhouses is occasionally located on the left rather than the right side, while Wood (personal communication) likewise reports that the Kamula floor plan is reversible along this axis.

6. Information necessary to extend this comparison to the Kasua and Onabasulu is unavailable in the sources. Neither Freund nor Ernst addresses the issue of menstrual confinement and its relation to gender segregation in longhouse design. Ernst (n.d.:12) likens Onabasulu beliefs concerning male depletion through intercourse to those of the Etoro, but also mentions that exposure to menstrual blood and the blood of childbirth has comparable effects on male vitality. As is generally the case throughout the Strickland-Bosavi region, gender segregation is not rigid or absolute, and women may occasionally enter the men's section on a casual basis as well as during ceremonial performances (Ernst 1984:226).

CHAPTER 2

1. Dwyer (1985c) describes the methods employed in arriving at these figures. Those for Bobole are based on a one-year period of observation, while those for Namosado are based on three one-week samples spaced out over a year. The estimates (represented by "E" in table 2.1) for cassowaries, small mammals, and "other" for the Bobole community are those provided by Dwyer, which he believes to be low. The estimates for domestic pig and cassowaries at Namosado are not given by Dwyer; I have inserted them based on the values for Bobole. Dwyer (1985c:113) notes that captures of cassowaries are thought to be more common at Namosado, so this figure would be low. There is no reason to expect that domestic pork consumption would differ by altitude (see Kelly 1988 regarding pig husbandry). It should be noted that no wild pigs are included in the figures for either community, although one was shot at Bobole outside the sample period and wild pigs were thought to be taken more often at Namosado. Data from Kaburusato, at about the same altitude as Namosado, would support this (Kelly 1977:34). Overall, the figures for protein consumption represent low estimates in both cases. The slight difference in total protein consumption between the two communities that appears in table 2.1 should not be regarded as significant. The main point that the table is designed to document is the differences in means of protein procurement by altitude, and the level of reliability of the estimates is sufficient for this purpose. The data are also sufficient to support the conclusion that the Etoro diet is adequate in terms of animal protein. The minimum estimate of 11 grams of animal protein consumed per person per day is about the equivalent of 2 ounces of beefsteak. Since the "persons" included in this figure include nursing infants and small children, adult consumption is higher. The diet is well supplied with vegetable protein, and there are no signs of nutritional deficiencies.

2. The figures presented in table 2.2 are derived from the following sources: Bobole and Namosado Etoro, Dwyer (1985c); Kaburusato Etoro, Kelly (1977:34); Gofabi Bedamini, van Beek (1987:app. B); Fagamaiu Kasua, Freund (1977:324). I

have used the following ratios, derived from Dwyer (1985c), to convert bag weight into edible weight for the Kaburusato, Gofabi, and Fagamaiu data: pig, cassowary, birds, mammals, frogs, snakes, and lizards, .75; fish and crayfish, .86; bird eggs, .93; insects, 1.0. Protein content would be the same percentage of edible weight in each case, making conversion unnecessary. It should be noted that the samples are for time periods ranging from 1.5 to 52 weeks. The shorter sample periods are subject to a degree of inaccuracy due to seasonal variations. Moreover, large game may be taken in unusually large or small numbers during sample periods. In the case of Namosado, fewer than average were taken (see n. 1), while in the case of the Gofabi Bedamini, a significantly greater-than-average number of pigs were procured during the sample period (van Beek 1987:143), inflating the proportion of large game in the total. An additional source of sampling error arises from underreporting of all sources of animal protein other than large game, since some of the smallest items are consumed in the forest or garden when they are procured, while midsize game may be shared out and consumed at garden houses rather than at the longhouse. The Kaburusato sample is subject to this source of error. Despite these caveats, these data reveal broad differences, particularly when the known direction of error is taken into account.

Although table 2.2 is concerned with the proportional dietary contributions of various sources of nondomesticated animal protein, the dietary contribution of domesticated pigs is known in three cases and may be noted here. Domesticated pigs supply 27.9 percent of all animal protein in the Bobole Etoro diet (see table 2.1), while the comparable figures are 32.3 percent for the Kaburusato Etoro and 42.7 percent for the Fagamaiu Kasua (Freund 1977:326).

3. The Namosado data are derived from three 1-week samples spaced over a year, (Dwyer 1985c), while the Kaburusato data are derived from a 52-week sample. Although wild pigs are procured at Namosado, none were taken during the sample period, so the proportion of nondomesticated animal protein derived from large game is understated. The Kaburusato data omit game not brought to the longhouse, so that the proportion of nondomesticated animal protein derived from midsize forest mammals is understated.

4. When a longhouse is abandoned and another constructed, there are often a substantial number of residence changes. Incoming residents include those who find the new house convenient to sago and other resources they wish to exploit, and residents of the former longhouse may go elsewhere for the same reason. Usually the new longhouse is some distance away from the previous longhouse since proximate sago resources will have been depleted. Discord arising from witchcraft accusations also promotes change of residence. In all, individuals join a new longhouse group about once every ten years (Kelly 1977:133–37).

5. Banana plants produce their first fruit in 12 to 15 months. However, after the stalk has been cut in harvesting, one or more already-present suckers begins to grow up in its place. A second crop may thus be produced in about 10 to 13 months. Bananas planted in the garden adjacent to the longhouse may continue to bear in this way for four years, although yields decline markedly. Bananas are generally planted near brush piles, and the nutrients released by the decomposition of the brush contribute to the production of a second crop.

6. Dwyer (1983) does not give figures regarding the extent to which individuals hunt singly or in pairs, but does note that for four pairs of individuals (8 of 31 hunters) he was "unable to separate the catch on an individual basis" (ibid.:147–48). Usually, multiple-day hunting trips are undertaken by a group of individuals, who camp out in the forest in a temporary shelter. They may then set out individually or in pairs, and the latter may split up part of the time. Dwyer's data indicate that at least a quarter of the hunters favor companionship and that the four pairs of hunters that can be identified captured less game per person-hour than the overall average (see Dwyer 1983:173), suggesting that hunting in pairs entails an inefficient deployment of labor.

7. Feil (1987:179–81) provides an instructive survey of the economic organization of the societies of southwest New Guinea, in which he notes that "the sexual division of labor is not rigid" (ibid.:179) and that, in addition, men are not strongly dependent on the productive activities of women (cf. Kelly n.d.; Ortner and Whitehead 1981:20–21). The material presented here is consistent with, and amplifies, these observations.

8. In making the points that the Etoro lack a concept of male and female tools, exclusive tasks, and inimical influences, I have in mind an implicit contrast with Irish peasants that might usefully be made explicit. Arensberg (1937:52–54) notes that male work and female work are largely confined to separate spheres of activity to which each gender is said to be "naturally" suited. Involvement in the domain of the opposite sex is "unnatural," and also "unlucky" and "dangerous" with respect to a favorable outcome of the endeavor. Women are forbidden to use male implements, and Irish countrymen "heap ridicule upon the thought of a man's interesting himself in the feminine sphere, in poultry, or in churning" (ibid.:52). Within the New Guinea context, the Raiapu Enga display a marked development of male and female crops which are segregated in two types of gardens that constitute male and female domains of productive activity (Waddell 1972:50–51, 98–101).

9. As explained in chapter 1, the longhouse is partitioned such that the men's section occupies the central area, along both sides of the main corridor, while the women's sections under the eaves border this on two sides. Viewed from a perspective that focuses on the longhouse as well as on the surrounding territory, the male spatial domain thus includes the center and the donut-shaped outer ring that encompasses the spatial domain of most female activity. The latter is continuous, extending from the women's section of the longhouse along the outer walls to the adjacent section of the bush containing sago stands and gardens.

10. See Kelly (1977:42–44) for a discussion of food taboos. The main point to be noted here is that there are very few game animals that a man can eat that he cannot also share with his wife. Leaving aside the hornbill and males of the sexually dimorphic cuscus *Phalanger orientalis,* both of which can only be eaten by elderly men, there are only 3 of 34 birds, 4 of 20 game mammals, 3 of 9 snakes, and 1 eel that a woman would be unable to share with her husband. The 3 birds and 3 snakes are very rarely taken; the eel, the small rat *Chiruromys vates,* and the striped possums *Dactylopsila trivirgata* and *D. palpator* are occasionally eaten; while only the cuscus *Phalanger gymnotis* is consumed with any regularity. The two striped possums and the cuscus accounted for only 10 percent of the 1,874 small game mammals taken by

Bobole residents over the course of a year (Dwyer 1982:531–32; scientific identification of Etoro taxa provided by Dwyer, personal communication). The remaining items in the diet, including the wild and domestic pig, cassowary, and bush hen eggs that are the most important sources of protein at Kaburusato (Kelly 1977:34), can all be eaten by women other than widows and, with one exception, shared between spouses. The exception pertains to a temporary prohibition on the consumption of domestic pork that is incurred when an individual's mature pig dies of natural causes; the prohibition is removed when this owner next slaughters a domestic pig and distributes it to others. As a result of this prohibition (discussed in more detail further along in this chapter), half the men are debarred from consuming domestic pork. Thus an estimated 93 percent of the animal protein in the diet is available to mature women, 65 percent to mature men who cannot eat domestic pork, and 99 percent to those who can, with an average of 82 percent for these two classes of married men. While most game can be shared between spouses, the net result of these prohibitions is to provide married women with a larger share of available animal protein. See note 21 of chapter 7 for an extended discussion of the derivation of these figures.

11. Both the Kamula and Bedamini, who extensively engage in focused hunting of large game, evidence ideologies that elaborate a connection between large-game hunting and masculinity (see Wood 1982; van Beek 1987).

12. Among the Miyanmin, "12 women killed 65 small mammals as compared with only 51 reported killed by 28 men" during a representative three-week period (Morren 1985:131). While the Miyanmin are similar to the Etoro in evidencing a significant level of female small-game procurement in foraging, and in manifesting a division of labor that Morren characterizes as "flexible" (ibid.), they differ in maintaining that hunting is an exclusively male sphere of activity and in the fact that they tell condescending stories about women's hunting (Morren 1985:130–31). The animals the women procure are smaller, and the net weight of the male contribution was thus greater than that of the female contribution in the above sample. Men also hunt large game such as pigs and cassowaries. Nevertheless, the importance of the female contribution to protein procurement is evident, and the Miyanmin are similar to the Etoro and Bedamini in this respect.

13. Ortner (1978:89) provides a somewhat similar analysis of Sherpa hospitality.

14. Van Beek's (1987:app. B) data indicate that women obtain 38 percent of these animals. My own data (1977:34) include only those animals brought to the longhouse and thus omit those consumed at garden dwellings. Since female captures often occur during garden clearance and distribution takes place at garden houses, I am unable to accurately quantify their frequency. Van Beek's data also show that women obtain 55 percent of the aggregate weight of the following items: snakes, frogs, lizards, spiders, larvae, grasshoppers, beetles, and dragonflies. Women procure 32 percent of the aggregate weight of all small and midsize items (i.e., 32 percent of the total bag excluding wild pigs).

15. In the distribution of mammals, Bedamini women favor boys over girls, i.e., sons over daughters. Girls are favored over boys in the distribution of snakes, lizards, and insects.

16. Among the Etoro, the distribution of midsize game is governed by food taboos, while van Beek (1987) does not mention food taboos in his discussion. Van Beek's data presentation also does not distinguish between family members and other kin. In the Etoro case, a man distributes portions of large and midsize game to other hunters, who then parcel this out in secondary distribution to family members and others (such as a deceased brother's widow) attached to the hearth group (and forming part of the production team). In the Etoro case, midsize game is thus typically distributed to women in secondary distribution. It is not entirely clear from van Beek's account whether the adult women to whom a man gives food include women other than wife, sister, and brother's wife (i.e., women of the hearth group), who are the recipients in the Etoro case.

17. Among the Bedamini this parallel is further accentuated by giving semen to pigs "in order to make them grow" (van Beek 1987:35).

18. It is important to note that the proportional contribution of sago to the starchy component of the diet is not reported on the same basis in each case. In some instances, sago consumption is measured in terms of dietary starch intake by weight (Kasua and Kamula), in other instances by estimated caloric contribution to the starchy component of the diet (Bobole Etoro), and in still other instances by the percentage of days of the year that it represented the principal starch consumed within the community (Kaburusato Etoro and Gebusi). Sago provides 285 calories per 100 grams, sweet potatoes 150, taro 145, and bananas 105 (Oomen and Malcolm 1958:140–41), so that sago's proportional contribution by weight is less than its proportional contribution in terms of calories. Daily consumption patterns are not directly translatable into either weight or calories but would also tend to underestimate caloric contribution in that an individual who is replete on a meal of sago will have consumed more calories than if he or she were replete on a meal of tubers. The figures presented in table 2.3 are those reported in the literature or estimated on the basis of ethnographic description noted in the text. These are rough estimates in nearly all instances, and it would be unwarranted to try to refine them by reducing them all to a standard measure. With the exception of Dwyer's estimate for the Bobole Etoro, they represent or more nearly approximate dietary intake by weight and thus underestimate the caloric contribution of sago to the diet. The main point of the table is to indicate the very substantial variation in reliance on sago, bananas, and root crops within the Strickland-Bosavi region, and the available data are adequate for this purpose. If caloric contributions were employed, the high end of the range of variation for sago dependence would be 91 percent of the caloric intake from vegetable foods for the Kasua, as opposed to 85 percent by weight (Freund 1977:325), and 91 to 96 percent for the Kamula. However, in cases in which the proportional contribution of sago is 25 percent by weight, its caloric contribution would increase to over 40 percent. Thus, the Bobole Etoro, among whom the caloric contribution of sago to the starchy component of the diet is estimated to be 32 percent (Dwyer 1990:223), probably represent the low end of the range of variation measured on this basis. However the rank ordering of cultural groups in terms of reliance on sago would not be altered by employing a caloric measure.

19. Families vary in the frequency of sago processing because some only process one-half to one-third of a palm at a time, sharing the sago log with one or two other

family work groups, while other families process an entire palm on their own. In other words, there is greater variability in the size of work groups than in reliance on sago, although the latter is also variable.

20. Data on labor expenditure in sago processing are based on detailed observations of the work done on one complete palm and partial observations of work on several others. The palm selected for the complete study was typical in its dimensions and was said by the work party to be neither particularly "hard" nor particularly "soft," so that I believe the data are representative despite the restricted sample. The palm contained 33.22 cubic feet of pith and produced 231.25 pounds of sago starch, or 6.96 pounds per cubic foot. This figure is close to the average of 6.26 pounds of starch per cubic foot for seven palms that Townsend (1969) reports for the Sanio-Hiowe, and this supports the assumption of typicality. The sago-processing operation required 119.05 person-hours, with 76 percent of this being female labor. The yield of the palm was 1.94 pounds (.88 kilograms) of sago starch per person-hour (or 2,522 calories of starch per hour). This yield is a little less than half that reported by Townsend (ibid.) and is low for New Guinea generally. However, since the Etoro yield of starch per cubic foot of raw pith is comparable, this must be due to differences in the effort required in processing rather than differences in the extractable starch per palm. This would be expectable, since slower maturing palms are known to be more fibrous and the rate of maturation of Etoro palms is retarded by the comparatively high altitude at which they grow (close to the upper limit for palms used as a starch staple). As noted earlier, the Etoro favor palms growing at 700 to 800 meters or less, with the palm studied coming from 750 meters. The Sanio-Hiowe data Townsend reports are for palms growing at less than 90 meters.

It is also evident from a comparison of the procedures involved in sago processing that Etoro palms are more difficult to process than those worked by the Sanio-Hiowe. The Sanio-Hiowe merely wash, knead, and squeeze the pith a few times after it has been placed in the troughs (ibid.), while the Etoro beat the pith with a stick, wash and knead it, beat it again, and then repeat the washing and squeezing. The additional task of beating twice plus the double washing add to the labor requirements and reduce yields per unit of labor, accounting for the differences between these two cases in pounds of sago starch produced per hour. Wood (1982:42) reports that the yield of Kamula sago palms is the same as that of the Sanio-Hiowe (e.g., 1.9 kilograms of starch per hour). Typically, the Kamula do not beat the sago, but put it in bags placed on a platform and, after wetting, tread out the water with their feet (a method also practiced by the Keraki, see Williams 1969 [1936]:422). Here, too, the comparative ease of processing accounts for higher yields per unit of time, and this is also associated with lower altitude palms.

21. As noted earlier, there are a number of studies that show that sago processing is much more efficient than gardening in terms of calories produced per hour of labor, with a ratio in the range between 2 to 1 and 3 to 1 commonly being reported (See Ohtsuka 1977:257; Ohtsuka 1983:135; Ellen 1979:49–51; Townsend 1974.) However, in the Etoro case, the returns per hour in sago processing are only half those of the Sanio-Hiowe and the people of the Oriomo plateau. If Etoro gardening were comparable to the gardening of these other groups in terms of caloric returns per hour, then the

labor efficiency of sago processing compared to that of gardening would be between 1.5 to 1 and parity. Although I have no data on caloric returns in gardening, a comparison of the time spent in gardening and sago processing in relation to their estimated dietary contributions is consistent with the probable range adduced above. A married couple spends 6.72 hours per week in sago processing and 11.63 hours per week in gardening (excluding harvesting, which cannot be separated from foraging). When the minor starchy crops such as pumpkins and the nonstarchy components of the diet such as pandanus, sugar cane, and various garden greens are considered, the caloric contribution of gardening is on the order of 55 percent and that of sago processing 45 percent. This suggests that Etoro sago processing is roughly 1.4 times more efficient than Etoro gardening (excluding harvesting effort) in terms of calories produced per hour of labor. This figure is presented, despite the limitations of the data, to attempt to answer a question that logically arises, viz., why do the Etoro process sago at all when the yields per unit of labor are so low compared to other New Guinea groups? They do so because sago processing is still somewhat more efficient than gardening in terms of caloric returns on labor, even with these comparatively low yields for sago processing.

22. These data are based on observations of three gardens. It should be noted that fencing requirements per acre vary with the size of the garden and the characteristics of the site (see Kelly 1977:53). The effort required for tree felling is greater on long-fallowed sites, while weeding difficulty is reduced. Crop selection affects planting time, etc. The figures presented are derived from observations in the typical sweet potato garden established in high second growth dominated by 80-foot oaks. The sexual division of labor differs somewhat from that reported earlier (Kelly 1977:50) due to the exclusion of harvesting from these figures. This is combined with foraging in figures presented subsequently. The somewhat greater female labor contribution in the earlier figures reflected women's harvesting in sweet potato gardens but omitted male harvesting in pandanus groves. Both are now reflected in the combined category of harvesting and foraging. Gardens made by bachelors (in which almost all labor is male) are not averaged into the figures presented. Although this would increase the overall proportion of male labor, bachelor gardens offset the somewhat greater number of female workers in the total labor force deployed in other (nonbachelor) gardens.

23. These figures for weekly labor time are derived by multiplying the .35 acres (or .14 hectares) cultivated per capita per year by the 274 persons in a sample of the age structure of the Etoro population (Kelly 1977:29) and multiplying the result by the 1,154 hours per acre required in gardening. This figure is then divided by 183 to give the hours required per worker per year. Those who do not form part of the labor force include 8 elderly individuals (aged 61 to 70), 64 children (under age 11), 15 boys (aged 11 to 14), and 4 girls (aged 11 and 12). In all, workers represent exactly two-thirds of the total population. Boys of 13 to 14, girls of 11 to 12, and individuals in their early 60s do a limited amount of work, but this varies from person to person and generally is less than half that done by the average adult. Observations of these younger boys and girls also indicate that they accomplish substantially less than an adult per unit of time and thus do not contribute as much to the completion of a task as an adult would. The figure of .35 acres (.14 hectares) cultivated per capita per year

is the midpoint of a range presented earlier (Kelly 1977:51). It also represents a slight downward revision of the extent to which small shares in gardens outside the community would increase the .3 acre per capita cultivated in the gardens made by Kaburusato community members. It should be kept in mind that the mix of sago processing and gardening varies by community, and the extent of land in cultivation likewise varies. At Bobole, where less sago is utilized, the four house groups studied by Dwyer cultivated .15, .19, .24, and .31 hectares per capita per year (Dwyer 1990:46).

My data pertaining to labor expenditure and the division of labor are based on close observation of the productive activities of 25 individuals who resided at Kaburusato throughout the 15-month fieldwork period. (One family that was estranged from the community due to a recent witchcraft accusation and resided primarily at their garden house is excluded from this residentially based sample.) These 25 individuals included 4 married men between the ages of 31 and 50 (Tuni, Weliba, Yeluma, and Ibo) and their 4 wives between the ages of 17 and 45 (Haboia, Wadome, Silo, and Akwadi), 5 bachelors aged 19 to 30 (Illawe, Hariako, Selagu, Nogobe, and Sawa), and 4 widows between the ages of 26 and 55 (Suaqua, Asigila, Yebua, and Pegome). Hariako and Suaqua were married during the fieldwork period, and Sawa married a woman from another community toward the end of this period. In addition, the community included 1 girl aged 14 (Saffara) who is counted as part of the labor force, a girl of 12 (Maya) and a boy of 14 (Igioto) who are not so counted (although both contributed somewhat less than half as much labor as an adult), and 5 children under the age of 10. Within this sample, workers represent 72 percent (18/25) of the labor force, as opposed to the 67 percent for the larger sample of 274 persons. The ratio of workers to dependents is thus slightly more favorable in this observational sample than it was in the general population, and the total weekly hours of labor recorded may therefore be slightly less than average. The ratio of male to female workers is balanced (9 to 9), and the observational data are therefore representative of a typical husband-wife (or bachelor-widow) work unit. In an average community, male workers would constitute 53.5 percent of the workers rather than the 50 percent of the observational sample. The additional male workers would be bachelors. As noted earlier, bachelor gardens offset the imbalance in the sex ratio so that female gardening labor is not increased by being distributed among fewer workers. The observational data should therefore be representative of the sexual division of labor between husband-wife pairs in other communities despite the fact that the sex ratio at Kaburusato was balanced rather than being somewhat imbalanced in favor of male workers.

24. The attempts that men make to construct, consolidate, and revise wider kin relations through betrothals and widow remarriage are sometimes impeded by a widow's efforts to bring about a union she desires. That widows often do attain their marital objectives is indicated by the fact that 47 percent wed bachelors. About 70 percent of these bachelors are betrothed to a young girl, and this betrothal is broken when they marry a widow. In other words, the marriage plans men have made are disrupted in a substantial proportion of these cases. An additional 29.4 percent of widows wed married men, 17.6 percent marry widowers, and 5.9 percent marry divorcés (Kelly 1977:302). These also include many marriages widows desire, but they differ in that male marriage plans are not upset. Although the marriages that

widows successfully bring about with bachelors disrupt betrothals, they are often consistent with the objectives of the deceased husband's lineage in other ways, as most are leviratic. Although a deceased husband's younger brother (or "brother") may marry a widow rather than the girl to whom he was betrothed, a marriage may successfully be arranged between this girl and another young man of the same lineage, so that exchange relations are carried forward despite the disruption. The conception of marriage as part of an exchange of women between lineages facilitates such rearrangements.

The attainment of male objectives in widow remarriage is also indicated by the fact that widows of agnatic parallel marriages are nearly always remarried in a manner consistent with the important external sibling and exchange relations of the lineage that are engaged in these cases (Kelly 1977:241). When particularly important issues are at stake, a widow will be unable to persuade a man other than her designated future husband to marry her, and she may be pressured into an unwanted match by both her natal lineage and her deceased husband's lineage. (See Kelly 1977:252–55 for a description of such a case.) However, these outcomes are relatively rare. In most instances, a widow's desire to marry one of her husband's "brothers" rather than another is either unproblematic or can be accommodated by the rearrangement of other unions. It may be that widows take cognizance of the degree of opposition that would be generated in targeting specific men for their advances.

It is important to note that both bachelors and married women see widows as being sexually aggressive in their efforts to secure a desired remarriage. Bachelors perceive themselves as being pursued by widows, who pose a threat to their betrothals and their spiritual vitality (through sexual depletion). The flirtations of younger widows were a common topic of conversation when bachelors talked together in my house. Married women also perceive their husbands to be the targets of widows' advances. On one occasion, when a number of women were gathered in my house, Ibo's wife Akwadi embarked on a long monologue on adultery in which she emphasized that *she* never engaged in this although *some* women gave no thought to soliciting intercourse from another woman's husband, deplorable as this was. Although ostensibly addressed to me as information on Etoro customs and practices, Akwadi fixed one of the widows present with a penetrating glance. She went on to say that although some women did not mind having a co-wife, she most certainly did and that Ibo would not take a second wife if she opposed it. (Ibo, who was off with other men gathering wild nuts, later confirmed this.) The point Akwadi was making was unmistakable. The married women of Kaburusato also took a leading role in the expulsion of a young widow from the community for sexual impropriety (Kelly 1976:44–45). Although the specific offenses involved a bachelor, there were indications that the women of the community suspected the widow of advancing her marital prospects on several fronts. It is evident here that the parties who have an interest in widow remarriage include not only the male agnates who seek to arrange unions and the widows who seek to exercise personal choice, but also the married women of the community. Cantrell (n.d.) provides very interesting comparative data on Gebusi women's perspective on matrimony.

25. The introduction of steel tools 12 to 15 years prior to ethnographic study has had less effect on the Etoro economy than one might suppose. Although a steel ax is

four times more efficient than a stone ax in cutting trees (as determined by experiments conducted in the field), many laborsaving techniques used in conjunction with the stone ax have been abandoned so that the realized advantage is only on the order of two to one. Formerly, the Etoro lashed several poles to the trunk of a tree so that it could be cut 10 to 12 feet above the ground, where the diameter of the trunk was about 20 percent smaller. Care was taken to insure that a felled tree toppled a number of others that had been partly cut through, while currently there is a tendency to cut trees so that the tops converge to form brush piles. Many trees were formerly ringbarked rather than felled. Overall, it is estimated that the tasks of fencing, felling trees, and clearing undergrowth take only half as much time with steel tools, but since planting and weeding have not been affected, weekly labor expenditure in gardening has only been reduced from 14.17 to 11.65 hours. The labor savings in the women's task of clearing undergrowth appears to have been comparable to that realized by the men in fencing and felling trees so that the proportional contributions of each gender changed only slightly, with the female contribution rising from 56.6 to 57.9 percent with steel tools. Labor expenditure in sago processing has not been affected by steel technology, as a stone tool is still used to pulverize the pith. The efficiency advantage of sago processing over gardening would be only marginally greater with stone tools. The time required to repair traplines for annual use was greater with stone tools, adding about .65 hours per week (or 34 hours per year) to the male workload. The taking of arboreal game by cutting the trees in which they had taken refuge would have entailed added male labor as well, but the increase is unlikely to have exceeded 2 hours a week. Cassowary snaring, fish poisoning, taking terrestrial game, and foraging are unaffected. The construction of longhouses once every four years would be more time-consuming with stone tools, but materials from older houses are no longer salvaged as they were in the past, reducing the labor savings provided by steel technology. Firewood collection may also have been somewhat more time-consuming. Overall, a recalculation of the figures in table 2.6 so as to reflect the increased labor expenditure required with stone tools would add an estimated 1.3 hours to male and female gardening effort per week and an estimated 2.65 hours to male hunting and trapping effort. This increases total male hours of labor per week to 25.52 and total female hours to 17.81. Male labor expenditure in subsistence food production thus would have been 58.9 percent of the total with stone tools as opposed to 55.8 percent with steel.

Although this recalculation is based on estimates and the precise figures may be inaccurate, the general conclusion that steel technology has not greatly reduced labor inputs or significantly changed the proportional labor contributions of each gender can be established with some certainty. This is due to the fact that sago processing, planting, weeding, harvesting, foraging, fish poisoning, cassowary snaring, and the excavation of holed-up terrestrial game are all unaffected. Moreover, most of the time expended in hunting is spent patrolling the forest, and most of the effort in trapping is travel time to check traps. Consequently, a doubling of the estimate of added labor required with stone technology would only increase the male labor component to 59.6 percent of total labor expenditures, compared to the current 55.8 percent with steel. Consideration of the possible effects of a change in the economic mix leads to similar conclusions, i.e., the consequences would be slight. It is possible that less sago was processed prior to depopulation (and the current abundance of mature palms this produced), while the garden acreage taken into cultivation per year was expanded to compensate for this. Suppose, for the sake of example, that sago-processing efforts were reduced by one-half and gardening efforts were doubled. This would only reduce the female component in starch staple production from 64.5 to 60.4 percent. If this were combined with the original estimate of the added labor required with stone technology, the male labor contribution would be 59.6 percent of a total of 49.65 hours of work per week. Although total weekly labor would be nearly one-third greater than at present, the sexual division of labor would have only shifted from male-female percentages of 60 to 40 (precontact) to 56 to 44 (in 1968). Thus, neither steel technology nor depopulation can have significantly altered the basic pattern of the economy.

26. Women bring small children with them to gardens and sago stands, so that tending them in these contexts does not add hours of labor other than those already recorded. In the longhouse context, younger children are often in the company of older children so that child care is considerably less demanding for parents than one might envision from an ethnocentric perspective.

27. As explained in note 10, 97 percent of the animal protein in the diet is available to mature women (aged 19 and older), while items prohibited by food taboos account for the unavailable 3 percent. As a result of the prohibition on pork consumption, 82 percent of the available protein in the diet is available to men aged 18 and older. Only 35 percent of animal protein is available to widows during the mourning period of two to three years prior to remarriage (Kelly 1977:45, 311). This would reduce female consumption to 93 percent if averaged over the course of a lifetime (see n. 21 to chap. 7). It is evident that men are not privileged in nutritional terms, although they are symbolically privileged in that they can consume certain rare but spiritually significant items prohibited to women. For example, the striped possums are the hunting dogs of the *Sigisato* spirits, and the hornbill is the corporeal abode of homicide victims, who constitute a special class among spirits of the dead (Dwyer 1990:15). Hornbill is eaten only by very elderly men; others are said to be afraid to do so. The striped possums can be eaten by men aged 18 and older, but not by women. It is said that in the past women who ate these sickened and died (as consumption invites a witchcraft attack). The terrestrial cuscus *Phalanger gymnotis* (*hatagaui*) and an unidentified snake (*kai nuba*) are likewise said to cause women but not men to become ill. The rat *Uromys candimaculatus* (*fagena*) is said to cause sterility in unmarried women, although married women can and do consume it. Consumption of the rat *Chiruromys vates* (*yesula*) is said to cause the waistband string of a woman's skirt to break, producing an event of acute public embarrassment. A woman's consumption of the red parrot (*akahelo*) or the sulphur-crested cockatoo (*ahea*) is said to have fatal consequences for any man who subsequently has intercourse with the woman. These two birds are associated with spirits of the dead (i.e., *Kesames*). Overall, these food taboos tend to convey the notion that the spiritual properties of certain animals cause problems for women but not men. These problems are related to witchcraft attack, sexual relations, and reproduction, which are all interrelated phenomena within the more encompassing Etoro cosmology of life-force transmission.

28. In the New Guinea Highlands, the social positions of Big Man and rubbish man originate out of economic activity. Moreover, the pig is both the epitome of cultural value and a reservoir for the accumulation of surplus agricultural production. Here the strategic focus on economic process recommended by Modjeska (1982) does provide a useful point of departure in analyzing social inequality and penetrates deeply into the topic. However, the very significant dimension of witchcraft beliefs and labeling as an aspect of social inequality has received little attention and Strathern's (1982b) important pioneering efforts to work out interconnections between witchcraft beliefs and aspects of production and exchange have not been followed up. I mention this in order to make the point that, while the Etoro and Highlands cases do indeed constitute different types of societies, amenable to different modes of analysis, there may also be similarities that are overshadowed by these different analytic approaches. Reay's (1976) intriguing article also suggests that witchcraft labeling and the political aspirations of Big Men as economic operatives are intertwined.

CHAPTER 3

1. This initial section is an elaborated version of an earlier publication, Kelly 1976.

2. The complicated matter of identifying the witch responsible for a specific death will be discussed in chapter 4. However, it may be noted here that acts of witchcraft are visible to *Kesame* and *Sigisato* spirits (who communicate this information to mediums) and to the victim himself at the point of death, when his *ausulubo* separates from his body. Acts of witchcraft per se cannot be seen in dreams, although convincing circumstantial evidence of their occurrence may be witnessed.

3. The Etoro maintain that the child of a witch and nonwitch will not normally possess this characteristic. The offspring of two witches are thought likely to be *kagomano* but are not necessarily so. These contingencies turn on the belief that a witch must copulate "as a witch" in order to beget a *kagomano,* and only a pair of them are likely to do so (perhaps because the lone witch would reveal his true identity to his "natural" spouse by such behavior). In addition, two natural parents may have a witch-child born to them if the woman is unknowingly raped by the *ausulubo* of a witch while she sleeps. The birth of a *kagomano* therefore does not necessarily implicate either parent. All physically large infants are presumed to be *kagamano* and are submitted to infanticide. (Thirty percent—3/10—of all children born during the 15-month period of my fieldwork met this fate.) Only witches are thought to preserve such offspring.

4. Josephides (1983:301) provides data indicating that stepping over a man is the symbolic equivalent of having intercourse with him among the Kewa. A man who is the victim of a potentially lethal form of sorcery can be cured if his wife either steps over him many times or has sexual intercourse with him. In this case actual or symbolic intercourse provides for the depletion or "flushing out" of supernaturally imparted substances. The male victim of sorcery is drained of the lethal substance through intercourse and thus cured.

5. The blows were administered by the (married) elder brother of the man and by the two "sons" (by an elder co-wife of the deceased husband) of the widow, one recently married and the other a bachelor in his early 20s.

6. This extension of the locational restrictions to canines is probably due, in part, to the Etoro view that dogs possess some humanlike qualities. There is, moreover, an explicit identification with respect to sexual behavior. The Etoro say that dogs are "like people" because male dogs sniff one another's genitals.

7. Both types of sexual relations are uniformly regulated by kinship. Wives and young male protégés should be selected from among those individuals who are within the kinship category *aua* (m.s.); husbands and inseminators are found within the reciprocal category *naua* (m.s. and w.s.). (See Kelly 1977:179–84 for discussion of this kin category.) The ideal inseminator (among those eligible by kinship) is a boy's true sister's husband or her betrothed; brother and sister will then receive semen from the same man (ideally a father's mother's brother's son) and be, in a sense, cospouses to him.

8. A predisposition toward development of the desirable characteristics of one's inseminator is also transmitted in the semen itself (rather than by tutelage). Some young men thus thought it conceivable that they might acquire the capabilities possessed by persons of Western culture (and hence the associated material culture) by ingesting their semen, and they asked me to make arrangements for them to go to the coast as contract laborers so that this experiment might be tried.

9. Institutionalized homosexual relations between women are reported for the Kamula (Wood 1982:191) but not for any of the other Strickland-Bosavi tribes. Cantrell, who focuses on the female life cycle, reports that such relations are absent among the Gebusi (Cantrell n.d.). It is thus possible that Etoro men's views concerning the mode of transmission of witchcraft between women is conjectural and has no basis in practice. Gender parallelism in beliefs concerning maturation is discussed further along in the text.

10. A. Strathern's early paper on kinship, descent, and locality (Strathern 1973) has been of considerable importance in drawing attention to the widespread role of food in cultural conceptions of the physical and spiritual constitution of the person and the construction of shared substance relations. For example, among the Siane, "food is one of the media through which a paternal spirit is instilled into clan members as they grow up" (Strathern 1973:30, drawing on material presented in Salisbury 1964). Among the Etoro, game is yielded up by the male *Sigisato* spirits associated with each lineage's territory. As noted in chapter 2, concerted hunting and trapping are thus carried out on one's own lineage's territory. However, the game procured is shared out among all residents of the longhouse community, including nonagnates. Thus while the growth of flesh, blood, and skin is attributable to game linked to lineage *Sigisatos* and lineage territory, this substance component does not recreate a distinctive relation of a person to a descent group. Paternal substance (bone) that delineates recruitment to lineage membership is immutable and entirely unaffected by food consumption. An initial maternal substance is mutable and comes to be progressively overshadowed by accretions derived from game provided by men (and *Sigisatos*) of different lineages. Thus a man is linked to his own lineage by bone substance and to

all men by flesh and blood substance. This parallels the spiritual community of males who share a common pool of life force. The differences between the Etoro and Siane thus conform to Whitehead's (1986) distinction between cultural systems that emphasize manhood and clanhood, respectively, in male initiation.

11. Schieffelin (1982:195–96) notes that participants in the Kaluli seclusion lodge assert equality with respect to the rest of society, but focuses on the conclusion that this precludes bestowal of a status change by the rest of society. He thus de-emphasizes the transition from dependence that this entails. However, the Kaluli also differ from the Etoro in that the lodge members are supplied with food by their fathers, and are therefore not entirely self-sufficient (Schieffelin 1982:164, 177).

12. Etoro beliefs and practices are not dependent upon the seclusion lodge for their continued existence. Thus bachelor gardens may be instituted outside the context of the lodge, and the anointing of a mature young man can take place as an individual event, in the context of a *kosa* ceremony. Both of these adjustments were practiced in traditional precontact times and continued in 1968–69. The Etoro did not express the view that the multicommunity seclusion lodge was a thing of the past, although the last initiation occurred not long before the first administrative patrols. Among both the Kaluli and Onabasulu, similar seclusion lodges were discontinued after the inception of sustained administrative and missionary influence in 1964 (Schieffelin 1982; Ernst n.d.).

13. The analysis presented here is relevant to a number of issues that have recently been addressed in the literature. Although discussion of these is beyond the scope of this work, some of the connections may be noted. First, the symbolic equation of shell valuables with semen has broad relevance for a number of issues pertaining to exchange. Wealth is clearly a detachable part of the male person (re: Gregory 1980, 1982; Strathern 1983). Maternal substance is an equally detachable part of the female person (although the capacity to bear children is not). The exchange of semen and wealth for female reproductive capacity and maternal substance therefore does not entail the objectification of women (re: Strathern 1983). Indeed, in the Etoro system, males and male substance are also exchanged (Kelly 1976:53).

The second point to be noted pertains to the matrilateral payments characteristic of the Daribi (Wagner 1967), Wiru (Strathern 1971b), and many Highland societies. The Etoro exchange of shell valuables (representing semen) for tree oil (representing female reproductive capacity under male control) can be juxtaposed with these cases following an insightful contrast M. Strathern (1983:169, 175) notes. However, neither recruitment to a patriline nor continuing matrilateral influence is at issue in the Etoro case. The transaction entails the reconfiguration of a substance relation as an exchange relationship, as explained in the section to which this note is appended. The extent to which this interpretation might elucidate aspects of the contrastive matrilateral payments of other societies might usefully be explored. It would seem that continuing matrilateral influence is bound up with the empowerment of menstrual blood as a supernaturally charged substance, paralleling and perhaps informing supernatural influence. The Kamula case is of particular importance since the Kamula share features with both the contrastive Etoro and Daribi cases (Wood 1982). Finally, the Etoro equation of semen with shell valuables does imply that wealth comes from men (re: Lindenbaum 1984:351; Feil 1987:194). However, this entails no conceptual basis for an appropriation of female labor, since none is involved in the generation of wealth. This will be established in chapter 6. The works cited here have all contributed to my understanding of Etoro transactions, and this footnote is intended to bring out and acknowledge these interconnections.

14. The fact that both hunting and heterosexual relations take place in the forest is probably of symbolic significance, although I lack the data to elaborate the nature of this interconnection. Among the neighboring Bedamini, hunters relate that a solitary wild pig hunt is instigated by a dream of a beautiful, full-breasted maiden who invites the hunter to come to her place in the forest. The hunter then repairs to that location in the predawn hours, where he finds a sleeping pig in its lair and kills it with an arrow fired at close range (van Beek 1987:69).

15. These prohibitions have less effect on consumption of available protein than the number of prohibited taxa suggests, since many of the latter are rarely or infrequently consumed. See nn. 10 and 27, chap. 2, and Kelly 1977:45 for further discussion of this point.

16. The point that a man is "indebted" to his father requires some qualification. As noted earlier, the self-sufficiency of the seclusion lodge marks the termination of a young man's dependence on paternal nurturance and life force, so that indebtedness to the father is only residual and the initiate emerges as a man among men. A comparison of Etoro initiation with that of the Bedamini and Kaluli brings out the Etoro emphasis on this egalitarian theme. Among the Bedamini, the importance of the father's role in the process of male growth and maturation is explicitly emphasized. When the initiates are assembled by a river to collect one stone apiece (to subsequently be fired to steam-cook the pigs killed for this occasion), a community leader proclaims, "I have eaten my father's cock!" (Sørum 1982:53). This conveys the notion that the ultimate source of life force is the father. The Bedamini initiation entails no period of seclusion and is not preceded by a phase during which economic self-sufficiency is demonstrated. Likewise, Kaluli initiates are supplied with provisions (other than game) by their fathers during the 15-month period of seclusion (Schieffelin 1982:164, 177), so that they are not entirely self-sufficient. The Etoro thus emphasize that the initiates are, in important respects, self-made men. It is significant in this respect that only uninitiated Etoro boys assume food taboos on the occasion of their father's death and that the taboos are lifted when the boys enter the seclusion lodge (or at the age when they are eligible to enter). This suggests that an initiate emerges as a man among men, an independent agent unencumbered by weighty obligations to his father other than deference and support in situations of conflict. There are no formal economic obligations to fathers. As noted earlier, young men provide assistance in felling trees to a wide range of older male kinsmen as well as performing this task for the benefit of widowed "mothers."

17. Although women clearly know the basic outlines of the doctrine of life-force transmission, which impinges on public life, they apparently do not know what transpires at the seclusion lodge. Men relate that a woman attempted to spy on the initiates during the most recent seclusion. She was spotted by one of the bachelors who was harvesting sweet potatoes in the bachelors' garden. He was entirely nude in accordance

with seclusion lodge practice. He chased her away, threatening to beat her with a stick since it is forbidden (*tobi*) for women to see the secluded lodge members. However, the latter were not outraged or even upset by this intrusion, but considered it a source of great humor. Indeed, men told me the story on several occasions, with considerable mirth. The humor derives from the men's view that the young woman (then about 25) had come to seduce one of the virginal bachelors, but instead received the just come-uppance of being driven away with a stick. The story thus confirms men's views that women are sexually predatory creatures, out to drain men of their life force. But the bachelor was steadfast in his commitment to the principles of the lodge, and this is the moral of the story.

18. Women in the kinship category *ame,* which includes mother, mother's sister, father's brother's wife, and mother's brother's daughter, play important roles through-out all phases of Bedamini initiation (Sørum 1982:59). These include manufacture of parts of the initiates' attire, lecturing the novices on adult responsibility (together with adult men), fetching the novices from a bush hut where they spend a day, and dancing. These elements are consistent with the themes of male-female complementarity and the importance of women in exchange relations that link groups (ibid.). The accounts of the Etoro seclusion lodge and emergence ceremonies I elicited were unaided by direct observation and lack this level of detail. Although Etoro informants did not include these features, they might well be present since the Etoro ritual encompasses the same themes. Parts of the initiates' attire (as they emerge from nakedness at the lodge) are probably contributed by their mothers, e.g., new net bags. This would be consistent with the unchanged mother-son relationship. The women welcome the emerged initiates in the opening dances and might well fetch them as well. If the initiates are lectured, I would expect that women would take part, since the initiates are becoming full members of the gender-integrated communal longhouse and now enter more fully into production organized by the gendered division of labor. How-ever, the anointing of the initiates is the final ritual act that not only culminates but also recontextualizes all that went before. The Bedamini lack both seclusion and this anointing ritual, so the two initiatory complexes are clearly different although they share common themes pertaining to gender complementarity.

19. The basic concept of a circular closed system entailing a reciprocal relation of life and death is manifested in other aspects of cosmology that are outside the scope of the discussion at hand but may be briefly mentioned. The spirits of the dead occupy the bodies of a certain fish (*abaso*) and reside in the rivers. The *Sigisatos* are descended from a primordial crocodile (and culture hero) and at times take this form (although they characteristically reside in the bodies of cassowaries by day). The crocodiles feed on the *abaso,* and this symbolically closes the circle of life and death inasmuch as the *Sigisatos* also implant souls in men. In other words, the *Sigisatos* symbolically con-sume "death" and also bring forth life.

20. The myth overstates the case with respect to immortality. In other contexts, the Etoro express the view that in the absence of witchcraft, a man would live to an advanced age and ultimately die from depletion.

21. "Mother!" is a shortened form of an expletive frequently used to express

astonishment. The meaning of the expression in this context is "as astonishing as incest."

22. The condition of being "alone" evokes pathos and trepidation to the Etoro. It connotes a social isolation that is the antithesis of the communal life they cherish and is also associated with vulnerability to the danger of both raiding parties and witchcraft attack.

23. The improbable manner in which the members of the *sa:go*'s community meet their death is of the nature of an ethnic joke. In this and in other myths the enemies of the Etoro are portrayed as dim-witted in the extreme. In this particular instance, the slashing also connotes the earlier episode in which the crocodile kills the members of the raiding party by slashing their throats. Thus there is also a sense that the crocodile *Sigisato* continues, even in death, to spiritually bring about the demise of his (and his age-mate's) enemies.

24. The term *aye negei* is literally translatable as "before placed" and may be glossed as "a good man of yore." The *aye negei* is invariably the principal character in any tale in which he appears, and the attributes that he evidences from one myth to the next are cleverness, skill, strength, and virtue. He is often a spirit medium. The use of the term *aye negei* thus signals a certain type of narrative in much the same way that "once upon a time a white knight lived in such and such a place" does. The hero of the *Sigisato* origin myth is also an *aye negei*. In the myth of appropriation to which this note is appended, it is important to know that the young man who is the main protagonist is a heroic figure of this type.

25. The Etoro taxa *mahabu* includes the cucumber and this wild fruit which is morphologically similar in possessing a rind, fleshy part, and soft, seedy center (which is reddish-orange).

26. "To polish his bow" is a male euphemism for intercourse, so that the association between the black palm bow and the phallus is quite explicit.

27. This maintenance of fundamental principles of order by the *Kesame* spirits parallels the action of the *Sigisato* spirits in other tales. Recall the story related in chapter 2, in which a *Sigisato* kills a woman for bringing a forbidden variety of sago (a low-altitude thing) into the upland primary forest, and thus conflating "low" and "high."

28. The role of boys as recipients of life force may create a problem of ambiguous gender identity in some instances. One boy of 13, who had come to the community in which I resided in order to be inseminated by his father's mother's brother's son, made a joke of donning a woman's skirt and draping it over the heads of men seated on the floor in my house. This public enactment of an apparent confusion of gender identity incurred a verbal rebuke from older men, although it also elicited embarrassed laughter from some male onlookers as well. That a boy should be feminized by his role as recipient of semen is the exact opposite of what is supposed to occur, although his role as recipient of semen is somewhat analogous to that of a woman.

29. Eileen Cantrell collected a very similar myth among the Gebusi. However, the Gebusi myth is part of a corpus that women relate in female-exclusive contexts, while the Etoro version is related in the communal section of the longhouse by individuals of either gender. The Gebusi women's interpretation of the analogous myth is consis-

tent with my presentation of Etoro women's perspective on the version presented here (Cantrell, personal communication). Although the authorship of a myth is indeterminate, I consider it probable, on internal grounds, that this Etoro myth is female authored.

30. Parentheses are here used to identify and mark off clarifications elicited after the myth was recorded and transcribed. The text is otherwise as close to a literal translation as I could achieve.

31. Amputation of a girl's finger joint is a component of mourning among the Dani of Irian Jaya (Heider 1970:238), but this custom is not practiced by the Etoro, nor are there any other real-life circumstances under which such amputation occurs.

CHAPTER 4

1. Since a "nothing" sickness will pass of its own accord and a witchcraft-induced illness requires a supernatural cure, the Etoro employ very few medicines. All of these are understood to alleviate symptoms rather than act upon the cause of disease.

2. The ethnographic film "Tidikawa and Friends," made by Jeff and Sue Doring (1971), depicts a Bedamini séance that is very similar to the séances observed among the Etoro. Knauft (1985a:88–93, 295–319), Sørum (1980:273–96), and Schieffelin (1977, 1985b) provide accounts of séances among the Gebusi, Bedamini, and Kaluli, respectively.

3. A *Sigisato* may appear to a man in a dream to inform him of his wife's adultery, reveal the whereabouts of a lost pig, or pledge to protect him from an impending witchcraft attack. Only the *Sigisato* or *Sigisatos* that are associated with a particular lineage (through co-ownership of a common territory) appear to lineage members.

4. The physiological consequences of psychologically induced stress were outlined by Cannon (1942) many years ago and have been much discussed and debated since (see Eastwell 1982).

5. The data presented in this chapter pertaining to curing, death, and witchcraft accusations are derived from two samples, a smaller representative sample and a larger sample that encompasses all cases known to me. The representative sample is confined to the 8 of 11 longhouse communities for which I have detailed genealogies and have established the age of all residents. These 8 communities are Ingiribisato, Kasayasato, Hilisato, Sarado, Kaburusato, Turusato, Katiefi, and Haifi. The 3 longhouse communities that are excluded are the eastern Etoro communities of Poboleifi (Bobole), Nemisato (Namosado), and Gemisato (see Kelly 1977:12 for locations). In 1966, four men of Poboleifi were tried and convicted of executing a witch and sentenced to five years in prison. This had no discernible effect on the less-contacted Etoro further west, except that the manner of executing witches was altered so as to preclude physical evidence (i.e., throat-slitting was substituted for crushing the skull with an ax so that the skeleton of a decomposed corpse revealed no signs of violent death). Although the indigenous system of practices associated with witchcraft accusations may have been altered in the eastern communities, there is no evidence of any significant alterations in the communities that comprise the sample.

The residents of the eight communities included in the sample constituted 71.5 percent (276/386) of the total Etoro population on May 1, 1968, and are representative of the entire population in terms of the sex ratio (see Kelly 1977:29, 172). I have no reason to believe that they are not representative in other demographic respects as well.

Within this 8-community sample I have data pertaining to 28 deaths that occurred between May 1, 1968, and July 31, 1969, while I was in the field. These 28 deaths comprise more than 10 percent (28/276) of the initial population of the 8 communities. This very high mortality rate was the result of an influenza epidemic (see Kelly 1977:30) and was part of a general pattern of epidemic mortality from introduced diseases that is estimated to have reduced the Etoro population by about 50 percent during the period from 1935 to 1969. The effects of this concentration of mortality within a brief period of time upon the witchcraft accusation process are discussed further along in the text. However, it should be noted here that the 1969 epidemic was not a unique event, but only the latest in a series of epidemics that had occurred during the preceding 30 years.

These 28 deaths included 15 of 121 females and 13 of 155 males in the initial (May 1, 1968) population of 276 persons. Of these, 11 females died of illness (10 during the epidemic), 1 drowned, 2 were executed as witches, and 1 sick child who was believed to be a *kagomano* (witch-child) was left unattended, without food or water, to perish. These 15 female deaths resulted in: (1) 7 witchcraft cases in which a total of 9 witches were named (including two pairs of coconspirators); (2) 2 death compensations paid for executed witches; (3) 6 cases in which no public action had been taken by the time I left the field and in which it appeared that no accusation would be made. These 6 cases included 2 child deaths, which typically entail no public action. Of the 13 male deaths, 9 died of illness (8 in the epidemic), 2 drowned, 1 was executed as a witch, and 1 sick child believed to be a *kagomano* was left to perish (with his father's brother's daughter, mentioned above). These 13 male deaths resulted in: (1) 10 witchcraft cases in which a total of 10 witches were named; (2) 1 homicide compensation paid for an executed witch; (3) 2 cases in which no public action had been taken by the time I left the field and in which it appeared likely that no accusation would be made. One of these involved a child death.

There was 1 case in which the same man (Nomaya) was named as the witch responsible for 3 drownings (2 males and 1 female) that occurred simultaneously, shortly before I left the field. This case was unfolding at the time I departed, and it was said by many people that Nomaya would be executed. I have no doubt that he was in fact killed within a few days of my departure, but I lack direct confirmation of this outcome. This case is mentioned here because it will be included in some tabulations of the rate of witchcraft executions.

In addition to the 28 deaths that took place between May 1, 1968, and July 31, 1969, within the 8 longhouse communities that comprise the sample population, I have data on 26 additional deaths that took place at these communities during the period from mid-1965 through April 1968. Twenty of these deaths occurred in the period from July 1967 through April 1968, which included an epidemic of similar proportions to that observed while I was in the field (in January 1969). Four of the 6 remaining deaths occurred in 1966 and early 1967, and 2 took place in the latter part of 1965. (These deaths could readily be dated in relation to the half-dozen government patrols that had visited the area since 1964.) All these deaths were fresh in people's memory, and the details of the resulting accusations were still topics of discussion. The age of the deceased was established in these cases by determining the identity of surviving age-mates, and the ages of other parties (witch, accuser, etc.) were determined by subtraction from their current age (in 1968–69).

This total sample of 54 deaths represents 17.9 percent (54/302) of the mid-1965 population of the 8 communities that comprise the sample population. These 54 deaths include 22 of 128 females (17.2 percent) and 32 of 174 males (18.4 percent). The fact that very similar rates of mortality for males and females obtained during this four-year period suggests that the data are reasonably comprehensive, and that there has been no significant tendency to remember more of the deaths of adults of one sex than of the other. (Child deaths that took place between mid-1965 and May 1968 were not systematically recorded.) Although male deaths constitute 59 percent of the total, the rate of mortality for males during this period is only slightly higher than that for females. The imbalance in the sex ratio is very marked among individuals below the age of 15 (Kelly 1977:29) and therefore is not attributable to the adult mortality that is the focus of concern here. (Child deaths are not of concern because they very rarely eventuate in witchcraft accusations.)

Of the total of 22 female deaths that occurred during this four-year period (mid-1965 through July 1969), 18 females died of illness, 1 drowned, 2 were executed as witches, and 1 sick child was left to perish (as explained above). These 22 female deaths resulted in: (1) 11 witchcraft cases in which a total of 14 witches were named; (2) 2 death compensations paid for executions; (3) 9 cases in which no public action was taken (including 2 child deaths). It may be noted that a substantial proportion (7/18 or 39 percent) of adult female deaths due to illness or accident do not eventuate in a witchcraft accusation. This is evident in both the prefieldwork (mid-1965 to May 1968) and fieldwork period deaths, indicating that the latter were probably not instances in which a delayed accusation might have been lodged after I left the field.

Of the total of 32 male deaths, 24 males died of illness, 3 drowned, 3 were executed as witches, 1 was killed in a dispute, and 1 sick child was left to perish. These 32 male deaths resulted in: (1) 24 witchcraft cases in which a total of 28 witches were named; (2) 4 homicide compensations paid; (3) 4 instances in which no public action was taken (including 1 child death). In all, 88.5 percent (23/26) of adult male deaths due to illness or accident eventuated in a witchcraft accusation (including cases resolved by both executions and requests for compensation). In addition, 1 male child death due to illness eventuated in an accusation (while the 1 comparable female child death in the sample did not). (Nomaya is counted as accused but not executed in this enumeration.)

These data provide a total of 35 witchcraft cases (i.e., 35 victims of alleged witchcraft) in which 42 witches were accused. Although this sample is representative, it includes 24 male victims of alleged witchcraft and only 11 female victims. This is due to the larger number of adult male deaths during this period, and to the substantially larger percentage of adult male deaths that eventuate in witchcraft accusations (i.e., 88.5 percent as opposed to 61.1 percent of adult female deaths). The use of a restricted but thoroughly known sample makes it possible to establish that the preponderance of witchcraft accusations stemming from male deaths is a property of the data, rather than the process of recording the data.

In addition to the 35 witchcraft cases that constitute the representative sample, I have knowledge of 9 other cases. Six of those occurred outside the sample communities, and 3 occurred within the sample communities but prior to 1965. Unless explicitly noted, the data presented in the main body of this work are drawn from the representative sample and exclude these 9 cases. They are primarily relevant insofar as they record past accusations lodged against accused witches included within the sample.

The data on curing presented in the portion of the text to which this note is appended are derived from the representative sample of 54 deaths. In 8 cases a cure was requested (with 7 refused and 1 performed), in 12 cases no cure was requested, and in an additional 12 cases this issue is moot due to sudden death from accident or homicide. In 22 cases, I have no data on this point. These are almost entirely cases that took place prior to the fieldwork period.

6. Both Nogobe and Kayago performed cures at other longhouses and garden houses during this period, but I do not have a complete record of these activities.

7. The median age of deceased males in the sample of 54 deaths (see n. 5) is 38 years, while the median age of deceased females is 48 years. These data are consistent with the fact that the sex ratio is nearly balanced among individuals over the age of 40 (see Kelly 1977:29), although it is very unbalanced below this age. These data are also consistent with the greater proportion of male than female deaths in the sample. Since women also marry earlier than men, deceased females tend to have adult children while deceased males tend to have younger children. Thus, a seriously ill woman is frequently attended by true and/or classificatory sons and daughters, while a seriously ill male is more frequently attended by true and/or classificatory brothers. Although 34 percent of brothers and sisters coreside and 43 percent of sisters coreside, 93 percent of brothers coreside (Kelly 1977:145–53). Since sibling groups are also depleted by mortality as they age, women are even less likely to be residing with a sibling at the time of death. These data are significant in that the individual who lodges a witchcraft accusation in the case of a man's death is generally a brother of the victim, while the principal accusers in the case of a woman's death are her son and/or husband.

8. Although the discussion I witnessed took place at Kaburusato while the witchcraft accusation was being formulated at Sarado, the testimony that incriminated Nomaya was discussed at Sarado as well. This was where Wasagaya's story was heard by Kaburusato residents attending the *guano*. Similarly, Ibo's dream was first related at Kaburusato but subsequently retold by others (many times over) at Sarado. Although Nomaya resided at Sarado, there would have been ample opportunities for open public discussion when he was absent from the longhouse during parts of the day (to harvest from his garden, for instance). This is indicated by a parallel case that occurred at Kaburusato, where the alleged witch being discussed was also a community member. Most accusations are against coresidents (as discussed further along).

9. This is particularly evident in the accounts of a close relative's death that informants provide some years after the event. These contain detailed descriptions of acts of witchcraft that could only be derived from the séances conducted during the

guano, since only the spirits could have reconstructed or witnessed what was said to have transpired.

10. There can be further instructions to employ a third oracle, using a tree python, but this did not occur in any of the cases with which I am familiar.

11. This calculation includes the impending execution of Nomaya (see n. 5). It should also be noted that these figures include instances in which the same person was killed in resolution of multiple accusations. The 8 (of 42) instances when an accused witch was killed involved the execution of 5 persons, 4 males and 1 female. One additional adult in the sample of 54 deaths was killed in connection with a witchcraft allegation, but this case is not one of the 42 as the accusation was made outside the sample area and I have very little data regarding it. The woman was later killed after she returned to the sample area. Another of the 54 deaths was also a homicide stemming from a wound received in a dispute over compensation.

In all, the sample includes 50 deaths of individuals over the age of 14, of which 7 (14 percent) were homicides. Five of the 7 persons killed were males and 2 were females, with the distribution being 4 males and 2 females for witchcraft executions. The sample of 54 deaths includes the deaths of 4 children over the age of six months. Three of these deaths occurred during the fieldwork period and 1 (involving a witchcraft accusation) during the preceding period. While the data are comprehensive for the fieldwork period, I lack comprehensive data on the deaths of children during the period from mid-1965 to May 1, 1968. However, 2 of the 3 child deaths during the period from May 1, 1968, to July 31, 1969, were homicides (see n. 5). Only one child died in the epidemic and none during the remainder of the period. This suggests that there would only have been 2 to 3 child deaths due to illness during the prefieldwork period (of which 1 was recorded). Assuming that there were 3, and that no child homicides occurred then, the total sample for the four-year period would expand to 56 deaths, of which 9 (16.1 percent) were homicides. The homicide rate would then average 2.25 persons per year for a population that averaged 276 persons (304 in mid-1965 and 248 on July 31, 1969). This yields an average homicide rate of 815 per 100,000 per annum for the four-year period. The homicide rate for the fieldwork period was 4.8 persons per annum for a population that averaged 262 persons, or 1,832 per 100,000 per annum. Among the Gebusi, the homicide rate is conservatively estimated as 683 per 100,000 during the precontact era (1940–62) and 419 per 100,000 during the contact period (1963–82) (see Knauft 1985a:376–77). Although these rates are extraordinarily high by cross-cultural comparative standards, they are comparable to rates reported for the Goilala (533) and Hewa (778) in other areas of New Guinea (see Knauft 1985a:379; Hallpike 1977:120; Steadman 1971:215). In figures for Western societies, warfare deaths and executions carried out by the state are not calculated as part of the homicide rate, producing rates that are lower but not comparable. During the U.S. Civil War, the total homicide rate would appear to approximate and perhaps exceed the figures for these New Guinea societies if this rate were calculated so as to include all deaths directly caused by other persons.

12. A substantial compensation was paid in this case (see table 6.4). A man who incurred a relatively minor ankle wound during a confrontation that occurred while I

was in the field also received a modest compensation of one pearl shell and three cowrie strings.

13. Nawadia was accused of causing the death of Pabu's and Taifa's son Talibago, who was somewhat less than two years old. There was, of course, no deathbed testimony, and the pig-organ oracle also was not employed. The accusation was based solely on the pronouncement of Araradado's spirit. It is very unusual for a witchcraft accusation to be made when a preverbal child dies, and I know of no other instances. This was the ground for considering the accusation illegitimate and thus refusing compensation. The compensation was refused by Nawadia's father and her husband Osopo, who was Pabu's father's brother's son's son. Nawadia was twice divorced before marrying Osopo, although she was only about 18 years of age at this time. She had been accused of witchcraft at least once before. She was also bestowed upon Osopo by her father with no payment of bridewealth, as it is disadvantageous to marry a woman previously accused of witchcraft. Although she and Osopo both desired the union, his kinsmen and coresidents at Turusato probably did not welcome it. The original accusation stemmed in part from the fact that Nawadia was known to be a witch and was also considered a difficult person (as attested by her marital history), but there were additional structural and political factors involved as well. These will be discussed in the next chapter.

The accusation did lead to a change of residence, as it usually does. Nawadia and Osopo went to live with her father at Kasayasato. However, she was again accused of witchcraft there when her father's father's brother's son Siari died. She subsequently gave birth to a male child, which was taken to confirm her guilt in both these instances. However, Pabu did not reiterate the claim for compensation. While I was in the field, Pabu killed Kulubido, who was named as the witch responsible for Taifa's death. Thus, I would adjudge Nawadia to be at risk, even though Pabu was not actively pursuing the compensation claim at this time. Although an individual may not press for payment of a refused compensation after the birth oracle later confirms guilt, letting bygones be bygones, Pabu was among those least likely to adopt this position.

14. As I now learned, my presence at the discussion at which this decision was taken signaled my support, just as Illawe's presence signaled his. On the way back from Turusato, Illawe initially assumed I would return with him and urged me to bring the shotgun I had recently acquired (in order to reciprocate the shares of meat I was regularly given as a resident of Kaburusato). Illawe accepted my declination, made on the grounds that Kayago was his sister's husband but not mine. However, he then asked to borrow the shotgun. This request being turned down, Illawe urged me to promise to lend him the shotgun in the event that Wato did indeed kill Kayago, so that he might more easily avenge the latter's death. On several occasions, I was asked to accompany a party of men going to another community to demand compensation. However, I was never able to do so because it was not possible to go simply as an observer without the connotation that I had taken sides.

15. It would seem that Wato might easily have deduced that Kayago and Waua would refuse to pay the compensation, since both were far from the scene of bewitchment and compensation is nearly always refused in such cases. Moreover, it would seem that Wato could have anticipated that Kayago would have strong support from

his coresidents in pursuing this course of action. The accusation is also difficult to comprehend because Habwili on one hand, and Kayago and Waua on the other, had moved in different circles throughout their lives. There was only one marriage between their respective lineages. The two accused men lacked any intelligible motive and had never previously been accused. It seems unlikely that Habwili named either individual in his deathbed testimony, and it was also said by Illawe that his own kinsmen at Haifi confirmed this. It thus appears that Kayago's and Waua's names were put before oracles and were introduced into the formulation of the accusation in this way. One might speculate that the individual behind this was Tsmari, who was married to Habwili's father's brother's daughter and resided with Habwili at Haifi when Habwili died. This was the single marriage between Habwili's and Kayago's lineages, as Kayago and Tsmari are distant agnates. About 19 months earlier, Kayago's mother Kebo died at Kaburusato where both Kayago and Tsmari resided. Kebo named Tsmari's wife, Waime. Kayago requested compensation on the basis of this deathbed testimony, without consulting his own spirits or those of the senior resident medium, Araradado, his mentor. Tsmari agreed to pay, but proclaimed Waime innocent, and expressed his confidence that the birth oracle would confirm this. The decision not to employ the pig-organ oracle or consult the spirits was evidently meant to facilitate complete reliance on the birth oracle. However, the accusation induced Tsmari to leave Kaburusato and take up residence in Haifi. He had been a *tafidilo* at Kaburusato, and the accusation undercut his effectiveness as a community leader both in itself and because it reflected tensions between community members and Tsmari's second wife, Waime. He had just married Waime, a woman who was previously twice divorced and twice accused of witchcraft. Tsmari thus lost his position as a community leader at Kaburusato and may well have blamed Kayago for this (although it was more accurately attributable to an inadvisable second marriage).

Moreover, there had been conflict between Tsmari and Kayago only a few months before Kayago was accused in connection with Habwili's death. Waime gave birth to a male child, which Tsmari took to indicate that she was not the witch responsible for Kebo's death. He requested that the compensation be returned, but those who had received shares when it was redistributed argued that it should not be returned. This view stemmed from the fact that the birth of the male child confirmed that Waime was responsible for Hamone's death. This was the first accusation against her, and it was argued that her first child born thereafter pertained to that death and not Kebo's. Even Tsmari's eldest son, Ayage, sided with his coresidents against his father on this point. Tsmari was enraged by this, and later that night he struck Ayage across the rib cage with the back of his steel ax while Ayage was sleeping, cracking several of his ribs. (This did not lead to any permanent breach in the relationship.) No one at all sided with Tsmari, indicating the complete erosion of his influence within the community in which he had formerly been *tafidilo*. This clearly rankled.

The following day Kayago offered Tsmari a pig, a pearl shell, and four strings of cowrie shells as a partial return for the pig, pearl shell, and ten strings of cowrie shells Tsmari had originally paid in compensation. Kayago provided this on his own, as those who had received shares of the compensation when it was redistributed were resolved not to return these. Waua (also Kebo's son) was among those who refused.

Given this background of recent conflict, it is plausible that Tsmari played a role in having Kayago's and Waua's names placed before oracles, leading ultimately to the accusation. After moving to Haifi, Tsmari continued to be regarded as a *tafidilo*, but his influence was considerably reduced. His wife's "brother" Habwili was a well-established *tafidilo* at Haifi. After the deaths of both Habwili and Kusuame (the *tafidilo* of Katiefi), Tsmari became the only *tafidilo* at the combined community that coalesced at Katiefi (at which Wato was also the only medium). Both as *tafidilo* and as Habwili's wife's "brother," Tsmari was in an excellent position to exert influence with respect to the names placed before the oracles and may also have taken part in the consultation of the pandanus oracle itself.

16. One case of refused compensation was structurally similar to those in which compensation was not requested. When Enoia died, his brother Waya requested compensation from the husband and brother of Heanome, who was the witch named. However, Heanome's husband was Waya's wife's lineage "brother," who felt the compensation should not have been requested and consequently ignored the suggestion that he pay it.

Five instances in which compensation was refused on the grounds that the accusation was not legitimate have been discussed. There was one additional refusal of this type that is of interest because it involved the only accusation against a man over the age of 40. Kusuame, the *tafidilo* of Katiefi, was accused of having killed the retired medium Sanimako by witchcraft. However, this accusation was not made by Sanimako's brother, Abama, but by a classificatory sister's husband (Kayupa). Abama maintained that Sanimako died without naming a witch and did not pursue the case by performing oracles or eliciting a medium's spirit pronouncements. Kayupa maintained that Sanimako had named Kusuame, his mother's brother, and that Abama suppressed this information because Kusuame was Abama's mother's brother as well. Abama flatly said this was a lie. The compensation was never paid. However, two years later Kayupa and his cross-cousin Ayage, who both resided at Haifi, became involved in an argument over the unpaid compensation with Kusuame's father's brother's son's sons Nafi and Porama, who resided at Katiefi with Kusuame. In the course of this argument, Kayupa and Ayage fired arrows into the ground in front of Nafi and Porama. There were rumors of impending conflict between these communities but nothing transpired.

In the two final instances in which compensation was refused, there were no grounds for disputing the legitimacy of the accusation. One of these cases involved Nomaya and the other involved Tame, two alleged witches who have been discussed in connection with other cases. Both responded belligerently to these accusations and flaunted the warrant for execution that nonpayment entailed. Both were accused again in connection with deaths that occurred not long thereafter.

17. Brothers invariably reside together most of the time but may be separated for short periods when each one resides with his respective wife's fathers (Kelly 1977:145–46). Nomaya had resided with his brothers at the inception of fieldwork but moved shortly thereafter to a community where he had no close kin or affines. His separation from his brothers was unique in this respect. Nomaya's closest kin at Sarado, to which he moved, were Ailoe and Maua, his father's brother's wife's

father's brother's sons (i.e., "mother's brothers"). But both these men died in the epidemic so that his closest kin at Sarado when he was accused were more distant "mother's brothers" who had not sponsored his residence there.

18. The witch and victim were coresident in 66.7 percent (28/42) of the accusations. Five of these accusations were resolved by execution, leaving 23 cases in which there was a choice to be made between remaining in the community or moving to another. The incidence of coresidence is somewhat higher (72 percent) in the expanded sample of all known accusations.

19. There was one instance in which an offer of compensation was initially refused, and the community of the deceased sought vengeance instead. A four-day armed conflict ensued, after which the originally offered compensation was accepted.

20. Others also left. These included two young men who were "sister's sons" of Piawe and Kusuame. They joined kinsmen at Sarado. Kusuame's widow, Kodi, went to Kaburusato with Kayari and his wife Yawa, who was Kodi's daughters. Udali's younger sister, Oname, fled to Turusato to live with her betrothed, Waua. Her younger brother Haimago (aged 8) went with her. Oname, who was 12, had been sleeping next to Udali when the latter's throat was slit by her father's brother, Kauhe. She was shattered by this experience but was very solicitously cared for by the men and women at Turusato. The accusation against Waua and Kayago was first lodged a few days before Udali was killed and Oname fled. Udali's and Oname's half sister, Nabulo (aged 14) remained at Katiefi with her brother Mugu (aged 6) and half brother Suno (aged 8). Nabulo was betrothed to Abama, the husband of Habasiome (who had accused Udali of witchcraft). Moreover, her mother Tina (widowed by Piawe's death) remained at Katiefi as well. As was mentioned earlier, Harogo's sister, Taniginiame and his father's brother's son, Aheo, were left to die when they became ill during the epidemic because they were believed to be witch-children (*kagomano*). The consequences of this epidemic of introduced disease (influenza), and of the aftermath of witchcraft accusations and executions that followed in its wake, were thus devastating.

21. Taifa was originally married to Kanamabe, a matrilateral sibling of Pabu. She left him to take up with Pabu (initiating a de facto divorce). Their union was one of a small number of romantic marriages (in contrast to the typical union, arranged when a girl is about 5 years old). They went to Huli territory and resided there for 12 years, returning only after Kanamabe's death. This background is also relevant to a second accusation Pabu lodged against Kanamabe's brother, which will be discussed shortly.

22. The individual most directly responsible for the deaths of the children Aheo and Taniginiame was Kayupa, who was their next of kin. He was Aheo's brother and Taniginiame's father's brother's son and resided with them. He and his wife Mebo had been responsible for caring for these children up to this point, together with two of Kayupa's unmarried brothers. Kayupa and Mebo had no children of their own as yet and were not overburdened. Contrary to sociobiological expectations, close kin were thus responsible for five of the nine homicides in the sample (i.e., these two homicides, and the executions of Udali, Samabe, and Sayaga).

23. The principle of "an eye for an eye and a tooth for a tooth" is often ethnocentrically misunderstood. From the vantage point of a tribal society that lacks formal judicial institutions, it constitutes an attempt to place narrow and just limits upon

revenge, and is counterpoised to two eyes for an eye (to extend the metaphor). The Etoro concept of compensation represents an even more humanitarian ideal in seeking to address the expectable emotional distress of an aggrieved person and quench the desire for retribution at its source.

24. See note 5 for a description of the sample to which the data presented in table 4.1 pertain.

25. This form of analysis has been advocated by Marwick (1964, 1965, 1967) and Knauft (1985a) for evaluating the frequency of accusations against individuals in particular kin categories. It is here extended to age/sex categories.

26. Infanticide is also grounded in witchcraft ideology in that large children believed to be *kagomano* are subject to this practice. The mother or a kinswoman in attendance presses the newborn's face into the moist earth so that it never draws its first breath. Technically speaking, infanticide thus entails an attribution of witchcraft (possession of a *tohorora*) followed by an execution. This is entirely in the hands of women, specifically the mother or some kinswoman acting on her behalf. During the 15-month period I was in the field, there were 10 births. Three infants were submitted to infanticide, including 2 males and 1 female. (Two other female infants died of natural causes within the first six months, bringing total infant mortality to 50 percent.) It is of interest that Waime did not allow her child to live even though she was 39 years of age and had no living offspring. The two other mothers were younger, but one also had no children and the other had only one. This indicates that infanticide is ideologically motivated; a child is killed because it is believed to be a witch and not because the mother is overburdened or seeks to rationally orchestrate her parental investment, as sociobiology would predict. The high rate of infanticide is also striking in light of the fact that the Etoro had undergone 50 percent depopulation in the preceding 25 years and expressed the view that they were dying out. Infanticide was clearly not a rational population control device, but it is ideologically intelligible because the Etoro attributed depopulation to an abundance of witches and sought to reduce their numbers.

I have not included the attributions of witchcraft that infanticide entails in table 4.2 because I lack data pertaining to infanticide during the two and three-fourths years' prefieldwork period. Moreover, the attributions of witchcraft that are included involve social processes entailing persons other than accused and accuser in a way that the mother-newborn attribution does not. Nevertheless, the proportional distribution of witchcraft attributions against children would obviously be higher if infanticides were included. The homicide rate for the fieldwork period would also expand to 2,748 per 100,000 per annum if these additional humanly caused deaths were included (see n. 11).

It should be noted that the average population of 276 persons for the four-year sample period is identical to the population on May 1, 1968, on which the age structure is based. The age structure is the same as that reported in Kelly 1977:29, with three emendations. There are 17 (rather than 15) males aged 31 to 35, 10 (rather than 11) males aged 36 to 40, and 4 (rather than 3) males aged 60 to 65, increasing the total male population to 155 and the total male and female population to 276 (from 274). The initial age structure was based on preliminary tabulations of the residents of eight communities on May 1, 1968, that were subsequently rechecked and emended to take into account changes of residence that occurred in April. However, the few changes made were not applied to the already completed age structure at that time. They are important in the present context because they have a direct bearing on the issue of proportional representation.

27. Although girls may be ceremonially married at 14 (and bridewealth transferred), they do not commence sexual relations with their husbands until their attainment of productive and reproductive maturity is celebrated, as explained earlier.

28. The distribution of witchcraft attributions by age among the Etoro is nearly a perfect inversion of the distribution of sorcery attributions by age among the Gebusi (Knauft 1985a:141). Among the Gebusi, the frequency of accusations increases with each successive age-group, such that 80 percent of living men and 28 percent of living women over the age of 45 have been accused while only 5.6 percent of living never-married young adult men (aged 15 to 28) and no living never-married young adult women have been accused. In the third column of table 4.2, I have tabulated Etoro witchcraft attributions as a percentage of population for each age category. These tabulations are not comparable to Knauft's, because his tabulation does not include multiple accusations against the same individual while mine does. This produces higher percentages in the Etoro case. For example, there were 3 accusations directed against the women in the 16-to-20 age-group, which includes 9 persons, so that the incidence of accusations is 33.3 percent of the population of that age/sex category. But all 3 accusations were directed against Udali, so the number of accused witches in this age category is 1 of 9, or 11.1 percent. Despite the fact that Knauft's tabulations are directed to a different purpose and are therefore not directly comparable to the data presented here, the stark contrast in overall patterns is apparent for senior men over age 40 (or 45). Senior Etoro men are rarely accused, while senior Gebusi men are frequently accused. However, the two ethnographic cases are similar in that more males than females are accused and more males than females are killed in both (see Knauft 1985a:117, 132–42). In a large sample, Gebusi males were accused in 68.6 percent (116/169) of all male deaths, in 37.0 percent (20/54) of all female deaths, and in 61.0 percent (136/223) of all deaths. These data show that among the Gebusi, as among the Etoro, more male than female deaths eventuate in accusations and that there is a tendency toward accusing a person of the same sex as the victim of supernatural attack. Among the Bedamini, death is attributed to male supernatural attack and illness to female supernatural attack (Sørum 1980). In the Kaluli case women are also very rarely accused of causing death by supernatural attack (Schieffelin 1976).

29. When Heanome's husband Ailoe died at Sarado, it was his half sister Suagua (living at Kaburusato) who was the source of the rumor that Heanome herself was responsible for both this death and the death of Ailoe's (and Suagua's) brother Maua that had occurred the following day. This exemplifies the point that women play a direct role in making incriminating statements about potential suspects. Suagua's indictment was especially incriminating since she was Ailoe's next of kin and was presumed to know his deathbed statement (although she was not present when he died).

30. The seven flawed accusations are predominantly those discussed earlier with respect to refusal to pay compensation. They include Tame's accusation of Hariako, Tsmari's accusation of Kayari, Wato's accusation of Kayago and Waua, Pabu's accusation of Kayari and Esopa, and Kayupa's accusation of Kusuame. Most of these were motivated by retaliatory interests. Only Pabu's accusation of Kayari and Esopa contained aspects of material interest, namely the recovery of valuables expended by Pabu in paying compensation for executing Kulubido. However, as was noted earlier, there was also bad blood between Pabu and Kayari stemming from the fact that Pabu ran off with Kayari's brother's wife, so that Pabu had emotional reasons to suppose Kayari harbored ill will toward this woman (Asifa) whom he was accused of bewitching. This was the only one of these accusations that resulted in payment of compensation. The expression of private interest in a retaliatory accusation therefore typically results in the forfeiture of compensation because the accusation fails to receive authentication. Pabu's accusation of Kayari (and Esopa) was also not authenticated, but Kayari paid out of fear for his life.

Three of the flawed accusations were among those I have labeled politically significant (i.e., those against Kayago, Waua, and Kusuame). Two of the accusations against a previously accused witch are also in this category, i.e., the second accusation against the medium Nasu and the accusation against the wife of the *tafidilo* Tsmari.

31. Marwick (1963:7–8) reports a parallel situation among the Cewa. While women are held to be more prone to supernatural attacks than men, this cultural generalization is not borne out by the actual gender distribution of accusations.

32. The execution of Yo illustrates the hazards of attempting to substitute a brother for a husband as protector. Yo's separation from her husband (and the problems in their relationship this betokened) led to his failure to come up with the half of the compensation that was his responsibility when she was accused of witchcraft. Her brother was in the process of bickering with her husband about this (so that payment was delayed) when she was shot.

33. This high proportion of unremarried widows is due to the early age of marriage for females and the late age of marriage for males combined with the tendency for males to die at an earlier age. Many women are widowed at some point, but subsequently remarry (as discussed in chap. 2). However, the proportion of unremarried widows in the population appears to be constant (Kelly 1977:310).

34. It would be useful to recalculate the proportional distribution of accusations against women, making a distinction between junior and senior females irrespective of chronological age but taking childbearing into account. In other words, women such as Waime, Nawadia, and Heanome would be classified as junior females. This would greatly inflate the ratio used to measure the proportional distribution of accusations for this category and reduce it for other categories. However, I cannot reliably distinguish between women who have never borne a child and those who gave birth to a child that died for all women in the sample. While table 4.4 shows that childless women of the first type account for 71 percent of the accusations against women, it provides no information regarding other women in the same position who were not accused (e.g., Wadome).

35. The case of Kabano's remarriage was well known to me because six men who resided at Kaburusato followed the negotiations closely. They were matrilateral siblings or "sister's sons" of Abenamoga who had contributed (or whose fathers had contributed) to his bridewealth payment when he initially married Kabano. They therefore felt they should receive a nominal share of one cowrie string apiece from the bridewealth Yakea redistributed. However, the prospective bridewealth of one pig, three pearl shells, and three cowrie strings was predesignated for Yakea, his brother, his father's brother's son, and other more closely related matrilateral siblings (including Abenamoga's wife's sister's husband, i.e., Kabano's sister's husband). These six men did not dispute the legitimacy of Yakea's prospective redistribution and had no quarrel with him. However, they felt the bridewealth was not sufficient and traveled to Sarado to make this case to Nomaya. He refused to accommodate this request. It would have been difficult for him to do so since no one contributed a single item to the bridewealth payment he eventually transferred (as discussed below). Nevertheless, this refusal was taken as yet another index of Nomaya's selfish and ungenerous nature and constituted another black mark against him.

A few months later, one of several chickens I had brought in from Huli territory in the Highlands disappeared and it was said that Nomaya's dog was responsible. I was urged to demand compensation for this loss but failed to do so. This would have provided yet another occasion for an angry confrontation with Nomaya, as my co-residents were eager to accompany me and press this demand on my behalf. Nomaya was thus repeatedly placed in situations where he came off as manifesting the archetypical selfishness and lack of responsiveness to others that are the hallmark of the witch. Moreover, virtually everyone had a grievance against him. Indeed, even I believed at the time that his dog had in fact stolen my chicken, although in retrospect this seems unlikely to have been the case. It also seems clear in retrospect that the nominal valuables sought from Nomaya on the occasion of Kabano's remarriage were not important in themselves but rather as symbols of stinginess.

It is of interest that no one contributed to Nomaya's bridewealth payment, which he accumulated by trade. It was the normative amount for a widow remarriage. Nomaya's first wife had died, and he was alleged to have been responsible for her death. This datum was one of the many negative remarks about Nomaya recorded in my notes. It is difficult to assess the degree of accuracy in these reports, given the ill regard in which Nomaya was held. However, it is of considerable interest that Nomaya's allegedly having struck his first wife was considered indicative of his evil and malicious nature, linked to possession of a *tohorora*. This wife beating also established a basis for the view that Nomaya's wife's death was due to his witchcraft (although he was not formally accused, since he himself was the principal next of kin). It established his intent to do harm. The allegation that Nomaya caused his first wife's death then provided grounds for not contributing to his subsequent bridewealth payment. This shows how the label of witch serves as a vehicle for negative sanctions against highly disapproved behaviors by providing grounds for disqualifying kinship obligations.

It is not easy for a thrice-accused witch to remarry. However, Nomaya was astute in selecting a prospective wife that no one else would seek to marry (due to her childlessness) and a woman who was not on good terms with her agnates (who would therefore not heed the objections virtually any woman would be expected to raise). Moreover, the marriage was advantageous to both Kabano's deceased husband's and father's brother's lineages in terms of a redefinition of sibling and exchange relationships. This compensated for the third obstacle to a thrice-named witch's remarriage, the fact that Nomaya was no more attractive as a potential affine than as a spouse. This liability accrued to Kabano's father's brothers, who now became Nomaya's wife's "fathers" (although Yakea was wife-giver). This is why they might have been expected, under other circumstances, to take Kabano in as she requested. But they did not desire her belated return to the agnatic fold, did not wish to countermand Yakea's legitimate right to arrange her remarriage (and thereby engender bad relations with him and his agnates), and foresaw advantages in laying the groundwork for future claims on women of Nomaya's lineage. When Nomaya was accused of causing the three drowning deaths eight months later, they did not support him or offer him refuge. The potential liability he constituted was therefore avoided in practice. However, it is well illustrated by this turn of events, which shows the undesirability of having a witch who is sure to be accused again as an affine, creating the potential for becoming embroiled in unwanted conflicts that disrupt other valued social relations. The disabilities associated with inclusion within the category of witch thus include difficulty in arranging a remarriage and access only to a pool of potential spouses others consider undesirable.

The case of Nomaya's remarriage to Kabano also brings out one counterbalancing advantage that accrues to the established witch. He or she is feared. Yakea was said to have feared that Nomaya would bewitch him if he (Yakea) did not accede to Nomaya's request but instead sought to arrange a different remarriage for Kabano or agreed to her suggestion that he marry her himself. Kabano was likewise induced to try to make the best of an unwanted union by fear of Nomaya's witchcraft. Both she and Yakea very likely welcomed Nomaya's impending execution eight months later. This view was universal. Indeed the case that Nomaya was a vicious wife-beater and an utterly despicable, selfish, and malicious person was so convincingly made and universally supported that I found myself having no qualms whatsoever regarding his impending execution. This led me to the conclusion that it was time to leave the field.

CHAPTER 5

1. Among the Gebusi, as among the Etoro, potential novice mediums are nominated by the female spirits of an existing medium and "persons generally *cannot* indicate themselves as prospective spirit mediums through dreams, altered states of consciousness, or recovery from psychological or physical illness" (Knauft 1985a:419). Gebusi novice mediums undergo induction at age 18 to 22, and a prospective medium should ideally be a virginal bachelor (ibid.:306). As among the Etoro, novice mediums may conduct séances and engage in curing but do not conduct inquests to determine the identity of the sorcerer responsible for a death (ibid.:306, 419). Gebusi spirit mediums comprise 14.7 percent of the initiated males in genealogies (ibid.:235), a proportion virtually identical to that for the Etoro (calculated on the basis

of the current population). The two ethnographic cases are also similar in that mediums are disproportionately drawn from descent groups of above-average size in both instances (ibid.). However, the Gebusi differ in that a novice medium is often a son or brother's son of a deceased medium (although trained by a mentor related to him as either agnate, affine, or matrikinsman (ibid.:419). Etoro mediums are not disproportionately likely to be the son or brother's son of a medium. Only 2 of 15 mediums (13.3 percent) are so related, this being less than the proportion of mediums in the population. Knauft's (1985a, 1989) analyses of séances and spirit mediumship have provided a general framework that has greatly facilitated the analysis of Etoro data pertaining to the same phenomena.

2. The protégés included in this table encompass all 14 living mediums in the eight-community sample, 2 recently deceased mediums from sample communities, and the 2 nominees (Sawa and Illawe) discussed earlier. Although the nominees did not (or had not yet) become mediums, their relations to the prospective mentors who nominated them are nevertheless indicative of the kinds of relationships that may obtain, and they are included to augment this somewhat small sample. The age that the two deceased mediums would have attained on May 1, 1968, is employed to determine the age differential between them and their protégés. The age of these deceased individuals was established by identifying their living age-mates.

3. One may also examine the success of each medium in training successors. Only Tofono trained 3 established mediums. He probably also trained a fourth, the deceased medium Abenamoga. Mugu, Piawe, and Nagubi each trained 2, but 1 of Nagubi's trainees was in the process of failing to make the grade. All these named individuals were deceased by the end of my fieldwork period. Of 5 remaining deceased mediums, 2 trained a single successor (Waroa and Arugwei), and 3 died without intellectual heirs (Sanimako, Maua, and Abenamoga). (Abenamoga does not appear in fig. 5.1 because his mentor is not definitely known and he trained no one.) Of the living mediums (in July 1969), 4 had trained a single successor, and 7 had not trained any as yet. Only Mugu, Tofono, and Piawe have thus succeeded in doing more than replacing themselves, 7 others have only achieved replacement, and 10 have failed to do so (at least to date).

4. I neglected to determine who trained Kago, who resided outside the sample communities. Kago played a role in only one witchcraft accusation during the sample period, being called in by Tofono to ratify the latter's pronouncement that Tahopi was responsible for the death of the medium Abenamoga in about January 1968. Kago thus might have been another of Tofono's protégés.

5. Mariabu was still considered to be a *tafidilo* but did not continue to function in the capacities associated with this status at Turusato because these roles were played by the established *tafidilos* Yora and Ahoa.

6. Kayago was responsible for confirming one other witchcraft accusation during this period. He was called to Kasayasato (which lacked a resident medium) when Siari died in late 1967. He confirmed the guilt of Nawadia in this instance. Kayago subsequently made three pronouncements in 1968–69, confirming Kulubido's responsibility for Taifa's death and later exonerating Kayari and Esopa. In early 1968, he also traveled to a small garden house settlement to confirm Tofono's deathbed indictment

of Tugaba. Araradado confirmed the oracular indictment of Tame as the witch responsible for Wayoro's drowning in 1966. The subsequent indictment of Nawadia in connection with Talibago's death in late 1966 was the last spirit inquest he conducted.

7. Nawa's mother was named as the witch responsible for Kukubia's sister's death. Some weeks after compensation was refused, Kukubia (Nogobe's father) went alone to a garden being weeded by Nawa's mother and her husband's agnate's wife Kebo. He killed Nawa's mother with an ax and cut out her heart, carrying it back to Sarado where he displayed it on a stake. He then shouted out to the residents of the neighboring community of Kaburusato that the heart confirmed the accused witch's guilt. He also promised compensation. The men of Kaburusato shouted back, announcing their intention to avenge this death (rather than accept compensation). The two communities fought on four successive days at a prearranged intermediate location in a recently abandoned garden. Arrows were exchanged at the relatively long range of about 100 feet, without the two sides closing. Each side was assisted by kinsmen from other longhouses. Katiefi longhouse was largely allied to Kaburusato, and Haifi was largely allied to Sarado (and the men of Haifi residing there, including Kukubia). In the evening intervals between combat, men of Katiefi and Haifi worked out a proposed compensation payment, and they urged their respective allies to accept this resolution. The latter agreed, and the fighting ceased. Nawa thus received the compensation for the execution of his mother that had been offered at the outset. No compensation was paid for wounds received in the encounter, as is typical. This is the only instance I know of in which the execution of a witch led to armed combat between communities. However, there was another intercommunity conflict between Kaburusato and Sarado stemming from reciprocal pig thefts that also led to four days of fighting. This occurred about nine years later (and six years before the fieldwork period).

8. *Sigisato* spirits reside in the bodies of cassowaries by day, and the capture of a cassowary in a snare thus entails a local spirit's rendering of his "flesh" to the community as a token of beneficence and goodwill, providing the occasion for a séance. The *Sigisato* spirit also indicates to the trapper where the snare is to be set, either relating this in a séance or appearing in a dream to a member of the lineage with which he is associated.

9. The Komo patrol officer routinely sought to identify one individual in each community to whom he could delegate the responsibility for building and maintaining three dwellings in each community to accommodate himself, the half-dozen native police who accompanied him on patrol, and the patrol's Huli carriers. This same designated individual was to see to it that latrines, trails, and bridges were maintained in good order, the longhouse kept free of refuse, etc. The prospect of becoming a designated "boss man," with a uniform and small annual stipend from the government was held out as the potential reward. Despite this, the position was not eagerly sought, as it entailed the responsibility of recruiting uncompensated labor to do work for the government that was resented. (When Kaburusato residents built their first "house kiap" early in my stay, they then intentionally felled a large tree on top of it and subsequently repropped the crushed structure with a minimum number of poles.) Tsmari had originally been impressed into this role as prospective boss man. However,

after cajoling resistant residents to build the required structures with less than complete success, he absented himself during the patrol officer's next visit, sending word that he was gravely ill. Nogobe then put himself forward in Tsmari's stead for a position no one wanted. Nogobe's reasons for doing so are addressed further along in the text.

10. I asked Illawe if Nogobe had spoken with the new patrol officer (via the government interpreter) about becoming boss man while he was at Komo. According to Illawe, he had done so, telling the patrol officer to be sure to bring the uniform when he visited Kaburusato.

11. Nogobe also pumped me for information before this séance. He had learned while at Komo that the Unevangelized Fields Mission missionaries stationed there planned to visit Kaburusato in the near future. He wanted to know if they would sleep in my house or in the guest house, recently constructed at the kiap's instructions to accommodate his visits. While the planned visit was by now common knowledge, this detail would not be known. One can only conclude that Nogobe was seeking to enhance the reputation of his spirits as knowledgeable and accurate predictors of future events. It may be recalled that Kayago obliquely predicted the execution of Kulubido. After this event took place, people specifically recalled the dire prophecy and were clearly impressed by the foreknowledge displayed by Kayago's *Sigisato*. This shows that accurate prophecy is reputation enhancing (as is success in curing and organizing fish-poisoning expeditions). Nogobe's attempts to extract information from me that might be utilized in such reputation-enhancing predictions reveal both his ambition and his efforts to match Kayago's success in this regard. However, unlike Nogobe, Kayago never attempted to extract specific information from me that might be utilized in making predictions. He did become extremely interested in a conversation I was having with Illawe in which I was relating how the moon revolved around the earth and the earth itself was a similar globe that revolved around the sun, such that the earth's shadow accounted for day and night. This information later found its way into a séance, in conjunction with typical astrological predictions about the waxing and waning of the moon. Mediums characteristically visit other communities frequently and make use of whatever information they may come to learn in predictions issued in subsequent séances at their home community. However, Nogobe went beyond this in his efforts to generate information, at least in his interactions with me. He seemed to be straining to generate reputation-enhancing prophecies.

It might be noted in passing that Nogobe never did receive the boss man's uniform during my stay. The patrol officer thought him too young and did not see the indications that Nogobe commanded the respect in the community that was an administrative precondition. Eventually, Nogobe would need to reverse a whole string of prophecies about becoming boss man, but this would have occurred after I left.

12. During October, while I was away on a field break, Nogobe was reported to have directed a successful fish-poisoning operation. He thus had one success to his credit prior to this occasion.

13. The medium Abenamoga was residing at Katiefi when Piawe moved from there to Haifi. Abenamoga moved to Katiefi in early 1966 following the breakup of the Nagefi longhouse community. He was married to two women of Katiefi, Piawe's sister (who had died by this time) and the *tafidilo* Kusuame's daughter. I neglected to

ask who had trained him, as he had died in late 1967 and was not among the practicing mediums. However, it is very probable that he was a protégé of Tofono, with whom he had resided for many years at Nagefi. The fact that he was Piawe's (deceased) sister's husband would have facilitated his coresidence with Piawe even though he was not his protégé. Abenamoga would then have been living at Katiefi in the latter half of 1967 when Udali was accused of witchcraft, although he himself died between November 1967 and February 1968. However, he is not reported to have had any connection with the accusation. Although the timing cannot be pinned down precisely, Abenamoga was evidently still living when Piawe moved to Haifi, but then died within a few months, leaving Katiefi without a resident medium.

14. Another known exception involved Abenamoga, discussed in the preceding note. Both Nasu and Abenamoga were close kinsmen of the mediums they respectively joined, and both were also closely connected to the leading *tafidilos* of each of the communities to which they moved. Tofono, the third medium who was displaced by the dissolution of Nagefi, moved to a garden house near Turusato. Tofono was a matrilateral sibling of the Turusato men, including the medium Taipa and the *tafidilo* Yora, but was not a close kinsman of either. However, he was the most widely renowned Etoro medium at this time, as will be discussed further along.

15. Tarume was consulted on one other occasion that came to my attention. This instance entailed determining the guilt or innocence of a person suspected of pig theft. The case is discussed later in the chapter.

16. The individual named by Abenamoga in his deathbed statement and subsequently accused, following authentication by both Tofono and Kago (of Sesimato), was Tahopi. Tahopi is the brother of the medium Nasu. When the *tafidilo* Kukubia died at Nagefi longhouse in late 1965, Nasu himself was named as the witch responsible, and Abenamoga authenticated that accusation. These two accusations suggest that there was competition and conflict between Tofono's two coresident protégés, who were contemporaries. Moreover, Tofono evidently did not intervene in this but implicitly sided with Abenamoga in stepping aside so that the latter could authenticate Kukubia's identification of Nasu as the witch responsible for his death. As senior resident medium, Tofono was in a position to exonerate his protégé Nasu but did not do so. Moreover, he subsequently authenticated the accusation against Nasu's brother.

17. In 1968, the Etoro adopted the use of a magical talisman (*huhubia*) to ward off the patrol officer. The bespelled leaf of an epiphyte was wrapped in another leaf and concealed in the wall of a dwelling where it would be in close proximity to the patrol officer during his visit to the community. This was supposed to have the effect of hastening his departure and precluding arrests for witchcraft executions. The *huhubia* was said to have been acquired from the Onanafi, who in turn acquired it from the Huli. It was reportedly used by the Huli to cause a pig to produce a litter as well as to ward off the ill effects of colonial intrusion. The Etoro also experimented with the *huhubia* by placing it in traps to increase their yield. The logic of this lay in the fact that certain forest mammals are the "pigs" of the *Sigisato* and *Kesame* spirits. The introduction of the *huhubia* came to my attention when Ibo asked me if he might place it in the wall of my house just prior to the patrol officer's arrival (a request to which I readily acceded). It was in this context that he explained to me how he had just

acquired this magic, not formerly known to the Etoro, and how he planned to test its efficacy in trapping in future. It was considered relatively efficacious with respect to the patrol officer, since the latter made no arrests in connection with the witchcraft executions that had recently taken place. The Etoro rarely employ magic, although there is one spell used to ward off rain during *kosa* ceremonies. This is recited while spitting at the clouds.

18. This sample differs from that in table 5.2 because it includes the members of lineages rather than the residents of communities. However, the main reason why mediums constitute 20.0 percent rather than 18.5 percent of the population is that the former figure is a percentage of all men 21 to 46 while the latter is a percentage of all men 18 to 45. The medium Piawe (aged 46) is thus included in the first calculation, augmenting the percentage.

19. One mythic story recounts a woman's visit to the spirit world of the *Kesames*, her reunion with her deceased brother (who is a medium), and her return. Her sojourn parallels that of an entranced medium's spirit. This tale is related as the exploits of a named woman who lived several generations earlier and differs from the standard myth in this respect. (The actors in the standard myth are the timeless and unnamed *aye negei*, or "hero," and persons designated only as "the old woman," etc.) It thus appears plausible that this woman represented as a historical figure was a spirit medium. Her spirit familiar may have been her deceased brother who was a medium. The one female spirit medium among the Gebusi receives the spirits of deceased individuals although, as among the Etoro, male mediums only receive the progeny of ghosts rather than ghosts themselves (Cantrell, personal communication). It is noteworthy that the Daribi *sogoyezibidi* is a type of shaman who has a relationship with a ghost that enables her or him to cure and divine (Wagner 1972:139). Seven of 11 *sogoyezibidi* listed by Wagner's informants were female, as were the majority of spirit mediums. The latter also entertain ghosts. This suggests the possibility that there may have been a distinct type of female shaman among the Etoro in the not-too-distant past, but that no one has recently been recruited into this position.

20. The capacity of male mediums to create a cultural world through séances includes the capacity to provide spiritual legitimation of innovations. The prophecy of Nogobe's spirits that he would become "boss man" of Kaburusato certainly brought this position within the compass of community leadership roles in an entirely novel way and also constituted an effort to vest it with culturally relevant meanings it formerly lacked.

21. It is noteworthy that the *kosa* ceremony derives its name from the mating dance of the red bird of paradise (termed *kosai*). The central performers in the *kosa* ceremony are also painted red and are resplendent with plumage that evokes the red bird of paradise. This symbolic association is explicitly made by the Etoro themselves and is also drawn by many other Strickland-Bosavi tribes that have variants of the same ceremony (Knauft 1985b:323). The figure that Etoro men aspire to symbolically emulate in their most cherished ritual is thus the spirit woman. (Compare the parallel drawn in Knauft 1989:72, 85.) To become the beautiful spirit woman in ritual parallels the attempted appropriation of femininity in myth. Among the neighboring Bedamini, paintings on bark depict corpulent female figures that recall the renowned Venus

figurines of the European Upper Paleolithic. (Some of these are shown in the movie "Tidikawa and Friends.") A religion like that of the Etoro and other Strickland-Bosavi tribes that focuses upon the spirit woman would be entirely consistent with the production of such female figurines. The reasons why the spirit woman is an idealized figure will become clear as the discussion proceeds.

22. Cantrell (n.d.) provides an extended analysis of the effect of the model provided by the Gebusi spirit woman upon women's lives and perceptions.

23. The sky world of the *Sigisatos* takes shape at night when they return to their longhouses after roaming lineage lands in cassowary form by day. I will come back to the significance of this nocturnal transformation further along in the discussion.

24. *Tafidilos* are prominent in all decision-making processes pertaining to social conflict, e.g., the decision to pay or refuse to pay witchcraft compensation, the decision to take up arms against a neighboring community, and the decision to conduct a retaliatory raid against a neighboring tribe. The exclusion of women from the role of *tafidilo* is intelligible in terms of the *tafidilo*'s substantial involvement in social conflict.

25. Ibo developed the idea that I was in some way like a spirit medium earlier in my fieldwork. He asked me if listening to the radio was a means of communicating with the spirits of my deceased relatives. He also thought writing was a magical act. There was in fact a precedent for his invocation of the paper oracle in that he once came to me and asked that I write down the name of a pig he could not find on a piece of paper so that he might locate it. On this occasion I went to considerable effort to explain that writing was a representation of the sounds made in speech and was a "picture" of talk in the same way the cassowary footprint design was a "picture" of such footprints. Ibo grasped this with no difficulty. However, when I was finished with this lengthy discourse, he said that the pragmatic aspects of word pictures did not address their magical properties. The *huhubia* was, pragmatically, merely a leaf, but it might nevertheless have magical properties. The thing about magic was that it involved a second, nonapparent level like the *ausulubo* plane of existence. Since I had to agree that Ibo was certainly correct in this, I could only say that writing had no such properties to the best of my knowledge. He then proposed that there was no good reason not to give him the piece of paper with his lost pig's name on it as it could certainly do no harm. Having no further arguments on which to base my resistance, I complied with his request and wished him the best of luck. He found his pig within a matter of hours.

26. The annual incidence of each of these decisions is: initiation .20, new longhouse .25, hosting *kosa* .50, affinal pork exchange .66, compensation decision .30, intratribal armed conflict .13, extratribal armed conflict .05, for a total of 2.09 collective decisions a year. During the fieldwork period, there were 3.2 collective decisions per year made at Turusato and Kaburusato (see following note).

27. The community discussions that I witnessed included the two described (regarding the pig theft and the compensation demand at Turusato) plus a discussion at Kaburusato as to whether to pay compensation to the Onanafi men who threatened to inform the government of Kulubido's execution. The latter discussion occurred early in my fieldwork, and I could not follow it in any detail. It took place before a séance

when a number of men from Turusato were present at Kaburusato. It was similar to those described in terms of the prominence of the *tafidilos* Ibo and Ahoa. However, it differed in that a number of young men spoke. They each expressed their readiness to take part in a raid against the Onanafi longhouse of the extortionists. I also have material on discussions at both Kaburusato and Turusato concerning the coordination of affinal pork exchange (described in Kelly 1977:223–28) and the construction of a new longhouse by Turusato community members. In the latter instance, several individuals initiated the discussion by suggesting that a new longhouse was needed. The women in particular favored new construction, and some of their husbands supported them. However, Yora and Ahoa wished to wait until the next communal garden was initiated, and their views prevailed. The decision by Turusato and Kaburusato to cohost the *kosa* ceremony brings the total community discussions to eight for two communities over 15 months or 3.2 per community per year.

28. When I first arrived at Kaburusato, I was accompanied by a 12-year-old Huli boy who was reputed to speak Etoro and knew a little pidgin English. As I soon learned, he did not actually speak Etoro, although a few Etoro men spoke enough Huli to make communication possible. I thus dispensed with his services after three months as I had then learned more Etoro than he knew (being materially assisted in language acquisition by my wife's work on the language). However, this "interpreter" designated Tsmari as the individual I should deal with in arranging for the construction of my house. Tsmari was at Kaburusato when I arrived, although his new gardens were at Haifi and he had largely shifted his residence to the latter community.

29. My house burned down at night under suspicious circumstances. The community had hosted a *kosa* ceremony the night before, and we had been up for 36 hours when we retired. My wife was awakened by the smell of smoke around 3:00 A.M., and we discovered the main room of the house was already engulfed in flames. The 25 gallons of kerosene I had on hand blew the house to pieces about five minutes later, before I had time to remove anything other than my field notes. Ibo and Illawe, who came running when I called that my house was on fire, got out one patrol box. I suspect the fire was set by Tuni, as we did not get along well and he did not welcome my presence at Kaburusato. In any event, Ahoa came down from Turusato to begin rebuilding the house on the same spot as soon as the ashes had cooled. He recruited nearly all of the men of Kaburusato and Turusato to complete the task. These men had no expectation of receiving any compensation for their efforts because we no longer had any possessions other than a few clothes (but no shoes), and it was inconceivable to them that we could resupply. Indeed, men now returned many things I had given them, saying (for example), "Take this ax that you gave me because now you have none." I was very moved by the generosity and assistance of my Etoro friends. They said they rebuilt our house because they wanted us to continue to live among them and thought that otherwise we would leave. In this type of fieldwork, one has friendly and unfriendly relationships as in any other social context, but the expression of both friendship and animosity followed cultural contours of greater amplitude than those to which I was accustomed. Ahoa's role in rebuilding my house was a striking example of his leadership ability, since this was a nontraditional task from which none of the participants expected to benefit in any direct way.

30. "To go painted" is a translation of an Etoro phrase. The use of face paint conveys that the visit is a formal one with a particular purpose. Different motifs convey the distinctive purposes of such visits, all black being worn for raids and black with red markings around the eyes when compensation is to be requested. A red-and-yellow motif signals invitation to a *kosa*.

31. The Etoro custom of compensating the next of kin of allies killed fighting on one's behalf is also found among many other New Guinea cultural groups including the Dani (Larson 1986), Jale (Koch 1974), and Enga (Meggitt 1977). The compensators are the two social groups that are principals in the conflict, sometimes described as the "owners" of the war. Although the Etoro do not use this phrase, they employ the concept. Tifanifi was the equivalent of the owner of the war on the Etoro side. The men of Tifanifi were also responsible for assuming the most dangerous task of covering the retreat. The Tifanifi *tafidilo* at the extreme rear received multiple wounds.

32. Alua was no longer considered a *tafidilo* in 1968, when he was 63, as he had become a *tole*.

33. There is no named status comparable to *tafidilo* accorded to senior women. However, these women enter into community discussion and may also play the important ritual role of publicly weeping and burning the dancers in the *kosa* ceremony. In six *kosa* performances for which data are available, 39 individuals played this role and 4 of these were women. Many of the other 35 individuals were *tafidilos*. A woman's social standing thus increases with age in certain respects, provided that she does not become an unremarried widow. The spatial restrictions that accompany widowhood compel a woman to remain on the periphery of the communal section so that a widow could not play the ritual role noted above. Senior women are thus divided into two groups by widowhood in the same way that senior men are divided into two groups by the *tafidilo*/non-*tafidilo* distinction.

34. In contrast, Pabu ran off with an already married woman, lived among the Huli for 12 years, and never made a bridewealth payment.

35. Kamula men, who also subscribe to a depletion ideology, are reported to consider a two-month interval between acts of coitus appropriate (Wood 1982). I never put this particular question to informants, but Etoro taboos prohibit copulation for an estimated 205 to 260 days a year.

36. Piawe is listed as a *tafidilo* but not as a medium in this table. The reasons for this will be evident from the comparisons drawn in the text. He is most usefully compared with others in his age cohort, which includes those eligible for *tafidilo* status.

CHAPTER 6

1. It should not be imagined that indigenous trade networks persisted for thousands of years before being disrupted by the Australians. On the contrary, it is quite likely that patterns of exchange were subject to periodic shifts and alterations due to the fact that key items were often available from more than one source. Stone ax/adzes and shell valuables are a case in point. In earlier times (before 1950), stone axes were manufactured by the Samo and Honibo who occupy tribal territories along the Strick-

land river about 25 miles due west of the Etoro (Knauft 1985a:10; Swadling 1983:89). These axes were traded eastward along a route from the manufacturers to the Gebusi, Gebusi to Bedamini, Bedamini to Etoro, and Etoro to the southernmost Huli. Shell valuables—particularly cowrie strings—moved in the opposite direction. However, stone axes were also available to the Huli from Highlands quarries via the Waga to their east (Glasse 1968:21). These Highlands axes were traded to the Onabasulu (the eastern neighbors of the Etoro) in exchange for cowrie strings, tree oil, and other items (see Ernst 1984:79–94). Cowrie strings were available to the Huli from the north and east (Glasse 1968:21) as well as via the Onabasulu and Kaluli to their south. The Etoro obtained cowrie strings from both the Huli and Onabasulu. Given these diverse sources of cowrie strings and stone axes, there are many possible patterns of exchange. For example, the Etoro could have acquired stone axes from the Huli in exchange for cowrie shells obtained from the Onabasulu, and abjured exchange with the Bedamini (with repercussions for the Gebusi, Honibo, and Samo further down the line). Alternatively, the Etoro could have either supplied axes to the Onabasulu (for cowrie strings) or obtained axes from them (for dog's-teeth headbands, manufactured by the Gebusi). It is evident that trade patterns are not narrowly determined or constrained, and it follows that shifts from one to another of several logical possibilities are likely over time.

2. Salt, tobacco, and cowrie strings in particular are widely exchangeable against many other goods.

3. Tobacco is grown in gardens made on the site of an abandoned dwelling, which has been burned to the ground to create a bed of ashes. It grows prolifically under these circumstances. I never observed tobacco interplanted in sweet potato or taro-banana gardens.

4. A young man's lack of dependence is due both to the character of the regional trade system and to the predominantly male labor component of the products that the Etoro do produce (as opposed to those they merely import and reexport). Middleman trade offers the potentiality to create wealth without engaging in production and is in this respect an analogue of the financing activities of some Highlands Big Men (Strathern 1969). The exchange items needed in order to obtain imports in the first instance can also be produced by young men themselves. In theory, a young man thus needs nothing whatsoever from others in order to accumulate his bridewealth. In practice, however, a young man will typically have some cowrie strings before he begins to trade, having received these from kinsmen (including his father) at the redistribution of social payments. He may also have inherited shell valuables from his father, if the latter is deceased, although the quantities are quite small for reasons explained further along. This start-up wealth obviates the need to engage in production, at least in theory, since a young man could exchange cowrie strings for tree oil with the Onabasulu and then trade the same tree oil to the Huli for a greater quantity of cowrie strings or for mother-of-pearl shell ornaments. (Or he might trade cowrie strings to the Huli for salt and tobacco and trade the latter to the Onabasulu for tree oil that was then traded to the Huli for mother-of-pearl shell ornaments.) However, young men typically do engage in the manufacture of exports during the period in which they are actively engaged in trade. In other words, young men characteristically deploy

some previously acquired shell valuables in trade and also produce items for exchange, rather than employing only one or the other of these alternative means of accumulating shell valuables.

5. One of these questions pertains to the devolution of rights to redistribute bridewealth. If Tabieme's father Tofono had been alive, he would have served as redistributor. Since Tofono was deceased, this right passed to his brother's son, Sawa. But why would it not have passed instead to Tofono's brother, Kayari, remaining within the senior generation? The main factor, in this case, is that Sawa's parents both died when he was relatively young and he was subsequently raised by Tofono and grew up with his "sister" Tabieme. He was, on these grounds, her closest male kinsman.

6. It should be noted that the Etoro, Onabasulu, and Huli all appreciate the relationship between exchange value and distance from source of supply. Ernst (1984:88) recounts an Onabasulu effort to use this to their advantage under postcontact conditions. The Huli have traditionally done so, passing through Etoro territory to trade with the Bedamini and through Onabasulu territory to get close to a source of supply for cowrie strings (Ernst 1984:89). Ernst (ibid.) also notes that Hughes's generalizations concerning distance of travel in trade within the interior of New Guinea are not borne out (see Hughes 1973:106). This is also applicable to Hughes's observations concerning the absence of middlemen.

7. The relationship between bridewealth and the maintenance of a supply of stone tools suggests several interesting hypotheses. Axes can be obtained for less, in terms of shell valuables, closer to the source of supply (Ernst 1984:88; cf. Sahlins 1972:281–82, 296–97), and one would thus expect fewer valuables and a much smaller circulating pool of wealth near the point of manufacture. This implies a small bridewealth payment. The Gebusi case fits these expectations. The Gebusi are the immediate neighbor of the two tribes that traditionally manufactured stone tools (the Honibo and Samo). The Gebusi also lack bridewealth payments, although a recently married man might give a gift of a single pig, shell valuable, dog's-teeth necklace, or stone ax to his wife's parents (see Knauft 1985a: 170, 411). The same general principle applies all along this trade route, i.e., Eastern Bedamini bridewealth payments are reported to be half as large as those of the Etoro. The Bedamini are located between the Gebusi and Etoro. Huli and Onabasulu bridewealth payments are both substantially greater than Etoro payments. I do not intend to suggest that the magnitude of any bridewealth payment is mechanically determined by distance from the site of stone tool manufacture. However, a bridewealth payment consisting of tokens of exchange value that are convertible into a commodity (or an analogue thereto) cannot be unaffected by factors influencing the exchange value of that commodity. Moreover, it is well established that distance from source of supply is such a factor.

8. Additional factors that affected the regional exchange system and indirectly played a role in Etoro bridewealth inflation should be elucidated here. It has been noted that the Australian colonial administration introduced very large quantities of mother-of-pearl shell into the Highlands. At the same time, the Australian patrol officers made a regular practice of confiscating the weapons of Highlanders who engaged in tribal fighting or appeared likely to do so. In southern Huli territory, a fair proportion

of the existing stock of black palm bows was taken out of circulation. These bows are one of the items the Etoro export to the Highlands. (They are a lower altitude product that is both manufactured by the Etoro and imported from the Bedamini.) Bows were thus in great demand among the Huli, while the latter possessed steel axes and ample supplies of shell valuables to offer the Etoro in exchange. Patrol officers' efforts to prohibit the trade in bows were entirely ineffectual (see Ernst 1984:86 regarding Onabasulu bow sales in 1970–73). These conditions enabled the Etoro to acquire steel axes without depleting the accumulated pool of shell valuables that they had formerly expended in exchange for stone tools. Shell valuables thus became items that were acquired in trade but deployed almost entirely in social payments (cf. Ernst 1978:190). Although it was said to be quite possible for an Etoro to exchange a mother-of-pearl shell ornament for cash ($10.00 Australian in 1968–69) with Huli or Onabasulu men, this seems not to have occurred. The pool of valuables thus increased, since young men continued to add to it, and bridewealth also increased. Although the circulation of wealth in 1968–69 (and traditionally) is the main concern of this chapter, it may be noted in passing that the bridewealth system has continued to evolve. Dwyer (personal communication) reports bridewealth payments of 5 to 7 pigs and 140 to 150 Kina (P.N.G. currency) during 1979. Shell valuables are no longer given.

9. In the Highlands case, Big Men had secured a monopoly in the exchange of certain shell ornaments that were an obligatory component of bridewealth, so that young men were dependent upon them to assemble bridewealth (Golson 1982:133). The Etoro lack Big Men who might hold a monopoly, and bridewealth has always consisted of readily available items.

10. Data pertaining to 11 additional bridewealth payments are available (Kelly 1977:217). However, determining the age of contributors to prior bridewealth payments and their proportional representation in the population (presented in table 6.3) would require reconstructing the age structure of the population in each case, which is in turn contingent upon precise dating of the time of each transaction. I have consequently elected to use a restricted sample representing the most reliable data. However, it may be noted that data pertaining to three mid-1960s bridewealth payments confirm the general patterns presented here.

11. Some grooms are in the 31-to-40 age cohort, so the contributions of all men 21 to 30 are a smaller percentage of the total when the groom's contribution is not segregated, as it was in earlier discussions.

12. In order to make table 6.5 comparable to table 6.3, I have omitted the one donor aged 11 to 15, as the inclusion of this donor would necessitate recalculating the percentage of individuals of each cohort in an expanded population of all males 11 to 60 (as opposed to all males 16 to 60). The percentage of total value shown in table 6.4 is thus recalculated in table 6.5, excluding the small contribution of this individual.

13. Sawa's case pointedly illustrates the degree and timing of reciprocity in these transactions. There were 15 contributors to Sawa's bridewealth (excluding Sawa himself). Of these, 5 had previously received items when Sawa distributed his "sister's" bridewealth and also when Sawa distributed the witchcraft compensation that had been paid on account of his father's brother's death the year before (listed under Tofono in table 6.6). Three other contributors to Sawa's bridewealth had received shell valuables

from his sister's bridewealth, and 1 other contributor had received a share of Tofono's witchcraft compensation. Of these 9 contributors who had previously received, 6 gave exactly what they got, 2 gave less, and 1 gave more. There were 6 other contributors to Sawa's bridewealth that did not receive anything in either of these prior distributions. These included 4 age-mates and 2 *tafidilos,* none of whom was close kin. These individuals may be seen as initiating reciprocal relations with Sawa, to which he would be expected to respond in future, by offering contributions to his bridewealth that were not specifically requested and which they were not obligated by kinship to give. In redistributing his sister's bridewealth, Sawa likewise gave items to 7 individuals who did not subsequently contribute to his own bridewealth (and to 8 individuals who did). Three of these 7 recipients were also young men with whom Sawa was initiating relations of mutual support, while 4 others were close kin (e.g., true mother's sister's son). All of these individuals would be expected to reciprocate at some future date. They might well contribute to Sawa's younger brother's bridewealth, for example. However, it is clear that reciprocity is not exact and need not be fulfilled at the earliest possible opportunity.

14. In table 6.7, the groom's contribution is included in the total value contributed to bridewealth (while it is excluded in table 6.3) because this contribution is relevant to the redistribution of wealth. The small contributions and shares of redistributions involving boys aged 11 to 15 are excluded for reasons of comparability, as explained earlier, and percentages of total value are recalculated to reflect this exclusion. Systemically, there are twice as many death compensations as bridewealth payments since marriage unites two individuals for whom death compensation will eventually be paid. However, during the fieldwork period, compensation payments exceeded marriage payments by a ratio of five to one due to epidemic mortality (see n. 5 to chap. 4). The weighted average of all contributions is thus constructed taking this into account. This predominance of compensations is relevant to the comparison of *tafidilos* and non-*tafidilos* since the latter contribute much more to compensation payments than to bridewealth. The redistribution of wealth effected through the cycle of accumulation and redistribution of social payments is thus more accurately portrayed through a weighted average that takes the frequency of witchcraft compensations into account (as well as the amounts contributed and received).

15. Older married men no longer go on triangular trading expeditions to acquire shell valuables. Although they may continue to trade to a limited extent, they tend to engage in exchange in order to obtain steel tools and consumables such as salt, Highlands tobacco, and recently weaned shoats. With the exception of the shoats, these items are frequently procured in exchange for shell valuables (as was traditionally the case with respect to stone tools). The pool of wealth in shell valuables that a young man accumulates is thus subject to shrinkage as a result of conversion to tools and consumables as well as through less-than-equivalent returns on contributions to social payments. The modest net gain experienced by men aged 41 to 60 is counterbalanced by these expenditures because these older men do not manufacture or import products to exchange for consumables (except insofar as they occasionally trade sago, produced by their wives, for shoats).

16. A contrast between the female roles of sister, wife, daughter, and mother emerges rather clearly in relation to male death. The brother-sister relation is commemorated in the public distribution of witchcraft compensation. The widowed wife and children (including daughter) are seen as partly responsible for the man's death and come within the most highly restricted categories in terms of food taboos (see Kelly 1976). A classificatory "mother" (often mother's brother's daughter) completes the last phase of a three-part burial and places a man's bones in a lineage burial cave with those of his ancestors (Kelly 1977:92).

17. The main Etoro intercommunity ritual places strong emphasis on the concept of compensating grief. This is the *kosa*, the Etoro version of the Kaluli *gisaro* analyzed by Schieffelin (1976) and Feld (1982) and examined from a comparative regional perspective by Knauft (1985b). Audience members who are moved to tears by the *kosa* performance are compensated, and this payment is also termed *su*. The concept of *su* as compensation for grief per se, apart from any admixture of rights pertaining to persons, is clearly one of the stronger messages conveyed by the ritual. It is arguable that this meaning of *su* predominates as a result of its prominence in ritual. These ceremonial *su* payments are discussed in a later section of this chapter.

18. Bridewealth can, of course, serve as a mechanism for promoting or perpetuating an unequal distribution of wealth if marriage payments are not equivalent for all social strata, and if redistribution is circumscribed and/or entails systematic biases (see, for example, Kelly 1985).

19. Compensation was paid following 20 of the 50 adult deaths in the sample specified earlier (see nn. 5 and 11 to chap. 4). This included compensation for 6 deaths due to homicide and 14 due to witchcraft. Compensation for 1 additional death was pending, and the results of the birth oracle could lead to the eventual payment of compensation that was initially refused in other instances. The number of accused witches who paid compensation was greater (i.e., 17) due to accusations against two coconspiring witches. The number of compensators was further increased (to 21 for witchcraft and 27 total) as a result of instances in which a husband and brother jointly paid compensation for a woman's witchcraft.

20. In this table an individual responsible for accumulating half a compensation (as a coconspirator or accused woman's husband or brother) is counted as a .5 compensator. The percentage of individuals of different ages in the population used to calculate the ratio in the last column is given in earlier tables (e.g., table 6.3). The percentage of individuals aged 16 to 60 accused of witchcraft during the sample period is 16.8 (16/95). The contrast between *tafidilos* and non-*tafidilos* entails individuals 36 to 60 when the young *tafidilo* Ahoa is a contributor or recipient in a social payment that forms part of the sample but includes individuals 41 to 60 when he is not. The variable age span from table to table is thus necessary to avoid distortions that would be introduced by unwarranted dilution or expansion of categories on grounds irrelevant to the specific data set (i.e., the grounds of consistency from table to table). Non-*tafidilos* aged 41 to 60 constitute 15.7 percent of the total population (of males aged 16 to 60) as noted in table 6.3. *Tafidilos* aged 41 to 60 constitute 11.6 percent (11/95) of this population. This age span is employed because Ahoa was not a compensator. However, it may be noted that *tafidilos* aged 36 to 60 constitute 12.6 percent of the

population and that employing this figure would result in a ratio of .63 instead of the .68 recorded in the table. In other words, the age span employed does not significantly affect the results with respect to the category of *tafidilos*.

21. The obvious (and quite Tylorian) message here is that relations of affinity and kinship following from intermarriage obviate latent hostility between communities. The presentation of smoked marsupials is part of one individual's ongoing affinal exchange. Grubs and pork are exchanged on other occasions (see Kelly 1977:222–28; Ernst 1978 analyzes similar exchanges among the Onabasulu).

22. Although many individuals weep during the course of a *kosa* performance, only a relatively select group among these also burn the dancers. Older men in general and *tafidilos* in particular are prominent among those who enact this role. Women may also play this role but seldom do. In six *kosa* performances for which I have data, women participated in the burning (and the more dramatic center stage weeping) on two occasions, constituting 4 of the 14 burners in these two instances combined, and 4 of 39 burners overall. Married women also perform an opening dance, in the cleared area in front of the longhouse, just before the display of mock hostility described in the main body of the text. Unmarried girls form a double row of dancers between which each *kosa* performer passes as he dances the length of the longhouse. The important role of burning the dancers is thus the only one that is not gender specific. Comparable age/sex distinctions characterize performers in the Kaluli *gisaro*. For example, Schieffelin (1976:172) notes that young men do not burn the *gisaro* dancers, but provide torches to the older men and women who do.

23. Schieffelin (1976:198–99) notes the predominantly affinal axis of the host-guest relationship. He also mentions (ibid.:207) that compensation does not go from dancers to those who burned them in any precise one-to-one fashion but rather tends to pass between relatives positioned as guest and host. In the list of actual payments he reports (ibid.:208–9), all shell valuables were given to classificatory wife's brothers and cross-cousins (i.e., passed between intermarrying lines). Beads, mirrors, blankets, and knives were given to a wider variety of kin, including outmarried "sisters," but some marriage-related connection is reported in all but one instance. The Kaluli also term this payment *su,* which Schieffelin (ibid.:206) translates as "compensation."

24. Exchange carried out in a festive public context is commonplace throughout Melanesia, and I use the term "ceremonial exchange" here to locate Etoro practice in relation to this regional pattern. However, the transfer of shell valuables in the Etoro case is not at all the main focus of the event, unlike the transfer of pigs and valuables in Highlands ceremonial exchange (Strathern 1971b; Meggitt 1972b; Feil 1978), and inclusion of the Etoro *kosa* in the same category as the Enga *Te* and the Medlpa *Moka* hinges on limited formal attributes. The differences are much greater than the similarities, although the latter are worth noting.

25. As noted earlier, *su* is intended to assuage the feelings that motivate vengeance (which is itself a transaction in the currency of emotion). *Su* may also assuage feelings that might otherwise find expression in witchcraft. The fact that those who weep most profusely in the *kosa* do not often personally receive the compensation is attributable to the collective nature of grief. Grief is located in a matrix of social relations and is always shared with kin.

CHAPTER 7

1. Van Beek (1987) provides exceptionally detailed data concerning game distribution among the Bedamini, and his analysis of these data has been useful in the development of my analysis of Etoro game distribution (although the two groups differ in some relatively minor details). Dwyer (1990:passim) also provides valuable data concerning Etoro distributions of game and domestic pork.

2. For an Etoro man to give game directly to a woman connotes an intimate relationship if the two individuals are not related in a way that directly precludes this (e.g., as brother and sister). Thus, a man cannot hand food (or, indeed, anything) to his brother's wife or his wife's mother but must give it to someone else to pass along to such women if he seeks to effect such a transaction (and vice versa). Van Beek (1987:152–53) also reports that sexual connotations inhibit an adult man from giving meat to an unmarried young woman (other than his daughter). It appears that such attributions of sexual connotations to meat sharing are widespread, and this may be a common corollary of the pattern whereby women primarily receive meat from husbands rather than obtaining it directly from hunters. One of the consequences of this general pattern is thus the minimization of conflicts arising from suspicion of sexual impropriety.

3. As Collier (1988:35) notes, these paternal contributions to child rearing are generally quite substantial in brideservice societies. For example, Hewlett (1991) reports that fathers among the Aka pygmies spend 47 percent of their day holding or within arm's reach of infant children less than 18 months of age. The movie "Tidikawa and Friends" (Doring and Doring 1971) depicts patterns of maternal and paternal child care among the Bedamini that are similar to those among the Etoro. It is important to recall that relatively few hours per day are devoted to subsistence. When at leisure, men are frequently with their children. Men often carry their young sons with them if they retire to the men's section in the afternoon or evening. Boys sleep with their fathers after about age five.

4. The ethnographic cases most comparable to the Etoro for which data are available are the Oriomo Papuans and the Minyanmin, both New Guinea hunter-horticulturalists. Men contribute 53.3 percent of the time devoted to food-getting activities among the Oriomo Papuans (Ohtsuka 1977:256), while the comparable figure for the Minyanmin is 51.9 percent (Morren 1985:89).

5. The Etoro are an exception to this, insofar as sago production does generate sufficient quantities of sago flour to distribute to all group members.

6. Hunting effort is specifically linked to marriage in one respect. A man whose wife has just given birth is obligated to supply her with a quantity of forest mammals. However, the wife herself is the primary beneficiary of this increased hunting. Moreover, it is a man's obligation to his wife and not the provisions she supplies that stimulate increased production.

7. It should be noted that Collier's argument that Comanche bachelors donated goods and labor to their in-laws is based on inference, as is evident from the following quotation:

In Comanche society, a bachelor *probably* lacked the ability to process a whole bison. It would thus *seem logical* for him to give his kills to his future in-laws, or to a polygynous "older brother" who let the bachelor live with one of his wives. Similarly, a Comanche bachelor *probably* gave away most of the horses he acquired on raids. A man who had no wife to feed and care for the captive and slave children who herded horses in Comanche society (see Hobel 1940:15) *probably* had no way of keeping more than a couple of animals. As a result, a Comanche bachelor who lived near his desired bride's kin *probably* did "hunt and raid" for his in-laws, in the sense that he regularly gave them the products of his hunting and raiding. (Collier 1988:32, emphasis added)

8. My interpretation of the Kamula data presented here differs from that of Wood in that he emphasizes the asymmetry that may obtain in practice. He also sees the wife's father as dominating and exerting authority over a dependent son-in-law (Wood 1982:120). However, this asymmetry is attributed to the fact that a man often marries the daughter of his inseminator so that he is indebted to his wife's father for his growth and maturation (ibid.:80). In addition, a wife's parents can curse their daughter, rendering her infertile, and a wife's brother can curse his sister's children, causing sickness and death (ibid.:101–3). A man is thus asymmetrically dependent upon the goodwill of his affines in order to have children. These asymmetries originate in parent-child and inseminator-inseminee relationships (that are analogous). If an inseminator (who is also a wife's father) is weak and needs labor assistance that he cannot readily reciprocate, this is seen as due to the transfer of life force. Moreover, the inseminee gains the strength to engage in productive labor that his inseminator now possesses to a lesser degree (ibid.:80). It is thus evident that deviation from a reciprocal exchange of labor between wife's father and daughter's husband is predicated on the inseminator-inseminee relationship and upon manifestations of depletion. Affinal relationships per se are ideologically formulated as reciprocal, other things being equal. This is why a wife's brother is obliged to reciprocate. The asymmetry in the exchange of labor that may eventuate is thus attributable to the inseminator-inseminee relationship rather than the affinal relationship.

It should be noted that wife-takers are semen-givers in the Etoro case while wife-takers are semen-recipients in the Kamula case. There is no relational asymmetry in the Etoro case because an inseminator receives his inseminee's sister in marriage. The Kamula arrangement aligns rather than counterbalances the wife-giver and semen-giver relationships, so that a young man owes a great deal to his wife's father. However, the main consequence is deference since the pig rump and cassowary thigh fat a wife's father receives in meat distribution do not constitute a material gain (as explained earlier), and labor assistance is reciprocated so long as the wife's father is healthy. Wood (1982:120) characterizes the latter as "a degree of labor service."

9. Rubel and Rosman (1978), Godelier (1982:32), and Andrew Strathern (1982b) have contributed to the development of a very useful distinction between types of societies based on the dominance of person-for-person exchange as opposed to the substitution of pigs or valuables for persons in transactions pertaining to marriage and death. Although the Etoro are an intermediate case, the distinction is nevertheless useful in analyzing the multifaceted nature of Etoro social transactions.

10. It is questionable that any hunting cultures regard the killing of animals as a form of "violence" in the sense that this word conveys in Western culture. It is thus doubtful that a rival could be intimidated in the alleged manner.

11. Marilyn Strathern (1988:13–15, 159–65) elaborates essentially the same point in her discussion of the "dividual."

12. Data are available concerning four female-initiated divorces, two of which fall outside the sample (which includes the unions of all ever-married Etoro men and women in which one or both parties were still alive on May 1, 1968; see Kelly 1977:299). In only one of these cases did the rejected first husband attempt to recover his wife. The woman and her lover took refuge with a neighboring tribe and returned only after the first husband had died 12 years later. The other three men philosophically accepted the dissolution of their unions. One expressed the view that there was no point in being married to a woman who disliked him, and the others (whose views were not elicited) apparently felt the same. All four men remarried with little delay. One wed a lineage sister of his first wife, provided as a replacement. Another wed a girl originally designated for his younger brother, while the latter married a lineage sister of his elder brother's first wife (also provided as a replacement). A third man married his elder brother's widow, obviating the obligation to provide a replacement. In the fourth case, two of the rejected husband's brothers were already married to lineage sisters of his absconding wife, and there were no other lineage sisters that could have been provided in the near future. However, the rejected husband obtained a wife from another lineage to whom promises of a future reciprocal exchange were made. These data suggest that a man whose wife rejects him for another man need not be concerned that he will have difficulty obtaining a replacement. Moreover, there is no evidence that a man's social standing is adversely affected. There is consequently no impetus to attempt to recover the woman other than a strong emotional attachment. A man's reputation is not at stake. The Etoro diverge from the brideservice model in that conflicts over women are rare. Nearly all overt conflict pertains to witchcraft accusations.

13. It should be noted here that there is very little characterological assessment of other persons other than the assessments associated with the distinction between witch and nonwitch. The concept that individuals differ in terms of personality traits is otherwise very weakly developed in comparison to Western culture. Others are primarily perceived in relational terms. A mother's brother is thought of as expressing affection and support by virtue of being a mother's brother rather than as a result of personality dispositions.

14. See Hatch (1989) for a particularly useful review of the literature on status systems. In most instances, the term "prestige" tends to be employed to refer to achieved virtues, while the term "status" is employed to refer to both achieved and ascribed virtues. The usage employed in this work thus conforms to an unformalized tendency in the literature.

15. More recently, efforts have been made to employ alternative grounds for specifying classes of societies that manifest comparable forms of social inequality. These include Woodburn's (1982) distinction between societies whose economies are based on immediate and delayed return and Collier's (1988) distinction between bride-

service, equal bridewealth, and unequal bridewealth societies. In both instances, the classificatory criteria employed are not intrinsically linked to the criteria for defining socially differentiated categories and allocating virtue in the societies that are classed together as members of a common type. This leads to various difficulties discussed earlier.

16. It is important to note that there is no necessary relationship between the form and extent of inequality. Although inequality may be restricted in form to principles of categorization, recruitment, and assignment based on age, gender, and personal characteristics, the degree or extent of inequality that obtains within this limited framework may well be greater than in societies with more elaborate forms of social differentiation. One of the principal defects of Fried's (1967) employment of the concept of "egalitarian society" is that he conflates limitations of form with limitations of degree.

17. It should also be noted that it is somewhat wide of the mark to designate "religion" as a source of social inequality, since the observed connections that prompt this conclusion stem from the fact that a religious system invariably entails a metaphysic. It is the latter component—rather than faith, worship, or ritual—that engenders inegalitarian consequences.

18. The line of reasoning that guides the preceding interpretation implies that sociocultural systems in which shamanism is open to both men and women would possess less gender-biased cosmologies. Although the development of this point is beyond the scope of the present work, an example may be noted. Among the Washo, who have both male and female shamans, there are two creation myths that account for the origin of the tribe. In one, this is attributed to Creation Woman and in the other to Creation Man (Downs 1966:90, cited in Van Zandt 1989). It is also noteworthy that male and female shamans are reported for several simple societies that are considered to be notably egalitarian, e.g., the Andaman Islanders (Radcliffe-Brown 1964:176; Ortner 1990) and the Montagnais-Naskapi (Leacock 1981:22).

19. The Washo (Downs 1966), Andaman Islanders (Radcliffe-Brown 1964), and Montagnais-Naskapi (Leacock 1981) provide three examples of gender-neutral shamanism in which female practitioners disappeared under contact conditions. The Baruya (Godelier 1986), Sambia (Herdt 1977), and Ona (Chapman 1982) exemplify gender-stratified systems. Male-exclusive shamanism is characteristic of the Strickland-Bosavi region and of southwest New Guinea more generally. Cases include the Etoro, Bedamini (Sørum 1980), Kaluli (Schieffelin 1977; 1985b), and Marind-Anim (Van Baal 1966). Among the Gebusi there is one female spirit medium (Cantrell n.d.; Knauft 1985b). Eliade (1964) provides information on an extensive body of cases. The cases enumerated above provide the basis for the preliminary comparative observations noted here. A more extensive comparative study would obviously be required in order to document and elaborate these observations. It should be emphasized here that the comparison is only applicable to simple societies possessing a distinctive type of prestige system. There is greater variation in the forms of shamanism that occur in conjunction with other types of prestige systems, including female-exclusive shamanism (see Kroeber 1925 with respect to the Yorok).

20. One could make a case for the proposition that every ideology is underwritten by a metaphysic, so that a uniformly accepted metaphysic entails not only a hegemonic ideology but the absence of any competing ideology. Given a uniform metaphysic, divergence from the hegemonic ideology is not at the level of a counterideology but of an interpretive point of view. This perspective is informed by the view that the ideological potency of Marx's critique of capitalism resides in its alternative metaphysic that reformulates the causes and processes that govern economic reality.

21. In calculating the percentages presented here, I have employed a life span of 60 years. Women who die young typically do not experience widowhood, while a substantial proportion of those who live beyond their childbearing years will be widowed and incur food taboos as a result. The average percentage of animal protein available to adult women annually would be increased if the calculation included women who never experience widowhood as a result of dying young. The calculation for men is unaffected by the life span employed, since it is based on data indicating that half of adult men are prohibited from consuming domestic pork at any given time. The animal protein in the diet available to them is thus the average of the 99 percent they can consume when not under this prohibition and the 64.6 percent they can consume when they are, or 81.8 percent (see Kelly 1977:45). Available data indicate that all widows below the age of 45 remarry (Kelly 1977:301). A woman who was widowed before this age would thus consume 97 percent of the animal protein in the diet for 39 of the 42 years from age 19 to 60 (inclusive), and 35 percent for 3 years, for an average of 92.6 percent. A woman who was never widowed would consume the full 97 percent. A woman who was widowed at age 50 and did not remarry would consume 97 percent for 32 years and 55.3 percent for 10 years, for an average of 87.1 percent. (The 55.3 percent figure takes into account the fact that a restriction on bush hen eggs is lifted for women past childbearing; see Kelly 1977:43–45.) It is evident from these calculations that the women who are most affected by the food taboos associated with widowhood still consume a larger percentage of available protein than men (87.1 percent versus 81.8 percent). Thus, the overall average for women will necessarily be greater than that for men. An overall average can be calculated by determining the number of women whose life experience approximates that of these three categories. Among women aged 45 to 70, 54.1 percent are married and have never been widowed. Another 16.7 percent are remarried widows, while 29.2 percent are unremarried widows. The latter have been widowed for various periods of time that average considerably less than the 10 years employed in delineating this category. A weighted overall average based on this distribution yields a figure of 93.4 percent. Employing a life span of 55 years instead of 60 yields a figure of 92.9 percent.

22. The reciprocal exchange of dinner invitations in American society also entails a symmetrical exchange of equivalents in which empirical differences between the dinners given and received are characteristically ignored. This example is useful in conveying the general sense of a symmetrical equivalent exchange in which the things exchanged are not precise equivalents in all respects but are regarded as such by social actors.

23. When I elicited the kin terms that Illawe applied to 159 women, he designated Esopa as his *nebabo*, the term applied to mother's brother (Kelly 1977:192). This

classification effectively defined Esopa as a sociological male in certain respects. It illustrates the specific form that masculinization may take in Etoro society. Sociological masculinity is always context specific so that a woman remains a female but plays the role of a male in particular areas of social life.

24. Efala composed and directed another pageant at Easter 1980 in which his spiritual authority was similarly employed:

> In one part of the church, young men played cards for money. Elsewhere, a fancily-dressed, town-experienced, heavily smoking man (played by the pastor Efala) interrupted a church service to spread largesse and lure men to the "good life." The community was progressively reduced to the elderly and to women and children. Finally, former residents reappeared as drunken louts and the people rebelled, evicting those who would not mend their ways and reconsolidating around former, community-centered, values. (Dwyer 1990:196)

In this drama it is revealed that recovery of the material well-being of Eden cannot be effected through labor migration, but only through the communitarian ethic now embodied in the church's congregation. It was in preparation for this performance that the partition separating the men's and women's seating areas was removed. Unfortunately, the subsequent development of Efala's essentially millenarian doctrine is unknown, as Dwyer left Bobole not long after this. However, the main thrust is clear. Moreover, Efala's willingness to employ his spiritual authority to shape the social construction of reality and influence the course of events is strikingly evident. The participation of the entire congregation in his construction gives testimony to his capacity to effectively achieve his objectives.

Bibliography

Arensberg, Conrad M.
  1937   *The Irish Countryman.* New York: Macmillan.
Barth, Fredrik
  1975   *Ritual and Knowledge among the Baktaman of New Guinea.* New Haven: Yale University Press.
Beek, Albert Gosewijn van
  1987   The Way of All Flesh: Hunting and Ideology of the Bedamuni of the Great Papuan Plateau. Ph.D. Dissertation, Anthropology, University of Leiden.
Berreman, Gerald
  1981   Social Inequality: A Cross-Cultural Analysis. In *Social Inequality: Comparative and Developmental Approaches,* ed. Gerald Berreman, 3–40. New York: Academic Press.
Beteille, Andre
  1981   The Idea of Natural Inequality. In *Social Inequality: Comparative and Developmental Approaches,* ed. Gerald Berreman, 59–80. New York: Academic Press.
Cannon, Walter B.
  1942   Voodoo Death. *American Anthropologist* 44:169–81.
Cantrell, Eileen M.
  1989   When Sisters Become Brides. Unpublished paper presented at the 88th Annual Meeting of the American Anthropological Association, Washington, D.C.
  n.d.   Gebusi Gender Relations. Ph.D. Dissertation draft, Department of Anthropology, University of Michigan.
Champion, Ivan
  1940   The Bamu-Purari Patrol. *Geographical Journal* 96:190–206, 243–57.
Chapman, Anne
  1982   *Drama and Power in a Hunting Society: The Selk'nam of Tierra del Fuego.* Cambridge: Cambridge University Press.
Collier, Jane Fishburne
  1988   *Marriage and Inequality in Classless Societies.* Stanford: Stanford University Press.
Collier, Jane Fishburne, and Rosaldo, Michelle Z.
  1981   Politics and Gender in Simple Societies. In *Sexual Meanings: The Cul-*

581

tural Construction of Gender and Sexuality, ed. Sherry B. Ortner and Harriet Whitehead, 275–329. Cambridge: Cambridge University Press.

Collier, Jane Fishburne, and Yanagisako, Sylvia Junko, eds.
1987   *Gender and Kinship: Essays toward a Unified Analysis.* Stanford: Stanford University Press.

Comaroff, John
1980   Introduction. In *The Meaning of Marriage Payments,* ed. John Comaroff, 1–47. London: Academic Press.

Creed, Gerald W.
1984   Sexual Subordination: Institutionalized Homosexuality and Social Control in Melanesia. *Ethnology* 23:157–76.

Dahrendorf, Ralf
1968   *Essays in the Theory of Society.* Stanford: Stanford University Press.

Diamond, Stanley
1974   *In Search of the Primitive: A Critique of Civilization.* New Brunswick, N.J.: Transaction Books.

Divale, W. T., and Harris, M.
1976   Population, Warfare and the Male Supremacist Complex. *American Anthropologist* 78:521–38.

Doring, Jeff, and Doring, Sue
1971   Tidikawa and Friends. 16mm ethnographic film. Sydney: Atlab.

Downs, James F.
1966   *Two Worlds of the Washo.* New York: Holt, Rinehart and Winston.

Dwyer, Peter D.
1982   Prey Switching: A Case Study from New Guinea. *Journal of Animal Ecology* 51:529–42.
1983   Etolo Hunting Performance and Energetics. *Human Ecology* 11:145–74.
1985a   A Hunt in New Guinea: Some Difficulties for Optimal Foraging Theory. *Man,* n.s., 20:243–53.
1985b   Choice and Constraint in Papua New Guinea Food Quest. *Human Ecology* 13:49–70.
1985c   The Contribution of Non-Domesticated Animals to the Diet of Etolo, Southern Highlands Province, Papua New Guinea. *Ecology of Food and Nutrition* 17:101–15.
1989   Etolo Traps: Techniques and Classification. *Queensland Museum Memoir* 27(2): 275–87.
1990   *The Pigs that Ate the Garden: A Human Ecology from Papua New Guinea.* Ann Arbor: University of Michigan Press.

Dwyer, Peter D., and Minnegal, Monica
1988   Supplication of the Crocodile: A Curing Ritual from Papua New Guinea. *Australian Natural History* 22(11): 490–94.
n.d.a   Hunting and Harvesting: The Pursuit of Animals by Kubo of Papua New Guinea. In *Man and a Half: Essays in Pacific Anthropology and Ethnobotany in Honor of Ralph Bulmer,* ed. A. Pawley, Auckland: The Polynesian Society.

n.d.b The Right Crop, The Wrong People: Banana Growing in the Tropical Lowlands of Papua New Guinea. Unpublished paper, Department of Zoology, University of Queensland.

n.d.c Hunting in Lowland, Tropical Rain Forest: Towards a Model of Non-Agricultural Subsistence. Unpublished paper, Department of Zoology, University of Queensland.

n.d.d Yams and Megapode Mounds in Lowland Rain Forest of Papua New Guinea. Unpublished paper, Department of Zoology, University of Queensland.

Eastwell, Harry D.
1982 Voodoo Death and the Mechanism for Dispatch of the Dying in East Arnhem, Australia. *American Anthropologist* 84:5–18.

Eliade, Mircea
1964 *Shamanism: Archaic Techniques of Ecstasy.* Translated by W. R. Trask. Princeton: Princeton University Press.

Elkin, A. P.
1964 *The Australian Aborigines.* New York: Doubleday and Company.
1977 *Aboriginal Men of High Degree.* St. Lucia: University of Queensland Press.

Ellen, Roy F.
1979 Sago Subsistence and the Trade in Spices: A Provisional Model of Ecological Succession and Imbalance in Moluccan History. In *Social and Ecological Systems,* ed. P. C. Burnham and R. F. Ellen, 43–74. A.S.A. Monograph No. 18. London: Academic Press.

Engels, Friederich
1942 [1884] *The Origin of the Family, Private Property and the State.* New York: International Publishers.

Ernst, Thomas M.
1978 Aspects of Meaning of Exchanges and Exchange Items among the Onabasulu of the Great Papuan Plateau. In *Trade and Exchange in Oceania and Australia,* ed. Jim Specht and J. Peter White, 187–97. *Mankind* 11(3).
1984 Onabasulu Local Organization. Ph.D. Dissertation, Department of Anthropology, University of Michigan.
n.d. Onabasulu Male Homosexuality: Cosmology, Affect and Prescribed Male Homosexual Activity among the Onabasulu of the Great Papuan Plateau. Unpublished paper, School of Social Science and Welfare Studies, Charles Sturt University, Bathurst. *Oceania* (forthcoming).

Evans-Pritchard, E. E.
1976 [1937] *Witchcraft, Oracles and Magic among the Azande.* London: Oxford University Press.

Fallers, Lloyd A.
1973 *Inequality: Social Stratification Reconsidered.* Chicago: University of Chicago Press.

Feil, D. K.
1978   Women and Men in the Enga *Tee. American Ethnologist* 5:263–79.
1987   *The Evolution of Highland Papua New Guinea Societies.* Cambridge: Cambridge University Press.

Feld, Steven
1982   *Sound and Sentiment: Birds, Weeping, Poetics, and Song in Kaluli Expression.* Philadelphia: University of Pennsylvania Press.

Firth, Raymond
1964   *Essays on Social Organization and Values.* London: Athlone Press.

Flanagan, James G.
1989   Hierarchy in Simple "Egalitarian" Societies. *Annual Review of Anthropology* 18:245–66.

Fortes, Meyer
1959   Descent, Filiation and Affinity: A Rejoinder to Dr. Leach. *Man* 59:193–97, 206–12.

Franklin, Karl J., and Voorhoeve, Clemens L.
1973   Languages Near the Intersection of the Gulf, Southern Highlands, and Western Districts. In *The Linguistic Situation in the Gulf District and Adjacent Areas, Papua New Guinea,* ed. Karl Franklin, *Pacific Linguistics.* Series C, no. 26. Canberra, Australian National University.

Freund, Paul Joseph
1977   Social Change among the Kasua, Southern Highlands, Papua New Guinea. Ph.D. Dissertation, Anthropology, University of Iowa.

Fried, Morton
1967   *The Evolution of Political Society.* New York: Random House.

Giddens, Anthony
1976   *New Rules of the Sociological Method.* New York: Basic Books.

Glasse, Robert M.
1968   *Huli of Papua: A Cognatic Descent System.* Paris: Mouton and Co.

Godelier, Maurice
1982   Social Hierarchies among the Baruya of New Guinea. In *Inequality in New Guinea Highland Societies,* ed. Andrew Strathern, 3–34. Cambridge: Cambridge University Press.
1986   *The Making of Great Men: Male Domination and Power among the New Guinea Baruya.* Cambridge: Cambridge University Press.

Golson, Jack
1982   The Ipomoean Revolution Revisited: Society and the Sweet Potato in the Upper Wahgi Valley. In *Inequality in New Guinea Highland Societies,* ed. Andrew Strathern, 109–36. Cambridge: Cambridge University Press.

Goody, Esther
1970   Legitimate and Illegitimate Aggression in a West African State. In *Witchcraft Confessions and Accusations,* ed. Mary Douglas, 207–44. London: Tavistock Publications.

Goody, Jack
1973   Bridewealth and Dowry in Africa and Eurasia. In *Bridewealth and*

Dowry, by Jack Goody and S. J. Tambiah, 1–58. Cambridge: Cambridge University Press.

Gregory, Christopher A.

1980 Gifts to Men and Gifts to God: Gift Exchange and Capital Accumulation in Contemporary Papua. *Man,* n.s., 15:626–52.

1982 *Gifts and Commodities.* London: Academic Press.

Hallpike, Christopher R.

1977 *Bloodshed and Vengeance in the Papuan Mountains: The Generation of Conflict in Tuade Society.* Oxford: Clarendon.

Hatch, Elvin

1989 Theories of Social Honor. *American Anthropologist* 91(2): 341–53.

Hays, Terrance E.

1988 Strickland-Bosavi Bibliography. Unpublished manuscript, Department of Anthropology and Geography, Rhode Island College.

Heider, Karl

1970 *The Dugum Dani.* Chicago: Aldine Publishing Company.

Herdt, Gilbert H.

1977 The Shaman's "Calling" among the Sambia of New Guinea. *Journal de la Société des Océanistes* 33(56–57): 153–67.

1984 Ritualized Homosexual Behavior in the Male Cults of Melanesia, 1862– 1983: An Introduction. In *Ritualized Homosexuality in Melanesia,* ed. Gilbert H. Herdt, 1–81. Berkeley: University of California Press.

1989 Spirit Familiars in the Religious Imagination of Sambia Shamans. In *The Religious Imagination in New Guinea,* ed. Gilbert Herdt and Michele Stephen, 99–121. New Brunswick: Rutgers University Press.

Hewlett, Barry S.

1991. *Intimate Fathers: The Nature and Context of Aka Pygmy Paternal Infant Care.* Ann Arbor: University of Michigan Press.

Hiatt, L. R.

1971 Secret Pseudo-procreation Rites among the Australian Aborigines. In *Anthropology in Oceania,* ed. L. R. Hiatt and C. Jayawardena, 77–88. Sydney: Angus and Robertson.

1985 Maidens, Males and Marx: Some Contrasts in the Work of Frederick Rose and Claude Meillassoux. *Oceania* 56:34–46.

1986 *Aboriginal Political Life.* (The Wentworth Lecture 1984.) Canberra: Australian Institute of Aboriginal Studies.

Hides, Jack

1973 [1936] *Papuan Wonderland.* Sydney: Arkon.

Hughes, Ian

1973 Stone-Age Trade in the New Guinea Inland: Historical Geography without History. In *The Pacific in Transition: Geographical Perspectives on Adaptation and Change,* ed. H. Brookfield. Canberra, Australian National University Press.

Jorgensen, Daniel, ed.
  1983   Concepts of Conception: Procreation Ideologies in Papua New Guinea.
          Mankind, Special Issue 14.
Josephides, Lisette
  1983   Equal but Different? The Ontology of Gender among Kewa. *Oceania*
          53:291–307.
  1985   *The Production of Inequality: Gender and Exchange among the Kewa.*
          New York: Tavistock Publications.
Kelly, Raymond C.
  1976   Witchcraft and Sexual Relations: An Exploration in the Social and Se-
          mantic Implications of the Structure of Belief. In *Man and Woman in the
          New Guinea Highlands,* ed. Paula Brown and Georgeda Buchbinder,
          36–53. Washington, D.C.: American Anthropological Association.
  1977   *Etoro Social Structure: A Study in Structural Contradiction.* Ann Arbor:
          University of Michigan Press.
  1985   *The Nuer Conquest: The Structure and Development of an Expansionist
          System.* Ann Arbor: University of Michigan Press.
  1988   Etoro Suidology: A Reassessment of the Pig's Role in the Prehistory and
          Comparative Ethnology of New Guinea. In *Mountain Papuans: Histori-
          cal and Comparative Perspectives from New Guinea Fringe Highland
          Societies,* ed. James Weiner, 111–86. Ann Arbor: University of Michi-
          gan Press.
  n.d.   Sanctions and Symbolic Domination: Patterns of Male-Female Relations
          in New Guinea. Unpublished paper, Department of Anthropology, Uni-
          versity of Michigan.
Knauft, Bruce M.
  1985a   *Good Company and Violence: Sorcery and Social Action in a Lowland
          New Guinea Society.* Berkeley: University of California Press.
  1985b   Ritual Form and Permutation in New Guinea: Implications of Symbolic
          Process for Socio-Political Evolution. *American Ethnologist* 12:321– 40.
  1986   Text and Social Practice: Narrative "Longing" and Bisexuality among the
          Gebusi of New Guinea. *Ethos* 14:252–81.
  1987a   Review Essay: Homosexuality in Melanesia. *Journal of Psychoanalytic
          Anthropology* 10:155–91.
  1987b   Managing Sex and Anger: Tobacco and Kava Use among the Gebusi of
          Papua New Guinea. In *Drugs in Western Pacific Societies: Relations of
          Substance,* ed. Lamont Lindstrom, 73–98. ASAO Monograph No. 11.
          Lanham, Md.: University Press of America.
  1987c   Reconsidering Violence in Simple Human Societies: Homicide among
          the Gebusi of New Guinea. *Current Anthropology* 28:457–500.
  1989   Imagery, Pronouncement, and the Aesthetics of Reception in Gebusi
          Spirit Mediumship. In *The Religious Imagination in New Guinea,* ed.
          Gilbert Herdt and Michele Stephen, 67–98. New Brunswick: Rutgers
          University Press.

1990   The Question of Ritualized Homosexuality among the Kiwai of South New Guinea. *Journal of Pacific History* 25(2): 188–210.

1993   *South Coast New Guinea Cultures: History, Comparison, Dialectic.* Cambridge: Cambridge University Press, forthcoming.

Koch, K. F.

1974   *War and Peace in Jalemo.* Cambridge: Harvard University Press.

Kroeber, A. L.

1925   *Handbook of the Indians of California.* Bureau of American Ethnology, Smithsonian Institution, Bulletin 78.

Landtman, Gunnar

1927   *The Kiwai Papuans of British New Guinea: A Nature-Born Instance of Rousseau's Ideal Community.* London: Macmillan.

Langness, L. L.

1974   Ritual Power and Male Dominance in the New Guinea Highlands. *Ethos* 2(3): 189–212.

Larson, Gordon F.

1986   The Structure and Demography of the Cycle of Warfare among the Ilaga Dani of Irian Jaya. Ph.D. Dissertation, Department of Anthropology, University of Michigan.

Leach, E. R.

1954   *Political Systems of Highland Burma.* Boston: Beacon Press.

Leacock, Eleanor Burke

1981   *Myths of Male Dominance.* New York and London: Monthly Review Press.

Lederman, Rena

1981   Sorcery and Social Change in Mendi. In *Sorcery and Social Change in Melanesia,* ed. Marty Zelenietz and Shirley Lindenbaum, 15–27. *Social Analysis,* Special Issue 8.

1989   Contested Order: Gender and Society in the Southern New Guinea Highlands. *American Ethnologist* 16(2): 230–47.

Lee, Richard B.

1979   *The !Kung San: Men, Women, and Work in a Foraging Society.* Cambridge: Cambridge University Press.

Lévi-Strauss, Claude

1971   The Family. In *Man, Culture, and Society,* ed. Harry Shapiro, 333–57. Oxford: Oxford University Press.

Lindenbaum, Shirley

1984   Variations on a Sociosexual Theme in Melanesia. In *Ritualized Homosexuality in Melanesia,* ed. Gilbert H. Herdt, 337–61. Berkeley: University of California Press.

1987   The Mystification of Female Labors. In *Gender and Kinship: Essays toward a Unified Analysis,* ed. Jane Collier and Sylvia Junko Yanagisako, 221–43. Stanford: Stanford University Press.

Locke, John
1978 [1690]   *Two Treatises of Government.* London: J. M. Dent.
Loupis, George
1983   The Kaluli Longhouse. *Oceania* 53:358–83.
Lowie, Robert H.
1924   *Primitive Religion.* New York: Boni and Liveright.
1947 [1920]   *Primitive Society.* New York: Liveright.
Marwick, Max G.
1963   The Sociology of Sorcery in a Central African Tribe. *African Studies* 22(1): 1–21.
1965   *Sorcery in Its Social Setting: A Study of the North Rhodesian Cewa.* Manchester: University of Manchester Press.
1967   The Study of Witchcraft. In *The Craft of Social Anthropology,* ed. A. L. Epstein, 231–44. Cambridge: Cambridge University Press.
Mead, Margaret
1935   *Sex and Temperament in Three Primitive Societies.* New York: New American Library.
Meggitt, Mervyn J.
1962   *Desert People: A Study of the Walbiri Aborigines of Central Australia.* Chicago: University of Chicago Press.
1965   *The Lineage System of the Mae-Enga of New Guinea.* New York: Barnes and Noble.
1972a   Understanding Australian Aboriginal Society: Kinship Systems or Cultural Categories? In *Kinship Studies in the Morgan Centennial Year,* ed. P. Reining, 64–87. Washington, D.C.: Anthropological Society of Washington.
1972b   System and Subsystem: The *Te* Exchange Cycle among the Mae Enga. *Human Ecology* 1:111–23.
1977   *Blood is Their Argument: Warfare among the Mae Enga Tribesmen of the New Guinea Highlands.* Palo Alto: Mayfield Publishing Company.
Meillassoux, Claude
1964   *L'Anthropologie économique des Gouro de Côte d'Ivoire.* Paris: Mouton.
1972   From Reproduction to Production. *Economy and Society* 1:83–105.
1973a   The Social Organization of the Peasantry: The Economic Basis of Kinship. *Journal of Peasant Studies* 1:81–90.
1973b   On the Mode of Production of the Hunting Bond. In *French Perspectives in African Studies,* ed. Pierre Alexandre, 187–203. London: Oxford University Press.
1981   *Maidens, Meal and Money: Capitalism and the Domestic Community.* New York: Cambridge University Press.
Mitchell, J. Clyde
1967   On Quantification in Social Anthropology. In *The Craft of Social Anthropology,* ed. A. L. Epstein, 17–46. London: Tavistock.

Modjeska, Nicholas
    1982   Production and Inequality: Perspectives from Central New Guinea. In *Inequality in New Guinea Highland Societies*, ed. Andrew Strathern, 50–108. Cambridge: Cambridge University Press.

Morren, George E. B.
    1985   *The Minyanmin: Human Ecology of a Papua New Guinea Society.* Ann Arbor: UMI Research Press.

Mukhopadhyay, Carol C., and Higgins, Patricia J.
    1988   Anthropological Studies of Women's Status Revisited: 1977–1987. *Annual Review of Anthropology* 17:461–95.

Murphy, Robert, and Murphy, Yolanda
    1980   Women, Work and Property in a South American Tribe. In *Theory and Practice: Essays Presented to Gene Weltfish*, ed. Stanley Diamond, 179–94. New York: Mouton Publishers.

Ohtsuka, Ryutaro
    1977   Time-Space Use of the Papuans Depending on Sago and Game. In *Human Activity System: Its Spaciotemporal Structure*, ed. Hitoshi Watanabe, 231–60. Tokyo: University of Tokyo Press.
    1983   *Oriomo Papuans: Ecology of Sago-Eaters in Lowland Papua.* Tokyo: University of Tokyo Press.

Oomen, H. A., and Malcolm, S. H.
    1958   Nutrition and the Papuan Child. South Pacific Commission Technical Paper No. 118. Noumea, New Caledonia.

Ortner, Sherry B.
    1978   *Sherpas through Their Rituals.* Cambridge: Cambridge University Press.
    1984   Theory in Anthropology since the Sixties. *Comparative Studies in Society and History* 26:126–66.
    1990   Gender Hegemonies. In *Discursive Strategies and the Economy of Prestige*, ed. Bruce Lincoln and Richard Leppert, 35–80. *Cultural Critique*, Winter 1989–90.

Ortner, Sherry B., and Whitehead, Harriet, eds.
    1981   Introduction: Accounting for Sexual Meanings. In *Sexual Meanings: The Cultural Construction of Gender and Sexuality*, ed. Sherry Ortner and Harriet Whitehead, 1–28. Cambridge: Cambridge University Press.

Poole, Fitz John P.
    1976   The Ais Am. Ph.D. Dissertation, Department of Anthropology. Cornell University.
    1981a   Transforming "Natural" Women: Female Ritual Leaders and Gender Ideology among the Bimin-Kuskusmin. In *Sexual Meanings: The Cultural Construction of Gender and Sexuality*, ed. Sherry B. Ortner and Harriet Whitehead, 116–65. Cambridge: Cambridge University Press.
    1981b   Tamam: Ideological and Sociological Configurations of "Witchcraft" among Bimin-Kuskusmin. In *Sorcery and Social Change in Melanesia*, ed. Marty Zelenietz and Shirley Lindenbaum, 58–76. *Social Analysis*, Special Issue 8.

1982 The Ritual Forging of Identity: Aspects of Person and Self in Bimin-Kuskusmin Male Initiation. In *Rituals of Manhood: Male Initiation in Papua New Guinea,* ed. Gilbert Herdt, 100–154. Berkeley: University of California Press.

Radcliffe-Brown, A. R.
  1964 *The Andaman Islanders.* New York: The Free Press of Glencoe.

Read, Kenneth E.
  1965 *The High Valley.* New York: Charles Scribner's Sons.

Reay, Maria
  1976 The Politics of a Witch-Killing. *Oceania* 47:1–20.

Reesink, Ger P.
  1976 Languages of the Aramia River Area. *Pacific Linguistics* A-45:1–37.

Rousseau, Jean-Jacques
  1938 [1775] A Discourse on the Origin of Inequality. In *The Social Contract and Discourses,* 155–238. London: J. M. Dent

Rubel, Paula, and Rosman, Abraham
  1978 *Your Own Pigs You May Not Eat: A Comparative Study of New Guinea Societies.* Chicago: University of Chicago Press.

Sahlins, Marshall
  1958 *Social Stratification in Polynesia.* American Ethnological Society Monograph No. 25. Seattle: University of Washington Press.
  1963 Poor Man, Rich Man, Big-Man, Chief: Political Types in Melanesia and Polynesia. *Comparative Studies in Society and History* 5:285–300.
  1972 *Stone Age Economics.* Chicago: Aldine-Atherton.
  1981 *Historical Metaphors and Mythical Realities: Structure in the Early History of the Sandwich Islands Kingdom.* Ann Arbor: University of Michigan Press.

Salisbury, R. F.
  1964 New Guinea Highland Models and Descent Theory. *Man* 64:168–71.

Sanday, P. R.
  1981 *Female Power and Male Dominance: On the Origins of Sexual Inequality.* Cambridge: Cambridge University Press.

Schieffelin, Edward L.
  1971 The Influence of Contact on the Agricultural System of the Great Papuan Plateau North of Mt. Bosavi, Tari Sub-district. Unpublished. Department of Anthropology, Fordham University.
  1975 Felling the Trees on Top of the Crop: European Contact and the Subsistence Ecology of the Great Papuan Plateau. *Oceania* 46:25–39.
  1976 *The Sorrow of the Lonely and the Burning of the Dancers.* New York: St. Martin's Press.
  1977 The Unseen Influence: Tranced Mediums as Historical Innovators. *Journal de la Société des Océanistes* 33(56–57): 169–78.
  1980 Reciprocity and the Construction of Reality. *Man,* n.s., 15:502–17.
  1982 The *Bau a* Ceremonial Hunting Lodge: An Alternative to Initiation. In

Rituals of Manhood: Male Initiation in Papua New Guinea, ed. Gilbert H. Herdt, 155–200. Berkeley: University of California Press.

1985a   Anger, Grief, and Shame: Toward a Kaluli Ethnopsychology. In *Person, Self, and Experience: Exploring Pacific Ethnopsychologies,* ed. Geoffrey M. White and John Kirkpatrick, 168–82. Berkeley: University of California Press.

1985b   Performance and the Cultural Construction of Reality. *American Ethnologist* 12:707–24.

Schieffelin, Edward L., and Crittenden, Robert

1991   *Like People You See in a Dream: First Contact in Six Papuan Societies.* Stanford: Stanford University Press.

Schlegel, Alice

1972   *Male Dominance and Female Autonomy.* New Haven, Conn.: Human Relations Area Files Press.

Schlegel, Alice and Berry, Herbert

1986   The Cultural Consequences of Female Contributions to Subsistence. *American Anthropologist* 88(1): 142–50.

Schneider, David M.

1980   *American Kinship: A Cultural Account.* Chicago: University of Chicago Press.

Service, Elman R.

1978   *Profiles in Ethnology.* New York: Harper and Row.

Shaw, R. Daniel

1972   The Samo of the Strickland Plain: A Cultural Sketch. Unpublished. Paper, Translation Department, Summer Institute of Linguistics, Papua New Guinea.

1973   A Tentative Classification of the Languages of the Mt. Bosavi Region. In *The Linguistic Situation in the Gulf District and Adjacent Areas, Papua New Guinea,* ed. Karl J. Franklin, 187–215. *Pacific Linguistics,* Series C, 26.

1974a   Samo Sibling Terminology. *Oceania* 44:189–215.

1974b   The Geographical Distribution of Samo Relationship Terms: Where Have All the Women Gone? In *Kinship Studies in Papua New Guinea,* ed. R. Daniel Shaw, 223–46. Ukarumpa, Papua New Guinea: Silprint.

1981a   Every Person a Shaman: The Uses of Supernatural Power among the Samo. *Missiology* 9:159–65.

1982   Samo Initiation: Its Context and Its Meaning. *Journal of the Polynesian Society* 91:417–34.

1985   The Good, the Bad, and the Human: Samo Spirit Cosmology. In *Worldview and Worldview Change: A Reader,* ed. I. Grant, 518–27. Pasadena: School of World Mission.

1986   The Bosavi Language Family. *Pacific Linguistics* A-70:45–76.

1990   *Kandila: Samo Ceremonialism and Interpersonal Relationships.* Ann Arbor: University of Michigan Press.

Sillitoe, Paul
   1985   Divide and No One Rules: The Implications of Sexual Division of Labor
            in the Papua New Guinea Highlands. *Man,* n.s., 20:494–522.
Simmonds, N. W.
   1966   *Bananas.* London: Longmans.
Sørum, Arve
   1980   In Search of the Lost Soul: Bedamini Spirit Trances and Curing Rites.
            Oceania 50:273–96.
   1982   The Seeds of Power: Patterns of Bedamini Male Initiation. *Social Analy-
            sis* 10:42–62.
   1984   Growth and Decay: Bedamini Notions of Sexuality. In *Ritualized Homo-
            sexuality in Melanesia,* ed. Gilbert H. Herdt, 318–36. Berkeley: Univer-
            sity of California Press.
   n.d.   *The Forked Branch.* Unpublished book manuscript.
Steadman, Lyle B.
   1971   Neighbors and Killers: Residence and Dominance among the Hewa of
            New Guinea. Ph.D. Dissertation, Department of Anthropology, Austra-
            lian National University.
Strathern, Andrew
   1969   Finance and Production: Two Strategies in New Guinea Highland Ex-
            change Systems. *Oceania* 40:42–67.
   1971a   *The Rope of Moka: Big-Men and Ceremonial Exchange in Mount Hagen,
            New Guinea.* Cambridge: Cambridge University Press.
   1971b   Wiru and Daribi Matrilineal Payments. *Journal of the Polynesian Society*
            80:449–62.
   1973   Kinship, Descent and Locality: Some New Guinea Examples. In *The
            Character of Kinship,* ed. Jack Goody, 21–34. Cambridge: Cambridge
            University Press.
   1982a   Two Waves of African Models in the New Guinea Highlands. In *Inequal-
            ity in New Guinea Highland Societies,* ed. Andrew Strathern, 35–49.
            Cambridge: Cambridge University Press.
   1982b   Witchcraft, Greed, Cannibalism and Death: Some Related Themes from
            the New Guinea Highlands. In *Death and the Regeneration of Life,* ed.
            Maurice Bloch and Jonathan Parry, 111–33. Cambridge: Cambridge
            University Press.
Strathern, Marilyn
   1972   *Women in Between.* New York: Seminar Press.
   1981   Culture in a Netbag: The Manufacture of a Subdiscipline in Anthropol-
            ogy. *Man,* n.s., 16:665–88.
   1983   Subject or Object? Women and the Circulation of Valuables in Highland
            New Guinea. In *Woman and Property, Women as Property,* ed.
            R. Hirschon, 158–75. London: Croon and Helm.
   1988   *The Gender of The Gift: Problems with Women and Problems with Soci-
            ety in Melanesia.* Berkeley: University of California Press.

Swadling, P.
    1983   How Long Have People Been in the Ok Tedi Impact Region? *Papua New Guinea National Museum Record* 8:79–95.
Terray, Emmanuel
    1972   *Marxism and Primitive Society.* New York and London: Monthly Review Press.
Testart, Alain
    1987   Game Sharing and Kinship Systems among Hunter Gatherers. *Man,* n.s., 22:287–304.
    1989   Aboriginal Social Inequality and Reciprocity. *Oceania* 60:1–16.
Townsend, Patricia K.
    1969   Subsistence and Social Organization in a New Guinea Society. Ph.D. Dissertation, Department of Anthropology, University of Michigan.
    1974   Sago Production in a New Guinea Economy. *Human Ecology* 2(3): 217–36.
Turner, Terry
    1979   The Ge and Bororo Societies as Dialectical Systems: A General Model. In *Dialectical Societies: The Ge and Bororo of Central Brazil,* ed. D. Maybury-Lewis, 147–78. Cambridge: Harvard University Press.
Van Baal, J.
    1966   *Dema: Description and Analysis of Marind-Anim Culture.* The Hague: Martinus Nijhoff.
Van Zandt, Tineke
    1989   Supernatural Power and Inequality among the Washo Indians of California and Nevada. Unpublished paper, Department of Anthropology, University of Michigan.
Voorhoeve, Clemens L., and Wurm, S. A., comps.
    1981   Western Province, with Gulf and Chimbu (Simbu) Provinces (Papua New Guinea). In *Language Atlas of the Pacific Area,* gen. ed. S. A. Wurm and Shiro Hattori, Part I, New Guinea Area, Oceania, Australia, Map 12. *Pacific Linguistics,* Series C, 66.
Waddell, Eric
    1972   *The Mound Builders: Agricultural Practices, Environment, and Society in the Central Highlands of New Guinea.* American Ethnological Society Monograph No. 53. Seattle: University of Washington Press.
Wagner, Roy
    1967   *The Curse of Souw.* Chicago: University of Chicago Press.
    1972   *Habu: The Innovation of Meaning in Daribi Religion.* Chicago: University of Chicago Press.
Weiner, James F.
    1988   Introduction: Looking at the New Guinea Highlands from Its Edge. In *Mountain Papuans: Historical and Comparative Perspectives from New Guinea Fringe Highlands Societies,* ed. James Weiner, 1–38. Ann Arbor: University of Michigan Press.

Whitehead, Harriet
    1986   The Varieties of Fertility Cultism in New Guinea. *American Ethnologist*
            13:80–99, 271–89.
    1987   Fertility and Exchange in New Guinea. In *Gender and Kinship: Essays
            toward a Unified Analysis,* ed. Jane Collier and Sylvia Junko
            Yanagisako, 244–70. Stanford: Stanford University Press.
Williams, F. E.
    1969 [1936]   *Papuans of the Trans-Fly.* London: Oxford University Press.
Wolf, Eric R.
    1981   The Mills of Inequality: A Marxian Approach. In *Social Inequality:
            Comparative and Developmental Approaches,* ed. Gerald Berreman, 41–
            57. New York: Academic Press.
Wood, Michael
    1982   Kamula Social Structure. Ph.D. Dissertation, Anthropology, Macquarie
            University.
    1987   Brideservice Societies and the Kamula. *Canberra Anthropology* 10(1):
            1–23.
Woodburn, James
    1982   Egalitarian Societies. *Man,* n.s., 17(3): 431–51.
Wurm, S. A., Voorhoeve, C. L., and Laycock, D. C., comps.
    1981   Southern Highlands Province, with Enga, Western, Gulf and Sepik Prov-
            inces (Papua New Guinea). In *Language Atlas of the Pacific Area,* gen.
            ed. S. A. Wurm and Shiro Hattori, Part I, New Guinea Area, Oceania,
            Australia, Map 11. *Pacific Linguistics,* Series C, 66.
Yanagisako, Sylvia Junko, and Collier, Jane Fishburne
    1987   Toward a Unified Analysis of Gender and Kinship. In *Gender and Kin-
            ship: Essays toward a Unified Analysis,* ed. Jane Collier and Sylvia Junko
            Yanagisako, 14–50. Stanford: Stanford University Press.

Index

595